Anonymus

The Ladies' Companion and Monthly Magazine 1861

Volume XX.

Anonymus

The Ladies' Companion and Monthly Magazine 1861
Volume XX.

ISBN/EAN: 9783742825513

Manufactured in Europe, USA, Canada, Australia, Japa

Cover: Foto ©Thomas Meinert / pixelio.de

Manufactured and distributed by brebook publishing software
(www.brebook.com)

Anonymus

The Ladies' Companion and Monthly Magazine 1861

THE

LADIES' COMPANION,

AND

MONTHLY MAGAZINE.

VOL. XX.—SECOND SERIES.—1861.

LONDON:
PUBLISHED BY ROGERSON AND TUXFORD, 246, STRAND.

INDEX.

NOVELS, ROMANCES, TALES, &c.

POETRY.

Printed by Bagster and Tuxford, 366, Strand, London.

RUTSON MORLEY.

BY JAMES B. STEPHENS.

Chap. XI.

Two days afterwards the "Capitole" steamed out of the harbour of Marseilles. The "Capitole" had steamed out of the harbour of Marseilles many times before, without any historical prestige or [illegible] [illegible]; but now the event was more personally interesting to me than Thermopylæ or Pompeii. I was a passenger on board of her, Italy-bound; and my fate was now very much dependent on the [illegible] plank of her, that hung off the [illegible] of the angry waves.

We had what sailors, [illegible] of [illegible] [illegible], call "dirty weather." All the morning long, Marseilles had been like a mere sketch of itself, no matter what the point of view. Now and again a few red umbrellas, moving in one direction and another, gave it the air of a thousand phantasmagoria seen through a curtain of dreams. With its great outlines dying into foggy distance, and all its pleasant details "swallowed up and lost" in the [illegible] of rainy dreariness, the whole city was reduced to a mere elementary lesson of perspective. But ere we had been many hours at sea, by slow degrees the curtain began to part asunder; and first of all in the far opening immensity the black mountains revealed their blackness, and the rugged cliffs their defiant ruggedness; and then the clouds, gathering themselves together more heavily, hung like curtain [illegible] between the topmost slopes and the now glistening city; then again, as if suddenly dismissed by the word of a Higher Power, broke into hurried thousands, that seemed to rush each to its own appointed home in the [illegible] of rocks.

And this was the Mediterranean — here mountain-crowned; there, [illegible]; and away beyond, blue with boundless distance! Shall I tell you what I thought of, as the mountains grew more vast, the city more glistening, and the sea more widely blue? Of the immutability of those hills, on which had gazed, thousands of years ago, many a "[illegible]-eyed" Greek, sensibly proud of, and delightedly [illegible] to [illegible], the infant colony, so full of brilliant promise? Of the many stately galleys that had swept into that harbour, with songs of joy, and [illegible] [illegible] from [illegible] [illegible]? Of the many languages, whose echoes, now circling far off in the infinite of space, still [illegible] from this as their eternal centre? Of the many changes in the character of its government, and in the gods of its worship? Of the many sailors that had [illegible] [illegible] to the chapel on the hill, to pray for their loved ones on the deep, and of the many dead that lay there? Of the many bloody deeds that darken its history, and the terrible song that [illegible] with [illegible] through the last moments of [illegible] [illegible]?

Yes; these and many more thoughts crowded upon me; but above all, and underneath all, was the joy with which I repeated to myself, again, and again, and again: "The sea is His, and He made it; the strength of the hills is His also."

The mountains were becoming more and more [illegible], [illegible], the city but dimly distinguishable above the water line, and the Château d'If, of Monte Cristo memory, a mere speck, utterly divested of terror, before I sufficiently recovered myself from the trance of beauty and of praise into which I had fallen, to look around on my fellow-passengers. So many curious circumstances had happened to me since leaving England, so many curious coincidences leading to curious discoveries, that I would not have felt it at all improbable that I might chance upon Herr Deicken. I had now washed my hands of blood; but I did not the less regard it as a sacred mission to pursue the mystery into the midst of which I had so strangely been thrown. It was, therefore, with no inconsiderable anxiety, that without any ground of hope except the simple fact that Herr Deicken had gone southward, I examined the faces of my fellow-travellers. But the result was disappointment. Some wore spectacles; some had earrings; [illegible] [illegible] [illegible] [illegible]; some had [illegible] chins with large pockets; some, perchance, carried snuff-watches

2

than one; and one gentleman I certainly heard speak with a lisp; but in no one individual were these characteristics so blended as to constitute the pictorial identity of Herr Dietrich.

The day wore on; the blue deepened into purple; and the purple softened again into the sober hue of night. The idea of sleep did not cross my mind, and that "brave soul-bringing freshment" was infinitely preferable to a close berth below. Accordingly I walked the deck, joyously filling in my new prospects with all sorts of leafing towers, cathedrals, highlands, blue skies and "purple Apennines." Pleasant work it was, especially pleasant to the lightsome sense of deliverance from danger and great sin. There was now a light upon my path—the old home-light, dim indeed, but certain to increase, brighter and better than that "light that never was on land or sea." And now to all this was added the sweet feeling of security in regard to my sister. I had heard from my mother before leaving Paris. The crisis was over, and my home was again happy. I could look backward with thankfulness, and forward with hope. What more could the heart of man desire?

How many times I measured the deck that night I know not. The glare from the engine-room frequently attracted my attention, and led me to compare the burning toil and self-consuming life below with the pure serenity of the upper air. Once I threw myself down on the deck, close to a grating which commanded a full view of the scene of action. Two men, all aglow, like fabled Cyclops, were busy at the time feeding the greedy furnace with enormous shovels of coal. Sweating, indeed, but yet "grinning, under their sooty load," their toil seemed a pleasure, to judge from the vigour they were displaying, as rather, poking out in delectation, each detachment of coal seeming a new effort of their Herculean frames. In one corner of the room, notwithstanding the overbearing heat, lay, what appeared to be the form of a slender young man fast asleep. His face was turned from me, but I was much struck with the beauty of his long black hair, which lay in waving masses on his shoulders. I watched him for some time, wondering what could have tempted any one with so apparently delicate a form to choose such a sleeping-place. I was just about to rouse myself, and resume my deck promenade, when I saw the man slowly turn upon his back, and then half turn himself as if by a slow effort. I waited to catch a glimpse of the face, but his hair had fallen over it, and I could not distinguish a single feature. I paused, however, when suddenly a brain, as if in a haunted dream. In the act of turning, his linen shirt fell open, from the neck; and there on his breast, flashing with the light of the furnace, lay a jewelled cross. It needed no nearer inspection to enable me to recognize the counterpart of what I had seen before.

I was at first half-annoyed at having my peace of mind again disturbed. The old whirl of perplexity renewed itself, sweeping round with it the ghastly forms of all the horrible thoughts from which I had so recently been delivered. Was this a Guarding Providence hemming up my way, or an Avenging Nemesis tracking my every step? Was it a gleam of hope, or a messenger of guilt? Was it a temptation sent to try if I was in earnest in my new obedience, and could at last resist the power of curiosity when it led into dubious paths; or was it a sign to follow on to the fulfilment of a mission, and the solution of a mystery which seemed fraught with grave issues? . . . . . And then Stephanie! Had I forgotten her? Ah, no! she was the earthly horizon of my new-born happiness, girdling it round and round. I did indeed look to a wider horizon, the far-off circuit of the Universe that is but the hollow of the Almighty-hand, and there, and beyond it, the "delegated spirit," bound to range with reverence and godly fear. But, of my earthly prospects, the love of this woman was indeed the widest boundary; and I deemed it a holy one, sanctioned of heaven. Therefore I pished, and waited, and watched, trembling with conflicting anxieties.

I was not the only one whose attention was attracted by the glitter of the jewels. First one Cyclops perceived it, rested his iron upon it, (here unfortunately mythology does not correspond), tapped his brother, pointed to the shining object, and then rubbed his own shining nose. The brother Cyclops struck his two black hands in unmitigated astonishment, looked at the first-speechless, and appealed to his own nose in a similar manner for a solution of the mystery. In their perplexity, the furnace door was left open, whence issued a red glare that communicated to the whole scene an air of infernal grotesqueness. Cyclop A was evidently the ruling spirit. His next movement, almost simultaneously copied by Cyclop B, was to kneel down by the side of the sleeping form, and inspect more closely, but without touching, the object of their curiosity. The inspection lasted for several minutes, and was terminated almost as simultaneously as it had been begun. A then jumped up and shut the furnace door; upon which B, likewise on his feet, went through the form of securing it more firmly. They then sat down on the iron steps immediately beneath me, and gazed silently at the brilliant puzzle.

"Do you think it is real?" at length hissed A.

"What do you think?" hissed B.

"I think it is."

"So do I."

Upon which they again put themselves in a devotional attitude before it, and mutually poked each other's ribs (A. of course, taking the initiative), with such evident intent to commit an offence in perfect good humour, that I was just about to raise an alarm, when a slight motion on the part of the sleeper sent them back both upright—quite simultaneously this time—like two clowns in a "tableau comique."

And now the features were revealed, and there below me lay, without the shadow of a doubt, the original of the portrait I had seen at Wiesbaden, and the perfect translation [illegible] of my own Stephanie. Beautiful—exquisitely beautiful, even in the lurid glare that struggled fiercely through the stoked door, and the undeserving, not [illegible], in the [illegible], would have been more capable of winning admiration. I did not wonder that Winston had loved him. The same beauty—softened but the same—but beyond the current of my misfortune. And as yet his eyes were closed; but I pleased myself with thinking that, when he opened them, I should see the old bewitching loveliness that had charmed me in my lost one. How was I to speak to him, and what was I to tell him? Perchance, what I had to relate would only complicate his difficulties, and add new mazes to the labyrinth. Perchance my story might be but a bunch of Tantalus fruit, ripe only with disappointment.

I was at the old purloining work again, and my brain was reeling as in days before; but I caught myself, and would no more of it. Another [illegible]—it was a prayer this time—and I had made my resolution. These calculations were clearly not built in vain. It was manifestly my duty to follow them up.

But to return A. and B. from their painful attitude of uprightness, which certainly continued as long as I have taken to set down my morbid recollections, their next move was to replace themselves on the iron steps, as if to ponder on the question and make sense of [illegible]. A short pause succeeded, when, in the language of human nature let it but suggest them, the following conversation actually took place:

A. "Did I not tell you he was something better than he professed to be?"

B. "N'me-or yes!"

A. "Isn't it too bad of us to keep him down here, when we can do his work between us?"

B. "N'me-or yes!"

A. "But don't you think we should button up his shirt first, to save his decency's [illegible] to know that we had seen this thing?"

B. "N'me-or yes!"

Upon the clear establishment of which pointed concurrence, A. again knelt down beside the sleeping figure, and cautiously performed the kind office he had proposed. B., supplementing his efforts, by way of fastening the [illegible] more securely, awoke the sleeper. He sprang up with a bound—his eyes full of anything but [illegible] [illegible]. His idea evidently was, that violent hands were being laid on his treasure; and accordingly he took his stand firmly in a corner, facing the innocent stokers with looks of defiant indignation that one would hardly have thought such soft lineaments capable of.

"Don't be alarmed," said A.

"Don't be alarmed," said B.

"We mean kindly," continued A.; and B. echoed, "kindly."

"Go up on deck, my friend, and take your sleep there. Your work has been too hard for you, and you are not used to this heat. We two will manage the work nicely between us. Don't lie down without your cloak over you, or you'll get chilled."

And the good soul patted him on the back, and half-pushed him up-stairs, diligently refixing all the slippers of the [illegible] but to express his thanks. B. gave the finishing stroke to the proceeding, and bid him "only dress" in half a minute.

Farewell A. and B., Cyclopean brothers! In the presence of other thoughts I forgot to seek you out when we reached our destination; but across gulfs of time and space I can join hands with you, and beg a blessing on your honest heads! Toil on, brothers, in the fierce glow of your furnace, and may your work be sweeter to your kind hearts than the luxurious ease of wealthy [illegible]! May the fire to which ye devote your lives become the altar of an accepted sacrifice, and the very burden of your labours be no account of reward! Toil on in patience; for ye shall yet see the place of your work in the long endeavour of humanity! Yes, look up now and again from the fiery glare—up to the blue [illegible] of Heaven, with [illegible] [illegible], and remember this verily: "there remaineth a rest."

As may be supposed, I was up and on the watch immediately. The [illegible] of the evening had evidently banished all idea of sleep from the mind of the young Greek; as, instead of laying himself on the deck according to his orders, he proceeded to pace it up and down with a hasty step. I placed myself against the bulwarks by the companion-ladder leading down to the engine-room, that I might catch the expression of his face in the dim light as he passed and repassed. He seemed melancholy in the extreme, and yet resolutely hoping against hope. Once and again, as he passed, his countenance seemed to brighten, as if with the dawn of a hopeful project. The next glimpse of him would forcibly recall the face of Stephanie as I had seen her at our second meeting. I was puzzling myself as to [illegible] when the knot of perplexity was cut asunder by the young man himself stopping suddenly opposite me, and inquiring with a quivering voice if I spoke Italian. I told him I did, and [illegible] to know if I could be of any service to him.

"I merely wished to ask," he said, "if you would tell me what I require to do in order to obtain a permission of residence for a short time at Pisa."

"I am going there also," I replied, "and as I shall have to get the same for myself, I shall be glad of your company. I have got full instructions as to all that kind of thing. I suppose you have got a passport?"

"Oh, yes."

"Then you will have no difficulty in obtaining a permission of residence. Have you been in Pisa before?"

"No . . . that is to say . . . you will think it very strange if I tell you that I am going to Pisa to see if I have been there before."

"Have you any relatives in Pisa?"

"I am not sure."

"Will you think me impertinent if I say that I am very much interested in you?"

"I shall only think that you are kind without reason. I do not know why you should be so."

"I shall tell you why. Heaven has thrown me almost unwillingly in your way."

"How so?"

"I shall prove it to you in the first place by telling you that your name is [illegible]."

You should have seen how he looked. You should have seen the sudden changes that his face betrayed from hope to fear, from fear to almost comical bewilderment.

"I am a friend of Mr. Winslow's," I said at length.

"Ah! I see now!" he cried, with a laugh of delight. "He has shown you the portrait, and has he forgiven me, do you know, for my [illegible] leave-taking?"

And thereupon I gave him a true and particular account of what I had witnessed of Winslow's feelings in regard to his departure. He was lavish in his expressions of gratitude towards him, and in praise of his noble and generous character.

"And now," said I, when he had ceased, "I believe that I have much to tell you; but what I do tell you will very much depend on what you have to relate to me regarding yourself. I saw your letter to Mr. Winslow. I know from that that you are a mystery even to yourself. Yet I know that you are in search of something, and before I say anything further, you must tell me what it is, otherwise what I have to say may only leave in disappointment."

"Will you put your hand in mine, sir, and say that you are really my friend?"

"There. Do you believe me?"

"I do."

"Then tell me what you seek."

"Perhaps, sir, it is only a vain dream, but I think I once had a sister; and I shall seek her all the world over until I find her—and if I find her not, I shall still seek her. And if it be only a dream, O it is sweeter than all certainty, and I should like to die in it. . . . . But this must seem to you very foolish, does it not?"

"Far from it. What do you recollect of your sister?"

"Ah, sir, that is the difficulty. I can hardly separate my recollections from my dreams. My first distinct recollections begin after my recovery from a long illness, which I was afterwards told was a brain-fever. Before that time I seem to see my sister, shadowy and transparent, as you may fancy a blessed child-angel; but the face remains with me still; and, as the years have rolled on, it has grown with my growth, from childhood to almost manhood. I have seen it watching over me in the dark nights, sometimes sorrowful, sometimes joyous, but always loving. It has been pale and sorrowful of late, and once I saw it weep. But the strangest thing of all is—I am persuaded that I saw my sister . . ."

"Where?"

"In Paris, just before I left.—But you smile sir, and. Tell me, sir, do you know anything of my sister?"

"Be patient a little yet. Perhaps I do, but tell me of the circumstance you refer to."

"I spent much of my time in Paris in rambling about from one part of the city to another. If you knew the style of my previous life, you would not wonder at the extraordinary pleasure this gave me. On the day I refer to, I happened to step into the Station of the Chemin de Fer de Lyon. The crowd about to travel were just waiting for the opening of the bureau when I entered. I waited awhile till it was opened, and then amused myself by listening to the names of all the different destinations to which the various individuals were bound. At length all were served with tickets but one man, who first of all asked for two tickets for Lyons, and then, as if changing his mind, asked whether he could not book right on to Marseilles. I did not hear the reply. Two tickets were handed to him, and then I saw him join a young lady who was waiting for him at the door of the compartment in which the third-class passengers are assembled before being admitted to the platform. A policeman closed the door after them, and so hurriedly, as to catch part of the lady's dress. On his re-opening it to release her, her face was turned towards me, and, as I live, it was the face that has been my guardian angel all my life through. I rushed forward at once, but the door was re-closed with a slam before I could attract her attention, and, as I had no ticket to show, I was refused admission. I entreated earnestly to be allowed to enter, if only for a minute. I said I was sure it was a long-lost sister of whom I had caught a momentary glimpse. At first I was told that it would not be permitted; then gradually the man softened, and said he would open, but bade me remember that he would keep his eye on me, so that I need not attempt anything in the way of pocket-picking. It was too late, however. The train was just starting as I gained the platform. I saw the man, who accompanied her, looking out of the window of one of the carriages, but nothing further."

"What was this man like?"

"A short, thickset, ill-looking man, with a great bushy beard. I grieve to think of that angel girl travelling in such company."

"And how did you get here?"

"Mr. Winslow told you about my departure from Paris. I had but little money—certainly far too little to admit of my travelling by rail. I knew Mr. Winslow would have helped me if I had asked him; but how could I crave money from one who had already been so kind, and for a quest which might after all be but a vain imagination? I could not bear, too, the thought that, had I never again been able to find him and to return it to him, he might think of me through life as a mere impostor. I resolved, therefore, to walk to Marseilles, though with only the shadow of a hope that this would be of any use towards the accomplishment of my object. It was weary work truly. I generally walked about forty miles a day, purchasing a little bread and fruit when I happened to pass through a town or village, and sleeping at night by the road side. I was frequently stopped and interrogated by gens d'armes, but I generally found my plain story compassionately received, and have been sent on with a blessing by more than one fierce official from whom I would have expected rougher treatment. On arriving, however, at Nuits-sous-Ravière, I was suddenly arrested and carried before the Prefect of Police. I sat for some time in a cell adjoining his bureau, tremblingly anxious as to my impending fate, [illegible] of his decision than of the utter destruction of my project which it would certainly bring about. The gens d'armes stood over me with such an air of defiant exultation that I am certain they mistook me for some great criminal. What followed convinced me still more of this. A bell sounded over my head, upon which the two gens d'armes seizing hold of me, almost dragged me to the door of the bureau, and then thrust me into the presence of a very benevolent looking old gentleman, who, on seeing me, to my extreme astonishment, threw himself back in his chair, and burst into a long fit of laughter, in which two or three clerks, when he had found it possible to say a few words to them, joined most heartily. When the Prefect had regained control over himself, he rose, and taking up a photograph which lay on the table, held it up before the gens d'armes with one hand, and pointed to me with the other, whereupon the whole company shrugged their shoulders, the gens d'armes in particular—which latter, with a flushed visage and a [illegible] smile, then retired from the room. The Prefect motioned me to [illegible], placed me on the bench, and said something in French, of which the only word I understood was the [illegible] time. I stammered out a few words in Italian, upon hearing which, he instantly established one of the clerks as interpreter. He asked me a great many questions about myself, and, as I had hitherto found the plain truth my best helper, I told him all I could remember. He seemed greatly interested. He provided me with a comfortable lodging for the night, and made me promise to remain in it till he would send for me the next day. I did so, and early next forenoon a servant came and conducted me to his house, where I found the Prefect, his wife, and the interpreting clerk waiting for me. He then made me go over the same story, particularly inquiring into all my hardships on the way from Paris. I again answered all his questions, thanked him as warmly as I could for his kindness, and begged to be allowed to continue my journey. I imagine that Italian must have been telling on my appearance, for he insisted that it was impossible I could reach [illegible] on foot in such a state of weakness, and, in spite of my obstinate resistance, forced upon me as much money as would defray the expense by rail. His wife joined her urgent offers to his, and I at last accepted their kindness, but only as a loan, which I have sworn to myself to repay if I live. I arrived at Marseilles a few days ago, and immediately set about making such inquiry as I could by means of Italian. I met with many rebuffs, many shrugs of the shoulders, many suspicious looks. I never before felt what a lost ocean a city is. I found myself a mere speck on its waters. After two or three disappointing days of disappointment—I gave up all hope."

"Then what has led you to take this further journey?"

"I used to make a point of going into all the shops where signs bore Italian names. I generally found people there with whom I could converse. The day before yesterday I happened to pass the shop of a worker in alabaster, over the door of which I read the name Bellamano. I entered it, and the first thing which caught my attention was a model of a leaning tower, which, somehow or other, seemed to identify itself with some previous recollection. I at once asked if it was modelled from a real tower, and where it was. 'It is the leaning tower of Pisa,' said the sculptor, 'and this is the cathedral, and this the baptistery.' 'And what is this?' I asked, pointing to a model of a beautiful little chapel. 'That is the Santa Maria della Spina.'

"Instantly clouds of shadowy thoughts seemed to me to assume substance and reality; I had seen these things before. 'Do you know if this little chapel stands on the margin of a river?' I inquired again. 'It does.' ...... I felt (and still feel) certain that Pisa is connected with my earliest life; and with that conviction strongly rooted in my mind, I was seized with the strong desire to proceed thither at once. I made all inquiry about the route, and finding that I had not enough money to take me thither, I offered to work my passage on board this vessel. I was at first refused, there being no necessity for an additional hand on deck; but it was at last agreed that I might assist in the engine-room. However, the kind fellows who are there insist upon taking my work on themselves, and have forced me on deck. I have now told you what you wish to know. I might tell you of my previous life, but I am dying with impatience to hear if you have anything to say of my sister."

I spoke to him of Stephanie **till** the stars came out of the sea. With such a subject, and with so eager a listener, the soft-winged hours floated away unheeded. I told him of the strange circumstances under which I had met her, of her yearnings after a remembered brother, of the face that visited her and grew with her, of her tenderness of heart and of her great beauty. I told him—I could not conceal it—how she and I loved one another, how our souls were now so intertwined that they could no more be separated, and how I now looked to him as to a brother. All this while he was lying at my feet, looking up into my face, flushed and entranced, as a saint may be in the first ravishment of glory. The proximity of several of our fellow-travellers, however, who now began to emerge one by one from the tomb of their secret, put a pleasant end to my volubility, and seemed likewise to rouse my companion to a keener sense of external things. His daily of subject began in this way to the play of many phases of thought. I never saw a face that more perfectly reflected the inner-workings of the mind. I could see that he was reviewing all the bearings of the mysterious story, and in quick succession building up hopes and pulling them down, planning and rejecting, rejoicing and sorrowing. At length he rose, and turned from me, and after pacing up and down the deck for some time, threw himself on his knees, with his face to the fast-appearing sun, and remained in this attitude, regardless of several astonished spectators, long enough to accomplish a very considerable prayer. On rising, he resumed his walk, and it was not until I, rather puzzled with his strange behaviour, made a move as if to go below, that he strode rapidly up to me, and taking me by the hand, showed a faint attempt to speak, in a flood of tears. I did not wonder that his pent-up emotion on a subject so sacred should have forced him, at length, to play the woman; and placing my arm in his, I turned with him, and we walked up and down for some time in silence.

"You will think me very strange," he said, at length—"very unmanly; but oh, sir, you will not take her from me!"

This was a view of the subject, certainly, which had not dawned on me till now. Within the pleasure and conceits of my own love I had entirely forgotten him, forgetting that I was an interloper upon him. His sister was his life-object; and the mere fact that she was to be happy with me would not satisfy him. And in spite of myself, many little selfish, but thoroughly positive and practical thoughts, drove me all of a sudden into a very calculating state of mind. For it did seem as impossible for me to yield up Stephanie to the other ownership of her brother as to enlarge the possibility details of the matrimonial establishment so as to include them both. Here was a dilemma, indeed and here I. Natural for him, after a life of weary waiting, of hope deferred and struggles endured, to desire to realise undivided possession; Natural for me, on whom had dawned the life of a higher love than that of brotherhood itself, to cling to the new revelation, and press on to its daily sanctities!

There was nothing for it now but to leave the matter to time. I would not shatter a brother's hopes; I could not disdain my own.

"You will not take her from me, will you?" he again inquired, with a heart-rending earnestness that constrained me to cast about for a speedy reply.

"We have not found your sister yet," was the only one that suggested itself.

"Ah, but we *shall* find her. I may not teach you, but why are all these strange lines, which begin at the outside, tending to a centre? Surely not to cross each other without purpose, and go out again into infinite darkness. I know little of the world; but I have read of the ways of God. You and I shall see her; but, oh, when I have only looked at her, you will take her away!"

"Nay, nay; it would be years before I could marry your sister."

"Then I yield you, when years shall have taught me to love her more and more—when, from being my hope she shall have become my joy—when, from being my distant beckoning star, she shall have become the sun of my life; then you will come, so much wiser, so much more to be desired than I; you will come to claim her promise, and take her away from me, and I shall be alone again!"

"I will not take her heart from you. It is possible for a wife to love a husband without abating her love for a brother. If you take her all to yourself, she will be nothing to me; but if in due time you yield her up to me, she will still be to you all that a sister can be."

"Do you believe this, sir?"

"I do."

"You will think me strangely ignorant when I tell you that I must depend on your word for many of the simplest things of life. I think I have generally found, in reading the lives of great women, that the name of the sister all but disappeared in that of the wife. Is it not so in common life?"

I certainly was a little puzzled to hear such a matter discussed with reference to reading, instead of ordinary experience. Notwithstanding I felt called upon for an explanation.

"Perhaps," said I, "that is owing to the imperfection of all history, which, dealing only in broad results, cannot reach into the inner feelings. These women you have read of are great because of something in which they differ from ordinary women; and if the husband is heard of, it is because the wife must bear his name, which thus shares in her celebrity. But the love of sister and brother—and my own heart bears me out here—is, thank God, so ordinary a thing as to be too ordinary for history."

I was glad to run into abstractions, however out of place at the time, to escape from the practical question that stood like a barrier between us; and by way of still further avoiding it, I begged to know how it was that he, at his age (which was not much less than my own), professed so little of the ordinary experiences of life.

"I think I may say," he replied, "judging from what I have read, and from what I have lately seen of the ways of other men, that mine has been singularly different from most of them."

Glad to get him on this subject, I expressed my anxious desire to know whatever he could remember of his previous life.

"I have not much to tell," he began, as we seated ourselves, not altogether unprepared, a considerable way out on the bowsprit, which unusual position we had chosen in order to avoid the disagreeable acquaintance with that most merciless of operations, 'washing decks.' "I have not much to tell, but what I do remember I shall relate to you the more readily, as it may help you to excuse in me much of what may have been unpardonable ignorance. I have already told you that my earliest recollections, if recollections I may call them, are but dim shadows floating confusedly through my mind, and often intermingling themselves with what I afterwards discovered to be the experience of others which I have picked up in books and paintings. I will not trouble you with them just now. I will begin with what appears to me like the first flash of my perceptions; at a time when I think I must have been not less than four years of age. I remember the scene very clearly. I was lying on a low pallet in a small white-washed room, all but bare of furniture. It was very bright, however; a brilliant sunlight streamed into it through a small window just over my head. There was a low stool in one corner of the room; in another, a great heap of mats, nearly reaching up to a shelf which supported a few books and a lamp. A rude fire-place, with a few charred sticks, and a massive door, on which was painted the picture of a figure bearing a cross, were the only other noticeable objects, save a jug of water which stood on the floor near my head.

"I tried to rise, but could not; my strength was quite gone. I tried to cry out, but it seemed to me as if I had utterly lost the use of my voice. I lay long in a state of utter amazement, and so weak, that I thought I should have died—until indeed I wished to die. I could not think what had come over me. I could not quite remember who or what I was. The very effort to think wearied me out, and I fell asleep again. It was dark when I awoke, and my state was more than ever a perfect blank to me. I was in a burning thirst, and remembering the jug of water I had seen near my head, I managed with a great effort to pass my hand over to it, and slide it a little closer to me. It was too heavy for me to lift, but I managed to tilt it down so as to spill a little of the water over my lips. I felt considerably refreshed, but in no way enlightened. I must have lain awake during several hours, which were past in fruitless questionings, when I heard a grating sound as of some one unlocking the door. It was very slowly and cautiously done, and presently the door opened, almost noiselessly, and a man entered bearing a lantern. After carefully securing the bolts inside, he turned suddenly towards me, directing the light full on my face. I was almost frightened to death by his startling appearance. He was a very tall, powerful man, fiercely bearded and armed to the teeth. His head was covered with a shawl of green and gold, wound round like a turban. Underneath a huge rough capote, beautifully mounted pistols and daggers flashed from a gorgeous girdle. A stiletto was lying by his side, and on his knees were plates of steel.

"When he saw that I was awake, he placed his finger on his lips, and, advancing towards me, laid down the lantern and lifted the water to my mouth. As he raised my head very gently to enable me to drink more easily, I began to feel a little reassured, though my first idea had been that all these formidable weapons were intended for my immediate destruction. After I had drunk freely, he laid me in gently back again, and then whispered to me in Italian, 'Sleep again, little one; you are going to be well soon.' He now sat watching me till he thought I was asleep, when he proceeded to divest himself of his arms, and his fine clothing, for which, to my further astonishment, he substituted a long coarse frock, with a girdle of rope, a hat like an ordinary hermit's, without rim, and shoes of the coarsest description. When he had completed his new attire, he next set himself to secrete the garments and arms he had just laid down. The garments he folded up and placed under the pallet on which I was lying; the weapons he hid deep in the heap of mats. In the weakness of my mind and body at the time, I was quite unable to adhere to any one course of thought, or any one course of observation; and just at this point I slid off into a state of wonder as to where such a quantity of mats could have been found, and then deep in a dream of a forest of mats, with numberless little children sporting on the heights, when, all of a sudden, I was startled by the voice of some one singing, and, looking up, saw the same man seated on the outer threshold of the door, swaying himself backwards and forwards as an accompaniment or attraction to one of the most mournful of imaginable chants. It was, indeed, a strange, wild song; and as I lay and listened to him in that dreamy half-state, which makes us see with half eye and ear and the other half dream, as he sang and swayed himself, and warped himself and sang, it seemed to me as if his voice were now moaning in rocky hollows, now quivering among the sobbing leaves of many forests, now bubbling in the plashes of fresh brooks, and now swelling with the murmur of the mourning sea. How long he sang I know not, for when I awoke from a dream that I was a lark, pursuing his voice through the heights of air, I found that he was lying in the straw pallet, and I on his breast. It was broad daylight, and I did hear a lark! Oh, how I longed to be up, and to climb up to that bright window, and to look out and see whither I had come! How I watched till the strange man would wake, that I might question him as to the things that were bewildering me! He did not seem unkind, and perhaps he would tell me who and where I was, and whose were the kind faces that I seemed to miss, and that were still more like shadowy spectres, which would not come nearer me to let me embrace them, nor yet leave me alone with the stranger. At length he awoke, and perceiving that I was awake also, put his finger to his lips, as before, and then stroked my head as gently as a mother might have done, saying at the same time, very kindly, 'Not yet, my little one. You must sleep to-day, still; and to-morrow we shall go out and gather flowers.'

"I was in a frame of mind to be satisfied with anything, and one of unquestioning obedience; so that when he rose, and kindled a fire with the flint and steel, and removed an unsuspicious stone from one corner of the floor, and drew from a wonderful little cavern beneath materials for coffee-making, &c., &c., and busied himself in the preparation of a comfortable breakfast, of which he made me partake, though sparingly, and then told me he was going to leave me for a little, but that I was on no account to stir—up to the last hour of all this, and all through that day, I was as silent and as peacefully guided as any child could well be. Towards the evening he came in again—not alone this time, but accompanied by three or four aged monks, clad very much like himself, but in much richer material, and one of them carrying a long silver-headed staff. They looked on me so kindly, and showed me so many little dainties they had brought for me, some of which they allowed me to taste, that I never dreamed of being afraid of them. They talked long with my friend, in a tongue then unknown to me; but I afterwards learned that he had told them of his having found me floating on the waves, and that they were then disputing as to whether this were not a special Providence which had sent this child to the holy hermit to be brought up for God. The hermit stood all the while before the lamp of stone, and seemed very much amazed with the result of their conversation, but still more so with their departure, which took place after each in turn had patted and stroked me, with saintly smile, that filled my dreams all the night long.

"Among other good things, the kind monks had made me take a little of some very choice wine, and they were not long gone before I was again asleep under the influence of it. It must have been long past midnight when I awoke, and then, as before, there was the grating of the lock, the light of the lantern, the flash of stars, and the green and gold. Then there was the slow changing and fading of these, and presently the same swaying to and fro, and in the misty windings of the song, the same moaning in the hollows of rocks, the quiver of sobbing leaves, the plaint of little brooks, and the moaning of the sea. I slept again, and awoke on his breast. The room was full of light, and I longed more than ever to look out on the freshness of the world. I felt myself stronger too, and much longed to play, though with a strange sensation of the absence of wonted companions.

"My wish was gratified at last. By gradual stages, and with the gentleness of a woman, the kind hermit half-carried me to the door, where he had formed for me a little seat of turf. As you may guess, I surveyed the scene with curious eyes. Just beneath me, and far as the eye could reach, the sea lay gleaming. All around where I sat were craggy rocks, rising abruptly from the water. Just over me, and luxuriating up into the very sky, woods upon woods towered gloriously, from the depths of which innumerable little streams ran prattling to the sea; and above all this, a great white rock, high and majestical, lifted its head into the azure heavens. I felt as if in fairy-land—and indeed, if there be a fairy-land, it surely cannot be more beautiful than Monte Santo!"

"Monte Santo!"

"Yes, that is where I have lived since the time I speak of, until lately."

"And have you actually passed your life among the monks?"

"Yes. I suppose this explains much that may have seemed to you strange about me. But I am glad you have interrupted me, so I was forgetting myself in the intensity of my own recollections. I must cut my story shorter. Suffice it to say, then, that I passed the next three years of my life as the hermit's child. Night after night I heard him sing his wondrous song, though it was only now and again that he appeared in the dress in which I had first seen him. I passed my days chiefly in the pathless woods, leading the life of a fawn rather than that of a child of man. And no wonder. Oh, sir, if you knew that land, the glory of its forests, and the purple of its vineyards—if you had climbed its highest peaks as I have done, and plucked the mosses that grow on its summits—if you had searched as I have the shadowy depths of its valleys, and found every day some new and curious nook, full of mystery and dreams—if, like me, you had daily enjoyed the companionship of its brooks, of its birds, of its flowers, nay, of the very breezes that whisper through its woods, you would not wonder that, before the world of books was opened up to me, I found more fellowship in the waving of boughs and the converse of waters than in the ways of men. A new cavern, moss-grown and lichen-covered; a new cascade, murmuring the same tale that all the waters told; a new gorge, dark and deep, with the fragmentary gleam of brooks flashing through capricious gaps in great regions of foliage; a new labyrinth of starladen boughs; a new flower, hiding its unasked beauty under the dripping canopy of projecting cliffs; a tree, heaven-blessed, stretching out its giant arms like a maniac suddenly conscious of nakedness, and grasping at the drapery of its rich-robed brothers; a withered trunk, whose heart the vulture-ages had eaten out, and in whose hollow I could sit and watch the grey-clad procession of the hours,—these, and such as these, were the incidents of my life. Besides, my uncle (as the hermit had taught me to call him) had cautioned me against being much in the company of the monks. In a land so thickly studded with monasteries, it was of course impossible to avoid them altogether; but I was strictly forbidden to answer any questions they might put regarding my uncle's way of life. I therefore, as I said, kept as much as possible in the pathless woods, and in the solitary places of the rocks. My uncle was very kind—never harsh, except when I questioned him as to how I had got there, and how long I was to remain. In a short time I began to learn that it was in vain to question him; and during the rest of the time that we passed together, we were as loving as father and son. But our parting came; and a sad one it was.

"One night, my uncle (whom I had observed to be very much agitated during the whole of the preceding day, and, contrary to his kindly wont, too much absorbed within himself to give heed to my most importunate demands on his attention), after having sat for hours, silently watching the approach of darkness, turned suddenly to me, and addressed me in a tone of nervous haste, such as he had never before used to me.

"'Boy,' said he, 'can I trust you with a secret?'

"'What secret, Uncle?' I asked.

"'No matter what. Do you love me?'

"'You know I do, Uncle,' said I, rushing forward and throwing myself into his arms.

"I felt a tear drop on my cheek, and looking up to his face, saw with astonishment that he was weeping. I did not know how to comfort him, except by embracing him all the more closely.

"'If I were to leave this place hurriedly and secretly,' said he at length, 'would you go with me, Ivaron?'

"(I should have told you that he had named me after one of the monasteries in whose neighbourhood we dwelt.)

"'I would,' I replied, '—most willingly—anywhere you like.'

"'But would you go if I told you it was a dangerous life I was about to lead, and that you would see none but rough and daring, though honest, men,—that you would many times have to hide with me in dark caverns, and to be often very hungry, and without anything to satisfy your hunger, and perhaps have to see blood shed, and well-known friends falling in fight, and, after all, see me carried away from you to die a cruel death, without being able to leave you anything but a bad name?'

"'But why are you going away, Uncle?' I asked, 'if all that is before you?'

"'I only say it is possible, Ivaron. I hope, my child, for better things—ay, for glorious things!'

"'Then if you go, I will go.'

"'But would you not rather stay with the good monks? They are kind men, and they all love you.'

"'Yes, but none of them love me as you do, Uncle.'

"When I said this, he embraced me tenderly, and said that nothing would separate me from him. He then told me to go outside the little hut, and down by a well-known path to the sea-shore, there to strike a light, and by that means to kindle a torch with which he provided me. This I was to hold until I should see anything unusual, upon which I was to hurry up to the hut again as soon as possible, and inform him of what I saw.

"I did so I was directed. It was a moonless night, but the stars were twinkling brightly, and the sea had no intervals more now and again a long-drawn sigh, that fell on the ear more like the moaning of an ancient sorrow than a sensible sound. I lit the torch, which emitted a strange green light that at first half-frightened me; but I looked at the stars and at the sea, and felt strong again. I sat down on a stone, and at first amused myself with dropping pebbles on the green reflection of the torch in the water, and watching the beautiful undulations. Then gradually as this ceased to be novel, I set myself (for the sake of shortening the time, which was now beginning to feel rather long) to count the faint recurrence of the low sigh that seemed to me to speak of some great grief hid in the heart of the ocean long ago. I thus fell into a dreamy state, in which I remained for a considerable time, when of a sudden I became aware of a boat at a very few yards from the shore. It was slowly approaching, and as the oars rose and fell without the slightest plash, it seemed like a spectral boat in a soundless sea. A man was standing in the bow making signs to me; instead of waiting to interpret which, I threw down the torch in dreadful alarm, and rushed wildly up to the hut. My uncle opened the door as soon as he heard my footsteps. I saw that he was dressed as I had first seen him, and that he had an air of defiant boldness, such as I had never seen him assume before. I told him of what I had seen, and that the boat was already by the shore.

"'It is well,' he said, calmly. **'Then you** may go to bed, my child.'

"'But am I not to go with you, dear Uncle?' I asked in alarm.

"'Not this night, Ivaron. I shall be back to this place before morning. To-morrow we will leave it together. Fear nothing, my child. The good God watches over such as you.'

"It was the first time he had spoken to me of God. I made some remonstrance; but he took me in his arms, laid me on my bed, and, kissing me affectionately, left the hut without a word. I felt that I did not dare to follow him, and being now quite accustomed to find myself alone in the darkest nights (for it had always been in the darkest nights that I had missed my uncle) I soon fell asleep without fear.

"I had slept for some hours, when the door of the hut suddenly opened, and my uncle, staggering in, threw himself, groaning, on the bed. I started up in great alarm, struck a light hurriedly, and held the lamp forward to his face. To my horror I saw that there was a great gash on his brow, from which the blood was fast flowing, and another stream of blood welling out on his beautiful girdle from some wound in his breast. I screamed out, and nearly fainted; but he raised his hand, and merely whispered:—

"'Hush, for the love of God!'

"It was the second time he had spoken to me of God.

"'What can I do **for you, dear dear Uncle?'** I said, striving to **control my agony of alarm** and sorrow.

"'Come near me, **my** child,' he said, 'for I have not long to live. The villains whom I should have slain have murdered me.'

"'Oh, Uncle,' I cried, 'do not speak in this way. Let me wash that ugly wound.'

"'It is too late. Come nearer me still. They will tell you bad things of me, Ivanoe . . . but I loved you, my child . . . I loved you indeed!'

"A long pause succeeded—I, sobbing like to break my heart, and the dying man, breathing harder and harder.

"'I cannot lift my arm, Ivanoe,' he at length whispered, with great difficulty; 'but do you put your hand . . . into my breast . . . a little further up . . . there . . . open my shirt, and . . . take that cross from my neck. . . . Nay, my boy, I cannot lift my hand . . . take my dagger and cut the string. . . . There . . . that is yours . . . wear it . . . it may help you to find out who you are. . . . I know nothing except that I took you from some . . . more wicked than myself . . . Come nearer me still, Ivanoe . . .'

"And I lay in his blood, pressed against his last heart-throbbings, and choking with my own tears. Suddenly, with a huge effort, he raised himself, held me from him a little way, looked with his grey eyes upon me for a moment or two, then clasped me to his bosom again, and lay down to die.

"'Ivanoe,' he whispered, with his last breathing, 'such as you can pray . . . say . . . God forgive him!'

"It was the last time that he spoke to me of God, and the words had hardly crossed my lips, when I knew that my uncle was dead.

"I was alone in that dreary hut with the bloody corpse of the only being I loved on earth. Oh, sir, I believe there have been many lifetimes spent in the busy world, without ever such an experience of terror and woe as struck and bent my childhood on that fearful night! Oh, if you had seen how awful he looked when the grey dawn paled the poor lamp, and set the seal of more terrible reality on the horror of his ghastly wounds! A ray from the rising sun lit up the diamond of the cross which was lying on the bed, and, remembering what my poor uncle had told me, I took and secreted it in my bosom. It was my first return to sober thought, and I began to reason, child that I was, as to how I should act. I thought that, if I told the monks what had happened, they might find wherewith to say evil things of him, and that I resolved should not be. I thought I would dig for days and days till I had made a deep grave in the floor, in which I would bury him, then go to the monks and tell them that my uncle had left me. But then I was afraid that, if discovered at the work, they would say I had murdered him while he slept. I was musing what to do, when I was thrown into new alarm by the sound of many footsteps rapidly advancing towards the hut. Presently the door was thrown open, and, looking out, I saw the Abbot of Iveron. I had seen him several times before; indeed, he was one of those who had visited the hut as I before related. He was attended by a great crowd of the brethren, one of whom, standing close to the abbot, carried what I at once recognized as my uncle's sabre, now terrible with blood. Those who were near enough to obtain a glance of the gory spectacle that the open door revealed, started back appalled, and a cry of horror passed over the whole crowd. I heard the abbot order them back, and then name a few of the elders who alone were to enter with him. I understood their language now. It was my uncle's language too, and he had taught it me. Three or four of the youngest of the lay brethren were then ordered to station themselves outside the door; the rest, with the exception of the four selected by the abbot, returned, as he had commanded, to their monastery.

"The monks having entered, and having closed the door, stood for some time in speechless horror. At length the abbot spoke to me. I was now lying on the heap of rags, with my face hid in my hands, greatly fearing lest they should think I had murdered him.

"'Come to me, child,' he said. 'Alas, poor boy, thou art bloody too! . . . . . . I will ask thee a few questions, and, as I am in the place of God, I charge thee, answer me words of truth.'

"'I will, father,' I replied, at once awed and encouraged.

"'Where is the holy hermit?'

"'That is he,' said I, pointing to the body.

"At this the monks looked at one another like men bewildered.

"'Hath the Lord permitted this?' said the abbot at length. 'Father Emmanuel, do thou wash the face, and see if this be indeed the holy hermit.'

"The monk did as he was desired, then slightly raised the head of the corpse, and showed the pallid features to the fathers, whose very hearts shook with fear, while they saw that it was indeed the hermit.

"'Who hath done this?' said the abbot, again addressing himself to me.

"'I know not, father,' I answered; and thereupon I told him some of the circumstances of the preceding night. The monks again looked at each other in blank perplexity, which was only interrupted by Father Emmanuel shifting the disposition of the bed-clothes, and covering the face of the dead.

"'Come with us, child,' then resumed the abbot. 'This is no place for one of thy years. Thou hast begun early to know how wicked the world is. And, of a truth, that its curse should find its way even to our land of holy retirement! Come, thou shalt henceforth live with us.'

"It was now that I became more than ever alive to the agony of parting. I flung myself on the bed, and clung frantically to the body; but was soon lifted and led out by the monks—not harshly, but firmly. The abbot closed the door behind us, and gave strict charge to the stalwart lay-brethren on no account to allow anyone to enter.

"'It behoveth us,' he said, 'to learn something of this mystery, and of the manner of his death, ere we can inter him in our holy soil.'

"'And of the manner of his life, too,' suggested one of the lay-brethren.

"'Ha! knowest thou aught, Philip?'

"'I cannot say I know, but I have sometimes thought,' replied the lay-brother.

"'Come thou also with us, then, and let us know what thou thinkest.'

"Accordingly we all proceeded to the monastery of [illegible], where a cell was appointed me, which I was to share with a priest to whom I had more than once spoken, and who begged hard to be put in charge of me.

"I know not what was the end of the consultation; but long afterwards they told me that my uncle had been an outlaw, the head of a terrible band of men who were ill-affected towards the Government of the country—that he had assumed the life of a hermit for the sake of concealment, and had so perfectly blinded the monks to his real character that they thought him a pattern of holy asceticism—that his wandering abroad in the night had led to the general belief that he sacrificed sleep to devotion—that all the while he had been the recognised leader of many rebellious movements in the country, which he had concerted, with other subordinate leaders, in secret midnight conferences held on the neighbouring promontories—that the authorities had obtained information of this, and a band of Government troops had surprised the rebels on the terrible night I have told you of, and had taken several prisoners; finally, that my uncle had escaped, though with his death-wounds on him, and had been rowed over by a few followers, who, however, had been taken on their way back, and had given such information as afterwards reached the monks. But they would never tell me what was done with his body; though, I think, from some hints I heard, that they bore it far out to sea, and buried it in the waters. Whatever he was, I love his memory; I am sure he must have been driven by force of circumstances to that wild life and that cruel death."

Just at this point of the story, the order was given to haul down the [illegible], and we were imperatively ordered off the forecastle. During the whole course of the young man's narrative I had been utterly insensible to external things. My eyes were immovably fixed on the water beneath us, rising and falling in overlapping masses on either side of the steamer's bow, like earth from a plough-share. But now I raised them on one of the fairest of cities rising up before us—a great amphitheatre of palaces, extending upwards, terrace above terrace, until lost in the beauty of mountains.

"What glorious city is this?" cried my companion, in the ecstasy of admiration.

I had never seen it before, but a thousand tokens taught me to answer at once:

"Genoa la Superba!"

A GLEAM FROM THE PAST.

BY HARRY A. CARTWRIGHT.

Touch'd with a soft and tender grace,
In the action, the word, and the tone,
He looks in her fair young face,
And the hard lines fade from his own.

Oh he listens with eager ears,
He answers with faltering tongue,
His mind is busy with by-gone years,
That come like the echoes of song.

Faint, faint sounds in the distance there,
Of music passingly sweet;
And the long past wakes in its lair,
And again youth's pulses beat.

And the old man, no longer grey,
Like the change in a fairy-scene
From the present has past away,
And the days come back that have been;

And his heart leaps up once more;
A moment he seems to rejoice,
And his being thrills to the core
At the sound of a woman's voice.

The sound of her voice and her smile,
Death, relaxing, yields to the charms,
And restores, for a little while,
A dear lost form to his arms.

He gazes—the maiden's cheek blushes,
All rosy and red, as she stands;
Nor can she divine why he offers
His withered and trembling hands.

"Like—like—so like," he murmurs
To her who sleeps under the ground?
Ah! she died in far-off summers,
But I [illegible]—thought she was found.

"Found! and the present vanished away,"
And memory loosened its hold,
Then a film his gray eyes stole away,
And he whispered—"Oh, old, so old,

"God bless you! forgive—forgive me!
Like—so like to the face I knew;
Oh let it again smile on me,
For the fancy seems still so true.

"Oh! a kiss from the lips so fair,
And the vision will pass from me!"
And the maiden stoop'd by his chair,
And she kiss'd his wrinkled brow.

SPIRIT-WORLD.

BY MERLIN.

Last night, when all the household slept,
The north wind blew so wild,
That I lay in my bed and wept,
Bitterly, like a child.
I know 'twas weak and coward-like;
Once I was bold and brave,
Ready to march, ready to strike,
Now I yearn for the grave;
Yearn to the souls of those above,
Who in God's light are furl'd—
To feel the bliss of re-awaken'd love,
And live in spirit-world.

I walk along, where fresh winds blow,
Dark like smoky [illegible];
And find God's world in beauty grow
[illegible];
I stand away and sit apart,
While all the world is gay;
In all the [illegible]
I go alone to pray;
And in the silent summer night,
When [illegible],
I watch the dying amber light,
And live in spirit-world.

When thro' the aisle and cloister dim
The ghostly twilight falls,
And sunset shadows flit and skim
O'er the sculptur'd walls,
Alone, I touch the organ-chords,
And bid the music roll,
And seem to hear an angel's words
Of greeting to my soul.
The music lingers round the halls,
Then seems to Heaven whirl'd,
And bears me upwards with the spells
To realms of spirit-world.

Weak, oh weak is my woman's will,
And goes from my control,
In vain I bid the tumult still,
Or peace be in my soul;
For never more is rest in life,
Or home on earth for me:
But evermore is endless strife,
And struggles to be free.
For life is shorn of love, one by one
My joys their sails have furl'd,
And those who with me voyag'd have gone
To dwell in spirit-world.

MANNERS.—In all the superior people I have met, I notice directness, truth spoken more freely, as if everything of obstruction, of malformation had been trained away. What have they to conceal? What have they to exhibit? Between simple and noble persons there is always a quick intelligence; they recognize at sight, and meet on better ground than the talents and skills they may chance to possess—namely, on sincerity and uprightness.—EMERSON'S "Conduct of Life."

THE CORNFIELD.

BY ADA TREVANION.

Here—while the gorgeous sunset's overflow
Touches the cornfield with the hues of Heaven,
And the west wind, in wand'ring to and fro,
Bows down the full ears, let us pass the even;
The scarlet poppies and the blue corn-flowers
Will smile us back again to bygone hours—

I call to mind a handsome August morn:
The lark was up and singing o'er the lea;
In the bright sun those rosy buds were born,
Which dye in radiance hill, and tower, and tree;
And gold-eyed moths flutter'd on glancing wings
Among the sheaves, which seemed the dark earth's kings.

Two constant hearts, that Fate had severed long,
That gracious morn were linked in one for aye;
Two lovers listened to the lark's glad song,
Poured 'neath the silver splendor of that day.
Then here they met; and here, with happy tears,
Love bound, in one full sheaf, the hopes of years.

Dear wife, sweet wife! you know how fondly placed,
Amid your treasures, are some dried wild flowers,
With the dew of their gath'ring o'er them traced;
More prized by you than blooms from fairest bowers.
Of our past days those blossoms seem to tell—
And of the morn when sorrow bade farewell.

Ramsgate, 1860.

SONG.

BY ANNE A. FREMONT.

I have no lands, I have no gold,
Nor woolly flock in crowded fold;
My only offering, love, will be
A heart that throbs and beats for thee!

I cannot bring thee jewels rare
To shine like stars in thy dark hair;
The wild rose, and the hawthorn sweet,
Will be for thee a chaplet meet.

Nor have I chains of gold, to deck
Thy queenly brow and graceful neck;
No, dearest! all thy chains must be
Such only as love weaves for thee!

For I have neither land nor gold,
Nor bleating flock in crowded fold:
A heart that throbs and beats for thee,
My only off'ring, love, will be!

AN ARTICLE WITH AN OBJECT.

BY JOVAN.

By the time this article appears, the over-worked and the under-worked will alike be thinking of their annual migration. The heat and glare of the city, becoming daily more intolerable, will drive them away, whether they rush forth greedy and eager in search of honest and wholesome enjoyment, or proceed in a stately and decorous fashion to "kill time" in the country, since time is beginning to kill them in town. The coast will again be invaded, by an army innumerable, irresistible, with endless balances at its banker's. Shipple, who now has one of the loveliest nooks in England almost entirely to himself—and who draws his honest little pictures in a solitary little way—will see, ere long, as he returns from his happy and innocent [illegible], the travelling-carriage, dire messenger of Doom. Next morning, the hats will be out and around him. As he sits sketching under the limestone crags, he shall hear merry tinkling laughter above his head; and, casting up his astonished eyes, shall see that the laughter emanates from beings whom to see is to adore—whom to hear is to become hopelessly enslaved. Not for thee, oh Shipple, are such beings: neither, oh Shipple, for me. Go on with thy pencil, my friend—even as I myself will agitate my eager quill: at a distance indeed we may worship and admire; but they? Serenely unconscious, they walk along their path of life—a romantic walk by hidden streams, that leads to an establishment and a position.

Yes, the crags, and the sands, and the glistening pebble-beaches receive their visitors once more. The god of the sea, even Poseidon the mighty, gives once more his grand "At Home," his summer party; whereof the name of the guests is Legion. Guests of all kinds these be: divisible, however, for my present purpose, into two great classes—those who have money to spare, and those who have not. The present article is intended for the former.

Have I, then, suddenly become a Millionaire? Has fortune opportunely slain my uncle in the Opium Trade? Have those shares of mine in the Cheap Great Dip Company (Limited) risen to a miraculous premium? I would it were so; but so it is not. Why, then, do I speak to the rich? Brethren, there dwells within me something of the Bohemian spirit, something of the Gipsy blood. I am nothing if not indecorous and unconventional. [illegible] to the rich I speak—to the rich by the seaside. Thou stately father, with "Marchmont" written on thine ample form, thine ample [illegible], come! I would fain clutch thee! Thou dignified and graceful individual, who art a ruler of [illegible], and hast coaches, and shooting-boxes in the heathery North, and country-houses in the Sussex weald; lend me thine ear, for I need it. Lady fair, with the silver locks, and the gentle look of a calm old age; [illegible] until you have heard me out. And let Arabella listen, for I am to speak of romantic Dora; and Walter, who looks languid, but has a heart in him and a brain—(I wish he would give them fairer play, but the one has a little laziness, the other thinks a little more freely); and Reginald, who was at Lucknow, and who was braver there than he is at Scarborough; listen, oh ye of the Upper Ten. My talk shall be full of reverence for you, for I would fain obtain monies from you.

"For myself?" says a rather grinning Cynic. Well, my P.C., when I do send round the hat, I shan't ask you!

I write this article with a definite object, apart from, and infinitely above, the merely professional feelings with which I am to supply a given quantity of matter for a given wage. It is one of the happiest privileges of a man of letters that sometimes, in the mere exercise of his profession, he may do solid and substantial good.

The cause which I am to plead is a very just and noble one, though I must first plead it in my own way—which is not a matter of course, or orderly way—if I am to plead it at all. Briefly, I want to tell those of my readers who have money to spare, these two facts:—

Fact the First, which is a sad one; in 1860 there were 1,379 wrecks on the coast of the United Kingdom, involving the loss of 536 human lives.

Fact the Second: the National Life-boat Institution depends upon voluntary subscriptions for extending its means of action.

I need not, I think, draw the deduction for you. It seems to me to lie very plain. I do not say that all these lives might have been saved; I do say that many of them might, had the funds of the Institution been more ample than they are.

Now, I know that the demands upon English Givers have lately been very large. When a few weeks of hard weather threw thousands of Londoners on the streets, the subscriptions that were raised were more glorious to this country than the gaining of ten battles. When, in the far East, men who had lately risen against us to slay us, lay starving—enduring a famine partly caused by their own default (as, indeed, the sufferings of the London poor were in no slight degree directly traceable to their own sad improvidence), the hand of England was up at the news, and her magnificent generosity again welled out, in the old free flood. Two such subscriptions have [illegible] to be made in a single year.

Nevertheless there are many, and amongst them, I know, there may be some who will read these lines, whose sympathy for doing good is still unaltered, but who, amidst the many applications for their bounty, hardly know to which request to yield. It is for those I speak; it is to them that I want to urge the claims of the National Life-boat Institution, and [illegible] to stay their hand and [illegible] in this [illegible] [illegible]. More or less, the dear old Irish ancestral has strengthened us all. More or less, it [illegible] through the [illegible] of every one of us. This [illegible] [illegible] [illegible], but [illegible] the [illegible] [illegible], and [illegible] in its [illegible]. Our dearest [illegible] have gained their glory from it. It has been the [illegible] of the [illegible] [illegible] [illegible] ever done by our race, and of the most terrible sufferings [illegible] endured. Sorrows, and [illegible], and freedom, and joy, it has brought to us from of old, and brings yet. Alas, it brings [illegible], and desolation, and despair. If I now say for myself, that the sea has given me some of my greatest joys, and has caused me one of my deepest pangs, there are thousands like me who can say the same.

And every guinea given to the Institution may help to save a Life; may not merely save the sailor himself from death, but the sailor's mother's heart from breaking, too.

I have here two little sea-pieces to place before you. In the first, you will see an English yachtsman's jollity and joy, out on the sea, sailing for pleasure and sport through bad weather as fair. In the second, you will see a little [illegible] "who had got wounded in the head and whose face was covered with blood." I have seen that face very often at night since I read the story.

It is a lovely morning in July, the morning after the Royal St. George's Regatta. Kingstown Harbour is bright and beautiful with the upper masts and snowy canvas of a whole fleet of yachts. An "ocean race" is about to begin, from Kingstown to Cork, a race that will try the mettle and the seamanship of those that take part in it. Seventeen yachts are to compete; the largest a schooner of 140 tons, the smallest a cutter of 25. At half-past ten they are off, with a fair working breeze from the North-west, and every stitch of canvas set. We—you and I, reader—are on board the Sybil, neither a [illegible] than any [illegible], but a comfortable yacht of nine-and-thirty tons. We are somewhat late in starting, for we are detained by a [illegible] that we have ordered for our [illegible]; but at last the noble fish is received on board, and when we round Wicklow Head we have made up for lost time and are in the middle of the fleet. There is rough work before us, for the wind has been drawing round off the land from North-west to West and has now settled down at South-south-west, "a regular dead noser."

There is dirty weather brewing. On and on we go, passing and outsailing other yachts, until at last the little Wild-flower alone remains to [illegible]. A fierce race it is, but at last we head her, and lead the fleet. Meanwhile, the weather has grown worse; the wind begins to [illegible], the sea rises, and the yacht "jumps like a greyhound in the slips." A rough night is before us, but we make everything fast on deck, and descend with a view to the saloon. "He appeared in fair [illegible] as he was [illegible] upon the table, but scarcely had the captain made the first [illegible] of the fish [illegible] than the little ship gave a [illegible] jump, [illegible] the saloon, with an [illegible] of the [illegible] jelly, [illegible] gentleman's shirt front and [illegible] on the nose. It and we were forced to polish him off [illegible], so [illegible] a bit of him was found, it [illegible] on the [illegible]."

And now, though the night drew on, and the darkness closed in, the little ship ran forth [illegible]. At half-past eleven the Blackwater Bank light ship "glimmered like a star through the haze of rain and wind-drift."

The full [illegible] of the Atlantic [illegible] is [illegible]. Our [illegible], from their [illegible], ought to [illegible] in such heavy weather. "Eager to hear [illegible] through the hours of darkness the [illegible] that could [illegible] the [illegible] of our [illegible]; but nought [illegible] save the howl of the [illegible] through the rigging, or the [illegible] white glare of [illegible] as we dashed it in [illegible] from the [illegible]. Dark and cold and weary were those hours, but we [illegible] our little bark was bounding along like a [illegible], breathing, living thing, frolicking with the storm as if in very [illegible]. At length an almost palpable darkness [illegible] made the [illegible] lose their intensity. [illegible] a cold [illegible] that reached the very [illegible]. The [illegible] of the storm was [illegible], colder and more [illegible], until at last it was a [illegible]—it was the dying [illegible] of the night. Up from the east [illegible] grey streaks; by and by [illegible] pillars of light [illegible] their heads above the horizon; golden [illegible] played [illegible] from wave to wave; then a great flood of glorious sunshine burst over the sea and up through the heavens; and the young day was born, as it were, in a moment. The change from that dark cold hour—thrilling in its touch as the hand of death—to the bright, life-imparting, balmy breath of morning, I shall never forget. [illegible] [illegible] seemed [illegible]. [illegible] welcome; ill-favoured cormorants [illegible], and guillemots and puffins, [illegible] themselves [illegible] the [illegible]." Now to work again. "Speedily the [illegible] the [illegible] little Sybil; her [illegible] of the night was swiftly cast aside, and as graceful [illegible] like some dainty beauty in Rotten Row, she was careering proudly over the long Atlantic swells." It was high time; for, at a few minutes past five, we [illegible] our two chief dreaded antagonists, the Kingfisher (50) and Peri (80), are visible—and a-head! Others are near us, but with these two will our last desperate struggle have to be. And now for a long day's work: we ran between the Saltee Islands with [illegible] little water; for two hours we are abreast of the Hook Tower light, near the entrance to Waterford Harbour, in a "terribly ugly cross sea," so that it is all we can do to hold our own, until at last we dash confidently "through a weak spot in the [illegible] waves," and are again away. "One second night's vigil commenced, and never was the first glint of dawn more longingly watched for. At two A.M. the wind flew round to north by west. At the first wink of daylight we discovered the Kingfisher and Peri just ahead of us. With a rattling cheer all hands were turned up, and now commenced the tug of war in right earnest; every rope and sail was overhauled, and not a precaution that could secure another inch of speed was neglected in our little ship." The contest is at length in sight: both Kingfisher and Peri are still ahead; the race seems lost. "In fact, to ordinary observers, it was all over but shouting; but we had a man at the helm who had not yet expended half his cunning lore of the sea. I have sailed many a match, but I never saw a more brilliant piece of helmsmanship in my life than on that morning. The race was won by [illegible] and [illegible]!"

Let us think—never mind the ruined [illegible], never mind the weary nights, the chopping seas, the howling winds; let behold the race is won, and behold here are the times at which we pass the flag-ship, goal of victory:

	H.	M.	S.
Sybil	5	29	0 A.M.
Peri	5	30	0 A.M.
Kingfisher	5	35	0 A.M.

We have sailed two hundred miles round the Irish coast, and we have won the [illegible] by [illegible] minutes!

I have been all the more liberal in my quotations for the reason that very few of my lady readers are at all likely to "take in" the periodical in which this fresh and graphic sketch appeared. It is a fine periodical of sport; it contains a great deal of vigorous, manly, and graceful writing, and its name is—*Bell's Life!*

I have given this sketch to illustrate one of the aspects in which the sea presents itself to us—its most pleasant and delightful aspect; with just enough of peril to spice the enjoyment. I maintain that we all like to read about races and regattas, whether we understand them or not. I am but a "land-lubber" myself, though I was never guilty of the painful impropriety of talking sea-slang (I leave that to you, sir!); but I revel in nautical books, and where their technicalities are most utterly unintelligible, my enjoyment of them rises to its highest pitch.

And now, leaving this joyous summer aspect of the sea, I have to suggest, by another sketch, the kind of scenes through which our life-boatmen pass. It is a sad, short, painful story; but, to my mind, very eloquent with the eloquence of fact. The vessel it concerns was called the "Lovely Nelly," of Seaham.

The year of grace 1861 closed in on our English north-eastern coast in storm and fury. For the two last days of the dying year a tempest had been brewing; and on New-Year's day, when we quiet city-folks were exchanging "compliments of the season," many anxious eyes were turned to seaward, and many an anxious heart grew sick as the wind rose, and rose, and still rose. Many vessels, southward-bound, put about, and had to run as far as Leith Roads for shelter. Soon after daybreak on the first of January, the coastguard men on Tynemouth Point, looking out to seaward, saw a vessel, deeply laden, with a flag of distress flying. She was struggling to get to the northward, but struggling in vain, and rapidly driving in upon the coast. The coastguardmen followed her along the shore, and, as they went on, the people of the villages turned out to join them; so that, ere long, each headland had its anxious crowd, looking, pitying, trembling. It was a very sad sight to see. The vessel's sails had mostly been blown away, and she grew more and more unmanageable amid the terrible seas that broke around and over her. At length, abandoning the desperate effort to get to the northward, her crew, as the last chance of life, ran her on the Whitley Sands. She was so deeply laden, that when she struck she was still three-quarters of a mile from the shore. It was impossible to reach her with rockets. Only one hope remained—the Life-boat! As fast as they could run through the driving wind and rain, coastguardsmen and fishermen made off for Cullercoats, where was stationed the Percy life-boat. Six horses were harnessed to her carriage, and down they came at a gallop to the sands. She was speedily manned—thank God no life-boat is ever useless for want of brave men to form her crew! The men pulled out as for their own lives, and not a moment too soon did they reach the ship, which was now broadside on to the sea, her crew in the rigging, and the waves breaking over her half-mast high. Cleverly and deftly was the life-boat laid alongside; the vessel was grappled, and the boat held to her by a strong rope. Instantly the crew made towards their deliverers; but even as they left the rigging, three of them were swept into the sea. The life-boat was handled with a glorious skill; two of the crew were at once picked up, and as the third man went down to his death a strong hand seized him, with a grasp of iron, by his hair, and dragged him up to life. Two other men were got into the boat; did any remain on board the ship? Yes; how overlooked, how [illegible] left to die, we know not—but the little cabin boy remained. The boy's cry for help grew very pitiful: "he had got wounded in the head, and was covered with blood!" One of the life-boat's crew has since said that every face could be seen white and sick, and tears rain from rough eyes like a child to chid them—"They clenched their teeth, and with their own lives in their hands" dashed in their boat to save him. The sea beat her back. They dashed in again, to be swept back once more. Again and again they tried. The poor boy, meanwhile, crying terribly in his great loneliness and despair. He was so young, and the boat was so near! But in another minute the vessel might part, and the fall of her masts would crush the life-boat. Then, making signs for him to leave going, a hoarse man gave the order, in a hoarse, broken voice, to "cast the rope!" In an instant she was swept away under the vessel's stern—not a second too soon, for at once the mainmast fell, with an awful crash, on the very spot she had just left, and the vessel parted in two. The boy—"his face was covered with blood"—fell into the sea. Clenched in agony or clasped in prayer, his little hands rose once—twice—thrice over the waves, the torrent swept away his poor boyish cry into the roar and tumult of the winds; he did not rise again. The life-boat was pulled back.

Imagine, if you can, how every heart on shore beat fast and hard, long straining to the life-boat, dashing into the surf, the men would drag her ashore; imagine, if you can, how the crowd would feel, and how the brave would bear after the lost . . . and answer me, is not such a work infinitely grand and noble? has it not somewhat special claims upon our aid?

This story is but one of many—very many. The engraving given with the present part of this magazine tells a somewhat similar tale. I have not been furnished with the exact particulars of the wreck to which it refers, and which took place near Scarborough; but the picture speaks for itself. Driving cloud, high wind, and a furious sea—a vessel rolling and labouring in her extreme need; and, cleaving through the waves with a strong, steady speed, the rough sailors, urging their life-boat to their duty . . . All these are plain enough, and all these are realities. In this very year 1867, which is but half over yet, nearly two hundred lives have been saved by the life-boats, under the management of the Institution, of which there are now a hundred and twelve, but of which there must be many more ere England can be said to have done her duty by her sailors. Miss Burdett Coutts, with that noble liberality which has made her name deservedly honoured wherever the English tongue is spoken, has given more than one life-boat herself. The maintenance of a life-boat station is one of no slight expense; it averages £50 a-year. The money paid in acknowledgment—I will not say reward—of services such as those I have described, amount to thousands of pounds. The Institution, I think, is growing in public favour, as it needs must wherever its aims are stated and understood. This pleading of mine is very weak, but stronger voices than mine will be raised again, as they have been raised before.

As a matter of business I should mention that contributions should be sent to Richard Lewis, Esq., Secretary to the National Life-boat Institution, John-street, Adelphi, London.

I would fain hope that these words of mine, being as backed by realities, may here and there do good. I have said that I appeal mainly to holiday makers. I know—how well I know!—the kind of vague, listless benevolent sentimental feelings which fill one often at the sea-side on a summer day. Here we see bright-eyed little fellows, with the keen glances that tell of clear head and brave heart—and have we not wished ourselves rich, to speed such a boy on his voyage through life? We—poets, artists, philosophers, musicians,—we have these feelings, and you also (is it not true?) you who have the worldly means of justifying such pure promptings? And, it may be, some of you, reading these lines as you rest under the cool cliff shadows, on the quiet beach—looking out dreamily over a sea so calm that these tales of tempest may seem mere stories of long ago—some of you, forced by heaven to feel that the howling of the gale over foam-crested waves may seem but a tradition; some of you, when you return to your pleasant homes, may take out that best possession of all, a cheque-book (would that you may insert the name of Richard Lewis, in that spell-enchanting volume, and if any bird of the air flies to the present writer with the tidings that you have done so, he will leap to the air with glee and clap his hands in virtuous exultation.

Modern Literary Recreations.—"In the present day, women commonly amuse themselves, and sometimes others, by works of history, or biography, or poetry, or fiction. We may find a lady writing a stupid work on navigation; another is the adventures of her age; a third immortalizes every English queen, bringing such regal interest so much to sentiment, that one can hardly avoid imagining that we have known the long dynasty in some other time. A fourth introduces to our minds intimate acquaintance with Princes of Wales that is to be kind; a host of lively [illegible] take us into Roumany; we are transported once to Bengal and back by the giddy girls; we have, too, in short, a taste, a wish, a weak sufficiency that the press does not, through an [illegible] kind of [illegible] supply. We go down at [illegible] —and to [illegible] modesty as gardening, [illegible] art. In [illegible] history [illegible]. For women of rank and [illegible] of publishing, which was generally done by [illegible] patronage, such as [illegible], [illegible], [illegible], in "some very hidden mysteries," in those of which happily, since there is now a [illegible], there was then a [illegible]. But a lady, with a vocation for scribbling, took out a sheet of letter-paper—each page [illegible], though small in size—and dipped her quill into ink—[illegible] to brave, so [illegible], in a hand not much inferior to that of any lady's maid, [illegible] on the wedding bill, indited a missive on politics, scandal, [illegible], or religion, which was [illegible] to [illegible] who could [illegible] the composition [illegible]."—The Queen of Society.

LET WELL ALONE!

BY MRS. ABDY.

"My dear friend," said Mrs. Forbes, as she entered the drawing-room of Mrs. Sandham, "I fear that something has occurred to depress your spirits, you look quite dejected to-day."

Now Mrs. Forbes expressed herself in a very flattering manner. Mrs. Sandham's countenance bore rather an unamiable than a dejected expression; in fact she looked very much as if she were sitting in a tableau vivant to represent an indignant fairy, moved to mischief by the non-arrival of a card of invitation from a crowned head!

"I am indeed much dejected," she replied in a faint tone of voice, "my dear brother has been making his will this morning, and Mr. Bailey, the solicitor, has been kindly paying me a visit to communicate its contents to me."

Mrs. Forbes privately thought that Mr. Bailey's particularly communicative disposition was scarcely a desirable qualification in his profession; however, she merely said;

"That accounts, my dear friend, for your depression; you have so much sensibility; but I doubt not you attribute dear Colonel Marston's wish to have his will made with the idea that his impaired health might suggest to him the wisdom of doing so, but really, you agitate yourself unnecessarily; the Colonel is in the prime of life; I met him in the village yesterday, and thought that I had never seen him looking so well."

"How can you make so ridiculous an assertion?" said Mrs. Sandham, raising her voice to a tone very inconsistent with the character of a nervous, anxious-minded sister; "my brother is not above forty-five years of age to be sure, but his constitution is impaired, his spirit is broken, and I do not consider his life worth two years' purchase. However," she continued, rapidly lowering her voice, "there is no use in lamenting that which is inevitable; we must all die."

"Unquestionably we must," responded Mrs. Forbes, "and the dear Colonel is doubtless aware of that fact, and has therefore judged right in making his will, to be prepared for whatever may occur."

"But he has not judged right in his manner of distributing his property," said Mrs. Sandham; "he has made an unjust will."

"Has he, indeed?" exclaimed Mrs. Forbes, "now do you know I always feared that the poor dear Colonel's excessive kindness of heart would lead him to leave a great deal of his money to public charities; he is intimate with two of the committee of the County Hospital, and our vicar, Mr. Staples, is always talking about the necessity of building a new school-house."

"You are quite wrong," said Mrs. Sandham, "my brother has left but a very small sum in charitable bequests, and you are so exceedingly unfortunate this morning in the whole tenor of your remarks, that I think it highly improbable you will be able to form any tolerable conjecture as to the manner in which he has bequeathed his property."

Somewhat mortified by this affront to her sagacity, Mrs. Forbes began to meditate as deeply as if she were endeavouring to solve a riddle in the "Family Friend." She reflected that Mrs. Sandham was in the enjoyment of a comfortable property, that she had one son, who was dependent on her, and who was "so devotedly attached to his dear uncle" that his mother had fixed herself in a pretty little ornamental cottage within five minutes walk of the residence of her brother, in order that the wish of Augustus might be gratified. Mrs. Forbes also called to mind that the Colonel possessed another nephew, who had been an orphan from his youth, he had a small patrimony of a few thousand pounds, and was an inmate of the Colonel's house. Perhaps, therefore, my readers will consider that Mrs. Forbes evinced no surpassing clairvoyance, when she said;

"I think it probable that the Colonel has equally divided his property between your dear son and young Arthur."

"And you actually have guessed the true contents of this nefarious will!" exclaimed Mrs. Sandham, "I could not have believed that anybody would have deemed my brother capable of such folly and injustice; yes, it is too true that such is the present distribution, but I shall not know rest till a new will is made."

"My dear friend," said Mrs. Forbes, "I cannot see why you should give yourself such unnecessary uneasiness; what need is there of a new will? surely it is wisest and best to 'leave well alone.'"

"It is quite evident to me," said Mrs. Sandham indignantly, "that you are bent on irritating and provoking me this morning in every possible way; are you entirely devoid of common feeling and common sense?"

Mrs. Forbes, applying a handkerchief to her eyes, sobbed out that "she hoped she was devoid of neither."

"Then, can you really think," pursued Mrs. Sandham, "that a young man like Arthur, who would be munificently provided for by a legacy of five thousand pounds, ought to be placed on an equality with one like my Augustus, qualified to spend the same number of thousands annually, and to find them very insufficient for his expenses at the end of the year?"

"To be sure," said Mrs. Forbes humbly and apologetically, "I did not think of that."

"You require somebody to teach you to think

on proud subjects," said the slightly mollified Mrs. Sandham.

"Very true, my dear friend," responded Mrs. Forbes, "and therefore I am happy to be instructed by one of your firm mind and strong point. I quite see now that it is a very urgent with so your admirable sense, but how can we get it altered? how can we get the Colonel to change his opinion of Audley?"

"I confess I do not at present see any way of doing so," said Mrs. Sandham.

"Are there no little debts or scrapes or entanglements that we might bring forward against him?" asked Mrs. Forbes.

"None that are not very slight and trivial," said Mrs. Sandham, surprised by the question into momentary candour, "and indeed less than might be brought against Augustus."

"Suppose he married a portionless girl," said Mrs. Forbes, "or one belonging to a family whom the Colonel disliked, would he not resent such an alliance?"

"I do not think he cares for riches," replied Mrs. Sandham, "or that he dislikes a person in the world excepting the lady to whom he was engaged twenty years ago, and who behaved unpardonably to him, married a cousin, and went off with her husband to India."

"I never heard any particulars of this wise condition," said Mrs. Forbes. "It has always seemed an unpleasant subject to you, my dear friend."

"Very much so," replied Mrs. Sandham, compressing her lips; "the girl was engaged to my brother, but her real preference was bestowed on a cousin of her own. This fortunate cousin was promoted unexpectedly to a good situation in India, and she then wrote to my brother, telling him that she had a great friendship for him, but that her heart was in the possession of another. I endeavoured to mediate between them, but without success; she married her cousin, and my brother afterwards forswore all love affairs lest he should meet with another fair, faithless Annette Leigh."

"Annette Leigh!" repeated Mrs. Forbes with animation.

"That is the name," said Mrs. Sandham coldly, for she was aware from long experience that Mrs. Forbes was one of those very tiresome persons who can never hear a name mentioned in society without seizing it with as much ardour and interest as if it belonged to the dearest friend they had in the world, till, at length, after a very tedious and unsatisfactory investigation, they decide that a few years ago they met at a party with a person of a similar name, only it happened to be spelt differently.

"Annette Leigh," resumed Mrs. Forbes, "was, I conclude, her maiden name; what was the name to which she changed it?"

"She never changed it at all," said Mrs. Sandham, "her cousin bore the same name."

"Then, I am convinced," exclaimed Mrs. Forbes, "that the beautiful Annette Leigh mentioned in a letter which I have just received from my friend, Mrs. Wynne, must be the daughter of the Colonel's faithless fair one. Mrs. Wynne says that the young lady who has interested her so much, was the only child of this couple in India, who returned to England two years ago, meaning to keep an expensive establishment, and to introduce their daughter to the world, but a series of misfortunes occurred. Mr. Leigh first lost his wife, then his fortune, which he had been persuaded to embark in an enormous speculation; his own death soon ensued, and Annette Leigh, left quite destitute, is now living a dependant on a bad-tempered and grudging distant relation."

"And do you imagine," asked Mrs. Sandham, who had listened to this speech with unwonted interest, "that you could easily obtain an introduction to this beautiful orphan?"

"It is all arranged that I should do so," exclaimed Mrs. Forbes with infinite delight; "you are aware that my kind friends often invite me to stay with them at Christmas."

Mrs. Sandham assented; in fact Mrs. Forbes did occasionally obtain a Christmas invitation, by dint of very plain hints about the dulness of her home, and about her facilities for making herself useful in a house full of guests; and to do her justice she performed all that she promised; she was always ready to talk to bores, amuse children, extol the accomplishments of young ladies, and make up rubbers for their mothers and aunts, in addition to which qualifications she showed aptitude for "Acted Charades," made flowers of coloured paper for decorations, and was skilful in dressing a Christmas tree.

"I am invited to stay with Mrs. Wynne at Christmas," said Mrs. Forbes, "and Mrs. Lutteridge and Annette Leigh are to be of the party."

Mrs. Sandham mused for a few moments, and then said:

"Mrs. Wynne is, I believe, acquainted with Audley."

"She is so," replied Mrs. Forbes.

"Do you think you could persuade her to invite Audley to be one of her guests?" asked Mrs. Sandham.

Mrs. Forbes paused for awhile, and then remembering that Audley was young, handsome, and that his name had just been put down as joint inheritor to a large property, she declared that she was sure Mrs. Wynne would be delighted to write him a note of invitation. "Not that I quite see, my dear friend," she said, "how this visit is to work out your plan for sowing dissension between the Colonel and his nephew."

"The results of the visit," said Mrs. Sandham, "will, I doubt not, fully effect my purpose."

After some more confidential communication, the friends separated, Mrs. Forbes having received as a present a ruby ring which she had often admired and coveted as it sparkled on the finger of her patroness; the dependant left quite satisfied with the success of her morning performance. Nevertheless, as she walked through a thick fog and drizzling rain to her little lodging in the village, she murmured to herself, "There may be faith and truly ... and ... they be objected to, and they be ..., but after all, where is the use of taking so much trouble to undo what has been so very quietly and ... done already? I must say that I think it is always the wisest way to 'let well alone.'"

* * * * *

When we last parted from Mrs. Forbes, she was wending her way under an umbrella over a muddy path in the faint light of a foggy afternoon; we meet her again in a very different scene. Arrayed in her best silk dress, and her most complacent smiles, Mrs. Forbes is sitting in an elegantly appointed and splendidly illuminated drawing-room, filled with gay guests. She sits by a beautiful and interesting young girl, whom she often eyes with admiration, but very seldom addresses; it is quite evident that she sits there in "play propriety," lest the engrossed young man constantly whispering in the ear of the beauty should be suspected by the company to be privately making love to her.

A precocious little girl, kept up unpardonably beyond the proper time, passes close to Mrs. Forbes, and she eagerly detains her, anxious that the lovers should feel themselves quite sure that they are unwatched. Mrs. Forbes attempts to talk about magic lanterns, and is rebuked by an account of the Colonial microscope at the Polytechnic; she endeavours to converse on the leading incidents in the lives of Rosamond, and Cinderella, but is sternly rebuked by quotations from the History of England which she is unable to answer; the juvenile prodigy inwardly opines that the cultivation of the mind might have been much neglected in the days of old, and passes along to a quiet corner where she overhauls a chess-table, having previously remarked that "she considers chess to be a very intellectual recreation."

Anon, an expedition to the music-room is proposed, the beautiful girl is eagerly seized on by half-a-dozen [illegible], and borne away from the drawing-room, followed by her attendant cavalier.

Mrs. Forbes then crosses the room, and takes her seat by Mrs. Lutteridge, an exceedingly peevish looking, unprepossessing old lady. Mrs. Forbes forthwith launches eloquent on the grace and beauty of Annette Leigh, and inquires if she resembles her mother, to which Mrs. Lutteridge replies that she is her living image. Mrs. Forbes compliments Mrs. Lutteridge on her generosity in taking charge of the destitute orphan, and Mrs. Lutteridge snappishly replies that she sacrifices a few luxuries to enable her to do so, but that she has the consciousness of doing her duty; which has always been her first aim and consideration through life. Mrs. Forbes highly extols this delightful sentiment; and ventures to hint that Mrs. Lutteridge is not likely long to retain the society of Miss Leigh, since an eligible match, the favourite nephew of a wealthy bachelor, is evidently waiting her acceptance. Mrs. Lutteridge meekly replies that we ought to be willing to part with our dearest companions if it be for their own interests that we should do so; and, warming with the subject, professes her readiness to accompany Miss Leigh to the altar at the shortest possible notice, provided only that the match be an unexceptionable one.

All at present seems smooth and cloudless in regard to the courtship of Audley and Annette Leigh, and Mrs. Forbes indites a long letter that night to her friend Mrs. Stapleton, "reporting progress," and hinting at the merits of her own exertions in bringing about such a happy state of affairs. Mrs. Forbes retires to rest, but somehow her dreams are not so satisfactory as might be anticipated; she hears wedding bells, but they sound discordantly in her ears, and she beholds the form of Mrs. Stapleton trampling on a wedding favour, [illegible] consolation to administer to her than to say: "It would have been better my dear friend, if you had taken my advice, and been content to 'let well alone!'"

A week elapsed, and the Christmas party broke up, but great events had occurred in the interim. Audley had proposed for Annette Leigh, and been blushingly accepted by herself, and graciously by Mrs. Lutteridge. The knot hinged at the approbation of Colonel Marston, but Audley assured her that the recommendations of person, mind, manners, and disposition possessed by Annette were quite sufficient to insure her a favourable reception from his uncle. Mrs. Forbes warmly congratulated Audley on his happiness, and said that she concluded he would not write to his uncle on the subject of his engagement since he was so shortly to see him in person; and Audley, who possessed that dislike to letter-writing which I suspect [illegible] in any one's character, coincided in her opinion; and, when he wrote three lines to the Colonel, mentioning the period of his return, did not warn him of any interesting information which he intended to communicate. Mrs. Stapleton was therefore left quite at liberty to sow the seeds of evil in the mind of her brother; and the day before that named for Audley's return she called on the Colonel, with sorrow on her brow and triumph in her eye, to enlighten him as to the proceedings of his nephew.

I must now introduce my readers to Colonel Marston, who was remarkably handsome and prepossessing in appearance, insomuch that certainly "the wish was father to the thought" in his sister's mind when she said that "she would not give two years purchase for his life." Colonel Marston's countenance was thoughtful and intelligent, and his manners grave and calm. An [illegible] writer observes, that "Life is a succession of lesser links"; but the Colonel had undergone one great disappointment in the discovery of Annette Leigh's falsehood, and had lived a very quiet life ever since. Many wondered that so highly-endowed a man as the Colonel should not reside in London, and gather around him all the literary celebrities of the age. But he replied that he had gathered them round him already, and made out his theory, in my opinion, very ingeniously. But Colonel Marston considered notwithstanding as the most gifted persons of the day, I can hardly think that in any occasion he could have mustered at his house a bevy of divines, philosophers, scientific men, historians, biographers, poets, dramatists, and novelists of the first order of merit; and I also greatly doubt that even the portion of them whom he might have succeeded in collecting would have shown themselves retiring, unobtrusive, putting forth their brilliant abilities when drawn out, and contentedly retiring into the back-ground at the will of their entertainer, guiltless of all rivalry with each other, and satisfied either to remain with their host through the "small hours," or to "go at eleven" like the abstemious guests of the methodical Dr. Kitchener. Yet all this excellent society did the Colonel gather round him at pleasure, because he possessed an admirable library.

Happy is the man who has a taste for books. Pope said: "As much company as I have kept, and as much as I love it, I love reading better. I would rather be employed in reading than in the most agreeable conversation." And her "fair foe," Lady Mary Wortley Montague, remarks: "No entertainment is so cheap as reading, nor any pleasure so lasting."

I might multiply quotations on the subject, but Mrs. Sandham is entering the library, and the bitter, mocking, chilling spirit of the world comes with her. "I am sorry, my dear brother," she said, "to tell you that I am the bearer of unwelcome news. It relates to the conduct of your favourite nephew, Audley."

Colonel Marston, laying down Tennyson's "Maud," with a half-sigh, replied, "You are fond, Louisa, of alluding to Audley as my favourite nephew; I assure you that I have quite as great a regard for your son; and, if you knew all, you would be fully satisfied of the reality of my impartiality."

Poor Colonel Marston; he little thought how much his sister knew, or how far she was from being satisfied with the knowledge she had obtained.

"I am fully aware of your kindness, my dear brother," said the affectionate sister, "and am sorry that it should be wasted on an ungrateful object. Has Audley mentioned in his letter to you that he is engaged to be married to a penniless girl, to whom he has lately been introduced?"

"He mentioned nothing of the kind," said the Colonel; "and I doubt not that a country-house flirtation has been magnified by idle rumour into a serious engagement."

"Far from it," said Mrs. Sandham. "Our worthy friend, Mrs. Forbes, assures me of the fact; and I grieve to add, that the young lady is one whom you will deem a decidedly objectionable connexion."

"As I am not conscious," said the Colonel, coldly, "of having any peculiar aversions among 'the rosebud garden of girls,' I must beg you to be more explicit."

"Have you not received a serious and cruel injury at the hands of a woman?" asked Mrs. Sandham.

"You allude, of course, to Annette Leigh?" said the Colonel, with a perceptible change of countenance; "but I am at a loss to conceive how the subject of my nephew's choice can be connected with her."

"The false Annette Leigh of your early affections is no more," said Mrs. Sandham; "but she survives in her daughter: a second Annette Leigh—designing, calculating and subtle as the first—has ensnared the heart of our poor nephew! It is yet in your power to save him. Let it be understood that all his hopes of inheriting any part of your property will be blighted by his marriage, and you may rely upon it that the mercenary Annette will immediately discard him."

Mrs. Sandham left the room, and Colonel Marston felt no inclination to resume the reading of "Maud"; a more potent spell was upon him than that of the poet's lay. Memory waved her wondrous wand; again he gazed upon the beautiful Annette Leigh, and listened to her assurance of affection. Anon his sister warned him of a rival, the power of her youth [illegible] on his account. He disbelieved the tale, till at length the [illegible] being excited by a [illegible] appointment, and the Colonel received a letter from Annette, declaring her return to her first love. His sister condoled with him, and suggested that Annette might already have repented of her letter—he had written reproachfully and vehemently in reply to it. His sister enclosed the letter written within one of her own, couched in a strain of milder remonstrance, and sent it to Annette. Neither received any answer. Annette married in haste, married her cousin, and went to India. All these images came like a melancholy dissolving view before the eyes of the Colonel; the smooth current of his life was suddenly disturbed; Annette Leigh seemed to have returned to haunt him—his warm-hearted, unsuspecting nephew was to be the victim of a scheming coquette, trained in artifice by a deceptive mother; till at length the consoling reflection came to him that Audley was yet unmarried, and that it was not too late to save him.

Poor Audley! he arrived at home the next day, anticipating a delightful interview with his uncle, in which he should dilate on the perfections of his beloved, describe her eyes and hair, and her songs and drawings, extol her temper and principles, declare that she was a fortune in herself, predict that he was about to become the happiest man in existence, and, in short, give vent to all the abstracted fooleries of the accepted lover. Little did he think of the storm of anger with which his "marvellous pleasant love-story" was fated to be received.

The anger of habitually mild and self-controlled persons has always something startling in it; and Audley had never witnessed any of the ebullitions of irritability with which the nephews of rich uncles are in general familiar. His youthful faults had always been reproved in the kindest manner; and he had never received any warnings against falling in love with a portionless beauty, since, as we have already shown, the Colonel did not consider a handsome fortune on both sides to be at all a necessary ingredient in matrimonial felicity.

Poor Audley! he heard the gentle, modest Annette Leigh designated as an artful adventuress! He heard the good and tender mother, of whom Annette had spoken to him with tears, represented as the most base and treacherous of women. No wonder that he retaliated with violence. The threat of disinheritance was held out by the Colonel; and Audley, when he quitted him, did what he had never thought of doing on any other occasion—he sought the advice of his aunt, Mrs. Sandham. She was very kind and soothing to him; said that his uncle was perceptibly breaking in health, which was sufficient to account for his unusual irritability; and that when Audley was once married, there would be no doubt that forgiveness would be very soon extended to him. Mrs. Sandham praised Annette Leigh, whom she said her friend Mrs. Forbes had described as truly charming and amiable; and she concluded by advising Audley to absent himself for the present, when she would undertake to restore the Colonel into a better and kinder frame of mind. Audley thanked her warmly, and wondered how he could ever have suspected her to be addicted to double-dealing and mischief-making.

Audley immediately returned to London, and took up his abode at an hotel in the neighbourhood of Wilton Crescent, where Mrs. Lattridge resided. His visit to the ladies proved less agreeable to each party than had been anticipated. He considerably softened the disapprobation of the Colonel, entirely omitted all mention of Annette Leigh's mother, and intimated that "the good old gentleman's views" of marriage, from which he had hoped his marriage [illegible] quite [illegible] had begun to throw his influence over him, and caused him to object to Annette's want of fortune; but that he trusted a very short time would work a change in his sentiments; and that he felt sure that, when his uncle once knew Annette, he would admire and love her.

Annette felt grieved and hurt, but she encouraged her lover to hope for better times. Mrs. Lattridge was angry and mortified; she had expected Audley to begin to talk about the drafts of the marriage settlement, and was in no mood to listen to the objections of mercenary uncles. Besides, although she never treated Annette Leigh herself with respect or kindness, she did not choose her to be ill-treated by any one else; and she considered that any one who had the honour of being a relative of her own ought to be received with open arms by any family. She did not, however, wish entirely to put aside all chance of this eligible match for Annette; but she signified to Audley that, although she should be happy to see him as an occasional visitor at her house, with other friends, he must not expect, under existing circumstances, to be admitted there on the footing of an affianced lover. Consequently Audley went there, by invitation, about once a week, and suffered bitterly under the torments of ennui in the intervals of the visits. Audley had not, like his uncle, a taste for musing. He was entirely dependent on society; he had been accustomed to it, and felt it to be a necessary of existence. He was one of [illegible] his friends in London, and soon began to accept every invitation and join in every party of pleasure that came before him. Audley had the very silly and dangerous habit of talking about his private affairs to every one whom he considered deserving of the appellation of "a good fellow;" and to several of these [illegible] individuals he imparted his engagement to Annette Leigh, and his uncle's disapprobation of it. He was unanimously advised "not to make a victim of himself;" the troubles of a poverty-stricken ménage were graphically depicted to him; he was told that "he was the last man in the world fitted to marry on two hundred a-year," the amount of his paternal income, and he laughingly acknowledged the truth of the impeachment. Then a pretty young heiress whom he had frequently met in society, and who had always behaved to him with frozen reserve, showed symptoms of a thaw in her manner, and Audley began to think that he had parted with his heart to Annette Leigh on too short a notice, and to reprobate the [illegible] and [illegible] of Christmas parties, and country-houses.

Mrs. Sandham had her spies in London, who informed her of her nephew's way of [illegible] the lonely hours which he was doomed to pass away from Annette Leigh; she trembled for the success of her plans, it was evident that the flame of affection was beginning to burn very faintly in the heart of the wavering lover of the beautiful Annette. Mrs. Sandham, however, like a spider, when she saw one of her webs demolished, immediately began to spin another. Annette corresponded with Mrs. Forbes, and to her had [illegible]. Mrs. Sandham immediately suggested that Mrs. Forbes should invite Annette to stay with her in the country. Audley might then return to his uncle's house, and enjoy daily interviews with Annette. Mrs. Sandham had no fear that the Colonel should hear of Annette's residence in his neighbourhood; his secluded habits and reserved manners placed him entirely out of the sphere of village gossip. Constant intercourse between the lovers, Mrs. Sandham thought, was the only way of [illegible] "the lamp of love into a [illegible] flame."

The invitation was given, and Annette accepted it with pleasure, for not being at all aware of the strength of the Colonel's objections to her, she imagined that it had probably been given at his desire, and that he was eager to become acquainted with her, and to judge whether she was likely to conduce to the happiness of his nephew. Mrs. Lutteridge viewed the matter in the same light, and graciously permitted Annette to accept of the invitation. All were pleased with the arrangement, except Audley, but as he saw that it was taken for granted that he should be pleased, he contrived to put on the semblance of satisfaction.

Mrs. Needham busied herself in adorning the apartment destined for Miss Leigh; she bestowed with unbounded liberality books, plants, ottomans, and knick-knacks on her niece-elect, and Annette, who was told by Mrs. Forbes on her arrival, that these offerings were arranged by Mrs. Needham's own hands, and sent from her own house, felt grateful for her attentions, and rejoiced to think that she might depend on one friend in the family.

It had been arranged that on the day after Annette's arrival in the village, Audley should return to his uncle's house, and Mrs. Needham contrived to be with her brother during a great part of the day, that she might exert herself in preventing that temporary pique between the uncle and nephew, which she hoped would soon be visible in them.

Audley did not arrive on that day. Two more days elapsed, and he was vainly expected. Annette feared for his health, Mrs. Needham for his stability, and Mrs. Forbes, who had hoped to receive much gratitude and some pretty presents from the lovers brought together by her means, felt herself in a false position, having a Juliet in her abode, and lacking a Romeo to come and court her.

On the fifth day, Mrs. Forbes sallied forth to call on her friend Mrs. Needham, and unburden herself in vain conjectures as to what possibly could be the reason of Audley's strange conduct. She had scarcely departed when the postman, "messenger of grief to thousands and of joy to some," arrived at the door. He was truly a messenger of grief to poor Annette. She received a letter from Audley, in which, after a number of flowery phrases, protestations of unchanged affection, and declarations that a very dark cloud was about to hang over the rest of his existence, he avowed that "although poverty had no terrors for himself, he could not endure the idea of seeing the object of his affections suffer from it, and therefore, with a breaking heart, he gave her back her truth."

Annette was deeply wounded and hurt by this letter; she had too much good sense to be deceived by the protestations of the writer that he was actuated in his views entirely from a consideration of her advantage; she now at once saw that she had inspired merely a brief and ephemeral passion, which required the sunshine of prosperity to keep it alive, and which drooped and died in the first chill blast of adversity. Annette was much to be pitied, she had no true friend with whom to counsel, no peaceful home in which to seek a retreat; she felt herself alone in the world, and remained an unconsenting [illegible] acquaintance and inmate of Mrs. Lutteridge, who was the only person on whose protection she had any claim.

When people are in trouble their first wish is generally to breathe the open air, and although it was the month of February, the sun shone forth as brightly, and the breezes blew as softly as if they were coaxing the world a premature morning visit. Annette Leigh took her way slowly and sadly to a little copse which she had visited the preceding day with Mrs. Forbes, and was approaching a rustic bench, when, perceiving that it was already occupied, and unwilling to encounter the observation of a stranger, she glanced on. Little, however, had she calculated on the effect that her appearance was to produce, had she been a spirit from the other world, she could not have excited a greater sensation in the mind of the occupant of the seat, who, hastily starting up, and extending his arm as if he wished to ascertain whether she were indeed a phantom of the air, tremblingly uttered the words—"Annette Leigh!"

Annette was astonished and indignant, she had no idea that the handsome, gentlemanly man, in the prime of life, who stood before her, could possibly be Audley's uncle, Audley having represented his relative as an old and decrepit man, and assured the relations of Mrs. Needham that "his brother's life was not worth two years' purchase!" Annette, like most ill-used persons, was disposed to fancy that every one was in a combination against her, and she imagined that the speaker was a friend of Audley's who took advantage of her deserted and friendless position to insult her; she therefore turned away from him, with much such a look of mingled sorrow and reproach as Helena in the "Midsummer Night's Dream" might have been supposed to have worn, when she said to Lysander,

> "Oh! that a lady of one man refused,
> Should of another, therefore, be abused!"

"Annette Leigh!" exclaimed Colonel Marston, "I conjure you to stay, I come again to gaze upon your mother: scarcely can I wonder that my nephew should have been infatuated with the fresh charms that worked such woe to myself."

"If your strange and mistaken speech," said Annette, with cold severity, "arises from the belief of your nephew's engagement to me, I can relieve your mind from all anxiety. I hold in my hand a letter received from him this morning, in which he bids me farewell for ever. But in regard to my late mother—the best, the kindest, and the most highly-principled of women—I can only say, in reply to your brutal allusion to her, that I consider it my greatest honour and privilege to be her daughter."

"I would that I could feel she had been innocent and faithful," said the Colonel; "but to you—to her daughter—she, of course, never mentioned the name of her injured lover."

"She never mentioned your name to me," said Annette; "but she once told me that, under the influence of misconception and wounded pride, she had broken off all intercourse with her first lover, under mysterious circumstances; and that she regretted afterwards she had not searched into them more closely."

"Little as I deserve it of you, Annette," said the Colonel, "I trust you will not refuse to reveal these circumstances to me."

"My mother," said Annette, "was on intimate terms with the married sister of her lover; from this lady she once received a letter, written kindly and affectionately, regretting that she was obliged to inform one from her brother, couched in terms of harsh and bitter reproach, and offering her services as a mediator on the occasion. My mother was shocked and surprised at her lover's letter, which appeared to allude to a/the communication, [illegible] by herself, of her preference for another; she immediately replied to it, assuring him that he must be labouring under a misconception, for that her affections were his alone; she enclosed this letter in one to his sister, who told her, in reply, that her brother had scarcely read through the letter when he destroyed it, and declared that he would never read another line written by one so false and treacherous. The sister insinuated that she had too much reason to fear that her brother had sought this conclusion to give an excuse for his own inconstancy. All intercourse ceased between the parties, and my mother's cousin, who had long loved her in secret, and for whom she felt the most esteem and friendship, now asked for her hand, and the union took place very shortly, in consequence of the necessity of proceeding to India. The marriage proved a very happy one; but my mother related these circumstances of her early life to me to caution me to abstain from forming hasty conclusions under the influence of offended pride. The cold indifference shown to her by her lover's sister after the termination of the engagement, and some derogatory and unkind remarks uttered by her, which had been officiously repeated by an acquaintance of both parties, having led her to suppose that the sister had probably had a great share in producing the quarrel which she professed to deplore and undertook to reconcile."

"It was entirely her own cruel work," exclaimed the Colonel. "Annette, I can clear myself in your opinion, I can show you that I am entitled rather to your pity than your blame."

Long and interesting was the conversation that ensued between the Colonel and his restored Annette Leigh, for such he persisted in thinking and calling her. He did not oppose her determination to return to London the next day, but said that he would write to Mrs. Luttridge, and spare her all the pain of an explanation.

Annette did not confide to Mrs. Elwin any of the events of the day, but merely expressed her thanks to her for her hospitality, and her wish to return home the next morning. Poor Annette! she had anything but "home sweet home" in her thoughts, when with a trembling step, downcast eyes, and throbbing heart, she entered the drawing-room in Wilton Crescent; but she had no reason to fear an unpleasant reception; the post had arrived before her, and Mrs. Luttridge had received Colonel Marston's letter.

What could that mysterious letter have contained? not only did it still Mrs. Luttridge's tongue on the subject of Audley, but it made her positively liberal and smiling. Annette was treated as a relative, presented with new dresses, and consulted on every subject. Had an enchanter been at work? yes, the greatest of all enchanters—money! The Colonel in his letter to Mrs. Luttridge had announced that he had recognised in Annette Leigh the daughter of one who had formerly been very dear to him, that he should henceforth consider her as his own adopted daughter, and while truly thankful that she enjoyed the protection of Mrs. Luttridge's roof, could only consent to her remaining there, by her kind relative agreeing to receive from him a yearly sum in consideration of her expenses.

What that yearly sum might be Mrs. Luttridge never told anybody, but doubtless it was with her entire approbation, for she returned a most courteous letter to Colonel Marston, extolling his generosity to her dear Annette, and hoping to have the honour of a visit from him whenever he came to town.

A year has elapsed, and many events have occurred in the course of it. Colonel Marston, after parting with Annette, had a long and distressing interview with Mrs. Sandham, in which she confessed that she had herself imitated the handwriting of Annette Leigh in the letter purporting to declare her affection for another; she maintained that she was actuated by the best intentions, feeling convinced that Annette could never make her brother happy; but in fact she had determined that her son should inherit the property of his uncle, and could not endure the idea that it should descend to children of his own.

Mrs. Sandham felt that after this discovery of her treachery, the neighbourhood of her brother was no longer a fitting residence for her; she repaired to London to meet Augustus, who had just arrived from a foreign tour, but, alas! the meeting was far from being an agreeable one.

Augustus had been welcomed to England by a host of Christmas bills, showing that he had been far outdoing his usual doings in the way of extravagant expenditure. All application to his rich uncle was of course out of the question. Mrs. Sandham paid the bills, and is now residing with her son at a cheap town on the Continent.

Audley is married. As soon as he had written his farewell letter to Annette Leigh, he wrote another letter, offering his hand and heart to the pretty heiress. She referred him to her uncle and guardian, who was the very kindest of uncles and guardians, giving his consent the minute it was asked for, showing no curiosity as to Audley's fortune, and saying nothing about the property of his niece being settled on herself; he was a silvery-haired, courteous old gentleman, and Audley was quite delighted with him. The marriage soon took place, but the honey-moon of the young couple was darkened and clouded [illegible] in its first quarter.

The name of his silvery-haired, courteous old gentleman appeared in the list of bankrupts, and the whole property of his niece [illegible] was absorbed in the crash. Audley therefore has been compelled to do what his friends and himself destined him to be so well fitted for—namely, to begin married life on an income of two hundred a-year.

Annette Leigh has become the wife of Colonel Marston. Shortly after his first acquaintance with her, he took a fancy to spend much of his time in London, and availed himself amply of Mrs. Lambridge's invitations to her house. He soon discovered that Annette Leigh was yet more charming than her mother, and Annette discovered that he was much better suited to her than his nephew would have been, even had the latter realised her first opinion of him.

The misanthropy of the Colonel has passed away, and he is delighted to accompany his charming bride into society. Colonel and Mrs. Marston treat Mrs. Forbes with kindness, justly considering that in her part she was merely the weak tool of the artful Mrs. Sandham. Indeed, Mrs. Forbes was never so happy in her life as at the present time. She had hitherto always entertained the misgiving that her friends considered her as a somewhat common-place person, with but a moderate portion of judgment and foresight; but now, that she has spread abroad through the village the history of Mrs. Sandham's dissatisfaction with her brother's will, and her own wise advice to her to "let well alone," she finds that her character for a prudent counsellor is established on excellent grounds.

It must be allowed, however, that Mrs. Forbes, like the author of a single speech, or the author of a single work, rather wears out the subject of her own cleverness, and sometimes introduces it at unseasonable times; the most uncompromising adherents to old fashions and customs, merely on account of their antiquity, could not have a greater horror of improvements than is felt and expressed by Mrs. Forbes; and if any of her village friends contemplate quitting their house to live in a better, exchanging their pony-chaise for a close carriage, or removing their children from an indifferent to a superior school, let them never venture to mention the subject to Mrs. Forbes—their communication will be sure to be met with the oracular response "Let Well Alone!"

THE VALE OF SHREWSBURY.

BY JOHN RANDALL.

A little more than a mile below Welsh Pool is Buttington; the battle-ground of Dane and Saxon, in King Alfred's time. Here the hardy Northmen, in their retreat before Alfred's generals, were brought to bay; and, in attempting to cut their way through the lines of the besieging army, met with severe slaughter at the hands of the Saxons, "aided by the sons of Powis." Buttington lies pleasantly at the foot of the Long Mountain, which terminates there, after having accompanied the river some miles along its eastern bank. It attains an elevation at the "Welsh-harp," above Buttington, of 1,200 feet above the sea, and is celebrated as the scene of some Border feuds. The Welsh who call it Mynydd, or Cefn Digoll, point to an old camp, near here, as the one where the heroes of the declining star of Cambria made a last stand against the collected force of the Lords Marchers, for the independence of the principality, but were overcome by the oppressors of their country in the year 1294. Descending its western slope, which is marked higher up by ancient tumuli, is that singular earthwork and bi-national monument of former times, known as Offa's Dyke. It continues its course past Buttington church in the direction of the river, where it is crossed, its followers coming up on either side the Briedden hills, dividing the two countries it was designed to separate.

There is something interesting in this old mud-wall, running over hill and dipping into valleys, and we followed it in its northerly direction across the Morda, to Llan-y-Blodwel—where it becomes quite a landmark, thence past Chirk Castle to the Dee, where it diminishes to a thread. Speed says that it was a barrier to separate the Welsh from the English, designed by Offa; adding, that a law was made by Egfrid at the instigation of his wife, that it should be present death for the Welsh to pass over this dyke; and that later under Harold, whilst it was ordained that what Welshman soever should be found with any weapon on that side of the limit should have his right hand cut off by the king's officers.

It is not often that in nature bordering on

what, otherwise, may appear a myth, or a little bit of fairy land, that history sheds such light on tradition; or that both are so closely confirmed by fact. Welsh writers, however, question the popular opinion founded upon the three—the legend, the historic statement, and the fact; and ask you, were their fathers pigmies, that they could be shut out by a wall of mud, or ought a fence stretching from sea to sea across the island be watched or made to bristle with spears. Without altogether denying the fact that this remarkable earthwork was the work of the distinguished Mercian King whose name it bears, they contend that it was an international line of demarcation, the mutual work of the two nations. Either way, as we see it climbing the hills and dipping into the valleys, or stretching its slow length across the plain, it is to lovers of antiquity an eloquent and significant memorial of times gone by, and one which, by pointing to the site of the ancient [illegible], serves to revive scenes and associations connected with an interesting phase of [illegible] history. And now that the whole nation is [illegible] and looking back to gather strength from a review of its eventful struggles, it seems strange that progress and agricultural improvements should lay hands upon it to mutilate it; still more so that it should be the victim of the spade upon the estate of a nobleman who is president of an Archæological Association.

Parallel with it, between the Severn and the Dee, is another ancient monument of the kind, called Watt's Dyke; and upon the right bank of the Severn, as it descends, is an old [illegible] bank raised against the encroaches of the latter by the monks of the Abbey of Strata Marcella. This monastery, which has entirely disappeared, was subject to the monks of Buildwas, on the river lower down, and was founded by a pious Welshman who gave "to God, and the Virgin his mother, and the monks for the good of his soul," the rich meadows we see before us, along the sunny banks of the vale. It is one of the most productive spots in the two counties, consequent upon the overflowings of the Severn which enrich the fat meadows, like the Nile, and which, heretofore, have given an alluvium to the fields that enables them to reproduce harvests of rich ripe grain many years in succession.

Above this alluvial flat, mapped out by hedge-rows, the familiar forms of the Breidden hills present themselves. Like the Wrekin and the Malverns, they are conspicuous for many miles along the river's course. You see them from its source, and from many minor eminences on its banks, their aspects changing as the point of vision varies. They consist of the Moel-y-Golfa, the Middletown, Bulthy, Bausley, Criggion, and Rodney's Pillar hills, together with several minor ones. The resemblance of the former to Vesuvius has often been remarked, and the conical outlines of others when seen from a distance are no less striking. The most imposing from the river, to which it presents a bluff imposing front, is the true Breidden, or Rodney's Pillar hill, so called from its summit being surmounted by a column commemorative of the victories of Lord Rodney over Admiral Count de Grasse. It was evidently the focus of that volcanic action which gave birth to the granite, and the centre of that igneous disturbance which elevated large tracts of country, of which the rounded summits of Moel Cliff, Pen Hill, and the magnificent ridges of Breidden stone, with their mineral veins of copper and cobalt, are results.

Like the Wrekin and the Malverns, they afford evidence of distinct periods of origination; the grey limestone to the West, indicating that the inhabitants of the sea in which they were then laid, were destroyed by sudden outbursts of volcanic matter; and the red sandstones to the East showing that they were elevated and thrown into their present position long afterwards. Their geological features may be studied in several quarries on the hills; and the [illegible] which their upheaval produced at points in the direction of Welsh Pool—where they have upheaved the Silurian rocks and exposed the two divisions of the system, one on either side. Rude stone walls and earth-works upon their summits intimate that they have also witnessed rival conflicts of human passion, of which others of these Welsh Alps have been the theatres; those upon the Rodney's Pillar, the Cefn Castell, and Bausley hills, being the strongest, and the others merely entrenchments. They are said to have formed the favourite resort of "Cymbria's Eagle Chief," Owen Glendwr; and their geographical position, with respect to the river and its fords, favours the view taken by some writers, that they may have been the scene of the great struggle between Ostorius and Caractacus. Mr. Hartshorne, whom we have quoted in favour of the claims of Caer Caradoc to this honour, admits the strong grounds archæologians have for fixing upon this spot. That the stern discipline of Mars were not unsuitable to the [illegible] of the position, may be imagined, from the writings of a bard and warrior of the twelfth century, who, stationed all night to watch one of the passages of the river, thus expressed himself:

> "I watched through the night with care, to guard the fords,
> Where the [illegible] waters [illegible] murmur in the fords of [illegible]:
> The green hillsides which bear a brighter green, have felt the stream,
> And are never playful on their even banks,
> With painted pictures gliding at their ease in [illegible] groups."

Their summits command fine views of the Severn and its tributaries, of the green livery of their sunny vales, dotted with homesteads and hamlets, and bounded by an amphitheatre of hills—sharp and clear in outline against the azure sky. They form the outworks of the Welsh line of Alps, the natural, [illegible] fortresses of the ancient Cymry, that guard the entrance to the inland vale beyond them. The botanist who may undertake the task of scaling the highest crag will find around its horizon (Potentilla rupestris), a plant, we believe, not known in any locality nearer than Cologne; and around the pillar which crowns its summit [illegible].

Near the foot of this remarkable group of lofty hills, the pretty little bridge of Llandrinio crosses the Severn; beyond it is Llandysilio, and still further on in the same direction Llanymynech. The latter name, in Welsh, signifies the village of miners; and that from very early times the hills have been perforated for lead and other metals, appears probable, from the primitive tools and ancient relics found in old workings; the latter including coins of Antoninus and other Roman Emperors. It is said that in a cave called Ogo, a bracelet of gold, some human remains, a Druid's belt, and a battle-axe have been found; and that the caverns, which extend some distance, present interesting appearances, from stalactites pendent from the roof. At Abertanad, the river Tanad falls into the Vyrnwy; and the latter, with the increased tribute it receives, enters the Severn, amid the rich pastures near Melverley. When heads fail the two rivers mingle their waters without turmoil or a sigh; but, at other times, when heavy rains have fallen along the banks of the Tanad or the Vyrnwy, the latter comes down with a rush, and boldly thrusts back the "Queen of rivers" along its side; then it collects its waters, and again returns to battle with its rival. [illegible] with the strife between Line and Shrewsbury, [illegible] the Severn or its tributaries by the colour of the River which it waters, the water being charged with sediment corresponding with the soil it passes in its course.

Below, where the Severn and the Vyrnwy meet, we feel bound to remind us that we are still upon the Borders, and amid the great Marches of Wales. Old fortresses and feudal strongholds are thickly sown, so much so that Fuller says, "Shropshire stands divided from Wales by a wall of continued castles." Churches are dedicated to warrior saints. War and religion then were paramount; fighting men and priests—those of stone, brass, and carving effigies—arranged in richer warlike guise. Spots where men agreed to drag and pray were marked; so that together or alone, even murderers, a crowning the bounds of the marches, obtained protection from their pursuers, as at Alberbury, where traditional superstition [illegible] Welshmen charged with murder found asylum till released by the [illegible] in time of war. Men also fought, and then founded monasteries to atone for sin. Like old Fitzwarin, who, as old chronicle states, "upon returning from [illegible] was in Ireland, and thinking that he had sinned by the slaughter of much people, sought remission of his sins by founding a priory in a wood on the river Severn." Of the old castle of Fitzwarin, at Alberbury, a portion of the walls alone remains; while Wattlesborough, another Border stronghold near, has been reduced to an old square tower and some portions of its wings.

There were but a few of the fortified houses held by Lords Marchers, who, from the difficulty of reaching the Welsh in their mountain fastnesses by means of large armies, it was found good policy to locate at once and hold by their retainers, as their own, lands along the borders. The more to encourage them to conquest, they were given a voice in Parliament, with their significant of the districts they subdued. In return for these possessions and privileges, they rendered military service to the crown—such as that of keeping their castles sufficiently fortified to withstand the Welsh, and of furnishing the King's army, in time of war, with men. There were at one time 134 of these lordships, with military governments, and customs so strange, that offenders in one would often find impunity in another, and escape the punishment due to crime. With such singularly fortified positions, and [illegible] by war and hardship, these feudal barons of the Marches were among the most powerful of the nobility, and their names stand prominent in history.

The local government of these districts continued in the hands of these men long after the circumstances which were supposed to warrant it had passed away. Alberbury is the property of Sir Baldwyn Leighton, whose present residence is Loton, a mansion pleasantly situated amid ancestral trees, and where the Sovereign George IV., when Prince of Wales, [illegible] to visit the country whence he derived his title, walked a mile from Loton Hall into the principality, and, having plucked a branch of oak, which he placed in his hat, returned. The [illegible], however, [illegible] to feel flattered by this short visit, and made due demonstrations accordingly. The bed of oaks, [illegible] carefully guarded, and a brass plate affixed to record the circumstance for the benefit of posterity. This parish is noted as having been the birthplace of Old Parr, who lived to the extreme age of 152.

Lower down the river is [illegible], the [illegible] of the Romans. Grey rocky terraces appear upon the slope, and the building itself is thrown into relief by a dark, sombre background of trees.

Leaving [illegible] we cross the river, attracted by the wild-looking ruins of Shrawardine. A shady lane, between banks of gravel, [illegible] the ferry to the village. The church, which is an ancient structure with a wooden tower, contains some brass and marble memorials, and a curious old font. Its proximity to the castle seems to have been anything but an advantage, as it appears, from an old parish register, to have suffered severely during the different sieges of the fortress. The crumbling remains of the old castle, which occupy a field opposite to the church, fitly symbolise the times when the country was wasted by Border wars. Raised to check the encroachments of the Welsh upon the fertile lands of the interior, many grants in aid of its repairs were made during successive reigns; and ten [illegible] were held, in the early part of the 13th century, on condition of service rendered in defending it. It was a Royal castle up to the year 1215; afterwards it came into the hands of the FitzAlans, and passed by purchase to Sir T. Bromley, in 1583.

Below Shrawardine, right and left of the river, are the villages of Ford and Montford, consisting of small clusters of houses and homesteads, whose populations have remained pretty much the same for centuries. We passed through Montford without seeing a single soul, excepting one old man, who was lame. It was during a sunny interval in the wet summer of 1860, and we imagine the entire population had gone into the fields to make hay. A farmer, whom we met afterwards, resting on his pitchfork, told us that the bold projecting mass of stone upon the adjoining hills reminded him of a load of hay; to Sir R. Murchison and others it conveyed a very different impression, namely, that of a ruined city. Montford bridge, one of the passages of the Severn, of great importance during the international disputes and quarrels of the Borders, is famous for being a parley between the representatives of the two countries. Henry III. here sought to entreat David, Prince of Wales, when he proposed that the Lords Marchers should meet him in 1243.

Preston-ford and Montford-bay are fishing stations, where an old fisherman told us he had known fifteen salmon caught in a day. Shrawardine-ford and Montford-bay also furnish good fishing. Below Montford bridge, the Perry—an industrious little river—having first done duty at the many village mills along its course, comes down to join the Severn. Like the villages and the village churches along its banks, those old clacking mills upon the Perry have histories of their own. For ages their lichened wheels have gone their busy rounds, many generations of millers have assisted their neighbours in turning village harvests into bread. To that of Fitz, between Perry and the Severn, the Haughmond monks not only brought their grist six centuries since, but also took toll of their neighbours' batches. For this privilege they were indebted to Robert de Girros, who gave two-thirds of this profitable mill, toll of his own wheat, sole ownership of the fishponds, common pasture for the millers' cattle, and turves to winnow corn, to the said abbey. At Bicton, close by, the Abbot of Haughmond also held land, with the privilege of his tenants cutting fuel at Bicton Heath. Below Bicton, and opposite to Fitz, is the Isle, 535 acres in extent, and enclosed by the Severn, excepting at a narrow isthmus, pierced to obtain water power for a mill. It is the property and residence of the Sandfords, to an ancestor of whom it was given by Queen Elizabeth.

Below the Isle is Leaton Knolls, wooded to the water's edge, and commanding views of the winding river, of the Breidden and other hills, and adorned by the modern mansion of John Arthur Lloyd, Esq. On the other side, lower down, is Rossall Hall; and opposite is Great Berwick, and Berwick House, the property, and the latter the residence, of the Hon. H. W. Powys. Along these thickly-wooded banks the gallant Percy halted, and lay encamped the night before the battle of Shrewsbury; and here, while partaking of the hospitality of the Bettons, of Upper Berwick, he left his sword—an incident which caused him some uneasiness prior to the commencement of the battle.

Opposite Berwick, formerly, was Shelton-ford, which Owen Glendower, it is said, should have crossed to join his ally. In a field above the river is the oak, from the topmost branches of which Owen is reported to have watched the course the battle took, prepared to advance or retreat as the case may be. Welsh historians, however, by no means admit the truth of a tradition which involves the good faith of their countryman. Owen, at the time they say, was in a remote part of Wales, and ignorant that his presence was either needed or expected till he heard of Hotspur's overthrow.

From the field-walks near Shelton Oak the town of Shrewsbury comes pleasantly into view, the towers and spires of the churches rising from the trough of the valley, and, seen through casual openings in the trees, afford good materials for the pencil.

Like many old towns of equal antiquity and importance, Shrewsbury, no doubt, owes its existence to its position. It occupies an eminence, on three sides surrounded by the Severn; and, from the disposition of its buildings, appears to have grown rather than to have been built. It has an aspect befitting the capital of an important county, and an air of antiquity which distinctly reminds you that it was formerly the metropolis of the Welsh. Its native poet (Churchyard) described it poetically three centuries since; and Leland (traveller and antiquary) has also sung its praises. Speed described its salubrity, Shakespeare the horrors of its battle-field; Camden praised its wealth, and others its beauty, its site, and its hospitality. An early British prince and bard speaks of it under the name of Pengwern, and refers to his countrymen having sought refuge here when driven from Wroxeter by the Danes. The Saxons, who drove out the Britons, called it Scrobbesbyrig—and that it was a place of sizable importance is clear, for, buried deep down in the market-square, the traces sought by antiquaries are still found.

The Saxons, with a chieftain whom a Welsh bard styles the hog, were in turn expelled by the Britons, who planted here their "clean king," and who, once more obliged to yield, retired to the other side of the Breidden hills. Scrobbesbyrig now became the capital of the Mercian kings. Instead of rude hovels and wattled huts, buildings of importance sprang up. The college of St. Chad took the place of the log palace of the "crowned king;" and the Lady of the Mercians founded St. Alkmund's. With the Norman Conquest it again changed masters—at least, after the Battle of Hastings made it prudent for it to do so. The posit

title, Earl of Mercia, now became merged in that of Shrewsbury; and the kinsman of the Conqueror, upon whom it was conferred, built the stout old castle on the isthmus of the Severn.

The history of the town, from this point, no longer borders on a myth; but, with the written record comes the accomplished fact, and old red stone ruins, like those leaning their broad back against "the mound," tell their own tales. How significant the old walls stand, giving frown for frown to the distant hills of Wales! How redolent of the olden time; and what distant periods they link together! The proud old keep, that bade defiance to the foe, is now a dwelling house; and its guard-chamber, formerly resounding with the tread of armed knights, is a drawing-room. The inner gateway, through which the last Norman Earl of Shrewsbury carried the keys to Henry I., is left. The inner chapel, dedicated to the warrior saint, where fighting men watched and prayed, has disappeared; while that of St. Nicholas, outside the court, used for retainers of the castle, has been converted into stables.

Shadows of the past fast flit before us as we contemplate the crumbling walls of the old building; still more so if we ascend the Laura Tower, rising high above the mount—itself 100 feet above the river—and look around us. Henry advances from the dark defile of Wenlock Edge; Stephen lays siege to the castle, which sacrifice itself in favour of the Empress Maude; Llewellyn wins back the heritage of his fathers, but is expelled by John, who, having reduced Oswestry to ashes, retakes the town; David, the last of the British princes, falls into the hands of Edward, and Parliament is summoned to Shrewsbury for his trial. The sentence it passes is severe, and the execution, which takes place on Pride-hill, an everlasting disgrace to the town. Members who witness it hasten to meet the King and his Chancellor at Acton Burnell, where Parliament sits in a barn. The Great Parliament (21st of Richard II.) is held here, the lords temporal and spiritual being sworn on the cross of Canterbury, brought here for the purpose.

Two years later, and the elements of rebellion culminate in the great Battle of Shrewsbury, where two thousand noblemen, knights, and gentlemen, and six thousand private soldiers fell on Battley-field, where the victor built a church over the body of the slain. The town is taken by storm under Colonel Mytton, of the parliamentary army; and after the Commonwealth comes the Restoration, when James II., having ascended the throne, comes here in the course of a tour he makes through his dominions. The corporation goes mad, and the mayor dumb, in presence of the King! They vote £300 for his entertainment, and make him a handsome present into the bargain; in return for which he condescended to exercise the gift of healing, by "touching" with the royal finger, for the king's evil.

The early ecclesiastical history of the place, to some extent, is brought before us by means of the same red-stone characters. On the opposite bank of the river is the Abbey, reared by the same founder, who in later years assumed the monastic garb, and was buried beneath its altar. Its abbot, who ranked with barons, had a seat in Parliament and carried the silver crosier. It was the depository of the body of the virgin Winifreda, whose decapitation, with other marvels attendant, caused her to rank high in the calendar of the saints, and her remains to bring much grist to the abbot's mill.

Only the church and some outbuildings now remain; but, in its broad and massive Norman tower is one of the finest windows in the kingdom; and its interior architecture, mural monuments, and altar tombs, with their quaint inscriptions, render it well worthy of a visit. In the precincts of the Abbey is a sculptured stone pulpit, formerly used in the refectory, it is supposed, by junior monks, who read to their brethren while at meals. A short distance from the Abbey, and near the Doric column commemorating the achievements of Lord Hill, is another memorial of the piety and philanthropy of past ages—a fine old church, dedicated to the patron saint of cripples. Its brown window has a representation of St. Giles, and its floor retains memorials of the masters of the hospital. A large hollow stone in the yard is still called the "pest-basin." Tradition asserts that it was filled with water, and used during the plague for people to pass their money through in their bargains with the countryfolk for provisions.

Crossing the handsome English bridge—graced by a goddess of the river and the father of the fountain on its centre arches—to the top of Wyle Cop, we find on the right St. Julian's, St. Alkmund's, and St. Mary's churches, and on the left St. Chad's. The modern structure of this name is the fashionable church of the town. It stands near the entrance to a magnificent avenue of limes, which form a public promenade, and intersect the sloping green sward of the quarry.

Next to the public buildings we have noted, the most striking features which meet the eye in passing along the streets are those presented by the domestic buildings of past centuries. Their white squares and black timbers, their lofty fronts and latticed windows, opening upon carved and highly-ornamented balconies, have a pleasing, suggestive aspect. They tell us that our ancestors, who built churches and endowed them, who fought stout battles and won them, had the love of home which characterizes our countrymen. At the head of these stands the Council-house, so called from its having been the occasional residence of the Council of the Marches. It was the residence, too, of Charles I. and James II. during their visits to the town; and at present forms several handsome private dwelling-houses. Its carved front, and highly-ornamented timber gateway leading out of the castle street, are relics of considerable interest in themselves. Many of these fine old houses of quaint buildings are to be seen in the direction of Mardol, and along High-street to the bottom of Wyle Cop. They project across and shade the flags in front; sideways they nod and lean, till they sometimes touch, forming dark arcades, locally known as Shuts. Many of these singularly beautiful, but now neglected structures, are to be found in out-of-the-way places, where they appear to shun observation. One faded mansion of this kind, with cloistered arches, ornamental upright brackets, and projecting stories, has been converted into shambles, and the beautiful ceilings, ornamented mouldings, panellings, fireplaces, and carvings of chambers have been torn down, and their outer shells made to serve as storehouses for bark or timber. In wandering through the dark passages of one we once met a brick-maker, who seemed as surprised at seeing any human being but himself amid the wilderness of rooms as Robinson Crusoe did in discovering other footsteps but his own on his solitary island.

Equally metamorphosed are the old guilds, or halls of the trades, where feasting, and no little tyranny, was practised by corporations of drapers, mercers, and others. Excepting the [illegible]—the members of which took the oath of allegiance before the mayor the other day—these corporate bodies no longer exist; but the old panellings, the quaint carvings, the portraits of the patrons and presidents, and the tables, may still be seen; and the modern pageant of Shrewsbury Show serves to recall the nature of the festivals these bodies kept up in former times.

With the foresight of Shrewsbury's most valued institutions—not including royal personages as well as private citizens—we find education and religion cared for. In some instances the funds of one were diverted to meet the wants of the other, as in the case of the Grammar School, founded by King Edward, and endowed by him out of the dissolved colleges of St. Mary's and St. Chad's. This valuable institution, enriched from time to time by subsequent endowments, has been fortunate in its masters, and eminently successful in sending out clever men, who have not unfrequently attained great eminence.

The Severn having completed its silvery crescent round the town, falls back into a narrow and graceful curve in the direction of Uffington, a little village, pleasantly situated, three miles from Shrewsbury. Behind it rises the wooded steep of Haughmond, crowned by a castellated turret on the side next the river. Down these steep rocks—so tradition tells—Earl Douglas leaped his horse and fell, after the battle of Shrewsbury. A dark thicket of fir upon its brow is still called the Queen's Bower, from a legend that Queen Eleanor watched the progress of the battle in which the fortunes of her husband were involved. Sundorn, the seat of the Corbets, with its lawn and lakes and ornamental grounds, occupies an opening in the dark mantling shade to the west. On the same side against the same dark background are the ruins of Haughmond, an abbey founded by Henry I., who gave its monks the pannage of the neighbouring woods, and rights of Weir and fishing in the Tern. They had, as we have seen, mills to grind and ovens to dress their food, and incomes from churches as far off as Coventry and Norwich; indulgences, too, were granted by Pope Boniface to penitents who should visit the monastery. Its chapter-house is a beautiful one of its kind. Archæologists visiting these ruins are pained to find how much they have been tampered with by modern builders, in taking portions down and "turning others to account."

Leaving Uffington, with Haughmond hill behind us, and passing Preston Boats, we find Longnor Hall on the left, the mansion of the Burtons, one of whom, an ancestor of the present House, was buried in the garden. He was refused interment in the family vault of St. Chad's because he had been so wicked as to die of joy upon the accession of Queen Elizabeth coming to the throne.

The village of Atcham, with its bridge, church, and well-known inn, are now before us. These, with Attingham hall—the seat of Lord Berwick, where the Tern comes down to join the Severn, are objects familiar to old travellers along the Holyhead road. On passing the bridge, the road winds caressingly round a grassy knoll, on which stands the quaint and quiet village church, whose form is reflected by its placid waters. The green mosses and of the luxuriant ivy, serve to conceal those which show the real age of the structure, tolerable indications of which, however, are to be found in the fact that stones forming portions of a Roman arch, and a portion of a sculptured Roman column, form a part of its walls. These, no doubt, were part of the ruins of the ancient city of Uriconium hard by. Among the relics the old building contains is the reading-desk, carved, it is said, by Albert Durer, the panels of which represent passages in the parable of the Prodigal Son. Atcham is celebrated as being the birthplace of an able Salopian author, who lived soon after the Norman Conquest, and who faithfully recorded the transactions of his time. The Rev. H. Burton, who takes great pride in this venerable fabric, has done much to improve and restore it. The river, after winding considerably, below Atcham, passes the site of the ancient city of Uriconium. The first thing which strikes you upon alighting on this rich bit of table-land, bounded by the graceful winding of the Severn on one side, and by the far-famed Wrekin, that once lent its name to the great city, on the other—is the situation. Verily the old Romans, or whoever selected it, must have had some taste for the beautiful, some liking for pure air—for air filtered by trees and purified by hills. Like Caerwys, it is the centre of an amphitheatre of hills, a position in harmony with the genius and daring of the people. Beyond the river, on whose waters the Britons paddled their wicker boats, are seen the long-backed Lawley, the pointed Caradoc, the round-topped Longmynds, the shaggy Stiperstones; and, higher up the valley, the stately Breiddens, the hills of Llangollen, and others meet the eye. And, if we except some forest-lands where red deer bounded and the wild boar stood at bay, the state of the country is not far different from the time when the sound of Roman trumpets and the shouts of Imperial legions broke the echo of the hills. From very childhood one has wondered at those hardy sons of Romulus, who faced the deep and came so far from home, conquering our nation, and leaving roads, cities, and forms of government as indications of their presence. And here is the quiet sunlight let in once more upon their streets, their foundations, their gods, their games, their personal ornaments, and the skeletons of the men themselves. You walk their streets, cross their thresholds, and stand where Roman sentry watched in their masters' chambers or parties of festivity, or council deliberating upon more serious matters. After a lapse of fifteen hundred years, during which the surface has many times changed owners, you tread their mosaic pavements, the ornamented passages of their mansions, handle their domestic utensils, admire their well-formed vessels, and see the very paint and plaster upon the walls of their apartments. The "old wall" that stood there for centuries, like some old world relic, has grown eloquent; a veritable sphynx by the roadside, suggesting enigmas to the passer by, it has found its interpreter in the excavations the pick and spade have made within reach of the vast [illegible]. From the very time when the [illegible] first fell down with a crash, the city has furnished plunder for the country round. The old monks, who loved to make take down the stones than to quarry new ones, built their churches with the spoil; whilst the old fragment to which we alluded, stood out as a perpetual advertisement of treasures buried around it. That an suspicion of the wealth which lay beneath its dark soil led peasants who knew little or nothing of its history to poach upon its precincts, is evidenced by the fact that it was only upon the ground that they had found nothing, that a party of treasure seekers, detected digging by night, escaped the censure of the Wroxeter manorial court in the thirteenth century. During the latter end of the past, and the first half of the present centuries much treasure has been removed; for, notwithstanding the jealous care taken by the lords of the soil to secure objects dug up or turned up by the plough, there is scarcely a cottager for miles round but has done a small but profitable trade in coins or other articles of value. We have been told, by farmers in villages near, of Roman people having been paid by their men in buttons, for which they said they were [illegible] by reason of their large size. To journey the [illegible] of the reader into the old town whose streets so long there have ceased to echo to the tread of its inhabitants, let us mark its ancient extent as indicated by the broad mound and hollow, and by its walls and foss—forming an irregular oval. We enter from that well-known Roman road, Old Watling-street, by one running at right angles, parallel with the Old Wall, and paved with small smooth stones, like many of our modern streets. North of this we come upon a beautiful tesselated pavement, highly ornamental, having an elegant border. Light and dark coloured stones of small size and oblong form, three-fourths long and one or one-and-a-half square at the surface, were employed to work out the design; but in the decorative border alluded to another of a red colour was added. A similar pavement was found at a short distance, indicating the existence of rooms of some pretension. A passage 14 feet broad, paved with bricks three inches long by one in width, set in what is called herring-bone fashion, leads from hence to a large rectangular enclosure, 226 feet in length by thirty in width. South of the Old Wall, where discoveries have been made, worn by time, we come upon the domestic apartments of the establishment, to which belonged the rooms on the other side, where are several apartments with hypocausts, for the purpose of warming the buildings, and from which the heat was conducted by flue-tiles to other apartments. These are in an excellent state of preservation, such pillars supporting the floors of the rooms, and portions of the flooring itself still standing. Upon a flooring of bricks are raised pillars of small square [illegible], at a distance of two or three feet apart. On the tops of these are others projecting till they meet, and forming bases to which are laid [illegible]. On these again is concrete—liquid mortar, and broken tiles—to form the flooring. One hypocaust had a room, with a semicircular recess over it, 37 feet by 20, communicating with another similarly provided. The hypocaust under the latter was approached by a stone staircase from without, and at the bottom of the latter, on a little platform, where the stoker of the establishment had accumulated, was found a mass of old pottery, glass, coins, hair-pins, bones of edible animals of the time—wild boar tusks, and deer horns, &c. Three of the rooms on this, the south side of the old wall, appear to have had vaulted roofs, and one is supposed to have been used as a store-room, judging from some bread which was found there. The human skeletons met with in different portions of the ruins are supposed to afford evidence of the massacre of the inhabitants. Two of these appear to have been pursued and slaughtered in an open court north of the old wall, and three others to have perished in one of the hypocausts, where they had fled for safety. One of the latter was evidently an old man, with whom the hiding [illegible] in death; for near him was a heap of Roman coins, 132 in number, and among them small nails and bits of decomposed wood, as though they had been contained in a box of that material. These coins were all, excepting one, which had been plated, of copper; and are exceedingly interesting, as exhibiting the character of the circulating medium of a period just prior to that of the Anglo-Saxons. These coins and other relics, including coal-heads of broken pottery, are to be seen at the Shrewsbury museum.

A PHOTOGRAPHER'S STORY.

I am a photographic artist. To prevent people from forming a mistaken conception of me, I may as well state at once that I do not pride myself on being an artist—that, in fact, I consider that term, as applied to myself, all fudge! I am a photographer, and not a bad one. If you want clear, sharp, brilliant pictures, I am the man for you. As for being an artist, I may confess here (nobody will know me) that I had much rather not be an artist. I should be very much ashamed of myself if I turned out such disgraceful smudges as artists delight in!

There was a man named Cox, a water-colour painter—perhaps my readers may have heard of him. Well, a lot of his pictures were exhibited in London some few years ago, and a friend of mine—one of our profession who sticks up for being an artist, and who does the art-articles in the "Photographic Dial"—this friend of mine persuaded me to go with him and see them. I think people are mad. To hear the ladies cry out, "How sweetly pretty!" and the gentlemen "What broad handling;" and my friend "What keeping! what skilful composition! what chiaroscuro!" I couldn't help thinking at first it was some farce, they were all acting, or that they had plotted together to take me in and laugh at me. But they really did it all as gravely as people go through the kneeling and the standing and the sitting at church. Some of them actually spoke out from the heart! I watched them, and saw it was not sham—for them I should prescribe strait-waistcoats!

These pictures of Cox's (will you believe it?) were things of which I could make neither head nor tail. You might have turned every one of 'em upside down and it would have looked just as well! The very paper on which they were painted was a lot of odd scraps pasted together—the coarsest stuff I ever saw in my life; full of chopped straw, and as rough as a nutmeg-grater! The colouring reminded me exactly of the blotting-paper on which I dry my plates out of the bath! It was nothing but a lot of dirty greys and greens and reds run into one another just as it happened! Now this Cox, they tell me, was a great artist—then I say I don't want to be an artist.

Just another instance of what an artist is, and I will begin my story. I went to the Brompton Boilers the other day. What I went for was to see the photographs with which Government is so shamefully underselling us. When I had done with those, however, I thought I would just take a turn round the building to see what was to be seen there; and I hit, first thing, upon the painting gallery. I don't mean to say there were not some pretty enough pictures in it. There were a good many of Landseer's dogs—I have nothing to say against them; but at last I came into a room the walls of which were all [illegible]. I rubbed my eyes; but I am generally quick at accounting for things, and I soon made up my mind what was the truth of the matter. I had seen in a long line of cases, down below, articles of food and their adulterations. There was coffee and roasted corn, chicory and dandelion seeds, and hundreds of things besides. Well, I got it into my head that this was the art-adulteration room. These, I thought, are hung up as a caution to the public! They may see here what bad art is, and guard against it when they furnish their houses. It seemed to me a good notion, and I amused myself by looking at specimen after specimen. All the Plagues of Egypt were there. I thought these sketches were fanciful ways of alluding to particular defects and tricks. My friend, the writer for the "Phot. Dial," has some books written by a man named Ruskin, which I could never make head or tail of; but I had learnt, from opening them now and then, that this polite way of attending one thing by calling it another was a grand highart dodge. I remembered the Seven Lamps of Architecture, and so knew very well what kind of meaning the Nine Plagues of Egypt might have. While I was looking at one after another, a man with moustachios and a beard came up to me. I mistook him at first for one of us. I think he mistook me (I also wearing a beard and moustachios) for a painter, which he turned out to be.

"I see, sir," he said, with a flourish of his hand, "that you too, are worshipping the immortal Turner! Let us offer up our devotions at the altar of art together."

I thought at first he was chaffing; but he was perfectly in earnest, and I let him go on, and pretended to agree with him, and so drew him out. I never heard such bosh before or since. The art-writing of the "Phot. Dial" is nothing to it; though I will say that the painter was in earnest while my friend only parrots the feelings and the knowledge that he writes about. Then I discovered that my specimens of art-adulteration were the works of "the immortal Turner!" "the glorious Turner!" Turner—pshaw! I knew they turned me sick! This Turner, then, was another great artist; and again I say I don't want to be an artist.

However, it is the custom of the trade to call oneself photographic artist, instead of plain photographer, just as she always puts Esquire at the end of a rich man's name; and so I style myself (as I am printed on my professional cards) a photographic artist. The "artist" does not mean anything, doesn't make my photographs a bit the better; but, since everybody else uses it, I may as well use it too.

Now I look upon Art as only another name for fancy and romance and imagination. Those who really believe in it I have generally found to be weak-minded men, and therefore not to be trusted in plain matters of fact. Those who pretend to believe in it are clearly not to be trusted; for, if they draw the long bow in that, they will draw it in other things besides. That is why I have been so particular in stating my views about Art before I tell my story. It is a mysterious kind of story, which I myself could never make out; and I don't wish to be accused of either weak-mindedness or drawing the long bow.

I have a partner in my business, and we have between us, besides our place in town, a travelling photographic gallery. "Hunkins and Scrudge" is the name of the firm; and I am Hunkins, at your service. I and my partner take it by turns to go out of town year by year, some time during the summer months. I have been half over England in this way; and I can tell you that this doing the provinces is a very pleasant sort of life, and pays well, too. We not only take portraits, but do a good bit of business in the stereoscopic line. Perhaps some of my readers know "Hunkins and Scrudge's views of Oxford and Cambridge?" Also we take, to order, views of the houses of the gentry round about the towns where we put up. Some would-be gentry, who live in little detached villas with little bits of garden to them, give us a good deal of trouble in this way. They can't be made to understand that one cannot take a photograph whose length is six times its height. However, this is what we do in our business now—and the things are very pleasant. We also [illegible] a number of fresh places each time; we get a good many negatives on hand, and among them an assortment of views which are worth any money to those who know how to use them. Altogether, doing the provinces pays—pays in the way of health, of pocket, and of new ideas; and I may quote the old line, and say that doing the provinces

"Is the way to be healthy, wealthy, and wise."

When I was out in the North on my summer trip a little while ago, I settled for a week in the small town of L—— (I will not write the name in full, for this may happen to come to the sight of the lady—Miss White I will call her—and she might not like old neighbours to know it). Handbills had been distributed some days before, and my first morning's work was a very full one. I had three pairs of lovers, and about a dozen children—lovers and children are always our most numerous customers, though not the most pleasant ones. Lovers will arrange each other, always preferring one particular side of each other's face or something of that kind; and children never can be arranged at all. Then lovers and mothers—both proverbially blind—are always inclined to grumble at the portraits when they are finished. However ugly and awkward the sitters are, they expect the portraits to be pretty and graceful. They never can understand that the eye of the camera can't be blinded like the eye of a mother or a lover. On this morning I had the usual trouble with both lovers and children. Lovers would put each other into the worst possible light and the worst possible position, would be full of flutter and blushing, would crack and disarrange everything just at the last moment, would stare each other when sitting out of countenance. Then some of the children were frightened and kicked and screamed, and some were in high spirits and jumped off and on the chair, and some were sulky and stiffened themselves so that they couldn't be got to sit at all. One baby woke up in the very act of having its likeness taken, and its portrait turned out very much like a [illegible]; of course I had several pictures of children with half-a-dozen eyes and any number of fingers; so that the average number of glasses I used was about three to each child. Photographers need have plenty of patience. Taking portraits is a very different thing to having one's portrait taken; and I can fancy, though I am not an imaginative man, that the feelings of the sitter are mild enough to those of the photographer.

Over and above the portraits, I had several orders for negatives. A rich young officer came to me to arrange about taking a group of the officers of his regiment quartered in the town. A fat oily dissenting parson wanted a hundred copies of himself, to be sold to those sitting under him at seven-and-sixpence a-piece, the proceeds to go towards repairing his chapel. The local actors wanted a group of themselves in the characters of a favourite piece. Two pretty young girls from the ladies' school wanted themselves taken together, with copies to give to all their school-fellows. Altogether I had done a good day's work, and as I brought in the swinging sign at the door of my van, I felt satisfied. I was knocking the ashes out of my pipe, when an old man in a sober groom's suit came up to me.

"Hunkins and Scrudge?" he said to me interrogatively.

"Yes, my man," I said, "Hunkins and Scrudge. What do you want with them?"

Thereupon he handed me a letter, the contents of which was as follows:

"L—— Vicarage.

"*Miss White wishes two views taken of C—— [illegible] tonight and an adjoining house. Will Messrs. Hunkins and Scrudge let her know what would be their charge for taking these photographs.*"

I wrote a polite note in answer, enclosing my charges. The groom took it back with him and in less than an hour returned with another letter:

"Miss White will thank Messrs. [illegible] and [illegible] to take the two views of C—— church to-morrow morning (if weather permit). Any hour most convenient to them will suit Miss White. She will have the photographs of the two views [illegible]?"

I packed up the necessary traps that night, and started with my wheel-barrow tent for the village of C—— a little after eight the next morning. The urchins of L—— cheered me out of the town somewhat derisively, having that sort of contempt for my wheel-barrow tent which anything unaccustomed excites in the [illegible]. Some of them accompanied me to C——, and the C—— children turned out in their [illegible], so that I left quite a crowd outside the vicarage-gate. The distance to C—— was not more than half-a-mile. I hoped to get my business done and be back again at my van in time for most of the portrait customers.

The vicarage was little more than a cottage, but pleasantly ivy-covered, and surrounded by a neatly laid-out garden. There was a lady in the garden, dressed in the deepest mourning. She advanced to meet me, whereupon I put down my tent and took off my hat.

"You are the photographer?" she asked.

She was a tall, spare lady, not very young. She was pale-faced, and her eyes were sunken and dull. She looked unhappy; but her voice was hard and her manner proud. I had learned that the vicar, Miss White's father, had died about a month before, so I could account for her black dress and her unhappy look. It is strange how differently different people take grief. You may not know that we photographers sometimes have grave offices to perform, and see not a few people in their sorrow. In cases of hopeless illness we are called in to perpetuate the pain-drawn features; more than once I have been sent for to take the cold still image of a dead face. In such ways I have seen a good deal of grief and observed how differently it affects people. It softens some and makes them beg, as it were, by gentle, softened looks and tones and manner for the human sympathy of even strangers and servants. It humbles some who have been proud before, making them feel, I suppose, how all—judges and [illegible], lords and beggars—are alike impotent in these [illegible]. But others it hardens. They cannot bear their fellow-creatures to know that they are down. They give way to their grief in secret, and come out from their chambers with defiant eyes and rigid mouths. They resent the presence of anyone, fearing that he has a hidden pity for them, and feel as an affront each common act or word of politeness.

Miss White, I saw at a glance, was one of this latter kind. I put on my hat, and said indifferently, "Yes, madam. Nine into seven, I think you said for the view."

"I consider your charge exorbitant," she said harshly.

I explained why I was obliged to charge what seemed to her a heavy price. This bit of business called me away from my portrait work; I lost a morning over it. Then, interiors were difficult, sometimes impossible, to be taken. It all depended upon the amount of light. Churches are the darkest buildings I know. As if the long narrow windows did not admit a sufficiently small amount of light, they fill them often with yellow and red glass, on purpose to bother us photographers. Well, I told her the reason why I was obliged to charge her very much more than I should for taking her portrait; and then I consented to lower my price a little.

Somehow I knew that she was poor. Her dress was scanty and [illegible], the [illegible] was brown, her gloves were [illegible] and mended. I knew that she would have to turn out of her old home, as parsons' families always have. I felt an extra pity for her because she was one of that over-sensitive sort that will not accept pity at any price. These reflections passed through my mind as I stood talking. It must not be supposed, however, that I lowered my charge because I pitied her. Feelings are one thing and business is another. If I were Jack Ketch I might feel sorry for the poor fellow with the rope round his neck, but I should do my duty all the same. We always allow a little for coming down, and are open to making bargains, in this branch of our profession. For instance, a gentleman says, "I can't give you this price for the front view of my house;" then we say, "Come sir, we'll take the back view in addition at half-price." This is the way we manage it. In the present case, I agreed at last to throw in a small positive of the vicarage for my original charge.

"I will show you the views I want you to take," says she, a little more graciously, when it was settled. She went in for the big church key, and then we started for the church which was close by. The tail of children followed up at some little distance behind us, taking up their position in rows on the church wall and the tombstones when we entered the church-yard.

Just within the gate, I pulled up.

"We couldn't do better than this, ma'am," says I. The view was capital. I know in a moment what will make a picture, and I knew that I shouldn't get a better view of the church than that.

"That view," said the lady, "will not do."

She went on round the church, and by-and-bye stopped.

"This is where it is to be taken from," she said emphatically.

Not a good picture; but I saw in a moment why she chose that spot. There was a new tomb—very handsome tomb—in the foreground, with an inscription; "To the memory of the Reverend Thomas White, M.A., &c."

"We are to take in that tomb, ma'am," I said.

She scowled at me, but her lips trembled.

"Yes. Now, I will show you the interior view."

So, we went into the church. The view she chose there would not do at all. She had no notion of the light and the dark side of a building. I found that she wanted the pulpit and the Communion-table, and a tall square pew (I suppose the vicarage pew) included in the picture. I managed to get them all from the opposite side of the church, and she said "that would do;" and then, leaving me the key, returned at a quick pace to the vicarage, while I followed more slowly, to arrange my traps.

First of all I took the house, finding all my chemicals to be in capital order. Then, leaving my dark tent in the corner of the garden, as the distance to the church was so short, I prepared to take the outside view. By the time that was finished, the sun would have worked round sufficiently for me to set to work at the interior.

The children teased me sadly, as they always do. The personal remarks they make one don't care for, nor for the shouts of laughter they set up when one puts one's head under the focussing cloth; but they are apt to rush before the lens, in pursuit of each other, while one is taking a picture; and one can't leave the camera at their mercy for a moment. However, I got the old person, who had brought the letter on the preceding night, to stay by the camera while I took the outside picture; and then I carried the camera to the church, and there it was safe enough.

The church was very dark. I had great difficulty in making out enough of a picture on my ground glass to arrange the camera by. However I got it fixed rightly at last. I wanted more light. The belfry-arch was filled in with woodwork in which were doors. These I opened, and found other doors beyond, leading out into a porch. The porch was closed in by a gate of open paling-work, which was locked; so I could leave open the second pair of doors, too, and get light through the locked paling gate, without suffering from the intrusion of the boys. It was just what I wanted.

I lowered my plate, which had been in the bath while I focussed, locked myself again in the church, put the slide into the camera, and uncovered the lens. Half-an-hour's exposure, I decided, or a little more.

The light was beautiful: the sun was just covered with thin white clouds; there was as much light as one could have without actual sunshine. If the sun would pop out brilliantly during the last few minutes of exposure, nothing else could be desired. I think we photographers come to have a sixth sense about light. We can measure it just as if our eyes were the two sides of a balance. Oh, I don't think it is our eyes that do; I think we feel light rather than see it. I know as well as can be when my picture is going on all right in the camera. I feel when a too gray darkness is creeping over it; I feel the moment when it palpitates into great white passion. I know, when I am about to take it out, the very fraction of a second at which it needs be had; and sometimes I can't hit upon the exact fraction, because my fingers are not quick enough for my inner action.

Half-an-hour in a church, with nothing to do, is a long time. The time passes slowly enough when the congregation are in the pews and the parson in the pulpit, but a church is still duller on a week-day. All I could do was to look about me, and even in this amusement I was sadly cramped. I could not move up the aisle far from the belfry-arch without coming into the range of the lens, so that I could take in but a distant view of most of the church.

The boys in the churchyard at first served to distract my attention. Of course they had discovered the open doors, and they collected round the porch-gate, looking between the palings, and saying one to another, "I see 'im, Bill—look'ee, there he is!" or catching me with the tempting question, "Who put his head into a bag?" But, after a time they became tired of looking through the palings into the church, and began to find it more entertaining to wage war among themselves. The L— boys and the G— boys, I suppose, had a standing feud between them, as all boys of neighbouring places have. There was much rushing round the churchyard in pursuit of each other, and much shouting of their respective war-cries, which consisted, I remember, of—"Who put the windlestraw in the pound?" on the L— side, and "Who hilled the goose?" on the other. Now and then one would flatten his nose for a moment against a low window, or would send a shrill whistle through the porch gate; but they ceased to take any other notice of me.

I am a good Christian, I hope, and I don't practise my trade (further than printing goes, which one must do sometimes under pressure of business) on a Sunday, as some I could mention do. But I must confess I am not often in a church. For the last two years, or thereabouts, I have been of the Baptist persuasion, and have attended pretty regularly the ministrations of the Reverend Habakkuk Sippletoberry, at Ebenezer Chapel. Miss Mary Jane Scrudge (sister of my partner), whom I hope next month to lead from the altar Mrs. Hawkins, junior, is of the Baptist persuasion and of a religious turn, which fact may account for my present belief. The Baptists have a notion that a church is an improper place, scarcely better than a playhouse, and, though we are to be married in church—the ceremony there performed being held to be the more binding—I am sure that Mary Jane would think the worse of me if I entered a church for any other than professional purposes. Before I began to make up to Mary Jane, I used regularly to spend my day out on the Sunday, thinking no harm of it then, though I know better now. But I have said enough, to show why I am not much acquainted with churches in the light of places of worship. In the way of business I have taken some half-dozen or more, and those pretty good samples of the various kinds of churches. I can never make out why they are so different from each other, when, as I suppose, all church-people worship in the same manner and believe the same things.

I have taken churches all tricked off with colour and gilding; the walls covered with painting, which, like a bad hand, couldn't be read by anybody but the man who painted it; the communion-table set out, like the sideboard in some grand house, with lots of plate, big gold waiters and candlesticks (which the Reverend Shuttleboro, preaching from somewhere in Revelations, proved to be the mark of the beast); the pulpit hung with damask jewellery; spread-eagles, with bookstands on their backs; tiles, with patterns on them like green-house pavements; gold stars on the ceiling at one end; pews very low—uncomfortable for the back, I found on trying them, and without doors—not so private as I should wish my pew to be. Well, that is one kind of church. There is a church in London (I dare say my readers have been to see it among the other sights), which was built as a pattern for this style. It is a regular show place, and very successful I should think. Whether they ever have service in it I don't know for certain, but I fancy not; they would be afraid of spoiling it. This style of church is harder to take than any other, because of the red and yellow glass in the windows.

Then there is another kind of church in London: big roomy galleries all round, supported on pillars beautifully painted to look like marble (that *size* is *art* I can understand); a great organ, all polished mahogany and gilded pipes, like a handsome clock-case; a mahogany pulpit with an octagon sounding-board, and no expense spared in the crimson cushions and fringes; high, square—what I call *comfortable* pews; the commandments printed very plain, so that one can't mistake them, and framed off from all the rest of the ornaments, as if to draw particular attention. (The architects of the style of church described in the last paragraph seem to me to use the commandments as if Heaven had expressly sent them to them as a nice odd bit of ornamentation, that may be zigzagged over their clean-scraped walls in endless varieties of shape and colour.) Then there are monuments of marble, black and white nicely relieving each other, with little fat cherubs' heads at the corners, and cherubims and hour-glasses carved in prominent positions. Over the communion-table there is often a picture, which, between the two square windows, looks of an uniform deep brown mouldy colour, except where, in the centre, some white face, with upturned eyes, starts out from the darkness with a sort of ghastly life.

Then there is the country church, of which the L—— church, now upon the carpet, may serve as a specimen. The country churches, I suppose, will not last long in their present condition, if this rage for restoring holds. Last year I took a view of a village church, which had been lately "restored," as the term is. I don't [illegible] of taste, but it did not seem to me to go well at all with the green grass and the blue sky and the bright sunshine outside. The colouring looked tawdry, like a pantomime drop the morning after. Everything looked too new and polished and clean, as if it had no affinity with those outside weather-influences, producing stains and damp and dust.

I walked up and down my limited space of aisle between the pews, watch in hand, seeing as much as I could see of the church. It was an old ramshackled building. Ages ago everything had been whitewashed that could be whitewashed—ceiling and walls and oak beams alike; but the weather had been taking the white out of it ever since, marbling the walls with streaks and patches of brown and grey, or vivid green. I could make out in those stains, dim confused landscapes, not unlike the productions of that great artist Cox, before-mentioned. In places the plaster had fallen from the ceiling. The pews were like a parcel of old packing-cases or orange-boxes. I never saw such pews before or since; though the owners seemed chary enough of them, in almost all, their names being printed in black letters on a slip of white ground. The flat square tiles of the pavement had been patched up with common bricks, and here and there a plank had been let in, the whole being intermixed by a coat of green mouldiness. Tiny plants were springing up in the interstices—in the belfry quite a nursery-garden of them. There was a row of high-pointed arches on one side and of low round arches on the other. A great painted arch led into the chancel. Squeezed up in a corner, between the arch and the first low round-headed arch, was the pulpit. An unwieldy dark corner—the parson must have had hard work to read his sermon there on a winter's afternoon. The pulpit, I thought to myself, will not come out well in my picture. The font was under one of the pointed arches, just opposite the door. The top of its lid was covered, for some reason or other, with a fool's cap. The lady had wanted me to include the font, too, in the picture; but it was simply impossible. Now, I may be wrong, but this is the notion I have of what was passing in the lady's mind. She was poor; she was going to leave the home where she had lived all her life, and she must have something to take away with her to remember the old place by, though she could not afford to spend much. Perhaps she would have chosen a view of the vicarage before anything (how her eyes brightened up when I proposed to figure in that little position!) but then it struck her that a view of the church would be more proper. There were the graves, she must have liked it any rate; then, there was the font where she was christened; and there was the communion-table where she had taken the sacrament, and where, at one time, for anything I know, she might have had a chance of being married; and there was the pew where she had sat Sunday after Sunday; and there was the pulpit her father had preached from. Women have a sentiment in these matters of religion. I know Mary Jane looks on Ebenezer Chapel as a sort of holy ground; and has a portrait of the Reverend Shuttleboro (which photograph I took myself) which she hangs up opposite mine.

Well, to go on with my description: through the chancel arch, the communion-table was to be seen; handsome worked cover to it, and rails before it, commandments very plain in yellow on a blue ground, high up on either side. The man who painted them didn't know that his yellow letters would come out black in a photograph, and his blue ground light. There were monuments on the chancel wall as elsewhere. On a pillar close to me was a large printed card stating that a man might not marry his grandmother, and so forth, which struck me as curious.

Exhausting that end of the church in twenty minutes and a fraction, I turned my attention to the other. Three painted shields of arms over the belfry arch. In the belfry an old iron chest, the trestles for funerals, a ladder leading up to the higher story, one bell rope a good deal worn. That was all. Through the porch gate I could see the village shop and the village inn; and as I stood there, a boy came suddenly round the corner upon me with a shrill whistle that made me start.

Twenty-five minutes. I watched a fat toad crawling slowly up the aisle. A robin, which had hitherto been flying to and fro, perched upon a beam over my head and began to sing. The sun popped out from behind the clouds and shone in through every window along one side of the church. The pulpit looked darker than ever behind the lines of light. I felt that my photograph was going on just right, but knew that Miss White would find fault with the pulpit. There would not be much of a pulpit to be seen.

Verging upon the half-hour. I paced back to the belfry and peeped out through the rails again, like a wild beast in a show. The minute-hand of my watch crept on. I have looked at it so often that I have learned to see it move. Time was just up. As I turned to go to my camera, I saw the bell rope swinging to and fro; and immediately after the heavy sound of the bell came thundering down upon the top of my head. I thought the bell, or the roof, or the whole tower was coming down on me too—it startled me so. The sound went trembling through the church; and outside of the church through the air, too, as I soon found from the rushing of the boys to the porch gate. However, I had my camera to think about just then, and couldn't stay to speculate on the ringing of the bell. I believe if a lion stood between a photographic artist and his camera when the time is up, the lion could not stop him.

Bringing my slide out of the church, I found the boys ready for me. The sound of the bell had aroused the villagers, and a good many of them were standing at their doors to see what was the matter. The only way I could account for its ringing myself was, by supposing that the wind had shaken it.

Miss White met me in the garden. I could see she was in a towering passion.

"If I had thought, Sir," she said, "that you did not know how to respect a sacred place where you were admitted on sufferance, I would not have employed you."

"Ma'am," I answered, for I was nettled, "as for respect, I took off my hat, though there was a draught like the wind from a blacksmith's bellows. I should no more think of touching the bell than you would."

"Don't add to your sin," she said, "make haste and finish your work, and let me be rid of you."

There is nothing riles a man more than a false accusation. I knew I should lose my temper if I spoke; besides, my picture was spoiling, so I turned on my heel and ducked my head into the dark tent.

I am afraid I am using a great many expressions which people who know nothing of photography will not understand. But there is scarcely a family now which has not an amateur photographer in it; some young lady who spoils her pretty little fingers, or some young gentleman who blackens his shirt cuffs and cambric pocket-handkerchiefs, and whose pictures are not quite worth the spoiling of either. However, for the benefit of those who have not a photographic amateur in the family, I will explain that, when I say I began to develope my picture, I mean that I poured on to it a certain chemical solution which brings out gradually all the details of light and shade which are already there, but unseen.

I began to develope. The windows started out in a moment, then came the patches of sunlight, then the white monuments on the walls, then the polished edges of the pews; and then, very slowly, the outlines of the arches, the round pillars, the walk between the pews, the details of the pews themselves, the communion-table with its railings, the commandments and the *pulpit*.

I have heard people talk about photography as if it were a very mysterious matter. I dare say that to a novice, the gradual coming out of a picture under development seems mysterious the first time or two. But it is the simplest thing in nature. It is the light and the chemicals that do it. Good light, good lens and good chemicals—these are your tools. I have seen in print a great deal of poetical nonsense about photography—waves of light, images thrown off from people and caught and retained by magic—"quædam simulacra, modis pallentia miris," (I copy that letter for letter out of a book;) "phantoms, strangely pale" it means as they translate it underneath. You may be sure that when anyone begins to write poetically on a subject, he knows nothing of that subject. There is nothing poetical to be got out of what one knows; and every photographic artist will tell you that there is nothing in the world more plain, and matter-of-fact than photography. Whatever there is in range of your lens, you will have in your picture...... But sometimes an extraordinary occurrence will happen in the most ordinary routine. An extraordinary occurrence happened in the development of my picture. I can't explain it in the least, but I am going to tell you what it was.

I had said all along in my own mind that the pulpit would not come out well. In developing, a space remained perfectly white in the dark pulpit corner between the two arches, while the rest of the picture was planning more and more detail every moment. This was natural, and what I had expected. Towards the last a pinnacle of the pulpit on the right side and the edge of the cushion came faintly into sight. Then suddenly a great blur made its appearance where the pulpit ought to have been. I had never known, in all my professional practice, a stain like this, or coming in the same manner. The stain came as if it were shot into the picture; sharp outlined, distinct, full of minute detail. I was puzzled. I held the glass up to the light. It was not a stain. It was a *figure!*

Miss White was angry that she could not have the photographs at once, and could not understand for some time that the negative-views of the church had to be printed. Of course, it was not likely that she would detect with her inexperienced eye, the figure in the pulpit. People never can make out a negative, where all the whites are black and all the blacks white. I promised to bring her the pictures on the next evening; and so packed up my traps and returned to the inn.

I printed that afternoon, watching the printing-frames in the intervals of portrait-taking. The figure came out wonderfully sharp and distinct—an old gentleman with white hair, dressed in a black gown, every fold of which was visible, with a pair of white hands hanging down over the breast. I hesitated a little whether I would not leave this figure out of the picture, which of course I knew how to manage. But at last I decided I would let it be as it was.

The pictures were very successful. I framed them neatly and took them to C—— Vicarage on the following afternoon, when it was too late for portraits.

I knocked at the door, and a servant let me in and showed me up a room where Miss White was. The house was all in disorder. They were evidently packing up for leaving. Miss White was overlooking a man who was putting an oil picture into a case. It was a portrait of a gentleman. Though the face was much younger, it struck me like lightning, that this was the same person as the figure in my photograph.

Miss White took off the paper in which I had wrapped the pictures. Of course she saw the figure in a moment.

She gasped out, "Papa!" and fell to the ground as if she had been knocked down. I caught the pictures as she fell, so that the glasses were not broken.

* * * * *

I keep the negative among my curiosities.

ROSE'S THREE TRIALS.

BY JAMES R. STEPHENS.

There are twenty years of sun and cloud
  Betwixt my Rose and me:
Oft have I toss'd her in my arms,
  To wake her infant glee;
I was vain of what was on my cheek
  When she was on my knee.

The world is wide, and youth is wild,
  The native soil is tame;
The sea is broad, and the blessèd God
  Is in all lands the same;
I prayed his grace, took heart, and sail'd
  For Fortune and for Fame.

I fought the anger of the deep,
  The perils of the [illegible];
I fought with Nature and with man—
  Her lands unknown before—
When [illegible] years had come and gone,
  I stood at Rose's door.

The gold of Ind was in my purse;
  I was a rich man now!
The badge of Fame was on my breast,
  Its shine upon my brow;
Yet a silvery voice [illegible] my heart,
  I know not why or how!
A little while and Rose was mine,
  By plighted word and vow.

But twenty years between us lay,
  A bridgeless, dark abyss!
Was my worn heart responsive
  To the passion of her kiss?
And could my heavy spirit love
  On tender love like this?

Her very laugh awoke my fears;
  I trembled when she smil'd;
Was hers the love of woman,
  Or the impulse of a child?
Was this the life-love of her soul,
  Or a freak of passion wild?

And when she shook her lustrous curls,
  So fairy-like and young,
Above my joy this darksome doubt,
  Like a foul vapour hung.
I was resolved to try her heart,
  E'en with a lying tongue.

One ev'ning when the twilight's breath
  Scarce stirred the leaves of June,
I led her forth, and [illegible] to her
  Beneath the mellow moon.
I told her I was deep in debt,
  And would be bankrupt soon.

"Wilt marry one with broken fame
  And broken fortune too—
Waste thy young heart with fever'd dreams
  Of penury in view?
I will not claim thy vows—unless
  Thou speak them all anew."

Oh, fair is the moon, when in nights of June,
O'er her sapphire paths she hies,
And softly bright is each twinkling light
In the chambers of the skies;
But none are half so beautiful
As the light of Rose's eyes!

This was the light that she turn'd on me,
And I read her soul thereby—
I could divine her inmost thought
Before she made reply—
"I am almost glad that thou art poor,
I fear not poverty!

"And now I feel more near to thee;
It was not so before.
Now I can be of use to thee
Thou'lt love me so much more.
Thou must not think how proud I'll be
To ride our lights along!"

I took the dear one to my breast—
Woman and child in one.
"I did but jest, but now I know
What thou'dst have loved and done;"
I thought my doubts were laid to rest—
They came back with the sun!

I sought her when the floods of storm
Swept o'er earth and main—
When thunders peal'd, and lightning's shot
Between the window-pane,
I chose the hour of Nature's growl
To try her heart again.

"There is blood upon my soul," I said—
The blood of one I slew;
Wilt waste thy heart with fever'd dreams
Of infamy in view?
I will not claim thy vows—unless
Thou speak them all anew."

Oh, how gentle and kind is the sweet summer wind
As it breathes o'er the perfumed land!
And how soft is the sleep of the silver deep
On the breast of the golden sand!
But nothing is half so gentle and soft
As the touch of Rose's hand!

This was the hand that she laid on me!—
"Tell me the tale, and I
Will take the guilt upon my head,
And for thy crime will die.
Only enshrine me as thy wife
Within thy memory."

I took the dear one to my breast,
Woman and child in one.
"'Tis true I slew him with this hand,
But the deed was fairly done.
It was a Russian soldier, Rose,
And I slew him at his gun."

"Tears are again. Another dawn
Would bring the nuptial day;
I found her sporting on the lawn,
She seem'd to me too gay;
And the fiend whispered in my heart,
She's but a child at play."

I tried her once again: "Sweet Rose,
The vows I've sworn to thee
When once another's, and her babe
Has sat upon my knee;
But I left them far away, Rose,
In a land beyond the sea.

"Wilt waste thy love on such as I,
With infamy in view?
I've jested with thee twice, Rose,
What now I tell is true!
I will not claim thy vows—unless
Thou speak them all anew."

Oh, swift is the flight of swift sky at light,
That issues from the gates of morn;
And keen is the blast o'er the ice that has past
In the lands where winter is born;
But nothing is half so swift and keen
As the glance of Rose's scorn!

This was the scorn that she flash'd on me,
From quivered my lip and eye,
"Live alone, and learn to loathe thy sin,
Live on, but let me die.
Pluck the last vestige of my love
From thy false memory."

She took a bracelet from her arm,
And flung it on the grass.
"Take back thy gift . . . . Sir, stand aside!"
"But hear me, Rose!" —— "Alas,
I dare not hear! . . . . Sir! stand aside,
And let a lady pass."

I took the dear one to my breast,
Woman and child in one,
"'Tis true I had another, Rose,
But our wedded life is done—
The pair they've slept within their graves,
The mother and her son."

And Rose forgave me.——Now, though I
Am older far than she,
Her thoughts are where her thine twine,
With all her childish glee.
Oh, could I only be to her
All she has been to me!

Love at Home.—When once a home is regarded by the young as only a place to eat and sleep in, the work is begun that ends in public-houses and a downward career. Young people must have relaxation and amusement; if they do not find it at their own hearthstone, it will be sought at other, and perhaps less profitable places. Therefore, at night, make the home cheerful and delightful with all those little arts that parents ought to understand. Don't repress the buoyant spirits of your children; half-an-hour of merriment round the fire-light of a home blots out the remembrance of many a care during the day, and the best safeguard they can take with them into the world is the unseen influence of a bright little home sanctum.—*Old Jonathan.*

THE WORK-TABLE.

NEW CROTCHET STITCHES.

(Especially suitable for Wool-work.) *

No. I.—Tunis Stitch.

This is begun exactly like Princess stitch, and with the same kind of hook. You make a chain of any given number of stitches, and work back on it, taking up each stitch and drawing the wool through, until finally you have all on the needle. Work back, by drawing the wool first through one loop only, and after that through two, till you have one only on the hook, which is the first of next row. So far the two stitches are precisely alike.

3rd. Instead of putting the hook in the upright stitch, insert it under the top, or upper part, between every two upright threads; and draw the loop through; so that at the end of the row, working from right to left, you have all the loops on the needle, the last one being made of a sort of loose thread at the end.

4th, or returning row, is like the second, but that you draw three off together at the last. Repeat these two rows alternately till sufficient is done.

This stitch is better adapted for making squares than stripes, as it works into a diagonal or slanting form, but can readily be pulled into shape.

A couvre-pied made of this stitch, in small squares of two bright [illegible] colours, would be very handsome, especially if each square was surrounded by a line of s c, worked in gold, or [illegible].

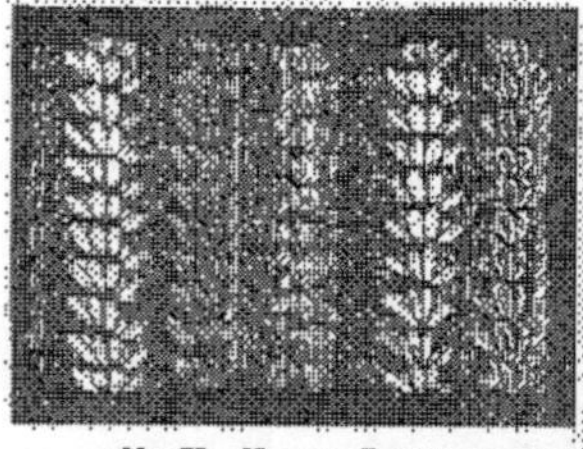

No. II.—Velvet Stitch

is made by putting the wool twice round the hook (as for t c), and then inserting it in the stitch to be worked. Draw the wool through this, and then through all the four loops and twists of thread together, which requires a somewhat fine needle. Do a chain stitch after every stitch; and in following rows insert the hook under this chain.

You work the velvet stitch on every alternate one only of the foundation chain.

This stitch is admirably suited for stripes of bright colours, divided by a narrow one of three rows, black, some [illegible] gold, and black again. The bright colours ought to be of not less than four rows; and five are more effective.

The [illegible] line should be done in [illegible] crochet silk; the wool used must be double Berlin.

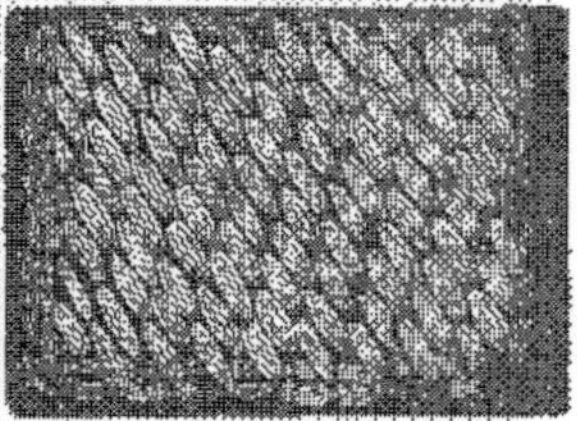

No. III.—Loose Princess Stitch.

This is a pretty and novel variety of the popular "Princess" (or, as the French have called it, Tunis) crochet. The only difference in working is, that when doing the forward row, after taking up one of the front stitches, and bringing the wool through it, you draw the wool again through the stitch just made, working on it, in fact, a chain stitch. Do this to every stitch in the row, working from right to left, except the first stitch, which, as our readers are aware, is merely the last stitch of the alternate or back row; and this must have a chain stitch worked on it.

It is somewhat lighter than the ordinary Princess stitch, and done in 4-thread Berlin is quite warm enough for a couvre-pied, or baby's blanket; but the stitches not being square, it is not suitable for embroidery.

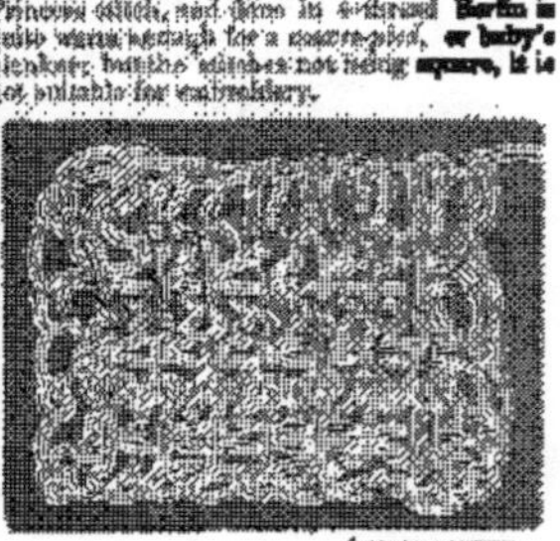

Aiguillette.

---

* Where it is desirable to use Cotton, we particularly recommend the Royal Boar's Head Crochet Cotton of Messrs. Walter Evans's and Co., of Derby.—Ed.

THE BUTTERFLY SLIPPER.

MATERIALS:—Black Cloth, Violet, Green, Crimson, and Blue *Ombre* Silks; Gold Thread, No. 2; Black and Ruby Cut Beads.

We can fancy that the design of this slipper may be *suggestive* enough to make it popular with many of our friends, who will think it a pattern especially *suitable* for some of their liege lords.

The butterfly is to be worked in chain-stitch, with the various shaded silks: the upper wings in green—the under in crimson, with blue spots. The body in lilac. On each side of the body a cut black bead may be put in every little loop, surrounded by gold-thread. This must be laid on each side of the lilac silk; but on the inner side only of the remainder. It is also to be employed for the sleeves. The eyes are to be rubies.

Braid may be used instead of the shaded silk; but the effect will not be so good. It is [illegible] [illegible], also, to draw the [illegible] of each through to the wrong side. If done in one colour only, much of the beauty of the design will be lost.

Black velvet would be a better material even than cloth; but it should have a lining of fine thin linen.

AIGUILLETTE.

THE ART OF SWIMMING.

We particularly recommend this article to our lady readers; for they should all learn how to swim. At some of our favourite bathing-places we have been pleased to see how many good swimmers and [illegible] are to be found among the lady visitors to those delightful places of resort.

As it is at this season that the healthy pastime of swimming may be pursued, we venture to give those of our young friends who may be inexperienced in the art a few hints which may serve them in time of need. Great caution is required in the commencement, for it is too often a failing in youth to brave danger, and incur risks (often fatal), from not having acquired the knowledge of avoiding them.

The tonic and reviving qualities of cold water are of the most remarkable character. How wonderfully refreshing it is to bathe merely the face and hands in cold water!

On first plunging into cold water, there comes a shock which drives the blood to the central parts of the system; but immediately a reaction takes place, which is assisted by the exercise of swimming, producing, even in water of a low temperature, an agreeable warmth. The stay in the water should never be prolonged beyond the period of this excitement. If the water be left while this warmth continues, and the body immediately dried, the healthy glow over the whole surface will be delightful.

To remain in the water after the first reaction is over, produces a prolonged chilliness, a shrinking of the flesh, and a contraction of the skin by no means favourable to health or enjoyment; for it is only in water thoroughly warmed by the summer heat where we may bathe for hours with impunity.

Certain precautions are necessary. Moderate exercise, by stimulating into action the powers of the system and quickening the circulation, is better than inactivity. We should never go into water immediately after a meal, nor while the process of digestion is going forward. Nor should we plunge into the water when violently heated or in a state of profuse perspiration. Such imprudences are often fatal, especially if the water be unusually cold. If too warm, the temperature of the body may be reduced by bathing the wrists and wetting the head.

Times and Places for Swimming.—Before meals rather than after, and especially before breakfast and before supper, are proper seasons for bathing. The heats of the day are to be avoided, but in very hot weather a bath is useful to cool the blood and secure refreshing sleep. If in the middle of the day, a shaded place should be chosen, or the head protected from the sun by being kept wet or by wearing a straw hat—as is practised by the fashionable French ladies at their watering-places.

The sea is the best place for swimming. Owing to the greater specific gravity of salt water than fresh, the body is more buoyant in it, as are other substances. A ship coming out of salt water into fresh sinks perceptibly in the water. The difference is nearly equal to the weight of the salt held in solution.

The bottom should be of hard sand, gravel, or smooth stones; sharp stones and shells cut the feet, weeds may entangle them. The swimmer must avoid floating grass and quicksand. The beginner must be careful that the water does not run beyond his depth, and that the current cannot carry him into a deeper place, also that there be no holes in the bottom. As persons are ever liable to accidents, cramps, &c., it is always best that boys or girls should be accompanied by those who are older than themselves, and who will be able to save them in an emergency.

Aids in Learning to Swim.—Probably one of the best ways of learning to swim is to go, with a competent teacher, in a boat in deep water; this supporting the body more buoyantly than that which is shallower, and preventing the constant tendency of beginners to touch the bottom, which here is, of course, impossible.

The teacher should fasten a rope securely around the waist,—better still—to a belt, which can neither tighten nor slip down. The rope may be fastened to a short pole. Supported in this manner, the pupil may take his proper position in the water, and practise the necessary motions, and the support of the rope may be gradually loosened until the pupil finds himself entirely supported by the water.

Corks and bladders are often used as supports for learners; but it is much better to begin without them. As, however, they may be a protection in some cases against accidents, and enable the learner to practise the proper motions for rapid swimming more carefully, they are not to be entirely condemned. Several large pieces of cork, uncut into stopples, must be strung upon each end of a piece of rope, long enough to pass under the chest and reach just above the shoulders; or well-blown and properly secured bladders may be fastened in the same way. Care must be taken to confine these supports near the shoulders, as by their slipping down they would plunge the head under water, and produce the very catastrophe they were especially designed to prevent.

A great variety of life-preservers have been invented, made of India-rubber and cork-shavings, in the form of jackets, belts, &c., which may be used like the corks and bladders; but, as their bulk is generally all around the chest, they hinder the free use of the arms and impede the velocity of motion. As life-preservers they would do very well if people ever had them on when they were needed, or had presence of mind enough to fit and inflate them in sudden emergencies. The best life-preservers are the self-reliance and well-directed skill of a good swimmer.

Swimming with the plank has its advantages. The young bather has always the means of saving himself from the effects of a sudden cramp, and he can practise with facility the necessary motions with the legs and feet, aided by the momentum of the plank. A piece of light wood, three or four feet long, two feet wide, and about two inches thick, will answer very well for this purpose. The chin may be rested upon the end, the other hand; but this must be done carefully, or the support may go beyond the young swimmer's reach.

A better method, as many think, than any of these, is for the teacher to wade into the water with his pupil, and then support him in a horizontal position by placing his hand under the pupil's chest, while he directs his motions. He may withdraw the support almost imperceptibly. But we do not see what advantage this method has over that first noticed with the band, unless it be that the teacher can better enforce his precepts by example, and, in swimming himself, give practical illustrations of his theories of propulsion.

The rope is another artificial support which has its advantages. A rope may be attached to a pole fastened (and mind that it be well fastened) in the bank; or it may be attached to a branch of an overhanging tree. Taken in the hands, the swimmer may practise with his legs, or, by holding it in his teeth, he may use all his limbs at once. The rope, however, is not so good as the plank, as it allows of less freedom of motion, and the latter might easily be so fixed as to be laid hold of by the teeth, and held securely.

The Cramp.—Those persons who plunge into the water when they are heated by exercise, and remain in it until they are benumbed with cold, or exhaust themselves by very violent exertion, are the most subject to attacks of cramp. The moment the swimmer is seized by cramp in the legs, he must not suffer himself to feel alarmed, but strike out the limb with all his might, keeping the heel downward, and drawing the foot as far upward as he can, although at the time these movements give him great pain. He may also turn on his back, and jerk the limb into the air, though not so high as to throw himself out of his balance. Should these attempts prove unsuccessful, he must try to reach the shore with his hands, or at least keep himself afloat until assistance can be procured. If he cannot float on his back he may swim upright, keeping his head above the surface, by striking the water downward with his hands near his hips, and thus make steady progress without using the legs. If only one leg be attacked, the swimmer may strike forward with the other; and, to acquire confidence in case of cramp, it is advisable to practise swimming with one hand and leg, with the hands only, or even with one leg.

Entering the Water—Striking Out.—We now come to the most important directions. As the pupil must gradually acquire confidence in this new element, he should not be urged to plunge in against his inclination. After wetting his head, he may wade in until the water is up to his breast; then, turning towards the shore, inflate his lungs, and, inclining forward until the water covers his chin. (The head should be thrown backwards, and the back hollowed, and the chest as much as possible expanded. In swimming, the feet should be about two feet below the surface. The hands should be placed in front of the breast, pointing forward, the fingers kept close together, and the thumb to the fingers, so as to form a slightly hollow paddle. Now strike the hands forward as far as possible, but not bringing them to the surface; then make a sweep backward to the hips, the hand being turned downward and outward; then bring them back under the body, and with as little resistance as may be, to their former position, and continue as before.

The hands have three motions: First, from their position at the breast, they are pushed straight forward; second, they sweep round to the hips, like an oar, the closed and hollowed hands being the paddle portion, and their position in the water and descent serving both to propel and sustain the body; and, third, they are brought back under the body to the first position.

Having learned these motions by practising them slowly, the pupil should proceed to learn the still more important motions of the legs. These are likewise three in number—one of preparation and two of propulsion. First, the legs are drawn up as far as possible, by bending the knees and keeping the feet widely separated; second, they are pushed with force backward and outward, so that they spread as far as possible; and third, the legs are brought together, thus acting powerfully upon the wedge of water which they inclosed.

The motion in the water should be as straight forward as possible, and the more the head is immersed the easier the swimming. Raising at every stroke—breasting, as it is called—is both tiresome and improper.

All these movements should be made with slowness and deliberately, without the least hurry. The learner will soon breathe naturally, and, as the motions are really natural, he will not be long in acquiring them. If he draw in his breath as he rises, and breathe it out as he sinks, he will time his strokes, and avoid swallowing water. Those who have been accustomed to fresh water must be particularly careful when they go into the sea, the water of which is very nauseous.

Plunging or Diving.—In leaping into the water, feet first, which is done from rocks, &c., the feet must be kept close together, and the arms either held close to the side or over the head. In diving head-foremost, the hands must be put together, so as to divide the water before the head. The hands are always a proper position for striking out.

It is wonderful how easy the swimmer directs his course under water. If he wishes to go down or come up, or turn to the right or left, he has but to bend his head and body in that direction, and, after a little use, he will do this almost unconsciously, as if his movements were the result of volition alone.

In descending in the water, bend the head so as to bring the chin near the breast, and curve the back in the same direction; in ascending, hold back the head and hollow the back. In swimming over the surface, look up to the sky; it is quite impossible to dive beneath the surface in this position.

Swimming in Deep Water.—In the swimming schools of Prussia, the pupils are taught in deep water, sustained by a belt and a rope attached to a pole, which the teacher holds as a lever over a railing. The motions of the arms, then of the legs, and then both together, are practised by word of command, like military exercises. The support is given as required. After a few lessons the pole is dispensed with, then the rope; but the pupil is still kept until proficient, within reach of the pole. This mode of learning to swim is like that practised in teaching boys to ride in the circus. A rope, fastened to a belt, passes through a ring in the saddle, and the end is held by the riding-master in the centre of the ring. If the boy falls, his teacher has only to draw upon the rope, and he is secure from danger, and ready to spring to his feet again.

Those who are learning to swim in shallow water, and without a teacher, may find an advantage in the following method: When the learner has acquired some facility in swimming, and wishes to try to swim out of his depth, he should first venture to cross a stream which may be a foot or two overhead in the middle. He must not be alarmed at not finding ground under his feet, or make quick and short strokes, and breathe at the wrong time, so that he involuntarily swallows water—all which mishaps, of course, increase the hurry and agitation, and make it difficult for him to get back to shore. Learners should, therefore, never venture out of their depth without having first tried such distances only as they are certain they can accomplish; for, if they can swim eight or ten yards without allowing their feet to touch the bottom, they can fearlessly attempt to cross a deep stream of only half this width, and so on, increasing the distance by degrees; they will thus progressively attain presence of mind, and find that the deeper the water the greater is its sustaining power, and the easier they will be enabled to swim in it.

Treading Water.—This is a favourite position in the water, and useful as a means of resting in swimming long distances. The position is perpendicular; the hands are placed upon the hips or kept close to the side to assist in balancing the body, being moved, like fins, at the wrist only; the feet are pushed down alternately, so as to support the head above water, and the body may be raised in this way to a considerable extent. While in this position, if the head be thrown back so as to bring the nose and mouth uppermost, and the chest somewhat inflated, the swimmer may sink till his head is nearly covered, and remain for any length of time in this position without motion, taking care to breathe very slowly.

Upright Swimming—System of Bernardi.—Bernardi, an Italian teacher of swimming, who has written a treatise upon the subject, warmly recommends the upright position in swimming as being in conformity with the accustomed movements of the limbs, from the freedom of the hands and arms, greater facility of breathing, and less risk of being caught hold of by persons struggling in the water.

Though this method can never supersede that taught by Nature and the frog—the best professor—it may be practised for variety's sake. The great difficulty is in keeping the head properly balanced, for whichever way it inclines governs the body.

Side Swimming.—In swimming on either side the motions of the legs have no alteration, but are performed as usual. To swim on the left side, lower that side, which is done with the slightest effort, and requires no instruction; then strike forward with the left hand and sideways with the right, keeping the back of the hand to the front, with the thumb side downward, so as to act as an oar. In turning on the other side, strike out with the right hand, and use the left as an oar. To swim on each side alternately, stretch out the lower arm the moment that a stroke is made by the feet, and work with the other arm on a level with the head at the instant that the feet are urging the swimmer forward; and while the upper hand is carried forward and the feet are contracted, the lower hand must be drawn toward the body. This method is full of variety, and capable of great rapidity, but it is also very fatiguing.

Thrusting.—This is a beautiful variety of this exercise, and much used by accomplished swimmers. The legs and feet are worked as in ordinary swimming, but the hands and arms very differently. One arm (say the right) should be lifted wholly out of the water, thrust forward to its utmost reaching, and then dropped upon the water with the hand hollowed, and then brought back by a powerful movement, pulling the water toward the opposite armpit. At the same time, the body must be sustained and steadied by the left hand working in a small circle, and as the right arm comes back from its far reach to the armpit the left is carrying in an easy sweep from the breast to the hip. The left arm is thrust forward alternately with the right, and by these varied movements great rapidity is combined with much ease.

Swimming on the Back.—This is the easiest of all modes of swimming, because in this way a larger portion of the body is supported by the water. It is very useful to ease the swimmer from the greater exertion of more rapid methods, and especially when a long continuance in deep water is unavoidable. The swimmer can turn easily to this position, or, if learning, he has but to incline slowly backward, keeping his head on a line with his body, and letting his ears sink below the surface; then placing his hands upon his hips, he can push himself along with his feet and legs with perfect ease and considerable rapidity.

The hands may be used to assist in propelling in this mode by bringing them up edgewise toward the armpits, and then pushing them down, the fingers fronting inward, and the thumb part down. This is called "winging."

The hands may be used at discretion, the application of force in one direction, of course, giving motion in the other; and the best methods are soon learned when once the pupil has acquired confidence in his powers of buoyancy.

OUR CORNFIELD FLORA.

BY CAROLINE A. WHITE.

There is no spot of earth so desolate or rugged but that Nature brings a bit of floral beauty to cover and adorn it. For every soil, for every situation, she has whole colonies of vegetable inhabitants, relays deep hidden in her fruitful breast, ready to be brought forth whenever needed, stored, it may be, from the beginning, but at any rate, instinct with life, and only waiting favourable circumstances to develope it. On many places of the coast, left bare and scarred by landslips, a spontaneous springing up of shrubs and grasses may be noted by tourists, clothing them from season to season with picturesque uncultivated grandeur.

Then again, observe (and we may do this nearer home) the railway cuttings of to-day, which a few months hence shall be glorious with indigenous verdure; and the brown earth-works, left in their rude and formal nakedness by man, upon whose steps follow close the pitying mother and wraps their bare and shelterless sides in garments of green turf. But for no locality has she prepared so bright-hued a progeny of flowers as for the corn-field.

Devotion, in the days of old mythology, could devise no more befitting or more glorious crown for plenty-bringing Ceres, than one of Poppies and blue Corn-flowers. With these the Greeks and Romans garlanded the statue of the goddess, and her priests wore crowns of them in honour of her at the autumnal ambarvalia. To-day, though the mother of Proserpine lives but in poetry, we find them glorifying (at the expense of good husbandry) the fields dedicated to the cereal crops. How beautiful they are!—those sun-flushed poppies, flaunting their scarlet banners amongst the blue-green stems of the bearded barley and the paler spears of wheat, or the drooping spikelets of the tremulous oats! Beautiful and matchless in exquisite contrast of colour, whether the fields be clad in vernal green or sunburnt to the golden brown of autumn!

We may find the Corn-poppy in many other situations than its legitimate one, but the Corn-bluebottle (*Centaurea cyanus*) seldom opens its azure eyes out of the precincts of the standing corn. Nor does the scentless May-weed lift its solitary white-rayed flowers, or fling abroad the hair-like segments of its sessile leaves, or the purple cockle open its velvet petals, or the golden discs of the Corn-Marigold glitter, but as exceptions in other localities. The same Power who sets bounds to the encroaching sea, limits the whereabouts of the simple flower, and entwines in these especial ones their destiny with the harvest sheaves.

The Poppy tribe (*Papaveraceae*) is said to have received its name from *pappa* (Celtic for pap), because, long previous to the invention of "Daffy's Elixir," nurses were wont to mix this plant with children's food to relieve pain and make them sleep. All this family abound with a milky juice of a highly somnolent quality; that of the *Papaver somniferum* yields us, under the names of opium, laudanum, and morphia, most valuable medicines. The ancients were well aware of the narcotic nature of this species; its inspissated juice was originally prepared at Thebes, and was called, from its beneficent property of allaying pain, *Manus Dei*, or the hand of Deity. Sleep was allegorically represented crowned with white poppies, and scattering them on the slumberous earth.

Our Corn-Poppy (*Papaver rhœas*) may be distinguished by the size of its broad scarlet petals, its short, almost globular capsule, or seed-vessel, and the spreading hairs of its flower-stem. Like others of its congeners, it hangs down its rough, egg-shaped buds, drowsily, till the time of opening them arrives, when the closely packed petals burst the two-parted calyx and flutter forth crumpled and creased from their confinement to flaunt their red flags on the serried fields, and herald the approach of the celestial Flora. We frequently find the base of the petals of the Corn-poppy stained with a dark mark, and its rayed stigma, like a star of purple velvet laid on a yellow ground, amongst its many stamens, adds not a little to the beauty of the flower. Though not accounted of any medical value in the present day, our forefathers gathered its green leaves for their soporific and cooling qualities, using them with the same intention that the heads of the Opium-poppy are used now, and also in soothing ointments. Certain it is, that the whole plant is powerfully narcotic, for the holding of the flowers in the hand produces headache and heaviness; and the same effect has been felt from their presence in a room when forming part of a bouquet of wild flowers.

In a recent visit to Southend we observed a little garden attached to a very humble wayside cottage, which, instead of the usual wilderness of sweet old English flowers, Clove Pinks, and Sops in Wine, Scabious, and Lavender, and Rocket, contained a monotonous crop of tall, dull Opium Poppies, with their straight-stemmed, grey-white flowers and glaucous green leaves. The plot of ground was too small to suggest their being grown for profit, and the lady, whose guest we were, set the matter at rest by telling us that for many years the same crop had filled the sombre-looking garden, whose owner laboured under a most painful and lingeringly careless disease, for which opium afforded her the only relief; but who, finding its purchase too expensive for her small means, had given up her little garden to the growth of the plant, which yielded a sufficient number of Poppy heads or capsules, to keep the poor sufferer in comparatively soothed and pain-deadened state.

This digression has led us wide of the waving corn-fields and their flowers. Let us now turn back and bind the Corn-bluebottle with our Poppy-buds. What can be lovelier in colour or in form than this frilled circle of deep blue florets, seated upon its pale green scaly wheel of bracts, with the dark thread-like anthers in the midst? Like the Knapweed, its near neighbour and relative (that other composite flower close at hand, that looks like a purple tassel set upright), its stems are tough enough to have gained for it in olden times the rustic name of "Hurtsickle, because," says our authority, "it turns the edge of the sickles that reap the corn;" but the Knapweed, with its tall-branched dark green stems, much more deserved this appellation, as any one may prove who attempts to gather its flowers. In fair rivalry with these gay blossoms the Mayweed spreads abroad its white-rayed stars, and may be easily distinguished from its fragrant companions, Wild Chamomile and Corn Chamomile (*Anthemis nobilis* and *Anthemis arvensis*), by the convex centre of its large-rayed flower-heads, each seated on a long naked stalk, whilst they bear erect stems, much branched, and each branch supporting a flower. The aromatic scent of these pungent leaves and blossoms will help to overcome the drowsy exhalations of the nodding poppies; and their palely radiant flowers will set off to great advantage the large handsome purple stars with which the Corn Cockle (*Agrostemma githago*), one of the showiest of the *Lychnis* tribe, crowns its straight downy stems. Close at hand we shall find the tall Field Scabious (*Scabiosa arvensis*), the "widow flower" of France, with bowed head, wearing from year to year her sad-coloured suit of delicate grey or lilac. Every one who knows the rich claret-coloured scabious of our gardens, the dark convex heads of which, with their velvet surface and many white anthers, were named by some of old "our lady's pincushion," will recognise its rustic relative. In by-gone days the juice of this plant, mixed with that of samphire and the powder of borax, was used by dainty women as a cosmetic to clear the face of freckles and morphew, and the whole plant was accounted full of healing qualities.

The pretty Fumitory (*Fumaria capreolata*), with its delicate green foliage and many-branched stems, at the tops of which, in the quaint phrase of one of our old herbalists, "stand many small flowers, as it were in a spike, one above another, made like little birds of a reddish purple colour, with whitish bellies," still loves the corn-fields, and cannot be left out of our rural wreath.

In the times just alluded to, when every baronial hall and manor-house had its "laboratory of flowers," in which the gentlewomen of the household were taught such portions of the chemist's art as the making of distilled waters, ointments, unguents, recipts for beauty, pomanders, and pomades, the Fumitory held a very high place amongst simples, not less for its cosmetical than its remedial qualities. The juice dropped into the eyes, though it produced pain and caused tears, cleared the sight and took away redness in them. Mixed with water and the honey of roses, and the mouth gargled therewith, it healed the soreness of the mouth and throat. The distilled water of the herb taken with treacle was good against pestilence, and the powder of the dried and cured melan-

cleanly! As a toilet lotion, the juice mixed with that of Dock leaves and vinegar took away sunburns and freckles, and with gum arabic dissolved in it, was esteemed an effectual depilatory. Nor does this list contain half the hidden virtues of the herb.

Winding up the stems of the corn, we find the mischievous but graceful Climbing Persicaria (*Polygonum convolvulus*), with its broadly arrow-shaped leaves and lateral spikes of four-whorled greenish flowers; it is a near relation of the common Buckwheat (*Polygonum fagopyrum*), which has recently been brought into cultivation as an excellent food for poultry. The whole habit of this plant so resembles that of the small Bindweed, that it sometimes requires a close inspection to perceive that it is not the parent of the pretty plaited, white, or rose-coloured cups of the *Convolvulus arvensis*, trailing upon the ground or looping little festoons of its wreathing stems from one plant to other, wherever it can find support. Full of fragrance on sunny days—and it opens on no others—it incenses the air with the peculiar odorous principle known as *Coumarin*, to which melilot, sweet-smelling vernal grass, the broad-leaved plaintain, and the flowers of many other plants, owe their almond-like sweetness.

We will not linger over the minor occupants of our cornfields—the common Speedwell (*Veronica agrestis*), with prostrate stems and small blue flowers; the Corn Salad, or Lamb's Lettuce (*Fedia olitoria*), which is extensively used as a salad-herb, and on the Continent cultivated for the purpose; or the modest Shepherd's Purse (*Bursa pastoris*), the "Poor Man's Parmacity" of our forefathers, with its diminutive cruciform white flowers, and its flat triangular seed-vessels, from which it derives its name. Nor is it worth while, unless a pet bird awaits our coming home, to gather more than a specimen of the common Groundsel (*Senecio vulgaris*), with its heads of dull yellow rayless flowers; or the Corn Sow-thistle (*Sonchus arvensis*), which is certain to find a home upon the field. The great Yellow Ox-eye (*Chrysanthemum segetum*), known in Gerard's time as the "Golden Floure of Valentia," will make a brighter contrast with the showy Corn Rose and the brilliant Blew Blue (for so the old masters of floral lore in England called the Poppy and the Cornflower, and we love to perpetuate these rustic names) than even that glittering member of the Composite brotherhood.

Here and there, trailing its branched stems upon the surface of the ground, the variable little flowers of the Heartsease (*Viola tricolor*) live their sunny life. Its prettiness has rendered it a favourite in every age, and being under the dominion of the celestial sign Cancer (according to the old belief in planetary influences) it was anciently held in high repute for its medicinal virtues. The rose herself has scarcely received more eulogy than this exquisite little wanderer, which is found in cultivated fields, on barren ground, and even on the summits of high hills. Sweetest names have been lavished on it, only Nicholas Culpepper, Gent., has ventured to stigmatise it as "that herb which such physicians as are licensed to blaspheme by authority, without danger of having their tongues bored through with an hot iron, call Herb of the Trinity." And having thus disburdened himself of his rising spleen against the old religious name its tripart colouring had given rise to, he tells us that it is also called "Three-faces-under-a-hood," "*Live in idleness*" (a probable corruption of Shakspeare's "Love in idleness," yet so exquisitely characteristic of the prone, sun-loving habits of the plant, that it sounds very like the original); it was also known as "*Cull-me-to-you*," a sweetly significant appellation in reference to its common one of Heartsease; and the old physician and herbalist adds, "in Suffolk we call them Pancies."

There are a few more flowers scattered upon our cereal fields that well deserve our notice, especially the Pheasant's Eye (*Adonis autumnalis*), with its thick green multifid leaves, its bright scarlet flowers, and its classic story. This is the "Adonis-flower" of the elder poets, who adopted the mythic fable which represented the solitary blood-red flowers, dropped as it were over the whole plant, to have fallen from the wounds of the dying youth beloved of Venus. In France it is called "Drops-of-Blood," which the bright red petals are freshly scarlet enough to resemble. Its beauty frequently introduces it to our gardens; but its "pheasants' eyes" glow brightest upon the yellow stubble-fields, in which Nature's hand has planted it—one amongst the fairest flowers with which Peace invests her cereal coronal of gold.

THE SUNBEAM.

BY J. G. TILDESLEY.

Gentle ray of sunlight, glancing
  From the bright and azure sky,
With celestial glory beaming
  Full of light, and life, and joy,
Gilding every hill and mountain,
  Smiling on their rugged side,
Cheering every crystal fountain,
  And the streamlets as they glide!

Tell me, is it not thy mission
  On life's gloomy path to shine!—
To give man a feeble vision
  Of those Heavenly rays divine?
Yes! to soothe affliction's pillow,
  And to banish earthly gloom,
Thine to cheer time's floating billow,
  As it bears us to the tomb!

THE LITTLE BREAD-WASTERS.

(Adapted from the German.)

BY HANNAH CLAY.

There were once two little children, named Godfrey and Emma, who lived in a nice house, with kind parents, and had every pleasure that they could reasonably desire. This little brother and sister were very kind to one another, and obedient to their parents. They were seldom corrected, for they had few faults; but one great fault they were constantly guilty of, and that was, that they were wasteful and extravagant about their eating. Their mamma had not been sufficiently strict with them in this respect; and they would leave such a dirty plate after every meal that you would have been quite ashamed to see them. Bread especially, that good gift of our Heavenly Father, they crumbled about them, threw aside into corners, or kneaded into all kinds of curious figures. Their father had often taken them into the fields, in spring, [illegible] and [illegible], and had desired them to notice how carefully the corn was sowed, ploughed, and reaped; but I am afraid that while he was talking, instead of listening, they were all the time watching the little birds in the hedges, or gathering the wild-flowers at their feet, or admiring the graceful waving of the ears of corn as they bent their shining heads to the breeze. Then, when the corn was ripe, these two children would follow the reapers in their merry work, drink buttermilk with them, and rub the brown rustling ears of wheat between their little hands to extract the grains, which they would parch at home on a shovel before the kitchen fire, their careless little hearts the while taking small heed of their father's wise words.

Thus the pieces of bread were still wasted, wasted, even although the children went to the farmer's barn to see the corn thrashed out by the great heavy flails, and to the miller's to see it ground, and to the baker's to see the flour made into dough, and baked in the large brick oven. They learnt no wisdom from all these curious sights; but the food, and especially the bread, at home, was still wasted as much as ever.

The kind and tender mother of Godfrey and Emma tried another plan. She thought to improve their young hearts by showing them the poor pale hungry children who came to the door to beg a bit of bread, and gave a hundred blessings for an old dry crust. At such times Godfrey and Emma perceived for a moment how wrong they were, and promised faithfully to be less wasteful in future; but when they were again satisfied with a good dinner and had a piece of bread before them, they forgot all their resolutions, began to knead it into birds and sheep and all kinds of figures, and finally threw it away.

One fine day in summer it was Emma's birthday; and the two children were taken by their kind parents for a short excursion into a beautiful wood near their house. There the birds were singing, and the green glades were enamelled with a thousand flowers; while the sunshine flickered through the tops of the tall trees, and made a golden network on the ground. Godfrey and Emma gathered sticks, and assisted their parents to build up a fire near a clear brook that ran through the wood. When they had done this, and had seen the coffee-kettle slung on a pole supported by two forked branches stuck into the ground, the brother and sister were at liberty to run where they pleased until the meal was ready. So they went about hither and thither, plucking wild flowers, until at length they became aware of a pretty reddish-brown squirrel, that sprang from tree to tree, from bush to bush, and endeavored by mischievous antics to attract their notice. "Oh!" said the children to one another, "if we could but catch the pretty creature, and take it home to live with us!" So they ran eagerly after it; but whenever they were apparently on the point of seizing it, it was off again, much too nimble for them; and at length it disappeared, with a few great springs into the thickest part of the wood.

Godfrey and Emma looked wistfully after the provoking little animal, but the wood in that direction appeared so dark and gloomy, that they dared not follow the squirrel; so they gave up the idea of capturing it, and sat down on a fallen trunk of a tree to rest themselves and recover their breath. As they gazed about them, they remarked with alarm that they were in a part of the wood which they had never explored before. They could neither hear the murmur of the stream, nor the voices of their parents conversing with one another; nor could they discern, beneath the over-hanging branches of the trees, nor among the tangled underwood, any beaten path by which to find their way back again to the place they had left. Poor children! a dreadful fear came over them; and they began to run about and call loudly on all sides, in the hope that their parents would come to their rescue. It was all in vain, no one replied; and the further they ran through trees and bushes, the more they became aware that they had really lost themselves.

The sun had now set, and it began to grow

dark. The songs of the birds had ceased; and nothing was to be heard but the hootings of the owls as they called to one another from the tops of the old trees. Tired to death with running, anxiety, and crying; faint with hunger, their clothes and shoes ragged and torn with pushing through the brambles; the wretched little ones seated themselves beneath a tree, and, with their arms round one another, fell into a kind of doze.

It appeared to them that they had not slept long, when Emma raised her head and cried: "Look! dear brother, look! is not that a light shining there?"

The brother looked, and really thought he perceived something shining through the trees. Full of hope that they might reach some cottage, or find some one who could help them in their sore strait, they stood up, tired as they were, and hastened towards the light. Before long they came to an opening in the bushes; and, looking through, they perceived something so wonderful that they stood stock still with amazement.

In a great open space in the middle of the trees, sat a tall and very beautiful woman, attired in a dark-green dress strewn with stars, whence shone the light that had attracted the children. Round this splendid queen or fairy were immense baskets, filled to the brim with little broken pieces of bread. All excepting one, which was heaped with grains of wheat, ripe and yellow. Now while the brother and sister still stood gazing and wondering, behold a troop of little ragged children, who advanced in a long procession from the opposite quarter of the wood. Each of these pale, sorrowful, barefooted little creatures carried a basket made of willows, and stepped in his or her turn before the beautiful woman. Then, as each child came opposite to her, the lady took a little piece of bread from one of the baskets, which changed in her white hand into a loaf, and this she placed in the child's basket with a friendly smile. The little ragged creature kissed her hand in token of thankfulness, and took its place in the retiring procession, which departed quietly as they had come. While this was still going on, a rush of wings was heard in the air, and an immense flight of small birds came and fluttered around the beneficent fairy. She extended her graceful foot, and with the pointed toe of her golden slipper pushed over the basket containing grain. The birds flew upon it with joyful chirpings, and in a few moments it was all eaten up.

Godfrey and Emma stood and watched this wonderful scene. Hungry as they were, the sight of the bread roused an intolerable desire to eat some of it; and by-and-bye they stole round through the trees, and slipped into the procession of starving children. The nearer they advanced towards the beautiful woman, the louder beat their hearts; until at length, when they stood in their turns before her, they hung their heads, and remained speechless, clinging to one another.

"What do you want with me, you little bread-wasters?" said the beautiful lady in a severe voice. "Do you know to whom you come? I am the Corn-seed Fairy. I wander through the whole world, and collect all the pieces of bread that careless people throw away, in order to feed the hungry with them. What do you want with me, you naughty children, who have so often spoiled and wasted the good gift of God! To punish you as you deserve you shall now, with hunger tormenting you at the sight of the bread which is denied to you, suffer all the sorrow felt by the poor starving children, who could often have satisfied their hunger with what you threw away."

She pointed to a mossy bank; and with flowing tear and conscience-stricken hearts the brother and sister sat down. Thus they remained for hours, watching the endless procession of famished children; and still more tormenting waxed their hunger, and still more sorrowful their little hearts.

At length they fell quite despairingly upon their knees. "Forgive! good Corn-seed Fairy, forgive!" cried they. "We know now how very wrong we have been; and never again will we be guilty of wasting bread."

Then the Fairy rose from her mossy seat, for she saw that this time the children made their promise in holy earnest. Bending compassionately over them she touched their eyes with the fringe of her golden veil.

* * * * *

Godfrey and Emma awoke as from a deep slumber. There were voices calling to them, well-known, beloved voices; and through the trees they saw their parents advancing towards them, accompanied by neighbours with lanterns, who had joined in the search for the missing children. With loud cries of joy, the little ones rushed into the arms of their dear father and mother. Their first delight over, they turned to look for the beautiful lady, but Fairy, children, and baskets had all disappeared. Could it have been simply a dream?

Dream or no dream, the effect of the vision remained. Brother and sister alike kept silence as to what they had seen, but from that day they never wasted food; and especially did they respect and honour bread, the best gift of God.

OUR LIBRARY TABLE.

POE AND HIS POETRY.*

—

"Sic animis natum inventumque poema juvandis."
HORACE.

—

The life of Edgar Allan Poe is one of the most striking and the most melancholy on record. Gifted with the brightest genius, and endowed with graceful and tender feelings, he unhappily succumbed to all the temptations which could allure him, and at last fell suddenly struck down in the prime of his life and genius. It is not our intention to write a biography of him, but some brief words of introduction are needed before entering on the consideration of his poetry. He married his beautiful and amiable cousin, Virginia Clemm, and she appears to have been possessed of every virtue which adorns the softer sex. She was throughout all his trials and his failings, the same tender, affectionate, loving wife to the end. Poe loved her, doubtless, with all the strength and purity of which his faulty nature was capable; and when she died, he gave vent to his grief in a little poem, which is, perhaps, one of the loveliest ever written, and which we shall presently mention.

The poetical writings of Edgar Allan Poe are remarkable for the love of the beautiful that pervades them, for the deep [illegible] that characterises so many of them, and for the extraordinary word-melody, if we may use the expression, which they possess. With regard to Poe's love of the beautiful, it is perfectly true though paradoxical, that plunging as he did into excess, no taint of [illegible] can be found in his poetry, which is so [illegible] ideal and lovely in its creation as to be utterly free from all sensualism. While the poet led a life of riotous debauchery with occasional fits of repentance, his genius burned with the purity of its flame unsullied. It seems through all his verses as if the spirit made amends for its earthly failings by soaring upwards into a region of undimmed radiance and [illegible] where the sweetest hopes are quivering on the verge of tears. The first quotation we will give as showing his love of all that is beautiful, is a verse from a little poem which is a gem of the most polished loveliness:

> "On desperate seas long wont to roam,
> Thy hyacinth hair, thy classic face,
> Thy Naiad airs have brought me home,
> To the glory that was Greece,
> And the grandeur that was Rome."

Can anything more keenly and tenderly express a love which might, indeed, be the inspiration of a poet? Another verse (from a different poem) which conveys as perfect an idea of the etherialisation of his mind is this—

> "Thou wast that all to me, love,
> For which my soul did pine;
> A green isle in the sea, love,
> A fountain and a shrine,
> All wreathed with fairy fruits and flowers,
> And all the flowers were mine."

To what shall his poetry be compared? To the chime of his own musical "Bells?" to the fresh bloom of flowers? to the ripple of a silver stream? But no one will find in his compositions any [illegible] of hidden feeling or solemn inward [illegible]. Non omnia possumus omnes, and to those who are content to take his poetry as it is, will be offered a noble gift, saddened by the recollection that the mind from which it came was so often and so sadly abused. The next quotation we have marked is one which unites beauty, melody, and sorrow; it is this—

> "Come, let the burial rite be read, the funeral song be sung!
> An anthem for the queenliest dead that ever died so young;
> A dirge for her the doubly dead, in that she died so young!
> * * * * *
> The sweet Lenore hath gone before, with Hope that flew beside,
> Leaving thee wild for the dear child, that should have been thy bride.
> * * * * *
> The life upon her yellow hair, but not within her eyes?"

The love which Poe had for his wife was one of his brightest and most redeeming qualities. She never had a reproach or cold word for him, often as he gave cause for them. And his grief when his Virginia died was such as might have been expected from such love. In the poem we are about to quote is embodied his affection and grief for his loved and lost one, whom he calls under the name of "Annabel Lee;" and thus runs the last verse:—

> "For the moon never beams without bringing me dreams,
> Of the beautiful Annabel Lee,
> And the stars never rise but I feel the bright eyes,
> Of the beautiful Annabel Lee;
> And so all the night-tide I lie down by the side,
> Of my darling—my darling—my life and my bride,
> In the sepulchre there by the sea,
> In her tomb by the sounding sea."

Surely never was sorrow of a stricken heart more touchingly told!

Poe's wonderful command of language, and the manner in which he weaves the melodies of words, cannot but strike the most cursory reader. Like a true poet, he with all his genius

* The poetical works of Edgar Allan Poe. (London: J. & C. Brown, Ave Maria Lane.)

was never careless, but each stanza was delicately finished and balanced. Perhaps the most obvious example we can give of this is the following verse from his "Ulalume"—

" And now as the night was senescent,
And star dials pointed to morn,
As the star dials hinted of morn,
At the end of our path a liquescent,
And nebulous lustre was born;
Out of which a miraculous crescent,
Arose with a duplicate horn,
Astarte's bediamonded crescent,
Distinct with its duplicate horn."

Of the "Bells" it is needless to speak; still more of the "Raven;" for these two poems would require an essay to themselves.

It may perhaps be allowed to compare Poe's poetry with that of Keats's, for both seemed only to long for and depict the beautiful, save that that of Keats is the most approaching to voluptuousness and is the more sensuous. As we have said, Poe shows no deep inward compunction or religious sorrow. But we would rather not speak of this, but be content to take his verse as radiant with all that is most delicate in beautiful ideality. Sorrow we must feel that such a genius was marred by sin. But he should be judged charitably, and not held up to posthumous reproach by dull scribblers, who—without having a spark of his genius, without knowing his temptations, without comprehending his nature—measure all men by their own standard of dull and pharisaical respectability. Not for one moment would we say a word that could be construed into advocating the pernicious doctrine that "genius must be allowed irregularities;" but remembering that Edgar Allen Poe was gifted and graced with brilliant powers, remembering that he lost his wife who was his better genius, and lastly, remembering that the tomb has closed over him, we would tell all his enemies and detractors that there never was a nobler or a sweeter motto, than that of, "De mortuis nil nisi bonum."

Thinking of him with powerful admiration, how can we better finish than with his own words—

" For alas, alas! with me,
The light of life is o'er,
'No more—no more—no more'
(Such language holds the solemn sea,
To the sands upon the shore),
Shall bloom the thunder-blasted tree,
Or the stricken eagle soar.

W. R.

SHAKESPEARE'S WORKS. Edited by Mary Cowden Clarke.—(*New York: D. Appleton and Co. London: Trübner and Co.*)—At a time when expurgated editions of Shakespeare for family reading are daily advertised, another edition, scrupulously revised, seemed scarcely called for, even though edited by one who so thoroughly comprehends and appreciates the poet as Mrs. Cowden Clarke. But the editor, in her preface, has reassured us. It is not an *improved* text, but the *pure text of Shakespeare*, so far as the experienced and discriminating judgment of one who has studied him so well and thoroughly, will enable her to discover what it really is. It is an edition in which "whatever corrections, undoubtedly proper, or with high probability of being so, have been suggested in the innumerable other editions, are given in the text: the reader is spared the process, and has the result." Whatever word in Shakespeare may now be obsolete, or whatever allusion there may be to old-fashioned custom, can, when the reader feels the need, be explained by reference to the glossary (a copious one), in which whatever was good in all the old rubbish of footnotes is given, and the poet is no longer buried under the mass of references with which his commentators have overlaid his text. The sonnets are included in this edition, which, for the convenience of purchasers, is published in one, and in two volumes.

THE TEMPERANCE SPECTATOR; THE TEMPERANCE DICTIONARY; ALCOHOL; WHY I HAVE TAKEN THE PLEDGE; THE TEMPERANCE STAR. (*Job Caudwell, 335, Strand.*)—We take this group of Temperance publications en masse, giving the palm of excellence in a literary sense to the Rev. Dawson Burns' Temperance Dictionary—a work which promises to contain a great deal of information upon other subjects than the one it is written to support. Here and there indeed the author, in his zeal for total abstinence, wrests his illustrations a little to one side; as under the word "Abednego," one of the four young Hebrew princes conveyed to Babylon with Daniel and his companions, where he refused to take the King's meat and wine, and exhibited in his subsequent appearance the *healthy* effects of an *abstinent diet*. In the text it is distinctly stated that it was to save themselves from *defilement* that the Hebrews refused to eat the King's meat or drink his wine, for the food of the heathens was an abomination to the Jews; but the argument pressed out of the passage might equally serve abstainers from flesh, and may be handed over to the Vegetarians. The "Temperance Spectator" we perceive has been for some time before the public. The present number we regret to say is chiefly occupied with *intemperate* abuse of persons and publications that differ in opinion from those of which it is the organ. It would be ludicrous if it were not painful to observe, in their efforts at one species of perfectability, how the ostensible leaders and supporters of this gracious virtue forget that charity to the weaknesses or mistakes of others which should of right belong to Temperance. Not by hard words, or phrases wrested from their real meanings, can the cause of this truly excellent movement be strengthened. It is rather singular that teetotalism requires a distinct edition of the Bible "with marginal readings and notes in harmony with the teaching of teetotalism." Hitherto, good men and temperate ones have thought it sufficient to make their lives har-

manner as much as possible with the teaching of the Bible.

MISCELLANEOUS POEMS. By Bota P. (London: Pitman & Co., 20, Ave Maria Lane.)—Why we should be favoured with this volume [illegible], as it appears, twelve months after publication, is as great a mystery as how it came to be written, or—a greater one still—published. That the author has the faculty of versification is evident. He expresses himself clearly at times, and in "Solitude," and in one or two others of the minor poems, is comprehensible, and even agreeable. But whenever a thought has to be sustained, as in the most ambitious poem in the volume ("Christmas Day"), we find the author wholly unable to control his Pegasus—the so-called poem a very chaos of words, a jumble of absurdity, with just sufficient elements to show the writer running through twenty-four verses with an idea which he or she does not know what to do with. Every line succeeding the last is a greater knot of verbal mystery, which the reader is totally unable to disentangle, except by [illegible], when the whole resolves itself into the unsatisfactory compounds we have named. Take the following verse, for instance, though any one would exemplify our meaning as well:

For not yet, is it not yet this day of days,
  This music-hall of men, this ground of peace;
[illegible], [illegible] all [illegible]
  Of Infinite Presence. Nay, not yet the [illegible]
[illegible] in [illegible] things; not yet may cease
  The din of discord; but it shall; the harp,
The bit-thought, it is given which all those
  [illegible] shall [illegible]. It widens; hark!
  His "It is finished" now [illegible] all which lies
    the dark.

Here we have the most extraordinary agglomeration of phrases—the "Music-hall" (whether the Surrey or Oxford-street is not stated)—"this ground of peace," an unexplained "man," "the din of discord," "the harp," "the bit-thought." Really it is painful, where a sacred theme is in question, to find it treated in a manner which excites only ludicrous ideas. But, lest we should seem to have wittingly culled an exceptional verse of this strange rhapsody, we take another one at random:

O, messengers, until [illegible] with [illegible] more!
  O long-excelled, that [illegible] [illegible]
    gems!
O [illegible] (for here, lo, the Christ is born!)
  [illegible] your [illegible] round the globe!
The Highest, oh, is here. Adown his face,
  [illegible] that is being [illegible]. Yea, if I
May [illegible] ye [illegible], the [illegible]
With [illegible] thought to life! But I will try:
[illegible] "Christ!" [illegible] Music [illegible]
    through His eye.

Really we are greatly tempted to continue our quotations, and, upon second thoughts, we will; but our specimen shall be from another poem. It is entitled, "Thou art no more!"

Thou art no more! Can this be so?
  My heart will not believe
The thought, but [illegible] with [illegible],
  [illegible] "not believe."
[illegible] of the lonely [illegible],
  A something [illegible] "death."
She [illegible] before [illegible]
  Out of her mouth [illegible] breath!
  Out of her mouth, up through the skies,
[illegible] her [illegible];
  And the [illegible]
The body of [illegible] "her presence."

Our readers will perceive that neither the laws of Lindley Murray nor those of metrical composition are of much consequence to Bota P., who in his great poem (longitudinally considered) tells us,

Ah! I begin
A cheerful thought to take, when I will do:
  This not the blessed angels [illegible] sing,
When their young [illegible] into their view
  Came the fair Child of Bethlehem? I think it is
    not!

Comparisons are proverbially odious, but we are compelled to say that less pleasant singing it has seldom been our misfortune to listen to. Here and there we find a strain modelled upon the quaint type of George Herbert's pious songs: take, for instance, "Content":

Ah! sweet Content and I are one!
  They heal and shine together—
And we will, no never, sever!
  Whate'er the kind of weather,
I make the show—Content's the motion.
  In these we walk
  With quiet talk,
With here and there a little laugh,
  The path of life together.

Here we have an attempt at the simplicity, the conceits, interpolated like an appoggiatura in music, the very rhythm; but where is the analogy to the subject, the relevance of the grace-note to the theme? Logically speaking, how can Content, which in the first four lines is treated personally, become leather in the fifth? And being the material of which the shoes are composed, how can Content be said to walk in them? Really Bota P. is determined to mystify us in every way; and we can scarcely forgive him, seeing that the "Music of the Winds," and other unpretentious compositions, exhibit (as we have before said) a facility for verse-making, an ear for rhythm and number, and an occasional prettiness of expression, which might have resulted in something better.

PERIODICALS.

MARGERY BROWNE: A [illegible] IDEAL. By G. E. Sargent. THE PEASANT'S HOME. By Mark Lemon. (Groombridge and Sons, 5,

Paternoster-row).—We have here the 13 and 14 numbers of this pleasant series of juvenile tales. Miss Sargent's second story is very much superior to "Hovering Hall," in the versatility and interest of its contents. It is a tale that young people, especially boys, will delight in: full of adventure and pretty descriptions of far-off scenery and strange objects. A Captain Hastings, after living some years in California with his family where he has amassed considerable property, takes the command of a vessel to England, glad of the opportunity of returning to his native land, and embarks with his wife and children. Unhappily, the crew is made up for the most part of renegades from other ships; in short, a desperate set of men, who plot to take the ship from him and make property of her cargo. The mate, with a few of the sailors, are faithful, but these fall victims to a fever which breaks out on board; and while the captain is still ill of it, he and his family are put into a boat and rowed on shore to a coral island in the Pacific. The black cook, "Guinea," and the dog "Neptune," swim from the ship and join them, and the former supplies the comic element of the story. The vicissitudes and expedients of the family, "all taken off" the island are very amusing and well described. The boys learn to be useful, and observant in self-reliance, and "Guinea" is a capital fellow—whose acquaintance we are certain our young friends will be glad to make.

No. 14 is a well-told story, but it can scarcely be considered to fall naturally into the series. The incidents and suggestions are not those with which we should desire to familiarize young people. The Pedlar's Hoard belongs, of right, to an older and more worldly-wise generation, who know how to appreciate Lucy Lightfoot's social obligations to Mary Gordon, and are perfectly awake to the craft and double-dealing involved in Mr. Withers' "Selling Off, Alarming Sacrifices, &c.," and who, without enquiry, know how to estimate the questionable calling of the London young gentleman—Mr. Simmons. We know that children in these days are more informed on such matters than we could desire them to be; but not even the amusing manner in which the story is told, can reconcile us to the introduction of such characters and scenes as fit ones to figure in, or form the superstructure of, a tale for children.

English Woman's Journal. (London: 19, Langham Place, *Regent Street*; *W. Kent and Co. Paternoster-row*).—The June number of our contemporary contains much excellent matter; an article, entitled "An Interesting Blue Book," affords a carefully written summary of the report of the education commissioners, and is followed by another instalment of the memoir of "Madame Luce, of Algiers;" but the paper that calls for most notice, and the subject of which cannot be too widely known, is that entitled "A Rural House of Bondage," which exhibits some of the wrongs existing under the system of "Statute-fairs," at which farm-servants are hired from year to year. As the fact itself may be new to many of our metropolitan readers we will transcribe the author's description of some, and, of our own knowledge, we may say, not the worst features of this truly "vicious and grossly demoralising system."

"At these 'statutes,' or, as the country folks term them, 'stattis,' hundreds of youths and servants-girls [illegible] regularly and [illegible] to enter year after year into annual compacts of slavery. Not so bad as American slavery; no, it is in a great measure voluntary, yet not altogether so. [illegible] have [illegible], and [illegible] servants, for as yet no Earl of Shaftesbury has inaugurated a great national system of general registry. What most strikes the [illegible] of this [illegible] and grossly demoralising system is, that to the young it is a day much looked forward to as a general holiday, though [illegible] frequently [illegible], [illegible] drudgery, and demoralising slavery. There is usually a change, but it is often a change from bad to worse. Farther [illegible] to our annual English slave-mart servants without [illegible], who can there get places without them; and heads of families, so well known in their own neighbourhoods, that their only chance of obtaining servants at all is by going to strangers at a distance. The bait by which the silly slave is most effectually [illegible] is what is called the 'arles,' 'earnest,' or 'fastening penny.' Sometimes two-and-sixpence or five shillings is thus obtained, and for this miserable sum they give up what Burns calls 'nerves, sinews, mind, body, [illegible] it may be, wit, conscience, [illegible] and [illegible] free-will into bondage;' for it [illegible] it was so in his day, and in Scotland also. I have long since [illegible] this [illegible] of the [illegible] [illegible] of the most demoralising of its [illegible]; [illegible] of the tyranny and drudgery, its [illegible] and natural results, [illegible] the young into premature marriages, and young women into haunts of vice,

"Any where, any where,"

out of the hands of their domestic foes, into debauchery and crime, crowding with early wickedness our prisons and our union workhouses."

If I remember aright, William Howitt has already broached the subject in one of his rural tales; but it is one of those deeply rooted evils which only yield to the force of public condemnation. We are glad to find, from a paragraph in a provincial exchange, that during the past month an influential meeting was held at Doncaster to promote the establishment of a registry office for farm servants. Mr. E. B. Denison, late M.P. for the Riding, took the chair, and was supported by the clergy of the deanery and many of the principal farmers of the district. The speakers admitted the evils of the present system of hiring, and, whilst doing so, they expressed an opinion that the plan of register offices should in the first instance be tried in the case of female servants, as it was regarded impolitic to carry out such a plan with regard to the men. A committee was appointed to carry out the object of the meeting. Here is a first step in the direction of the very measure suggested by the writer of the paper referred to, and we heartily hope it may be followed up with the earnestness and firmness that it calls for. The unnamed writer of "Fruits in their Season" continues his pleasant gossip upon his very fruitful subject.

AMUSEMENTS OF THE MONTH.

Really there is little theatrical news for a critic's pen to record as the result of the last month. To a certain extent, the intense heat of the weather has thinned the audiences, though managers have little to complain of in that respect. At

THE ADELPHI,

the famous "Colleen Bawn" has been running as usual, and, therefore, all the intelligence as to that house is summed up in a line. At

THE HAYMARKET,

Mr. and Mrs. C. Mathews have made their appearance in "The Overland Route," and other pieces in which scope is given for the peculiar talent of these favourite artistes. At

THE PRINCESS'S,

Mr. Fechter and Mr. Phelps have been alternately delighting the numerous and brilliant audiences. The play of "Werner" has been revived, and we are promised "Othello," which will enable us to have some material for our readers' amusement in the way of description and criticism. At

THE OLYMPIC,

Mr. Robson, having recovered, has been performing in "Ticklish Times," and a new comedy from the French (about which French adaptation we shall one day, when it is time for such, say a word), called "A Charming Woman," has been produced, Miss Amy Sedgwick playing the chief part. At

THE STRAND,

The comedy of "The Old Story" has been running. With all deference to its author, who holds the first place as regards a prolific pen in burlesque writing, we really cannot but think the piece, amusing as it is, scarcely deserves the honoured name of Comedy. The characters are all old ones, though very amusing. The dialogue is, of course, very smart and pleasant, as all is from the author's pen. The burlesque, "Aladdin," is still running.

THE FANCY FAIR OF THE DRAMATIC COLLEGE

Takes place at Sydenham on July 20th, and we trust it will be productive of large results to the treasury. It is in aid of an object most praiseworthy. We certainly hope to succeed in seeing the "brilliant galaxy" (to borrow a fashionable euphemism) of stars that will officiate as vendors at the stalls, and will say a little thereon in our next.

VOCAL ASSOCIATION.

ST. JAMES'S HALL.

The last concert of the season took place on the evening of the 10th ult., and was, as usual, fully attended. The entertainment presented a varied and liberal programme, the chief novelties being the appearance of Miss Anna Whitty and the re-appearance of Mr. Aptommas, the harpist, after seven years' recess. Amongst the solo singers were Miss Stabach, Mdlle. Koch, from Leipsic; Miss Messent, Signori Belart and Ciabatta, and Herr Della Anno—a German baritone, of whose powers a single hearing scarcely warrants our pronouncing an opinion. Of Miss Whitty's voice much has been said, and we are inclined to endorse all that has been reported of its fulness and flexibility; her notes are generally so pure and finished, that, while her vocalism has improved, we regret that she has something to unlearn, and especially counsel her to restrain the exhibition of unnecessary power, which provincial singers (especially from the northern districts) are so prone to indulge in. The facility and gracefulness of her vocalisation were very pleasingly displayed in Rossini's delicious air, "Non più Mesta," which, with the exception of the last few notes, was carefully and exquisitely executed; in these a vainglorious desire to astonish by the power of her voice, almost overcame the finesse of its elegant execution. Again, the appearance of labour—the action which gives the impression of forcing the voice from the larynx is not pleasing, and should be got rid of as soon as possible. The delightful solo and chorus, "With the carol on the tree," from Dr. Bennett's "May Queen," was given, con amore, by Miss Stabach and the choir, for the first, and, consequently, the last time this season. The "Ave Maria," from Mendelssohn's posthumous opera of "Loreley," which so often delighted the frequenters of these concerts.

during last year's series, was also reproduced; the chorus of women's voices, in sweetness and richness, painfully contrasting with the singing of the solo part so exquisitely and devotedly rendered by Madame Catherine Hayes, but to which Miss Messent's voice and style is by no means equal. Rossini, always melodious and healthy, found an agreeable exponent in Signor Belart, who sang, with much taste, the aria "Pria che spunti in Ciel" (*Matrimonio Segreto*), as well as the duet with Belletti—"Ah! bliss da quel Mercato" (*Il Barbiere*), and the buffo aria "Papataci," into the droll comedy of which he entered fully. As for Belletti, always rich in voice, and genial and at home with his audience, his singing was sympathetic, and resulted in an unavoidable encore. Miss Stabbach gave Haydn's sweet canzonet, "My Mother bids me bind my hair", very charmingly; and Mdlle. Koch essayed one of Mozart's delicious arias. If we except Mendelssohn's delightful part-song, "Oh hills, oh vales" which we have not correctly [illegible] to require some [illegible], the choral gems of the evening were J. S. Bach's "God is our refuge in distress," and "Behold how glorious is yon sky" (Grosse), both performed, for the first time, but with remarkable precision, and devotional expression. It has more than once occurred to us, through the concerts of the present season, that the progress of the choir was most observable in sacred music; this is probably owing to the growing popularity of oratorios, the frequency of their occurrence, and the demand for auxiliary force on festival and other occasions. A very delightful feature of the evening was the performance of Mr. Aptommas, an artist whose playing appeals not only to the admiration, but to the hearts of his audience—a need in music, too often lost sight of in these days of muscular force and showy manipulation—and which, very late in the evening, awakened real enthusiasm in the audience, who broke into a very *furore* of applause, which Mr. Aptommas gracefully acknowledged by returning and delighting them yet more with the simple plaintiveness of "Poor Mary Ann." Of the performance of Miss Alice Mangold, a very young and carefully taught pianist, all we have to say is summed up in these phrases: we could wish that something more of mind could be infused into her playing, which is rigidly correct, very clever, but at present soulless. In our last notice of the Vocal Association we mentioned the spirited performance of the "Garibaldi Chorus," by the choir, but neglected to name the composer, Mr. W. Spark, of Leeds. Our review has already exceeded our privileged space, or we should have been tempted to enter into other details relating to these concerts, and [illegible] to last month's [illegible], which is however passed at this date.

BURFORD'S PANORAMA,

Leicester Square,

Is a place particularly adapted for a visit this sunny weather, as the contemplation of the pictures, especially "Messina," with that lovely scene too, carry the spectator's mind far from this smoky and unbearable city to regions of beautiful scenery and fresh air. W. R.

LONDON AND MIDDLESEX ARCHÆOLOGICAL SOCIETY.

A meeting of this Society is fixed for to-morrow, July 2nd, at the church in Austin Friars, at 11 o'clock at noon precisely. The history of the church, which was granted by Edward VI. (all but the choir and chapels) to a congregation of German Protestant refugees for religion's sake, will be given by the Rev. Thos. Hugo, whose antiquarian research and interest in all that remains of ancient London is well known and appreciated. The members will also visit Sion College, where the Librarian, the Reverend W. H. Milman, M.A., will give an account of the library, and a selection of the MSS. and early printed books will be exhibited. The meeting will terminate at the Artillery Ground, where a brief history of the company will be given, and the armoury, &c. exhibited.

THE TOILET.

(Especially from Paris.)

First Figure.—Dress of grey *barège*. On the skirt nine flounces, bordered with mauve silk. A plaiting of *barège* forms a heading to the upper flounce. Body high and pointed, trimmed with a plaiting edged with mauve and two bows, *rosettes*, *macarons*, or whatever other ornament is adopted. Wide sleeves, with an opening edged with a plaiting. A single shawl of black lace. Muslin under-sleeves and *chemisette*. Bonnet composed of white and mauve crape; the front and curtain of the latter colour, the crown white, puffed, and covered with spotted black *tulle*. The only ornament on the outside is a drooping mauve feather, inside a *bandeau* of Parma violets; mauve strings. Swedish leather gloves.

Second Figure.—Robe of emerald green silk, made in the *redingote* style, and simply

ornamented from top to bottom with silk bows edged with narrow black lace. Sleeves wide and open. Muslin collar and under-sleeves. White muslin skirt, trimmed with a deep flounce, headed with two rows of puffing. Bonnet with a loose crown, made of spotted white tulle. The front is [illegible], the curtain white crape, covered with black lace. Branches of fuchsias are placed in the middle of the front, and hang down at each side; inside a [illegible] [illegible] of black blonde, with a narrow white blonde border. White blond down the cheeks. [illegible] parasol of [illegible] [illegible].

TOILET FOR A LITTLE GIRL.—A toilet for a little girl about six years old.—Skirt and jacket of embroidered white [illegible]; [illegible] collar and under-sleeves. Hat either of the Tudor, or bell-shape, of Italian straw, trimmed with flowers. Maroon kid [illegible] boots. Blue parasol.

At length the light colors belonging to the season have made their appearance; the most popular are foulards, gardenias with flounces, like mulls and the chintzes, piqués and mixed fabrics in linens. Tarlatans, silk grenadines, muslins, and French lawns, sprinkled with sprigs of diverse colors, such as pale-yellow, blue, green, rose, &c., the grounds preferred being white or pearl grey.

Shawls and mantelets of muslin bordered with flounces, embroidered or simply trimmed, are again in vogue; and shawls of lace, China crape, white embroidered with black, or gold colour and black; shawls of grenadine, plain, or bordered with lace; in brief, shawls of all sorts of light fabrics, are the rage for the present summer.

I give you notice of a grand simplification in the toilet, and no more. We have now only few [illegible] or [illegible]—the form is becoming more supple and more natural, and, after having metamorphosed women into individual [illegible], Fashion, by a reverse [illegible] of her wheel, decides that they shall return to the appearance of women, and become simple, graceful, and [illegible].

In the meanwhile, the actual style of toilet demands a certain harmony in the figure which forms its [illegible], and the new fashions and new forms would require a longer space to describe them than I have at my disposal. A short time since we were content with a cambric petticoat bound merely embroidered or garnished with lace. As [illegible] as English [illegible] to [illegible] [illegible], the [illegible] which [illegible] grey, with [illegible] of black, or [illegible], or violet, are much in vogue, while, for the [illegible] and the sea-side, I have seen a mixed fabric [illegible] white and black, bordered with black velvet, and trimmed with a broad band of black silk, forming a galloon above it; with this [illegible] [illegible], a white one is a [illegible].

PASSING EVENTS RE-EDITED.

"Sensation songs," "sensation dramas," "sensation ballets," and the alarmingly sensational performances of Blondin at the Sydenham home of science and the fine arts, are just now the current vogue. When eighty thousand persons collect to see a man play at chances, not only with his own neck, but with that of his own child, it is a sign that at least the hazard has its charms. The sensational hazards of the performance had not reached half their expected [illegible] when the interference of Sir George Lewis stopped the [illegible] exhibition in the bud, and reduced the altitude of the acrobat from two hundred to ten feet from the ground. We look back with disgust at the spectacle of Queen Elizabeth and her ladies on various occasions visiting the bear-gardens, and having one or more bears baited for their delectation; and shudder at the barbarity which makes the Spanish bull-fight a royal and national sport. But, though of course there is all the difference in the world between witnessing the brute courage and skill of the Matador, pitted against the brute strength and ferocity of the animal he means to slay, and the show of a daring rope-dancer wheeling a [illegible] child along an inch-and-a-half rope two hundred feet above the heads of the spectators, the child the while [illegible] scattering flowers along his aërial course, it must be granted that the secret of the popularity of both exhibitions is the same—a taste for horrible excitement—for thrills out of the ordinary range, to which an element of [illegible] [illegible] gives a zest—and which, however remote in the performance, excites the sensations of the spectators to the very acme of apprehension, and gives the feat the air of an impending catastrophe.

This taste for excitement was full fed on the evening of [illegible], when the [illegible] of the most frightful conflagration that has happened since the Fire of London gathered the [illegible] [illegible], and drew half the inhabitants of the metropolis to witness the horror, grandeur, and devastation of the scene, to which the sad death of the brave and good chief of the Fire Brigade, Mr. Braidwood, imparted a tragic gloom. The fire which broke out in the waterside warehouses of Messrs. Scovell at Cotton's wharf, has destroyed property to the prodigious amount of £2,000,000. It was lower-water, and the ships moored at the wharves could not be moved, but were included in the fiery ruin.

Amongst the noticeable events of the past month is the death of Lord Chancellor Campbell, of presumed rupture of one of the great arteries in the region of the heart—so suddenly and quietly that no alarm was given, though the event is supposed to have taken place about six o'clock, A.M. His lordship was eighty years of age, and was one of that group of talented Scotchmen who, as he was fond of quoting from Wilkie, "born in the Manse, had all a patent of nobility." As a judge, we read that he was one of the most notable that ever sat in the Court of Queen's Bench. As a literary man, his "Lives of the Chancellors," and the "Lives of the Chief Justices" which he subsequently wrote, afford a valuable addition to Biography.

Dr. Rodet, the chief surgeon of the Antiquaille at Lyons, is said to have made the valuable discovery that a solution of the perchloride of iron destroys the virus of hydrophobia with certainty, if applied within two hours of the infliction of the bite. The solution of perchloride of iron may be obtained of most chemists, and any person can apply it, which is far from being the case with the only other known preventive, the application of the actual cautery, which scarce anyone but a professional man has the nerve to use effectively or without danger to the patient. In cases of cow-pox, Dr. Rodet has also used the solution, and finds that it completely destroyed the virus. Glancing over the same paper in which this announcement is made, I see it stated that Mr. Simon has reported to the Privy Council, that owing to the indifference exhibited by the poorer classes on the subject of vaccination continual epidemics of small-pox have occurred in various parts of England during the last three or four years, and that wherever vaccination falls into neglect small-pox tends to become the frightful pestilence it was previous to the days of Dr. Jenner. If the solution of perchloride of iron is found efficacious in destroying the virus of cow-pox, is it not worth while to make an experiment of its efficiency in killing the malignant virus of small-pox; surely the experiment is worth trying?

Amongst the free exhibitions in London, especially interesting to our lady readers, I may suggest half-an-hour's investigation of the Messrs. Wheeler and Wilson's sewing machines, at 462, New Oxford-street, to which my own attention was drawn through a paper in the last month's number of this magazine. The visit must convince all but the most resolute believers in the self-sufficiency of the past to the needs of the present, that the only real way to assist our needle-women is to furnish sections of them with a machine which may help them to compete with the outfitters who at present monopolize the labour of the skilled women who have learned to use the machine at but a small advance upon their wages as hand-sewers, while they themselves reap all the advantages of the greater neatness, punctuality, and rapidity of the invention. We have heard of thirty and forty machines being purchased by one house, and yet ladies, as practical in some things as they are philanthropical in others, attempt to make a stand on behalf of distressed needle-women, whose only chance is in equal power of production with the day-workers in wholesale houses. It is in the order of things that manual labour shall yield to machinery, and the occupation of the sempstress is no exception. For years the employment has not (as a rule) yielded daily bread to a moiety of those who make it a business. And now, close upon the heels of the middle-man and woman, who cut closer and closer into the miserable earnings of those by whose starvation they enriched themselves, drives up the cleanly, frugal, tireless sewing machine, clearing the ground year by year of hopeless needle women, and steadily advancing from the warehouse to the genteel makers' work room, till now it may be seen in its rose-wood or walnut-wood frame, making an article of drawing-room furniture, and effecting in two or three days the plain work of a family.

C. A. W.

ANSWERS TO CORRESPONDENTS.

Books *for review*, Music, MSS., &c., must be sent in by the 10th of the month to be noticed, and replied to in the following number.

Poetry *received, with thanks*: "The Golden Wedding Day;" "Passion."

Madame de Genlis, Bentley: The sender is thanked for the offer of the translation, which is declined. The MS. has been returned as requested.

Willenhall: Our correspondent is thanked.

E. F. B., Knutsford, Cheshire: The article shall appear in our next. With regard to our correspondent's queries, we cannot tell, from the *titles* of papers, whether they are likely to suit us or not; but every attention shall be paid to the manuscripts, if forwarded, and an answer given in our next.

J. M., Greenock: Our correspondent challenges his fate; we yield to his request and publish his verses—the poetry and originality of which will, we have no doubt, surprise our readers as much as they apparently satisfy himself:—

IN REMEMBRANCE.

The flowers that thou gavest me are faded and gone,
How rich in beauty were they!
Sweet emblems of purity, love, and delight,
I cherish them e'en in decay.
They speak to me softly of those happy hours,
When fondly I strayed with thee,
'Mid Nature's wild grandeur, round thy native home,
Dear treasures unto me.

Is it possible that J. M. regards this piece of metrical patchwork as his own? We are tempted to print the whole, but one verse affords a fair example of the entire.

We cannot undertake to return articles unless stamps are sent with them.

Manuscripts *received, but not yet read*: "Fergus and Henry;" "Forest-bank Lodge."

Printed by Rogerson and Tuxford, 246, Strand, London.

RUTSON MORLEY.

BY JAMES B. STEPHENS.

CHAP. XII.

I need not record my impressions of Genoa. My new friend and myself did what we could to exhaust it in the few hours during which the steamer lay in its harbour; but nothing that we saw or heard had any reference, either direct or indirect, to what was uppermost in our thoughts. Yet how fain I am to speak of its glories, sea-embraced and hill-o'er-canopied—of princely palaces and gorgeous cathedrals—of its treasures of art and its treasures of nature! ... It is not needed. Has it not been already photographed into English literature, in words that are as near to the realities of marble, and nothing, and life, as words can come?

Late in the afternoon we again went on board, and in a short time Genoa was a tale to be told. Fearing that my companion would resent the discussion so vitally affecting my hopes in regard to Stephanie, I took the first opportunity of again entrapping him into the story of his previous life. He had made several appeals to the Cyclopean firemen below, but in each instance had been vigorously ordered aloft out of the engine-room.

"I told you," he resumed, when we had managed to secure an uninhabited corner of the ship—"I told you of my introduction to the monastery of [illegible]. Some other time, perhaps, I shall tell you more about the place, and about the manners of the monks, which I now know are very different from the ordinary life of the world. But in the meantime it will be sufficient to say that after entering a great isolated gateway, and passing a curiously painted verandah, I found myself in what is rather a little town than a single building, the most characteristic feature of which consists in an intricate confusion of projecting windows wonderfully old and [illegible]-looking. How I wish Mr. Winslow would go there, and bring it all back in his portfolio!

"I was fortunate in a companion. The priest to whose care I had been committed was as kind to me as my poor uncle had been. He had been a sailor in his youth, and had not lost the love of his former life. On the very first evening I spent with him in the monastery, he took down some old books which he had on the shelf of his cell—works on navigation, containing, in addition to many accompanying diagrams, pictures of ships, which he showed to me, with [illegible] explanations of the different parts of them. It was now that the light of books first dawned on me. The priest, whose name was Father Peter, was only too glad to find his [illegible] earnestly to be taught the use of them. For days and years the good man laboured at the work of my education, and I never tired of my tasks. Day after day, the mystery became clearer, and the pleasure wider and richer. I did not confine myself to one language, but mastered several, especially the old Greek, which was my chief delight. At last the third thousand year seemed to be a toil, and reading became a passion with me. But Father Peter's books were few, and I found, one day, to my great sorrow, that I had come to the end of the shelf. I began again at the other end, and had done so again and again, before I became aware that the gratification was not such as it had formerly been. And when a change was wrought so strangely and suddenly within me; a new curiosity had grown up within me, and, without the means to meet it, life seemed empty and dreary. For a while I betook myself to my old wandering ways, but without the former relish.

"I was much given, too, to basking in the verandah, and to lying in the chapel, dreaming of all that must be somewhere. Father Peter had told me that there were many more books in the world; and what I chiefly wished for, was to have books that might tell me of the lives of all the great old saints that were painted on the chapel walls, and whose figures were as familiar to me, and so much a part of my life, as those of the living fathers around me.

"'My son,' said Father Peter to me, one day, 'I have observed that of late, that thou art different from thy former self, and that there lurketh the [illegible] that becometh thy years. I think I know the burden that weighs on thy spirit. I have bid thee to a [illegible], whence thou hast seen a goodly land flowing with milk and wine and honey, but thou art denied an entrance into it. Is it not so, Ireton?'

"'It is,' I replied, seeing that he had indeed penetrated into my inmost mind.

"'What wouldst thou give me now, were I to open up to thee treasures of learning that all thy years could not contain?'

"'If it were not sin, I could fall down and worship thee!'

"'But hast thou considered the danger? Hearken, Ireton; even when I sailed on the deep, loving my ship and the open sea more than the home of my nativity, I yearned after the higher life that drinks its nourishment from the fountains of learning. After many years I retired hither from the world, trusting to dwell during the rest of my days in the calm of study and of worship. But I found ere long that (for me at least) the two paths led in different directions. I found myself losing the God I had innocently worshipped on the sea under the stars; I was losing him in the hopeless labyrinth of learned disputation. Instead of fearing the God to whom my mother taught me to pray, I found myself compelled as by a charm to seek out his unrevealed essence, and to strive after such heathen visions of eternal light as I read of in the volumes of ancient lore. I know not where I would have stopped. Perchance I would have striven on to blasphemous questions, did heaven not blasted me with righteous fury. But a holy brother, long since gone to God, perceiving that my prayers were less frequent and my former sympathies less keen, and knowing in himself the refined temptations that Satan uses through learning, counselled me with words of saintliest persuasion to return to the simplicity of worship. After much fasting and prayer, it was given unto me to die, and from that time I have restricted my study to the few books which thou and I have read together. I fear for thee, my son; for thou art quick in heart and eager desirous to know more. Yet I fear also to imprison the immortal mind that lives within thee. Thou art old enough now to judge for thyself. I give thee thy choice. Wilt thou, for the sake of knowledge, enter upon a new world of temptation, or wilt thou live as I live, a simple worshipper of God? Think how glorious all this is!' and he waved his hand over one of the fairest of scenes. 'The whisper of the leaves will not pervert thee from thy God. The little brooks have no doubts wherewith to darken thy soul. This great chasm beneath us doth not tell its danger, and its awful depth hath no temptation to the sound in mind. The great sea worships in unquestioning silence, and only rises from the repose of adoration to do the behest of Him who made it. And this great mountain talks reverently of the years of the right hand of the Most High; and, though it seems almost to touch the heavens, yet clings with its firm foundation to its appointed place on earth. But in the sphere to which thou aspirest, which is peopled with the thoughts that are the offspring of a fallen race, there thou shalt find confusion, doubt, perversion, the casting off of allegiance, and blasphemy. It is the ground—ah, how fair indeed!—on which earth and hell meet, and where their forces, alas! so frequently mingle, that it is sometimes beyond the keenest vision of man to distinguish them! Ireton, my son, mingle thy deliberation with prayer, and make thy choice.'

"I was not slow in choosing. Indeed, what Father Peter had said to me, only confirmed my choice. I relished the idea of attaining to great learning all the more, because there was danger to be encountered. When I announced my opinion to the good father, he said:

"'It is God's will. Let Him defend thee. Come then with me, and I will show thee thy heart's desire.'

"I then accompanied him to another part of the monastery, and ascended with him a broad old staircase, terminating in a massive door, strongly secured. He then produced a ponderous key from his girdle, and admitted me into a small room which contained the earnest of what was coming, in the shape of loose leaves of parchment scattered hither and thither on the floor. Then with another ponderous key, which was secreted in a scarcely perceived crevice in the wall, another massive door was opened . . . . I have read in fairy tales of mortals being taken by powerful genii into the heart of the giant mountains, and being there dazzled, even to fear, with the revelation of the riches of many mighty kings—mounds of gold and silver, rich robes and sparkling crowns, rings and jewels and chains, heaped together in careless profusion. I think I must have felt somewhat as that one felt, when I beheld before me more books than I had ever believed to be in the world, ranged shelf above shelf, and heap upon heap, more to be prized than all the treasures in the heart of the earth! And such books, many of them! Massive, tinted with the mystery of centuries, and richly encased, as by the reverence of men lavishly devoted to the shrine of wisdom, how imposing they looked!—almost too grand to be handled. I clung in a kind of terrified delight to the robe of Father Peter, and asked, hesitatingly, if all this were really open to me now.

"'The kind Abbot hath permitted it, though after much entreaty, he knowing the danger. All this is henceforth to be thy charge. The key is to be in thine own keeping. Thou must be answerable for every loss. Thou must watch therefore, for these are precious. . . . Ah, how precious! God forgive me, but I would fain close the door, Ireton, and throw myself again into the arms of this ancient father!'

"And as he spoke he seized a ponderous old manuscript, and pressed it to his heart, sighing like a man bereaved of a friend.

"I cannot describe my wandering joy; nor shall I dwell on the months and years during which I revelled in this exhaustless banquet of delights. I know, sir, from your face, that you, too, have known the frenzy of love, that will repay the devoted hours and the aching head. My special delight was in deciphering old Greek manuscript. The more difficult, the more welcome, as I felt that the [illegible] would be all the longer. Had not Father Peter compelled me to daily exercise, I should long ere this have been among the angels of the other world. Such continued to be my life until what I calculate to have been my sixteenth year. At length my tastes were turned into a new channel, and in this way:

"An English artist, who had been travelling through the greater part of Turkey, happened to reach our peninsula. By the time he arrived at our monastery, both he and his servant were so weak with fever as to be unable to proceed on their journey. The monks gave them shelter, and I was appointed to minister to the artist himself. I rejoiced in the office, and worried for his recovery—not only, I confess, for his own sake, but because I longed to satisfy my curiosity about that other world of which I had heard so much. It was some weeks before he was able to converse; but I was selfish enough to appropriate the first fruits of his strength. We had many conversations together, much to my satisfaction. A kind of friendship sprang up between us; and when he was sufficiently strong, he began to apply himself to his professional pursuits, by making a few sketches of the scenery and the surroundings. I longed to learn his art, yet I feared [illegible] that I had not courage to ask him to teach me; but having one day [illegible] employed his materials in painting a rude portrait of himself, which accidentally came under his notice, he professed to see some merit in it, and, on the day of his leaving, left me a gift—as he said—in acknowledgment of my attentions to him, a large supply of colours, brushes, canvas, &c., of which he affirmed that he had no further use on account of his intention of returning at once to England.

"My time—at least all the time I could spare from the chapel, in which I performed duty daily as a chorister—was now divided between books and painting. I taught myself, but with little success; and I soon devoted myself to copying the great paintings of the saints and martyrs that adorned the walls of the chapel. In this I found great pleasure. When my hand became a little more skilful, I tried to embody my faint recollections of her of whom we have spoken. I made many attempts before I succeeded in pleasing myself, the difficulty being that whenever I tried to fix my thoughts on the [illegible], many other faces, equally [illegible], mingled themselves with the one I sought, rising from and blending into one another as do [illegible] in the clouds. At last I seemed to myself to have succeeded, and since that time the face has been more constant and more real.

"This kind of life continued till I must have reached my eighteenth year. During all the years I had lived on the peninsula of Monte Santo, I had never seen the face of woman. To me she was a beautiful mystery—a something that would mingle sweetly with the [illegible] of that future to which our life of retirement pointed. You are doubtless aware that no female is permitted to dwell in any part of the peninsula, and that the law extends even to the brute animals. Between Father Peter and myself this was a forbidden subject; and I never heard it spoken of among the monks without a shrug of the shoulders and an allusion to the story of the fall. But I could not shut my eyes to the pictures of the female saints which every day [illegible], nor my mind to the tales of their beauty and of their noble deeds to which the many histories the library contained bore each ample testimony. Above all, the thought of her kept alive within me that sense of pure affection which seems to be reckoned the dearest feature of womanhood.

"One day, as I emerged from the library into the open air, to perform one of my various duties, namely, to sound the hour of noon, which is done, as are all the calls to prayer, by beating with a hammer upon a suspended board, I was startled by the sound of the sweetest laugh that had ever greeted my ear. I listened, and the silver notes were repeated with tones more [illegible] than before. They seemed to stir some long silent chord in my heart, which now thrilled as at the touch of an angel. I rushed out eagerly into the front court whence the sound seemed to come; and, looking up at the verandah, saw, to my astonishment, the Abbot and several of the monks in conversation with a company of strangers, among whom were two ladies, both of them far more beautiful than any of the pictures of the saints that had hitherto been my ideal of loveliness. From where I stood I could see also the ship in which they had come, and at the landing a boat drawn up, beside which stood several sailors in bright uniform.

"Father Peter was among the number of the monks who were conversing with the strangers. I saw him attract the attention of the Abbot to me, who then beckoned me to him. I ascended the few steps which admitted to the platform of the verandah in great trepidation, wondering what could be wanted with me.

"'Ingram,' said Father Peter, when I had joined them, 'be thou interpreter for me, while I go and make arrangements for the entertainment of the strangers.'

"How my heart thrilled when I found myself face to face with such beauty, and saw the ladies stretch out their hands to me with looks of kindness such as I had only read or dreamed of before! I had to conduct a long conversation between the Abbot and the visitors, the chief part of which consisted in the apologetic explanations of the former in regard to the strictness of monastic rule, not permitting him to receive the ladies within the monastery. Indeed he had gone to the utmost verge of his power in admitting them so far as the verandah. In a short time the Abbot, thinking that all would now be ready for their entertainment, demanded of me the key of the library, and then led the gentlemen off, leaving me in the verandah with the ladies, at their own request. The number and minuteness of their questions soon made me alive to another quality in woman, of which I had heard the monks make mention; but I did not find it at all disagreeable, worshipping as I did every expression of their faces, and every tone of their voices. You smile, sir; but I see no reason why I should be ashamed to confess that I was in a state of beatitude. We conversed in Italian, which they spoke beautifully, although, as they informed me, they were English.

"After smoking a pipe with the monks (this was not against rule), partaking of some refreshment, and seeing the sights of the monastery, the gentlemen cut short our interview, and bore the ladies off to the boats; but not until, to my great delight, they had promised to renew their visit on the following day, as they had not had time to examine so minutely as they wished some of the manuscripts in the library. The ladies, too, asked permission to sketch for an hour or two from the verandah, while the gentlemen would be pursuing their more learned researches: which permission was of course readily granted.

"I retired to bed that night, not to rest, but to ruminate on an idea that had taken entire possession of my mind. Among other things, the ladies had told me of a great gathering of all the arts that was shortly to be held at Paris. When I heard of the great doings that were then going on in the grand world that had so long been closed to me, a sudden distaste of my own life had taken hold of me. I had many times before, as you may suppose, conceived the idea of stealing secretly away from that land of solitude to some other part of the world. But the question of *whither*, had always baffled me. Now, it occurred to me that if I could prevail on these strangers to allow me to work my passage to Marseilles, to which city I understood from them they were next bound, I might take my paintings with me, and perhaps obtain a place for them in the palace of the arts of which they had spoken, and thus open the door to a new way of life. As I had seen so few paintings, and as my own were certainly equal to the best of those in the chapel, I confess I had a very different idea of them from what I have now. I ruminated long on the subject, and at length formed my resolution.

"Next day, when the party arrived, the gentlemen were again conducted into the monastery, and I was, as before, ordered to be in attendance on the ladies. As they told me that they were to sail next day, I saw that no time was to be lost, and accordingly took advantage of the earliest pause in their run of questions to tell them a little of my story. I said nothing about the paintings, as I had still some doubts in regard to their merits. I merely mentioned my earnest desire to escape from my present mode of life, and to work my way in the busy world. I felt encouraged to press my wishes, from the evident relish with which they were listened to. The young ladies fervently promised to use the utmost extent of their influence with their father, the owner of the yacht, to have me taken on board. When I told them that the matter would require to be managed very secretly, I think really that they relished it all the more. After a conference, during which many extraordinary suggestions were started and rejected, it was at length concluded that I was to be on the beach at ten o'clock that same evening, and that if I observed the sudden extinguishing of a light in one of the ports of the yacht which was pointed out to me, exactly at the last stroke of "four bells," which I could easily hear from the landing-place, I was to consider the matter as settled, and to prepare myself to mingle as stealthily as possible with a boat's crew, which was to be sent on shore some time afterwards on the pretence of a sudden necessity for a supply of olive oil, in which article our monastery was superfluously rich. The great difficulty was to settle the capacity in which I was to be received. At length one of the ladies suggested that the yacht was much in want of a 'steward's mate.' It was unanimously agreed to, by the second member of the party, that the yacht was in need of a 'steward's mate;' and though I was in utter ignorance of the duty either of the steward or of his mate, I at once professed my utmost readiness to execute the functions of the office indicated.

"I need not detain you, sir. You see how I am here. The family—let me bless them, as I leave off mentioning them—were determined to touch at Gibraltar on their way to England. I had managed to bring what I thought the best of my paintings with me; and fascinating as their kindness was—even to a 'steward's mate' —the purpose with which I set out was more fascinating still. I left them at Marseilles, with many regrets. I wonder if I shall ever meet them again! But if a cup of cold water shall not fail of reward, how great must be the recompense of those who turn the whole river of a human life into a new and better channel! When I meet my sister I shall tell her all the tale of their bounty.

"You seem to know the rest. I have told you much—more than ever I told to any one else before: yet how little it seems! Moment by moment made up the years that have made my life. Each moment has had its feeling, its fancy, its phrensy. The present end is—I am here; but ah! where is she?"

Chap. XIII.

Fine......"Fine morta."

Morta indeed; but still the residence, chosen or otherwise, of [illegible] living members of humanity, according to statistical accounts published by A. Zuccagni Orlandini, and quoted by the excellent Du Pays. Whether, considering the resemblance between flesh and grass, the said a Zoo, &c., is still prepared to swear to the odd 2, is more than any dare determine. If, however, the odd 2 were beggars, and especially if they were afflicted with some loathsome and visceral disease, I have not the slightest hesitation in affirming that they are still alive and begging.

My first day in Pisa, spent in passing from street to street, and from house to house, with the view of obtaining a suitable abode for the Dolly's, left with me an overwhelming impression of such beggary as itself beggars description. Was this the Italy of my dreams? . . . . . I had need of all my romance to shut out the importunate present—the palsied, leprous, [illegible] present, and of all my stoicism to shut my ears to complaint and my eye to foul disease, in order to realize the historic associations of the streets I was treading.

Our first day's search was unsuccessful. I say "our," because my new friend was still with me. By neutralizing myself with a [illegible] had [illegible] than Mr. Dolly in his liberality had provided for, I found myself able to retain Ferrara's companionship without intrenching on his slender means. Truly loath he was to yield to any such arrangement; but as I threatened an instant dissolution of partnership in this great matter between us as the penalty of contumacy, he was fain to submit.

Next day Fortune was more favourable.

On the [illegible] side of the Arno, close to the Church of San P. . . , stands the house which I selected as the future residence of the Dolly family. A gloomy, unpromising street-door, or rather gate, opens into a long corridor, the vaulted roof of which is fantastically decorated with broad bars of black and white. At the end of the corridor was a [illegible] staircase, the walls on each side of which were of a pale blue colour, adorned with the loves of Diana and Endymion in exquisite white relief. "Never saw I Spirituals likely to repent themselves." The gaunt vaulted corridor, full of echoes that seemed to [illegible] from far-off cloisters, had given me the idea of unmitigated [illegible]; but when the door that admitted to the staircase was flung open, the great flood of Italian light startled so many white figures into life and beauty that it seemed to me as if the rigid, calculating nineteenth century was but a cold intrusion upon the lively fancies and brilliant vivacity of the [illegible] days of old, when nature was all in all, and not, as now, the fleeting privilege of a hard-earned holiday. The apartments upstairs were equally contradictory of the gloomy corridor. Everything was pleasant, flowery, festive. Everything was lightsome, [illegible], [illegible]. A more incongruous combination of [illegible] and [illegible], of classic and Arabesque, of Athens and Alhambra, could not easily be imagined.

On either side of the staircase a [illegible] opened into [illegible]. On the one side a few steps led down into a garden full of orange and lemon-trees, in all the [illegible] of [illegible] ; in the midst of which a fountain, ever leaping into life from the heart of a marble basin, showered perpetual blessing on glistening multitudes of gold-fish, that twinkled ceaselessly amidst the dancing waters. On the other side, a similar number of steps conducted to more ornamented ground, a flag-paved court, where stood a little octagonal chapel of red brick, the roof of which commenced about six feet from the ground, and then tapered upwards to a most disproportioned distance. Seven arched niches relieved the monotony of the outer wall, in which the [illegible] forms of of old effigies were still discernible, though whether they had represented Christian saints or heathen [illegible], Time and the elements had rendered indeterminable. Within the door, as in most continental churches, hung a heavy quilt of stuffed leather. The first sight of the interior, which was dimly lighted from above, showed that the chapel was in reality a tomb. The centre of the floor was a richly emblazoned marble tablet, bearing the following inscription:

Hic jacet
[illegible] [illegible] [illegible],
In [illegible] [illegible].
[illegible]
A.D. [illegible].
[illegible] [illegible], [illegible]
[illegible] in Pace?

In the opposite recess stood an altar, with its complete equipment of ceremonial appurtenances: but rust and neglect were over all. What had once represented Holy [illegible] had become dim and inglorious: the candlesticks were mere [illegible] of rust; and the lace of the altar-cloth hung, faded and torn, among the rank weeds that grew in the chinks of the broken marble steps, and that derived half their life from the water which dripped from the roof in times of rain. Above the altar hung a faded Madonna, that, in spite of an [illegible] [illegible], still bore the stamp of genius and [illegible] art. The walls had once been hung with tapestry which had evidently told some historic tale; but the greater part of it was now lying on the floor, displaying a violent confusion of heads and limbs, that was more like the result of [illegible] [illegible] or tailoring disaster than the slow work of time.

My first idea on surveying the place was that the terms of residence would be much above the sum which I was authorised to offer. To my astonishment, I found that they were considerably below it. I was even so undiplomatic as to inform the old man who was in charge of the house that I thought it worth a great deal more.

"Ah, Signorino," said he, [illegible] [illegible], "it has been empty so long, so very long!"

"It is on the wrong side of the Arno, for one thing," I answered; "but I don't see how that can make so very much difference."

"Ah, no, Signorino, it is not that."

"If the house were haunted I don't see how it could be cheaper."

"Ah, then, the Signorina has heard the story!"

"What story? I know of no circumstance whatever connected with the place."

"Ah, then, perhaps I should not tell it you."

"If it is haunted, I shall take it all the more readily?"

"Well, then, Signorina, one night, when I happened to be living in the house alone—it was a dark and dismal night—I saw strange lights in the chapel."

"Well, I hope you went to ascertain what lights they were?"

"No, I was too much afraid! . . . . And, Signorina, they have been seen since—by others!"

"Who was the last inhabitant of this house?"

"Salvestro Gigini, the younger brother of Count Gigini, who is now the richest man in Palermo. The family is descended from the Prince who is buried in the chapel. Signor Salvestro was in the habit of repairing thither at midnight, to pray for the soul of his ancestor, from whom the family derived their wealth. He always went alone, and locked the chapel within."

"Was he a pious man, then?"

"I did not know him. The people here say that he was a miser; but he seems to have left very little except his house, which in reality belonged to Count Gigini, who at one time lived here along with his brother."

"How long is it since Salvestro Gigini died?"

"It is not known, Signorina, whether he be alive or dead. One night, at the accustomed hour, he shut himself up within the chapel. A favourite servant, who waited up for him, observing that he remained beyond his usual time, became anxious, and at length ventured to knock at the chapel-door. No answer was given. He knocked again and called his master. Still no answer. The other servants were then called, and the lock was forced; but they found nothing—not even the key. Salvestro Gigini has never been seen since!"

"How long is it since this happened?"

"Some fifteen or sixteen years ago."

"Did he leave no child?"

"Only one daughter—an infant of two years."

"And is she still alive?"

"Ah, Signorina, that brings me to the saddest part of all. Little more than a week after her father's disappearance, she and the son of Count Gigini—likewise a young child, and, like his cousin, motherless, who had been for upwards of a year in Pisa under the charge of a faithful nurse—set out for Palermo, accompanied by this nurse and her husband, who was in command of Count Gigini's yacht, in which they sailed. It was calm as it is now when they left Leghorn; but, ere long, furious gales sprang up, and as none of the party have since been heard of, it is supposed that the little yacht went down with all on board."

"It is, indeed, a melancholy story," said I, quite mechanically, for the mention of Count Gigini had showed me that I was again on the mystic track, and at once my mind whirled with the old bewilderment, and seemed to become full of moving diagrams, of circle wheeling within circle, of lines diverging and converging, yet all concordant to some all-interpreting principle to me unattainable. It was an old speculative state of mind, conjured up from dead University days, and linking itself strangely to practical circumstances.

"Is this all you know?" I asked at length.

"All that can throw light on the mystery."

"And who are you, if I may ask?"

"I was once the house-steward of Count Gigini, in Palermo. The loss of his son, his brother, and niece, weighed so heavily on my master, that he has never been like his former self since. He soon became unable to manage his affairs, and left everything in the hands of a Frenchman, who had lived with him for some years as his secretary—a designing, evil man, whose whole aim plainly is to make himself entire master of the Count's mind, and no doubt to influence his last testament in his own favour. His first policy was to get rid of all the old dependents of the Palazzo Nio—this was Count Gigini's house, of which I had charge for twenty years. It is out a little way from Palermo, a grand old Moorish palace. Ah, how I gloried in it, Signorina! . . . . . . I was the last who was sent away, and as my good master would not consent to part with me altogether, I was sent here ten years ago, to take charge of this house, and to let it, if occasion offered, to strangers. But it has got an ill-name, and in good truth I little care whether it lets or not, as this was a mere excuse for my banishment. But I have kept it well, for my master's sake; and, if you would like it, it is in excellent order."

"Stay a little," said I, under the influence of new light. The circles were more still, and more nearly concentric; the lines became less aimless, and seemed to tend more to one fixed point. "What is the name of this secretary?"

"In truth he is no secretary now. The Count has already given him much of his wealth; but still he retains him, yet always in such a way as to make it appear that it is the Count who follows him, since he manages to keep ever before the poor foolish old man's mind that he is on the track of his lost ones; and also, as I have reason to believe, using his wealth and name to form and foster dark plots which he pretends are to lead to the freedom of Sicily, and to the establishment of Count Gigini at the head of that state, but which are doubtless designed to serve his own evil ends."

"But you have not yet told me his name."

"His name is Blot."

The circles became still, and the lines radiated towards a common centre.

"Tell me next," said I—"for I am interested in this—did you ever know a man named Herr Dalcken?"

those beautifully-wrought chairs, and placing them in array on the pavement in front of an old-fashioned inn-door, waited till they were sold; and then, turning his horse, set off towards the primitive woodlands once more. One of the most pleasant recollections of my childish days is the purchase of a set of these chairs by those I dearly loved; and I am happy to say that the whole eight are still as good as the day they were bought, and rubbed to a degree of brightness dazzling to see. Their form is elegant, and does great honour to the hand, so long passed away, which wrought them.

I and a brother used to watch from the low window of the dining-room in the house where we lived, in great expectancy, for the coming of the old chairmaker. A month or two weeks would often elapse between one visit and another; and when it came it was often noon when his primitive cart stopped before the inn-door. His first job was to bring some hay forth for his horse; and then, whilst he unpacked his chairs, and set them in order along the pavement, his wife—as quaint and as old as himself, and habited in a perfectly bygone costume—opened a basket of viands. They then sat down together beneath the wall of the inn, leaving the passers-by to admire, or to buy if they willed—but never once asking them to do so. They were ignorant of modern puffing. The old man had made the goods himself, and he knew his work was worth the money he asked.

One autumn afternoon, soon after the chairs were set out—and they seemed more elegant in shape than any we had seen hitherto—I saw a neighbour, whom I loved, cross the street, and ask the price of them. The bargaining was short enough, for in five minutes the old man began to carry his goods across the street in the wake of his new customer. Wild with delight, I ran out of the room to ask leave to cross the street and see the purchase; and this being granted me, I was soon in the most ancient of kitchens, my small hand holding an aged hand, and an earnest listener to all that was passing. All present admired the chairs; and great was the old woodman's pride to be placed in arm-chair on either side the fire.

"Those of my make," he said, gravely, in reply to some question, "have for five or six generations been working in cherry and other woods, and for a time longer than that we have been dwellers in the old woodland where I come from. For forty years I have carried goods about this county, and those adjoining; and many a man knows me—master and tradesmen. My work has a good name; and these chairs (this was the very word) will, with ordinary usage, long outlast the hand which made 'em." This was a true prophecy.

The old man went, and that night I had the delight of seeing those I dearly loved sit on either side the fire, each in an arm-chair. The one smoked his pipe, grave and contemplative, whilst I sat upon his knee, the other in her dove-coloured Quaker bonnet—her eyes were weak, and she always wore one—spoke with mild voice, and plied gently her diligent knitting-needles.

Years passed by—perhaps twelve or thirteen—when I went and made a lengthened stay in the very country whence the old chairmaker had come from. It is a country of hills, occasionally of dense woods, and is solitary and primitive in a peculiar degree. One day, in spring, I happened to pass through a large orchard abutting on the village churchyard; and there I saw the farmer to whom it belonged. His men were felling some dozen or more old gnarled fruit-trees. As I knew the owner, I stopped to speak, and a natural question arose as to the use of the wood he had in hand.

"Why, ye see," he answered, "the trees ha' done their duty, and only cumber the ground. They've borne fruit for many a generation; and now the best on 'em 'll serve the use of old ——— the chairmaker, who lives a bit from here. The rest 'll do for the charcoal heap, for he and his lads make off many a load to the glass-houses and steel-houses, and many a place o' that sort, where it's found to answer a deal better than coal."

The individual he had mentioned, in connexion with the cherry-trees he was felling, brought to my recollection the chairmaker of my childish days, and I questioned him.

"Aye! I dare to say it's the same. Old John used to travel to ——— with his chairs, years ago. But he's an old man now, and don't go far from th' chimney-corner; and, what's more, folks now-a-days like to buy furniture in a shop wi' plate-glass windows, and be waited on by a talking shopman, instead o' buying chairs off a cart at the door, or off the market pavement. I don't think the things last as well; there's more o' the glue-pot, and less of a man's honest hand work. But folks like the polish and the plate-glass, and so they soon 'bide wi' the twiddle-down trash they get for their money."

"But old John, I should fancy, would never do bad work."

"Not he—he comes of an upright race. All on 'em ha' lived in the same part, generations without count, and everybody knows 'em. Time was when trade was better than it is now, for a lot o' things that used to be sold ha' gone clean out, and no one knows 'em. Crockery now-a-days is in everybody's house; but when I was young, wooden cups and bowls was to be seen on every board about here, except it were the parson's or the doctor's. Old John and his fathers made trenchers by the score; but that trade's done for, as many others be."

"What does he make, then?" I asked.

"He? why, he does nought but sit i' the chimney corner, or warm himself in the sun; his day o' work's done. But his lads carry on a trade in chairs, which they send to the big towns; the goods going in a cart 's [illegible] for, and when they get wood that's likely they make what's called 'rustic work,' and send it away to London. A lot o' this old cherry-wood here 'll do for that sort o' thing. At times, when they get oak or walnut timber, those young

Cuore 'll do a deal bit o' carving; and this goes to London, too, and passes off for work, I am told, done three hundred year ago. But the cleverest of old John's lads—him as carved the best—got disappointed in some love affair, and so 'listed. His regiment was sent off to India, and many a day it was before the old man lifted up his head again. It's said the brothers ha' been working hard and saving money to buy him off, unbeknown to old John; and to-morrow, when they comes here, I'm likely to hear some news."

"To-morrow, are the young men coming?"

"Aye, wi' their timber wain, to fetch the old trees. If thee'rt coming this way, thee'll see 'em in the orchard, about noon. Or if thee'd like to see the woodiest country about their dwelling, thee mun't; for there'll be an empty seat i' th' gig when I drive that way next week, and the old wooden house o' th' [illegible] worth seeing, for it holds many a curious thing, thou'lt see no where else."

"Indeed then I'll gladly accept your offer. The country is new, I want to see for its wildness, and the old wheelwright's face will bring me pleasant recollections."

So the following week I accompanied the old farmer on his solitary drive. Leaving a picturesque mountain village, and winding round the base of a hill, clothed in woods, and varied here and there by immense masses of lichen-covered granite, we began to enter upon a wooded tract, broken by [illegible] of [illegible] uplands. At last we struck into a forest tract—strictly such—and which, climbing as it were a hillside, brought us to a narrow upland, wild and weird beyond description. On either side descended from it some miles' breadth of trees; whilst this high range of land, itself comparatively bare, was covered by long and wind-swept grass, varied, at intervals, by enormous clumps of hollies, of vast age, as one might see by their thick stems and twisted branches. All beyond this upland was a sea of trees, some yet leafless, and others hastening to show their vernal glory. Not a sound was to be heard; the very gig-wheels were silent, as they passed along the [illegible] grass; but a bird's note broke the intense stillness, and if sound there were, it was that of the tall grass, as dried by the March winds, it moved ceaselessly to some impulse of the light, soft breeze. The scenery reminded me of some passages of a descriptive kind in Walter Scott's "Ivanhoe," and gave a very good idea of what English woodland scenery was during the middle ages, when baron or abbot hunted his "hart of grease," and churlish hinds passed their days amidst the gloom of trees.

Descending from this upland into a more ample road, the ruts of which were worn deep by woodman's wain and remnants of traffic, we struck deep into the forest, where the shadows were of sombre depth, though as yet the trees were but partially leaved. For two miles or more we followed this road, and then, on a lower level amidst the trees, a long, low, deeply-eaved thatched house, with many detached outbuildings or working sheds around it, came in view. It was built of wood, the interstices plastered in; and, as though one generation after another had built a part, it was of different sizes and elevations; here was an old stone buttress, there a gable, a little further on a deeper-dipping eave of thatch. There was a surrounding garden, a narrow shallow brook making its way across its thick grassed roots of trees; and, as if those who lived by handicraft in wood loved the old forest too well to live away from its shadows, vast oaks dipped their as yet bare branches on to the very thatch, whilst a picturesque group of black trees [illegible] the garden hedge.

The sound of hammers, and of saws worked by a water wheel, and grew more and more distinct as we approached the homestead, and then [illegible] it was louder still. The old farmer, on our little journey, had told me that the soldier-brother had been bought off, and was now on his way home; and that, fearing the sudden surprise, the aged father had been told his joy beforehand. It seemed so; for the old man, sitting in the sunny porch, had more than the peace of this world resting on his [illegible] sightless face. We went up to him, he put forth his palsied hands to greet his visitors—one he did not know—and then with the garrulity of age and great happiness, he began to tell about his son.

Presently we entered a long, roomy, very large kitchen, where a young woman—one of the sons' wives—bustled about, preparing dinner; whilst another, still younger and apparently a visitor, for she was dressed in her Sunday's best, was nursing one of the old man's grandchildren. In the garrulity he at once gave us to understand that this was his returning son's sweetheart, that she had not married after all, and, penitent for the lovers' quarrel which had driven him to so wild a step, had come some dozen miles to see his friends, and thus lead the way to reconciliation, as soon as he was home once more.

The old man being too feeble to be our guide, one of the sons—a smart man of forty—was called from the workshops, and he led the way. In the dwelling house there was not much to see, but in the next, where all sorts of gnarled stumps and twisted branches of trees and orchard trees were collected, the sight was rather curious. The man then went forward, up a dilapidated flight of stairs, into some old chambers, where were collected the last relics of a hundred bygone English customs; old spinning-wheels, reels, distaffs, spindles, then old wainscot cradles, vast oak boxes, meal chests, bowls and trenchers. From time to time the men sold occasional specimens of the former articles to antiquaries, or persons who still cleaved to bygone customs; but the trenchers were never parted with. It had kept the staple produce of this ancient race of wood-wrights, and they seemed to have a pride in the preservation of these antique relics of their forefathers. There was the square trencher and the round trencher, and the trencher with a brief legend on the rim, thus anticipating our modern bread-plate. There were dishes on a few of these articles, which are asked for into the nineteenth century.

Returning to the open air, and looking round the environment of the old woodwright's house, nothing could be more picturesque. Except for two mere lane roads, by one of which we had reached the house, the shadow of woods lay for at least a breadth of three miles around it, but extending, in many parts, thence that distance. The little croft, with its thin crop of springing barley, crisp, as it were, beneath the trees, and the few fruit trees in the garden could have little sun to ripen either cherry or damson; yet all the vegetation looked healthy, and not a sickly face was to be seen within doors.

We had not yet entered the parlour, but this we were presently conducted; and here the old woodwright's daughter had set forth refreshment. The room contained some old furniture, and some tolerable wood-carving, the work of the son who had enlisted. One of the old man's satisfactions was that his "lad would come back and work at the old trade; for," as he quaintly said, "none of his race had a ready hand at aught else."

Be this as it may, here was a quaint old English craft, well nigh gone, or, at least, diverted into far different branches. Birmingham had superseded the wooden trencher and the wooden bowl; the spinning jenny, the distaff, and the wheel; and other appliances, due to discovery, had replaced also the bellows, the tinder-box, and other old-fashioned articles. Thus every generation, as it uncovers the hidden secrets of Nature, and utilises them to its use, prepares the way for the succeeding generation to sweep what it used and treasured aside, as things obsolete and of no account.

ROUND THE LAMP-POST.

I wonder if they think it was put there for their especial benefit. But they think nothing about it; they are not come to the age of cavilling; they make no effort to separate the real from the ideal; it is in effect to them not an invention of science for lighting the streets, but their lamp-post, their rallying point when national-school doors give up their prey, and little urchins run out from cottages to join their bigger brothers and sisters round the lamp-post.

And there is a joining of hands and singing and shouting; a merry-go-round would be nothing to it. And occasionally a lifting up of some small voice in tears, and an argument as to who did or did not give Tom a black eye.

As I hear the noise and put down my pen in despair, I wonder who would live opposite a lamp-post. And then, looking at the children, and the merry faces, the sort of joyful abandon which there is in that dancing chain, strangely enough my sympathy is with the noisy ones in spite of their noise. Children must play, and perhaps they have no other place to play in but the street. What a beautiful thing that pole is, in their eyes! How the fattest of the troop runs up, and clasps it with a triumphant sense of being first! As I watch them, so many reflections arise within me. I sit down to write a tale. What in the world is it to be about? There is a perfect pall of unfinished ones before me, but they look stale and dead, stereotyped sort of things, which I cannot go on with to the accompaniment of a merry-go-round lamp-post. And now there is a shrill-voiced woman interrupting and whose "no place like home" all down the street. I wish she would try it, if it is so nice. But that is a mere spirit of impatience, because I have got to write a tale and she worries me. Write a tale indeed! But I know I must do it: it is my trade. Ah, before I made a trade of my pen how I loved it! I love it still, but the breadwinner has not the beauty of the first love. Just the way with us all; we want what we have not, and when we get it the charm is no longer the same. But what to write about? Good tales don't take; I suppose people don't like goodness, because it is unnatural. I could give a sort of skeleton picture of my own life. There is not much in it, when I come to reflect; very little indeed; but it is one thing, like the particular sketch, it would not worry me with its incongruity. What I have the contented lamp-post.

I was born—

"Be it ever so humble, there's no place like home."

The refrain comes in appositely. No, I was not born here opposite that post, but in the country, a blessing on it!

I think I see it now, and hear the unfinished chime of the mill stream, and see the sunlight on the water, glancing over the stones of the river and the moss grass. And I see the wood anemones down in the ravine, and the celandine and the violet; and the beautiful green young leaves, promising wild hyacinths in plenty. And above my head in the budding trees the thrushes are singing.

Oh, you boys round the lamp-post! this queer sensation which rises in my throat is not for you; but I wish you had such a place to [illegible] each other in, for once, as that coppice by the mill; and I wish—how I wish!—I could go now, and lie down holiday, with a cup of leaves, by the trickling brook that falls into the mill stream.

I ran away, boys; more shame for me. My step-father thrashed me, and I grinned in his face, and told him he never should do that again; and I ran away from home.

I never stopped to think of my mother, or to look at her; with my parcel box, and [illegible], I started for the school which I never reached, never meant to reach, on that April morning long ago! No need to reckon.

There are streaks of white in my hair—shining tokens, into which the colour has retreated, and the [illegible] will never rise again.

How the sun shone on that morning, and the birds sang in the trees that morning! You would think me foolish if I said what they all seemed to be saying; but I have never heard the birds in the spring-time without remembering it. How one whistled out "Do it, do it, do it," and another "Stop a bit, stop a bit." But I would not stop a bit; I went on, red-faced and panting, thinking how I should be revenged for that beating. As if I were not taking vengeance on myself—cutting off my own nose to spite my face, as the saying is.

And I spent the first night under a hedge, hungry enough. I had emptied my money-box into my pockets, and had taken a piece of bread, but that went at noon by way of luncheon; so there I was, hungry and weary and alone, lying under a hedge, and looking up into the stars.

You begin to think it was time to find my senses and go back, perhaps. If I had—why then my story would have been different; or I might not have been here to tell it. No, I was not going back. Tears came into my eyes and rolled down my cheeks as I thought how lonely it was; but I only grew more angry with my step-father, who, I said, had caused it all, and more determined to punish him.

I pictured myself dying of hunger and exhaustion there, where no one would see me perhaps till I was quite dead. I smiled at my own conceit, and looked in upon the mourners to see how sorry they were. But then I thought of my mother; and my sobs broke out loud and thick, in spite of my manly clothes, and the big jacket I was so proud of. Still I would not go back. I built fine castles about "the wanderer's return," setting forth myself as a triumphant hero in moustaches; I had not quite made up my mind as to the profession in which my glory was to be won, but I was decided about the moustaches. And then my mother would fall on my neck, and weep for joy; and as to my step-father, of course I should raise him from his knees, after the fashion of magnanimous conquerors, and forgive him. But there is no need to linger over my dreams, waking or sleeping, for in spite of the cold I did sleep, and did not catch my death. I managed to get to London, and with marvellously few trials, considering all things, I got there.

You would wonder now what an awkward country lad like I was could do in the great crowded streets, where the tide of people marches on steadily about its business, and every one looks straight before him into some future which concerns himself alone, and which he only sees. Well, I wondered myself, somewhat dismally, and I stood looking on with a heart that was growing heavy and hopeless, when an idea struck me. There were two boys about my own size squabbling about some [illegible] and [illegible] the [illegible], and I had been watching them with some interest.

"Keep your hands, Bill!" exclaimed one, thrusting out his fist, which by the way was not a clean one.

"No, there's a big dog!"

"Aint I. Who's a coward?"

"Coward yourself, granny!" was the quick retort; and the two lads began to fight vigorously. Then I saw some one stand somewhat before a basket which one of the boys had put down. The fight was over in the twinkling of an eye, and the basket-owner was crying out "Fair straight!" as [illegible] as though he [illegible] had never been [illegible] in the [illegible]. He could not [illegible] private feeling to interfere with business. As I said, this gave me an idea. I bought a basket, which I took into a confectioner's shop, and with my remaining money I filled it with the most tempting articles I could select, with the view of commencing street business in a small way.

It was hard work, but I went on perseveringly, and had actually earned a few pence, when I sat down to rest for a minute on a door-step. The houses began to swim before me, and the figures of walking men and women to dance up and down in a marvellous manner as I stared at them, and listened to the ceaseless murmuring of the human hive.

By-and-bye I awoke, and my basket was gone, contents and all. As I had put my earnings in the basket, I was there alone in London without a farthing, in the morning of beginning one. That was comfortable. With the tears of weariness and disappointment trickling down my cheeks, I went back till I found the shop where my basket had been filled. I told my tale, and they laughed at me; they did not believe it. Then the tears dried on my cheeks, for they were burning with anger and shame; and I said to those who mocked me: "Well, I don't want your help, I will do without it. I have told you the truth; I would not lie to save my life. Some day perhaps you may see me again."

It was a high-sounding speech, and the shop-men laughed all the more, but they were lucky words for me. There was a gentleman sitting at one of the tables with a newspaper, and as I spoke, he looked over it at me quickly. Then he put it down and came forward.

"Rather a lad, my boy. You wouldn't lie to save your life, eh?"

"No, sir," replied I. "At least I hope not."

"Ah, that's better. Where do you come from?"

"That I shall not tell anybody."

"Indeed!"

"I have never worked for my living yet. At home I—I had plenty of everything, but I ran away, because my step-father beat me, and I will tell no one where I came from, for fear they should send me back. I mean to get something, when I get rich."

There was a suppressed titter all round the shop, but I never raised my head: I didn't mind it then, for the gentleman did not seem to be making fun of me.

"And you are willing to work—hard?"

"Indeed I am."

"Your name?"

I hesitated. "If I tell you, you will not try to find out where I came from?"

He smiled. "No, my lad; I have something else to do."

"Robert West, sir."

"Very well; then come with me, Robert West, and I will see what you are good for."

My work was little enough at first. I was an office boy, and was only trusted to a certain extent. Besides which, whenever my master happened to be in the outer office, I saw that he watched me closely. One day I looked up at him, and caught his eye upon me as usual.

"I don't care, sir," I said, boldly; "you will trust me by-and-bye."

He laughed, and said I was a "queer chap!" and the next day sent me up on errand of such importance that I felt myself already on the way to greatness.

That was the beginning—a fair start in life—and it was all I wanted; I meant to succeed. I would have worked myself to the bone for success, and I got what I wanted. In one way or other we most of us do get what we really strive after! which is a thought at once of encouragement and warning; for if we go out of the way of duty after what we want, though we obtain it, the sin shall not go unpunished. I rose to be a clerk, well salaried; and then those dreams of ambition which never would let me rest, urged me on to the pursuit of something which had as yet been only a distant hope, a hidden beauty—I mean authorship.

All these years I knew nothing of my mother or my stepfather. Often a miserable longing arose within me to take a holiday, and go down to the old mill. Holidays I had in plenty, but they were all devoted to the new ambition. While restless nights I have paced my room, when the visions of the grand day were still, struggling with that desire to see my mother's face and hear her voice again. But I said, "It is not yet time. I will be rich first—great and independent; then I will see her, and she shall be proud of her son."

And then, as my pen grew facile, and my thoughts came forth in a stream that flashed and sparkled, and filled me with delight, I threw away the trade of clerkship, and struck out boldly into the field of literature. I progressed. Looking along my path, I felt inclined to cry out, "It is wonderful: it has been like magic!"

When a book by Robert West, which had reached a third edition, lay on my table, I thought the time had come at last. It was April, as it had been when I ran away and slept under the hawthorn hedge. I packed my trunk, no longer struggling, but full of a joyful excitement. I looked over the grimy housetops, and the smoke and the chimneys, and thought of the dairy dippers and the mill-stream. I went in the street the crowd that journeyed on, for ever hot and dusty, and thought of the fresh air blowing through the trees, the sunlight on the water, and the birds. Restlessly, tremulously happy, I packed my travelling-bag, and turned in thought the noise of the street into the whirr of the mill-wheel. I started home again, no longer a weary truant sleeping under hedges, but comparatively rich—a man of fair prospects and great hopes. I reached the town where I used to study a little and play a great deal at school. There were those which I recognised, but none knew me. There were improvements, too; I might have had a "fly" (formerly an unknown luxury), but I would not. I would walk through the coppice, that I might see the pleasant woods shadow had so often fitted before me in the heats of toil and weariness. I did see it. I could have thrown myself in the grass and sobbed aloud as I caught sight of the mill and heard the wheel. But we Englishmen are ashamed of our feelings, and smother them. I crossed the footbridge quickly, and my hand was on the gate leading to the front door. I stopped. I would go in the back; it was a little further round, and my heart beat so painfully. How natural it all looked, even to the old water-butt with its green slime, and the fowls that were scratching themselves and picking at stray morsels.

I could not look in at the windows, for the sun beat upon them; and the blinds had been drawn. The door stood open; I went into the passage, but no one was to be seen; then into the parlour. An old dog rose with difficulty, and snarled at me; when I spoke to him he wagged a feeble tail and lay down again, as if I were of no consequence at all, and it was too much trouble to notice me further. At the right there was another parlour. I turned the handle noiselessly, but it would not yield. Then I went upstairs, and stood at the door of a room where my mother had been used to sit sometimes when she was not well. I knocked, but there was a strange sinking about my heart as I did so. No one answered, and I went in.

Yes, she was there. At least the face I knew so well, and had so longed to see was there; but the lips were never going to speak to me again.

It was another cause than sunshine that had

drawn down those blinds. Not one word, not even forgiveness! Does it seem too hard a punishment, too bitter an after-taste of the apple of rebellion?

Oh you children, you boys and girls, think of it. You may not do as I did, but then those hasty words that you utter and forget; the rebellious temper, and the acts of disobedience; forgotten long, they do come back to us when they are past recall or atonement; when there is no more any breath in the dead lips to utter forgiveness.

* * * * *

The flowers may blossom in the coppice, and the sun shine over the water, but not for me; for the old mill is sold, and I am alone in the world. This is my tale; my sin and its punishment which rose up before me almost in answer to the shouting and merriment of those noisy urchins who are capering and dancing round the lamp-post.

LOUIS SAND.

LAST WORDS.

BY ELIZABETH TOWNBRIDGE.

Mother! they say I blame you as one who came between
Me and my early, happy dreams of all that might have been!
But, Mother, I do not blame you; against you do not rebel;
No; though I loved one better, dear Mother, I love you well!

You believed you did but your duty, as we were both so poor—
Alas! the world holds suffering worse than Poverty doth endure!—
Besides, it was late, it was too late, when we were bade to part.
I spoke the words as you told me; but, O Mother, they broke my heart!—
The timid heart which since that day doth cold in my bosom lie:
I had not strength for the bitter strife—I could only yield and die.

The words, perhaps, may sound strangely towards her through whom I live;
But one day it may be a comfort to know that I do forgive—
Forgive you the hours of anguish that into my short life came;
That, dying, I love you dearly, and never mean to blame.

I forgive all that bitter parting which gave his bosom pain:
One grief, at least, is spared me; for he now is happy again!
He thought I was false, cold-hearted. No matter: it is as well;
For a wife and a smiling infant in his heart and home now dwell!

For me all has long been over. Never, ah! never more
Shall we stand, 'neath the quiet starlight, loitering outside the door;
Lingering in the soft twilight, or the moonlight, fair and pale,
Listening the story of his love, like a child to a fairy tale,
Under that broad blue heaven which I never again may see,
His loving words and his clasping hand making earth a heaven to me!

You have but one other daughter—a gentle, loving child—
This morning she smiled upon me, and asked why I never smiled:
I could not tell her the reason, or cloud that open brow;
But, Mother, I charge you, never let her die as I die now!

Love her—I know you love her—but let that love be told:
When she turns to you in her little grief, do not seem so stern and cold:
If one wins her love, do not part them!—forth to the Battle of Life
Let them pass, 'neath thy shielding blessing, a husband and a wife!

And should children gather round them, at a table poorly spread,
He who fed ravens in the desert will send those children bread!
They will be round her when she dies—when her golden curls are grey!
Daughters to weep, and sons whose hands place her lovingly in the clay.

You weep, and your hand clasps my hand, to give me the pledge I claim;
But remember, Mother, I love you, and never mean to blame!

PRACTICALITY.

My clever friend, your sage advice is good:
"Be practical," you say, "and cease to trouble
"Your brains on matters never understood
"By mortal, priest or layman; cease to brood
"On wind-eggs—chickens never spring from bubble."

Your sage advice is good, my clever friend:
To Daemon, sure, a spectacle for laughter
Is Socrates, when post-devils suspend
The Satyr, squatted (O ye gods purpend!)
In a basket-basket, from a rotten rafter,

Half-way 'twixt heaven and earth—by both abjured:
Poor Socrates! a dolorous condition!
Such are the bitter fruits of being lured
By Siren-Chatter.——My clever friend, I'm cured,
And will repent in practical contrition.

J. A.

OUR INFANT SCHOOL—ITS RISE AND PROGRESS.

A squall—a scream—a crash.

Our carriage stops suddenly, we let down the glass quickly, and, popping out our head, inquire—

"What is the matter, James?"

"Only one of those confounded brats under the horses' feet again, ma'am," exclaims our coachman.

"I'll not have one of my children [illegible] and swore at and called a confounded brat by you, you nasty vulgar fellow! You've been the death of this little un, you have, with your careless driving!" was screamed out by a shrill female voice.

Now, as our ears informed us that the child most certainly was not killed, we got out of the carriage to make ourselves acquainted with the real extent of the injury, and found a sturdy boy of four years old struggling and squalling in the arms of a woman, just fresh from the wash, and who was most energetically bestowing upon our luckless coachman every epithet which her fancy suggested as suitable to the occasion.

As soon as we could obtain any admission to ourselves we ascertained that the little one was not in the least hurt, but that its screams proceeded from fright and a sense of injured dignity. It was extremely dirty from its fall in the road, and its pinafore was torn, but that was the extent of the evil. To this fact we for some minutes endeavoured, in vain, to call the mother's attention; for she, generally a decent well-spoken woman, and one of our especial village favourites, had on this occasion completely forgotten her manners, and would not cease in her abuse of James, who, in reality, was not to blame, as the child was making dirt-pies in the road, and had run directly in front of the horses, which was [illegible] by [illegible].

When we could make ourselves heard, we tried to show her how disproportioned her anger was to the extent of the mischief; and, at last, pacified her with the promise of two new pinafores on the morrow, provided she would promise to keep the child out of the road. Finding that, so long as we remained, she would return to her abuse of the coachman, we thought it advisable to let her cool; and, saying we would call again the next day, we left her to wash and comfort the little squaller.

This violent altercation had quite put out our coachman, and he mutteringly observed to us, that "[illegible] not only of his life, but of everybody else's like that travelled along the road; they was always in the way. He was sure that there was nothing for it but to kill one of 'em, and then, perhaps, the mothers would take some care of 'em."

Now, we perfectly agreed with James, as to the great annoyance that "them brats" were to all travellers; but we also fancied that the evil might be remedied without resorting to the extreme measures recommended by him: we therefore set out the next morning with two new pinafores, to see what a little quiet talk to our friend, Mrs. Cooper, would effect.

We found her very busy, ironing. She was quieted down, and seemed rather ashamed of her outbreak of the previous day, but still disposed to throw all the blame upon the coachman.

"But why, Mrs. Cooper," said we, "why was the child in the road? You have a nice garden for it to play in, and a gate which might be kept shut."

"Why, you see, ma'am," she replied, "I have got a lot of extra washing to do for a gentleman as is staying at the Parsonage, and I had not the time to be a looking after him; so he got out a-playing with the Jones' and Simpsons'. You see I be like to be doing summat; I can't be always a-gate of minding the children after they can walk; they must mind theirselves; and the lane is so good a place for 'em to play in all together [illegible] as far as I can see. If so be the drivers wouldn't be so careless, and I must say your James is the carelessest of 'em all; he is allways a-knocking down summat, and then he calls out 'Oh! it's only dirty [illegible]' says he. If he had only the cleaning and washing of all the frocks and pinafores, he'd sing a different song, and not laugh about it, I'll be bound."

Finding she was going off in the same strain as yesterday, we hastily presented the new 'pinnies,' and, requesting her to be more careful in future, rose to depart, when she said, more humbly—

"Thank you kindly, ma'am, for the pinnies!—I'm sure I wish I know'd what to do with the children—I did try last week, and kept Caroline at home to mind 'em, but the parson's lady called, and asked why she was not at school; and when I told her the reason she shook her head, and said, 'That will never do, Betty, for ruining the girl.' She said, besides, [illegible]. So, what be I to do? I did think of sending the little un there to the church school, along with her sister; but Mrs. Watkinson says that she cannot do with such babies, they're more trouble nor they are worth. What be I to do? My master was very angry with me last night about it, he said; the coachman had been complaining to him about 'em. What be I to do?"

Mrs. Cooper's melancholy despairing "What be I to do?" rang in our ears all that day, and for many succeeding ones. It was a very difficult question to answer, for how it was to be answered was not at once clear to us; and we had come to no decision on the matter, when news was brought, that one of the little Simpsons' had really been run over by a tiny [illegible], and that one of its legs was broken. Now, as the broken leg was not so easy to mend as the "torn pinnie," we felt that the case imperatively called for prompt and active measures,—it was decidedly serious.

"Oh!" exclaimed one of the mothers, with whom we were discussing this untoward event, "if we had only an Infant School in this parish, as they have in some places, we should know where the children were."

"An infant school, to be sure!" we mentally exclaimed, "that is the very thing!" We wondered that we had not thought of it sooner. The idea, however, once started, rapidly took form, and an infant school we determined to establish.

The plan was mentioned to the mothers, who hailed it gladly; they would willingly, they said, pay so much a fortnight to get the little ones taken care of. It would pay, they were sure, to keep them, for they could not keep an eye on what they would, when they were playing about all day. Two "pinnies" a week was enough for the girls that went to school; while those that stopped at home wanted a clean one every day. Oh, yes, they would send them, and thank you, ma'am.

This was encouraging; we determined to set up a school directly.

When the subject was broached among our own friends, we were met with shakes of the head. "An infant school! a nursery for fools! a hot-bed for idiots!" More than one school-teacher declared that the greatest dunces they had ever seen had been brought up in infant schools. While others, more leniently, said; "You will find it very expensive, as you will require a trained mistress, who understands the system; and then the apparatus will cost a great deal."

This was not encouraging, and we began not to see our way quite clearly.

But, as we are not easily baffled when we have set our minds upon a thing, we had no intention of giving up our scheme for ameliorating the condition of the children; we only determined to set to work cautiously.

The epithets applied by our friends to infant schools in general, rather puzzled us; as we supposed "what everybody says must be true," and that there must be some foundation for the uncomplimentary remarks; what the foundation was we are not ourselves to discover, as we could not understand why keeping children out of the dirt and from under the horses' feet should have a deleterious influence over their mental faculties. We had been kept clean and tidy in our juvenile days, and we did not think, whatever our friends may say, that our intellects had suffered in consequence; we therefore inquired of all sorts of people, visited schools, and, at least, satisfied ourselves that we had discovered the rock upon which infant schools had split, and which had caused the regular infant-school system to be so frequently the subject of animadversion.

We found, that in some not the enforced absence of dirt-pies and the risks of the road that was [illegible] to the children, so much as the routine of tuition which was substituted. The lessons and amusements appeared to us to be carried on with such mechanical precision, that the thoughts—*i. e.* the intellects—of the child might be with yesterday's dinner, or to-morrow's rice-pudding, without the slightest hindrance being occasioned in his present occupation. We do not wish to be thought captious and fault-finding with those, no doubt, more than ourselves, who invented this system; we only wish to give our reasons for going out of the beaten track.

We think that unmeaning manipulations, and songs which it cannot understand, is injurious to the mind of any child, as laying the foundation of a habit of repeating by rote, while not employing the understanding—a habit which we have repeatedly seen to be a very difficult one to conquer in after-life—a habit, in which the memory, instead of acting in concert with the reasoning powers, is encouraged to act quite independently of them, which practice induces a careless way of doing things; and the exclamation we so often hear, "Oh dear! I was thinking of something else," is the consequence.

Feeling all this, we determined, in our school—for a school we would have—to try a different plan, and to go more upon the system of a well-regulated nursery than that of a school.

We kept our own counsel, as we had been so quizzed that we did not like to run the chance of any more jokes upon our failure, if we did not succeed, and set to work quietly. After some deliberation we settled upon a system, for the success of which we felt sanguine. Having a promise of a sufficient number of scholars to make a trial with, our next step was to find a teacher. We had two reasons for not sending to a training school for one: firstly, we could not afford the wages; secondly, we did not want the system; so we set to work to train one for ourselves. We felt that, to carry "our system," much, very much, depended upon our choice in that respect, and we steadily said no to every applicant of any age, and ultimately selected a middle-aged matron, who had trained a large family of her own—a well spoken, good-tempered woman, who read correctly, and could sew and knit well. She did not apply; we sought her out; and, on her offering [illegible] the [illegible] replied, "I am afraid, ma'am, that I should not give you satisfaction; for I know nothing about teaching, and there are such new plans since I went to school, that I do not think I should make anything of it," &c. &c.

A little explanation soon overcame her objections, and convinced us both that we should get on very well together. We came to terms accordingly; we agreeing to find everything required, and to pay her a certain weekly sum, taking her children's money ourselves, thus guaranteeing her from any loss, and preventing all temptations to favouritism, &c.

A spare room in her cottage was speedily cleared out, and our simple materials for school-keeping collected in it. A couple of low benches and a table and chair for the mistress comprised the furniture; while for school apparatus, we had a dozen similitudes, a box of letters, a large sheet alphabet, a few pictures of familiar animals and birds, a book of easily understood stories, and another of childish (not silly) songs, two slates, pencils, thimbles, and patchwork: with all these, the best of their kind, we opened our school.

We began with six specimens of "perpetual motion," varying in age from three to five years, and at the end of six months we were entirely satisfied with our experiment. The school was found to answer, not, we beg leave to observe, in the common acceptation of the word, for it did not pay its way, our outlay being at twopence a week (our charge); but it answered its object—the children were kept clean and happy, they acquired good, quiet, orderly habits, and some little reading and working; the parents were satisfied and so were we. We have since progressed steadily, and our numbers have so much increased, that we have found it necessary to enlarge our room, send in extra benches, and raise the mistress's wages. Friends have ceased to laugh; the master and mistress of the parish school have complimented us upon the good conduct of our "superannuated," which have been passed on to them; we have the pleasure of seeing "our school" is appreciated; the small sum which it yearly costs us brings in a rich harvest in orderly children and grateful mothers; and we have every reason to congratulate ourselves upon our steady adherence to our determination.

We have so many times boasted of the superexcellence of "our system," that it is incumbent upon us to say a few words in explanation of it, in order that the reader may form a fair estimate of its merits. In arranging our plans we kept in memory the last verse of the "Busy Bee:"—

"In books, and work, and healthful play
Let my first years be past,
That I may give for every day
Some good account at last."

and we bestowed as much attention upon the settling of the "healthful play" as upon either of the first two elements. The elements of reading were taught, but not pushed, as we consider that there is no fear now-a-days that a person will not learn to read, and that art may be acquired at any age; whereas if the use of the fingers is not taught early, excellence in either working or writing is seldom attained. This was one reason for our bestowing so much more attention upon the working and knitting; and another was, that with a very little trouble working may be made an amusement; but no one ever made the alphabet or primer really attractive. We therefore devoted very little time to them.

Generally speaking nothing pleases a child more than making something; i.e. putting into shape that which before had none. A bit of coloured stuff, needle-thread, and we ask to form a bag or pincushion, will amuse a small thing at work far sooner than the endless hem of uninteresting white handkerchief, which is so often a child's first performance: we said coloured stuff, because their unaccustomed eyes do not easily catch the stitches on white; and they like to see how they get on. Then, again, until a pupil takes an interest in her work, and can handle her needle properly, we never give her hemming to do, as it is one of the most difficult stitches to do nicely; and nothing sooner disgusts a child than a hem, in which the stitches are that she pricks her finger and loses her temper.

A little before we drew our pen under "all the best of its kind;" for this reason; We do not consider it fair upon a young child to make it set its first stitches with a stump of a needle, a long piece of knotty cotton, an ill-fitting thimble, and a bit of hard calico; and then expect it to learn quickly and delight in its employment. Yet we have frequently seen children so treated by mothers, and nurses, who ought to know better if they gave themselves the trouble to think at all; but whose favourite maxim is "anything will do to learn upon; it is a shame to waste anything good upon a child." Now as we happen to differ in opinion from these worthy women, we also differed in our actions; and provided for our little ones bright needles, as the best adapted to their short fingers, smooth cotton, well-fitting thimbles, and silk bits of patch-work; and with these good materials we were satisfied with the progress made, and the pleasant faces of the little work-women.

On the same principle we taught knitting to both boys and girls, with short, straight needles, and cotton that would not easily split. Among our employments was the manufacture of kettle-holders in cross-stitch on coarse [illegible] canvas, which work was very popular with the pupils, and always made a great favour of by them; also the tearing up of waste letter-paper into shreds for the stuffing of pillows, some of which served as beds for the very small to take an hour's nap upon, and others were given away. And we may remark, that these pillows are much appreciated by bed-ridden people on account of their coolness.

The next thing we must touch upon is the "healthful play," which is divided into two parts; the noisy, either indoors or out, according to the weather, and the quiet play. To assist in the latter the slates proved most useful.

"Slates!" we think we hear some one exclaim, in whose mind's eye nothing pleasanter regarding a slate is presented than Long Division or Compound Multiplication. "Slates!"

Yes, slates, dear reader, slates made subservient to healthful play, for no arithmetic is taught by us.

Slates are, we flatter ourselves, an original idea; and we use them thus:—

When a piece of the "raw material" comes into our hands, the first thing we do is to persuade it to sit still for a few minutes without crying. Pictures are but little use; for a completely uneducated mind cannot appreciate a picture; it cannot derive any knowledge from it, unless some one points out the various parts of the picture; but, with a slate and pencil, the child immediately discovers that it can make a white mark of any kind or shape it pleases; and scratching upon [illegible] becomes a most fascinating employment. In a few days the scratches resolve [illegible] through [illegible] an unpractised eye would not [illegible] discover what; but the young artist will delightedly inform you that so and so represents a pump or a tree, and such and such a cat or a cow. Though not offended by your simplicity they are ready for any suggestions to improve the likeness; and, if you were to set them a copy you will win their hearts.

It is in copying that the slates afford an intellectual employment (grand words for an Infant School!). For in copying the minds of the children become interested, their attentions are absorbed, and they are imperceptibly taking in fresh ideas. Thus: You give a cow for a subject. Several draw cows upon their slates; on examination Tommy's cow proves to have only three legs, and Sally's no eyes. You inquire "Who ever saw a cow with only three legs?" The children stare, you point to the copy, and count the legs, making the children count after you; then make Tommy count the legs of his cow he sees the difference; so do the others. Next you draw Sally's attention to her "poor cow without eyes" and ask her how the animal could see to walk about the field without eyes? &c., and finish your remarks by showing that they will look at the cows in the lane and count their legs. Another day a duck or a horse may be the lesson, and comparisons made between them and the cow. In a short time the animals in the fields and yards will be invested with quite a new interest for the little minds, and afford much conversation among themselves and those at home, who always hear what has been doing at school. By this simple process two very important intellectual powers are developed — Observation and Comparison. Having taught a child to observe and compare, a great step has been taken towards general education. The habit of observing accurately once attained, it is seldom lost; and to that habit early acquired, many self-made men owe much of their greatness and success.

Simple songs, and pretty stories read to them are among their other amusements; but we take especial care that nothing shall be learnt by rote that they are incapable of understanding, and [illegible] their [illegible]. "Whatever is worth doing at all, is worth doing well," is a very favourite maxim of ours, and our mistress fully shares our feelings.

Having thus divided our time among "books and work and healthful play," a small portion of the first two, to a large one of the last, our system was arranged, and we had only to superintend and watch its progress, which has continued steadily and perfectly satisfactory. We see that the mind and intellectual development is advancing; though we have not one prodigy — not one child that is made to stand up and say its lesson to "the lady," and in so doing losing a great share of the child's best ornament — childishness — and putting the component parts in [illegible]; we never show them off, except in a mass. We do not expect that the genius of a Turner or a Stephenson will be that of one of "ours;" but we do expect that, as we have tried to educate them on a rational system, they will grow up educated men and women, and do their duty in the "station to which it shall please God to call them."

The success of our school has been mainly owing to our mistress; and we repeat our firm conviction, that the best training school for an Infant School mistress is her own nursery.

The economical reader may accuse us of extravagance in using every thing of the best; but, allowing for knots and breakages, we do not think the good costs more than the bad materials; and though there is no Royal road to learning, yet we believe there is both a rough and as well as a straight one, and we prefer the latter. We do not approve of removing every obstacle always out of a child's path; but we see no policy in permitting obstructions which do not necessarily belong to the business in hand, and thus rendering that business more distasteful than it need be.

Lest some reader might remark as a neighbour did, "you teach no religion in your school," we must say that we consider a knowledge of right and wrong, a consciousness that God is always watching them, and that He will reward the good and punish the evil doers, is as much religion as a child under seven can understand; and the [illegible] has a great moral attached to them; but, as we dislike hearing texts mumbled through, we give them none, preferring that Bible words should come fresh to them when of an age to understand them; and, believing that the old proverb "familiarity breeds contempt" is as applicable to Scripture as to anything else, we do not venture upon that holy ground.

Now, kind reader, it is time that we lay down our pen; and, in thanking you for your patient attention, we only hope that our hobby has not proved more tedious than hobbies are in general. The reader who mounts up behind us, on our hobby, should prepare himself for the fact that however the animal may kick, plunge, [illegible], shy, start, or run away, no hobby-horse was ever yet found to be short-winded.

Can she spin?—A young girl was introduced to James I., as excelling even learned men in classical acquirements. "Well," said the monarch, "now tell me what this paragon can do?" He was informed that she could speak and write Latin, Greek, and Hebrew. "Ah," replied the king, "these are rare attainments for a maid! but can she spin also?"—*Old Jonathan.*

LE PUY, HAUTE LOIRE.

(From the Note-Book of an English Lady.)

After a week's sojourn at D——, our house hired and furnished, our luggage not yet all arrived from Paris, a Government order ordered us to pack up again and return to the metropolis (more than two hundred miles by diligence), and then to proceed to Le Puy, Haute Loire, in the south, some four hundred miles farther—a perfect Siberia in winter, we were told, with a broiling sun in summer; and in the midst of a bigoted race as wild and uncouth as the mountains, amongst which they are lost, from the rest of the world. Others, indeed, gave us more cheerful prospects; and I confess that my repugnance vastly diminished at the thought of seeing a mountain, and that a mountain of the Cevennes, where streams of Protestant blood had once flown in the cause of religion, and where it will be strange if we do not find some traces of Protestantism.

We were also told that this capital of the ancient Velay is a very curious old place—that it is surrounded with ruined castles, so that there will at least be some sources for amusement, if it only consists in letting the imagination wander back to days of yore, on the very spot where "minstrel sung to lady fair of love true knight-like," and where I will conduct you, kind readers, if you do not find the ramble too tedious.

We have often in D——, leaving our things to the mercy of strangers, to be sold or sent after us; but my worst grief was the distance that would soon separate me from England—a grief which my husband guessed, and by his tenderness endeavoured to soothe and overcome.

I will pass over our journey back to the metropolis, with which in these days of easy transit so many of my readers are well acquainted. It was night when we entered the railway carriage for Lyons, so that we were deprived of the views of those rich vine-clad hills of Champagne and Burgundy that yield such joy to the heart of man, but which man is wrong to quaff too copiously at any time, and more particularly so when he is going to be married, and has to travel by that "cursed English invention," a railroad—which verity you will appreciate, after hearing the sad dilemma of a bold young Gaul, somewhat less in stature than those described by Cæsar, but the colour of whose hair and beard declared him a descendant in direct line. We had comfortably arranged ourselves for the night, when, at a few leagues from Paris, this gentleman entered our carriage, with Bacchus at his heels and in his head, disturbing us all with his noise and perpetual motion, now on this side now on that, now drawing the window up, now letting it fall down, his tongue striving to reveal the wisdom of his brain—the same appeared inclined to listen to. At last a fellow-traveller beside him, feeling the night-air too keen, requested him to shut the window. Our Gaul was enchanted at the sound of a human voice. Oh certainly, with the greatest pleasure; although for himself he felt very warm; but he always made it a rule to be obliging, were his head to burst even with the heat. And up went the window, making us all start from our seats with the noise.

"A little sleep would do you no harm," interposed the traveller, turning directly round.

"Sleep, my [illegible]—sleep! when to-morrow is my wedding-day! I assure you I have not the slightest inclination; I feel much too gay for sleep. Fancy a hundred thousand francs, and [illegible] expectations, with a pretty girl into the bargain! There is a chance for you! I that have nothing but my profession—and that, between us two, not over-brilliant! . . . I sleep, when at ten I am to be married! And if I passed the station, what then? 'Julie would not die with grief,' you may answer. Very probably; but [illegible], I tell you. Julie would not be ready a second time—girls are so susceptible!"

Then perceiving that his companion dozed, or pretended so to do, and casting a despairing glance around on all the other slumberers, he with a sigh resigned himself to silence, and in a few minutes gave audible proof that he could sleep, in spite of the wedding-day on the morrow; and we, far from troubling his slumbers, respected them, as those who lost their own repose at least.

On, on we rolled, each one dozing, or buried in his thoughts, and already "[illegible]," when suddenly our bridegroom elect started awake. "Jesus, Maria!" cried he, with bewildered looks, daylight already! Where are we, gentlemen? where are we?"

"Near Macon," answered Victor.

"Near Macon? grand *Dieu! grand Dieu!* I am lost!" vociferated he; and, putting his head out of the window, he howled like one frantic.

On, on rolled the wheels; shouts and cries were in vain.

"A midday train will convey you back," said Victor, quietly consulting a time-table.

"At twelve, and I am to be married at ten! I shall go mad, I tell you! Oh, the cursed English invention, to rattle on at this rate!"

And he gnashed his teeth with rage. Then, with gestures and words he gave vent to his fury—so grotesquely, that it was absolutely impossible to remain serious; and, if truth must out, I fear our commiseration in the misfortune of our night's disturbance was not so prolonged as it might have been; and we felt that the bride, timid as he had intimated, would not be very sorry to have a pretext to keep her person and fortune for another.

We left our inquiring companion at a station before we reached Mâcon, he crying loudly in anathema, declaring that back he must go immediately, as he was to be married at ten; the station-master shaking his head quietly, repeating, "Impossible! impossible!"

I saw the gentleman still; that made us all laugh so heartily as we sped on towards Mâcon, where a sumptuous breakfast awaited us, with twenty minutes to regale ourselves. "Oh, the [illegible] refreshment-rooms!" exclaimed I, as we entered; "and what a delicious meal after last night's fatigue! See how the table groans with good things! The sight alone gives me an appetite."

"Make haste!" answered Victor, who was already seriously at work; "or you will get nothing."

But, instead of obeying, I amused myself in watching a jolly-looking priest opposite me, who, although it was Friday, studiously avoided all meagre dishes, which the waiter as studiously persisted in offering him; and that without losing time, he most probably knew from experience the length of twenty minutes there.

"Make haste!" repeated Victor again.

But, just as I was on the point of beginning, the signal of departure sounded from the platform, and "Six francs each," from the waiter, to whom I protested that I had eaten nothing. Victor paid his twelve francs, and ready we rushed to our places, I as hungry as when I entered. I was, however, [illegible] Nature's [illegible], at the sight of those luxuriant hills covered with vines, or with patches of different crops of various shades that met our gaze as we approached Lyons, and that stretched out far and wide before us, resembling a gracefully waving sea of verdure, though by first possessing the [illegible] beauty of the Haute Loire.

We had a few hours to remain in Lyons, and we ran through this ancient capital of Gaul with true delight, admiring its noble squares, public works, superb edifices, and winding rivers; and thankful should we have been had our journey ended here. But on—on, on we must go, and at night did we bid adieu to the charming city, and set out for St. Étienne—black St. Étienne, with its [illegible] manufactories and coal-mines—a town that appeared to us particularly dirty and gloomy. Happily we had only the rest of the night to pass there, and at sunrise we started on diligence for Le Puy, Haute Loire.

Oh, magnificent Haute Loire! with what exclamations of delight did we hail thy glorious mountain-tops! now lost in the clouds, now smiling in the morning sun! My heart palpitates again with renewed wonder and emotion as I write, and recall the first view of a mountainous country. Huge wild rocks, hurled, as it were, one on the other, arose in solemn silence before us, and struck us mute with awe; for man seemed entirely banished from the scene; and it was only as we advanced further and further that small patches of cultivation denoted his presence somewhere. Here, with one and there a stray cottage, or small village, now half-way up, now at the foot of these stupendous heights.

We had a whole day's journey before us, for fast travelling is impossible in these mountainous regions; nor were we sorry, for it enabled us to admire at leisure the majestic grandeur—so novel to us both. And who can explain the sweet emotions that pervaded each of us, as, for the first time, we felt ourselves alone in a new world, our hearts animated with the same joy that the sentiment of the beautiful inspired in us, and made us feel more and more one?

My exclamations of surprise and rapture greatly amused our companion in the coupé—a fat, rosy, good-natured-looking curé, who, flattered at our admiration, hastened to acquaint us that he was a son of the Velay, by doing the honours of his country with great amiability. But we soon perceived that Le Puy had not the honour of having given him birth, but that Brioude, a town on the opposite banks of the Haute Loire, was the Mecca before which the capital even ought to bow. We of course readily acquiesced, not being acquainted with either, particularly as he also assured us that the streets in Le Puy tremble with dirt, and that the wine there is detestable. "Think a Ponot" (name given to the inhabitants of Le Puy) "to touch it when he can get any other," said he. "A young Ponot, with his [illegible], being at Bordeaux, determined to regale himself, he ordered a [illegible] to dine, and the [illegible] ordered the waiter to bring him a bottle of the best wine—*vin du cru*. 'Which wine?' asked the waiter. Now *vin du cru* for the waiter was a very different thing to *vin du cru* for the Ponot. The first was the best Bordeaux, while the latter was sour Le Puy wine. '*Vin du cru!*' indignantly answered the Ponot; 'do you imagine that I came all this way to drink *vin du cru*? No, no, I have enough of that at home; bring me a bottle of the best Bordeaux.'

"And yet they have the mania of cultivating the vine," continued our informer. "And you will see with what perseverance they plant it all round the town in every direction, and with what perseverance, also, the vine refuses to [illegible] its fruit."

"Has the town any particular industry?" asked Victor.

"Lace is the support of the poor, and the making of the rich. A vast deal is yearly exported to England; that is the only occupation of the Velay; and a [illegible] it is for the working classes, who gain [illegible] their meals a day; and the very best hands never exceed ten sous. Few there are who arrive at that price, as their skill [illegible] frequently [illegible] their [illegible] country. Well, well, the people are habituated to it. They are very frugal, living on black bread, soup, and potatoes; and I dare say they are as happy as the rest of mankind—besides, they have a horror of what the world calls progress. That feeling is fostered in them by the clergy, who persuade them that railroads, electric telegraphs, and all kinds of machinery are inventions of the devil, sent to mislead mankind; and that if they wish to go to heaven they have only to believe all the priests tell them, and go to mass; nothing else is necessary even for happiness in this world also. And most of them believe it."

"I suppose we shall see plenty of monks and friars?" I observed.

"You will, indeed, Madame: scarce anything else in the streets of Le Puy, for one counts hundreds in all possible congregations and orders. We have the largest establishment in France for Jesuits, in a village called Vals, which village is under the protection of the Black Virgin."

"And pray, who and what is the Black Virgin?"

"The Black Virgin! Have you never heard of Our Lady of Le Puy — the marvel of the middle ages? But I am a bad narrator. You will soon get initiated into all the miracles she has wrought. I cannot remember half of them. If my wife were here, she would tell you all about it, and make volumes to suit; for I leave all that to her. Miracles and saints, confessions and penitence, that is her affair; she has nothing else to do, we promised for us both." And he laughed—a very unorthodox laugh. "Madame is Protestant, I presume?"

"Yes, thank God!"

"Amen! Had I been born a Protestant I certainly should have remained one; but one must keep to the religion in which one was born."

"Why so?" said Victor.

And then began a discussion between the two that made my soul thrill with delight, to hear my French husband compare the pure doctrine with Romish corruption; and again and again did I mentally thank the Giver of all good for this inestimable good to me. But our audience soon declared his incapacity to argue on such a subject, and his conviction that Monsieur was right; yet, in spite of all, "one ought to keep to the religion in which one was born. My wife," added he, "would a thousand times rather see me a heathen, a Jew, or anything rather than a Protestant; and I caution you to be on your guard when at Le Puy, or you may encounter many disagreeables. The clergy are all-powerful, and have spies everywhere; but here we are at Monistrol; and if, like me, you cannot live on air, I advise you to alight and refresh yourselves. You will find bread and cheese, with wine as new as [illegible]. I warn you that we shall get nothing else before we reach Le Puy, at least eleven to-night."

We followed our jovial friend's advice, and descended between two or three [illegible], and as many children—only symptoms of life in this town. However, I am bound to say that, if the wine was sour, the cheese was excellent, flavoured as it was with a good appetite; while mine hostess, a plump, dark-eyed little woman, was overflowing with politeness, assuring us that, if we had been two hours later, we should have found a first-rate dinner—which, as we could not wait to verify, we chose to believe, in spite of the incredulous smile of the courier, who had provided against casualties, and held between two pieces of bread an enormous sausage, which he appeared to devour with great gusto; while, with the importance of some one arrived from afar, he related the news of the day to the inquisitive landlord and gendarmes, a troop of half-clad urchins standing before him with doleful faces and voices, both made for the occasion, begging "the petit sou pour l'amour de Dieu!" all in the same tone. But crack again went the whip, and round went the wheels, and soon Monistrol was far behind, with its [illegible] for young priests, [illegible] in the pride of the Virgin, and the [illegible] for good [illegible], and has been so for years. "How well do I remember it in my college-days, and our rival when at Le Puy! They paraded the streets with us, in all the religious ceremonies, which Government compelled us to take part in to please the clergy. How we strove to triumph in noise, if not in harmony with each other! . . . Ah! those were happy days! And the thoughts of the [illegible], where I spent a year, and left for the College of Le Puy, recall many a bright hope before me. My mother, being ambitious of having a priest in the family, and persuaded by her confessor, sent me to this establishment, where I was fattened, and allowed to do as I pleased, as I did nothing, and soon became weary and disgusted, particularly as I felt no vocation for the life laid before me, and positively declared to my mother that I would not embrace it. She then placed me at Le Puy, and there I spent four of the happiest years in my life; and, in spite of all I have been saying against it, I then thought it the gem of cities, and that because the pretty Adèle was born and lived there."

"And who was the pretty Adèle?" asked I, astonished, but a little amused to find sentiment in our satirist, and that so soon after the unsentimental sausage!

Our loquacious companion was delighted. "Who?" replied he, "why one of the sweetest little creatures imaginable, with whom I fell desperately in love at first sight. You smile, Madame: do you, then, think I never felt this all-engrossing passion?"

I protested.

"I assure you I have, and that many a time; for I have always had a very tender heart, although I remained single until forty years of age; but then no one would have me" (this smile said, "You cannot believe that!"). "But at eighteen I was exceedingly susceptible to the [illegible], and was ever sighing after some [illegible]. But the passion for Adèle was really serious; and she was often the cause of my quarrelling with my professors, who never could persuade me that Latin verses would ever be of any utility to me. I once did try my poetic skill in French verse; but, alas! the rhyme was never reason in spite of Adèle's vision before me: so I gave it up, and instead of allowing my genius to soar on high, I kept it close down on earth, to discover for me when and where I might probably meet Adèle. I lodged opposite the lady of my thoughts, and passed my whole year of rhetoric watching her window, turning every shadow there into Adèle: and, if happy chance showed me Adèle and her mother going out, away I ran, darting down all the bye-streets, to be able to turn and meet my love as if by hazard. I quite edified the old lady with whom I lodged by my constant attendance at mass and vespers, Lent and *Mois de Marie*. 'Look! look!' would she say to her refractory nephew, 'what an example you have before you—the pious young man!' Alas! the poor nephew had no Adèle to attract him there! The sequel of my tale was sad, and cured me for some time of falling in love; for, being with Adèle's brother one day in their drawing-room, I slipped—as a precious relic—into my pocket a large pin I thought I had seen in Adèle's shawl, and that I imagined of no intrinsic value; and, oh the blissful dreams it that night brought to my enamoured soul, as under my pillow it laid, a talisman of felicity! Alas! alas! fond illusions, how soon you all vanished and filled me with horror, when, the next morning, my friend Henri related to me the distress of his father, who was in despair at the loss of a very valuable pin he had left on the drawing-room table the day before, and now could find it nowhere! I trembled at what I had done, and, as soon as it was dark, I carefully sealed up the stolen article, and went into the street. 'Here, my lad,' said I, to a boy who happened to pass me—'here, take this parcel to that house opposite, ring the bell, put it into the servant's hand, and then run away!' The child obeyed me, while I stood watching him. My fright greatly cooled my passion, and a day or two after I left college and Adèle!"

"Did you, then, hear no more of your adventure?" asked Victor.

"And what became of the pretty Adèle?" said I.

"Well," answered the *notaire*, his face shining with satisfaction at having interested me—"see how oddly things often turn out: for more than twenty years I never heard a syllable more either of Adèle or the pin, and the event was almost effaced from my memory, when, one day, weary of living alone, I resolved to marry, and asked a friend who was fond of making matches to find me a wife. 'Young, rich, and pretty, I suppose?' inquired he. 'Well, yes, as much so as I can find. I possess so much, and should like about the same in a wife.' 'Come and dine with me on Sunday, for I think I have just your affair—only fifteen, and not ugly, I assure you.' Bref: I dined with my friend, and, to my great astonishment, who should the mother of the young girl be but Adèle herself, whom I soon recognised; and during the dinner the tale of the pin came out. Its disappearance and reappearance had ever remained a mystery to the family; and I, confessing all, made my former love laugh heartily at my youthful passion—unsuspected by her, although she remembered well that at the time she had observed my constant attendance at church, and our frequent encounters in the streets: and if, Monsieur and Madame, you ever pass through Brioude, I should be most happy to introduce you to Adèle and her daughter—now my mother-in-law and wife! But excuse an old man's loquacity, for I impose on your amiability in withholding thus your attention so long from our beautiful mountains; and night is fast approaching, and will soon mask them from you: a misty vapour commences to encircle them already. Do you not perceive it?"

"Yes; and how dreamy it renders the scene!"

At that moment the *diligence* stopped. "Would the travellers be kind enough to walk up this mountain to ease the horses a little?" asked the postillion.

"You must excuse me, friend," answered the *notaire*—"with my load to drag up I should sink under the weight!"

Victor and I alighted with pleasure, and, while the *diligence* took a circuitous route, we scrambled over bramble, bush, and rock, almost perpendicularly, up to the summit: and well were we recompensed for our fatigue and haste. Such a sight I never beheld! An immense panorama was at our feet. Mountain upon mountain, rock upon rock, now rugged and bare, now covered with every shade of entangled hue gilded with the burning rays of a setting sun gradually becoming fainter and fainter, and with which woods of fir trees, here and there contrasted their sable darkness, while ever and anon streams, that in winter are torrents, fell boisterously down, and rippling in capricious windings, ran quietly into the Lignon and the Loire that here meet in a bed of rocks, trees and bushes, bed that they appear to have dug between huge masses of granite which, for a short distance on either side, tower in most fantastic shapes perpendicularly above them, and then the two rivers branch out again in different directions, meandering and meandering, now appearing, now disappearing, until completely lost amidst the picturesque valleys through which they wander.

As hand-in-hand we stood and gazed in silence, an indescribable feeling of awe crept over us. Not a sound reached our ears, save the distant rumbling of falling waters, the tinkling of the horses' bells and the rolling of the slowly advancing vehicle. We looked, and the shades of night gradually enveloped the scene with her misty mantle, slowly and slowly, tree, rock and mountain melted and melted away like fairy-wrought scene.

At that moment the dying sounds of a vesper bell issuing from the vale beneath, and carried away by the embalmed gale, swept past us, taking up, as it rushed along, our crowning admiration also to the mighty Creator of such marvels; and as our souls cleared the space a momentary glimpse of the fatherland, of fair Albion, sparkling amidst the waters, added another joy to that blissful moment, and brought a tear of love and devotion to our glistening eyes.

The approach of the diligence awoke us from our reverie and we turned to pursue our route. The vast horizon on the opposite side was one sheet of fire. The glorious orb of day had finished his course, and had just sunk behind the chain of mountains that separated us from the rest of the world, throwing out with magnificent beauty the majestic contours of those opaque masses, now black as night. We paused for a moment, as if in presence of something supernatural: our hearts beat almost audibly.

"What is the matter?" inquired the postillion, who was walking beside us, and who also stood still, his glance following ours, and then returning to our faces to discover why we halted, carrying with it as much surprise at us, as at the spectacle before us.

"Look!" exclaimed Victor.

"At what?" demanded the postillion.

"At the sun and mountains!"

"At the sun and mountains, as if I did not see them every day without looking! What comical folks travellers are to be sure, they all fall into ecstasies before what I should never think of looking at, except to see whether it will be fine or fair weather to-morrow. Why about a month ago, an odd kind of an Englishman gave me a franc to wait five minutes for him, while he stood like a post on this very spot, and when I, as I thought to please him, and to gain my franc better, offered to point out to him the solitary house in which a prefect of the Haute Loire and his family were all murdered, 'Hush! man,' said he angrily, 'do not talk of murder to me now!' Well every one to their taste!" and the postillion shrugged his shoulders in pity.

"You would rather see a bottle or two of wine or brandy, would you not, before you?" laughed a traveller.

"I should think I would, after mounting such a steep as that we have just come up."

How strange, methought, that beauties amid which we are born and daily behold, should so often lose their charms for us! and thus it is for us all to a certain extent, though one must be a "postillion" I imagine to have one's senses as obdurate as those of our "postillion."

We again resumed our seats, again our companions chatted; but we were too much lost in the immensity we had just contemplated to enter into conversation again, and we all gradually became silent.

We passed through another town, called Yssingeaux, more miserable in appearance than Monistrol; and as we rolled down one of its streets, the moonbeams offered to individual dwel- to perceive small houses, with mud floors and rags stuffed in broken windows, inhabited by men, women, children, pigs, and fowls, all pell mell together; and not once in our day's journey had we seen a rosy healthy face, or a sprightly country lass, like those in Normandy or in England—all looked sickly and indolent. Numerous lights apprised us that we were drawing nigh to Le Puy; but, as it was now quite dark, we could see nothing but those lights, climbing as they did, from the high and low town, offering a very singular aspect. After mutual thanks, expressed and received, we bade adieu to the "Rentier," and, according to his recommendation, we took up our lodgings here—"Hotel des [illegible]," situated on a handsome square, Place du Breuil, and having one side on another smaller square, where the market is held. So now, after whirling over three parts of "la Belle France," we may, I presume, plant our foot here in security for some time, and in our calm future to increase, if possible, our mutual affection, mingling with it love for those whose thoughts will daily seek us in spite of mountains or distance.

THE PAST.

BY ANA [illegible].

Tell me not of the rosy Present, smiling,
  And of the Future with her [illegible] charms;
But while you speak, I turn from their beguiling,
  To watch a pale form lying in my arms.

It is the shrouded Past, with her have perished
  My girlhood's dreams, and all my sunny hours;
She was so much a part of thine, so cherished,
  That I have strewed her bier with fairest flowers.

I do not breathe her hushed name to remind you
  Of our past love, which is as dead and cold;
Nor do I seek to know the ties which bind you,
  Stronger and happier than the ties of old;

I only ask you, now that she is sleeping,
  To spare to me at least her burial day;
Since she will never waken for my weeping,
  To yield her hushed secrets to the day.

The Present holds for you a thousand pleasures,
  And the vague Future golden gifts in store;
Leave me the dead Past, with her shadowy treasures,
  Leave me the Past—for I have nothing more!

[illegible], 1860.

AN UNEXPECTED AUDIENCE.

(From a Pastor's recollections.)

When first I settled as pastor in the parish, where I have now resided for so many years, it was my wont to go on foot to pay most of my parochial visits. Some of these visits were made at a considerable distance, but I did not enjoy them the less on that account; for I was then young and active, and preferred walking exercise to any other; and I remember how delightful those long walks used to appear of a fine spring morning, when I rose with the lark, and pursued my way through the green lanes and along the pleasant paths which lay across the fields; the early morning at that season has charms peculiar to itself, everything looks so fresh and bright, and seems to bear the very impress of gladness; the light gossamer, as it hangs from branch to branch, gemmed with dewdrops, which sparkle in the morning sun like diamonds; the wild violet, so elegant in its growth; and "the pale primrose" glinting forth on the green banks; while the air hangs on its wings the rich burden of odours—the first offerings of the season; and the birds sing their songs and hop about merrily, in their happy companionship, among the branches. In later years, when I have been borne on such occasions by my trusty horse, or conveyed, as now, in my little four-wheeled carriage, I have often cast a longing look towards the intricate paths and wide fields which I used to tread.

In those days I often bent my way through the tangled bushes and by the winding stream, to call on the inmates of the humble cottage which overhangs its banks, but which I now approach by a less circuitous route, and in a less laborious manner. Among my first parochial visits in that direction, I often call to mind those which I made to a family of the name of Mansfield. I soon felt a great interest for these poor people, which has continued unabated for nearly half a century, for such among them as have been spared; and I frequently call to mind the worth of those who have been removed from the present scene; they won upon my regard not only by their many excellent qualities, but from the respect with which they at once treated me, which I knew was due only to my office, for I was a young man when I came among them, nor was it owing to rank or fortune, for many in the neighbourhood possessed both in a much higher degree, and yet were not held in the same consideration. I felt that it was owing to my office, and the veneration which they had for it placed me in a very peculiar position with respect to them, and the circumstances which afterwards occurred drew still closer the sacred ties by which we were united. The family consisted of four—the father and mother, a son, and a little girl many years younger. By a sad accident poor Mansfield's leg had been broken, and he had fallen into an infirm state of health, and was utterly disabled for work; but his son laboured hard to support them all, and, by his skill as a carpenter and his steady industry, he was able not only to provide all that was necessary for the family, but to lay by a little for a store. His workshop was close by the house, and there he might be seen, at the first dawn of day, busy with his tools, and whistling or singing some lightsome air as he went cheerfully about his work. The neighbours used to remark that John had a right to a light heart, for there was not a better or a kinder son through the length and breadth of the parish; they were indeed a happy family, blessed with affection and content. Little Nanny—a merry little elf—was the plaything among them; but John, as he well might, was the special darling. I loved to linger for awhile at his workshop, and to have a little chat with him as he worked. His mother would often venture to the door and peep in, that she might indulge herself with one look at John, and then John would always hurry to place a chair for her, and invite her to sit with that natural politeness which, always pleasing, is so lovely from a child to a parent. I often admired the lively turn which he gave to our chat when she was by, that he might have the pleasure of seeing her amused. Poor Mansfield, too, helped on by his crutch, would make his way to his son; and it was interesting to see the intense delight which he took in his work, and to hear the many questions respecting it, to which John gave explanatory answers, which left an evident impression of his genius on the old man. "Sure," his mother would say, "the blessing of Heaven is on our John, for there is nothing he takes in hand that does not prosper. When he comes in of an evening from his work, he sits down by his poor sickly father, and pets him like a little child; and before we go to our rest at night, he often opens his Bible, and reads out a chapter for us; and we all feel the better and rest the better for hearing it from his kind voice." John was continually planning something to add to their means, and had himself built an addition of two rooms to their house, which he proposed to let. It was not long before he got a tenant for them, in a man who arrived in the neighbourhood for the purpose of setting up a day-school; he was a person of quiet and retired habits, seldom stirring out after the school broke up. When the vacation enabled him to shut up school for a short time, he took the opportunity of going to see his friends, who lived in a distant county.

saying that he would be back in a month, when holidays were over, at which time he promised to pay the rent due for the rooms. The time that he had fixed for his return passed over, and week after week went by, and still he did not come; at length John gave up all hopes of his return, and he determined to have the rooms put in order, and to look out for another tenant. He broke open the doors, which the lodger had locked up before he went; and to his surprise found a crucible, and all the implements for coining; some base money was lying on the table, which John carelessly put in his pocket. In a few days after this, it chanced that a quantity of wool was stolen from a neighbouring mill, and a warrant was issued for searching all the houses in the hamlet. On entering the rooms rented by the schoolmaster, the constable discovered the crucible and instruments for coining, an offence at that time severely punished. Suspicion immediately fell on John, and he was apprehended in the neighbouring wood, where he had gone to fell some timber which he had purchased; he immediately bethought himself of the base coin which he had so heedlessly consigned to his pocket, and, dreading the trouble into which its discovery might bring him, hastily put it into his mouth, as the only way in which he could conceal it; but the action was noticed, the money found; and this circumstance, along with the fact of all the implements necessary for coining having been discovered in his room, was sufficient evidence against him, and considered quite conclusive of his guilt. He was taken to the assize town, put in gaol till his trial came on, when the circumstantial evidence was so strong, that a verdict of guilty was brought in against him, without any hesitation; and, indeed, the confidence in his innocence which his previous character and conduct might have warranted, was sadly shaken in the minds of many of his friends. However, for my part, I never doubted the explanation of the matter, and therefore was not deprived of the greatest source of consolation which I could urge upon his afflicted parents. I had often gone to them while the trial was pending, and they, assured as they were of his innocence, could not bring themselves to think that it would not be clear to all the world; but the sad news did come—he was found guilty and condemned to die. On hearing this melancholy intelligence I hurried to the poor afflicted couple; my heart grew heavier with every step I took, and though I was anxious to reach them as soon as possible, I involuntarily slackened my pace as I got nearer; and had to pause when I reached the door, to endeavour to gain some degree of composure before I entered. Poor old Mansfield lay stretched on the bed, quite overcome by the shock and the grief. I moved noiselessly in, with that instinctive dread of breaking in upon the grief which I held so sacred—which every one has felt. As I advanced Mansfield glared on me with an air of wildness. Alas! he thought in his agony that every one who approached him was the bearer of still more bitter news.

"Is it all over with our John?" said he, turning ghastly pale; "is it all over with our boy?"

As well as I could speak I told them that he had still some days to live.

"And so," said he, with that bitter composure which inevitable calamity sometimes brings, "they will hang my good and brave boy like a dog—and there is an end of us. Ah! sir, sir, it is hard to believe it; to think that we are never again to hold the hand that worked so hard for us—the hand that it was natural for us to think would close our poor eyes. Oh! sir, how can we bring ourselves to believe it? how can we think that the step for which we so often listened will never cross the threshold again—how can we think that the laugh, and the merry songs that so often delighted our very hearts, will never be heard any more within these walls! This poor woman—the poor mother", added he, gently laying his hand on his wife's arm, "ought to see him once more, ought to take her last leave; but she is loathe to leave me in such an extremity, for my life is wearing fast, fast away; grief can bring down the strongest to the grave, and why not one weak and worn as I am?"

A violent burst of agony from the poor woman, was the only answer which she made; she looked imploringly in his face, and grasped his hand tightly in her own, as if she feared to lose him if she loosened her hold.

"Sir, sir," resumed Mansfield, "pardon us, and ask pardon for us, if we are flying in the face of Providence; but such a good child, such a comfort, such a pride! Ah! sir, it is hard to part with one like him."

"My own darling, my own darling," interrupted the poor woman, "if we could see him (as if apostrophising her child) in his bed dying of some sickness sent by Providence, we could make up our minds to the parting; but oh! sir," added she, turning towards me, "to have his natural days cut short—to have his eyes close upon a world so pleasant to him! Oh! sir, it is hard to think it: my poor darling that I nursed upon my knees, that used to follow me about as soon as he could use his little feet, in and out, from place to place, wherever I went. My poor darling that worked early and late for our sakes ever since he grew up. Ah! sir, our hearts be n't stone: they must break!"

I tried to speak a few words of comfort, and to raise their thoughts to a world where friends may hope to meet, never to be parted.

"Ah! sir, it is much to think all that," said Mansfield; "and our boy may be with us in a happier place than this poor world; and yet we would give our heart's blood to have him here but for one hour—one little hour."

"My dear people," said I, taking a hand of each, and letting my tears fall unrestrainedly on them, "my dear people, think how good

John was; how he strove to please God; how dutiful and tender he was!" I was obliged to stop, for the recollection of all the kindness which I had so often seen him bestow on them affected me deeply.

"Do you think, sir—do you think there is no chance—no chance for his life," interrupted the poor mother, who still clung to hope in spite of all; "a king might well pardon such as he is. Oh! if he did but know how good he is—how true! Oh! if he did but know that a lie had never passed his lips, he would not but believe him on his word."

To work at these false hopes, which were only laying up more bitter disappointment, was indeed a painful task. To reason with those in an agony of grief is unavailing; it was only by the gentlest, heartfelt sympathy, and by withdrawing their minds from secondary causes, that I could in any degree soothe them. These poor people were strong in faith, and the hope was not lost on them which I brought forward to prevent the sinking of the terrible agony inflicted by the idea that but for [illegible] the bereavement would not have been. I left them sorrowfully indeed, but trusting they were not sorrowing as those without hope. What an anxious journey was that which I was planning [illegible]. I had left the unhappy people, as I went on my way with all the haste I could command—the agitation into which I had been thrown—the dread that my speed might be retarded by accident or obstacle, that a physical impossibility of seeing him who would alone aid me, might lose the object of my journey! He might be ill, he might be absent. All these misgivings that my mind had added to my anticipation. These anxious hours appeared as if peopled by a harassing dream; and even at this distance of time, when the excitement under which I then was, has so long passed away, the recollection of that wild tumult of perturbation seems as a troubled vision. Sometimes, disappointed in procuring a chaise, I mounted a horse, and galloped on to the next stage. When driving on, as I am now sure at the utmost speed, it appeared to me that the horses lagged lazily, and that the vehicle moved heavily and slowly. Several times I was on the point of alighting, thinking I could have got on more quickly on foot, and fancying that I was equal to run at my utmost speed the whole way. At eleven o'clock the next night, just off my journey, splashed, and spent with fatigue and anxiety, I stood at the door of England's Prime Minister. When the servant had shown me into a waiting-room near the entrance hall, I requested to see his master, and though he replied that his master was engaged with company, and that he could not be seen till ten o'clock the next morning, when he would be ready to give audience to all who called on business, I said I could not possibly go without an interview, and taking my card from my pocket, wrote underneath my name, "on a matter of life and death," and directed the servant to put it into his master's hand. He returned in a few minutes, and, showing me into a library, said that his master would wait on me immediately. During the time which elapsed before he appeared, I might have amused myself in examining some of the various specimens of art with which the room was adorned, and in which he was well known to take special delight; but my heart was too full, and my mind too much engaged to admit of any interest, but that which already occupied it. The door opened, and the Premier entered. I impatiently rushed forward: "I have taken the liberty of breaking in upon you, sir," said I, "at a most unseasonable hour; but the importance of the business which brings me will best plead my excuse."

"I am at your command, sir," replied the Minister, with much suavity; "I am ready to hear whatever you may have to communicate."

"It is in the matter of John Mansfield, who is now confined in gaol, under sentence of death, having been found guilty at the last assizes of coining."

"A case of coining, my dear sir," said he, impatiently interrupting me, "is one in which we never interfere; nor do I recollect at this moment a single precedent of the Royal Prerogative having been extended to any such. I am sorry, sir, but it is absolutely out of my power to serve you; and it would only be to the waste of your time, and the disappointment of your hopes, were I to hold out the least encouragement."

"But my dear sir, I do not come to solicit mercy—I come to ask justice; and if you will permit me to detail a few circumstances—which I will as briefly as possible—you will at once see that immediate steps must be taken. The execution is ordered for Saturday, and this is Wednesday."

The Premier motioned to a seat, in which I placed myself, and he took another, while I entered circumstantially on the subject in which he soon appeared to take an interest. "After I had returned yesterday evening from visiting the poor people," continued I, minutely narrating all that had occurred, "I found a messenger at my house waiting for me. He informed me that a traveller had been taken suddenly ill at a neighbouring cottage, and was dying, and that he had expressed great anxiety to see me without delay. I lost no time in going to the sick man, whom I found, as had been stated, in a dying condition.

"'Sir,' said he, 'I dare say you do not know me, but I have often seen and listened to you of a Sunday. I ought I know to have profited more by what I heard from you, and not have acted the cowardly part which I have done. All I can do now is to tell the truth, the whole truth. That money, sir, by the distribution of which, who might, if they kept [illegible] of it, be respectable by their industry; but, happening to fall in with [illegible] I became deeply interested, and listened with breathless attention). "I joined myself with them, and always having been of an ingenious turn, I was able to be of much use in the business; I fixed on Mansfield's lodgings, from their secluded situation, where I thought the more securely and uninterruptedly carry on the work. I brought the crucible and things necessary with me. I had hours to myself, when I worked hard, and struck off much money, which we passed here and there, and up and down through the country, no one suspecting us all the time. When my school broke up for holidays, I went home to see my own people, meaning to be back in a month. I left the crucible and some of the coins by it, carefully locked up in my bedroom, and took the key with me. A long fit of illness prevented my returning when I had intended; but, getting uneasy about the crucible and what I had left in the room, I set out before I had gathered sufficient strength for the journey. I was taken ill here, where I have been lying some days, as you see me, sir, at the very last ebb. I have heard all that has happened—I hope it is not too late—I hope the young man, the innocent young man, is still in life, and that with my dying breath I may save him." All this relates what poor John Mansfield has counted all through; and here, my dear sir, is the dying man's deposition; there is now but barely time to save the young man."

I need scarcely say that, all things being found to corroborate my statement, a reprieve was of course granted, and I hastened from London to poor John Mansfield in his prison. I was truly astonished to see the self-possession and the fortitude of the excellent young man. His voice faltered, indeed, when he spoke of his parents, and a few natural tears fell; but he was not long in regaining his composure, and he spoke of the closing scene, which was near, as he believed, so calmly, and of the happy and bright anticipations which lay beyond it.

"John," said I, grasping his hand fervently, "you are not to leave us; a good Providence has watched over you—your innocence is no longer doubted—a reprieve is on its way, a release will follow, and before many hours you will be restored to your home." The being who had stood before me, undismayed, with the grave, as I may say, yawning before him, now that the tension was removed, and that he was restored almost miraculously to life, was fearfully overcome—every limb trembled, a ghastly paleness overspread his face, large drops of perspiration burst out upon his brow, and he gasped for breath; I found, though I had made some little delay in the communication, that it had, after all, been too sudden; and I, too, felt painfully agitated. But his colour came again, and he burst into tears, and, fervently clasping his hands, he exclaimed, "Thank God—thank God!" and fell upon his knees, and in silent prayer poured out the feelings of his heart; then he continued to talk of his home, and to ask question after question about his parents, which he had not dared to trust himself to do before. A few hours passed thus; it was, in truth, a scene of surpassing interest to me, the more particularly as I had been the happy instrument of averting his fate.

When the hour came that, according to the prison rules, all strangers were to quit the gaol, John lost all self-command, he became like one nearly frantic, and, clinging wildly to me, declaring that I must not leave him, and exclaiming that if I went his heart he would be lost; it seemed that if I were to stir from his side, the happy vision would be dispelled beyond all hope of its being ever realised; it was with the greatest difficulty that I soothed him into a more composed frame of mind; but I did succeed in calming him before I took my leave of him for the night. The order for his liberation came in the middle of the next day; it would be a vain attempt to describe his rapture—he kissed my hands over and over again, he laughed, he laughed, he cried by turns. I really feared that his brain was turned; but he gradually became more composed. We travelled on towards the hamlet where his heart lay; the moon had just risen as we reached the stream, and was shining in all its calm lustre on the pure waters, as they glided along by the cottage. Poor John's transports were renewed at each familiar object, that he had never expected to see again, and his eyes. I went in alone to break the news to his parents; the poor mother looked in my face to read there the disastrous news of John's execution; the old man wrung my hand without speaking.

"My dear good people," I began, breathless with agitation; feelings utterly failed me, and I sank down, exhausted and overcome, into the nearest seat. When I could again speak I went on; "My dear good people, you have been patient and submissive to the will of God; he has looked with pity on your affliction"—I again felt choking, and was obliged to pause—"with great pity," I resumed, "and in his mercy he has seen fit to restore that which was lost; and, my dear good people, I have brought John back to you."

John was soon in the midst of them. The poor old man threw himself upon his breast, and gave way to a passionate burst of tears; the mother had fallen on her knees in humble thankfulness, and grasping John's hand, kissed it in wild ecstasy, while tears of joy fell fast. Little Nannie's joy was exhibited after a merrier fashion, for she danced round John with childish glee. As for me, I had taken my seat at the farthest end of the cottage, where I cried very heartily in all the joy of my heart. Having given them my parting benediction I left them to give expression to those feelings without the restraint which even my presence might have imposed.

GENEALOGY OF JEWELS.

There is nothing new under the sun. Imagine not therefore, dear ladies, that your most cherished ornaments have the least novelty about them—even if you can produce the newest fashioned necklace, bracelet, clasp, chain, or locket. From the beginning of the world women have always fixed their affections on these trifles; and you, also, in valuing them so highly, only follow the track made by thousands of the daughters of Eve who have gone before you. For instance, in the patriarchal tent, gold and gems were well known. Abraham's servant presented Rebecca with earrings and bracelets; Judith prepared for her fatal visit to Holofernes by taking off her sackcloth and adorning herself with jewels. The prophet, also, reproving the daughters of Israel with their vanity and love of finery, says: "In that day the Lord shall take away the bravery of their tinkling ornaments, their networks, their crescent-shaped jewels, their chains, their bracelets, their spangled ornaments, and the pearls that overhang their brows."

All the surrounding nations of Israel supplied the prophet Isaiah with examples of this pageantry. The Egyptian tombs disclose to light jewels as remarkable for cunning workmanship as for intrinsic value; the golden scarabæi, necklaces, rings, and bracelets, engraved, chiselled, or enamelled in a thousand different ways. Cleopatra's famous pearl, and its fate, is remembered by every one. The women of Nineveh, Media, and Persia, lavished gold and pearls upon their garments. The Grecian women, according to Homer, were well acquainted with cray golden girdles, rich clasps, crescent-shaped earrings, and bracelets, adorned with precious stones. All these figure in the toilet of Penelope. Amongst the Grecian jewels the ring of Polycrates is the most celebrated. Amasis, king of Egypt, having heard Polycrates described as the most fortunate of men, sent him this caution: "Your prosperities fill me with alarm; for the jealous gods suffer not that any mortal should enjoy unchanging felicity. Endeavour to bring upon yourself some loss, or misfortune, to counterbalance the dangerous favours of the gods!"

The tyrant of Samos, struck by this advice, threw into the sea a ring on which he set great value. Some historians declare it to have been an emerald, adorned, by a skilful engraver, with a lyre surrounded with bees. Pliny asserts that it was one entire sardonyx. The ring in question, having been swallowed by a fish, made its appearance three days after on the king's dinner table!

The ladies of Athens sometimes wore a golden grasshopper in their hair; and stones, cunningly carved, formed an important part of their costume. They served to clasp the tunic upon the shoulder, the girdle on the bosom, to confine the folds of the veil, and to fasten the sandal.

The Romans wore jewels even during the republic. The ring among them was a sign of nobility. It is well known that, after the battle of Cannae, three bushels were filled with the rings of the knights. As for the Roman ladies, their love for jewels amounted to infatuation. The riches of the world, the spoils of vanquished nations, flowed through their hands in every variety of decoration. Diadems sparkled in their black hair; their robes were brilliant with the starry gleam of jewels; their purple mantles were adorned with golden palm-leaves, and sometimes also with precious stones; rings glittered on their fingers, bracelets of gold and pearls encircled their arms, and they wore chains and necklaces with pendants. These latter were sometimes formed of coins or medallions.

Lollia Paulina, the repudiated wife of Caligula, is said by Pliny to have appeared at a simple family repast, adorned with pearls and emeralds worth forty millions of sesterces. Her head, breast, arms, and fingers were loaded with the spoils of the provinces. Precious stones were sometimes chiselled into the form of a cup and used at table.

The Roman matrons borrowed from the women of Gaul their blond tresses; from the eastern women their taste of gold tissues and jewels. And the men themselves, when the empire was declining, gave themselves up to these frivolities. Heliogabalus appeared in public with an embroidered tiara, and a flowing robe adorned with jewels. Incredible sums were given for engraved stones, mounted as seals or rings; and the iron circlets of the Roman knights were replaced by rings set with the most costly gems. There were rings for summer and rings for winter. The women had balls made of amber to rub between their hands, as it was imagined that the friction had an invigorating effect. A few of the patrician families remained faithful, nevertheless, to the ancient customs, and wore no other than ornaments of iron.

The barbarians had a strong appreciation for this splendour which made such eloquent appeal to the eyes. The moveable huts, and tents of skins, belonging to the soldiers of Alaric and Attila, were filled with treasures. The Goths had obtained possession of no less than a hundred basins filled with gold, pearls, and diamonds—a plate of gold weighing five hundred pounds, and a table formed of one single emerald, surrounded with three rows of pearls, and supported by massive golden feet inlaid with jewels.

Charlemagne succeeded in recovering some of

those inexhaustible treasures; he, having vanquished the Saxons and Huns, to discovered the secret caves where these grand-children of the barbarians (former conquerors of the world) had collected the spoils of their forefathers.

Eginhard relates that the soldiers of Charlemagne entered by torchlight into the citadel of Pannonia, and there found heaps of gold and silver. Armour enriched with rubies, sceptres, and ancient crowns, the heritage of a hundred nations, collected in former times. The chief part of this wealth was bestowed upon the churches and abbeys of France, since plundered at the time of the revolution. The jewels from the tombs of martyrs, the wealthy spoils of the convents, passing through many hands, are at length melted and scattered in commerce.

Our Gallic neighbours also adorned themselves with jewellery. Necklaces and bracelets were worn by the men; they ornamented their helmets with branches of coral. The women fastened their hair with curiously-fashioned pins; and in their ancient burying-places specimens of these rough ornaments were found. The early queens of Gaul crowned their long flowing hair with a circlet of fine gold, or a crown composed of gems and pearls. But if the material of these ornaments was precious, the workmanship was not only simple, but clumsy—as may be judged by the seal and the sword lately found at Tournay in the tomb of Childeric.

In vain did the kings make sumptuary laws against the luxuries of finery, and the rage for jewels. Noblemen and peasants alike vied in transgressing them. The women wore golden chains, jewelled crosses, rings, and purses. The men adorned even their arms with precious stones; they wore round the neck heavy chains of gold, from which sometimes a precious reliquary depended. The Byzantine jewels were thick, straight, clear, adorned with enamel and foreign stones, curiously engraved.

The Crusades served to increase this love of finery, by disclosing to the Europeans the riches of the Orient. At that time (so considerably is ours) linen was extremely scarce, though jewels abounded; and if a grand lady adorned her corsets with rubies and sapphires, the peasant's wife also had her ornament of gold, her rings and amulets. Louis (king and saint) presented Queen Margaret with a ring, bearing an engraved cross surrounded with lilies and daisies (Marguerites), with this inscription: "Hors cet anel pourrions trouver amour?"

The inventory of the rings and jewels of Charles V. proves that this king possessed forty-five rubies, nine sapphires, twenty emeralds, and ten turquoises, all mounted in rings; specimens of workmanship in cameos, pendants of pearls and sapphires, talismans or stones engraved with Hebrew characters, endowed by the credulity of the age with supernatural virtues; also twenty golden crowns garnished with diamonds and rubies, five cups of gold adorned with pearls and fine brooches, and fourteen girdles with jewelled clasps belonging to the queen; without counting candle-boxes, cups, and larger vessels, whose jewels glittered upon the massive silver and gold.

Diamonds were well known during this age. History relates of Peter the Cruel that he gave all the diamonds he had with him to the pilot who conducted him to Tunis, when he was hard pressed by the troops of Henry of Transtamare. But at this time no extraordinary value was set upon diamonds, because the art of cutting them was not known. A young nobleman of Bruges, named Louis Berghem, first remarked that two diamonds rubbed together would polish each other; and thus he early learned the art of making "diamond cut diamond." The first cut diamond, called the "Sancy," was worn by Charles the Bold, who lost it at the battle of Nancy. It was found on the field, and sold for almost nothing to some poor shepherds; then to a priest for three florins. It afterwards passed into the hands of Harley, of Sancy, and now belongs to the French crown.

It was not until the reign of Charles VII. that women began to wear the brocade formerly appropriated by the men. The Dukes of Burgundy, who were great lovers of pomp and prodigality, had amassed vast treasures of jewels and golden vessels. The collar of the Order of the Golden Fleece sparkled with gems; and it is well known how strange was the contrast between the magnificence of Charles the Bold, the splendour of his raiment, and the jewels of his ducal crown, in comparison with the mean doublet, and the little images of lead, with jewels of Louis XI.

The discovery of America brought treasures into Europe, by which, however, it has scarcely been enriched. In one night a captain won in one and lost the famous gold chain suspended in the Temple of the Sun, at Cuzco; and his companion paid 2,000 golden pesos for a cake of Indian wheat. Fernand Cortez lost in a shipwreck, on the coast of Algiers, five emeralds of inestimable value, cut by the Indians into the shapes of a rose, a horn, a fish, a bell, and a fish. Perhaps one day they may be found beneath the sands of that shore!

The foreign mines of wealth caused the jewellers to increase still more. At the court of Francis I. the ladies wore girdles of wrought gold, with chatelaines set with diamonds. Numbers of jewels were chiselled for them by Benvenuto Cellini.

The queens of the house of Valois are generally represented as glittering with pearls and precious stones. Marie Stuart, in her portraits, is often adorned only with the pearls of her beloved Scotland; but Elizabeth seems to bend beneath the weight of her jewels; and even in her old age she had a passion for this kind of decoration.

Henry III. had a womanish admiration for trinkets, and wore necklaces of pearls beneath his open doublet. Queen Anne of Austria added to the treasures of the crown, a string of splendid oriental pearls, which her son, Louis XIV., wore over his dress at great festivals. The ladies of the court used their jewels for embroidering their robes. The men wore jewelled shoe-buckles and garters; every button on their coat was a precious stone; and often even their hats were adorned with gems. Louis XIV. was said to be the most simply dressed person at court, excepting at a grand festival or a marriage ceremony, when he would be covered in jewels worth nine millions of money. At the reception of the Persian ambassador in February, 1715, this king wore a coat of black and gold, laden with twelve million brilliants, and so heavy that he was obliged to disembarrass himself of it, before dinner. A nobleman of Genoa, having offered to Louis XIV. a pearl of singular shape, bearing some resemblance to the bust of a man, that king had it set in such a manner as to represent a Roman warrior. Apropos of the reign of Louis XIV., we must not forget the emerald ring, given by the Duchess of Orleans on her death-bed, to Bossuet, who, in his funeral oration dedicated to this princess, makes a delicate and touching allusion to the gift.

The system of Law, which dispersed so many fortunes, gave fresh scope to luxury. The peers had melted of silver articles of furniture, and gems of fabulous value. St. Simon—who advised the Regent to obtain for the crown the famous diamond bearing his name—gives us the following description of a pearl belonging to the kings of Spain, seen by him during his embassy. "This pearl, called 'la Peregrina,' is of the finest water, shaped and marked precisely like those small, musk-flavoured pears, called 'sept-en-gueule,' which arrive at maturity after the strawberry season. Their name is intended to indicate the smallness of their size, since no human mouth could contain more than four at once. The pearl is as large and long as the small pear of this kind, and larger by comparison than any other pearl. It is therefore unique, and is indeed declared to be the companion of the identical pearl dissolved in vinegar and drunk by Cleopatra, in an extravagance of folly and love."

Now we cannot vouch for the truth of this genealogy; nevertheless, all famous diamonds have their history. The "Sancy" was found on a battle-field; the "Regent" belonged to the Pitt family before it became the most magnificent jewel of France; the diamond now adorning the sceptre of the Czars was formerly the single eye of an Indian god. But the diamonds of the fatal necklace of Marie Antoinette are all dispersed, and Napoleon I., on his marriage with Josephine, could only boast a diamond ring of very ordinary value.

In Germany each precious stone is invested with a symbolical meaning; and every month of the year is said to be under the influence of one of these stones. We furnish our readers with a list:—

January	Garnet	Fidelity in friendship.
February	Amethyst	Control of the passions.
March	Bloodstone	Courage and discretion.
April	Sapphire	Repentance, and the Diamond, Innocence.
May	Emerald	Happiness.
June	Agate	Long life and health.
July	Ruby	Oblivion of grief.
August	Sardonyx	Conjugal felicity.
September	Chrysolite	Preservation from folly.
October	Aqua marine	Misfortune, and the Opal, Hope.
November	Topaz	Friendship.
December	Turquoise	Success.

Thirty years ago, rings were made with precious stones, of which the initials formed a name or a word. For example, the name of Sophia would be expressed by the following jewels: a Sapphire, Opal, Pearl, Hyacinth, Jasper, and an Amethyst. This was at once an ornament and a souvenir; for we all like to have something dedicated to the memory of those we love.

The unhappy princess of [illegible] wore a necklace of malachites, engraved with the names of her eight children; and when she fell a victim to her maternal love, this ornament alone enabled her remains to be recognised.

We will not enumerate the ornaments of our day. This is a question of fashion; the fashions are subject to change, now, as in olden time.

Recent researches have made mention of a ruby ring, which forms a microscopic stereoscope, and in its depths can be distinctly seen the portraits of two of our most distinguished princes—a strange union of modern discoveries with gems dating their origin from the foundation of the world! And where are they, now, all those treasures of old?—the spoils of pagan temples, of Christian churches, of the palaces of Greece and Rome? A part has been destroyed by fire, buried in earthquakes, or overwhelmed in the depths of the sea; the rest perhaps, melted a hundred times in the crucible, pass at last into our hands under the form of money, plates, cups, and jewels of every description.

So, through manifold transformations, the metals that are now become precious thus transmit to our keeping the gold and gems with which they were once adorned, when the pulse of life throbbed in them as now in our own, till we also—ceasing to long for the glittering pearl, the lustrous emerald, or the flashes of the keen-glancing diamond—shall in our turn relax our grasp, and consign our treasures to succeeding generations.

LEAVES FOR THE LITTLE ONES.

THE TALKING DOLLS.

(Adapted from the German).

You think that dolls cannot speak, do you? Listen, then, to the story which I have to tell.

Three little girls lay sleeping in their small white cots, with the white curtains shading their little curly heads. Outside shone the moon, very brightly; and as she rose higher and higher, her beams fell aslant through the window-blinds on the three white counterpanes, and gliding up to the snowy pillows, roused the children from their slumbers. The curly heads turned from side to side, the rosy lips murmured some indistinct words; then the three pairs of bright eyes, black, blue, and hazel, opened widely and gazed around them.

Very still was the great house, for it was past midnight, and all the inhabitants had retired to rest. But through the stillness came a tinkling voice, very sweet and very small, like the trilling music of the tiniest of musical boxes.

"Oh dear!" it tinkled, "I am so miserable! My little mistress, Georgie, knocked a hole in my head, which hurts me dreadfully; yesterday my nose fell to pieces; my whole body is full of blue spots; I have no sound place about me! Who would have thought, when I lay dressed so beautiful as a doll in the Great Exhibition, that I should come to so miserable an end! Little Mary lets me fall every minute of the day; and to-night, when I am so ill and wretched, she has not even put me to bed, and I must sleep on the hard floor in this dusty corner!"

The tinkling little voice ceased, and another began.

"Ah! Miss Polly, you need not grumble so, you are better off than I am. You have some of the prettiest clothes in the world; and when little Mary takes you out in the morning, and puts you on your beautiful hat with feathers and your lace veil, no one will see the hole in your head or your broken nose. My mistress, Emma, has lost or soiled all my clothes; and I only lie in bed now, and not, as usual on the ground, because this afternoon, when she washed me, she took off my last garment and mislaid it, no one knows where. What will become of me to-morrow, when all the little girls will dress their dolls and go out to enjoy themselves, because it is a holiday. I think I shall be obliged to be wrapped in my sheet, and be carried about like a sick ghost! If I had but known this two months ago, when I belonged to a royal child, and lived in splendour and luxury day and night!"

As the small voice finished thus, there came from another doll's bed a low sound of laughter; and out popped the head of a baby doll, with a clean-washed china face. It had on a snow-white cap, trimmed with pink ribbons, and its brown glass eyes glimmered in the moonlight like glow-worms.

"Well, you little dwarf, why do you laugh so?" chirped one of the other dolls. "One would think you were laughing at us."

"Yes," squeaked the baby-doll—it had a spring in its body, and could only squeak—"I do laugh at you, and I cannot help it. You are, both of you, continually boasting; the one that she has belonged to a princess, and the other that she was at the Great Exhibition. Yet look at you, what sad figures you are! maimed and scarred, and almost blind, not a feature perfect; one would think you had been in the wars. I am but an ignorant baby-doll, have never lived anywhere but in this house, and never belonged to any one but my own dear little mistress, Lily. You thought I hadn't an air of distinction, and have seen nothing of the world beyond our dusty square. I am nursed and tended like a princess. My mistress washes and dresses me every day, as well as she can; she does not take me out in wind and weather, but remains quietly at home with me when the day is not fine; and carries me so gently up and down, that I shall remain young and beautiful for ever. You with your worldly experience will soon be destroyed, or given away wounded and ragged to some beggar-girl, who will leave you to die on a dunghill. Ha! ha! ha! I shall always have the best of it, I that am only an ignorant baby-doll. Ha! ha! ha!"

Thus spoke and laughed the baby-doll, and it was not very kind of her to triumph over her unfortunate companions, though they had been vain enough in boasting themselves above her. But then it is well known that dolls have no consciences, and do not distinguish right from wrong, like little boys and girls. The two larger dolls were quite discomfited by the satire of their small companion, and did not say another word.

Meanwhile the three children had been listening eagerly from their beds, and had heard everything that had been said. The two elder girls were so much ashamed at what they had heard, that they got up by the light of the moon to make their neglected dolls more comfortable. Mary took up her poor wounded Polly, put her on a little frilled night-gown and cap, and covered her carefully up in bed. Emma sought about until she found a small chemise. She put it on her doll for the present, intending to awake at five o'clock in the morning and make her a new dress and bonnet in time to go out with her little mistress and enjoy herself like other dolls.

The two girls henceforward took the best care of their dolls; but nevertheless, unlucky Miss Polly was compelled to go about her whole life long with a hole in her head and a broken nose, although she had been at the Great Exhibition.

THE WORK-TABLE.

COUNTERPANE, IN CROCHET.

TO BE WORKED IN SQUARES.

MATERIALS.—Messrs. Walter Evans and Co.'s Knitting Cotton, No. 6 or 8, with a suitable Hook.

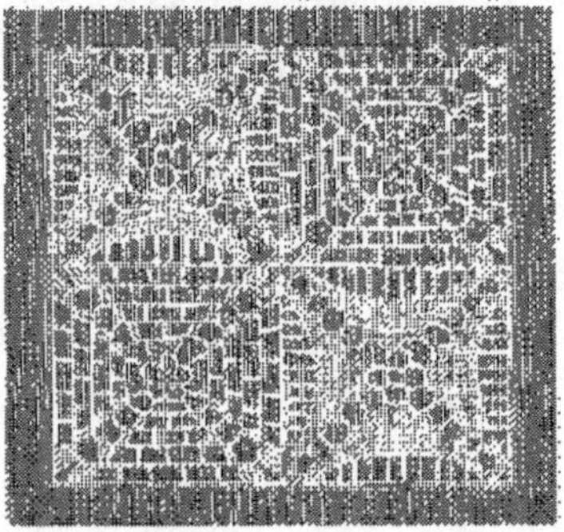

This counterpane is to be worked in squares, alternately close and open, arranged as in a chess-board, the open of one row joined to the close of another, and vice versâ. They may be sewed together, but I prefer connecting them with a crochet-hook, one line piece by piece, and the next line to it when completed.

THE CLOSE SQUARE.—6 ch close into a round.

1st round.—× 5 ch, 1 s c under the chain of 6 four times, slip on two of the first set of 5 ch.

2nd.—× 3 s c under chain of 5, 5 ch × four times.

3rd.—4 s c, 3 on 3, and 5 under the chain of 5 beyond, × 5 ch, 7 s c on 5 s c and two chain at each end; × three times; end with 2 s c, to make the first five seven.

[N.B. All the s c stitches are taken either under the chain or under the two sides of the s c stitch; and in the following rounds, as in this, the cross stitches can only be worked at one end of the first side in beginning the round, which is finished by doing them at the other end of that side.]

4th.—11 s c worked as the 7, with 5 ch after them, four times.

5th.—15 s c.

6th.—19 s c, with 5 chain after them, four times.

7th.—In this round a s c stitch is worked, as before, in every one of the former round, and 7 s c under every chain of 5.

8th (and last round).—S c on every s c at the corners, working two in one stitch; and along the sides, × 1 ch, miss 1, 1 d c; × as often as may be required.

THE OPEN SQUARE.—4 ch, close into a round, 5 ch, × 1 d c, 2 ch, × four times.

2nd round.—1 d c, 2 ch, 1 d c, 2 ch, all under the chain of 2; the same under the chain of 2 three times over.

3rd.—× under the next chain of 2, 2 d c, 3 ch, 2 d c (which forms the first corner), 3 ch, 1 d c under the next chain of 2, 3 ch, × repeat all round.

4th.—× 2 d c, 3 ch, 2 d c, all under the 3 ch, between the two pairs of d c; 3 ch, 1 d c under chain, 3 ch, 1 d c under chain, 3 ch, × four times.

5th.—× 2 d c, 3 ch, 2 d c, all under 3 ch at point, 3 ch, 1 d c under chain, 3 ch, 1 d c under chain, 3 ch, 1 d c, under chain, 3 ch, × four times.

6th.—× 2 d c, 3 ch, 2 d c, all under 3 ch at point; between point and point work as before, but with one repetition more.

This design is extremely pretty done in double Berlin wool, of two colours, for a couvrepiede, or baby's blanket.

AIGUILLETTE.

SPOTTED CROCHET,

ADAPTED PARTICULARLY FOR ANTIMACASSARS.

MATERIALS: To be worked, always, in hard-twisted Cotton. Nos. 4, 6, 10, or 12, of Messrs. Walter Evans and Co.'s Boar's Head Crochet Cotton will be found adapted to any kind of Antimacassar, from the large one intended to be thrown over a couch, to the tiny or table-d'oyley sorts.

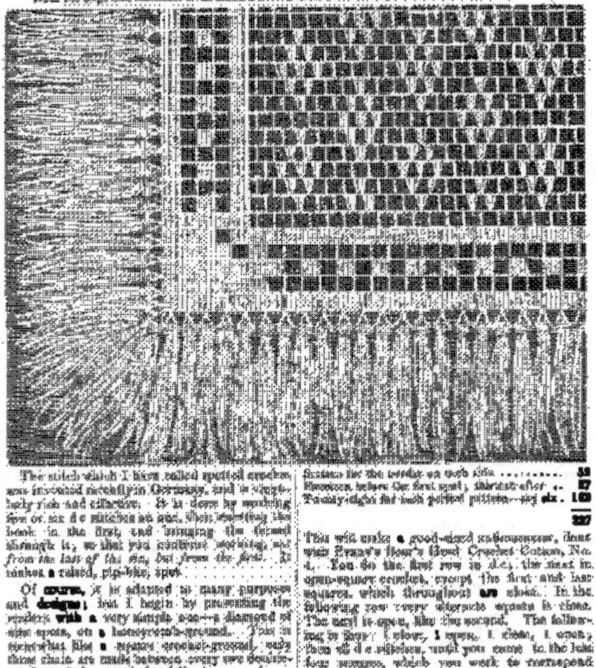

The stitch which I have called spotted crochet was invented recently in Germany, and is singularly rich and effective. It is done by working five or six d c stitches as usual, then inserting the hook in the first, and bringing the thread through it, so that you continue working, not *from the last of the six, but from the first.* It makes a raised, pip-like, spot.

Of **course,** it is adapted to many purposes and **designs**; but I begin by presenting the readers **with a** very simple one—a diamond of nine spots, on **a** honeycomb-ground. This is somewhat like **a** square crochet-ground, only three chain are made between every two double-crochet stitches, and the following row always has the d c stitches on the centre of the three chain; not on the d c stitch. At the beginning and end of this ground, in alternate rows, you do one chain, instead of three, to throw the d c stitch into its right place.

As a stitch in spotted crochet takes up no more space than any other d c stitch, it does not interfere with the groundwork at all. The six d c forming the spot are to be reckoned only as one.

The design now given requires the foundation to have the following number of stitches.

Sixteen for the border on each side	32
Nineteen before the first spot; thirty-eight after ..	57
Twenty-eight for each spotted pattern—say **six** .	168
	257

This will make **a** good-sized antimacassar, done with Evans's Boar's Head Crochet Cotton, No. 4. You do the first row in d c; the next in open-square crochet, except the first and last squares, which throughout **are** close. In the following row every alternate square is close. The next is open, like the second. The following is four: 1 close, **1** open, 1 close, 1 open; then all d c stitches, until you come to the last four squares, which you work to correspond with the first. The border afterwards is of five squares; the first and last always close; the middle one close in every alternate row; the rest open.

One row of **honeycomb must be done before the spots are commenced. The engraving will show where they come.**

A plain row must be worked before the border at top.

FRINGE.—1 d c, 3 ch, 1 d c in same, miss six equal spaces, except at the corners, where miss none. Knot a rich fringe into the loops.

AIGUILLETTE.

TRIMMING FOR A PETTICOAT, IN EMBROIDERY.

MATERIALS: Stout Long-cloth, with Messrs. Walter Evans and Co.'s Perfectionnée Embroidery Cotton, No. 20, and Boar's Head Crochet Cotton, No. 40.

This is a very handsome and effective embroidery pattern, and is easily and quickly worked. It is in a succession of wheels, united above and below by a single scallop, and the embroidery is done entirely in button-hole-stitch, except the double rows of barred button-hole, which form the lace-like borders to the inner side of the scallops.

The centre of each wheel is a double circle of button-hole-stitch; one worked towards the inside, and the other towards the outside. From the latter spring eight leaves, or spokes, button-holed round the edge, and with a small bar down the middle of each, likewise worked in button-hole-stitch. The points of the leaves are united by double scallops; the two forming the actual edge being considerably deeper than the others. As in the centre of the wheel, the inner row of this double scallop is worked with the edge to the inside, and the muslin cut away from between every pair of leaves; then the double line of Brussels edging is done, each over a thread, which gives the design a particularly rich and lace-like look. AIGUILLETTE.

CUPID A "MEDIUM."

BY SHIRLEY GERARD.

I had been knocking about the world, here and there and everywhere, for—no matter how many years; and having reached Paris at last I had a very bad attack of home-sickness. The result of this malady was that I found myself in the smoke and fog of London in December—the month, of all months, when London is most dreary.

I never felt more miserable. That New Zealander, to whom the ruins of St. Paul's are to sit for their likeness, will not feel more completely out of his element while taking his sketch than I felt out of mine as I walked along the deserted streets. Every face was unknown. Even the language did not appear so familiar as I reasonably expected it would have been. I suppose there was something outlandish in my appearance, for at one time I was followed for the length of a street by a set of grinning and ragged boys, who leered into my face, and jabbered at me, and danced round me like so many imps. They also pointed me out to each other with, "I say Bill; look at this 'ere chap! Ain't he a rummin' Wotsername? Don't want no drill neither, not he!" These speeches were so much High Dutch to me; I was not aware of the Volunteer force which had arisen upon my countrymen.

Being an Englishman, I should have found comfort in the reflection that another week would bring us to Christmas. But what was Christmas to me? I am a sociable animal, and the prospect of solitary roast beef and plum-pudding was not inviting. It is true, I had a "place" in Derbyshire; but, bad as London was, that would be unbearable. A great empty house, which no amount of fires could warm into comfort. I saw myself at the head of an immense dinner-table, a wilderness of mahogany stretching out before me, and the sound of my own knife and fork painfully audible. I recalled former festivals in that house before I had been "head of the family," when warmth and light, and bright faces and glad hearts were to be found beneath the dear old roof.

But death had made many changes among us. I found myself at two-and-twenty master of Wilmote Hall; but, unable to build up new pleasures amid the ruins of the old, I left England, and wandered over half the globe. I had kept up a correspondence with some of my College friends—with Charlie Neville especially—for a time; but my rapid changes of residence made the reception of letters a mere chance; so that when I arrived in England in December, 18—, I did not know how fate had dealt with my old companions. Poor Charlie! What a dear light-hearted old fellow he was! How well I remembered the day I had seen him last! We had come up from the Priory, his father's place, by an early train. I was to start for France on my way to the East that same night; Charlie was returning to Oxford, and the scene of our farewell was not the most sentimental in the world. It took place on the roof of an omnibus in the Regent's Circus. Just a grasp of the hand, and a "Well, good bye, old fellow! don't get eaten up alive anywhere," as he swung himself down into the crowd. I watched his tall figure and broad shoulders, as he strode off, as long as they were visible; and then I began to whistle, for, somehow, I was not very old, or hard-baked at this time, and I could not bear to say "good bye!"

I began to whistle again, as I thought of all these things, and the confounded fog must have got into my eyes, for I ran blindly against a gentleman who was rushing out of a shop, and into a "Hansom," which was waiting for him in the street.

"Hillo, look out, will you!" he exclaimed.

"What! Charlie, my boy! don't you know me?" I cried; for it was Neville himself. He stared at me for a moment, then with the one word—"Heathcote!" his fingers seized mine, and we shook hands like Englishmen.

"Where did you drop from? How long have you been in England? We thought you had been cut to pieces in the East, or swallowed by a crocodile in the Nile! I am delighted to see you, old fellow!" and with such expletive we shook hands again.

"And what are you going to do with yourself now?" he asked, as, having dismissed the cab, we walked along arm-in-arm.

"I suppose I ought to go home," I replied a little dolefully. "Christmas will be next week, you know."

"And a lively Christmas you'll have at Wilmote by yourself, certainly!" said Charlie laughing. "No, no; you must just get your hair cut, order some civilised clothing, like a pair of gloves, and come away with me to The Priory. They'll be delighted to see you. It was only last week my mother was wondering what had become of you."

"But I haven't spoken to a woman these hundred years, and you have no end of sisters and cousins."

"Not a bit of it. Lucy and Julia and the rest of them that you remember are all married long ago. The only one at home is little Violet. There will be some cousins though with sisters and brothers for Christmas I suppose; but we'll hunt or shoot all day, and they won't hurt you. It's all settled now; not another word. I'll write to Violet to-night, to make sure that you have a place to sleep in."

The prospect was really too tempting to be resisted; so I ordered the clothes, bought the gloves, got my hair [illegible], and then, of course, we dined together.

I am sorry that to outsiders the latter fact is almost synonymous, for Englishmen always dine together. Before they part for an indefinite time; when they meet after an indefinite time; when they get first honours at Brasenose; when they are plucked at Trinity; when they marry or they are ruined, or are cut off with a shilling, the result is invariably the same—a dinner! And why not? Why should not much health and champagne be a suitable accompaniment to the congratulations of success, or the condolences of failure?

We enjoyed ourselves amazingly. Charlie was the same light-hearted fellow as of old. I was more matter-of-fact, and prosy, but still no disciple of St. Simeon Stylites; so we got on admirably. I had a host of questions to answer about my travels; he had a host to answer about mutual friends. Then came a short cessation while we smoked [illegible] they were not cigars; we had a [illegible], and then we fell into conversation again; but this time it was upon the topics of the day.

"I am rather behind the times, as you may suppose," I said, as Charlie, in his brisk, off-hand manner, tried to [illegible] with current events. "You have had an international exhibition, a war, and a mutiny, a big ship built, a submarine telegraph attempted, a prize fight, and no end of volunteering and national defences since John Bull and I parted company—how many years ago now?"

"You need not be precise as to dates," replied Charlie; "intellect has certainly been marching in double-quick time since you turned wandering Gentile! but more wonderful things have taken place than any you have mentioned."

"What could be more wonderful than a ship as large as the ark, or—"

"Pshaw!" interrupted Charlie," "that's nothing—a mere every-day natural occurrence. What do you say to ladies and gentlemen in acknowledged communication with the other world?—mediums we call them. What do you say to spirits passing into mahogany tables, and keeping up a conversation with a roomful of people? What do you say to poetry written from the dictation of Byron and Shelley, and songs set to spiritual music?"

"Ah! come, old fellow," I said, "you look solemn enough, but you cannot 'do' me. You think I shall be deluging you with 'traveller's wonders,' and you want to take the initiative."

"Very good," he replied; "be as sceptical as you please; you always were an unbelieving dog! But if you do not mean to join a volunteer rifle corps, and believe in spiritualism, you may as well pack up your carpet-bag again, and go back to the bush; you're not the man for Gotham."

"Are you really serious, Charlie?"

"Am I serious? Of course I am. It is not a matter to jest about at all, I assure you. I could take a blowing-up from my mother or the governor, but I would not answer for the consequences if one of the round tables lifted a claw, and commenced to harangue me for my incredulity. I don't see why they could not do a scolding as well as any other kind of talk."

"Charlie," I said, soothingly, "how many glasses of champagne did you drink?"

"What? do you mean to insinuate that I am—'not to put too fine a point upon it'—that I am—drunk?" he asked with a comical twinkle of his brown eyes.

"Well, I don't think you are; and yet—"

"Ah! you only look upon the matter in this light, because you have not properly 'ventilated' the subject. I hope you notice the new application of that word? It is all the *fashion* now. I was a sceptic at first; but when one finds the science upheld by some of our cleverest men, what can one say? There is that *Whatever Magazine*; the editor is a man of established reputation, the magazine itself has a circulation of a hundred thousand, and in a recent number there was a strong article, written by an eye-witness of some most remarkable manifestations. My dear friend, there is no help for it; you must believe."

"Never!" I replied, stoutly. "There is no such thing as a *medium*! I don't believe it, and I never shall."

"I shall make a note of that," said Charlie, gravely, drawing out his tablets, "and bring it up against you the day you acknowledge your conversion."

"I hope your paper is indestructible and your pencil indelible," I remarked sarcastically, "for the lasting power of both will be strongly tested."

"Oh! you think so now; but I assure you you have no idea of the length to which the thing has gone. In another year or so it will be as firmly established, as one of the institutions of Great Britain, as the House of Commons or Greenwich Hospital. It is as usual now to ask a young lady if she is a *medium*, as to ask if she can sing. *Séances* are displacing *thés dansants*; and they are an improvement in many ways, for, as there is no light, your eyes are spared much wear and tear; you may wear soiled gloves too, or no gloves, if you please, and instead of asking a young lady to waltz, you beg that she will invoke the spirit of your grandfather. Now, for lovers of novelty, what can be more delightful?"

"Charlie, are you mad?"

"Now, Heathcote, do be reasonable. It is really painful, in this enlightened age, to find any one so wedded to old-world prejudices. You have plenty of excellent common-sense if you would only bring it to bear. Let me recommend you, as a friend, to take a few lessons in *mediumology*; you can have them for a guinea an hour, and at the end of six months you will be able to bring up all your own spirits without the aid of a professional. It appears rather a large outlay, certainly; but then, consider all you gain. Let me see; you can do it cheaper, I think. Some one told me there was a *Medium* made-easy in the press, compiled by the celebrated Mr. Parris; he is the man to whom Byron and Shelley dictated their poems. By-the-bye, I heard that Phelps is in treaty with Shakespeare, through Parris, for an original five-act tragedy for the "Standard"; and there is also some hope of getting Addison to edit a rival to the *Whatever*. The only fear is that his style may be a little too stilted and old-fashioned for these run-and-read days; but the mere rumour of such a thing has so frightened the editor of the *Whatever*, that he has engaged Charles Lamb, at almost fabulous pay, to write an essay for him every month."

"Do you know, Charlie, I am getting afraid of you."

"Don't be, in the least, my dear boy. I am not a spirit myself yet; and I assure you I have only given you a mere outline of the affair. It is only in its infancy. There are to be professorships in mediumology attached to Oxford and Cambridge, and papers on the subject read at the British Association. There are to be mediums appointed to the Royal household; they will take precedence of the chaplains, and are to be chosen by competitive examination. The medium to whom the spirits appear most attentive, and for whom the tables clamber highest, will get the post. Rather a good thing too—a thousand a year, and the privilege of communicating with all the Kings and Queens who have departed this life since the Conquest."

"Delightful privilege, truly!" I replied. "Anything more?"

"Well, you know I have not studied the subject very carefully myself, as yet; so my information is limited. Keep—it has been suggested to her Majesty that she need not have any trouble in future with her Ministers; but when they are beaten on the Budget, or have a squabble about Reform, she is to send for Pitt, and give him the reins of Government; and in the event of an invasion from France, the Duke of Wellington is to resume his old post of Commander-in-Chief—I hear that the Duke of Cambridge is furious at the prospect of such a slight; and Nelson will take the direction of the Channel Fleet, and—"

"Oh! for mercy's sake stop!" I cried; "you will drive me mad! Are you sure that I am in England—in London?"

"If you have any doubt upon the subject, come out and I'll show you the Thames. But you really do look scared. Take another weed, old boy, and submit to the inevitable. I should be most unhappy about you, were I not convinced that you will be a convert before my prudence. You will hear nothing else talked of at The Priory. Violet is a first-rate medium. The tables and chairs would do anything for her. I shall leave the honour of your conversion with her."

"Charlie, I repeat you will drive me mad! You don't mean that your sister is a medium?"

"Of course I do—the best in the world. I don't know what we should do without her. But she dresses like other people, and all that, you know. Do you remember her at all?"

"Oh, perfectly. A pretty little girl with long curls. I remember she gave me a rose and a kiss the day I left The Priory. I suppose she is a young lady now, with crinoline, and all that sort of thing? I warn you, Charlie, you have not predisposed me to like her by telling me of this rubbish of mediumology, or whatever you call it."

"Very well, please yourself, and you'll please me. You will find plenty of amusement at The Priory without spiritual aid; but I know you will not be able to withstand the evidence of your senses. It is all very well to condemn a thing in theory; but practice knocks a fellow over at once. And now it is verging towards the small hours, suppose we adjourn the debate?"

I complied, and with a cordial "Good night" we separated. We remained in London until Christmas Eve, and the short daylight of Christmas Eve itself was over when Charlie and I reached The Priory. I followed him, slightly dazzled and bewildered, into the warm and lighted hall. There was a sound of doors softly opening, and gleams of light began to stream down the staircase and to issue from unexpected places. Then there was a rustle of crinoline. I saw Charlie's arms round a girlish figure, while golden curls floated about him, and in a moment I found myself face to face with—

Very! If I go into raptures about Violet Neville, you will only laugh at me; but she was the prettiest creature I had ever seen.

As Charlie had predicted, the family mustered strong for Christmas. There were three married daughters with their husbands, one married son with his wife; while after dinner, every day, I thought the file of babies in white frocks, and with sashes of every colour under the sun, would never come to an end! How the mothers recognised their respective darlings is a mystery to me to this moment!

I had not taken Violet "in" to dinner, but Charlie had contrived that we should sit together. He had introduced me to her, and to the whole family, as a blind sceptic in the doctrine of "Spiritualism," but added that I was "open to conviction,"—which, as you know, was a gratuitous falsehood on Master Charlie's part.

I was determined to be agreeable, and Charlie says I succeeded; but, do what I would, I could not inveigle Violet from the absorbing topic of spiritualism; yet she looked so pretty while defending her theory, that, after a time, I was quite willing to listen; and, whether it was that I was infected by the universal belief apparently held in the science by the entire family, or that Violet being, as Charlie told me, a medium, exercised some influence over me, I know not; but the whole affair did not appear so absurd as it had done at first.

I felt exceedingly happy when I awoke on Christmas morning, and heard the bells of the village church pealing through the frosty air. It was really delightful to know that I was in dear old England once more! And I lay, drowsily tracing the outline of the leaves and sprays which the frost had formed upon the window-panes, feeling that I ought to get up, but not knowing well how to begin, when Charlie burst in, in his dressing-gown. He pulled me up without mercy, announced that the children were getting their Christmas-boxes in the dining-room, and said there was already such a good savour through the house, that he thought the plum-pudding would be for breakfast!

That Christmas-day at The Priory was the happiest I had spent since I had outgrown jackets and lollypops. We all went to church, and after luncheon we went to walk; Charlie and his sister and I went together to look at some view; but, on our way, he declared it was very uninteresting to talk to one's sister, and attached himself to a very pretty cousin. Then Violet and I had really quite an interesting conversation upon spiritualism; and I was surprised to find how the subject bore investigation, and how much she found to say about it! I said that I should like to see some "manifestations," and she promised to gratify me if possible; but added, laughing, that the spirits were sometimes sulky; so that I must not expect too much.

So engrossed were we in our discussion, which branched off now and then to other topics, that we took a wrong turn, and it was not until all trace of our companions had vanished that we discovered our mistake. It was quite dusk when Charlie, who had been sent in search of us, met us returning leisurely towards the house.

"Well, I hope you saw the view and enjoyed yourselves," he said, taking Violet's arm, and desiring me to "go on out of the way." "Were you geologising or botanizing? or what were you doing?"

"We were 'spiritualizing,'" I replied; "I begin to think that the subject is worth investigating."

"Ventilating, you mean. Did I not tell you that to 'ventilate' a subject was the correct term now? See, there is the second bell. Off with you, Violet, or you will never have your curls arranged before dinner. And so you were 'spiritualizing,' were you?" he said to me, as we separated in the hall to dress. "I shall make you apologise for all the hard names you called me that night we met in London," and, snapping his fingers in my face, he sprang upstairs, whistling "Sweet Spirit," from Lurline.

Away flew the days. We danced the Old Year out and the New Year in. On Twelfth Night we had a regular jollification! A ball for all the children in the county, with lots drawn, from a huge cake, for King and Queen; and games until they could play no longer. And all this time I was becoming more and more convinced that there was something in "spiritualism," and I was never tired of conversing with Violet upon the subject. To gratify my curiosity there were several attempts made to let me see some "manifestations," but somehow they were always unsuccessful. I thought they did not go to work with sufficient seriousness; Violet said there was a "disturbing power" present, which was a hint at my incredulity. They little knew that but for dread of Charlie's ridicule I would have declared myself a convert.

Towards the end of January the merry party at The Priory began to dissolve. Every day our circle was narrowed, and at length I felt that I must also tear myself away. I was very miserable, for the prospect of solitary state at Nilbore was more distasteful than ever, the more so as I must leave behind me one with whom even a desert would be a paradise. I had, during my travels, encountered dangers fearful enough to make the stoutest heart quail, but I confess I could not muster sufficient courage to ask Violet Neville to be my wife. She had grown so shy with me of late, too, and our long discussions upon "spiritualism" and other topics had gradually, but decidedly, ceased.

Well, my last day came; we had spent the entire afternoon skating upon a small lake within The Priory domain, only reaching home in time to dress for dinner. I went into the library to get some of my belongings, which I knew were scattered about there. It was lighted only by a wood fire, and, to my surprise, I saw Violet sitting on a low stool before it, her hat thrown upon the ground, and her face hidden by her curls.

"I beg your pardon," I said, advancing to her side; "I did not know you were here. I fear you are over-tired; it is natural to—"

"I am not tired, but very cold," she replied, with a slight shiver, and the curls fell lower.

I felt I must say something. "Miss Neville," I began, and I actually did not recognise my own voice, it shook so much—"I have spent a very happy time at the Priory; I shall be far away to-morrow, and——"

"How far?" she interrupted, looking up at me.

I don't know to this hour how it was. It must have been something in the expression of her eyes; but it all came out. I found courage to ask the momentous question, and you may infer the result, when I tell you that the second dressing bell rang unheeded, and we talked on in the dubious firelight—not about spiritualism however—until the gong announcing that "dinner was served," caused Violet to start.

"Oh! what shall I do?" she cried.

"Go and make yourself presentable," said Charlie's voice, at the open door. She darted past him like a hare, and he turned the light of the candle he held upon my face.

"So it has come to this with you, has it?" he said.

"We were only holding a little private séance," I replied, quickly. "You know the spirits prefer darkness. I have renounced all my errors, and proclaim myself so firm a believer in the mysterious science, that I am about to place myself upon a footing with Royalty, and attach a medium to my household."

"Humph! I see," said Charlie; "and Violet has consented to accept the post. You see I was right, old fellow; I knew you would be a convert before six weeks. Well, you have my blessing and approval." And we shook hands, and laughed at each other in the most confused fashion.

I did not leave The Priory the following day, and in three months there was another gathering of the clans; for in those months Violet and I were married. I have always felt it a cowardly act to shrink from confessing an error, so I shall just state that the belief I acquired in spiritualism at The Priory, at that Christmas time, has not since diminished. And I would strongly recommend all single gentlemen, if they wish to be happy, to supply themselves with a medium without loss of time.

My dear wife is a "medium" still; she is the "medium" through which every pleasure and every happiness has come into my life; she is the "medium" through which I have learned to value many things I was disposed to criticise before; and, with such qualities, I am more than contented to allow the fabled power of communion with the other world to pass into the oblivion it deserves.

A GRAVE SUBJECT.

BY GOLDTHORN HILL.

Prone as we very generally are to provide ourselves with necessaries, and something more, there are one or two essentials, certain to be required by every one of us, who hopes to make a good end, and exit calmly and decently from the present scene of our existence, which, as a rule, we are content to dispense with purchasing, and shift the trouble on any other shoulders than our own.

Occasionally, we hear of an individual, who, after the manner of Chinamen, sets up his coffin while his appetite is still good, and his general health unaffected. But the case is exceptional, and, instead of winning approbation, the exhibitor of so much practical foresight renders himself the subject of suspicious gossip touching his sanity, and of newspaper paragraphs which circulate from county to county for months afterwards.

Nor does it often occur that we buy a little freehold on our own account, with a view to building on troglodyte principles. Anybody may purchase that estate, and place that mansion for us! we set aside our personal interest in it, in the most disinterested manner, and leave the affairs to our executors or next of kin. Even those of us who are eligible to the dignity honours of the "family vault," have no great appetite for its present occupancy; we enjoy the privilege best through a long perspective, as both a few or at a distance? But we are quite ready to stand aside, and let another take precedence of us. The company of all the Capulets hath no argument in it for our being of their present guild. With Juliet, we have no stomach for the bones of our buried ancestors. Love itself can give no fragrance to them; we would rather be their survivor on this side, and spend our days like Old Mortality in tracing the inscriptions on the door of their allied abodes of moss and lichen, than be ourselves the substantive article of the stone-cutter's *Hic jacet!*

But, however distantly as individuals we are content to regard such posthumous honours and possessions, a relative interest in them is another matter; and, in all ages of human history, and amongst all peoples, the homes of the dead and the rites and ceremonies of sepulture have engrossed a large share of attention.

These rites, neither commanded by religion, nor made incumbent on the survivors by acts of law, have their root in the affections of our common nature, the sympathies of a common fate; and we bestow in love, or reverence, or pity, that crowning act which gives back earth to earth, in the certainty that when Nature claims her part in us, some hand will be found to provide us with a bed of clay, and such cold hospitalities as be needful!

Yet are these preliminaries [illegible] whose graves are in question. Various nations have had various methods of disposing of their dead; some have them still, though civilization is gradually assimilating them to one single pattern, and no people now, that we know of, cast the bodies of the dead to the dogs, as did the ancient Bactrians, or feed the fish upon their bones with them, like the piscivorous Ichthyophagi of Ptolemy and Herodotus; or solemnly commit them to the deep, as the Norsemen their warriors and vikings. The cairn, the cave, the catacomb, columbarium, holy crypt, and saintly churchyard, have all been dedicated to the service of the dead. The Jews, while a nomadic people, made use of the rent rock; the heap of stones over the place of sepulture not only served as a memorial, but warned strangers of its purpose, and prevented their polluting themselves by disturbing it. At other times, they buried their dead in natural caves, or hollowed graves in the rocks, and the practice prevailed, as we learn from a notable instance, long after they had become a settled nation, and appropriated fields to sepulchral purposes.

The earliest family tomb we meet with is the Cave of Machpelah, which Abraham purchased to bury Sarah in, and wherein Isaac and Rebekah were laid, and the weak-eyed Leah, and in which Jacob, ere he gathered up his feet into the bed, and yielded up the ghost, solemnly commanded his sons to carry him.

All through the Old Testament we find the recurrence of this sentiment; kings and judges, and other great men, as they die off, are "gathered to their fathers," or "buried with their own people"—a sentiment widespread as the human family, and inherent in many savage tribes, as well as amongst civilized peoples.

Graves in cliffs and mountains were common in the land of Egypt, where the embalmer's art [illegible] lending immortality to the [illegible] corpse, which demanded an enduring depository. Hence, those old-world wonders, the pyramids; which, whatever scientific and ingenious [illegible] may discover in their geometrical proportions, were the tombs and monuments of kings.

The locations of many of the graves, which perforate the Libyan and Arabian mountains, as well as those extensive sepulchral galleries and chambers hewn in the limestone rock on the western bank of the Nile, are adorned with pictorial representations of the domestic customs, religious ceremonies, and sepulchral rites of this ancient people, whose language is a mystery, but whose social history the tombs have kept sealed for the scrutiny and research of modern times.

Many of these illustrations of antique life are in a state of marvellous preservation, the colours fresh and bright, as if the artist, who must have laid aside pencil and pigments more than two thousand years ago, had only recently left the scene of his labours. Nor were the guests for these still chambers less carefully prepared or brilliantly ornamented.

The toilet for the tomb was of the richest, as any one may perceive who looks into the wall and table cases of the Egyptian-room at the British Museum. The ear-rings, and bracelets, and necklaces of gold and silver, of emerald, amethyst, and cornelian, the finger-rings and figures of deities, the amulets and engraved gems, the gilded ornaments, the fragments of garlands, sepulchral sandals, and the silken, painted, and net-work coverings of the mummies, all show the extraordinary care bestowed on the adornment of the dead.

That the Egyptians looked for the resuscitation of the body seems certain from the pains they took to prevent its destruction; and we could almost imagine that a loving and foreseeing tenderness thus surrounded the dead with familiar things and pictured circumstances, that when, like the sleepers in the Ephesian cave, they should awaken, they might look upon their long sleep as a dream, and be unamazed by Pharaonic surroundings.

According to Pomet (quoting, of course, from Herodotus and the elder historians), three modes of embalmment were practised by the Egyptians; and rank and wealth were thus enabled to purchase a longer immunity from dust and ashes, than those whose relatives were obliged to content themselves with bestowing on them a second or third-class preparation. Hence the greater number of the mummies in the Egyptian-room are those of priests and officers of state; and if the superstition still prevalent in simple places, that the soul cannot rest till the corpse returns to the earth, were more than a superstition, could any worse purgatorial retribution be devised for a bold infringement of the laws of Nature than the tardy crumbling of King Men-ka-ra and the courtly company around him?

The first and most expensive mode of embalmment was valued at a talent of silver—a measure variously estimated from £138 to £200 sterling; and to this cost, in all probability, those swart, slim mocks of men and women, many of whom held priestly offices at Thebes three thousand years ago, owe their appearance in metropolitan glass-cases at the present day.

When a person of the first quality deceased, I should not wonder if the city article in the current "news" quoted a rise in the price of palm-wine, and other aromatic liquors, or that the event affected the spice and drug markets to the advantage of the Arabian merchants, whose riders must have sent them home full sheets of odoriferous orders for a month afterwards. Wax, too, and flowers and all sorts of fragrant herbs went up, and the vendors of sweet-scented essences and oils and ointments found a quicker sale than usual for their goods.

In the meanwhile three functionaries proceeded with their offices upon the corpse. The first marked the parts of the body where the necessary incisions were to be made; after which the dissector (a profession who appears to have been regarded as infamous and held in general reprobation) stole in, and with a knife made of an Ethiopian stone (Pomet) cut through the flesh, "as much as was necessary and as the law permitted, and immediately fled away with all the expedition imaginable; because it was the custom of the relations and domestics of the deceased to pursue him with stones, and do him all the injuries they could, treating him as an impious wretch and the very worst of men. Afterwards the embalmers (who were reckoned as holy men) entered, to perform their office."

The received account of this process (which occupied thirty days), the nature and description of the viscous baths, the fragrant gums, spices, odoriferous herbs, oils, unguents, and essences used in it, the swathing of the body, and its after-ornamentation, are known to every one. Nevertheless, the arcanum of the embalmer's art has never been discovered; but remains a "dead secret" to this day.

When a man or woman were thus mummified,—wrapped in cerated cere-cloth, cased with bitumen, or enclosed, like a fly in amber, in resinous gums, and subsequently enveloped with a network of bugles, or covering of painted or blue linen, with gilded figures of the divinities, or scenes from the great funeral ritual depicted thereon. The face painted after the most approved cosmetical fashion, or, if suffering had rendered it *facies Hippocratica*, covered like that of Kath-ti, princess of Amoun, with a gilded mask. A garland or diadem upon the head, a necklace of sacred symbols round the throat, the arms and hands adorned with bracelets, and finger-rings set with scarabæi (or figures of the gods), the breast covered with a pectoral plate, charged with the same sacred images—he or she frequently became of more value to the survivors than they had been during the whole course of their lives. A gabbara, or mummy, had a money-value in the market; it was negociable at sight. Its presence was better than a policy of insurance in a house—a man might pawn it, or mortgage it, or otherwise raise property upon it, the embalmed body of his relative becoming a more reliable security than the two living bondholders demanded by the customs of usury in the present day; "for the debtor who could not redeem this pledge was reckoned unworthy of civil society, which engaged him indispensably to find out ways to recover his kinsman in the time limited."

In bygone years, mummies, real or pretended, had an actual place in the pharmacopœia of European physicians; and the Jews, who chiefly exported them, may have thus indemnified themselves by the most terrible form of retribution that could befal the ancient Egyptians, for the sufferings of their forefathers—those hard-used brickmakers, whose labour is traditionally said to have been expended on the materials used in building certain of the sepulchral pyra-

aside. During the Greek and Roman-Egyptian periods, the same modes of embalmment and sepulture continued; but though we subsequently find embalmment practised in many nations, in the case of royal and great personages, the method of withholding the body from decay for many centuries has been, comparatively, unknown out of Egypt.

In ancient Greece cremation was the general mode of disposing of the dead; it was enjoined by law upon the Athenians. But interment in the earth was likewise practised, and it may be that some traditional modification of the Egyptian customs crept into and lingered in their ceremonies. It is curious, in connexion with the pigments and gilding used by the embalmers, to find the late Dr. Chandler, in his travels in Greece, adding that in the City of Saints, he saw a woman in a house bewailing her little son, whose dead body lay by her, dressed, his hair powdered, and the face painted, and [illegible] decked with leaf-gold.

Those of our readers who have visited that interesting, but too little known, collection, the Soane Museum, in Lincoln's Inn Fields, will remember the beautiful alabaster sarcophagus, discovered by Belzoni in the Valley of Tombs, Biban el Melook; and from this and the black granite chest which enclosed the mummy [illegible] of the royal scribe Hapimen, now in the Egyptian Saloon of the Royal British Museum, we form an idea of the care and wealth of workmanship bestowed on these receptacles of the dead, by those old worshippers of the principles of vitality and renewal, so evidenced to them throughout all nature.

Glass coffins are also said to have been used by the Egyptians, and recent discoverers have found that the Babylonians [illegible] those articles [illegible] the [illegible] of their predecessors, and coffins of glazed earthenware have been found at Warka, very slightly injured, except from external violence, which Mr. Birch believes date back to the days of Nebuchadnezzar. The early Greeks, as I have before said, the Romans, the Gauls, the ancient Germans, and various other nations, consumed the bodies of their dead by fire, and afterwards collected the bones and ashes into urns. Amongst the Greeks and Romans these were frequently of the most costly workmanship, adorned with mythological and historical subjects, sometimes in relievo, and at others painted; but those found in the tombs of poor and undistinguished persons, are usually of dark-coloured or black earthenware, and [illegible] intended, more for the [illegible], and a simple expression of sorrow. Cinerary urns are also found in the graves of the ancient Britons, amongst whom, in all probability, the practice of cremation existed long before their conquest by the Romans.

It has often occurred to the writer of this paper, that at some future time, when wisdom shall be stronger than prejudice, we shall return to this classic mode of relieving the living from the ever-present and ever-increasing burthen of the dead. In whose [illegible] or [illegible] body, however compactly we may make them, lurks and lurks the germ of old and new diseases, ready to exhale in unseen forms, to spring out at the touch of the sexton's pick, and spread themselves abroad upon the [illegible] winds, or attach themselves to the garments of the passer-by, or to enter into him with the air he breathes. Such contingencies were disposed of utterly on the funeral pyre of the ancients; and though affection or ostentation might encumber the ground with family sepulchres (columbaria), with a separate niche for every urn, and into which even the ashes of favourite slaves were admitted; or magnificent mausoleums altogether disproportionate to the requirements of the handful of dust, into which even a Mausolus, or a Hadrian resolved themselves out of his flesh. Yet, in this harmless and purified condition, all that was left of the beloved in life might be placed in any chamber, or enshrined in the garden of our home, with nothing to repel us from its presence, or to make its contiguity either above the earth or within it dangerous; the corresponding [illegible] of this [illegible] is [illegible] a source of deadly epidemics, [illegible] in the [illegible].

Probably, in contradistinction to the funeral practices of the heathen Greeks and Romans, as well as that the bodies of their friends (martyrs or otherwise) might escape desecration at the hands of their persecutors, the primitive Christians buried their dead in the subterranean catacombs, which are said to extend twelve or fifteen miles under and around Rome.

These passages and chambers, penetrating from the church of St. Sebastiano, in the direction of the [illegible] Hills, were originally formed by the ancient Romans, who took thence the pozzolana sand for their buildings. In all probability the whole of the excavations are due to the same cause, and are supposed to be the Puticuli of which Horace speaks, and which Varro and Festus Pompeius also mention, where the bodies of slaves and those whose means would not admit of the expense of cremation were interred. There are, however, places for cinerary urns, and as it is well known that, even before Christianity was recognised, the Romans occasionally buried their dead, it is possible that persons of higher rank were occasionally deposited here.

In these gloomy chambers many evidences of ancient [illegible] traditions are found in the paintings on the walls, the presence of [illegible], as, as they are now supposed to be, [illegible] beside the door; and, instead of the pictorial plate with gilded images of the gods, the piece of painted linen laid upon the breast, with the pictured face of Christ, or of some saint (often St. John); or, it may be, the device of two doves on a cross, with the monogram of Christ, surrounded by a wreath as [illegible] on sarcophagi and funeral monuments. Sometimes it is the cross; though the presence of this symbol is by no means an unerring sign that the occupant of the tomb on which it appears was a martyr, or even a Christian; for the cross was an Egyptian emblem of eternal life, and is often present on Egyptian tombs, as well as in the temples of Serapis.

The true indications of martyrdom are too often the cup of desiccated blood placed at the side or feet of the remains; the insignia of the death suffered, or the mark "☧"—a compound character, from the Latin and Greek alphabets —to signify the emphatic epitaph, "Pro Christo!"

With the advance of Christianity at Rome, the "Bustum" gave way to the burial-ground, and funeral pyres were quenched. Only the flower-strewings and the garlands, the purple roses of the spring, and fragrant lilies that Virgil sings of—

> Tu Marcellus eris. Manibus date lilia plenis:
> Purpureos spargam flores; animamque nepotis
> His saltem accumulem donis, et fungar inani
> Munere— [*Æneidos* lib. vi. 883.]

which decked the old Roman columbaria and funeral monuments, were still continued—a simple rite, full of pathos and poetry, and which appears to have suggested itself very early to the human heart. There are nosegays represented in each hand of the mummy-shaped coffin of the princess Kafb-ti—she with the glittering mask, and the ivory studs in her hair—to whom I have already referred amongst the Thebans in the Egyptian-room of the British Museum.

The Greeks crowned their dead with flowers (roses especially), and laid wreaths of them upon the graves; and in Britain the same practice, if not native, took deep root upon its introduction by the Romans, and has never since been wholly lost. The Britons marked their graves (as is still done in Ireland, where a suicide is buried) by a heap of stones. The conical shape of these cairns has led an ingenious writer on sepulchral customs to suggest an affinity between this form and the Egyptian pyramid; but as a load of stones or earth, thrown down promiscuously, immediately takes this shape, the first handful cast upon the spot would decide the form, and every future stone would help to build it up, or adjust themselves by the law of gravitation into a conical shape.

The Saxons, as is proved from writings still extant, planted flowers upon graves, and interred their dead in fields and cemeteries apart from the towns; but on the introduction of Christianity, a desire on the part of the people to be buried where saints and holy men had lived and died, or where their relics were deposited, led to the practice of burial in churches.

The first Christian place of sepulture in England was the present site of Canterbury Cathedral, formerly outside the walls of the city, and between 750-'60, occupied by an idol temple, which Ethelbert, first King of the Saxon heptarchy, granted to Austin (or Augustine), a Roman monk, as a burial-place for himself and his successors. Burial within churches preceded burial in church-yards; but as the Saxons simply laid the body upon the surface of the earth, or in a very shallow grave, and raised earth and stones over it, the floors of the churches soon became encumbered with these little mounds, and, from other causes, so unfitted for the celebration of Divine service, that many of them were obliged to be abandoned; and canons were decreed forbidding sepulture in consecrated buildings to any but saints and priests, or those who would enrich the church by heavy fees for the privilege; nor even these, unless deposited in graves at a proper depth beneath the pavement.

Hitherto our ancestors (wiser than their descendants by many generations) had forbidden burials in cities; but although the cost of interment within sacred edifices of course contracted the numbers who benefited by the privilege, the superstitious desire to share in it was not weakened. It was doubtless with the hope that his example would effect a revolution in this feeling, that the good St. Swithin desired that his body might not be laid within the church, but where the drops of rain might wet his grave, and where passengers might walk over it. We have all heard how munificently his desire was granted; how, for the forty days his remains were permitted to rest under the vault of heaven, the pluvial July clouds poured down their rich warm showers, till the monks of Winchester, fearful that as long as the saint bishop lay there the rain would never cease, *pro bono publico* removed the body to the interior of the cathedral.

During what are called the middle-ages, the rage for costly tombs and funeral pageantries reached its *acmé*; and the descendants of a people whose only monument had been a rude heap of stones, and whose coffins (when they used any) were a rude oblong of unhewn and unornamented stones, or a bull's-hide, or, at a later period, a sheet of lead, now revelled in elaborately sculptured tombs of marble and alabaster, or carved work glorified with gilding and bright colours; or marked the resting-places of their friends, beneath the consecrated pavements, with sepulchral brasses of the richest designs and most exquisite workmanship.

Puritanism, at the period of the Revolution, gave a severe blow to this fashion of posthumous magnificence. The most beautiful tombs were despoiled, and the brasses torn from their sockets; and henceforth the richly ornate altar-tombs and monuments, dating from the twelfth to the close of the fifteenth, or commencement of the sixteenth century, gave place to memorials of a less elaborate and costly nature. Doubtless the filling up of the churches with pews had a great deal to do with the extinction of these splendid monuments, which, as commerce and riches increased, were no longer confined to nobles, county magnates, and distinguished men, and hence mural monuments multiplied.

In the meanwhile, though a species of embalmment was almost always practised in the case of great or wealthy people in this country till comparatively very modern times (a circum-

cians not without its effect upon the air of the crypts or vaults in which such bodies were interred), pestilence upon pestilence lurked up the town and city grave-yards, which [illegible] the [illegible], and disseminated far and wide the seeds of pestilence and fevers. Every few years (and it is worthy of note that one is not recorded in this country previous to the days of burials in church-yards, and that the earliest broke out at Chichester and Canterbury, the precise places where the custom of placing the bodies of the faithful within the precincts of the church was first observed) the plague appeared. London soon takes pre-eminence in the history of this fearful epidemic, the return of which occurs curiously enough at proportionable intervals to the growth of its dead and living inhabitants. For some time it seems to have confined its visits to a customary appearance; but during the fourteenth [illegible], four different visitations are recorded; three in the fifteenth; four in the sixteenth (the last of which carried off the fourth part of the inhabitants); and two are chronicled during the seventeenth. But, in reality, we learn from official accounts of the last—emphatically the Great Plague of 1665—that the city had not been clear of the plague for twenty-five years before; and only free from contagion three years in close [illegible]; so that the dreadful disease appears to have permanently established itself in the metropolis.

From this period; or, rather, from the purification of the Great Fire which followed it, we may date the growth of sanitary improvement in the city. One of the first measures of the King and College of Physicians had been the covering of the church-yards two feet deep with fresh earth; and, as the fire destroyed eighty-nine of these overcrowded charnel-houses, and their [illegible] must have cleansed the very [illegible] then, the [illegible] of these sources of miasma was, for the time, lessened. But in 1778, almost midway between the Plague-Year and our own times, the state of the [illegible] of the city [illegible] for [illegible] from the public [illegible]. Nor did these complaints die out, but, as complaining is a natural institution of the English, it continued from time to time for a hundred years without notice, and was only regarded, long subsequently, when the outbreak of that modern pestilence, the Cholera, with its marked predilections for bad drainage, corruption, and [illegible], forced the attention of Government to the condition of these burial repositories of the dead, and happily resulted in the closing of their gates for funeral purposes, and the Act for extra-mural burials. Thus, at the close of more than a thousand years, we return to the fashion of the past—a fashion from which [illegible] Oriental nations have never deviated.

In the meanwhile, private enterprise had established, for many years, the slow [illegible] of the [illegible], and suburban cemeteries, replete with the [illegible] solemnity of shade and quiet, and that pensive beauty which the admixture of monumental pillar and sculptured urn with the dark cypress and other evergreen foliage, and in which the neatly-kept paths (bordered mostly by [illegible] or [illegible]), the carefully-trimmed lawns, and lively garden-ground, contributed. Norwood, Nunhead, Putney, Highgate, and (earliest of its date for its grand size) Kensal-Green, rapidly became popular. But, while every year has added something to their positive beauty in the growth of the trees and the luxuriance of the flowers, Time has also taken much from their salubrity and the appropriateness of their situation. Look where we will, Town is rapidly approaching them. The value of ground in the neighbourhood of London leaves man no choice; they must build—must meet the demands of the living for house-room, even though they tread on the threshold of the dead; so that the out-of-town cemeteries of a score or more years since, seem fair to become themselves intra-mural.

I know but one of these funeral gardens, in choosing the position of which such contingencies have been calculated to meet the requirements of its solemn purpose a hundred, ay, hundreds, of years hence, though all the dead of London were deposited day by day in separate graves beneath its healthy hillocks. That large cemetery, whose central division, had it pleased the Directors, might have extended miles in a straight line across Woking Common; but which, at present, only intersects four hundred acres of the five thousand one hundred appertaining to the Necropolis Company.

The plan is almost too vast, too grand, to be quickly and popularly appreciated. The wildness of its surroundings, the far-extending moorland, stretching beyond all the eye rests upon the ridges of the Hogsback and the wooded Frimley Hills—only the waters of the Basingstoke Canal silently stealing through the whole—has a pathos of its own, in its vastness and similarity. In presence of which the solitude of the grave, its utter seclusion and isolation of all human interest, becomes suddenly and terribly realizable. To members of a population accustomed, as a rule, (till very lately) to bury their dead at their very doors, or beneath the floors of their family pews, I can imagine that the very circumstances which give such especial fitness to this spot for sepulchral purposes, are regarded by the majority with lingering prejudices in favour of London clay, and proximity to the habitations of the living. As if the dead were better lodged for their nearness to us; or, that the constant observation of mortality had any influence, save that of blunting our impressions of it!

The distance of the Necropolis from any town should be regarded as a concession to sanitary science, which renders necessary the dead compatible with the preservation of the public health. The aridity of the ground is another most important point in its favour, in some measure ascribable to a thorough system of drainage; but more so to the nature of the soil—

a surface of peat-earth upon sand, or gravel. Then, too, the fresh sweet air, coming and going over undulating miles and miles of heath-land golden with furze thickets, or purple with ling, and scented with the exhalation of thyme and other aromatic plants, which form, upon the highest parts, so large a portion of the herbage. The wild open that margins it; the very silence, unbroken but by the lark's song, or the plover's cry—make as a fresh pure part, leaving its path upon the distant landscape by soft grey vapour-wreaths—are surely objects more consonant to humanity, to religion, to the tenderness of native grief, than those that greet the mourner who lays his dead in the dank and already over-crowded cemeteries in our metropolitan districts.

The arrangements, too, from the first reception of the corpse at the Station of the Necropolis Company, in the Westminster Road, to its final lodgment in the grave at Woking, are conducted with a simplicity and quiet decorousness that leave no soreness on the minds of the observer. If we have no plume-crowned hearses, or feather-tufted horses, no mutes, no [illegible] stepping undertakers' men, with wands, neither have we the tittering and small jokes of those so-called silent gentlemen, behind the well-craped cambric beacons (reversed) which they carry; no simulated grief, being decently dry, the frequent application of white handkerchiefs to wipe the dew of festive potations from the lips of the [illegible] men in black, who sit round them the passages before the lugubrious cortège moves away.

The utmost silence prevails; each coffin is placed in a separate compartment of the funeral carriage, and firmly strapped round to prevent disturbance from vibration. The carriages for the mourners and friends differ only from those on ordinary lines in having everything about them black; as are all the fittings-up of the waiting-rooms at the terminal. The carriages are divided, as elsewhere, into first, second, and third-class, and the funerals are classed in the same way, with a corresponding rate of charges.

The cheapness of this tariff (as everyone has seen who reads the Times)—a first-class grave in perpetuity, inclusive of the conveyance of corpse, funeral service, and interment, £[illegible]; that of a second-class grave, inclusive of the same items, £[illegible]—might have been borne with; but when the Company, though leaving it optional to the persons concerned, offered—when a [illegible] ceremony was desired from the house of the deceased to the London premises—to provide responsible undertakers to perform this portion of the funeral, at comparatively moderate charges, it aroused considerable acrimonious feeling on the part of some of the modern Libitinarii, who, at first, very fiercely opposed the Company; not in the fairest way, perhaps, but by writing about the most disgusting and frightful reports, infinitely calculated to terrify the credulous, and keep alive the prejudices of the humbler classes.

We remember, when the beauty of what was then called the general cemetery at Kensal Green was first talked about—ten years, I find, since its first opening—how soothing was the effect of a visit to it; and what a relief the thought occasioned that now there was no longer need to dread the hideous hole in a crowded, reeking, desecrated nook, built round with the most unsightly houses, where the children brawled all day; or in those gaunt expanses, where the tombstones fell over one another, white and bare, and not a branch waved, nor a flower grew, as in Bunhill-fields and old St. Pancras, but all was ghastly and full of noisomeness and horror; how we talked of its 40 acres and its capacity for no end of funerals; and yet at that very period, [illegible], it already held 6,000 occupants. What of it, now, after a lapse of nearly twenty years? Of Highgate I scarcely like to speak; for who desires to speak ill of that which they have once well loved? and yet, on most warm days, the exhalations from the gratings in Swain's Lane have made us reel with faintness, and, for all the wealth of flowers and their perfume, the digging of a grave [illegible] from one end of a walk to the other, so saturated is the soil with the products of decay. Other cemeteries in the neighbourhood of London are lovely to look upon, in the fullness of their summer foliage and the luxuriance of their flowers; but in winter there is the water, and the black slippery clay, and we do [illegible] a violence when we bury our dead out of our sight under such conditions. Better a pauper's grave within the precincts of the wind-swept common, where every occupant keeps his narrow bed, apart and undisturbed, and Nature is left, without profanement, to her solemn work of elemental resolution!

Some years have now passed since the grounds of the Necropolis were planted, and by this time the thousands of trees have assumed shade and stature. The travellers by rail across the common can see the gleam of marble column and monumental stone shining amongst the evergreens, and avenues of limes and [illegible]; but we must go nearer to perceive the beauty of its arrangements, and to see the innumerable roses and the cream-tinted flowers of the magnolia, and the many-coloured garden-beds, quite apart from those of the sexton's planting. There the ashes of the dead may hope to remain unmolested, and the living find a tender pleasure in visiting, from time to time, a spot made doubly sacred by the sanctity of its solitude.

OUR LIBRARY TABLE.

FRAMLEY PARSONAGE. By Anthony Trollope. (Chapman and Hall, 193, Piccadilly.)—It is as yet by no means decided what a novel should be. There is a growing inclination to restrict the domain of the novel within narrower and narrower bounds. Novels with a direct moral purpose, or a historic purpose, or a scientific purpose, are sure to be carped at by the critics. An essay, they say, is the right form in which to embody these high purposes; an author ought not to foist his speculations upon the public in a manner necessarily so unnatural and incomplete. Then, tragical subjects are said to be unfit for novels. To choose a tragical subject is instantly pronounced to be a mark of ill-taste. An intricate plot is decried as impossible in real life. Carefully elaborated characters are held up as burlesques of human nature. Altogether, it will be found that unfavourable criticism generally points to the fact that the novel-writer has aimed at too much. His plot, or his characters or his speculations are overdone. To say that the novel shall represent, without overstepping the modesty of nature, real human life, is no longer a sufficient definition. We are beginning to restrict it within very much narrower bounds. Some years ago we read in a critical journal a definition of what the novel should be, which, perhaps, most of our modern school of critics would accept. The writer stated that the only proper subject-matter for the novel was the manners of the time in which it was written. With great ingenuity he proceeded to show how invaluable such books would be to historians of later ages, who would thus have documents ready to their hands from which to cull those historical flowers which so pleasantly bestrew their weightier pages. "Tom Jones" was cited as an example of this orthodox novel—"Tom Jones," from which book we learn that swearing was more common in those days than in these, and that the higher vices were not so strictly kept behind the veil as they now are. If we accept this definition of the novel, viz., that it shall represent solely the manners of the time in which it is written, then "Framley Parsonage" is a model novel. This, with the other statistic works of Mr. Trollope, will be hailed by after-ages as a priceless possession. From its pages the future antiquary will learn, among other curious facts, that the contemporaries of Mr. Trollope were accustomed, under all circumstances, whether of joy or grief, to drape [illegible]. Surely, Mr. Millais, when he drew that personification of crinoline representing Lucy Robarts in a state of woe, was in an humour of grim satire. There could not have been better emblem of the book than this picture. The pretty [illegible] face and clasped hands and little [illegible] feet (though this must be hoisted in a horse-[illegible] fashion) squeezed into odd corners to give due prominence to that mountain of flounces, are as the touches of real human nature which Mr. Trollope has sparsely scattered on the outskirts of his huge mass of conventionalism. The story turns upon the inconveniences caused by a bill-acceptance, and the disquiet arising from a love-affair between a rich lord and the sister of his parson-friend. The bill, with all its attendant expenses, does not exceed a thousand pounds. Mark Robarts who accepts it has an income of fifteen hundred a year; moreover, all his friends are rich and are eager to lend him or to give him the thousand pounds in question. One does not quite see why the affair should end in bailiffs taking possession of the parsonage furniture, save that the exigencies of the story demand that little piece of excitement, and that a moral is thus pointed how very much more shocking it is for a clergyman to suffer such misfortune than a layman. With regard to the love-passage between Lucy Robarts and Lord Lufton, the only difficulty is that Lady Lufton, his mother, is supposed to be hostile to the match. Lucy will not accept Lufton until the consent of his mother is gained. The mother never could in that manner [illegible] anything, and so, when he asks her to consent to the marriage, she does consent. Why Lucy should in these cries upon the scene [illegible] in crinoline does not sufficiently appear. There are the usual questions of casuistry in the book—the struggles between duty and pleasure which lie at the bottom of all human stories. Here these take the form of casuistries as to what a parson ought to do or ought not to do. How far may he extinguish the voice of his patronage? Ought he to ride a [illegible]-duke? Does the presence of his bishop with him in questionable society render that society innocuous to himself? May he ride to the meet with a friend, and, if so, may he cross one field after the hounds, and, if one, how many more? By how much is the wickedness of having anything to do with a bill increased by the party being clerical instead of lay? We know of old that Mr. Trollope takes a great interest in the clergy. He tells us somewhere in this story, with a somewhat grandiloquent gravity, that his mission towards them extends only to consideration of their social relations, not of their public or clerical business. We are glad his mission is so far limited. In another place he hints that he has a scheme for the equalizing of ecclesiastical incomes, which scheme would seem to us to be an interference with ecclesiastical business in its most vital point. However, we are spared the unfolding of this scheme in "Framley Parsonage," and so we have only to look at Mr. Trollope's mission according to his own proclamation—a mission to reclaim gently the "social condition" of the clergy. "Spare the rod and spoil the child," quoth Solomon; and Mr. Trollope when, after mild castigation, he relegates this child to a fool's cap and the corner, perform these activities ostensibly with an eye to the child's good. We have often wondered what he proposes in these continued mild satires. We get always now, in his books, a flourish of trumpets while he is going to trot out a parson. He has schooled him for that trick, and it is always printed in his bills, in the largest letters. Mr. Trollope in his famous act of parsonship is received with loud applause at the threshold of the arena, and probably hisses would follow if he substituted any other performance for that time-honoured one. The lady part of his audience, especially, appreciate this poking of fun at their pastors. Bishop Proudie turned into an old pantaloon is meat and drink to them. The wickedness of making fun of a bishop gives an exquisite edge to their delight. We could understand that applause of this performance would make Mr. Trollope repeat it, also that habit would make him repeat it—it would be very easy to do what he has been doing for half a life, but when we find him gravely hinting a high moral purpose in these exhibitions, and referring to his labours past and to come as giving him a claim to the gratitude of his countrymen, we recur with doubtfulness to the old consideration—what is his object? Is he a special enemy or a special friend to the parsons? Did a parson once injure him, or are all his relations in the church? Does he think the parsons the only men worth reviewing in this wicked age? or does he think them the only men foolish enough and defenceless enough to be lashed by satire? Or is it that he has some natural sympathy or antipathy against them? Some men are strangely affected by a cat or the singing," the [illegible] of a bagpipe. Any how the parsons would be well rid of him. That the question of parsonism, in its social as well as its other relations, is a difficult one and becoming more and more difficult yearly, is pretty generally acknowledged. But poking gentle fun at the manners and customs of the clergyman will not help towards a settlement of the question. It has long ago been pointed out that the pet parson holds, as it were, an intermediate position between the male sex and female—he is a weaker man, he is a stronger woman, and it is against this anomalous condition, which has been forced upon our manhood gradually—now by [illegible]—now by [illegible]—that our [illegible] have placed in revolt. Such discussions as Mr. Trollope brings forward—how far a clergyman is justified in yielding himself in the way of worldly amusement—whether his virtue is pure enough to resist seduction and strong enough to repel temptation—whether the ecclesiastical attitude of gathering one's garments about one is not the most becoming and the safest attitude for him—such discussions take for granted the semi-feminity of the clergy, and propose only to decide what golden mean between brazenness and effeminacy would be their most fitting garb. Another novelist is fond of touching upon this vexed question—touching upon it in its social light, and in an honest manner. If Mr. Trollope has not got cured of his [illegible], he would do well to study George Eliot's treatment of the subject. To return to the hypothesis of Manners being the proper subject of the novel. Accepting this, we must inquire, what Manners are. In the sense of our definition, Manners are the conventional habits of Society. Society lives in London for so many months of the year; at country-seats for so many; hunts in Leicestershire during this season, fishes in Norway during that, shoots in Scotland or travels on the Continent during another. Society has its boxes and stalls at the opera, its entrance into certain houses. It consists of lords and commoners, and of some few out of the lower world who gain admittance into Society by means of their great wealth. Higher dignitaries of the church are in Society, and during the country-seat season parish-parsons gain entrance, on a lower footing. Sometimes an apothecary or a lawyer, in default of these, but oftener to [illegible] a burlesque manner. Ladies'-maids and footmen and grooms play the broadly comic parts, speaking a language peculiar to themselves alone. The country-seat has its attendant village, and so on [illegible] pauperism and Mrs. Podgens's baby. The town has terrible designs upon its innocents, which wild young men tempt, and so we are introduced to the Tozer family. Society consists of a few thousand people who all agree to live much in the same way, and to do the same things. Probably among these few thousands there is genuine tragedy and farce enough to form the basis of as heart-moving a human story as has ever been written. [illegible] Duke, [illegible] of [illegible], and Miss [illegible], we have them all in their higher walks of life, made by the same Maker, tramping on the same earth, differently only in that their clothes are finer and their grammar more genteel. But their deeper considerations [illegible] the [illegible] of Manners. Love-sick Lucy, [illegible], and the Duchess are the chief humours of the novelist. We want description of the savage's war-paint, not speculations as to his thirst for blood. To say that there are no touches of nature in "Framley Parsonage" would be untrue; but we do say that they are almost lost and swallowed up in the overwhelming floods of conventionality. Lucy is pleasantly drawn, and something like satiric diatribe against herself appears as well as can be her bitterness of heart. The devotion of Mrs. Robarts in the [illegible] is touching. The spice of poetry that exists in Society gains instant acknowledgment in every heart as true. The pride of Crawley, in its first conception, is excellent; but then Mr. Trollope has chosen to burlesque it with his flippant wit. There are passages in this book so truthful, so pathetic, so humorous, that they move those who are not admirers of the author to a tearful impatience of the mass of trouble in which they are buried. The standard which the story sets up for itself is a false one. There are no men and women in "Framley Parsonage;" they are never viewed as men and women, but only with regard to their relations to Society. The only conscience in the book is, "What will the world say?" the only morality, "Such conduct does not become such a position." Unlock Mark Robarts and he [illegible] not exist. Deprive Lord Lufton of his title, Miss Dunstable of her wealth, and they cease to be. No doubt the accidents of life affect men greatly; but men do exist apart from these accidents. We can take Hetty, strip her of her lowly circumstances, and raise her to the rank of a lady, and she will remain the same Hetty. In Maggie Tulliver we have the very type of a nature always at war with the circumstances surrounding it. But can we imagine Lucy Robarts lowered to the station of Hetty? Does she not disappear entirely when we take from her her educated sharpness of tongue and her conventional notions of propriety? It is because Mr. Trollope's characters are not men and women, but effects of given circumstances only, that he errs so greatly in bringing them again and again upon the stage. He has not the wonderful insight to show a Beatrix Esmond developed into a Baroness Bernstein. * * * * We have said enough about Mr. Trollope to show that we differ from all the world in our estimate of his novels. He is now, perhaps, the most popular of our modern novelists; his name (Heaven save the mark!) is coupled with the best of English Literature as literary [illegible]. (Is novel-writing the highest branch of Literature? and have we no Dickens or Thackeray to represent it, if it is?) Rumour promises us another novel from his hand in the pages of the Cornhill. His Orley Farm, illustrated by an artist, once our first, is on every drawing-room table. Mr. Trollope is at the height of his fame. We prophesy that he will live to see his novels rated at their worth. That we should return to an admiration of the fashionable novel, long since buried beneath worthier fictions, now resuscitated in all its dinner flunkeyry, is not a good sign.

J. A.

MARGARET; OR, THE MOTHERLESS. By Mrs. Pfeiffer. (London: *Hurst & Blackett*.)—A novelette in verse, with a really interesting story, sweetly and gracefully told—so naturally, that at times the reader has difficulty in believing that it is not an actual narrative. Without rising into the higher realms of poetry, the author's verse is neat, smooth, and often elegant. Margaret is an orphan, left to the care of a light-hearted woman of the world (Juliet), who wearies of her task in a day or two, and hands over the poor infant to be cared for by one very little adapted to the office—

> The Nurse's countenance with [illegible], [illegible] and [illegible],
> Must mould a child of Eden still the same,
> Hard, grudging, [illegible] into [illegible] and [illegible],

"The girl grows on apace—grows beautiful,

. . . . . . with wonderful brown eyes—
Now bright, now [illegible], as in a [illegible]
Of young [illegible]."

She has intelligence and aspirations, a kindly heart, longing for sympathy and filled with keen desires for a more loving life than the [illegible] of the farmer and his wife afford her. Meanwhile Julia has "failing health;" and, being about to visit Italy, remembers her friend's child, and takes her with her. The character of Julia is very cleverly sketched; as are those of the group of all countries and professions, that, as a lover of the arts, she draws about her. Amongst other German visitors, comes "Albrecht," who exerts a sort of fascination upon everyone; but chiefly upon Margaret. Briefly, his Highness (for he is a Prince) falls in love with the young girl; who, robbed of all her dower of love through life, loves in return—or thinks she does—and they are married. The next scene is a "grey old castle," in Germany; and Margaret has already discovered affection on the part of her husband, and she, in "poverty of heart, a loveless wife." Undisciplined in mind, she submits very ill to her great sorrow. Her jealousy is roused by his attentions to his cousin; her patriotism insulted by his scorn of her country; and his intention to take an active part against it, by heading a band of soldiers in the interest of Russia (it is the period of the Crimean War), renders her malignant. This portion of her story is supposed to be written by Margaret. The sentiment of the following lines will find ready sympathy:

> "Let us have with the [illegible]," I said;
> "I love my country, and [illegible] ;
> Bondage is hard for those, who, [illegible]
> In freedom, [illegible] doomed to pass
> Beneath a yoke: and the free sons,
> Or daughters, of a generous soil,
> Will keep some hold we [illegible],
> Some liberty of thought and speech;
> Some [illegible] never to be [illegible],
> And which no tyrant can despoil."

Subsequently, the diary of the lady falls into her husband's hands; and, as she has written all she thought and felt, these revelations end in a [illegible] and the final separation of the pair. Margaret returns to England; a dishonoured wife, [illegible] looked upon by those who knew her, and has come to seek a livelihood.

> Time for every ear, there appears
> The sound of all sorrow and [illegible];
> The [illegible], for one, is [illegible] heavy with thoughts;
> A [illegible] which [illegible] for him.
> But the time has come, when the Battle of Life
> Must be fought by woman; and often alone
> [illegible] a woman has [illegible] to wife,
> And many a mother's heart [illegible]
> Over the children she never has known;

By-and-bye, we find her again under the roof of her friend Julia, whose dangerous illness introduces us to a young doctor and a nurse, who exercise much influence for good on her future life. But we have no space to follow the windings of the tale. The following verses will acquaint the reader with the author, though not with her skill; and had them, we hope, to read this truthful story and graceful poetic [illegible].

They stood together, with [illegible] eyes,
 [illegible], [illegible] with [illegible] being;
Not daring to [illegible], by [illegible] or sight,
 Or words, however [illegible] thought [illegible],
The [illegible] consciousness that, holding [illegible]
 With [illegible] theirs, their [illegible] [illegible] them;
[illegible], [illegible], no more to part.
 [illegible] [illegible] was [illegible] with [illegible], and [illegible] were [illegible],
And their [illegible] within, with the [illegible] light
 Which gilds the Eternal City day and night.

And ever after, thinking on this [illegible]
 [illegible], they were [illegible] to [illegible]
The steps by which they [illegible] in their dream;
 Or [illegible], of [illegible], [illegible] on their [illegible].
There only [illegible] the [illegible] and the [illegible].
 Before them, [illegible] the [illegible] of their [illegible];
And, strangely, though their [illegible] were [illegible] known,
 The [illegible] grass and [illegible], spreading wide
Behind them, with the [illegible] [illegible],
 [illegible] their [illegible] everywhere between.

PRISON BOOKS AND THEIR AUTHORS. By John Alfred Langford. (London: William Tegg.)—Considering the great number of men, illustrious for their virtue, ability, and learning, who, by the exercise of their genius, have glorified the dungeon—into which bigotry and tyranny, in one form or another, had cast them—there cannot be a worthier theme for a book than that offered by the history of their lives and prison restrictions; and scarcely one which, to do sufficient justice to, entails a heavier demand upon the highest qualities of authorship. Mr. Langford has the merit of always selecting subjects for treatment by his able pen, which, from the [illegible] of their bearing on the highest interests of humanity, must ever command attention, and be profitable to all; and which, interesting as they are in themselves, are, in his case, rendered still more so by the great ability, learning, and breadth of view he brings to the task of discussing them. And to indulge in this commendable exercise of judgment, as it is exemplified in his present work in particular, with any degree of success, is no easy matter. It requires much more than learning or mere undisciplined talent to do so. To make it productive of anything merely good and [illegible], a writer must possess not only learning and ability, but also great critical acumen and habits of [illegible], patient industry, and research—all of which Mr. Langford evidently has in no mean degree; and as the result of their exercise we have one of the most pleasant and instructive books on the interesting subject to which it relates that have yet been contributed to [illegible] literature. To say our author has written it in a manner and spirit worthy of his theme is high praise, but we can honestly give it to him.

He is one of those [illegible], comprehensive, and disciplined intellects which seem intuitively to know all the merits and defects of any subject they take in hand, and have the happy faculty of placing them so [illegible], and without any apparent effort, in the precise light which will best make them understood and appreciated. And this valuable faculty is exemplified in the work before us in a remarkable degree. The space devoted to the prison books and their authors treated of is necessarily very limited in extent; but it is quite sufficient to enable our author to give an accurate and satisfactory idea of both—of their excellencies and faults, of everything indeed; that, at least for the purpose of [illegible] those [illegible], is needful to be known about them; and we rise from his account feeling that nothing more is needed to enable us to pronounce judgment on them, and that they have become permanently engraved on the memory. The worth of his sketches and criticisms, &c., is enhanced by the charm of his style, which is one of the most easy, natural, and flowing of any we have met with, and harmonious in every way with his subject. Of course he has been compelled to confine his attention to only a few authors, it being impossible within the limits of one book to deal with more than a few of the great number entitled to notice; but he has chosen some of the most [illegible]—amongst whom are two or three [illegible] [illegible] in England [illegible]—[illegible] in his introduction to the work that he is prepared to extend the list should it be found necessary to do so. The book is divided into twelve chapters, each of them being devoted to a separate author—the chief events of whose life are given along with an analysis of, and extracts from his most remarkable prison works. The authors treated of are:—Boethius, the Earl of Surrey, Cervantes, Sir Walter Raleigh, Robert Southwell, the Martyr; George Wither, the Puritan; Richard Lovelace, the Cavalier; John Bunyan, Dr. Dodd, James Montgomery, Leigh Hunt, and Thomas Cooper—all of whom have written more or less, and most of them their best productions while in confinement. The chapter on Boethius, the last great representative of the classic mind as it flourished in ancient Rome, and his celebrated work, "De Consolatione Philosophiæ," written in prison shortly before his infamous execution, occupies the place of honour, and from it we take our author's estimate of his character and the spirit of his book, which may also serve as an illustration of his powers of critical analysis:—

"By possessing of all the learning of the times, [illegible] [illegible] for himself the praise of the [illegible] of his own and all succeeding ages. Cassiodorus, speaking for his master Theodoric, thus speaks of the many [illegible] of his friend's genius: 'Through him Pythagoras, the musician; Ptolemy, the astronomer; Nicomachus, the arithmetician; Euclid, the geometer; Plato, the theologian; Aristotle, the logician; Archimedes, the mechanician—have learned to speak the Roman language.' Like all other truly great men, Boethius did not forget the [illegible]

than Ollapods. This is one of the great centres of [illegible] over the hearts of men are most moved, and more permanently influenced, by anecdote than by any other form of [illegible].

We must now take our leave of this most interesting and ably-written work; and, in closing our notice, we may remark that it is embellished with excellent portraits of some of the authors depicted, is beautifully printed in antique type, and, altogether, is got up in a style of much elegance and taste. It has, as it deserves, our heartiest commendation; and we trust it will meet with that large measure of success to which its great merits entitle it.

PERIODICALS.

THE ENGLISHWOMAN'S JOURNAL. (19, Langham Place, Regent Street; W. Kent and Co., Paternoster-row).—The July number of our contemporary opens with an article from the "Journal des Economistes," of October last, entitled, in its present form, "Women and Commerce," in which the vexed question of women's labour is discussed, and the arguments for and against its employment in those trades already occupied by men, are carefully summed up by M. Joseph Garnier, who, however, concludes that the ideal amelioration is to be found rather in the diminution of the necessity of woman's presence in the manufactory, field, or workshop than in the growing need of her presence: a conclusion in which we fully agree. That thousands of women must live by their own labour in the present day is but too patent to us all, as it is equally so that thousands of men block them out from certain in-door and womanly occupations for which they are, by right of taste and feeling and natural ability—to borrow a phrase from another science than social economy—eminently adapted. Let us hope that the spirit of emulation and manly enterprise, which our volunteer system bids fair to bring about, may result in the need of worthier occupations for a large section of the young manhood of this country than the unfolding of silks and muslins, the fingering of artificial flowers, and the measuring of tapes and ribbons—aye, or the sale of soaps and essences, or the dressing of ladies' heads—and this while thousands of their fellow-countrywomen have to seek the means of livelihood at the sacrifice of home and friends and country, in distant colonies. But the fact that

—the competition, on a large scale, of women, whose remuneration is always less than that of men, must exercise upon the general rate of wages a real depression—

should, in the humble opinion of the writer of these lines, make us pause before throwing them into competition with male workers in manufactories or other undertakings, which unsuits them for home occupations, and render them less valuable as housewives and mothers. The very interesting memoir of Madame Luce, of Algiers, is brought to a close; "Dykes in their Season" is continued, and among other papers is one entitled "Emerald Green," which reveals unimportant dangers lurking in the seemingly simple and graceful art of flower-making. In the colouring of certain kinds, substances are used of so dangerous a nature that the persons employed in manufacturing them are seized with what the least practised hands suppose to be a violent cold; it is especially the case with the foliage of green flowers, from which the poisonous powder which gives the colour, is never rinsed, as is the case with other colours; and though the young girls and women work at them with handkerchiefs tied over the ears and mouths

—the green powder will smash into the mucal organ. To-morrow there will be a discharge of blood and mucous, and, as the cold is gone, boils will break out upon the face, and, especially within the ears and nostrils, there will be inflammation.

Surely our lady readers will pick up, and to this frightful wrong—this system of slow poisoning—by abandoning the wearing of green wreaths, and dissuading others from doing so after the details so strikingly set forth.

MARRYAT PRAISED—THE STORY OF NELSON. By W. H. G. Kingston. (London: Groombridge and Sons, Paternoster-row).—Mr. Kingston is so well known as a writer of pleasant books for boys, that his name upon the title-page is sufficient guarantee for the excellency of the present narrative. Especially at home in nautical matters, he takes his young readers through the most stirring incidents of Nelson's life, and, with a pleasant facility, compresses into the pages of this little book an amount of interesting anecdote and adventure which will make many a boy's heart beat with emulation. The story is supposed to be told by an old Greenwich pensioner, who, as man and boy, had sailed with Nelson all his life; and who is so pleased to relate his reminiscences of the heroic Admiral, as his auditor, an embryo midshipman, is to listen to him; and as we are sure all manly boys will be to read his story.

[We regret that want of space obliges us to hold over our notice of Mr. Bird's pleasing book, "Something for Everybody"; "The Odd Fellow's Magazine"; "Report of the Royal Life-Boat Institution"; "Workmen's Visitor's Journal"; &c., &c.]

AMUSEMENTS OF THE MONTH.

But little has taken place in the way of theatrical novelty during the past sultry month, and the heat of July always renders a close theatre less inviting than at other times, although, on the whole, managers have had little reason to complain. At

THE ADELPHI,

The "Colleen Bawn" has been for a time withdrawn, and the thrilling "Dead Heart" revived. Mr. Webster's fine impersonation of the hero, Mr. Fisher's finished and striking portraiture of the remarkable *Lecour*, and Mrs. A. Mellon's touching rendering of *Catherine*, render the drama most attractive. One of those ephemeral farces that this theatre delights in has been produced, yclept "The Pretty Horsebreaker," the plot of which, such as it is, consists in a wealthy gentleman, whom the titled mother of some charming [illegible] is angling for, preferring the humble cousin of the family, under the impression that the title of the piece is her proper description. At

THE HAYMARKET,

A new comedy called "My Lord and My Lady" has been brought out. Passing to

THE PRINCESS'S,

We see Mr. Fechter's "Hamlet," has been, as usual, drawing crowds. The performances, during the earlier part of the month, by Mr. Phelps of "King Lear" drew good audiences. We were greatly pleased and enthralled with his reading of the character, which was at once powerful and touching. At

THE OLYMPIC,

"A Charming Woman" has been running, followed by "The Wandering Minstrel," in which Mr. Robson moves to the utmost the risible faculties of his appreciative audiences.

On the 20th July, the Crystal Palace, lovely with its green lawns, masses of brilliant flowers, and sparkling fountains, was the scene of the

FETE OF THE DRAMATIC COLLEGE.

The stalls of the Fancy Fair, at which presided most of the popular and charming fair members of the histrionic profession, were crowded with eager and admiring purchasers. The Richardsonian Drama, one of the cleverest exhibitions possible, also drew great numbers, as did the burlesque performed by the Savage Club. Aunt Sallies, Raffles, Temple of Mystery, and a Post-office presided over by a charming Post-mistress, played their part in lightening the hearts and pockets of the thousands of pleased visitors. So excellent an object as the Dramatic College deserves every encouragement, and we sincerely hope that year after year the Fête will increase in its successful enterprise, and, judging from the last one, it bids fair to be, next to the Derby and the [illegible] Meeting, the most popular annual assemblage in London.

W. H.

LONDON AND MIDDLESEX ARCHÆOLOGICAL SOCIETY.

A very interesting meeting of the members of this Society and their friends took place on the 2nd ultimo, at the church of Austin Friars, where the meeting was addressed by the Rev. Thomas Hugo, who entered very lucidly into the past history of the church—one of the few which escaped the great fire of 1666, and which has been since the time of Edward the Sixth in the possession of the Dutch congregation, to whom all the present monuments in the church belong. Formerly the church had been rich in beautiful monuments and brasses, of which but only the indents remain; while no vestige of the effigies or tombs of the Blondells, and Giffards, and Courtenays, and the Greenfields, and many names of mark and likelihood exist. Whatever escaped the rapacity of the Marquis of Winchester, son of Sir William Paulet, who for the pitiful sum of £100 "disposed of the pavement thereof, with all the magnificent sepulchral monuments of the nobility," fell subsequently before the iconoclastic spirit of the Cromwellians. Nothing can be plainer than its present appearance; yet, standing on the raised platform on which the communion-table is placed, the appearance of the long line of beautiful arches which remain attests to its former beauty; though neither the roof nor even the tracery of the walls are of the same period; indeed, there was nothing to prevent the rapid rotting of the former, for the Marquis had stripped it of the protecting lead, and had ingeniously converted the fine church of the Friars Eremite, which Humphrey Bohun, Earl of Hereford and Essex, had founded, into a stable. The carving on the front of the organ gallery is in the renaissance style, and has been painted; while that of the oak-panelling behind the communion-table was pronounced by the learned Chairman to be Jacobean. A discussion arose touching the date of the windows, Lord Talbot de Malahide, who presided, being inclined to consider them of the Flamboyant style, and Mr. Hugo's opinion leaning to a later period.

It had been stated in the programme of the day's proceedings that the Society would, after leaving the church of Austin Friars, visit the Armourer's and Brazier's Hall; but, upon its being understood that the visitors would probably number two or three hundred, the worthy company thought it prudent to cancel the honour of admitting a scientific society within their gates; and in consequence, instead of having to chronicle the plate, charters, &c., of the Brewer's Company, we found ourselves in the Merchant Taylor's Hall, which reminded us, by its quaint magnificence, its carved festoons of fruit and flowers above the doors, its richly-ornamented ceiling, and painted windows, of some of the ancient city guilds in Belgium. Here, not only the hall and library, and kitchens, but the curious old crypt (now used as a cellar), were thrown open for the inspection of the visitors. The hall itself, with its emblazoned walls and festive memories—for a banquet had recently been held in it—was a pleasant sight; but treasures of another kind, and far more interesting to the archaeologist, were conveniently displayed upon the tables. Here a golden bowl of rich workmanship, weighing [illegible] ounces, another of silver-gilt, almost as massive—dishes of the same now used for rosewater at the dinners of the brotherhood—and a loving-cup of the precious metal, capable of containing three quarts. Amongst other objects of antiquarian interest, was the standard yard-measure of the realm, of solid silver, and which in former days it was imperative on the cloth-merchants and drapers who attended Bartholomew Fair to send for before selling a portion of their goods, and for the loan of which 4s. 1½d. was charged. A very curiously wrought silver hour-glass was also exhibited, the gift of Thomas Roberts. And, turning from the festive insignia, memorials of a very different character, but quite as gorgeous in their way, met us in what Londoners call the ancient mortuary belongings of the company, two of which, however, were [illegible], suggestive of funeral pageantry far more magnificent than we moderns have any notion of. One of crimson velvet, embroidered with gold, exhibits round the border the arms of the Company, and the history of St. John Baptist, the patron of the fraternity. Another, of cloth of gold, has the same emblems wrought in colours in the border. From hence the Society proceeded to Sion College, on the ancient site of Elsing Spital. The college owes its foundation to Dr. Thomas White, who left £3,000 to purchase and build the same, with almshouses for 20 poor people—10 men and 10 women—besides making provision for their support by liberal endowments. A selection of curious MSS. on vellum, and rare books was exhibited, of which the spacious library contains a number; one with a chain still appended to it, by which, in former days, such treasures were attached to the walls of libraries, as well as to the reading-desks of churches. The Rev. W. H. Milman, M.A., Librarian of the College, gave an interesting account of the treasures in his charge, some of which belonged to the Jesuits, and others to the old library of St. Paul's. The library itself, with its nooks for quiet reading, the pleasant glimpses of its fittings up, and its unexpected wealth of books, (which are open to the public by the payment of a small yearly stipend), and the courtesy of the curator, are amongst the pleasantest reminiscences of a pleasant day.

The meeting terminated in the upper hall of the Hon. Artillery Company, where the minutes of the Secretary were read by the Hon. Secretary, [illegible], Esq., and exhibited the growing popularity of the Association.

C. A. W.

THE TOILET.

(Especially from Paris.)

First Figure.—A Pompadour serge dress. On the skirt, one deep flounce and four small ones, the last of these headed. These flounces are bordered with green silk. Body high; waist round. Dolman sash of green ribbon. Sleeves plaited at the top; loose at the bottom, and trimmed with lace frills, beginning at the shoulder. Plain black poult shawl decorated with bands of black velvet and bordered with lace. Tulle under-sleeves puffed. White crape bonnet, having a deep crown covered with black tulle. Green crape blonde, the curtain of black tulle spotted with jet. For ornament three tufts of green feathers and white jessamine.

Second Figure.—Dress of pearl grey barège. Body high. Sleeves with large plaits at top; wide at the bottom. On the skirt, and running upwards to the body, a plaiting of the material five inches wide. White muslin chemisette, trimmed with two frills, having a wide hem and three rows of lace insertion; above the top frill a plaiting with a transparent of pink. Head-dress, a Greek net and a broad brimmed Tuscan hat, trimmed with black velvet and roses.

Third Figure.—Toilet for a little girl nine years old. A buff quilting skirt and jacket, with worked muslin collar and under-sleeves. Tuscan hat, bordered with Prussian-blue velvet, with a tuft of blue corn-flowers. There is a small pocket on each side of the jacket.

Simpler dresses, and flounces running in front and round the side, are much worn.

Ribbons are the favourite trimmings. They

are gathered, and placed at the bottom of the dress, either sloping or in lozenges, and are sometimes of two colours in alternate portions, about a quarter of a yard in depth. Front trimming of bows of ribbon of the same colour as the dress, passing one above another from the bottom to the point in the centre of the corsage. A bow of the same ribbon is worn instead of a brooch at the top of the corsage.

Sleeves, of course, continue wide and open; those in the bell-shape are pretty, looped up in front by a strip of silk, edged with lace, under which plaits are formed. Puffed sleeves also continue in favour.

Dresses for young ladies are generally made low, in order to wear with them the very pretty spencers of white muslin just now in fashion. They are either embroidered or puffed; the puffs running lengthwise or horizontally, according to taste. Some are puffed only to form a yoke, when the style allows of it. Black ribbon velvet inserted longitudinally has a very pretty effect; rose or ribbon may be introduced instead, so as to vary the toilet when desired; the puffings may be separated with little bows. Most of the sleeves are puffed to the wrist; but they may be made either long or short.

Black and white lace spencers are also worn, and are very pretty for evening, especially over a Spanish corsage of black or bright-coloured silk. The general form of head-dresses partakes of the diadem and the [illegible], connected by a very narrow wreath on each side.

The newest wreaths are of two kinds of flowers, and the round tuft in front and at the back continue to be worn; the latter is sometimes separated, so as to either enclose the hair or to be placed under it. The coiffures are of the same forms as described in our last. The colour Isabelle is much worn in mantles and cashmere shawls; but black is greatly in vogue. At the sea-side and watering-places, the cloaks are generally circles, with large hood, lined with silk and trimmed with heavy tassels. White, blue, and fuchsia-coloured mantles of cashmere, with a sleeve puffed in the style of Henry VII., and trimmed with gold passementerie, are also a very effective wrap.

PASSING EVENTS RE-EDITED.

While might be still fresh for the loss the literary and artistic world have sustained by the death of Mrs. Jameson, a wider circle is made sorrowful by the passing away of one who has been pronounced, without a dissentient voice, so far as we have heard, the greatest English poetess of this or any other age. Elizabeth Barrett was the daughter of a country gentleman, who, after leaving Cambridge, purchased an estate in Herefordshire, where we presume his gifted daughter was born. Few particulars of her life or [illegible] are given in the notices we have seen of her death; probably her father's sympathy for intellectual cultivation and literary pursuits encouraged her predilections; for it is denied that she owed much to the influence of her kinsman, John Kenyon, or to the Greek scholar, Mr. Boyd, with the last of whom her correspondence did not commence till she was thirty years of age, [illegible] attained a position of some fame. In brief, it is claimed for her that she was a self-taught and self-sustained artist, though not in the simplest and strictest sense of those [illegible]; [illegible] position, education, the sympathy, companionship and correspondence of learned and intellectual friends were hers from the first. It would appear that Miss Barrett never enjoyed robust health, and that her sight suffered so much that she was confined for some time to a darkened room. But her mind appears to have soared the wider and higher for these physical limits; and the most intrepid thoughts, and noblest and most courageous aspirations and sympathies, enshrined themselves in her heart and found an utterance in her verse, that kindled them in others. It is twenty-four years since she wrote "Virginia's Tomb," a [illegible]; and then she was famous. Few who read it can forget the womanly pathos of the poem; but the strong tenderness, and pity, and scorn of wrong that was the best part of her nature; and the grand power of her verse overflowed years afterwards in the "Cry of the Factory Children," the passionate pleadings of which echoed and re-echoed through all England, in town and village, and helped forward their emancipation. All she has ever written has been remarkable for power and originality; but the most powerful and most original of all her works—the master-piece—is her brave, pitiful, sublime novel in blank verse, "Aurora Leigh." The marriage of the poetess with Robert Browning, a poet, whose instincts and sympathies were fully in accordance with her own, is said to have proved a most happy one; while her removal to Italy must have enabled her to enjoy existence much more than her fragile health would have admitted of in a less genial climate; and at the same time, by its new life and [illegible] of associations, to have invigorated and added power to her imaginations. The death of the poetess took place at Florence, on the 29th of June.

To recall ourselves to the events of the past

month at home, melo-dramatic horrors have abounded. In Northumberland-street, Strand, at noon of a summer's day, with people passing, and others actually in the house. Pistol-shots are heard, and a deadly struggle takes place, which ends in the death of the would-be assassin, and the wounding of his intended victim without causing inquiry or interruption. The Vidil case is also without parallel in this country; and, while we sympathise in the silence of the son, who, despite his written statement, has since refused to proceed against his father, we must sincerely hope that the Baron, who, after riding out on a mid-summer's afternoon to pay visits to Royalty, decoys his son up a shady lane, and then endeavours to knock out his brains with a hunting-whip, may not be allowed—in a land where justice is presumed to be blind to rank and wealth—to escape her inexorable hands.

On the 20th ult., the Annual *Fête* and Fancy Fair in aid of the Dramatic College Fund, took place at the Crystal Palace, and was most numerously attended. All the principal actresses had stalls, and assumed the characters of saleswomen with felicitous earnestness—asking and obtaining unheard-of prices, and in some instances, where trusting individuals had neglected to obtain change outside the stalls, more than the prices. But then, charity thinketh no ill; and the fair faces and persuasive eyes of the extortioners made willing victims even to the proverbial juggles of the wheel of fortune. On the part of the actors, it was whispered to us, that they dealt more in "sells" than in sales; but their strategy was of a less subtle description than that practised by the stall-keepers; in fact, on the part of Messrs. Toole and Paul Bedford, it was broadfaced to a degree, and yet everybody appeared thoroughly to enjoy it. Forsaking the legitimate drama for the day, these gentlemen and their compeers turned aside to the picturesque outskirts of the stage, if I may so express it, and converted themselves into proprietors of Punch and Judy, the Peep-show, Aunt Sally, and Cheap Jack; or revelled in all the boundless ABANDON of their art on the platform, or the stage of Richardson's show. In front of which, the clown and lady in the low bodice and straw hat promenaded as of yore, the former eagerly handed the company up the orthodox steps, and making the proclamation: "All in, all in!" "just a-goin' to begin!" and the gong, that surely we have all heard, sounded with tremendous effect on vacillating spectators. Indeed, though the performance was announced to take place every ten minutes, the theatre filled to overflowing; and we confess, such was the fascination of the unique performance, that we found ourselves twice slipping with our friends through the side-door at which the press were admitted. Subsequently the Savage Club took possession of the stage, and performed the original burlesque of Valentine and Orson, written by Messrs. Planché, Talfourd, Byron, Halliday, L. Buckingham, and W. Brough: the acting of the latter gentleman, Mr. Lionel Brough, and Mr. Byron was excellent, and the performance, which was repeated to a more than crowded house on each occasion, must have produced a very handsome item to the proceeds of the day. The whole of the amusements were repeated on the [illegible], and we have heard that the Dramatic College Fund has been largely increased by the active exertions of the managers, actors, actresses, and gentlemen connected with literature and art, who succeeded in sending home delighted audiences on both days of the entertainment.

C. A. W.

ANSWERS TO CORRESPONDENTS.

Errata: In the article "Our [illegible] Flora," in the last month's part, a mistake has occurred through the dropping of a paragraph, by which "[illegible]" takes the place of "[illegible]" in the description of the [illegible].—Ed.

[illegible] received, with thanks: "[illegible] the Rain;" "Fancies."

Declined, with thanks: "Gertrude;" "The Parting;" "At Florence;" "To a [illegible];" "[illegible]." "Sonnets," by R. D.; [illegible], by Amelia; "[illegible] the Fair," [illegible].

Manuscripts received: T. L., [illegible]. Had the author not stated that the first part was the [illegible] of the tale, we should not have put him to the trouble of sending the remainder, which is three times as long, and would require much more space than we can afford. "The [illegible];" "The [illegible]." As soon as read, the authors shall hear from us. "Our Sunday [illegible]." The similarity of the subject, and its treatment, to an article at present publishing in a contemporary journal obliges us, with much regret, to decline the unknown contributor's favour.

D. M., [illegible]: Our temporary absence from home prevented our receipt of this correspondent's note till too late to answer it by the address given. In reply to his inquiry, the magazine may be had to order of all booksellers. We hope to find space for the first portion of "[illegible]" in our next.

Books, Music, &c., for review in this magazine, must be sent by the 10th of the month.

Notice: We cannot undertake to return rejected MSS. unless stamps are forwarded for the purpose. Authors are requested to retain copies of their articles.

Printed by Rogerson and Tuxford, 246, Strand, London.

RUTSON MORLEY.

BY JAMES B. STEPHENS.

(Concluded.)

CHAP. XIV.

It was very faint indeed, if it was a light at all. Perhaps it was that the words of the old steward had taken so strong a hold upon my mind that the dim imaginings of a dream had assumed the reality of open-eyed perception. It was gone at once, only as if a mere memory of light had flitted over the world, and had then passed away into forgetfulness.

Yet there it was again! Indistinct as before, dim and faint as if the remote reflection of a distant's wing, hovering on the confines of sight! Again it passed. Where had it been? In the chamber, or outside? Or had it been at all?

A third time! More clear, but more steady. Iverson sits up in bed, and I know that he too is gazing on it, and that it is not a creation of phantasy. We look for some time at the window in silence, for the light is now plainly outside, till it disappears, and then only we question each other of what we have seen.

Each had seen a light, three distinct times. Each had suspected his sight until the third time; but now we were quite agreed on the point of its accuracy. Accordingly we rose as stealthily as possible, and proceeded softly towards the window, which, as I said before, looked out on the chapel. We waited there for some time, when at length the faintest possible glimmer showed the only window of the chapel which our point of view commanded. The light was unmistakeably in the chapel and was moving slowly to and fro. My first feeling was that eerie sense of the supernatural which will sometimes make the stoutest heart aware of its own beating. But my curiosity was stronger than my superstition, and the abiding impression that we had been sent here for the unravelling of the mystery that had wound itself around us, impelled me to instant investigation.

We dressed ourselves as quickly as we could without light, and were finding our way noiselessly down stairs, when Iverson, in a whisper, prudently suggested that we were unarmed. I remembered the pistols which I had purchased, and which I had left on a cabinet in the old hall. I soon found my way into the hall, where the dying embers of the log fire made the darkness only more visible and more insufferable than the utter blackness without. Finding the pistols where I had left them, I rejoined Iverson, to whom I intrusted one of them, and a few steps more brought us to the glass door that led out into the chapel-yard. The key was in the lock inside, and attached to it hung a much larger one that even in the darkness I divined to be the counterpart of that which had been lost when [illegible] had disappeared. [illegible], and hand-in-hand, we glided over the flagstones without waking the ghost of an echo. As might have been expected, we found the chapel-door closed. With the utmost caution we inserted the key we had brought, into the lock, and found to our great satisfaction that the door yielded noiselessly, and that nothing was now between us and the interior but the heavy leathern quilt. Here we came to a standstill, hardly knowing whether to burst in suddenly, or to proceed cautiously. The latter appearing the safer method, we pushed forward one side of the quilt, at something like the rate of a hair-breadth a minute, till at length the gap was sufficient to admit a head. Being next the opening, I was the first to look in. The first glance showed the unexpected existence of a light proceeding from some place underneath the altar. It was clear that a light was burning somewhere, and that what I saw was but a faint escapement through an intricacy of minute apertures in the decayed ornamentation of the woodwork. It was clear, also, that we could gain no further satisfaction by standing where we were, and we entered the chapel with the same caution we had hitherto observed. We were just about to proceed to the altar to pursue our investigations, when the light became brighter, as if approaching nearer the altar from within, and our excited ears caught the sound of slow stealthy footsteps.

"Behind this tapestry!" I whispered hurriedly, and drew Iverson beside me under the damp mildewed folds that nearly choked us with the falling mould of years and years of decay. I could see the light from where I stood. It continued to approach and to brighten. Shall I be ashamed to confess that each felt the other's trembling, and that we stood hand clasping hand, each trying to keep up the courage of the other by a succession of friendly squeezes!

At length the footsteps ceased. The light was now unmistakeably just within the woodwork of the altar. All was silent for a moment or two, when suddenly the whole front of the altar opened up perpendicularly, and the figure of a man became visible in the light of a lantern which he held before him. He crept out slowly on his knees, and when he had fairly emerged, raised himself, gradually let down the altar-front which closed with a slight click as of a spring, and then pulled down over it the faded remains of the cloth and lace, which he disposed as nearly as possible in the manner in which I had seen it on the previous day.

I knew him at the first glance. Pale and haggard, hair and beard dishevelled more than ever with night terror, shading with his hand the lantern which he had now placed on the altar, along with a pistol which he had also carried, there stood Guiseau, shivering visibly. He stood for some time, peering from under his glowing brows into the dark recess of the tapering roof. Soon the motion of his beard indicated that his mouth was shaping itself to words. I strained my ear to catch any sound, and at length caught a few detached whispers—deep gasping whispers.

"So often and for nothing now! . . . . . Shall I try once more? . . . . . If the bones were not round it! . . . . . If I could even lift one bag without disturbing him! But the rattle of his bones would bring all hell around me! . . . . . And yet why should I be afraid? . . . . . I did not intend to kill him! . . . . . No, I did not. . . . Once more then? . . . . . Ah, well! Perhaps to-morrow night if it be as dark as this . . . . . But I must see to the stirrup."

At this point he placed his handkerchief over the lantern, and then moved to the side of the chapel opposite us, where he knelt down and employed himself in replacing a small marble slab which had been removed from its position. "Guard the door," I whispered to Iveson, and at the same time crept quietly to the altar, lifted the handkerchief from the lantern, and seizing the other pistol, stood with them both presented at the terror-stricken miscreant, who had sprung to his feet in an instant, and was making for his pistol, when the sight of the two barrels levelled at his head made him wheel towards the door. Here, however, Iveson stood firm, his pistol likewise ready; but it was evident from the convulsive shudder that seized the wretch, and the sudden hiding of his face in his hands, that the features of the youth, ghastly even as they were, were more terrible to him than the deadliest of weapons. Gradually he sank on his knees, his face still hid. Never was wilful as thought in villany, or more paralysed by its discovery. His body was literally writhing, as those of the lost had done in the torchlight a few hours before. It behoved some one to speak, but it was some time before I felt conscious that I could command my voice sufficiently well to conceal the fear that possessed myself as well as him.

"Guiseau!" I managed to say at length.

He started at the mention of his name and looked up at me. Evidently he preferred looking in my direction to that of the door. It was plain, notwithstanding, that he did not recognise me, and his terrified perplexity seemed piteous to pity.

"Now," said I, struggling to be firm, "your choice lies between us and the authorities. You will probably find us the more easy of the two to deal with; but your only hope lies in exact obedience to anything we request you to do, and in answering faithfully any question we may put to you. Do you promise this?"

"What power have you over me?" he asked, seemingly reassured by the mention of a hope.

"You murdered Salvestro Gagini."

"I did not intend to kill him! But stay! How do you know that?"

"It is in vain to parley with us. I have told you already that your only hope lies in strict obedience. Touch that spring, and lead us at once to where his body has lain for fifteen years. Go before us. Remember we are two to one, and both armed. Any suspicious movements, and I shall maim you with a bullet, and then deliver you up to the police."

"Do not ask me, sir, to look on him again. Oh! it is awful; though I did not intend it!"

"Quick!" I said, "or I shall put a bullet in your right arm!"

Forced to yield, the craven touched the spring, and then moved towards the altar. I lifted the lantern and allowed him to open up the concealed door. We crept in cautiously, keeping our eye on his every movement, and found ourselves in a small recess, where was another door that Guiseau opened with a small key which he produced from his pocket. A flight of stone steps was now before us, leading down into a dark vault, into which we descended, notwithstanding that the unwholesome atmosphere nearly stopped our breathing. When we had reached the floor, Guiseau, hanging back, pointed to a corner of the vault, and signed us to go forward. I pointed one of the pistols at him, and insisted that he should still keep his position in front. We then moved on a few steps, and holding forward the lantern, I saw what I had heard darkly hinted at on the night which had led to so many strange events. A similar iron chest stood in the corner, on which, and with its gaunt arms round it, lay a human skeleton. It was what I had expected, yet the reality struck me with horror, and at the same time with such furious indignation at the guilty villain beside us, whose hand had quenched the light of a human life, that I felt my finger tremble on the trigger, in a manner which it needed all my self-command to restrain.

"Look here!" I cried, holding the lantern to Iveson's face. "Look here! guilty wretch, and tell me whom you take this to be!"

"It is the face of a Gagini."

"Now," said I, "I am in possession of several

points of the story that hangs round all this; but I want no fear, telling us every particular; and if in any one point you falsify what I already know to be true, I shall disregard the whole, and give you up to justice. Tell it quickly, too, for this atmosphere is not healthy to stay long. Sit down on the ground there, and tell it as you shall have to tell it on the Judgment Day!"

The wretch let himself subside in a heap, and his story—once interlarded with exclamations for his own too-obvious guilt—was to the following effect:—

His first acquaintance with M. Biot began in Palermo in a court of law, before which Guiseppe was tried for a crime that he did not name, but which I had little doubt, from the hold that M. Biot had over him, must have been something flagrant and bloody. Through the thin thread of his evasions I could learn that M. Biot had witnessed the act for which he was tried, but had appeared, furnished with a fictitious story, as a witness in his favour. His evidence had been the means of Guiseppe's acquittal, and in this way he had bound to his sanguinary [illegible] the cowardly miscreant over whose neck the sword of justice was ever hanging by the slender thread of this man's caprice. At that time Guiseppe was a common sailor, but had shortly afterwards been put in command of Count Gaglia's yacht.

He had not long held this position when M. Biot propounded to him a villanous scheme for getting rid of the children of the brothers Gaglia, the son of the one and the daughter of the other, who, it seemed, were betrothed in early infancy. After the death of Count Gaglia's wife, in accordance with the story I had heard from the old steward, his son had been sent to Pisa under the charge of an old nurse, as the Count, whose mind, naturally weak, was much shaken by his bereavement, was ordered to travel for some time by way of restoring both mind and body. After the child had been removed a year with his uncle and cousin, M. Biot persuaded the Count, who had by this time returned home, to send for his son, and, by way of reciprocating his brother's kindness, to [illegible] the little niece being with him. The yacht was accordingly sent to Leghorn to convey the children to Palermo, Guiseppe having orders, with the promise of a large reward, and with ample means placed at his disposal, to discharge the crew at the former port, to have the yacht newly painted, and to engage a new complement of men, with whom and the children he was to sail for Alexandria. On arriving there he had orders to deliver the children into the hands of a villain like himself, also, for some reason or another, dependent on M. Biot; then to discharge his second crew, and dispose of the yacht as best he could.

After arriving at Leghorn he proceeded to Pisa to declare his mission. Some delay in the preparations necessary for the children's departure caused him to be established as an inmate of the Casa Preli for some time, during which he had ample opportunity of observing the habits of life of Salvatore Gaglia. Combining the report of his being a miser with the circumstance of his nocturnal visits to the chapel, Guiseppe suspected the truth. He had sent the [illegible] to ask Signor Gaglia to allow him to see the interior of the old chapel, which request had been granted, doubtless for the very purpose of avoiding suspicion. Making the most of his opportunity, Guiseppe had taken an impression of the key [illegible], so that a night or two afterwards he was able to conceal himself behind the tapestry of the chapel, and watch the motions of the ill-fated miser.

Then came the final tragedy. Suddenly struck with the desire to share the treasures contained in the chest, Guiseppe, with the intention of merely stunning the owner of them, struck him a blow on the back of the head with the butt end of a pistol which he had carried with him. Salvatore Gaglia fell forward on the chest, which closed with his weight, and lingered it with the rigid embrace of death. Horror-struck at what he had done, probably for the second time, the guilty wretch had not the courage to lift the body of his victim from the position in which death had fixed it. He left the chapel as poor as when he entered it.

Conscience-stricken, and at the same time afraid of M. Biot, he resolved to secure for the children a milder fate than had been designed for them. Placing the daughter of Salvatore Gaglia under the charge of his wife, who had accompanied him to Leghorn, and who was only too glad of a substitute for a daughter whom they had recently lost, he embarked with the boy for Alexandria, under the idea that he might there [illegible] with the agent to whom M. Biot directed him and thereby learn something of the previous life of the latter, which might give him equal power over his fate, and enable him to throw off his iron yoke. On his way thither, however, he was attacked by Greek pirates, who took possession of the yacht, and sailed off, leaving him far out at sea, and blind, in an open boat. He had no idea what became of the boy and crew. As for himself, he was picked up by a French vessel, and taken to Marseilles, from which place he communicated with M. Biot, who immediately furnished him with the means of making his way to Paris, where he was shortly afterwards joined by his wife and their supposed daughter. Here he was kept in employment by M. Biot, who had won himself the very highest influence among the Ultra-Republican party, whose most secret plans were all conducted by him. Guiseppe had been his agent, though not by any means his only one. In spite, however, of his occupations, he had contrived on several occasions to make his way to Pisa, and at dark midnights to face the scene of his guilt. But his courage had always failed him, and he had never been able to turn his crime to any profit.

The last of M. Biot's plots, most of which had hitherto been unsuccessful, through the over-caution of many of his party, was one for taking away the life of the Emperor of France

In this he had persuaded Count Gagini to join him, filling the old man's mind with the notion that this was the necessary step towards the freedom of Sicily, of which the Count was made to believe himself the probable future ruler. Guisnac being disappointed of his reward (which he had demanded beforehand) for the share he took in it, and weary of the profitless yoke, refused to take back the girl, informed M. Biot of her real birth, and threatened to put Count Gagini in possession of the whole story unless M. Biot would at once grant him the stipulated sum. M. Biot instantly adopted a different line of policy, produced the money, and only bargained that Guisnac should instantly start with the girl for Marseilles, and wait there till the plot was carried out, when he would join them, and supplement the reward with a permanent provision. This conference, so far as I could learn, must have passed between them on the morning after my last interview with Stephanie. Guisnac, as soon as the necessary arrangements could be made, complied with the desires of M. Biot in the matter, and remained at Marseilles until his arrival there. A day or two after, having sent Guisnac on a message, which had ostensible reference to the promised grant, M. Biot disappeared, and Stephanie at the same time, though whether she had accompanied the dark schemer, or had been separately disposed of, Guisnac could not say. With such means as he had, he made his way again to Pisa, intending, as he had several times before tried to do, to lift the remains of his victim, and appropriate the contents of the chest. However, as on each preceding trial, his courage had failed him, and, at the moment of his discovery he was about to retire with the same empty result.

"And can you give us no clue," I demanded in frantic anxiety, which had been ever increasing as the narrative progressed, and in which I was even exceeded by Iverson—"no clue to what has become of the lady?"

"I can; though a slight one."

"Then, for heaven's sake, let us have it."

"Not so fast, sir. Now that I have told you all, what are your intentions towards me?"

Iverson and I looked at each other, and knew not what to say. Was it duty to God and man to let such a miscreant loose upon society?

"Remember," continued Guisnac, "in spite of all I have told you, you cannot find the girl but for me. I am sure I could find her, but I am tired of this sort of thing, and all I want now is to sail for America, in a ship which leaves Leghorn in a few days, and to have a little means to begin with in a new way of life. That is what I came here for to-night."

"Tell us at once," I cried, infuriated, "or you will be a helpless burden in a moment!"

"Ha! ha! I know too well the value you attach to the secret! I make this the price of my liberty."

What could we do! But perhaps he was only deceiving us; and, indeed, I thought I perceived a flaw in his story.

"Stay," I said; "how is it that M. Biot never remarked the likeness of Stephanie to the Gagini family, since it must be so striking?"

"He did remark it: but my wife's daughter was born when she was in Count Gagini's service; and it was on condition of my marrying her that the Count put me in command of his yacht. M. Biot had not heard of the death of my wife's child, and consequently was in no way surprised at the likeness."

My only doubt was answered, and I believed the story. What, then, as I had asked myself before, was to be done? I read Iverson's sentiments in his face, and found that they agreed with my own. I was no minister of vengeance. Was it not more binding on me to save than to destroy?

"You shall have your liberty," I said at length, "on condition that you put us on the lady's track. But you shall not touch the smallest coin of this treasure, if treasure it is: and if what you have to say does not recommend itself to me by its consistency with something that I already know, I shall disbelieve it; and your fate remains in our hands."

"Will you lay your hands on that skull, and swear that you will let me go free if I put you in possession of information likely to be useful?"

We did so, and Guisnac proceeded.

"I remained some time at Marseilles after their departure, spying into every hole and corner, in the hope of finding some trace of them. One day I chanced upon an old man who had once had charge of Count Gagini's private museum, but who had left the family on account of the enmity of M. Biot. In my rage at my old employer's treachery, I confided to him the whole story of his crimes. I thought he would have gone mad when I had narrated the circumstances; and he kept on continually exclaiming, 'I know where to find him: I know where to find him'! Repeating this again and again, he rushed out, frail as he seemed, from the café in which I had met him, and disappeared before I had time to pursue him, leaving on the table a half-finished letter that he had been engaged in writing when I entered. Here it is!"

I seized it at once. It was in French, and to the following effect—

"My dear Mr.— Mr.— (I forget your name, but I daresay I will get at it before I need to address this), I fear I treated you rather uncourteously last time I saw you; but I know you will excuse an old man's peculiarities.

"As to the matter in hand, no luck as yet, my boy; but if you wish to communicate with me, address to me within the next month, to the care of Signor Andrea Bronzino, Casa Pesti, Pisa, whence, good permitting, I intend ——"

And here the letter stopped. As I read it, the clock of a neighbouring church sounded the hour of four. There was no time to be lost, if the wretch was to escape.

"Is this, as you live, the only clue you can give us?"

"As I live it is!"

"Can an oath bind you? If so, swear as we

here sworn, with your hand on this skull; and if you break your oath, may this bloody business haunt you for ever with all the horrors of irreparable hell! Nay, trembling coward! You *must* touch it!"

How he shook, as his hand touched the murdered head! How his whole face twitched convulsively, as I made him repeat, after me, the words of an oath, that he would carry himself and his iniquity to the other side of the globe, and there commence a new career of honesty!

* * * * *

We have done with Guiscard, and the world has done with him too—the ship in which he sailed never reached the destined haven. With many brave men, he shared the sepulchre of the sea. Where many a staunch heart is still, where many a manly form only quivers with the moving of the waters; where many a [illegible] eye, that once was the star of joy in some one's world, is quenched in the darkness of billows, where the once precious hair—brown, or black, or golden—that another's hands have smoothed, and loving fingers twined, floats living and dead from the "Grandless head;" where purity, and tenderness, and truth, and all that is lovely and of good report, have as often found a grave—as the murderer, ancient of [illegible], in chains, or sunny dales!

Chap. XV.

The winter is past, and the summer is here—here, on a fair Italian hill by the sea. Half the heaven is alive with the breathing splendour of a sunset, so vivid and so varied, that one might fancy it an embattled armament of ambers and trinkets toward the mountains. The other half, intensely peaceful, softens toward the mainland into a depth of repose, where only dreams in the pale serenity of azure. A silver sea sleeps on a golden shore. That mighty mountain to the south, robed with all the azures, and crowned with eternal snows, where, [illegible], for ever ascending, tells of the immemorial might that still slumbers in its bosom—that crimsoning peak that seems to rejoice with the lofty joy of a God in the [illegible] waves of unapproachable light, is the awful, the beautiful Etna. All around us and over us is the grandeur of Sicilian hills. Nor are we in desert places, alone in solitary halls of Nature. Wherever our eyes turn, the view of human habitations meets them. Down on the beach below us are cottages of fishermen, at the doors of which sit the fishermen themselves, each with his face to his boat. On the brow of the hill are ruins of many picturesque dwellings, from which an old wall runs about up the face of a cliff till it ends in a pile of ancient buildings, that look down from their inaccessible rocks with a majesty worthy of Etna itself.

The winter is past, and summer is here, whispering over us zephyr-accents of wondrous peace, as we lie lounging the hours through the broken colonnades of an old Greek temple.

On the fragment of a fallen pillar sits Count Guglielmi, with one hand locked in that of Lenora, and the other hid in the raven tresses of Stephanie, who both recline at his feet, gazing upon each other with looks whose intensity concentrates the "long result of many weary wailings and much hope deferred." At some distance sits Herr Dulcken, his whole existence manifesting itself in a continuous alternation of pinches of snuff and low chuckles, the latter accompanied with succulent rubbings of his knees, and his outer appendix to all the three watches in regular succession. I have seated myself beside him, and heaven knows, I am doing the best I can to enjoy both the sunset and the family picture.

"It is all your doing, Mister—Mither Murray!" exclaims Herr Dulcken, at the end of one of his chronological appeals.

"All my doing, Herr Dulcken! I was just about to observe that it was all yours!"

"Black my [illegible], then, all I did was to live till it happened!"

"If we had not seen you in Pisa, and if you had not directed us here as the most likely place to find M. Biot, we would never have got on his track. It is true he wasn't here after all; but it was here we got the clue to his movements, which has led to this happy result."

"Positively yours, positively yours. But no matter, my boy; tell me how you did after leaving this palace—you and Guiscard?"

"When the fishermen told us that M. Biot had hired a boat, and had sailed with Stephanie—I mean the Lady Fanny—for Syracuse, we proceeded thither at once, and had no difficulty in ascertaining that a party answering their description in every particular had but recently left that place for Malta. At Malta, after much inquiry, we learned that they had sailed for Alexandria in an English steamer. You remember what I told you in Pisa of the mysterious friend of M. Biot, to whom Guiscard had been directed to deliver the children. The idea of him flashed upon us at once when we heard Alexandria mentioned, and added to the interest of our pursuit. We embraced the first opportunity of a passage thither, but it was long ere we obtained the slightest indication of any tendency towards success. At length it occurred to us to find out and visit the various owners of the Nile boats which are let out to tourists, and to ask a description of the parties who had hired them for the season. We did so, and learned from one of them that M. Biot (there could be no doubt it was he) had proceeded up the Nile in one of those boats—but alone. Moreover, he had paid the whole expenses of the voyage beforehand, remarking that, as he did not intend to return by the same route, the dragoman was to bring home the boat. We were now at our wits' end. We did not doubt that the children had been placed in the hands of the wretch of whom Guiscard had spoken. These horrible possibilities almost reduced us to despair. Either

her existence had been put an end to, or she had been forced by [illegible] of those [illegible], or [illegible] in some slave-market, had her [illegible] bargained for by [illegible] wretches who—"

"Now, my dear Mister Morley, if you please, [illegible] of that [illegible]. Come to the point [illegible] as you can. We'll get all the [illegible], and all the little adventures by-and-bye, for the Count [illegible] you are not going to [illegible] in a hurry?"

"Our next resolution, then, was to make a tour of the principal towns in the east, with a view to inquire [illegible]. To come at once to the point, if you will have it—we found her in a slave-house in Damascus. The very magnitude of the sum which her owner—perceiving her rare beauty—[illegible] for her had been her safety. We appealed at once to the French and English Consuls, told them all our story; and through their means obtained her liberation—not, however, without making some compensation to the wretch who claimed her, which we were able to do, as you remember we had drawn largely on the treasurer of the [illegible]. After the first excited bewilderment was over, and when they began to realise—"

"Now, my dear [illegible], if you please, [illegible]. [illegible] I haven't gone through it all myself fifty times, both before it happened and since?"

"Well, [illegible], if you are satisfied with my story, tell me, did you find the Count [illegible] after you left us at [illegible]?"

"Indeed I did not. He had got it into his head that he had a share in the [illegible], and remained long in Vienna till last month, when I learned from that good [illegible], Andrew [illegible], who, like me, [illegible] to be [illegible] in the old way, that he had written to him to have the [illegible] in [illegible] ready for his [illegible]. I waited for him there, and when the first natural bewilderment was over and we began to realise it there, didn't I astonish him with your wonderful [illegible]?"

"You have never told me yet how you thought of directing us here."

"I knew, and only I, that [illegible] had [illegible] the good old man over this bit of [illegible] estate. It was never formally given over, but still [illegible] looked on it as his own, and drew the [illegible] of it; and, as it is rather out of the common route, I felt there that the villain would [illegible] himself to that retreat. Depend upon it, he had heard of your inquiries after him, or [illegible] of your approach, or he would not have left just on the very morning on which you had determined to invade the old mansion."

"And what about the jewelled cross, [illegible] [illegible]? That is another thing I have always intended to ask you."

"I found the crucifix I showed you in an old curiosity-shop in Perth. I knew that it was one of two that had been presented to [illegible] and the little lady Teresa, on the day of their infant-betrothal. I purchased it, though it could ill [illegible] all I had. I wrote to Count [illegible], informing him of the [illegible]. My [illegible] was answered by [illegible], who informed me that the Count was obliged to me for the trouble I had taken, and that if I would [illegible] the crucifix, I would be indemnified for all [illegible]. I saw plainly that if once the crucifix got into [illegible] hands, it would soon be got out of sight, in some way or other, [illegible] I kept it. I [illegible] this wicked [illegible] had [illegible] it off the lady Teresa's [illegible]. But come, my boy, this ground may be all very [illegible] and [illegible] in your [illegible], but it is hardly the thing for gout. Let us join the 'petite [illegible]' over there."

* * * * *

"And I—what am I, now? At what goal have I arrived?"

When we were in Damascus, I stood for many [illegible] [illegible], while they were in each other's arms. Was I wrong in imagining that she at first shrank from me as if I were the [illegible] of her new-found happiness, and that when she did approach me it was with something like constraint? I am too proud—and I am proud that I am too proud—to blindly her, and to recall the past to her, and to press my suit, and in concert with her, and to try to show her that her cousin [illegible] may still love her, and enjoy her love in the [illegible], although she become what she [illegible] in her [illegible]? And now that my poor [illegible], whom I hoped to elevate with myself, for whom [illegible], and not my own, I had girded and nerved myself for such a battle with life as could only end in death or victory, now that she has become the Lady Teresa—the Lady Teresa!—between whom and each of I the only [illegible] can be [illegible] . . . [illegible], [illegible]! What is this institution called rank?—this distinction [illegible] upon beings fashioned in the same image of God?—what is this, that it, and it alone, should [illegible] and eclipse all else, as if it were the great principle and foundation of society; as if love—ay, love, and honourableness, and manly independence, and all the noble attributes that [illegible] the [illegible] of life should [illegible] before the gaudy [illegible] of heraldic [illegible]—I do well to be proud. Why, all the [illegible] in Sicily could not light up a more [illegible] [illegible] than my own unsullied name, that a line of honest men have borne! It is I who would condescend; but still, the world would say it was she. What is the world to me? Alas, I cannot ignore it. I am a part of it. It then would be [illegible] by my side. How could I endure to be spoken of as "the Englishman whom the Lady Teresa has married?" And she would come to feel all this, too. Innocent and unsophisticated as she is now, when her ear shall have become accustomed to [illegible]—when the [illegible] of flattery shall have passed into her [illegible]—when the companionship of her peers shall have made her become [illegible] of noble blood, what may be the recoil of loathing that shall drive me from her. Memory, and show me as I am—a poor, ignoble stranger! . . . It will not be. I shall anticipate indifference by indifference; and, if need be, scorn by scorn. I will have none of her; no, not if Salvator himself should come to me, and say, "She is yours by promise!"

* * * * *

Was it not I who told them they were cousins, although the words scorched my throat? Did I not mark the first strange sadness, the gradual dawning of possibilities, the culminating joy of mutual understanding? Did I not misapprehend the language of her eyes—I, on whom they had looked with the same love, and trust, and promise? Shall I blame her for the coldness with which she turned to me, the embarrassment of her manner, the slowness of her speech? Why did she not spring to me, instead of to him—to him, who was dying for a touch of her hand? . . . Let him have her!

* * * * *

What raving is this! As if I do not know that it is all a lie! As if I have not known all the while that it is only the selfishness of jealousy, of envy, and foolish pride! As if I do not feel that I love her passing well! As if I do not worship her! As if I am not willing to kiss her very feet!

* * * * *

"Emily, I loved you, and I won your love. But it was by deceit. I pretended to know a secret which gave me power over your suspicious father. I saw dimly that the dying woman, while revealing half the story, yet felt constrained to throw from her soul the hidden knowledge of blood. But when I professed to know this, I merely suspected it. You were helpless, and I took advantage of your helplessness. You were surprised into loving me. Your circumstances are now very different; and there is one with you who has in every way a more just claim to your love. He will make you happier than I could. When you come to understand what family honour means, you will find that you would have been poorly mated with me . . . . Though you weep so bitterly, I see that you feel the truth of what I say. Your love for him is the love of a life-time. Why should my past dreams stand in the way of your and his happiness? . . . . Nay, I will not remain longer. 'You know not what to say to me'! Is not, then, your silence enough! . . . . One last kiss, Stephanie—ever Stephanie to me—one more touch of your hand! What can I do more for you, dearest, than sacrifice my own happiness to yours? Yet once more, my sweet! There, and there! . . . . Farewell!"

* * * * *

It is a strange, strange feeling, like the feeling of a great bereavement. As when death has visited a house, the full sense of separation comes not till the loved remains are carried from the door; so it was with me: I felt as if I had some hold upon her till the last Sicilian hill had faded from my sight, and now I know that she is lost to me for ever. What is this that I have done? Might I not have avoided it? Was it not my accursed pride? And shall I no more twine that dark hair round my fingers, no more play with those little hands? Is she indeed dead to me? Dead, dead—as good as dead!

Who was this Stephanie that sometime filled all my hours, and unconsciously taught me more of the true blessedness of life, and the true nature of the central love than all the doctrinal training of my early years? Was she a living, breathing being?—Yes, I held her to these arms. Oh, it is true, [illegible]; true indeed—too perfectly true! I know that I am on the deck of a ship, that we are furiously steaming for Naples. I know all that. I know all the geography of it, and the topography, if you will. Yet I know not where I stand. There is something gone, something beautiful, something vital, gone. Ah, surely there is fatality in the love of a woman; for how could a little figure, with dark hair and drooping eyes, account for all this misery? I see all that is going on before me. Far from being dreamy and abstracted, I am most wretchedly observant. I have watched that cigar in that gentleman's mouth, detecting and deciding till it diminishes so that he does not burn his moustache with the cherished end. There is a lady opposite me, reading, who has turned over exactly sixty-three pages since I sat me down here. I cannot tell what has impelled me to count them, except that I am glad to take refuge in anything. I am glad to observe; and every new observation calls up a thousand reminiscences, all fleeting sadly round the loved and lost.

As good as dead! Yes, I doubt not she is happy. At least, a little while and I shall be forgotten, and the real love of all her lifetime will fill her heart, and she may be happy. Why should I feel this half unpleasantly? Did I not wish to be forgotten? Was not the storm of thunder, in the midst of which I parted from them all, a positive gain to me? Did I not wish that I had slipped out of sight unperceived! . . . . Ah yes, I hope she will remember me, and name my name, when, by night or by day, her mind rises on the wings of prayer to a sphere where there is neither marrying nor giving in marriage.

* *

I ask myself, as before, what is this mysterious bond that it should thus become to me the all-in-all of the universe? Was my former life a mere negation, my former happiness a vain delusion? Or had I reached a culmination in my individual life, towards which the course of years and the inevitable laws of that great nature of which I am a part irresistibly carried me, against the advent of which it were as vain to struggle as against increase of stature or the hoariness of age? Was then this heaviness here only what, in the philosophy of my college days, I would have called the [illegible], and not the [illegible]?

If this be so, why such despair? If I have reached a period when womanhood becomes a [illegible]—when the soul, opening up to the [illegible] [illegible] of all things towards unity, becomes conscious of its own isolation, and, [illegible] visibly and sensibly to embrace the infinite love, clings in default thereof to the mortal type, and finds satisfaction in what is after all only the shadow and the foretaste—if years and inevitable development have brought me to this, why confine my aspirations to one impossible object, as if there were not other hearts equally full of goodness, and equally responsive to the longing of a worthy [illegible]? Is my own [illegible] [illegible] not full of beauty, and [illegible] [illegible] the [illegible] path to [illegible]? Why should my heart be desolate, as if the world were dead, and my poor moan the last syllables of recorded time?

* * * * *

One arrow, my [illegible], from the quiver of Stephanie pierced this panoply of philosophy. It needed not to seek the joints of the harness. Right through the breastplate it sped, till the winged tip was wet with my heart's best blood.

* * * * *

In what then shall I [illegible] refuge? In [illegible] likewise the [illegible] philosophy of [illegible]?

Nay. There was One who lived it—sanctified it—glorified it.

* * * * *

[illegible] again; the second time since I heard from Mr. [illegible] at [illegible] that Mrs. [illegible] was dead, and that he purposed returning to England with his boy. [illegible], [illegible], [illegible], [illegible] and [illegible], the [illegible] [illegible], is full of my [illegible] that he [illegible] in [illegible] is an [illegible] thing to tell me that [illegible]'s portrait, exhibited in the "[illegible] [illegible]," has gained him a name and something more substantial. [illegible] again! How the time has fled, with all the burden of events that it has borne along with it! Has it brought no lesson with those joys, and all those griefs? Yes, the great lesson, now written on my heart as with a pen of diamond: the straight path, the path on which the old [illegible] [illegible], is the path that leads farthest from temptation.

* * * * *

How strange it seems to be the same little bed in the same [illegible] of [illegible]! Have not my old dreams proved prophetic, my dreams of just a year agone? Have not I been a slave in that [illegible]'s hands, who now [illegible] I know not whither? Has not this poor machine been wound round and round, and [illegible]? And now comes the sunlight streaming into the same little chamber, gleaming on the polished floor, and [illegible] me up to look on the same sparkling sea, beyond which are still all that my soul prizes—all alive, and well, and smiling! Thank God! Thank God!

Did I say *all*? Time, which [illegible] many [illegible], will yet enable me to say *all*.

—

MY CHILDHOOD'S PAST.

A life gone by and hid,
Eve's [illegible] curtains spread
To shroud the dying day;
A [illegible] drooping head
Beneath a coffin-lid,
At rest for aye!

Such is my Childhood's Past.
But stay awhile, old Time,
And let me lift the pall,
And while the midnight's chime
Rings out o'er wood and [illegible],
My youth recall.

The drapery of the shroud,
Each little pleat and fold
I draw aside with care.
How fixed and still and cold
Those features once so proud!
How damp the hair!

I take the rigid hand,
I hold it in my own,
I press it to my heart:
But clenched and cold as stone,
It [illegible] me as I stand,
And bids—depart!

I have no [illegible] [illegible]
Upon the dead old Past.
Once to my quivering voice
Glad hearts beat [illegible] fast;
But that was long ago—
Its bygone joys.

Once eyes looked into mine,
Laughed in my hours of glee,
Basked in my [illegible] bliss:
Or, when grief came to me,
Met me with answering brine,
With tears—like *this!*

But now the eyes are glazed,
The plaintive voice is hushed,
The warm lips chill with dew,
My [illegible] low and crush'd.
Yet God above be praised—
I had *these*!

And in my deep-down heart
There is a hidden pool
Fringed by the moss of years,
Where, as an unborn soul,
Mirrors a higher part
Or present tears!

Heaven is up above;
Heaven looks down on me;
And my belov'd ones come
Softly and tenderly,
Flinging their shadowed love
Over my home!

F. C. B.

THE MANUSCRIPTS OF OUR FOREFATHERS.

BY C. RUSSELL.

The drawings which have preceded writing remain an established fact, since it is more natural to reproduce by a figure, however uncouth, the object we wish to remember, than to express its name by conventional signs, which could only be used when the circle of ideas and wants was sufficiently enlarged to necessitate the creation of a graphic language which could represent something beyond material images. However this may be, there is in the human faculty, and in the bias springing from our requirements and intelligence, nothing more marvellous than the possibility of fixing the fugitive word by characters, and immortalizing, by the stroke of a pen what would otherwise be transitory; engraving elsewhere than in the memory of man the history of the past, and corresponding with our equals without oral communication. The wise of former ages believed that the art of writing was given to men by their Creator at the same time as the gift of speech, so far did its invention seem to transcend the genius of the sons of Adam. St. Augustine supported this opinion, while St. Cyril attributes its invention to Moses; the Greeks gave the honour to Cadmus, the Egyptians to one of their kings, Mizraim; so we may safely decide that the origin is totally unknown.

As we have already stated, the most ancient writings are figurative, and draw the material object. If this was insufficient they represented it by a symbol—the cock being the sign of vigilance; the lion, of strength; the rose, of beauty; migratory birds marked the seasons of the year; a serpent biting his tail, in a circle only, eternity, which has neither beginning nor ending. Syllabic or phonetic writing was probably the next step, representing by a sign the different syllables of a word, [illegible] nearly like the rebus of the present day. For example, figurative writing, to express the word bellhanger, would draw the man at work; but the phonetic would give a bell and a hanger; thus making writing a more secret thing in the days when the priests of Egypt kept learning to themselves.

The alphabetical writing—which gives a letter to every sound, and allows of our tracing not only names, dates, and positive facts, but also ideas which spring from the world of thought, and for which it acts as a conductor—was adopted by every nation, as the most ancient monuments prove. The invention is attributed to the Phœnicians. The Egyptians knew three kinds, which they used simultaneously. The Romans seem to have employed figurative writing in the most ancient inscriptions on their temples; the Mexicans and Aztecs also knew this primitive writing; and even the savage tribes of North America traced with colours the remembrance of their wars and hunts on the skins of bisons; and we may also add the tattooing which is practised by the South Sea Islanders as another proof that a certain number of arts and sciences are the common patrimony of the sons of Adam.

All imaginable substances have been employed for the transmission of writing. The most ancient pages of history are written on bricks, stone, or marble, as proved by the temples and pyramids of Egypt, the ruins of Persepolis, Babylon, and Nineveh, many of which have been discovered in our own day; and where incalculable masses of bricks lie covered with characters, the history of these departed nations is there; but who can decipher it? The tables on which the ten commandments were engraved were of stone; the marble walls of the Grecian and Roman temples were loaded with inscriptions; and in the north of Europe, in Denmark, Sweden, and even Ireland, rocks have been found inscribed with runic characters. Of the same description are those wonderful rocks in the desert of Sinai, supposed to have been the work of the children of Israel during their long sojourn in the wilderness, and which are just now engaging the attention of the [illegible] philologists in England and Germany, in the hopes of finding powerful confirmation of the Mosaic records. As they are high up, above the reach of touch or sight, it is proposed to take photographs of them. The faithful stone has preserved the characters that the chisel traced on it; but the memory of man has lost these ancient languages, so that the bricks of Nineveh, as well as the wave-beaten rocks of the British, are a mystery to our race.

Metals were also used to preserve written records. The laws of the Twelve Tables, which formed the foundation of Roman jurisprudence, were engraved on tables of brass; the works of Hesiod were preserved on leaden plates in the Treasury of the Temple of the Muses in Bœotia; the high priest Aaron and his successors wore on the tiara a plate of gold, engraved with the words, "Holiness to the Lord;" and the names of the twelve tribes of Israel were on twelve precious stones attached to the ephod or sacerdotal vestment; the Jews also used rolls of leather. The Sibylline leaves were written on linen; and the Athenians inscribed the names of the soldiers who died for their country on a silk standard, which they hung in the Temple of Minerva. The laws of Solon were traced on oak boards. Every nation has written on the leaves of trees. Of vegetable substances the Egyptian papyrus was the most generally employed. When King Ptolemy Evergetes forbade its exportation the learned were in dismay; but necessity is the mother of invention, and the Kings of Pergamus, Attalus and Eumenes, who, above all others, cultivated and protected literature, imagined a new method of preparing the skins of animals, and fabricated parchment, which entirely superseded the papyrus. This article, rolled around a rod of wood or ivory, was used for the transcription of long manuscripts or correspondence; whilst for daily notes the ancients used tablets of ivory or wood, smeared over with wax, that the writing might be effaced at will, and for a pen they used the style or bodkin. This style often became a dangerous instrument; Cæsar, in defending himself against his murderers, wounded one with a blow from his; and Cassian, one of the early martyrs (a schoolmaster), was given up to the malice of his scholars, who killed him with stabs from their pens.

It is a curious distinction of race, that while the Greeks and Romans, with the European nations of the present day, write from left to right, the Jews, and all people of a Semitic origin, do it the contrary way. The ink which the Romans used was a composition very similar to our own; but they also employed gold and silver ink. The emperors of Constantinople signed with a purple-coloured ink. The distance between the lines used to be half-an-inch; then it was tripled, and it has gradually lessened. The most favourite binding was of cedar-wood; its incorruptibility preserved the manuscripts.

The most celebrated public libraries of antiquity were those of Alexandria, founded by Ptolemy Soter, 300 years before Christ, which was burnt by the Caliph Omar in A. D. 640; it contained 700,000 volumes; that of Pergamus; the Palatine library founded at Rome, by Augustus; and the Ulpian library. The invasion of the barbarians would have destroyed all these, had not the monks preserved a part. Great numbers of Syrian MSS., some of romantic age, have within the last thirty years been brought to Europe from that ancient seat of Pagan idolatry and Christian asceticism, the valley of the Natron lakes, in Lower Egypt. The contents are very various. Some are translations of the Greek philosophers and fathers, others biblical and liturgical—a mass of unarranged matter, which Dr. Cureton, our greatest Syriac scholar, has been deciphering for some years past. One large quarto, which was bought by Archdeacon Tattam, belongs to the fifth century, and has been put together by an ignorant monk, from four different copies; the only guide being that he took leaves as nearly the same size as possible, without caring for their being intermingled. In the re-organization of this, Dr. Cureton has found a very ancient copy of the four Gospels, written in the vernacular tongue in which our Saviour and his disciples spoke.

We are indebted to the Arabs for a second revival of Greek literature. They became acquainted with it in the beginning of the eighth century, and immediately translated the philosophical and medical works into their own language; so that "the royal library of the Fatimites," says Gibbon, "consisted of 100,000 MSS., elegantly transcribed and splendidly bound, which were lent freely to the students in Cairo." Yet this is moderate compared to the library of the Ommiades, in Spain, amounting to 600,000 vols. Cordova, Malaga, Almeria, and Murcia gave birth to 300 writers; and above 70 public libraries were opened in Andalusia. For 500 years Arabic Spain was the fountain-head of learning for Europe, where students from France and Italy repaired to complete their education.

The illuminated MSS., which are to us the most interesting, because of the place they occupy in the history of painting, and the historic hints they supply as to the manners and occupations of mediæval times, were entirely the work of the monks and nuns. As the art of illuminating is again revived, and so fashionable among our fair sisters, it will not be uninteresting to them to know something of MSS. which have a world-wide fame, and which are within the reach of many of them. A convent without a library, it was proverbially said, was like a castle without an armoury; and in every large abbey there was an apartment called the scriptorium, where many writers were constantly busied in transcribing not only the servicebooks of the choir, but books for the library. Estates were often granted for the support of the scriptorium. A monk of Hyde Abbey is mentioned as having in one year transcribed Terence, Boethius, Suetonius, and Claudian, illuminating the initials and forming the brass bosses of the covers with his own hands; and the scarcity of parchment alone prevented a much larger increase of MSS.

The style of these earlier works, which belong to the sixth and seventh centuries, was evidently of the Byzantine school, to which at this time artists of all countries looked for instruction; the chief features of which are extreme intricacy of pattern, interwoven with animals, and terminating in the heads of serpents and birds. They are adorned with plates of gold, and sometimes with emeralds, sapphires, and pearls. "Not being able to make them beautiful, they made them rich."

We have a splendid example in the "Durham Book" of the end of the seventh century. But when we reach a later period, we find the art of illumination more cultivated than ever. Artists of first-rate talent were employed in adorning books with exquisite miniatures, many of which are preserved as gems of art; the best coming from Flanders, whilst the most elegant initial-letters are found in Italian MSS. The Latin Gospels were a *frequent* subject for illumination. Two very fine examples are in the British Museum; one richly gilt, on purple vellum, with figures of the Evangelists, the blank pages being covered with elegant mosaics, reminding us of Roman tesselated pavements. On the outside of the other is a relic of its ancient binding—an early carving in ivory, in high relief, representing the Crucifixion, surrounded by four compartments containing an angel, eagle, and two animals, emblematical of the four Evangelists.

One of the most valuable treasures in the British Museum was bought from Joseph Buonaparte, in 1840, and is a large folio, on vellum, containing a comment upon the Apocalypse, executed in the monastery of Silos, in Old Castile, and completed in 1109. The style of the drawings is half Saracenic; the elegance of the ornaments contrasts strongly with the childish rudeness in the designs of men and animals—a circumstance which reminds us of the repugnance among the Arabs to drawing men and living beings. The architecture of the buildings is altogether Moorish, the walls covered with arabesque ornaments and horseshoe arches, and proves clearly the intercourse which existed between the Moors and Christians in Spain. It occupied not less than twenty years in writing and illuminating.

Many of these MSS. contain drawings representing an author presenting his book to his patron, and so furnish us with portraits of the literary men, as well as of the kings and princes of former days; for few gifts were more acceptable, or more frequently offered among princes and nobles (they only being able to give such expensive articles), than a richly illuminated book. A volume of the Romances of Chivalry, made by order of the Earl of Shrewsbury, the "stout and warlike Talbot" of Shakespeare, was presented by him to Margaret of Anjou. At the beginning of the book is a superb miniature, representing Talbot dressed in the robes of the Order of the Garter, offering it to the Queen, who is seated beside her husband, Henry the Sixth. It is accompanied by a dedication in French verse, in which Talbot, among other things, says that the volume was made for her instruction and entertainment, and that it was written in French; that, "after she had learnt English, she might not forget her native tongue." The first story relates the conquests of Alexander and his wonderful adventures; this is followed by the marvellous romances of Charlemagne, of Ogier of Denmark, of King Pontus, of Guy of Warwick, &c.

Another very interesting series of illuminations which our national library possesses belongs to the writings of Christine de Pisan. The opening picture contains the portraits of two celebrated women, Isabella of Bavaria, Queen of France, and the poetess herself offering the identical volume which she had received the queen's order to write for her, and therefore had caused it to be written, flourished (i.e., adorned with initials), and illuminated in the best manner. We have the representation of a royal room in the fifteenth century, the ceiling supported by elegant rafters of wood, the couch (then a rare article of furniture), the carpet thrown over the floor, and, above all, the singular dresses of the queen and her ladies, the head-dresses being of the large two-horned fashion, then so common. A bed is in one corner of the apartment, at the foot of which lies a greyhound, and on the queen's robe sits a pet lapdog.

Christine was one of the most remarkable women of her time. She was the daughter of Thomas de Pisan, a famous scholar of Bologna, who in 1368, when his daughter was five years of age, went to Paris at the invitation of Charles the Fifth, who made him his astrologer. He grew rich by the munificence of his royal patron, and educated Christine, greedy of learning, with the greatest care; so that she became celebrated as one of the most learned ladies of the age. She married a gentleman of Picardy named Stephen de Castel, whom the king appointed one of his secretaries. But the prosperity of this accomplished family was doomed to be short. Charles the Fifth died, and with him the pension of the father ceased, and, reduced to poverty, he died broken-hearted. A contagious disorder carried off De Castel a few years after, leaving his widow and three children in poverty. From this time she dedicated herself to literary compositions, and by the facility of her talents gained patrons. She was thrown on dangerous and troublous times, and, though a woman, did not hesitate to enter into the controversies which tore her adopted country. On one side she took an active part with the celebrated Chancellor Gerson in writing against the "Roman de La Rose;" and on the other by her political treatises. She attempted to arrest the storm which was breaking over France, and welcomed the appearance of the Maid of Orleans. Her writings, which are very numerous, are collected in the Imperial Library at Paris, all adorned with illuminations.

Of the "Roman de La Rose" we may say that, for nearly three centuries, scarcely any literary production, if we except the English poem of "Piers Ploughman," enjoyed so great a popularity. It was begun by a French poet named Guillaume de Lorris, who died in 1260, and was continued by Jean de Meun—a man of rank and fortune as well as a poet of high reputation—in 1305. The work frequently transgresses all our notions of delicacy. But this was not the prevalent taste in the age when it was most read. It is also filled with bitter satire against the monks, and contains many opinions on politics which were more liberal than were then likely to be agreeable. The consequence was that the book was at times prohibited, and one of the great pillars of the church said that "he would as soon condescend to pray for the soul of its author than he would for that of Judas!" It was partly translated by Chaucer. The manuscript copies are numerous, and it would be impossible to point out any miniatures more beautiful than those of the splendid copy in the Harleian MS. The plan of the romance is uninteresting. The dreamer finds a gate which is opened to him by Idleness, and he enters a beautiful garden. While he is contemplating the beauty of the ladies in the court of Pleasure he is pursued by Love, who is armed with five arrows. The fugitive arrives at a fountain, sees a beautiful rose-tree, and is seized with the desire of gathering a rose; at the same moment he becomes an easy prey to his pursuer. The rest of the poem is employed in relating the troubles and disappointments which the lover experiences in his attempts to obtain the rose; but, being befriended by Love, and his mother Venus, he finally gains his object. Our old poet Gower, in his allegorical poem, the "Confessio Amantis," imitated this romance. A fine vellum MS. of this work is also in the British Museum. It is a singular monument of the poetry of the age, and was written by command of Richard the Second, and first printed by Caxton, the father of English printers; but the verses are heavy and spiritless compared to his great contemporary Chaucer, who shines like a sun amid the small stars surrounding him.

The history of Thebes, with that of Troy, the wanderings of Æneas, and the conquests of Alexander, were the *four* stories of antiquity which figure most among the middle-age romances. The first three were considered members of the same cycle. The prologue to an old MS., in French, of the story of Thebes, describes it as "Li Roumans de Thebes, qui fu ancias de Trois la grant." It appeared early in French verse; at a later period, in the thirteenth century, it was given in French prose in a book which was long popular, and of which the MSS. are often richly illuminated. John Lydgate appears to have been the first who translated it into English. He was the immediate successor of Chaucer, and the MS. was written towards the latter end of the fifteenth century. The interest felt in "Troy the Great" was not only because of the fame of chivalry connected with it, but because most of the people of Western Europe had begun to lay claim to a fabulous origin from some of the Trojan chiefs, who were supposed to have wandered over the world after the ruin of their country. We frequently meet with anonymous accounts of the Siege of Troy in old manuscripts, and it finds a place in chronicles which pretended to trace back the history of the country, to which they relate, to its origin. About the middle of the twelfth century there was composed in England a very long and curious Anglo-Norman poem on the Siege of Troy, extending to upwards of thirty thousand lines, by a trouvère named Benoit de Sainte Maure.

It will easily be imagined that all these writers on the Trojan war had no great acquaintance with the works of Homer, which they considered of little value or authority. This Sainte Maure, after telling us that Homer was a "mervellous clerk," assures us that, living more than a hundred years after the event, he could not possibly know much about it.

There is a splendid illumination of the re-building of Troy by Priam, after it had been sacked by Hercules, on an unusually large leaf of vellum, now in the possession of M. Debruge, at Paris. Although the whole is full of exaggeration and fancy, yet its parts are curious examples of the domestic architecture of the age. The houses and shops are particularly interesting. In front is a richly embellished gateway, the right side of which seems to be occupied as a chemist's shop. Under one arch the chemist or apothecary is weighing out his drugs, in another his man is employed in pounding them in a mortar. The wares exposed for sale in the row of shops in the street are not so easily determined. One of them is occupied by a merchant, who appears to have on sale shoes, stockings, hats, and caps.

Among the most beautiful specimens in our British Museum, and which is considered so valuable, that the leaves have been separately mounted, and covered with glass to save them from accidents, is a MS. purchased of Mr. Newton Scott—one of the *attachés* to the embassy at Madrid, who bought it there. It is a genealogy relating to the regal house of Portugal, and appears to have been executed about 1507, in the time of the Emperor Maximilian. It is certainly the work of Flemish artists. Among the many interesting portraits it contains, not the least so is that of Constantia, the second wife of John of Gaunt, elder daughter of Peter, King of Castile, in whose right he assumed the title, and in the reign of Richard the Second invaded *Spain*, in order to obtain his kingdom, but by treaty abandoned his rights for a sum of money. She is represented in a crimson velvet robe, cut square on the bosom, a turned head-dress richly ornamented with jewels, and a lap-dog in her hand. Another remarkably beautiful portrait is that of her eldest daughter Philippa, who married John the First, King of Portugal, in 1387. The period of this international alliance was one of the most splendid in the annals of that kingdom, and Queen Philippa seems to have infused some of the enterprising spirit of her countrymen into her children; for her third son was distinguished by his love of science and travelling, visiting Africa, Asia, and Europe; so that when, after a long absence, he returned, his countrymen looked on his appearance as miraculous, supposing he had dropped down from heaven. The fourth son (Henry) was a great navigator, and made many discoveries and conquests on the distant coasts of Africa. Isabella, her daughter, was married to Philip the Good, Duke of Burgundy.

In the famous library of the Duke of Roxburghe, was a MS. which appears to have been written in the time of King Edward the Third, and has since been purchased by the British Museum for the sum of two hundred pounds. It contains a copy of the French romance of "King Meliadus," who, according to the romance of the "Round Table," was the father of the famous Tristam, one of Arthur's knights, and a "preux chevalier." His story, being a series of combats and hardy adventures, differs from that of Tristam, in the fact that the latter is a tale of love and chivalry; while the brave acts of Meliadus originated from no other stimulus than his own attachment to noble actions: "Quar ce que il fist, il ne fist mie par force d'amour, mais par force de son cuer semle-

[illegible] It is not surprising that the illustrations consist of battle-scenes and tournaments. The latter are always accompanied by numerous figures of ladies seated in the balconies, and furnishing us with every variety of head-dress, both in form and colour, which afforded a never-failing subject of satire. The pictures are interesting as artists' studies in various stages of progress; some only sketches, others half-finished. Here and there some subjects of interest are introduced, as views of towns, and the curious interior showing of a group of card-players.

Froissart's Chronicles were another favourite subject for illustration; a fine copy is in our museum. One highly-finished illustration in it refers to a tragical event which occurred at a masquerade in the reign of Charles the Sixth of France, in 1393. One of the Queen's ladies, a widow, was to be married; and in that age the marriage of widows was celebrated with the most riotous mirth, every one being permitted to say or do what he liked. One of the King's favourites, Hugh de Guisay, suggested that the King and five of his knights should be equipped as satyrs, sewed up in coats of linen, and externally covered with a coating of resin and pitch, on which tow was attached to make them look like goats, their faces being covered with hideous masks. Thus disguised they rushed into the banqueting hall, howling like wolves, dancing and leaping about in the most uncouth and extravagant style. In the midst of the confusion the Duke of Orleans and the Comte de Bar arrived, and thinking to add to the merriment and frighten the ladies, they set fire to the hairy covering of some of the masquers. The pitch and resin caught the flame, and the satyrs became in a few seconds so many blazing fires; as the dresses had been sewed on it was impossible to free them, and they ran round and round in the most excruciating agony. The young Duchesse de Berri threw her robe over the King, who was at the moment apart from his companions, so that no spark could fall on him, and he was thus saved. One of the knights, with great presence of mind, rushed into the kitchen and threw himself into a large tub of water, and thus saved himself; the others being almost half-consumed, two died on the spot, and two afterwards. The King was thrown into a long fit of madness, to which he was subject. This plate shows the ladies of the Court and the masquers, and the tub of water has also been brought into the hall by a kind of pictorial license, and it seems inexplicable why they could not all have been saved by plunging into it.

It is well known that prayer-books, bibles, and psalters were among the most precious of these illuminated MSS. A very beautiful one goes by the name of Queen Mary's psalter, and is embellished with an extraordinary number of pictures; as the old embroidered cover is preserved, with the brass corners and straps, it is kept in a case. The contents are—first, a series of pictorial illustrations of the Bible, described in the French language, as it was spoken in England in the fourteenth century; second, a calendar, with illustrations at the heads of the pages; third, the psalter and litany, in Latin, each page of which has a drawing in the margin, some consisting of burlesque designs of natural history, fables, sports; and others, illustrations of lives of the saints, which seem much more appropriate. The history of this MS. is somewhat curious: in the unsettled times of the Reformation it was on the point of being carried over to the Continent, but was seized at the Custom-house, and presented to Queen Mary, who had just ascended the throne; a Latin inscription at the end states the fact. One of the illustrations represents a feast, and a harper is seated beside the table; the minstrels or jongleurs forming a very important part of a banquet in the amusement of the guests; they recited the ancient romances of chivalry, or the exploits of the master of the feast, or his family; and when the party were merry with drinking, they sang laughable stories called fabliaux, which were of a very gross description, great numbers of which are preserved. The minstrels were also called in [illegible] in the monasteries and halls of ecclesiastics, but we may be allowed to suppose that there they sang pious subjects, the religious fabliaux or Contes dévots, which are also common in old MSS.

In the Imperial Library in Paris may be seen a rich collection of these mediæval relics of literature and art. The library of the Louvre contains the celebrated "Book of Hours," given by Charlemagne to the city of Toulouse; it is written in letters of gold upon purple parchment, and covered with red velvet. Petrarch's beautiful manuscript of Cicero's "Epistolæ ad Atticum" is still to be seen in the library at Florence; it is bound in an old-fashioned fashion, with heavy bosses of steel or brass, that by frequently falling on his left leg it so wounded him that he narrowly escaped amputation. The poet was the means of a [illegible] his beloved MSS., which, while they gave him delight, contributed to the revival of literature and civilization in Europe. His favourite, Virgil, is interesting for the marks of constant familiarity with its author; the margins and vacant spaces being full of annotations, and contain his pathetic lines on Laura. The curious miniatures by which the work is illustrated were executed by his friend Simon Memmi, the celebrated painter of Siena.

The value of such books was immense; grants of land, cattle, flocks of sheep, were not too high a payment for them. We read of a Countess of Anjou in the tenth century purchasing a single MS., "The Homilies of Aymon of Halberstadt," for two hundred sheep, fifteen quarters of corn, and a number of marten skins. The Bible of 1481, presented by Lorenzo to the [illegible] of Florence, presented him, in return, the gift of a [illegible]; and, at the very time the printing-press was in vogue, Panormita sold an estate in Sicily in order to buy a Livy, beautifully copied by Poggio. Perhaps the highest price ever given was in our own day, at the sale of the Duke of Roxburghe's collection in 1812, when the contest was between Earl Spencer and the Marquis of Blandford for the Valdarfer Boccaccio of 1471; the sum of £2,260 was paid by the latter nobleman for a volume which his opponent bought some years later for £918 15s. A century before, it had been purchased by the Duke of Roxburghe's grandfather for £100; it is probably the only complete copy in existence, that in the Ambrosian Library being deficient in one leaf, and that in the Imperial Library at Paris wanting three.

France has always been the favourite home of illustrative art, and Francis the First was a monarch who much advanced the civilisation of his subjects by giving his patronage to science and literature, and by showing his personal avidity for knowledge and instruction. He spent an immense sum in collecting MSS. from Italy and Greece, and was in frequent correspondence with the most learned men of the age. His own library bore traces of the same love of display which made the Field of the Cloth of Gold so memorable; his books were stamped with gold, with his device, and figures of the salamander and fleur-de-lys were covered thick with illuminations.

But it was the gallant King's treasurer, Grolier, who was the acknowledged prince of "fine copies," for he profited by his intercourse with Italians, Venetians, and the Aldus family, to make one of the largest and choicest collections of MS., books, and medals ever possessed. In his long life of eighty-six years he amassed treasures of a literary and historical interest that would have been inappreciably valuable could they have been kept together until now; but they were all dispersed by the hammer, after his death, in 1575. A contemporary collector was the fair, but frail, Diana of Poitiers, who ruled the King and the Kingdom of France in the days of Henry the Second, Francis's son. Her talents and beauty were so great that Rome and Pasquier said she owed her influence to magic. All her volumes were elegantly bound, and are known by a cipher—the double D interlaced with H—accompanied by her devices, the bow-hand crescent, arrow, and crowned H.

The illustrious De Thou was born with the spirit of a collector; the amusement of his boyhood was the illumination of scraps of old vellum, and he formed one of the choicest libraries in Europe. During a period of forty years, amid the pressure of onerous public duties, and the wars and disasters of the League, he laboured to make his collection the first of its kind, sparing neither pains nor expense, purchasing several copies of the same work, that he might select the best leaves from each. He expended no less than 20,000 crowns on binding alone, and left strict injunctions that his library should be preserved; but in vain; they were dispersed by auction just before the Revolution, three of the vols. being bought by Col. Stanley for £128.

One of our earliest and most munificent collectors was Humphrey, the good Duke of Gloucester, the groundwork of whose library began in 1425, when the English took Paris, and seized upon nine hundred volumes of MSS.; they were preserved in three chambers in the Louvre, which were wainscoted with Irish oak, and ceiled with cypress, curiously carved, the windows of painted glass, and fenced with iron bars. About 1440 he gave to the University of Oxford 600 vols., only 120 of which were valued at £1,000; they were the most splendid and costly copies that could be procured, finely written on vellum, and elegantly embellished with miniatures and illuminations. Only a single specimen of these valuable volumes has been suffered to remain; it is a beautiful MS. in folio, of Valerius Maximus, enriched with exquisite decorations; all the rest, looked like missals, and, conveying ideas of popish superstition, were destroyed by the pious visitors in the reign of Edward the Sixth, whose zeal was equalled only by their ignorance.

The Earl of Worcester, who lived in the reign of Henry the Sixth, and was put to death by Warwick in 1470, was an ardent lover of books, and contributed nobly to the young library at Oxford. On his return from a pilgrimage to Jerusalem, after spending some years at Padua and Venice, making great purchases of MSS. in both places, he repaired to Rome to satisfy his longing curiosity with a sight of the library of the Vatican, and drew tears of delight from Pope Pius the Second by a Latin oration he pronounced before him. To the gallant Anthony Woodville, Earl Rivers, the commonwealth of learning was greatly indebted; he was brother to the Queen of Edward the Fourth, and was beheaded, most unjustly, by Richard the Third, in 1483; he was one of Caxton's greatest patrons, and in a manuscript copy of one of his translations preserved in the Archbishop's library at Lambeth, there is an illumination, in which the Earl is introducing Caxton to Edward, his Queen, and the Prince. But the subject is endless, and we must close with an anecdote or two.

There are some curious entries in Lord Coke's library at Holkham, in the course of which are to be seen sundry volumes, which were used in the time of the civil wars as receptacles for money and jewels. Stories of books being employed as banks are not rare, and some of our readers may recollect hearing of the difficulty of certain executors in administering to the will of a deceased friend the sum of £700, which was noted as being "in Til." The deceased not having kept a list, the money was given up for lost, until it was remembered that a folio volume of Tillotson was among the books that had been sold. The bookseller's shop was visited in haste, the volume repurchased, and, though a clergyman had had it away for inspection, the sum in bank-notes was found intact.

That many of these valuable MSS. are abstracted and sold away from libraries is a well-known fact. M. Birez, the librarian at Rheims, used to say that no man was to be trusted alone with rare and curious books that did not belong to him. "My dear sir," said he one day to a collector, of whom he had the greatest mistrust, "when you come to the library you shall sit at this table close by me; my pen, ink, and paper shall be at your service; I have such a regard for you that I cannot bear you out of my sight." The gentleman took the hint, and troubled him no more. When Courtois, of the National Convention, so notorious for the abstraction of Marie Antoinette's will, visited the Rheims library, this same M. Sérot, who kept a keen eye on the visitor and his companion, opened a "Horae" of the fifteenth century—one of the gems of the collection. He said nothing until the two were about to depart, when he locked the door, put the key in his pocket, and said: "Gentlemen, have you heard what a suspicious sort of man I am? I have the horrible idea that one of us is a thief. Pardon me the thought: perhaps it is myself; let us see, then, are my pockets emptied? Now it is your turn, M. Bernet." This was the companion of Courtois, who submitted with a good grace; while Courtois himself was turning round and round, coughing, grimacing, and stamping down. "Do not stir, M. Courtois; your turn will come." "Allons," cried the thief, "quel diable d'homme, voilà!" (I see I must give it back), and threw the volume on the table. "Why were you not as capable of your 'Council of Trent?' François de Neufchâteau would not then have made a trophy of it before the First Consul."

THE YOUNG LADY ON A VISIT.

(*A Reminiscence of Lothario Lovemall.*)

BY JAMES M'GRIGOR ALLAN.

"I know a maiden fair to see—
Take care!
She can both false and friendly be—
Beware! beware!
Trust her not—
She is fooling thee!"—LONGFELLOW.

I am still a susceptible man; "but time was," when as a youth I first looked out upon the world from a beautiful American village on the banks of a broad river, that a "young lady" comprised in my mind the sum of all earthly blessings. To see and dream about this exquisite compound of angel and mortal, to know that such beings existed near me, was sufficient to fill my cup of happiness almost to running over—not quite, however. I had "The Pleasures of Hope," a heaven of anticipation to increase my present felicity. My "*tailor*," my "*summum bonum*" would arrive, when I should attain to the privilege of knowing young ladies—of becoming acquainted, through a regular introduction, with those dear *creatures* (what an expressive word creature is, applied to young ladies!) who now flitted about me, "like phantoms of delight," and were discerned dimly through a mist (of bashfulness) in my daily walks abroad, at church, at parties, and at picnics. Thus I should be supremely blest—a man "*totus teresque rotundus*"—equally removed above the storms of adversity, and the vain discontent which disturbs the bosoms of ordinary mortals.

But this bliss was not impatiently desired, but waited for, even as the sensible orthodox clergyman, while painting Paradise in the most alluring colours to his flock, personally enjoys this sublunary world, reconciles himself to the will of Providence, and is in no hurry to quit it for a better. I pass my time, therefore, in delightful reveries, in which I attempt to analyse the probable state of my feelings when I am admitted to the acquaintance of grown-up young ladies. What! shall I dance, promenade, talk, ride, perhaps flirt, with young ladies, and be like other men who can do these things, and still live?

* * * * *

I am older. I am approaching the termination of my fourth lustre. People have begun to call me Mr. Lovemall. I am not vain, I am not conceited; but I am self-reliant, and I wonder that young ladies do not look into my heart and discover the hidden treasure laid up there for somebody. I am getting acquainted with young ladies. I find all my most sanguine anticipations realised; but I have done nothing rash. I have shown no symptoms of the unsettlement of my reason from sudden joy. I question my heart as to the cause of this strange tranquillity, and a voice whispers it is because I am not in love. So I make frantic efforts to fall into this enviable state of feelings. I go out whenever I am asked; I accompany young ladies in walks, in geological and botanizing expeditions. When I hear of a new beauty arrived in T——, I make Herculean efforts to obtain an introduction. I write verses in albums; I accept politely-worded invitations, which, in my ignorance of the world, I do not know are never intended to be accepted; and I go out to the country, and stay for a day or two—ay, sometimes, for the gratification of the young lady or ladies who have bewitched me,—though the old folks wish me decently anywhere else: and I also accept invitations of another kind, which are meant to be accepted, and go for a week and stay a month; and then come partings, which, to quote my favourite poet, Byron,

"Press the life from out young hearts."

Well, these things are not to be done with impunity. I certainly have heartaches occasionally, and I rather think ladies' heartaches on [illegible]; but, unaccountable as it may seem, Cupid's bolt still passes on, leaving me

"In maiden meditation, fancy free."

But who can control his fate? When I least expected it—when I had become proud of the immunity I enjoyed—when with the most [illegible] intentions and the most exalted opinion of my own powers of pleasing I was endeavouring to make myself generally agreeable (imitating the little busy bee in roving from flower to flower, and consequently, I must confess, earning from ill-natured people the character of "an arrant flirt," "a male coquette," "a would-be lady-killer," "a vain coxcomb," "a conceited puppy," "a heartless trifler with female affection," "a gallant gay Lothario," and other titles of a similar complimentary nature)—I fell a victim to "a young lady on a visit!"

"The young lady on a visit" belongs, if I may so express myself, to a class especially dangerous to the peace of mind of susceptible bachelors. Our hearts are proof (at least I know mine was) against beauty which we see periodically, daily or weekly; but beware of "the young lady on a visit!" She is the enslaver, the conqueror, the destroyer! But let me tell my sad tale methodically. Most susceptible men possess refined minds and artistic tastes. Need I say that such was my case? I was in the habit of making pencil-sketches of my friends, which were generally considered happy likenesses. I had long promised to do one for a married friend, a Mr. Jones, and had omitted to fulfil my promise. One day he politely reminded me of the circumstance. I blushed at my forgetfulness. Let me confess, however, that I then discovered that a very beautiful stranger, a young lady, whom I had frequently seen walking with a younger brother of my friend, was staying on a visit at his house. He had mentioned her name more than once, and I, in my dulness and stupidity, had always pictured a maiden-lady of fifty. Who could have imagined that "Miss Primmer" was identical with the young and beautiful stranger? I fly home, I take my sketching materials, and rush to my friend's house. If I thought Miss Primmer beautiful in her walking-dress, what do I think of her now that I behold her in all the ravishing effect of evening costume!

I sit down to my task diligently, perseveringly; I make the sketch of my friend. It is handed about; it is admired. Miss Primmer languishingly remarks she would value such a sketch of herself—"oh! ever so much!" "Aha!" I say to myself, like the war-horse in Job:

"Upon that hint I spake."

I offer, then and there, to take her likeness. Miss Primmer will be delighted, if it is not too much trouble. Then ensues a slight deliberation between Mr. and Mrs. Jones about the propriety of allowing her down, and doing something to her hair, which I overrule. I would not have the graceful arrangement of the hair disturbed on any account.

I am rapt in my delightful occupation. I take no thought of the lapse of time. I make an elaborate drawing. How shall I attempt to render the fair oval face, the large almond-shaped eyes, the ruby lips, the winding raven-black tresses? I spend in a week sketching Miss Primmer, and sigh that I had finished there. At last it is done—that is, I am obliged to say it is finished. Though it is the best I have yet made, on a three-quarter of Bristol-board, with a delicate tinge of carmine for the lips and cheeks, of blue for the eyes, and sepia for the hair, I am quite dissatisfied with it as I look at the incomparable original. I feel how far it comes short of her. But everybody thinks it "beautiful" and "so like;" and Miss Primmer actually has the audacity to say she thinks I have flattered her. I intended to pay her a compliment, but my heart was too full to say more than "Impossible!"

Miss Primmer puts her sketch on the piano, and looks at it admiringly, and says, "I'm sure I don't know how to thank you, Mr. Lovesall, for your kindness."

"Perhaps," says Mr. Jones, "Mr. Lovesall will give us the pleasure of his company to dinner, and spend the evening with us, if not better engaged, and then you will be able to show your gratitude by giving him some music."

On that eventful evening I became Priscilla Primmer's slave. Every song she sang forged a fresh link in my chain. When she sang "Arise, arise, Zuleika," I felt there was little fear of my proving a "false Abdallah" to a Zuleika like Priscilla. She put such expression into "Fly to the desert, fly with me," that I really thought she meant it. I am convinced she was fully persuaded of the truth of those lines—

"For oh! the choice what heart can doubt,
Of tents with love, or thrones without?"

All her songs were about love, which is a ve-

markable peculiarity of young ladies' singing in general; and each seemed to portray more perfectly than the preceding one the state of my own feelings towards herself.

I am generally a pretty acute observer, but I confess, with the exception of Priscilla, what she sung and what she said, I remember nothing distinctly which took place that evening. I have a vague reminiscence of a weak and abortive attempt to play a rubber of whist; and even this would have entirely escaped my memory, but for the vivid anguish that was impressed on the countenance of my partner. Priscilla gave me her hand at parting, and she said: "Good-night, Mr. Lovegall, and thank you again for my picture." These may appear common-place words to the reader. I only know they comforted me exceedingly, for the manner in which they were spoken led me to imagine there was a deeper meaning underneath. So true is it, that women have a way of saying the most trivial things, which gives them a great value for us. I go home repeating those farewell words of Priscilla, occasionally singing scraps from "Zarifa," and other songs to which I had been listening, utterly indifferent to any opinions which passers-by might form as to my sanity.

I lie down "to sleep, but not to rest;" I dream that Priscilla and I, mounted on a swift dromedary, are flying from the pursuit of enraged parents and guardians across the Arabian desert. We are overtaken, not by our parents, but by the simoom, which has also been pursuing us (indeed the whole world appears to have turned against us), and just as we were about expiring, wrapped in a last embrace, I was awakened by the voice of my sister, calling from the bottom of the stairs, "Are you never coming down, Lothario? we have nearly finished breakfast." I go down, at length, humming—

> "Fly to the desert, fly with me;
> Our Arab tents are rude for thee."

"What put that into your head?" says my sister, and a laugh goes round the table. But when did love meet with sympathy from the world?

Several weeks elapse, during which I have seen Miss Primmer daily. It has not escaped my penetrating glance that the younger Jones, a boy, a *stripling of seventeen!* actually presumes to ingratiate himself with Miss Primmer; and that she, as young ladies will do, is very well pleased to watch the unfortunate and ill-starred youth falling desperately in love with her, and even sometimes to flirt with him, when she cannot get a better substitute. Poor fellow! I pitied young Jones, for I soon saw how the case stood, and that she cared nothing for him. It would indeed have been strange to prefer a beardless boy of *seventeen*, to a young man who in another month would complete his twentieth year. But, then, *boys* are so conceited! In spite of the compassion I feel for the poor youth, I reflected that it would serve him right, and prove a good lesson to him.

I and young Jones have been indefatigable in showing Miss Primmer the environs of our beautiful town or village of F——. On the eventful day fixed as the last of her sojourn, we went to look at the College, which is situated on an eminence, and commands a beautiful view of F—— and its noble river. I had Mrs. Jones on my arm, Harry Jones conducted Miss Primmer. Once, as I happened to look behind, I noticed him—impudent young monkey—under pretence of assisting her over a stile, squeezing her hand, which she was endeavouring to get away from him. On our way home we stopped at the public gardens, and here Mrs. Jones left us, either desirous of giving me an opportunity of conversing more unreservedly with Miss Primmer, or "on household cares intent." Then, I rather think master Harry was "nowhere." I must, however, do him the justice to say he was very goodnatured and not at all jealous. He seemed only too glad that I should join my entreaties to his to persuade Miss Primmer to prolong her visit.

Here, then, we made common cause together, and our united eloquence evidently shook Miss Primmer's resolution. Amongst other white lies, my coadjutor completely demolished the character of the captain of the steam-boat the which Miss Primmer was to take her departure that evening: according to his description, the Captain was terribly given to drinking; he had been seen to-day more than "half-slued," and he doubted not that before seven o'clock he would be regularly "spifflicated,"—such was the terrible word by which the narrator expressed the *ne plus ultra* of intoxication.

Poor Miss Primmer turned appealingly to me. "But is it true, Mr. Lovegall? Harry never hesitates at a little embellishment to serve his turn." This was a delicate way of hinting at a fact, which she had long since discovered, that my young friend was a most accomplished fibber. Harry was, meanwhile, winking most furiously at me to support his statement. The Captain was a very handsome dog. I replied: "I am not personally acquainted with Captain Missalequick; but common report certainly describes him as dissipated and *fast*. I will not vouch for the truth of the story that he once sacrificed a valuable cargo of hams to make the fire burn brisker when fuel ran short; nor, that he ever invited his passengers to sit on the boiler to keep it from bursting. These may be fabrications to his discredit, but I believe that, in common with most Yankee Captains, he shares in the prejudice that the safety of human life is not to be weighed against the reputation of making quick trips. I should certainly recommend you to wait till the day after to-morrow, and go with Captain Slowman."

This last shot of mine told pretty well. It was settled that we should leave the matter undecided—that Miss Primmer should return and consult Mrs. Jones. So we spent the intervening time in sauntering about the garden *tête-à-tête*, *à la* Marguerite and Faust. Harry was our Mephistopheles. It was not his policy to interrupt or intrude upon us. He evidently trusted to my influence to persuade Miss Primmer into staying, and, as she lived in his brother's house, he would reap the greatest benefit. No malignant shadow of impending disaster dashed the happiness of this parting interview. What I said, what revelations passed between us must be left to the reader's penetration. I cannot describe our conversation. Her last words, before we arrived at the house, were, "See, poor Harry does look melancholy. You must keep up his spirits, Mr. Loveaall, when I am gone; for I do really think he loves me very much."

The die is cast. Miss Primmer is going. I cannot tell which looks most miserable, Harry or myself, as I bid her farewell on the deck of the steam-boat; I can only get out this sentence—

"I—I—should be—at C—— soon, may I—call?"

"Oh, certainly, I shall be most happy to introduce you to my relations, and I am sure Mr. Jenkins will be delighted to make your acquaintance."

I did not reflect at the time, but afterwards I found myself frequently asking the question—"Who the deuce is Jenkins?"

Women have much greater power over their feelings than men. Miss Primmer was smiling sweetly, as I then fondly imagined, striving to hide her grief by an appearance of good spirits, when the boat swung off from the wharf. She stood at the stern, and waved her handkerchief. I dashed off at full speed; I ran panting and sweating, regardless of wind and limb. I cleared the town, I gained the open banks of the river, and, as I got some head start while the boat was getting under way, I managed to keep up with it for some distance. At last I flung myself, exhausted, on the shore, and watched the last flutter of the handkerchief, and strained my gaze on that receding form, till the steam-boat was lost to view by a winding in the river. The state of my mind might then be described by the words from the opera of La Sonnambula—

"[illegible]"

I never saw Miss Primmer again. Oh, that I had never heard of her! About three weeks afterwards Harry James rushed into my room in a very dishevelled state. He laughed wildly and hysterically as he pointed to a paragraph in a newspaper. I read as follows:

"Yesterday, by the Rev. Mr. Wright, Mr. John W. Jenkins, teacher in the High School of C——, to Miss Priscilla Primmer, only daughter of the late Peter Primmer, Esq."——

I read no more. The perfidious woman had been engaged to the miserable Jenkins all the time she had been flirting with Harry and myself. Harry had now recovered his speech: "And to a poor devil of a schoolmaster, as ugly as he could be, and blind of an eye. I have seen—the villain!"

That day I made two memorable resolutions—to give up all female society, and to die a bachelor. I adhered strictly to both these resolutions for the space of a fortnight, at the end of which period I renewed my acquaintance with a young lady, between whom and myself a mildness had arisen ever since my infancy with—

THE YOUNG LADY OF A VISIT!

LOST.

Gone overseas, and gone from me!
 Break, break, poor heart, and be at rest!
Wild-birds come from over the sea—
 Home, home, home, each one to its nest,
And the sea-birds flash into the waves,
 And the clouds they grow dim and grey!
Ripple and rush, the waters leave
 The sands at the foot of the bay,
And the night comes down like a dream,
 And the world is hushed into sleep;
And a thousand star-lighted gleams
 O'er the waters, who watch and weep;
And Death is the hope of despair;
 And Life only a long, long pain:
Oh! sad heart, and brain with care,
 He comes not—oh, never again!

Bitter it is to question, still,
 If ever more heard of his fate;
Bitter the years that then not kill,
 Bitter a life so desolate!
Oh for the power of the mighty seer!
 To lift the veil of time to his view!
Oh, God! for a voice that I heard,
 Days long gone, to make answer now!
Is he buried far under the dark wave?
 Or lies he [illegible]
Whisper it once, in broken breath,
 Of a love that was once my own!

Gone, gone, gone! Wake up, wild wind—
 Up, till the [illegible] have died away!
Oh! for a voice beyond my kind
 To pour my words and end my prayer,
In song, their [illegible]
 Should [illegible] to the place of repose.
And [illegible], if the power be given,
 [illegible]

Mine—oh! I loved him! And his love
 Was mine. In many a rosy dream
I saw the sunlight break above,
 And the days shone in its gleam.
Oh, but I loved him!—still I ask
 Of [illegible], and then, and hope I guess:
My idle soul [illegible]
 And my life's [illegible] strong and brave;
Fearlessly I [illegible] to him,
 And that, though all the world had gone!
Fearlessly hoped and lived with him,
 Though Fortune's darkest [illegible]

Oh, but I loved him! and he's lost—
 Lost overseas, and lost to me!
Waves are breaking beneath the coast,
 And the wind wails over the sea;
And I listen, listen, listen,
 Here at the close of the day,
And ever they seem to whisper
 Of the loved and the lost away!

H. H. C

REVERSES; OR, THE STRIKE.

(A Tale.)

BY JOHN D. CARTWRIGHT ("MERLIN").

Gilbert Glennan had risen from the workman's ranks, by the aid of energy, skill, industry, self-denial, and long-enduring perseverance. Early in life he made the attainment of wealth an object—in wealth he saw the "open sesame" to all that is desirable upon earth, the ladder by which he might rise to greatness, fame, and a fuller comprehension of the universe. He went bravely to work, and he succeeded. Success is in itself ennobling, if it be achieved by legitimate means—and the good qualities of Mr. Glennan's nature were developed by it.

All men, I think, agree in respecting their successful fellows; just as a schoolboy likes a fellow who has thrashed him. The [illegible] necessary for success are themselves sufficient [illegible] of a man's [illegible]. Be this as it may, there was not a man in Waberly who did not greatly respect Mr. Glennan, both as an honest man and a successful, upright tradesman. His rise was a work of many years, and only achieved by very slow, almost imperceptible degrees.

At his father's death, which occurred when he was sixteen years of age, he might have been seen passing to and from the factory, morning and noon and night, with the other operatives; or sitting with his mother, after work-hours, in a low-roofed, dingy house, whose rooms scarce held the necessaries of life. A few years later and we find him working—in the [illegible] of a [illegible] operative, in the busy time when [illegible] are in large demand—for an hour, or sometimes two, at night, after the factory is closed. And then, with these little hard-won savings, he changes from the factory to a house of his own furnishing, except the [illegible], which is but hired. He has been, with keen foresight, schooled to himself employment, while there is any trade, by cultivating his capacities till his work might be favourably compared with the best [illegible] in Waberly—and this was, perhaps, the greatest adjunct to his ultimate success; for it was the interest of his employer to keep Gilbert Glennan's [illegible] going; but [illegible], by stopping it in a bad time of trade, should he care it in the good one also. Thus there was seldom a time when he had not work to do—it was but the meet reward of his ability and [illegible]; for it was a rule of his, never to break a promise it was in his power to fulfil. Already was the mother proud of her son, as she went to and fro with his work to the warehouse; and it was a still prouder day for both when the last sum was paid for [illegible].

It is not with the rise of Mr. Glennan we have to do in these pages; and we shall not stay to chronicle the events that marked it. With the qualities we have shown him to possess, the reader cannot doubt his ultimate success in life, unless some unexpected event should occur to mar it. Neither will he doubt that it was the result of much self-denial and the work of many years.

At the time our narrative opens, he has succeeded, and is the proprietor of a factory in Waberly—a master, but still a workman in his new sphere, who has the interests of the operatives as much at heart as any man among themselves. Late in life he set himself to study, and cultivated his intellectual, as he had hitherto his business faculties—not, perhaps, with a [illegible] success, but yet sufficiently to ensure himself against the vulgar prejudices and manners which are so prominently the characteristics of men who have risen from workmen to masters. With pure and simple tastes, and but little education, he still knew sufficiently the value of letters, and felt keenly enough his own early wants to ensure an excellent education for his children, of whom there were three; and these, at the time our story opens, together with his wife, form Gilbert Glennan's household. His mother, who had lived long enough to see her son rewarded for his industry, was dead—and well it was, for the subsequent events in his history would have caused her many a bitter pang; and, as it was, she died happily and contentedly, with him she was so justly proud of by her side.

It will readily be admitted, that a man of the temperament we have endeavoured to show Mr. Glennan possessed, was likely to be no rash speculator; nor was he. Shrewd, liberal, with where merit deserved it, generous to the extreme, he was yet a man who [illegible] chances [illegible], and unless there were a few to his favour, nothing would induce him to invest; and this was the cause, the only cause, he gave to many of whom there were not a few in Waberly, capable of saying evil things of him; but they had no influence on his actions; and, let there be ever so many names down to a charity, or a new company, unless he approved the aim and saw the other a safe investment, nothing would induce him to give or to buy. Nevertheless, at the time our tale opens, his entire capital is being consumed in the erection of a new factory and improved machinery, which alone he knows can enable the men of Waberly to compete with those [illegible] of other places in England, or foreign [illegible]. He, therefore, sees in this a ready way to double his own pital; because he will be first in the market—because, without these improvements, Woberly will go to ruin.

"We must keep up in the march of trade, as in that of life," Mr. Glennon said to a large proprietor, who would not embrace the opportunity, and kept his out-of-date modes in operation, while already vigorous capitalists in the North were bringing the improved goods into market and destroying the Woberly trade.

"Why, yes, that's true," said the tardy capitalist; "but we'll wait and see."

"To-morrow we start the steam," said Mr. Glennon, as he sat down to dine with his wife and eldest daughter. "It has been a long work, and an anxious one, too. I was at one time afraid it would stand for want of capital, or that I should have to borrow—and it's overlate in life for me to begin that, when I have done without for so many years, and all uphill work, too; but I should like to purchase the Close, and build my operatives houses."

"Indeed, papa, I do wish that were possible. Aunt Milner and I have been distributing to-day along the lower town, and I am sure we shuddered before the doors, the houses were so dirty!" said Mary, and her father looked with delight on her fair face as she spoke.

It was a face to fill all beholders with delight, sweet, innocent, and beautiful as the face of a flower. Once seen—though it were but for a moment—in the street, such a face would never be forgotten! It seemed to beam with bashfulness, love, and womanliness.

"Ah, I knew it would please you, Mary," her father said; "and it is needless to say how I regret it can't be done—that is, not at present. By-and-bye, when this new place has returned me tenfold, as it must, why, then it shall; and you shall help me when you can."

"Oh, if I could really help in it, do it now, I would give up Paris, music—anything to help it on!" Mary exclaimed; "for I am sure there are hundreds of children die every year through those nasty, crowded, unhealthy houses! Why don't they build such one a house in itself?"

"They do now, because the law compels them; but it will be a long time before those built are taken down, Mary."

"Yes; but why don't they go and live in the new ones, then? I never shall understand it all; but you must not think me tiresome, papa"—and Mary went round to where he sat, and kissed him—"you won't think me troublesome, will you? And I do want to know all about it."

"No: I like you to inquire, Mary, and to feel an interest in these people, with whom my sympathies will always be; for I am, as it were, one of themselves," said her father, passing his fingers down her curls. "But, you see, their earnings are small; and they, not so frugal as they might be, cannot afford to pay the larger rents asked for the new houses—at least, they cannot easily understand that it would be cheaper, as it certainly must in the end, for it would give them health to work on, and save the cost of medicine often."

"Oh, yes, I can understand that; for there is nearly always somebody ill down there; and Milly Shergstone—you know Milly?" said Mary, pausing for her father to answer, and then continuing—"well, Milly's brother Tom is dying of consumption; and I am sure it's all through the nasty place he lives in. Oh, I am so interested in Milly, poor girl! She's been waiting to get married for months; and first her mother dying, then the strike, and now Tom, have put it off; so she will have to wait yet."

"I fear she will, Mary; for trade gets worse instead of better; and Milly is not the girl to get married blindly."

"Of that I am quite sure," said Mary; "and they are so poor now, it takes all the little she might save to get things for her brother."

"Well, when her father goes to work at the new place, we must see about getting them into a new house, where Tom will have a chance."

"And you start to-morrow, pa'?"

"Yes, the steam is getting up now for the first time. It has been a long and anxious time to me, and I have had fears about its success. But I am reassured; and, if trade will keep good, it must succeed."

"And shall you have work for all the old hands?" asked Mary Glennon.

"Not at first; but before long I hope. You see, with this new machinery one loom will do the work of three old ones; and therefore the rate of wages may be, if not increased, at least kept up to the old standard."

"I am so glad of that, pa'; for I am sure the men and women earn little enough now."

"Ah, but they are reducing them now; and there is talk of another strike!"

"I hope there will never be another," said Mary; "for the way they groaned and hooted through the streets quite terrified me. And then all the suffering besides. Oh, I do hope they won't strike!"

"Ah, so do I; but I fear they will. As a body the weavers of Woberly here are behind those of other towns in understanding the interests and workings of their own trade. The manufacturer is, in such a time as this, compelled to pay less for the labour he employs; because it is uncertain when he will sell—because, of all manufactures, this has the greatest risks; and a little caprice of fashion may render his goods valueless in the market. But come, this is not talk for you, Mary: play me some music."

"Oh, papa, don't say it is not talk for me! I want to know all about it, and like it better than music," said Mary, sitting down to the piano, for they had gone from the dining to the drawing-room; but, after playing only a short while, she was again at her father's side, leading the conversation back to the weavers; for somehow this subject was uppermost in her mind. "Millie said Johnson had broken the list; but I did not understand what the list was; though, from her manner, I thought it was a great calamity."

"The list, Mary, is a fixed set of prices, below which all the men have pledged themselves not to work; and a more injurious thing, both for masters and men, could not well be devised; for the price of labour, like the price of silk or any other marketable article, must rise and fall according to supply and demand; if there be no demand, then it will be a drug, and only speculators will purchase it at a reduced price, to ensure an extra profit [illegible] will counterbalance a probable loss. If the weavers understood that old proverb, which tells us 'half a loaf is better than no bread,' they would at once see it was their wisest course to lower the price; for only by this can manufacturers be induced to employ them in all times of depression, and the same hour that brought a new demand would be sure to raise their wages again to the old standard."

"Oh, thank you, I can understand now; and that is why Miller spoke so bitterly about Johnson's breaking the list."

"Yes; and it is sure to be followed by a partial strike—nothing more, I hope; and, as I shall pay more than the ordinary list prices, they will not dare to compel my hands to strike: if they did, it might ruin me. This is the curse of trades' unions—that they will not, sometimes, let those who will pay have work done; and it is the greatest injustice practised in England. As a means of obtaining legitimate ends, and carefully guarding their own interests, a trade union is a blessing; but it is too often made a curse. They get a limit which will barely support life, and are not unfrequently persuaded by crafty [illegible] men to strike where there is no real cause for it, and every strike is the loss of thousands of pounds in the wealth of the country, to say nothing of the many who die—if not of direct and positive starvation, at least prematurely, from disease induced by the want of a sufficient amount of food; when, all the while, but for these existing unions, they might be peaceably at work, promoting their own interests and the wealth of their country—and they are not unfrequently all the while persuaded into the belief that they are suffering martyrdom in a noble cause. The late strike here sufficiently showed this, and the evil that may be worked out of a seeming good; it impoverished the town and drove away the trade; another such strike, and Wakely would have become bankrupt; for there was not a house in the town but suffered by the withdrawal of such a sum as is paid into workmen's hands, and from them weekly into the tradesman's till."

Three weeks later than the conversation we have related above, the streets of Wakely were again filled with men and women, who paraded daily in a body through the streets to their place of meeting, where they heard reports, passed resolutions as to their determination of "holding out till the last," and denounced their employers as "petty tyrants, who would trample them into the dust," and such like phrases.

The masters were losing their orders, credit, and cash; the strike was not half, though this was made the pretext of the contemplated reduction in the list.

The weavers themselves suffered more than it would be well possible to describe: winter had set in with frost and snow, and they had little enough money for bread, none for firing; yet the strike continued, and their cause was right; but few men would admit the righteousness of it, on account of the means they took to enforce it. To band together and intimidate individuals, to stop every loom around the town, was not the way to gain their ends, only to drive away the trade. Yet, under I know not what penalties, they compelled every man to stay work, and down at New-place, where larger wages were paid than had been for years before, they would not let any man work.

"If this continues it will ruin me," said Mr. Glennan, as he entered the drawing-room with a pale, agitated face, and sat down by his wife; "every hour of delay jeopardizes the sale of my ribbons, and there is not a loom going."

Just as he had finished speaking there was a terrific hiss and groan in the street, below the window. His wife ran to the window and looked out.

"Wife, for God's sake keep from their sight; they are infuriated. As I came through the streets they howled upon me like a legion of fiends rather than men."

Mr. Glennan spoke bitterly, as indeed he had cause.

"On you, papa!" exclaimed Mary; "but you do not ask them to work for less wages than before."

"There is the injustice, the malice of it, I say, and am willing to pay even more than now: the improvement in my new machinery will enable me to do it; but this is looked upon by the weavers as a crime, and they treat me, who have ever had their interests at heart, as though I were their one of themselves—as a common enemy to their cause; I, they say, am the cause of this strike. God knows, I have been hitherto their friend; but henceforth—"

"Don't say what you will be in the future, papa," said Mary; "if they do you wrong now, they will see it one day; and, oh dear, it is but a want of education to teach them better. Even in this blindness and stupidity, I think we should pity rather than blame them."

"Perhaps you are right, Mary," said Mr. Glennan—"right, at least, so far as my hands are concerned, for they desire to work; but the laws of their affairs committee-men will not allow them, and, in the meantime, for me there is nothing but ruin."

"Absolute ruin, papa?"

"Yes, positive and absolute bankruptcy. All my money was absorbed in the building and the machinery; indeed, there are some debts; and the materials, for which I owe, and must presently pay, are losing in value every hour. If they had been quickly in the market, they would have returned me profits [illegible]; now they will be too late for the season, unsaleable, and I shall be ruined; the looms may, very probably will, have to be sold to pay for the silk."

Gilbert Glennan was not a man of giving impulses, but the present almost and terrible position of his affairs worked him beyond him-

wife. He got up and paced the room. The procession of the weavers was still moving past his house, and, as they saw his figure by the window, again they groaned and hooted. He sat down and buried his face in his hands, his lips were pale and firmly closed, but his whole frame was shaking with passion, anger, and sorrow. For a long time he remained thus. Mary crossed the room, and sat down by her father, but [illegible] to him as [illegible]—nothing [illegible] to him. But the voice [illegible] unheeded, and the silence was for a long time unbroken. When he did raise his head again it was evident he had been weeping. He was not a man one would think likely to weep; but he one, aye, even the strongest and most stoical of us, in the hour when a great passion has the mastery over our whole being, are thrown to contemplate the altered prospects of the future, and the chances are that, after a struggle, our passion will find vent for its relief, and we shall weep like a child.

So it was with Gilbert Glennan: no petty fear for himself that night had a place in his breast; but, as he sat, the contemplation of a future he had looked forward to with large hope and trust, changed, and he saw the balance of a life likely and [illegible] in a strangely altered sphere.

It is probable, very certain, that in the anguish of the moment his danger and the chances of his ruin were exaggerated; but, with the impending slackness of trade, and the strike, hope was [illegible] him.

"How do they associate your name with the cause of the strike?" asked his wife, when he was calm again.

"It is but the pretext for breaking the list, to meet the indifference of buyers," said Mr. Glennan, "and to combine a few grasping manufacturers, with whom it originated, to realize a larger profit. They say it is impossible for them to pay the present price and compete with the improved machinery. This was the [illegible] given for the general withdrawal of names from the list they had themselves helped to frame and sign a week before. But this was only the pretext for forcing the operatives back to the pernicious weekly wages system, which makes the good and bad workman nearly equal, and does nothing to promote the interest and improvement of our trade. But let us forget it for to-night, at least; to-morrow it must return to our thoughts. I had forgotten, it is Polly's birthday. How old?"

"Eighteen, papa, and almost a woman."

* * * * *

Our scene changes, from Mr. Glennan's house in the new town, to Mr. Hepworth's in the old, of whose daughter [illegible] the previous mention has been made.

It is our object and most earnest endeavour in this narrative to present the reader with a faithful picture—nothing more—of two homes and two families, whose all depends upon the welfare of each other; to show not so much our own view of an ordinary and distressing condition—which is, unhappily, of too frequent occurrence, and has of late years grown from a local distress into a national calamity—as the views of the master and the man.

There is something wrong in the system that does not allow our operatives to profit by improvements, as well as masters and capitalists, and which is always tending to the diminution, instead of increase, of the workman's wages; and, in the scene I am about to sketch, I am sure the kindly-hearted reader will admit that the wages, which is barely sufficient to support life, under such conditions must not be reduced.

Wadsley has grown, in a comparatively short time, from an unnoticed, obscure place, into a densely-populated town, with a multiplicity of interests, but mainly depending on that manufacture which the caprices of fashion do so much towards increasing or destroying. It is distinguished, one part from the other, by the adjectives Old and New; and, to a stranger, it would be difficult to realize that they were part of one place, so different are they in their buildings, streets, and character of the inhabitants.

Reader, who hast been with us in Glennan's in the New Town, accompany us now to Hepworth's in the Old. In the former, you had a slight though fair representation of the house-hold and sentiments of a master, an unpretending, worthy, self-made man; and now it is our purpose to show you the home and the opinions of a man who belongs to the operative class of Wadsley, and is "on strike."

The streets look, not less than he was, the change in passing from the New Town to the Old. The very air seems changed, and crowded, like the families, into a space too little for its well-being; the narrow streets, with the upper storeys of the houses bulging out, and darkening the pavement in the brightest day, are full of children, who shout and scream—some at play, some crying, some kissing, quarrelling, or fighting; while a little baby is let down to squall upon an adjacent doorstep, others sitting, or flattening their noses against the dirty glass of a huckster's window. In such a street, so surrounded, abode Millie Hepworth and her father. The bare naked walls were unconcealed by the few pieces of furniture, which were strewn about the floor, some of which had suffered loss of limb, or infirmity of some kind; the windows were patched with paper, and the little fragment of looking-glass which rested against the sash was half hid in cobwebs. In one corner of the room was a rude kind of couch, on which lay Millie's brother Tom, and his pale emaciated face told unmistakably of the malady which was gnawing at his heart. Millie was near the fire, intent over some household work, from which she ever and anon turned to look if Tom were still asleep; she had all a girl's love of neatness and order, but it was impossible to keep order there; for there were none of the adjuncts,—nothing to help to order. There was an unnatural, careworn expression in her features, which gave her the appearance of a middle-aged woman rather than a girl of twenty years; her hair was neatly braided in two plaits, indeed all connected with her appearance was neat, and her face, but for its troubled expression, might have been called pretty, as justly and certainly it was interesting. She was still hovering about the fireplace, when a little bare-headed, ragged child, whose face had evidently not known the wholesome influence of soap and water for a very considerable time, came rushing in.

"Hush," said Millie, looking toward the couch; "hush, Willie!"

The child stopped, looked at the sleeper, and then, going softly up to Millie, said, "Davis says he'll come to yer." After which he crept stealthily to the door, and ran into the street, with a shout and a laugh. Presently there came a knock at the door.

"Come in," said Millie, gently; and a dingy, [illegible]-like man, with his sleeves rolled up, entered.

"Oh, Mr. Davis!"

"Father at home?"

"No; he's gone to the meeting," said Millie, looking sorry towards the sick man, who moved round and opened his eyes. "Will you come to the door, and I dare say I shall do as well as father." Then, when they had reached the door, so as to be out of hearing, she continued: "I didn't want him to hear. It grieves him and makes him worse."

"You see, I'm sorry," began Mr. Davis (who was a baker), "but the missis's been this morning, and he says I must pay."

"Yes," said Millie, who had guessed rightly the cause of his visit, and partly from want of anything better to say.

"You know I ain't begun long, an' if he won't let me 'ave flour, I can't—though it goes agin the grain—let yer 'ave more bread. I says to him, says I, They're on strike; but he says that ain't no reason to him, and if I don't pay, he won't send me not another sack o' flour. It's very hard on him, very."

"Yes," said Millie again, while her face assumed a more careworn expression than ever.

"Well," says the baker, I thought it best just to come myself, because it wouldn't seem so hard like to me. You'll tell your father? Good morning."

He turned away with a sharp stop, as if he couldn't trust himself to look longer at Millie's troubled face. When he had gone a little way he turned to look back; she was still there, and he returned.

"If you could pay me for a little on now."

Millie assured him her last shilling had gone for Tom's medicine.

"Well, send the chap back; only you must pay when you get it from the fund. What does it run to now?"

"Seven shillings a week. Good morning, and God bless you, Mr. Davis!" said Millie; and the little urchin was recalled with difficulty from a noisy group of his playfellows to go back to the shop again; from whence he returned with a loaf, of which he was trying the quality as he came along.

"What'll come of us all, to be sure?" sighed Millie, as she re-entered the house. But her brother was coughing so badly she had no time for the solution of that terrible question.

Poor Millie's sorrows and troubles were many. The day for her wedding with George Hughes had been twice appointed: first the strike took all the little they had saved; then, when trade got good and there was plenty to do, they had to pay what "was run bad," before they could save again; and when they had done that, Tom got worse, and of course Millie stayed to nurse him. And now the looms were all still again, and likely to remain so for a long time. Her brother grew worse and weaker day by day.

"Oh, what'll become of us all, in the winter?" this was the thought that by day and by night haunted the brain of Millie Hepworth.

Her father and George came in from the meeting together, and Millie finished as she placed chairs for them, cut out the loaf, about which Davis had been thinking, and which was their only chance of dinner, before them.

"Are you going in, George?" Millie asked.

"No; [illegible] it [illegible] time we [illegible] since we first struck," said George. "How's your cough to-day, Tom?"

Tom appeared to [illegible] to speak; but did not utter half-a-dozen words ere his cough [illegible] and gave no more answer.

There was a silence after this, and then Millie asked again, "What do the committee say about it?"

"Just the same as yesterday, only they have sent deputations to Derby and Coventry for subscriptions, though I heard it's worse at Coventry than here," said Mr. Hepworth. "Ghosses's got out a paper saying why his hands are forced to strike with the rest, when he pays the list."

"Well, it does seem a shame," said George; "an yet it's 'bliged to be; they'd never come in, if we let some of 'em go on while others were out."

"They say it'll ruin him," said Hepworth, "though all he's bin spendin' lately, that he never broke the list yet."

"Ah! but he's signed agen it. Here's his name next to Johnson's," said George, pulling out a paper, with a list of names, and a few paragraphs on it, "and the committee say he's as big a tyrant as any on 'em."

"What does it say, George?" asked Millie.

"Well, mostly, as they want free-trade in labour—which means no list; so they can lower the wages."

"I don't believe that's it with Ghosses; leastways he allers payed me well, and seemed to take an interest in all on us as well as Wood."

"They're single workers as have been workmen themselves," said George, "though they make such a fine talk of our interests and all that."

"It be said as the French Treaty's doing it all; but, Lor', ain't we bin without work, and had to strike when we wouldn't be trampled on afore ever the treaty was thought about at all."

said Hepworth; "and if we let 'em beat us now, we'll never be what they have been—and we don't now get as much as our fathers did, when they couldn't make half so much or half so well hot as we can."

"How much are they going to allow out of the fund this week?" inquired Millie.

"None till next. Subscriptions haven't come in, and the committee says they can't pay."

"What'll become of us all, to be sure!" said Millie, and then told them what Doyle said.

Truly the prospect was terrible, with that sick, dying brother there, and without money for food and medicine. The doctor came without pay, else, thought Millie, he might have died before this—and then (God forgive her for the thought!) she wished he had, and she too with him. The world seemed to her not to have food enough for them all; and waiting, weeping, and watching had wearied her out. It was winter; the cold was intense, and there was no hope of George or her father getting work of any kind to do.

Every day there were meetings and speeches on the common, where thousands assembled. The masters would not meet the men while they adhered to the list. The hunger and the cold gave evidence of its work by swelling the bills of mortality, yet they refused all offers of lower prices, and suffered on, even to the extreme of deadly suffering; indeed, so firm were the men and women of Wolverly, that they looked upon themselves as martyrs in a noble cause. If here and there an operative commenced work without consent, and broke the list, he was hooted through the streets. The "petty tyrants" (as manufacturers were too frequently called) never appeared without receiving marks of displeasure; but these never extended to violence. The whole city suffered; and the pale, wan faces and shrunken forms of the weavers told their own sad tale.

"Millie, I'll go for a soldier," said George, as they were parting one night.

"A soldier, George?"

"Yes; and if they kill me, so be it. 'Twon't be half so bad as this. I can't stay to see you like this any longer, and I'll go for Queen and Country."

"Oh! not for a soldier. Anything but that. Spring is coming, and you might get work in the country, on a farm—or——"

"No; it's a soldier I'll be, Millie. We may wait and wait here till it kills us before we shall get married. Why the Lord alone knows how we have lived since Christmas, and I can't stand it any longer. Hark, there's Tom coughing again. I'll be in to-morrow."

Millie was weeping. Her tears fell upon his cheek as he kissed her "good-night."

"Good-night, George. You'll come before you go to—to——"

"Be a soldier? Yes," said he, moving away, while Millie went into the house.

George came in the next day. Tom was dead—and that day he forgot his idea of becoming a soldier.

That day Hepworth, coming home from the meeting, met George.

"Glennan is a bankrupt," said he, sadly.

"Poor Tom is——" said George, in a wild sad voice.

"What?"

"Dead."

*

The strike is over. The looms are again as noisy as ever. Men have lost the whole toil of their lives uselessly; others have perished in the struggle. The masters have not triumphed; the men have not maintained their list; but both have suffered—suffered beyond the power of words to describe.

Mr. Glennan, reduced in circumstances, has returned to his old place; and the new one (on which he spent so much anxious thought, and for which he had toiled many days and nights) has gone to benefit some wealthy man, sold for scarce half its value.

"Thank God it is only loss of money—not honour," said Mr. Glennan to his wife and daughter; still he felt severely that, which we all find so difficult, the first step down the ladder of fortune. But he was far from the bottom. When every debt was paid, he had a good residuum wherewith to start again.

"Oh! never heed it, father," said Mary; "it is but six years' work."

"Six years, Mary, of walking over the ground we have once successfully trodden is weary work."

"Not to the man of good faith."

Two days later than the conversation recorded above, Millie Hepworth came to Mary Glennan.

"You were always so kind," said Millie, "that we come to you, Miss, instead of to your father."

"You know I will do anything I can for you."

"Yes, I do know it, and thank you I'm sure. George and me, you see, Tom's dead now, and it's no use waiting till we are better off, because it would never be at all if we did."

"What would never be, Millie?"

"The marriage. George says if your father 'ud let him have the house near the factory, he'd be a sort of protection like to the place, and father 'ud help pay the rent."

"I can promise you so much, Millie."

Three weeks later, Millie and George stood by the altar on a sweet spring morning, from whence they came forth man and wife.

Thus, dear reader, we will leave them. May it be long ere there be another strike at Wolverly! The strike-system is the most hateful and pernicious one [illegible] as practised in England. It impoverishes the locality, ruins the capitalist, and not unfrequently kills the workman. Six years hence and the consequences of that one in Wolverly, which lasted six months, will still be felt by both workmen and master; for more than [illegible] years' toil was utterly destroyed by it.

THE WIDOW OF THE LAST OF THE STUARTS.

On the 17th of April, 1772, a marriage was celebrated in the chapel of the castle of Macerata, near Ancona. The day was Good Friday—a day of ill-omen, especially in Catholic Italy, for such a ceremony. The black draperies of Lent had been replaced by hangings of cloth of gold; the canopy, beneath which the bridal pair were to receive the nuptial blessing, was surrounded by the royal arms of England, and the blaze of innumerable tapers flashed back from the jewelled vestments of the officiating cardinal and his attendant priests. Notwithstanding all this pomp, however, the little chapel looked strangely sombre, as if in keeping with the wedding-party, who awaited before the altar the bride's arrival. Among that group the eye looked in vain for those bright young faces which most especially befit such an occasion. It was almost entirely composed of persons past the prime of life, and, excepting the few Italians who came prepared to look on with curiosity or indifference, of faded Jacobite gentlemen and their wives who shared the exile and blasted fortunes of the last of the Stuarts. The bridegroom was Charles Edward himself, but his person had preserved hardly a trace of the "tall youth of a most agreeable aspect," at whose first appearance in the camp of Preston Pans, some twenty-seven years before, Æneas Macdonald had found his heart "knit to the very throne." The grandson of James the Second was now fifty-two, his features were bloated by long habits of intemperance, and he was so listless and gouty that he could hardly rise without assistance at the approach of his bride, who, accompanied by her mother and a few attendants, entered the chapel by a side door. We can hardly believe but that at that moment the mother at least must have been painfully struck with the contrast between her beautiful daughter and the man on whom she was about to bestow her. The biographer of the Princess Louise of Stolberg draws a very prepossessing picture of her at the period of her marriage. "She was," says Von Reumont,* "charming, graceful, and vivacious, fond of literature, without pedantry, and of art, without a shade of affectation; she was of middle height, her hair fair, she had very lovely blue eyes, with the dazzling complexion and carnation bloom of a nymph in one of the paintings of her favourite master, Rubens." By her father's side the Princess was sprung from one of the noblest families in Thuringia; through her mother she claimed descent from Robert Bruce and the ancient Kings of Scotland. So distinguished by her birth, beauty, and talents was the young Countess, whom the policy of Louis the Fifteenth had called, in her nineteenth year, from the love and admiration of all who surrounded her, to a foreign country, to be the companion of a man more than thirty years her senior, a Prince broken in reputation and fortune, and sunk both in mind and body through degrading indulgences.

A few days after the ceremony, the newly-married couple made a semi-royal entrance into Rome, to take up their residence in the Palazzo Muti, the palace which had been the home of the Stuarts for upwards of half a century. Here the son of James the Second had kept up an imposing Court; the Papal troops mounted guard and saluted him when he left the palace, by order of the Pope, who formally acknowledged him as King of Great Britain. But times were changed since his death. The Hanoverian succession was now firmly established, and the present Pontiff felt no inclination to embroil his Government by recognizing the claims of the exiled family. In vain Charles Edward notified the arrival of the King and Queen of England [illegible] formally notified to Clement the Fourteenth. The Pope ignored his title. In Rome he was to be plain Charles Stuart, or, at most, the Count of Albany, the name under which he always travelled.

With this blow to her ambition, at the outset of her marriage Louise's unhappiness began. At the very least she had expected the honours of Queen, and found it a bitter disappointment to sink at once into a simple countess. It was, too, all the more bitter, because her pretensions to a higher title shut her out from the salons where she must have reigned through her charms and her talents. At that period the high society of Rome was unusually brilliant, while the young wife languished in solitary state, shut up in the dreary Palazzo Muti, her sole companions an uncongenial husband, and the few Jacobites who made up the shadow of his court; her sole amusement to listen, for the hundredth time, to the story of his Scotch adventures. But Louise need not have found life at the Muti palace so intolerable as it speedily became to her. The duties of her situation might have called out all that is at once most lofty and most tender in the nature of her sex. There have been women, in whom the spectacle of a man so fallen and so wounded by fortune as Charles Edward, would have awakened the deepest sympathy, women whose unselfish affection might have allayed the bitterness of personal disappointment, and sweetened adversity itself; whose companionship would suffice to arouse a man's better nature, and to strengthen him to meet the ills of fortune in a manner befitting his dignity. Had Louise de Stolberg been one of that sisterhood, her presence would doubtless have exercised a most beneficial influence over the remaining years of the last of the Stuarts. But

* Die Gräfin von Albany, von Alfred von Reumont. 2 vols. Berlin, 1860.

her character was cast in a very different mould; ambitious, selfish, and shallow, eager for admiration and applause, she refused every duty, the fulfilment of which was irksome, and which offered no gratification to her vanity or her self-love. She took no pains to hide her weariness of the restraint and tedium of her life, and her husband soon became the object of her cold aversion. So greatly disappointed in his last hopes, the unhappy prince fell again into the intemperate habits which he had shaken off on his marriage. Violent when he was drunk, and miserable in his sober intervals, he became, within a few years, almost as contemptible to himself as to his wife, whom he often ill-treated in his paroxysms of rage.

In 1774 the Pretender removed to Florence. The letters of English residents in that city are filled with details of his miserable state. His disorders had considerably damaged his health; he had become an object of pity and contempt to all who saw him, was rarely sober, and was frequently carried out of the theatre by his servants in a state of intoxication. "Every one sees that he is odious to his wife, whom he locks up and mistreats in every possible way," writes Sir Horace Mann, from Florence, in the November of 1779. Even then the countess was meditating her escape; but this was no easy matter to effect, for her husband compelled her to be constantly with him, and whenever he left the house without her, [illegible] locked her up till his return. At length, however, in the December of the following year, Louise and her confederates laid a plan for an evasion, which was carried out cleverly enough. One morning her chief confidante, a certain Madame Orlandini, proposed, at the breakfast-table, that the countess should go to see some extremely beautiful needlework at a convent near Florence. Louise made a show of asking her husband's permission. He gave it unsuspectingly, and himself accompanied the two ladies. Arrived at the convent, an Irish gentleman, who was in the secret, rang the bell; the countess and her friend entered, and the door instantly closed upon them. The gentleman returned to the carriage, from which the Pretender was slowly descending.

"Upon my word, Sire," he cried, with affected indignation, "these nuns don't understand manners, they have absolutely shut the door in my face."

Charles Edward still suspected nothing. "They will open it to me," he said, as he knocked loudly; but after knocking repeatedly, he became alarmed and angry, and shook the door so violently that the abbess herself appeared at the wicket.

"Signor," she said, with the utmost calmness, "the Countess of Albany has taken refuge in our house; she is here, under the protection of her Imperial and Royal Highness the Grand-duchess of Tuscany."

With this short explanation the wicket was closed, and the Abbess disappeared, leaving Charles Edward to digest the announcement as best he might.

During the following day, while the Pretender was addressing complaints and entreaties to the Arch-duke Leopold, Louise, on her part, was not less busy, and with much better success than her husband. The reply which her brother-in-law, Cardinal York, made to her appeal for his protection and an asylum at Rome, is still extant. He writes in a tone of grave and indignant sympathy, promises her his countenance and aid in the most affectionate terms, and offers, under the approval of his Holiness, the fugitive a home in the Ursuline convent at Rome, where his mother had passed many years. A papal brief confirmed Cardinal York's offer, and as soon as she had received this the countess prepared to depart for Rome. Under so august a sanction, and protected by an escort of the Tuscan troops, she might fairly have pursued her journey in broad daylight without fear of interruption. But the vanity and romance of Louise's disposition were flattered by a mysterious departure at nightfall, by a guard of mounted cavaliers, who surrounded the coach, and the protection of two gentlemen, who took their places on the box, disguised as coachmen, and armed to the teeth. One of these had played his part at the scene before the convent at Florence; the other was no less a personage than Alfieri, the poet-noble of Piedmont, whose life was afterwards to become so fully identified with that of Louise d'Albany. In 1777, three years before the flight of the countess, Alfieri, after wandering through Europe, settled once more in Florence, with the purpose of learning the pure Tuscan tongue, then almost a foreign language to his countrymen. He first saw the royal countess, then at the age of five-and-twenty, in the zenith of her charms, at the theatre, obtained an introduction, and forthwith became a frequent visitor at the Palazzo [illegible]. He it was who had persistently urged Louise to abandon her husband; who had secretly arranged the plan of her escape, and had procured the Grand-duke's protection. Of this side of the affair Cardinal York was kept in total ignorance, or he would never have sanctioned the step his sister-in-law had taken.

Louise had now gained all the substantial ends of her flight; she was secure from her husband's brutal ill-treatment, had been received in Rome by the cardinal with every mark of affectionate respect, and installed in the Ursuline convent. But to her the convent was merely a temporary refuge, and she speedily became quite as anxious to escape from the tutelage of her brother-in-law as she had been from the violence of her husband. Early in the following spring she took advantage of the cardinal's absence to regain her liberty, and, under the pretence of ill-health, exchanged the cloister for his splendid palace in the suburbs of Rome. Up to this period the woman, beautiful, young, and unhappy, who had been driven by the brutalities of her husband to take refuge in a religious house, had excited universal sympathy; but now, even Roman society, tolerant as it was disposed to be in such matters, was scandalised to see the [illegible]

[illegible] Cancellieri damaged with [illegible], and the wife not only holding a court as if triumphing in her abandonment of her husband, but receiving the daily visits of Alfieri, who had taken a villa in the neighbourhood. Degraded as Charles Edward had become, he was not insensible to the reports which reached his ears. He wrote to his brother at Frascati, entreating his interference; Cardinal York returned to Rome, and obtained a papal brief for Alfieri's banishment from that city. In the winter of 1783 the Pretender procured a formal separation from his wife, who profited at once by her liberty to join Alfieri on the French side of the Alps.

Few human histories better deserve the name of a social tragedy than this, now, for the first time, completely unravelled by Von Reumont's historical researches. Its characters: a prince, degraded to a miserable drunkard; the poet, who drove so grandly a guilty passion; and a woman, who refused that restraint of the moral law, without which there can neither be true dignity nor real happiness.

From such gloomy considerations we turn gladly to the light thrown upon the scene by the reappearance of the daughter, who came forward to fulfil those duties which the wife had abandoned. More than thirty years before, Miss Walkinshaw, a Scotch lady of rank, with whom Charles Edward had made a left-hand marriage, had given birth to an infant, who received the name of Charlotte Stuart. This daughter he had not seen since she was a child of six years' old. To her the desolate old man now turned, as the single hope left to his cheerless age. For the last time Charles Stuart exercised his royal prerogative in legitimising his daughter, under the title of the Duchess d'Albany, and then summoned her from her convent at Meaux to superintend his household. With her arrival in 1784, brighter days came for the unhappy prince. The duchess was one of those gracious and high-souled women, whose very presence is salutary. She reinstated the Pretender's disorderly household, and wrought a still more beneficial change in her father's habits. Her filial piety surrounded him with every care, and had a certain influence over his last years. Accompanied by his daughter, Charles Edward paid a last visit to Rome in the winter of 1785. Her intervention brought about a reconciliation between him and Cardinal York, who had quarrelled with his brother, and procured him a reception both respectful and friendly from Pius the Sixth. In spite of the tender care bestowed on him, the old man's health was fast declining. His intellect became clouded at times. He seemed to live only in the recollections of his youth. It is touching to observe how incessantly his thoughts turned to Scotland, as the scene of the brilliant promise of his youth. He was possessed by a desire to visit the Highlands once again, and after his death a casket, containing twelve thousand sequins, which he had set aside for this purpose, was found under his bed. Soon after Charles Edward had reinstalled himself in the Muti palace, an Englishman, a friend of Fox, paid him a visit. The stranger led the conversation to the events of '45. At first, says Von Reumont, the prince kept reserved, cold and distracted; but, as his interlocutor went on, his demeanour suddenly changed. A light came into his eyes, his whole face grew alive with feeling as he began the history of his campaign with the enthusiasm of youth. His marches, his battles, his wanderings, and adventures, the broken-down old man was once more the hero of them all! But when he dwelt upon the devotion of the Highlanders, of the melancholy fate which befell so many who had taken into the field his badge—"a throne or a grave," the words died upon his lips, Charles Edward fell back in his chair and fainted away under his emotion. In 1788, on the 30th of January, a day fatal to his house, Charles Stuart expired in the arms of the Duchess Charlotte. She herself fell soon afterwards into a lingering illness, and in the course of the next year, followed her father to the grave. We dwell with a loving regret on the memory of this true Cordelia, who left the silence of the cloister for the fulfilment of so high a duty, and having fulfilled it, sank into the silence of the tomb.

It is time we should return to the brilliant countess, who had now fixed her residence in Paris. Here the news of her husband's death reached her. Alfieri himself says that she was deeply affected by it, and we can well suppose that the contrast between her own conduct and that of the duchess, the thought that her place by that death-bed had been filled by another, might sting the faithless wife into some access of remorse. However bitter her feelings at the moment [illegible] was not the woman to cherish them long; indeed, she seemed bent upon forgetting them amidst increased stir and gaiety. Hitherto she had led a retired life, much more in accordance with Alfieri's misanthropic disposition than her own; but from this date she threw open her hotel to the literary and aristocratic world of Paris. Charles Edward's widow was now free to marry Alfieri; but, paradoxical as it may seem, her pride forbade this step. Faithless to her marriage vows, she was clinging [illegible] to the shadow of royalty they had bestowed upon her; she glorified herself as the "adorata persona" of the poet, who, on his part, flattered his vanity with the love of a royal Beatrice, and by no means wished her to resign her sounding title in his own. Charles Edward's widow styled herself Queen of Great Britain. Her servants wore the royal liveries, and addressed their mistress as "Your Majesty." In her principal saloon stood a throne, with a canopy, surmounted by the Royal Arms of England.

In 1791 our self-named queen paid a visit to England, and her conduct on that occasion strangely marks, as it seems to us, the hopeless confusion of false sentiments as regarded true dignity. We need not trouble Herr Von Reumont for some details of her visit, we have them before us written with a far lighter pen than any German ever handled. Let us see how Horace Walpole gossips over her in his letters to the

Miss Berry. "The Countess of Albany," he says, "is not only in England, in London; but at this very moment, I believe, in the palace of St. James's—not restored by as rapid a revolution as the French, but, as was observed last night at supper at Lady Mount Edgcumbe's, by that topsy-turvyhood that characterises the present age. Within these two months the Pope has been burnt at Paris, Madame du Barry mistress of Louis Quinze, has dined with the Lord Mayor, and the Pretender's widow is presented to the Queen of Great Britain. That curiosity should have led her here, I do not quite wonder, still less that she abhorred her husband; but methinks it is not very well-bred to his family, nor very sensible. Well! I have an exact account of the interview between the two queens from one who stood close to them. The Dowager was announced as Princess of Stolberg. She was well-dressed, and not at all embarrassed. The king talked to her a good deal, but about her passage, the sea, and general topics; the queen in the same way, but less. Then she stood between the Dukes of Gloucester and Clarence, and had a good deal of conversation with the former, who perhaps may have met her in Italy. Not a word between her and the Princesses, nor did I hear of the Prince; but he was there, and probably spoke to her. The queen looked at her very earnestly. It is not a piece of her going to court that she ends with the royal arms."

On the 3rd of June, a few days afterwards Walpole is writing again: "Well! I have seen Madame Albany, who has not a rag of royalty about her. She has good eyes and teeth, but I think can have had no more beauty than remains, except youth. She is civil and easy, but German and ordinary. Lady Aylesbury made a small assembly for her on Monday, and my curiosity is satisfied." So far the malicious letter-writer of Strawberry-hill.

On the 11th of the same month we find Hannah More telling a friend how "the Bishop of London carried me to hear the king make his speech in the House of Lords. As it was quite new to me, I was very well entertained; but the thing that was most amusing of all was to see among the ladies, the Princess of Stolberg, wife to the Pretender, sitting just at the foot of that throne which she might once have expected to mount; and what diverted the party, when I put them in mind of it, was that it happened to be the 10th of June, the Pretender's birthday, 'I knew the accent to be very much like her.'" Dear old single-minded prim Hannah More! To our mind, "the thing which was most amusing of all," to repeat her words, must have been the strong likeness between the Muse of the Italian tragedian and the discreet friend of Bishop Porteus.

Madame Albany, as Horace Walpole calls her, did not realise the expectations with which she had crossed the Channel. She had hoped to meet the same deference from the highest English society as she had received among the aristocracy of Paris. But she found herself completely disappoint-ed. The Royal family looked coldly on her. The Whig nobility had little sympathy for the Pretender's widow; those of the other party who still entertained a leaning to the Stuarts, felt still less for his faithless wife. This explains the severe judgment which Louise passed upon England after her six months' sojourn there. Neither taste, love of art, nor charm of society, she declares, are to be found among us. "If it were not for political liberty, the only advantage the island enjoys, England would be the last country, the English people the lowest nation in Europe." So writes the countess upon her return to Paris in October, 1791. She entered with double zest into the life and brilliancy, then at its zenith, of its society—a life and brilliancy still undarkened by shadows from the terrible events close at hand. Even after the first outbreak of the Revolution, she lived in her circle of literary and political friends; while Alfieri shut himself up in his study, continuing, as he said in his memoirs, to know nothing and know nothing of this tragical farce ("questa tragica farsa") of the French Revolution. With a self-absorption, intensely characteristic of the poet, he occupied himself with his autobiography, while the whole framework of society was breaking up about him, while his personal acquaintances were daily being dragged off to prison, and the guillotine. Not till after the massacre of the 10th August, 1792, was the tragedian brought to consider that the Revolution might not be equally disposed to ignore him, in return, and that Madame d'Albany and himself might be numbered among its victims. They now resolved upon flight. Alfieri procured passports with some difficulty, and on the 18th of that month, they started for Belgium.

At the barrier they were stopped by the National Guard, the passports were examined, found in rule, and the sergeant gave the order for the two coaches which held them and their attendants to pass. At this moment a troop of sans-culottes turned, half-drunk, from a neighbouring cabaret, drew themselves up about the carriages, vociferating: "Here are the rich carrying the bread of the poor away from Paris!" At this cry the populace came pouring down from street to street; a mob of furious faces stopped and crowded round the fugitives. The sight of great danger, the voices of the crowd, hoarse with rage, their threats of setting fire to the carriages, and the ominous yell—"A la lanterne les aristocrates!" "A l'Hôtel de Ville les aristocrates!"—overpowered the countess. She fainted away, and would have been dragged from her coach, had not Alfieri leaped out among the mob—"Look at me well," he cried, in a voice of thunder; "here is my passport. I am not French, but Italian—look, this, my hair red. I come hither to-day to pass, and I swear, by heaven, that I will pass!"

The poet's calm bearing, the prestige of his lofty air, awed the sans-culottes. For a minute the throng gave way under that influence, so subtle and so wonderful, of the man of genius over the many—a power to which the populace of Paris are eminently susceptible, and to which they yielded in some of the wildest scenes of the Revolution. By this momentary lull Alfieri profited; he threw himself into the carriage, gave a signal to the guards, the barriers flew open, and the horses left Paris at full speed. Nor had the escape been made by any means too soon; only two days afterwards a troop of National Guards appeared at the hotel, with an order to arrest Louisa Stolberg, Queen of England. The fugitives were enrolled on the list of emigrants, and the property they had left behind declared confiscate. All Madame D'Albany's plate and furniture, Alfieri's magnificent library, and the splendid stud of English horses—which the poet loved almost equally with his books—were sold by auction, and the proceeds swept into the public coffers.

After a short stay in Belgium, the Countess fixed her residence in Italy. Her house, in Florence, is still known as the Casa d'Alfieri, and bears the inscription—

"Here Alfieri,
Prince of Tragedians,
Lived and wrote his plays:
Here he died."

He added a theatre to the house, and all the first society of Florence flocked to the representation of his tragedies, in which the author himself took the principal character. Here he devised those sonnets in which he idealises his passion in almost mystic language. If we are to believe the poet, not a shade of jealousy or mistrust ever darkened the serene happiness he shared with his royal Beatrice. But the reality differed somewhat from the poetic fiction. Louisa de Stolberg was not to be spared the bitterness in store for every woman who forsakes her duty. Alfieri was by no means faithful to her, and she found him, after his own fashion, almost as much of a tyrant as Charles Edward had been. His morbid sensitiveness and irritability of disposition kept her in constant disquiet. There were constant storms to be appeased; she was compelled to subscribe to all his opinions—even to appear to sympathise with his frenzied aversion against the French, whom she loved in her heart as much as Alfieri hated them. In vain Louisa strove to make herself the centre and the queen of Florentine society; her companion was often so brusque and sullen in his manners that she had the mortification of seeing many who came with the deepest admiration for the poet, leave the Casa d'Alfieri in disgust at the haughty rudeness of its master. The dramatist troubled himself little enough about society; his chief pleasures were his studies and his horses. The Florentines used to see him, day by day, wrapped in a large scarlet mantle, his long red hair flying in the wind, driving furiously four-in-hand through the quiet, unfrequented roads near Florence. After many hours of this violent exercise, he shut himself up in his study till far into the night, allowing scant repose either to body or mind. At the same time, he regulated his diet, as he did everything else, according to his own strange caprice, refusing all aliment except of the lightest description; and this even he would only take in small quantities, under the notion that food clogged his imagination. As might be expected, Nature was not slow to assert her laws when violated so recklessly. In 1802, Alfieri was prostrated by an illness. It returned in the following year with still greater severity, but his state was not thought dangerous. On the 7th of October, in the early morning, he felt better; he raised himself in bed, and just as the first rays of the sun fell upon his noble wasted features, sank gently back. The poet had died, in Madame d'Albany's own words, "without a struggle, without agony, without knowing that it was death."

After Alfieri's decease, Madame d'Albany's inconsolable sorrow for her poet was the topic of Florence. Many people were charitable enough to believe her privately married to him, and those who did not could still in an age and country of lax morality respect the love which had been faithful to its object for more than a quarter of a century, and had now received the consecration of the grave. To the letters of condolence addressed to her, Louisa wrote in reply that death would henceforth be a real happiness. "I detest life," she says, "the world, and all that passes in it. I lived for one object alone, and that has been taken from me." She survived Alfieri only for the purpose of erecting the stately monument over his remains, which she engaged Canova to execute, for the sake of preparing his manuscripts for publication—and then, her work fulfilled, she was ready to follow her hero to the grave. So much the world looked for as the climax of the romance; but within a few months, the world laughed to see a French artist, François-Xavier Fabre by name (a man the junior by many years of Mdme. d'Albany), established in the Casa d'Alfieri as the poet's successor. She appears speedily to have reconciled herself to the loss of Alfieri, and no doubt rejoiced in secret to be free from the restraints imposed upon her by his rugged misanthropy. From this time she became, as Lady Morgan says, "the Queen of Florence." Distinguished foreigners from all parts of Europe, literary men and women, painters, poets, and sculptors—all were welcome at the Casa d'Alfieri, and all confessed that charm of manner which the Countess retained to an advanced age. Few women have been gifted with more social genius than Charles Edward's widow; she had a vivacity of expression, joined to a certain gracious dignity which suited well with her pretensions; she enjoyed conversation, and had not only the art of talking well herself, but the far rarer faculty of making other people talk their very best. But the person of the once-beautiful princess had lost, as Walpole says, "every air of Royalty." Chateaubriand, who saw her in 1803, thus described the Countess in her old age: "I knew Mdme. d'Albany in Florence," he says in his Mémoires. "Old age had produced an effect entirely contrary to

[illegible]

L. F. P.

THE WAITING WIFE.

BY JAMES [illegible].

[illegible]

[illegible]

AFTER THE RAIN.

BY MRS. ABDY.

[illegible]

LE PUY, HAUTE LOIRE.

(*Continued from page* 81.)

We have searched on all sides for a house to ourselves, but have been, at last, obliged to submit to the custom of the country, which, as in Paris, consists in occupying apartments. Each floor forms a complete dwelling; sometimes, even, when the house is very spacious, as ours is, two or three families inhabit the same storey. Thus, we have on one side of us an inoffensive old gentleman, and on the other a bland, smiling, [illegible], prying old maid. Our house is situated on what was once the principal square, the heart of the old town. Our landlord, Monsieur le baron V——, occupies a part of the house in winter; so you see we are in good company. But to give you a correct idea of our locality, I must first describe this curious old town, so famous in the annals of the Velay for its Black Virgin, and for the persecution of the Protestants during the religious wars in the Cevennes.

Imagine, then, what was once an immense lake, closed in by numerous extinguished volcanic peaks; in the middle of that lake, fancy a mountain—Mount Anis—at the base of which and all up its declivity on one side is built Le Puy, crowned with its cathedral, and the rugged rock, called "Rocher Corneille," that towers over all. This rock, the loftiest summit for many leagues around, is perceived at a very great distance, and the bishop, they say, contemplates erecting a colossal bronze statue of the Virgin Mary on it, so that she may be seen far and wide by her adoring people, which fills the clergy above, and that [illegible], to make the [illegible] and glory of the inhabitants of the Velay. Place Martouret is at the immediate foot of this mountain, and leads to the new town, that stretches itself out all along the valley on this side Mount Anis. My windows, looking out on Place Martouret, give me a side-glance of "Rocher Corneille," and straight in front I command a full view of not only the [illegible] [illegible], but also of "Roche Arnaud," that raises its superb head at some distance behind the Loire opposite, and of the country around it, which forms a very pretty landscape. Other windows of my abode look into a street, in which the egg and butter market is held twice a week; and, from an opening between the houses, I can just see the frowning peak of Mount [illegible], whence, alas! many a triumphing soul of a poor martyred Protestant has soared into eternal bliss. And now, reader, holding firmly to these iron bars, placed in the walls on purpose to aid those who ascend or descend the steep, dirty, narrow, crooked, badly-paved streets, come with me to the cathedral, and, as you pass along, just cast a glance on those high scowling walls, with here and there a grated window, so old, crumbling, and [illegible], as antique and ghostly as the most enthusiastic reader of old novels can desire. Alas! alas! many a poor heart has here sighed for liberty, and, perchance, broken in despair; for we are now amidst convents; methinks that now, even, a low, plaintive sound strikes mine ear—the wailing of some troubled spirit of ages past! From the depths around, one might almost imagine so; or, is it rather the moaning of the wind, struggling to escape through the vaulted street we are now entering? It was getting dark when, after many ups and downs, [illegible], we arrived at a small side-door of the cathedral, [illegible], only the shadows of two or three priests of [illegible] through the twilight from their evening prayers. A sudden [illegible] closing the door behind us made the ancient pile echo again, and the [illegible] of [illegible] [illegible] us, and [illegible] [illegible] the [illegible]. A glimmering light shed here and there a ghostly hue over the old knights or bishops on their tombs, and faintly showed us the [illegible] above. Suddenly we both simultaneously stopped, I drawing closer to V——; a low whispering sound began as if from amid the tombs. I expected nothing more or less than that we [illegible] of [illegible] a spectre [illegible], and summoned up all my courage to [illegible] it; for methought that already the old knights and bishops stirred. The whispering ceased, and two phantom-like [illegible] past us towards the door, a penitent and father confessor. We continued our ramble without uttering a word, and soon, attracted by a brighter light, we stood before Our Lady of Le Puy—a black wooden image, arrayed in false jewels and gold, and surrounded by numberless burning tapers. The charm was broken; the feeling of veneration and awe, that almost withheld our breathing, now vanished. We were no longer in the temple of the Invisible God, whose Spirit, filling and sanctifying the space around us, [illegible] His hallowed presence, so to raise our souls into [illegible] with Him. A [illegible] seemed to fill the atmosphere, and we turned away.

"This is what they style the triumph of Christianity," said Victor; "Diana might certainly recognize herself in her old haunt; for on this very spot [illegible] suppose she was [illegible]; many antique stones in the walls of the cathedral, found here when the edifice was constructed, denote the former presence of a temple to that goddess."

The Druids also are supposed to have adored here before the Roman sway. However that may be, the present building is dedicated to the Virgin Mary; it is in the Byzantine style, and attributed in part to the [illegible], and other parts successively down to the 12th century. When approached by the principal entrance, up to which nearly a hundred steps lead (the whole width of the cathedral), it has a very noble appearance.

"But the legend!" I hear you exclaim. "Can there be a Roman church without a legend, in that religion of legends!"

Certainly not. In these parts, where what they call a pious fraud (as if a lie could ever be anything but a lie) must ever have been an easy matter to impose upon the people, shut out as they are from the rest of the world, ignorant of Nature's laws, and inhaling from their mountains an air saturated with mystery and wonder.

Some crafty priest, in ages past, forged this pious fraud, like many others, doubtlessly to fill the church's coffers—aim, direct or indirect, of all their miracles. Once upon a time, says the legend, there dwelt at Ceyssac, a village near Le Puy, a rich widow, who, afflicted with some dreadful disease, had spent half her fortune in useless remedies, and only grew worse and worse. One day, however, lulled to sleep, in the midst of excruciating pains, by some invisible power, lo! a vision glittering with unearthly brightness appeared before her: "Cease thy groanings, daughter," said the heavenly messenger, "and away with thee to Mount Anis. Good tidings await thee." The slumberer awoke, and immediately ordered her servants to transport her to the spot indicated. There, seated on a stone (stone that is still preserved and shown!), gentle sleep again gradually came over the afflicted woman, and, as she dozed, behold soft music, as if descending from above, struck her ear; nearer and nearer the sounds approached, filling the air with the sweetest harmony: then, lo! a celestial woman, issuing from the clouds, slowly descended, and at last stood suspended in the air before her, surrounded and followed by such an angelic host that the azure space above was covered with their silvery wings. Her snow-white robes, as they fluttered in the balmy breeze, dazzled the sick one as she gazed. The heavenly strains ceased, and brighter and brighter grew the halo of glory round the Virgin's brow. "Daughter," said she, graciously smiling, and her voice, like a renovating balm, thrilled through the whole frame of the diseased one, "thou art healed; and, in sign of thy gratitude, build me a chapel on this spot: a stag shall trace the outlines in the snow."

The Virgin never works a miracle gratis. The Saviour says: "Go, sin no more;" but Mary has ever an eye on the substantial. Then, again, the angelic choir broke forth, as slowly the Virgin soared on high, accompanied by her heavenly train. The widow awoke perfectly cured, of course; and, although it was summer, the place all around her was covered with snow, and a stag had already traced the outlines of an edifice. Masons were soon set to work, and in a short time a chapel was constructed, dedicated to the Virgin. Then miracle after miracle was wrought; for, as Madame de Staël said, when she heard of St. Denis carrying his head in his hands, after it had been severed from his body, for more than a league: "It was only the first step that cost"! Pilgrim after pilgrim hastened to the far-famed abode of the "Queen of Heaven," and soon a cathedral displaced the chapel, become too small to contain so much glory. Then another miracle, a kind of finishing stroke, sanctified the new temple. When the choir was completed, says the legend, the funds were exhausted, and the cathedral not achieved; the bishop set out for Rome to crave the Holy Father's charity; but on the road two young men, of more than human beauty, suddenly accosted him: "Return," said they, "the blessed Virgin herself has sent thee aid." The bishop returned, and, as he entered the town, behold! the bells of the new edifice broke forth in triumphant sounds, its doors sprung open, the choir blazed with thousands of burning tapers, while hosts of celestial voices swelled forth into one universal strain of triumphant glory! And yet not a human being was within its walls. The angels themselves had consecrated, as well as finished the cathedral, and the choir is still called The Angel's Choir; two of the miraculous tapers are still preserved in the cathedral, with divers other relics.

Before we quit this haunt of superstition I will give you the history, more wondrous even than of her earthly abode, of the Black Virgin, who, during the middle ages was famed through Christendom; whom Popes, Kings, and Queens visited and invoked, and who never required to be implored twice, when supplications were accompanied with vows of substantial gratitude; thus riches flowed in, while fame flowed out. This lady boasts of an origin rather more ancient than you perhaps may expect. The prophet Jeremiah carved her sable brow, God having revealed to him the features of her who was destined to bear the promised Saviour. I certainly cannot compliment the prophet on his abilities in the art of sculpture. She was given by Saladin to St. Louis, when in the Holy Land, and that monarch presented her to Le Puy, where she immediately commenced her miracles, by according to the prayers of her royal donor a son, he having promised her a rich reward. She was often invoked by that mixture of crime and superstition, Louis the Eleventh, who made no scruple of threatening the different goddesses of his creed if they did not accede to his wishes; he had their images, in lead, on his hat—Our Lady of Embrun, Our Lady of the Deliverance, Our Lady of Le Puy, and Our Lady of Chartres—two black and two white; and when he was on the point of committing a crime he would place his hat before him, kneel down, and say: "Pardon me again this one little crime, I promise not to commit another;" and, if Our Lady of Le Puy refused the accomplishment of what he asked, he would implore Our Lady of Embrun, or the others, to revenge him on her, and vice versa. Our Lady of Mount Anis, the old historian says, rarely deigned to quit her sacred abode; but when she did, and allowed herself to be paraded about the streets, so dense was the throng to catch a glimpse of her benign countenance, that once, after a peak, several hundreds of poor creatures were thrown down, trampled on, and killed in the procession. I think she might have wrought a miracle in their favour, particularly when for a child in jeopardy she achieved such marvels. It is true that a Jew was to be punished in this case, and how could she allow her priests to miss an occasion of torturing a Jew, without counting the spoil that the Israelite withheld from Mother Church's coffers? Amongst the chorister boys was one who attracted the attention of all, by his beauty and angelic voice. At the *fête* of the Virgin, one year, while the procession passed a Jew's house, the child disappeared mysteriously, and nothing could be heard of him, in spite of the most diligent inquiries. The year rolled past, and again the Virgin was carried forth; her black majesty, this time, amid chanting, banners, priests, guns, candles, and incense. At the moment the choristers reached the Jew's house, but a heavenly voice issued from it, and startled the multitude, and their astonishment increased as the lost child, clad in snow-white apparel, came forth, took his accustomed place amidst the boys, and went on singing, as if nothing had happened. He was questioned; the Jew, of course, had enticed him into his house, had starved him, and had then put him into an oven. "But," said the boy, "a beautiful lady came, she, taking me into her arms, she carried me into a lovely garden, filled with fruits and flowers, that went so merrily while angels, that never ceased singing, surrounded this lady; I sang with them, and was fed with the most delicious fruit, until your voices reached us in the garden, and the lady brought me back, and bade me take my place with you."

"A miracle! a miracle!" shouted the priests. "A miracle!" resounded through the crowd. "The child has been in heaven; he has seen the holy Virgin!" and in a moment the whole throng was prostrate before the black doll, while hymns of adoration rent the air, and the boy was carried in triumph before the idol by the enthusiastic people. On a pedestal a fountain a young boy is carved, which is said to commemorate the Jew's victim; the inhabitants pretend that this fountain was raised on the very spot where the crime was perpetrated. This legend of a Jew stealing a child and torturing it is a very common one; I have heard a similar tale in so many places. It appears to have been a favourite accusation, during the middle ages, in the mouth of a poor, or rather a rich, Israelite. Was it because such an accusation was easy to impose on the people, still imbued with the ancient Roman belief that the Jews ate a child at their feasts? But the Romans also accused the Christians of the same thing, on account of the body and blood of Christ in the Communion. However that may be, this Jew, says the legend, expiated his crime—of which I have not the slightest doubt, no more than that gold was the cause of the accusation and suffering. "Oh good old times!" will people exclaim.

The more I hear of the good old times, the more I bless them, and love the age in which I live—age in which attacks are made, and I run no risk here of being roasted; for those walls can no longer ring with Te Deums for the torturing of a Jew or Protestant, as in days of yore. And as we turned, to leave this monument of a past crumbling power, "Oh! blissful civilisation," thought I, "thou hast, at last, the iron fetters in which Romanism held the Christian world, with such a greedy grasp, and also poured into nations thy vivifying rays of liberty—liberty, whose germ, although so long dormant among those gloomy middle-ages, yet was there hidden in our native soil, amongst the German race, whence, at last, she shot forth full of sap and life, under the name of Protestantism, spreading her refreshing branches far and wide. On, on she goes, pervading the old world, and distinguishing every nation that receives her by industry, riches, well-being, morality, and life. On, on she goes, and who can say where she will stop? Only when this edifice, and all that resemble it, shall ring with the Redeemer's praises alone, and the bright sunrise already glimmer at the horizon."

But to finish the exploits of the prophet Jeremiah's masterpiece, behold how all earthly greatness fades! for alas! the reign of our Lady of Le Puy was limited. The revolutionists hurled her from her throne, pulled her down, blasphemers by dragging her in the dirt, and then threw her into the flames, to mockery amidst their scoffings and jeerings. However, like the phoenix, she again rose from her ashes, and her people still believe that by miracle, the present one is the very same, although somewhat modernised in form and feature.

As we intended leaving—for the evening was remarkably fine for the season—we could not help observing the number of unfortunate creatures lurking about these silent streets near the cathedral. "It is an odd place," said I, "for Vice to choose her haunts—so near a sacred edifice, amid convents and priest's dwellings."

"Odd to you," answered Victor; "but very ordinary to me, for there it is everywhere. When Nature's legitimate sentiments are tyrannically repressed, illegitimate ones ever replace them, in spite of popes and laws."

When we entered home, we found a very pretty bouquet of violets, sent me by my smiling musical neighbour Miss G., who, it seems, has a particular affection for nice quarters—"the same young English lady and her amiable husband," whom she hopes to be acquainted with—so says my maid; who, it appears, lived with this lady's cousin, and knows her well. This rather annoys me, as there is no end to the gossip-telling servants, and those of this lady's character, I have already been warned to be aware of her. Her reputation is anything but agreeable. They say she is half a nun—that is, that she has taken the vows of celibacy. Slanderers whisper that such a thing was quite unnecessary—that her tongue alone would frighten away all loving swains! She is never to be seen without a little black dog—her whole and sole delight—whose age, although advanced, she remembers better than her own. She is indispensable in all religious ceremonies; decorates the altars, scolds the sacristan, declares the organist spoils the organ (he once behaved rudely to her pet, barking at his heels). She dines with the curé, threatens the vicar—is acquainted with all servants, knows all that is going on in every house, sometimes more—takes snuff, makes and breaks off marriages, arranges and deranges everything and everybody, and is the terror of all who have children to marry, and with whom all try not to quarrel. She is what they call a "bigot" in perfection. In a word, this virgin appears to be as famous in the town as the black one herself, and that in the highest and lowest ranks.

During the past four months I have had various opportunities of studying the world around me, and appreciating the society into which I am fallen; and if you do not absolutely put your "veto" on a little gossip, we will this afternoon have a regular intimate chat—although, as I write, I almost shiver with cold, in spite of my close proximity to a good fire—and that on account of the absurd custom in this country of having as many doors and windows in a room as the walls around it can contain. Thus, in my little drawing-room I have three doors and three windows, through which the wind almost whistles! Roche Arnaud, opposite, is entirely covered with snow; it freezes hard out-doors, and scarce a person is to be seen on Place Martouret, except the indispensable market-women, crouching over small iron or earthen pots containing their charcoal fires; some warming their feet or hands, others boiling black-bread soup, or—what they are reputed to relish infinitely more—taking "coffee" much in the style that "Mrs. Gamp" takes "tea"—and, in good truth, they certainly require something to keep out the cold. Now and then an explosion of indignation bursts out amongst them, for they are of very combustible matter, and all, perhaps, do not drink "fairly." However, the police-office is opposite them, and the commissary appears to be a very benevolent soul, and is arbiter in all their quarrels. He discusses the pro and the con, gets rather angry at times himself, but generally contrives to appease the storm, and goes away laughing. Here and there amongst them a wooden cradle is to be seen, in which is strapped down a coarse woollen bundle containing a little human form, whose puny face may be just perceived peeping from it. This bundle seems immovable. There, on the mother's head (they carry everything on their head), it is transported to market every morning—there the babe is suckled, fed with soup—there it sleeps and cries, cries and sleeps, until it appears quite accustomed to it. This unwholesome system of penning up the young limbs, and depriving them of air, must be the cause of the remarkable number of lame and deformed we have observed in the street. We one morning counted that forty passed our house in ten minutes! It is true it was on a Sunday. I should think that at least one-fourth of the population have some visible bodily defect. Some attribute this misfortune to bad nourishment and dirt, which most probably have also their share in the unhealthy appearance of the peasants; but, as the opulent are not more exempt from this infirmity than the poor, I infer that the privation of exercise and air in infancy is the real cause; added to which, they put the children's feet into clumsy sabots (wooden shoes) as soon as they can toddle, which must weaken and turn their ankles very much.

No mother, I am told, that respects herself, ever nurses her child. A few of the richest take a wet nurse in the house, but the generality send their infants as soon as they are born to poor women in the town, who, on their side, confide theirs to still poorer women in the country. These take them for almost nothing, often nursing two at a time. The town nurses are thus, by the sacrifice of their maternal yearnings, enabled to earn a few francs per month, and make quite a trade of it. I cannot comprehend how parents in easy circumstances can permit their offspring to pass the first year of their infancy in a hovel, frequently inhaling the nauseous breath of three or four in the same small room, without, at times, counting the pig and the fowls!

I have already told you that the only commerce here is lace. This branch of industry, both in the town and in the country, descends from the middle ages—perhaps from a more ancient date: and it is very curious to read an old historian I have just turned over, and to observe that, amid all the changes and revolutions around them, how little the female portion of the population has changed. The men have fought and bled, first in this cause, then in that; their trades, once so flourishing within the antique city, have quite disappeared. The only vestige left is the names of their streets, all denoting rich and important trades; and the race seems to have expired with their wealth and glory; for, if I may believe what I am told and what I remark, a set of drones now vegetate on the soil, their only occupation being to saunter from *café* to *café*, from wine-shop to wine-shop, from billiard-table to billiard-table, to smoke and drink, and to receive, now and then, gentle *strappandas* from their better-halves at home, who reign supreme. If, perchance, an electric spark of enthusiasm influences them at the remembrance of their former greatness in their country's annals, it is but the effervescence of a moment. They repel every notion of progress as a dangerous innovation that might derange their little affairs and trouble their vegetation. To the weaker vessel alone seems to have fallen the nerve for life's battle; and almost all the commerce and labour is achieved by the women. Those who have no shop to attend to, assemble just as they did two centuries ago, ten or twenty together, to work at their pillows: each woman has one. In olden times, their numbers were increased during winter by the inhabitants of the mountains, who, driven from their abodes, not only by the snow, but also by the birds of prey that continually hovered round them, and that inhabited the numerous castles around, abandoned their huts as soon as the first wintry blast announced the urgency of protection. Then on all sides, from the heights, every road and every path leading to Le Puy literally teemed with peasantry, driving their flocks and herds before them, going to seek protection from Our Lady of Le Puy, within the strong walls of that then formidable fortress, of which the bishop was feudal lord. Their women safely lodged, the men found work in the different [illegible] in the towns; some strayed as far as Lyons.

The women formed societies of ten or twenty; each society chose a patron saint, whose protection they daily implored. One woman in each society was entrusted with the direction of the whole, from every member of which she claimed obedience to rules they had agreed upon. They hired a spacious room, and all day long might then be seen (just as I have seen them now, in the solitary parts of the town), their feet on a chaufferette, their pillows on their knees, working, laughing, chatting, crossing themselves, and repeating Pater-nosters and Ave-Marias all in the same breath. They often work until midnight; and then, for economy, one candle or chandelle serves them all. It is placed in the middle of a round table, with six or eight glass globes, filled with water, surrounding it. These globes collect the luminous rays, and cast sufficient light on each pillow for the workwoman to conduct her bobbins. And in spite of the agility of her fingers, she is an envied one, indeed, who succeeds in gaining ten sous (fivepence) a-day. My maid, Madeleine, who is my "oracle" in all that concerns this class, pretends that the women only meet in these "working parties" to gossip and scandalise their neighbours. She went once or twice to see, but has soon sufficient of them. So you see I have a treasure in my house — a servant enemy to gossiping! and this in a country where that talent seems to be so highly cultivated; for, from what I hear, the chief occupation of servants and mistresses is to be initiated into the most trivial points of their neighbour's affairs. That arises, I imagine, from the very limited education bestowed on women; and, if Madeleine is so exemplary as a servant, my neighbour, Mlle. G. is the reverse; for she assured me that she always makes a point of giving her good advice every time she meets her — this tells you that I have been obliged to visit this lady in spite of my repugnance; and, if I introduce her to you again, it is because she is a type here, and one of the springs of the society, insinuating herself everywhere, and frequently causing great strife in families; for all listen to her. I could not help smiling the other day, on being told that her only complaint against us is that we always speak English before our servant! She is, however, in ecstasies at my never preventing my maid going to church, and has reported all to "Monsieur le Curé," who is perfectly edified, and has conceived a latent hope of recalling a schismatic Englishwoman within the church's bosom. A lady acquaintance has already commenced operations, and, to prepare the way, has lent me several books of miracles. But before I introduce this lady to you, let me give you a little insight into the society of the higher classes, where I met her. For that come with me to the Prefecture, a handsome building in a noble square (Place du Breuil, the rival of Place "Mercouer,") from which it is only separated by the row of houses on the right of us. This Place is the beginning of the new town, and occupies the flat part of the valley. Besides the Prefecture, it contains handsome public walks, behind the museum and its garden. This walk is in the shape of a horse-shoe, hence its appellation, "Le fer à cheval"; and is planted with lime-trees, with the Museum behind it. All this is very modern; but, as you delight in antiquities, let me tell you that numerous Celtic and Roman relics were found while digging in this once immense meadow. Breuil is the Celtic word for meadow; and many Celtic tombs and [illegible] Roman bricks, found on the spot where the residence of the chief magistrate now stands, prove that a Roman edifice once occupied the same locality. But here I am, far from my ball at the Prefecture, to which I promised to lead you, and in which I know you are dying to go, in spite of your taste for the antique.

Well, soon after our arrival [illegible] — as is the fashion in France — to the Prefet, and to other public functionaries; for, in spite of our wish to live very retired, we were obliged to do so, or to run the risk of being considered enemies to the existing power — a thing that no one holding a government appointment would desire. A few days after our visit we received a card of invitation for the ball, to be held [illegible] Christmas and [illegible] to which we replied with alacrity, for we had found the Prefet's wife a very charming, ladylike person, doing the honours of her house exquisitely; and she gave us a cordial reception.

The Prefet, they say, is not much liked. He [illegible] those that are heartily [illegible] the [illegible] and that rules them. We found him rather stiff and cold, affable by fits and starts. He speaks English well, and seems to be a clever man. He is at open war with the clergy both in town and country, and has a strong party against him, for which his quality of a stranger is sufficient. The Ponots, like the generality of people little habituated to intercourse with those beyond the precincts of their mountains, entertain a great antipathy for all who were not born under the protection of their black Madonna. So marked, indeed, is this division between them, that it seems quite natural to speak of the "French" and the "Ponots."

I find that I have the honour of representing the Anglo-Saxon race, and am a subject of curiosity. But to the ball. At first I found it a very dull affair; however, after sundry yawnings between me and Victor at a distance, both longing for one corn dressing, I managed to enjoy myself very passably; although that want of introduction to those with whom you dance renders chatting with your partner very difficult, particularly to a new comer like myself. However, England furnished a favourite topic with those with whom I danced; and I was much amused at hearing the current ideas in France concerning us. A Frenchman always begins by telling you that Englishwomen are charming; and then he imagines that he has carte-blanche to say what he chooses of our fathers and brothers; and this is what I could deduce from the numerous remarks made to me:—Englishmen sell their wives, torture the Irish, *font leur tour*, in the ruins, are snobs—they never produce such a thing as an artist either in music, painting, or on the stage; and, if they have never been on the Continent, they finish their mortal career with the spleen, or in a consumption, without ever once beholding the sun, except through a dense fog! Their laws are as abominable as they themselves. A nobleman may plunder, murder, and commit any other crime with impunity. One gentleman told me that he had had his pocket picked when walking in London, and the policeman refused to seize the thief! "The thief was a nobleman, most likely," answered I.

Do not imagine that I exaggerate in what I say; for nineteen Frenchmen out of twenty believe this, and would not for the world have a different opinion. But the twentieth does exist, and I have had the felicity of finding him; and while I sat, sipping a cup of tea, and wondering why the men in France always stand together in the middle of the ball-room, hat in hand, between the dancers, like a black cloud hovering over a garden of flowers, an old, gentle man (Mr. F.) approached me. We had already been to a [illegible] at his house—so that I was well acquainted with him, and hailed his arrival near me with real pleasure; for he is one of those witty, amiable, gentlemanly men of the "ancien régime" who is ever delighted to chat with. He speaks English, and has had frequent intercourse with English families.

"Well, Madame," said he, "what do you think of our balls? Are yours in England as gay as this?"

"I think so," answered I.

"A nice chandelier," recommenced he, smiling. "You dance for your pleasure, while we dance officially. Here we are nobles and non-nobles, looking daggers at each other, and would be much better at separate balls. You see that row of armchairs yonder—they are occupied by the members of the nobility, who have condescended to dance in the same room with the magistracies and *parvenus*; but they form quadrilles apart, and I have just heard a young man (Comte de V.) ask Mademoiselle de B. (his partner) whether she would condescend to have for '*vis-à-vis*' a little 'nobody,' for he could find no one else, and that loud enough for the 'nobody' to hear, who, greatly irritated, refused the honour of being *vis-à-vis* to Mademoiselle B.! The Prefet, also, has just received a young man out of the ball-room; a lady—the wife of a *parvenu* this time—having recognised in him a young tradesman in the town, and, highly scandalised that the Prefet should invite 'such people,' complained. The Prefet had not invited him; he had obtained a card through some one, and was begged by the Prefet to retire—which, in truth, was but just, as he had no business to intrude. But this will prove to you what our boasted equality is! But the great topic of scandal here is the manner all have for gambling, both men and women; and, in that drawing-room you see at the end of this, thousands of francs have already been lost this evening, in spite of the Prefet's dislike to gaming. Then observe how the women eye each other's magnificence! Look at their velvets and their satins! I wonder we do not have a minister instead of a priest!"

"Tell me," said I, "who are all these ladies then?"

"I will not only tell you who they are, but what they are, if you wish," answered he, with a malicious smile.

"No scandal, monsieur!"

"Scandal! would or could I be guilty of such a thing?"

And then my amusing companion passed in review all that fell within his "ken;" and truly, I presume, lost nothing in passing through his lips. The relation certainly did not raise the society of Le Puy in my opinion; and, strange to say, that all anecdotes thereupon here are always connected with the presence of a priest!

"I shall allow largely for embellishments," said I.

Mr. F. declared that all was perfect truth.

"Then truth is very ugly."

While we were thus chattering, a pair of elegant moustaches lounged past us.

"Who is that?" asked I.

"That is Monsieur le Comte de V., the very personage I spoke of to you, who was so insolent to the 'nobody.' He is a would-be scion of the old nobility, though if you probed deep into the past, you might perchance find that the founder of the family gained more money than glory, and handled less more than the sword. The present head is, however, a Comte, and is a staunch 'Legitimist' both in religion and politics. The son (the moustaches that have just passed) is half a renegade, and is suspected of having a tinge of Bonapartism just now, as he had of Republicanism under the Republic, and of Orleanism under Louis Philippe. He is one of those happy mortals, of the *ci-devant* tribe, whose coldest nerve [illegible]. He is the humble admirer of that smiling dame opposite us, who is longing to find the quality of your lace, I can see by her frequent glances at it. That lady, Madame D., is said to be on very friendly terms with an ecclesiastic in a high position here. He has a rich niece to marry, and the right ear of the Emperor when a place is to be given away; and the [illegible] are in quest of a rich dowry and a Government place."

This lady Madame D., although no longer in the prime of youth, possesses the [illegible] imaginable; her dark hair, coquettishly arranged, appears in the evening to be powdered. I felt quite attracted towards her, and was vexed in hearing, from Mr. F., that she and her husband (a tall spectre-looking man of fifty) are the [illegible] of society, and that to [illegible] and vanity she adds extraordinary [illegible]. At the Revolution in 1848 she panted to be the wife of a representative in Parliament, although her husband did not possess the requisite [illegible] in [illegible]. The lady, however, intrigued and manoeuvred so well, that at last they purchased an estate, which ruined them, and her husband was not elected. She, however, still keeps up appearances, and toils indefatigably to [illegible] what all know.

Mr. F. introduced me to her, and I soon found out that, according to Madame de Girardin's opinion, this lady was born to be a milliner. My "toilette" was examined; my hat felt and inspected, its price asked, and every possible and impossible question put and answered in the shortest space imaginable. Satisfied with this inspection, Madame D. sees at home every Monday, and would be happy to receive us. We have since been to see her, and she has [illegible] my [illegible], and, to pass the [illegible], has lent me the books of [illegible] I have spoken to you of. She has issued cards for a soirée next week, to which, of course, we shall go.

There are several other parties pending here; for it is the fashion here for all to give one grand entertainment—a dinner and soirée—every year, in which great luxury and magnificence are displayed by those who possess the means. For their dinners they send to Paris or Clermont, as provisions here are of the worst quality, on account of the [illegible] of the country.

Many of the rich inhabitants give [illegible]. Victor went to one the other evening, where there were more than forty men; the lady of the house was the only one present. There were real Pouzzi, and everything was in the greatest profusion. A magnificent supper was served at midnight—a thing which I have never seen in France (at the Professors' there was nothing but occasional refreshments). After supper the guests again sat to cards, and gambled for large sums until breakfast was served; those who were weary reposing on different sofas.

Victor of course did not prolong his visit until daylight; but we were told by another who did, and who left them again playing after breakfast; so that I do not know how long the soirée lasted.

A lady, exasperated at this exclusion of our sex, resolved to revenge us; and for that she gave a grand entertainment of ladies, which they say went off marvellously well. I cannot expatiate on its delights, as I was not known to the lady, therefore not invited; but I see very well that the Lords of the Creation cannot digest their exclusion, although they try to laugh at it; so that you see we are revenged.

So much for the [illegible] of the town at this time. The Carnival is fast approaching, when, I am told, there are wonderful things performed.

A gleam of sunshine brought us out the other day, and we visited several curiosities. Amongst others, the museum, which contains the human fossil, of which there has been so much said. I do not know how learned you are in geology, so I will just tell you that all savants deny the existence of a human fossil, or that man existed at that antediluvian period when the earth was inhabited by those extraordinary animals whose bones have been extracted from the bowels of the earth, and whose species have quite disappeared; and this because a human fossil had never been found! This was a decidedly scientific point, when all at once a great rumour was heard in the learned world that a human fossil had been dug out of the volcanic [illegible] near the crater of Mont Denise, near Le Puy; and the Pouzzi cried "Victory!" The learned geologists and naturalists of the locality (and there are many) soon wrote pages of arguments to prove the authenticity of their fossil; and to prove it to the world the [illegible] discovery [illegible] that the most celebrated professors from Paris and England came to examine it, and went away as incredulous as when they arrived. But that has not shaken the faith of the Pouzzi, who cling to their human fossil enthusiastically.

It is reported that a [illegible] workman, to console himself at the expense of the savants of Europe, imagined the joke of placing the bones in the block where they were found. Of course I am not competent to decide the question, and can only tell you that there are the fragments of human bones incrusted in the block of volcanic matter we saw in the museum, and that the facetious workman must have been a skilful deceiver to have so well succeeded.

After examining the fossil, we passed over several stones, ornamented with inscriptions that denote the sojourn of the Romans in the mountains of the Velay; some were secured to record the presence of a god unknown to the Romans. We lingered a long while over these last crumbling traces of the conquering and the conquered; for to me there is something very attractive in the work of the past, and its inscription is like a voice echoing down the long vale of years that separate us from those remote ages—a voice that warns us of the fragility of all earthly things.

The museum is very rich in relics of the middle ages, and that prove the past importance of Le Puy, such as coins with the arms of the Bishop of Le Puy, who then possessed the privilege of coining. There are also various precious stones of great value found in the [illegible], a [illegible] near Mont Mézenc, which still furnishes zircons, garnets, and other crystallisations at times.

From this museum we wandered to that belonging to the cathedral, rich in religious relics,

There we saw the famous tapers brought by the angels at the consecration of the choir. They are very black, and in a decaying state, but have nothing in them remarkable. A piece of the real cross also blesses this sanctuary; and the Holy Lance is here, entire; although I remember, when visiting the Sainte Chapelle, in Paris, the guide informed us that that edifice was once honoured by the possession of a piece of the Holy Lance, but that it had been transferred to Notre-Dame.

Some one objected, as having seen the whole lance at Le Puy. The guide was puzzled.

"Oh," said a facetious *Frenchman* of our company, "what does that prove? The piece in the Sainte Chapelle was probably like the hair of the Holy Virgin, which a priest had shown for many years to the faithful; until one day, a contrary bumpkin pretended that he could not see it, and exclaimed, "'Where, Father Abbot? Where is it? I cannot see it.'

"'*See* it!' indignantly answered the monk; 'you see it! when I, that have shown it for this last thirty years, have never yet had that joy!'"

The Holy Lance here is, however, authentic, as far back as the first crusade—and I cannot refrain from giving you its prodigious history, as I read it in an old chronicler the other day:

"At that momentous period when Peter the Hermit preached the first crusade, and, by his overpowering eloquence, put all Christendom in arms, the spark of enthusiasm, wafting through the mountains of Le Velay, enflamed its chivalrous sons, with the Bishop Adhémar at their head. The Pope, Urban II., was at Le Puy, and, at the feet of Our Lady of Mount Anis, conferred the title of Legate of the Holy See on the valiant Adhémar; who, with four hundred knights, set out for the Holy Land, and so distinguished themselves there, that Tasso himself has immortalised them. Adhémar was thus the spiritual guide of the first crusade, and to great courage he added a lofty soul and an enlightened understanding: thus he had had little taste for superstition. After the Christians had taken Antioch, aspiring for repose (so great had already been their sufferings), the Turks returned with renewed force, laid siege to the town, and threw them into a state of consternation unimaginable. In vain was every means employed to compel the infidels to retire—all failed; and famine, pestilence, and despair raged amidst the crusaders, while the people threatened open revolt. In this extremity a priest, named Bathelemi, one morning declared that in the night he had had a vision—an angelic messenger had revealed to him the spot where the lance that had pierced Our Saviour's side when on the Cross had been buried, and that the angel had ordered him to dig it up, and to place it in front of the besieged army, to whom it would ensure victory.

"A spark of hope once animated the soldiers, and accordingly they immediately hastened to the locality (near one of the gates of Antioch) indicated by Bathelemi. Alas! there was no lance, in spite of all their efforts to find it. The priest, however, insisted, and they repaired to the spot again the next day. Scarcely had they recommenced operations when a cry of surprise was heard, and Bathelemi triumphantly drew out the lance. In an instant the news, like an electric flash, flew from rank to rank, filling the souls of the discouraged army with enthusiasm. 'A miracle!—a miracle!' they shouted, and following Bathelemi (who carried the lance), they rushed like an impetuous torrent sweeping through the enemy's ranks, routed them, and returned in triumph to the city.

"But in spite of victory the Christians were divided in their sentiments as to the veracity of the vision, and many suspected Bathelemi of being the fabricator of it, and that he himself had placed the lance where it was found. Amongst the incredulous was Adhémar himself. He rightly attributed their success to the enthusiasm of the soldiers, rather than to the cause of that enthusiasm; others firmly believed the priest's history—and so great was the contention created by the Holy Lance, that it was at last decided that Bathelemi should go through an ordeal in order to prove his truth, and thus God himself would settle the question! Accordingly, a fire was kindled, and before the palpitating army the poor fanatic was immolated. He passed through unshrinkingly, and expired a few hours after in exquisite agonies. The sacrifice availed nothing; for his having issued alive from the burning pile was sufficient to maintain his followers in their faith. An historian of his party who records the fact, states that he proved his sincerity; and that, if he did expire a short time after, it was wholly from another cause.

"In spite, however, of the division of sentiments, the lance continued to be the standard of the crusaders until they conquered Jerusalem, when it was placed in the Church of the Holy Sepulchre, and honoured with the greatest veneration. And whenever success appeared doubtful, it was still carried in front of the army that never once was vanquished with it at its head; until the Turks, believing it to be a fatal talisman against them, fled at its approach. It was at last transferred from Jerusalem to the treasury of the cathedral here, in homage to the valorous Adhémar, killed at Antioch."

"Strange, incomprehensible middle-ages!" methought, as I stood and gazed on this once mighty lance, and the history of the crusaders unfurled itself before me. "To think that this obscure piece of metal then possessed such magic powers; and that that age of heroism was the exact period when harmless inanimated objects reigned supreme!"

We left the lance in its obscure corner, and turned towards where lay a Bible, of the ninth century, which as well as three handsome standards ornamented with precious stones, attracted our notice. The standards were saved from the great fire in Moscow, by a French soldier, who, in gratitude to Our Lady of Le Puy, for having permitted him to behold again his beloved mountains, deposited them at her feet.

We did not push our walk any further; so you must wait until my next for further amusement.

THE WORK-TABLE.

SOFA CUSHION, IN PRINCESS ROYAL CROCHET, EMBROIDERED.

MATERIALS: 6-thread black and white Pearl Wool; blue, crimson, green, and amber 6-thread Wool, and any short pieces of colours; also a coarse hook of the kind already described for this stitch; Cord and Tassels.

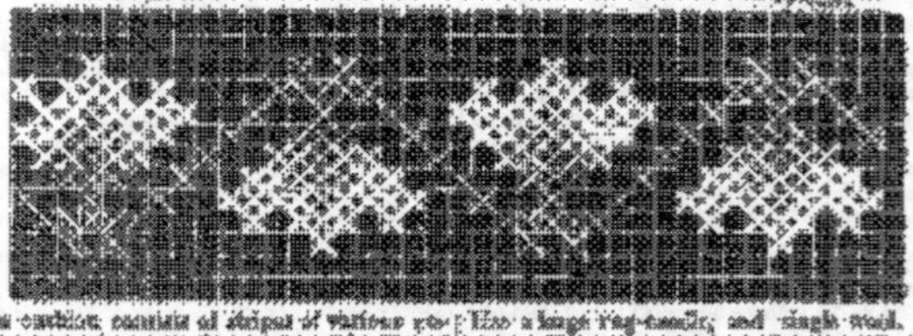

The cushion consists of stripes of various colours, arranged so as to harmonize with a line of pearl wool between every two, and also all round the cushion. For this you begin and end with this wool, and afterwards work two lines, to form the other two sides of the square.

With the pearl wool work a chain of 70 stitches, and do one row forward and one backward, to make one pattern of this stitch. Join on a coloured wool, and work thirty rows, making fifteen patterns; then the two pearl-wool rows again, then another colour, until you have five coloured stripes and six narrow pearl lines. Do a pearl line at the top and bottom.

The pattern is worked in cross-stitch, which is done on this crochet as easily as on canvas, with a large rug-needle, and single wool. The zig-zag line is in one colour, brown or black, the flower in three shades of bright colour. It may be worked entirely in one set of tints on each stripe, or each flower in a different one, according to taste. In the latter case you can use up any spare bits of wool you may have on hand; but the effect is, perhaps, better the other way. Suppose there are five stripes of the following colours—scarlet, blue, crimson or scarlet, green, and the design be worked on each in three shades of the colour following it, only with green on one amber stripe and blue on the other, it would look very handsome. The tassels to be made of wool of the leading colour, like those to the round cushion recently given.

AIGUILLETTE.

COLLAR AND CUFF, IN RAISED EMBROIDERY.

MATERIALS. Fine Book Muslin, Valenciennes Insertion, and Messrs. W. Evans and Co.'s Embroidery Cotton, No. 80.

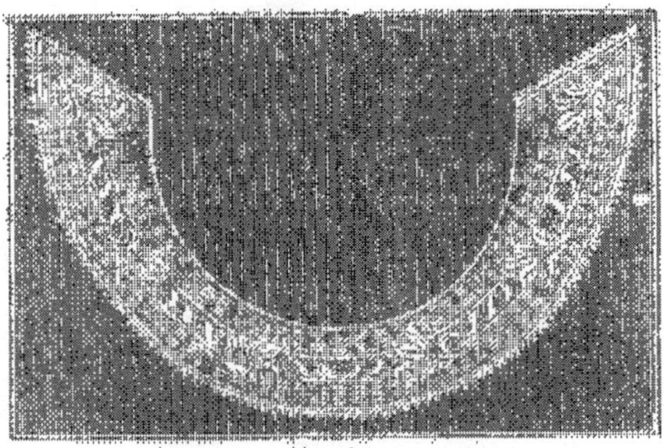

THE CUFF.

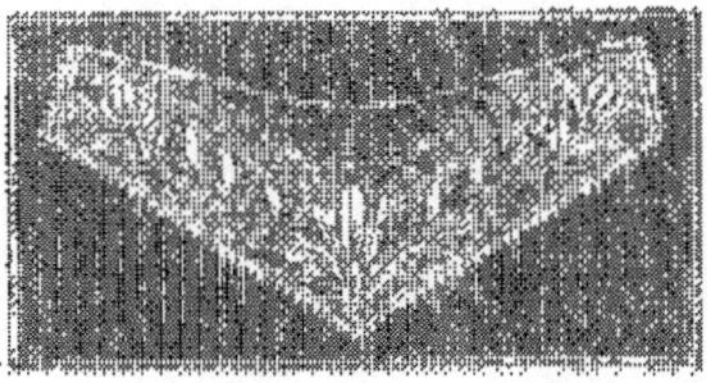

The peculiarity of this embroidery consists in the fact of the flowers being all wrought with the natural number of petals, and hollow or cup-like in form, as when growing. For this purpose the design is marked perfectly on the muslin; and, besides this, the upper part of each flower is traced separately, as will be seen in the section given of the cuff. This upper part, being worked heavily in satin stitch, is connected with the corresponding part of the flowers, by a row of button-hole stitch, through both, done along the outer edge, after they have been traced together. It will be seen that this upper part is not quite so large as the under-part of the calyx; and it is not intended entirely to cover the latter. With the exception of the flowers and leaves, the design is of a very simple character. The Valenciennes insertion (which must be laid under the muslin, and joined to it by a line of fine button-hole stitch, and a row of spots at each side) forms no inconsiderable portion of the collar; and on each side of it the pattern consists merely of spots and short bars simply sewed over. The insertion is laid under instead of over, as usual; because the tulips, being heavy, require the additional strength of foundation acquired by the double thickness. The stems, and parts of the leaves and petals, are much raised; but of the two latter some parts are filled with *point de sablé*—very minute spots, worked close together.

The border is a simple scallop, raised down the centre.

AIGUILLETTE.

CAVOUR.

BY W. W. [illegible]

Low lies earth's noblest head:
Cavour is dead!
White, and cold, and still he lies,
Whom Italy [illegible]
From where, beneath the Austrian's heel, she lay
With [illegible] in [illegible] to [illegible] dead!
Woe for the day
When those dread words each grief into all [illegible];
While, in their fear and grief, and with surprise,
Italy, the one thought that shuddered through each soul [illegible] road?
He is gone. Who now shall be the mighty guard [illegible]
Through the [illegible] dangers of her onward way?—
Through the dark future that before her lies?
Low lie the will so strong, the brain so wise;
Low lie the [illegible] arm, the [illegible] hand:
Cavour is dead!

Who [illegible] said—
"Cavour is dead!"
His spirit seeks God's [illegible]; but never dies
The [illegible] him gathered from his eyes,
Nor the great thoughts he [illegible] of [illegible]—
The mighty hopes he [illegible] to [illegible]!
While all that [illegible] caused,
Has [illegible] to be [illegible],
He, with [illegible] and wisdom [illegible],
[illegible] to powers before earth's [illegible],
Till dazzling light from the grim darkness [illegible]
The glory of his [illegible] from [illegible].
Which, while [illegible],
As in the old days, on the world's [illegible],
Unto our eyes that glory still he [illegible]
For aye to live.

Yes, to live on, and know
[illegible] no more, but [illegible]
And brightest [illegible] in the [illegible] of [illegible];
To light to glory [illegible], and [illegible],
Until the [illegible] of coming ages [illegible]
To [illegible]—
Lives mighty as of old.
Whose deeds by [illegible] shall be told;
And for Columbus, whom [illegible] shall sing
While round the sun the whirling earth is rolled,
And Galileo, [illegible] to [illegible]
That mightier Virgil shall, [illegible] of gold,
And [illegible], sing
Glory to him who such great days shall bring,
Who, with [illegible] might the [illegible],
That the great Future might [illegible]."

Yes; [illegible] he [illegible]
Lies there, to be seen no more!
To Death, [illegible] and the mighty soul
That [illegible] a nation's [illegible]
Has passed away
To that eternal day
That, soon as him, shall gather in the whole
Who wander darkly through this mortal way;
From the [illegible] slave who feels the despot's [illegible]
To him who treads the necks of nations down,
And [illegible] with peoples, as with toys, to play.
Unto the [illegible] lips; [illegible], O [illegible],
Give the cold form in glory to repose
Where coming centuries shall stand and say—
"No nobler life than this e'er reached life's goal!
Rest be his soul!"

Crown him with glory's palm
Stadeant [illegible] song to his high [illegible],
Whose life was noble as his deed was grand!
Who gave his great [illegible] with all [illegible] to stand

Co-equal, and [illegible]
Their [illegible] the voice.
May speak in thunder, and again [illegible]
[illegible] as of old, may be a power to [illegible]
The [illegible] the world [illegible] in [illegible] fight,
Or [illegible] from [illegible] that Zion—
The path of greatness, which before us [illegible]—
The [illegible] slipped [illegible] with [illegible] delight!
Chief and patriot, [illegible], as of old,
[illegible] the [illegible];
[illegible], in the [illegible] sight,
Thine is the glory none shall delight!

And [illegible] earthly [illegible],
[illegible] to [illegible] that [illegible] down,
Unto the [illegible] end of the still grave?
[illegible] of [illegible] hopes shall [illegible],
For [illegible] in the high [illegible],
Where he [illegible] new [illegible],
For [illegible] that have [illegible],
In [illegible] hearts, beneath a happier sun.
[illegible], whate'er his [illegible],
[illegible] in death,
We [illegible] to shine [illegible];
The presence of the All-Good, whose will by him [illegible]
Led! [illegible] and [illegible];
Through all [illegible] shall be [illegible]!
And with a hope [illegible], Cavour,
We [illegible] him up to the [illegible]!

IRREVOCABLE.

Ah! maiden, let me lay my [illegible] hand,
So dull with pain, upon thy [illegible] breast;
And, when my [illegible] are said,
[illegible] that [illegible], [illegible]
That [illegible] all the [illegible] and the [illegible].
And, even now, my soul begins to see
That joy which is the portion of the blest;
And of the [illegible] and [illegible],
When [illegible] Life's [illegible] forth [illegible]
Before the [illegible] of the great [illegible]!

What [illegible] pleasures [illegible] youth!
When [illegible] brought forth [illegible],
[illegible] hearts, [illegible], and [illegible],
[illegible] their [illegible] a dark alloy?
The [illegible] happier than [illegible] boy,
[illegible] was a king and [illegible];
[illegible] of [illegible] strong
[illegible] on the purple [illegible]
[illegible] would [illegible] to stay;
Alas! I [illegible] the [illegible] the [illegible]!

And I have [illegible] and life,
And [illegible] the poisoned cup down to the lees;
[illegible], in [illegible] and [illegible],
The [illegible] my [illegible];
And in [illegible] and [illegible]
Have [illegible] the precious years, but [illegible],
While [illegible] the [illegible]
Of that [illegible] which never [illegible],
And, [illegible], seek [illegible]
For the sweet [illegible] which I sigh!

But [illegible], as I am now,
I [illegible] that [illegible]!
[illegible] the [illegible] brow
Is [illegible] a [illegible];
And I can [illegible],
For [illegible] on the [illegible],
While I [illegible] to [illegible],
Although the [illegible] now [illegible]
For nothing [illegible] e'er [illegible]
From that [illegible] which is the [illegible] and [illegible]!

W. S.

AN OFFICIAL RAP.

On the 8th of April last the British nation was engaged in the unusual operation of "putting itself down," not perhaps exactly in the manner which neighbours over the water would wish, but nevertheless in a thoroughly effective fashion. John Bull, having put himself down, and conjugated, in full chorus, the verb "to canvass," his door received an "official rap," and a man, "dress'd in a little brief authority," took away his confession, which Mr. John Bull had made not always in conformity with his own desire, but under the direction of the Act of Parliament 23 and 24 Vict., c. 61. I was the man who gave that "Official Rap;" for, although the number of enumerators was legion, in every particular street it was the enumerator; therefore I may as well assume to myself the title of the original and only collector of the returns. I am not disposed to follow the example of some persons who have given any but the right reason for their making an appearance in public, but boldly avow that filthy lucre was my primary inducement for accepting temporary service under Her Majesty's Government. It must, however, be also understood that another object, in undertaking the office, was a vague expectation of amusement to be derived from the meeting up and totting of the British nation.

I have called upon the universal collector of census papers, but what I am about to relate occurred in a suburb of London, which, when the population was previously numbered, was, with its dust-covered fields and broken hedges on the one hand, and heaps of bricks, scaffolding, and rapidly rising walls on the other, in that peculiar transitional state between town and country, which, like the east wind, is "neither good for man nor beast;" its houses affording neither shelter for bipeds, nor its unoccupied space food for quadrupeds. Ten years have, however, worked a change; and the district is no longer a desert, but a thickly-populated thriving little world; in fact, having its priests and sextons, builders and barristers, cabmen and clergymen, drapers and dramatists, fundholders and fishmongers, jewellers and journalists, lawyers and labourers, musicians and magicians, surgeons and sweeps, tailors and tapsters, warriors and washerwomen, [illegible]; indeed a complete colony, representing every branch of trade, nearly every profession, and possessing its social climbing scale, descending from an aristocratic few to a plebeian multitude; furnished also with its administrative machinery, its county and police courts, its vestry-rates, its fire engine, its rifles, and its gallant band of volunteers; so that if the district were cut off from the greatness of which it is an integral portion, it would be found ready to undertake the task of self-government. A portion of this flourishing locality I traversed on the 8th of April last, collecting schedules from house to house, and announcing my advent by "an official rap;" a public-house being my alpha and another public-house my omega.

With the dignity befitting an enumerator, but with the guilty feeling of a respectable man who is seen going into a public-house at nine in the morning, I entered the "Sir Isaac Newton," and commenced my duties by informing the very fascinating young lady behind the bar that I had called for the census return. My communication was apparently of so facetious a nature that she immediately began to giggle, then to snick[illegible], and finally honoured me with a coquettish toss of the head, and a long stare, as if I were altogether a very novel and amusing object to look at. I don't know, but possibly there may have been some connection between the altered behaviour of that young woman, and the age assigned to her by the schedule; for as I glanced down the paper her giggling grew worse than ever, and then, without the smallest provocation on my part, she folded her arms, and, resting them on the beer-engine, looked me steadily in the face, and with the most horrible smirk exclaimed: "Now you wouldn't have thought I was as young as that, would you?" I can only say that my [illegible] in reply to the query was most emphatic, and I turned upon my heel with alacrity, and just got outside the door in time to hear a voice from the bar-parlour shouting, "Ask the gent, Sarah, if he won't take anything." The offer, however, came too late; the gent had flown, and was busy in the street of which the "Sir Isaac Newton" formed the corner house. It was a long street of shops, from which the gloss of newness had not worn off; the gilded legends over the doors were bright and glittering, and the varnish and paint were so recent that it seemed doubtful if they were quite dry. Down this street of commerce I marched, stepping in and out of the shops, and receiving the returns, in most instances, with a slap on the counter, as if the amount of business daily and hourly transacted was of a most extensive nature. Each schedule was properly filled up, and the collecting began, I must confess, to be rather monotonous. I suspected, after visiting twenty-four houses, that I was merely playing the part of an amateur postman, with the slight difference of receiving instead of delivering missives. I felt small, and to add to my discomfort I was attended down the street by a small cortège of young children, who followed at my heels, congregated round the door when I entered a house, and resumed their march after me when I came out. There was no silent admiration of the enumerator; they passed their remarks freely upon my personal appearance. Tom requested Bill "to twig my boots;" Bill desired Tom to look at my "portfolio;" Dick pointed me out to Harry "as the cove with the hat;" and Harry, having to enter a shop, took his leave by executing, a short distance in front of me, an eccentric dance, shouting at the same time, "Oh isn't I a Cure! ain't I a Cure!" I must own, too, that when I recognised a lady of my acquaintance on the opposite side of the way, and took off my hat in a style of which I am rather proud, my dignity was not increased by Tom and Bill mimicking the performance, amidst shrieks of laughter from their youthful audience. I felt losing my temper, when, fortunately, a policeman hove in sight, and Dick having called out "Here's the Bobby," the whole lot decamped; but, before ridding me of their presence, Master Tom made a pounce at the schedules in my hand, uttering the request "Give us one, mister." In reply I raised my umbrella in a threatening manner; but he had vanished, and my sole consolation was a grumbling remark from an old gentleman, whose nose I had nearly hit, respecting "persons being more careful in the streets, and should not swing things about in that manner." I had a great desire to ask him what he meant, but abstained from doing so, and marched on, savagely determined to pounce down upon the first man who had made a mistake in filling up his return. To this end, at the next shop I sternly demanded if it were properly filled up. The proprietor, a very small man, with hair stiffly standing up from the top of his head, eyed me contemptuously, then, straddling out his two absurd little legs, and sticking his two thumbs in the arm-holes of his waistcoat, fiercely told me that he was surprised at my asking such a question, as "none but a born idiot could fail to understand the Government instructions." He glared at me after uttering this opinion, and then drawing himself up to his full height (five-foot-one), walked down the shop, leaving me fairly extinguished. I regret to say that an examination of this fiery gentleman's return proved that all the information demanded had been carefully supplied; but subsequent investigations gave birth to the belief that a large percentage of my fellow-countrymen are "born idiots," and I would suggest that at the next census a column should be especially devoted to this particular chronic mental affection. Though disgusted with that shopkeeper, he certainly broke the monotony of my rounds, and the very first "official rap" I gave, on arriving in a street of semi-genteel houses, where the householders principally described themselves as "keepers of lodgings," was answered by an invitation into a parlour, where a majestic lady received me with a dignified bow, and deliberately placed in my hand a sealed packet.

"There, sir, is my paper."

I bowed, and was proceeding to break the seal;

"Surely it is not your intention to open it?" was the surprised inquiry.

I intimated that my instructions obliged me to do so.

"I then must observe, sir, that it seems strange, not to say unaccountable, that my word is to be doubted; and I can hardly think that the authorities would sanction such a step."

Although my dignity was hurt, I politely informed the lady it was absolutely necessary that I should see that the returns were properly filled up.

"There cannot be the slightest fear on that point," rejoined my companion, casting withering glances at me, and then adding, in a very sarcastic tone, "Perhaps you will admit this, when I tell you that for eighteen years I kept a first-class boarding school; fifty guineas a-year, Italian and music extra."

Certainly I could not see the connection between the boarding-school and the census return, and I was proceeding to break the seal, when she laid her hand upon my arm, and in a stern voice said: "Promise me one thing."

I stammered out, that it was impossible to make promises, but she interrupted me by adding: "Promise me, sir, that none but the Registrar General and yourself shall know the contents of that paper."

I bowed, and entertained some doubts of the lady's sanity; but she gave me little time for reflection.

"Remember, sir, there are reasons—delicate matters—which should not be made public; and I, therefore, if you have authority to open that packet, beg it may be placed by your hands in those of the Registrar General."

It was with the utmost difficulty that I could refrain from laughing, but I did manage to keep my countenance, and gravely assured the lady that her wishes should be complied with to the letter.

"Then I am satisfied, sir," was her reply; "I believe you only do a painful duty in opening this packet, and I thank you. Good morning."

She bowed me from her room, and I was so tickled with that unmarried lady's feverish anxiety, when I looked at the age she had inserted in the return, and remembered her almost antediluvian appearance, that my first "official rap" was characterised by small—[illegible] sounds, and, as if to make the burlesque more complete when the door was opened, the man who acted as porter went to the foot of the stairs, and shouted, loud enough to be heard half-way down the street, "Molly, Betsy! here's the gent come to know your age!"

From the street of lodging-houses I proceeded to one of the most nondescript description; every door-post was ornamented with a regiment of bell handles; carpenters had settled in the attic and the cellar; in one house a general shop-keeper kept his emporium in the front kitchen, and in another a tailor had established himself on the ground-floor; washerwomen and sempstresses abounded, and about the houses, squa-[illegible] and children there was a general look of dirt and industrious poverty. Diving down the area of the first house my descent was announced by an urchin shouting, as he passed, "Milk, below!" and then, playfully tapping my hat, he bestowed the remark that he supposed there "was nothing in it," which it must be owned rather ruffled me, and ill-fitted me for the calm performance of my duties, my was I much re-composed when a troubled face confronted me in the shop, and a voice exclaimed:

"Oh sir! I'm so glad you've come; such a dreadful accident."

Evidently I was mistaken for the doctor, and I informed the woman that I was not a medical practitioner, but the enumerator, who had called for the census paper.

"That's it, sir."

"Yes, sir, that's it," observed a red-faced woman, bustling up, and joining in the conversation. "Poor dear, she['s] [illegible] had a child [illegible] her husband [illegible], too, only two months old, and he took the pledge three year ago, and never broke it afore."

"That's true, Mrs Johnson," cried the other; "and it all comes of them statistics."

"Ah! it all the cause of this, Mrs. Giles! Heaven knows the trouble I've had with my old man. What with beer, baccy, and such like, I have almost been worritted out of my house. Only let them give me the making of the law, and I would show them what for."

As the latter part of this philippic was addressed to me as if I were connected with them, and as I was somewhat mystified as to a baby, two months old, having taken the pledge three years ago and broken it, and was with an accident in consequence, I again ventured to suggest that I had called for the census schedule, and had no sooner done so than the woman who had opened the door again began:

"That's it, sir; and only to think that of all nights in the year, he should have done it when that were in the house—and what, sir, we're to do no more than I can say."

"Ah! my dear, that's true enough! and if he was sent to prison it would only serve him right; for, as I read with my own eyes on this my own schedule, which, sir, it is properly wrote in, as my own daughter is a scholard, because I had little enough of that when I were young—and I am not ashamed to confess my age, which is forty-nine last Michaelmas. It is five pounds, and what you are to do, Mrs. Giles, if he's taken, and the blessed infant only two months old, is more than I can tell."

"Really I cannot see what this has to do with me."

"Of course, sir," continued the voluble Mrs. Johnson; "for a gent. like you it is not to be supposed that you should, sir; but if so be it is a case for the police-courts, for her sake, sir, and not for him, I will not say but what I would speak to his worship as to character and without saying more than as is truth. I have occupied this house ever since it were built, and paid my rent regularly; for which there are in that old tea-pot my receipts."

"I do not in the least doubt that; but I must really request you to hand me the schedule."

Upon making this demand in rather a peremptory manner, something resembling a coherent explanation was obtained. From this I gathered that Mr. Giles, a cooper, and so quiet a man that he had taken and kept his pledge for three years, had been so worked upon by some [illegible] advocates of the "cause" that he returned home the previous evening in a hopeless state of intoxication, and, much to his wife's horror, lighted his pipe with the schedule, at the same time exclaiming he was not a-going to be dictated to by any of them ere State secretaries, eating up the working man's money, and he should like to meet with anyone who would tell him he must do so, he would serve them the same way. Hence the wife's fear of drink, and the landlady's good-natured but [illegible] interference on her lodger's behalf. A fresh form and a few strokes of the pen soon got matters to rights, and elicited the remark from Mrs. Johnson, as I went up the street, that I was "a very pretty spoken gentleman, and others, that ought to know better, might have something from such [illegible]."

The sound of my "official rap" was much heard in a mews, and, if I were disposed to make a bad pun, I might remark that if this particular mews was not poetic, it was at least prolific. I never met with a more densely packed population than was discovered in the [illegible] windows of the rooms over the stables. Mothers and fathers, grandfathers and grandmothers, sons and sons-in-law, daughters and daughters-in-law, "lodgers" and "visitors," nephews and nieces, aunts, uncles, and cousins were all so closely stowed away, that it gave birth to the belief that the horse's manger by day was the baby's crib by night. And of the [illegible] it might be said it was like the chest of drawers in "The Deserted Village":

> "The chest contrived a double debt to pay—
> A bed by night, a chest of drawers by day."

There, too, I had an opportunity of seeing the spread of education amongst the lower orders. Every boy and girl under twelve was a "scholard;" as a large [illegible] the same day a full-blown "scholard" must learn from the mews, to be crowned with bays. Nowhere in those habitations of many people was the rule, and not the exception; and the noisiest of all was the one in which resided a buxom housewife, who told me that, during the last ten years, she had increased the population of the mews by nine; and that, when the previous census was taken, her family numbered four children: thus making a very pretty sum-total.

As I left the mews, a cabman, leaning near the brush-door, calmly smoking a long clay pipe, winked at me in the most knowing manner, and, indicating with his thumb a policeman who was standing at the corner, exclaimed—

"I say, master, you'll get at 'em, between you, this time!" and then, with another wink, took a long draw at his pipe, looking very much as if he had hit the right nail on the head. I suppose he imagined I was obtaining a return of the thieves. Perhaps the policeman thought

I was one myself, as he favoured me with a long stare until I got close up to him; and then, apparently satisfied of my respectability, resumed his slow heavy walk down the street.

Proceeding to an adjoining street, about which hung an air of struggling gentility, my "official rap" had only been repeated at the first house—not number one, as number one had yet to be built—often enough for me to acquire a greater amount of black lead from the knocker than was altogether agreeable, when a thin, middle-aged lady, dressed in rusty black silk, and her eighty gallons of crinoline, opened the door, and invited me into the front parlour.

"This way, if you please. This is my apartment."

She glanced round the "chair-lumbered closet just twelve feet by nine," and I did likewise, but failed to discover anything remarkable in it.

"I repeat, this is my apartment—at least for the present—and here is my return. You will find everything properly filled up. My age I have stated to be above forty; and that I assure you is correct—I am above forty."

I felt tempted to remark I didn't doubt the fact, but refrained, and simply said it was necessary to have more precise information.

"I can't give it. I won't give it, neither for the Registrar-General nor for the Home Secretary. I can make that answer or none at all. I have also filled in my occupation as 'Claimant of property.' That is my occupation, and it has been my sole one for the last ten years; and will continue to be until I die or gain my rights. I have been wrongfully defrauded, by the combinations of wicked persons, of my just and lawful rights; therefore, I maintain, I can only describe my occupation as that appertaining to a claimant of property. And I have only to remark that I have made this explanation to you away from the people of this—this place—which, for the present, I am compelled to inhabit. I have nothing further to add. Should you desire to know more, I can refer you to gentlemen of position who are perfectly acquainted with the circumstances of my case, and can vouch for my respectability."

I assured this gentlewoman that I never for a moment doubted her respectability, but that I should have wished for rather more precise information as to age and occupation; but finding that my request only produced a relapse into the argument touching her property and "the machinations of wicked persons," I left her to resume her worrying employment as claimant of property.

Another turn brought me into a street of third-rate lodging-houses, packed full of families, the heads of whom followed all kinds of precarious callings. Every front door was fitted with a latch-lock, and round most of the keyholes the paint was worn completely off, the walls of the passages were dirty, and every vestige of pattern had been trodden out and shuffled off the oilcloth. There was a perpetual bustle of persons up and down the stairs, and when I got occasional glimpses of the dirty little back yards I came to the conclusion that "little washes" were continually being carried on by some of the occupants of these "teeming" and not over-cleanly "hives." At one house in this street my "official rap" was answered by a little drab of a girl, who, on putting a bundle of returns into my hands, asked me "to step up to the second-floor front for their'n." I complied with the request, and, having achieved the feat of ascending the steep and narrow staircase, entered a room in which the most admired disorder reigned; wearing apparel was scattered in all directions; one chair bore the unwashed cups and saucers that had been used at breakfast; a teapot stood on a window-sill, flanked by a brass candlestick on one side and a half-quartern loaf on the other; some torn and dirty books were heaped upon another chair, and on one side of the fireplace was a clothes-horse, on which were hung about some minute articles of baby attire; whilst on the other side was the small owner of the property, lying asleep on the lap of a pocket edition of a maid-servant. And this small householder announced my arrival by a shrill cry for "Mammie"! In answer to the demand, a door communicating with the back-room opened, and a person dressed in a singularly ample, but rather ungraceful wrapper, made her appearance. She was not strictly handsome, but a large pair of brilliant, restless black eyes, which rolled and flashed incessantly, gave striking effect to her face; and, whether from her eyes, or her short, intermitted speech, I could not help associating her with a shadow of a young lady in a melodramatic print which hung over the fireplace.

"Will you take a seat?" she asked, in an undertone, a voice as if she was preparing me for the news of a poisoned cup; and seeing that all the chairs were occupied, she glided across the room, swept the books from the seat they occupied, and motioned me to the table, which was partially covered with the fragmentary remains of a banquet. I sat down, and was then asked "if I would be so obliging as to fill up the form?" I signified my willingness to comply with the request, and suggested that pen and ink were necessary. Unfortunately I had asked for articles most difficult to find, and a search for which entailed a complete rummage of the room, resulting in the required implements being at length dragged from a cupboard, where they were keeping company with the remains of "half a hundred" of coals, and a gridiron! How many balls that pen had, or of what peculiar pasty composition that ink was made, I do not pretend to say. A little hammering of the former, and a judicious admixture of cold tea to the latter, enabled me to perform my task. With a slow enunciation, and with the black eyes rolling and flashing, the heroine in the morning wrapper gave me her own, her husband's, and baby's names, their respective ages, conditions, and sexes, and where they were born; but when I asked the rank, profession or occupation of the "head of family," she

absolutely blessed, and their owner unclaimed.—
"That, sir, I decline to state."

"But really I must—"

"I cannot inform you."

"Is he in trade?"

"Again I say I decline to give any information in the matter."

"Are you aware that your husband is liable to a penalty?"

"We must take the consequences," was the reply, with an awful flash of the eyes.

I was fairly nonplussed; but, thinking she might be less reticent in regard to herself, I inquired if she followed any occupation?

"I cannot reply to that question," was the only answer vouchsafed; and although I tried my hardest, my only reward was an absolute persistence in the *Non mi ricordo* style of giving evidence, and increased stiffing of eyes. Finding all my efforts fruitless, I left this heroine, and on quitting the street-door was accosted by the landlady, who, catching me on the arm, asked me in a low tone of voice, "Can you tell me, sir, what he is?"

A jerk of the head indicated the direction of the second floor.

"If I did know I certainly should not tell you; but I don't."

"Well, really, I thought I should find it out now," sighed the landlady, as she closed the door after me; and I descended the step, thinking that perhaps, under the circumstances, her curiosity was a little excusable.

As it was now growing dark, I hastened to finish my rounds, and my "pillared eyes" succeeded each other with considerable rapidity, and at length I came to the last street, formed of two lines of semi-detached houses arranged in pairs, and all so alike, that it is to be hoped none of the "heads of family" are given to dining out, as a slight difficulty might be experienced in finding their respective homes. At the last house but three, in this most neat and most respectable street, I was received by a boy in buttons, who conducted me to the dining-room. It was neatly furnished, but bore unmistakable traces of the hand of the upholsterer, who had evidently been called in and requested to furnish the house. I had scarcely surveyed the contents of the room when the page requested me to "walk into the drawing-room;" where I was shown into an apartment lighter and brighter than the other. Standing by the fire was a stately lady, who claimed to be the "head of family," although, from the simple fact of her "condition" being "unmarried," there was no "family" to be "head of." I am not vain, but I do attribute the courteous of the smile which greeted me to the fact that I am not altogether bad-looking, and not to my official capacity of the enumerator.

"Pray be seated, and do let me ring for some wine," was the greeting I received; and I complied with the former but declined the latter request. "I am so sorry to trouble you, but I am so dreadfully stupid in all business matters—poor dear papa used to say he couldn't think what I should do without him."

I bowed, and wondered what the poor dear papa of that simple flame was like when alive!

"I am sure, then, you won't mind filling up that dreadful paper you left here the other day! I am almost ashamed to ask you; I am sure, when I saw you delivering them on Wednesday, I quite pitied you for all the annoyance you would have to undergo."

She had seen me, then! Which was it—my whiskers, or my general military bearing?

"I wonder where I put that paper!"

"It is of no consequence," I said; "I have plenty more."

"How very kind! I'm sure we all ought to be so much obliged to you! Oh, the ink; pray don't move—my stupid head! I think you will find everything there," she added, putting a handsome silver inkstand on the table, and seating herself opposite to me.

I could not help feeling something like a photographer, or perhaps a clerk in a foreign consul's office, about to finish a pen-and-ink portrait for a passport. The name was given correctly, but the relation to head of family elicited the exclamation—"Dear me, I suppose as the house is mine I am 'head of family.'"

"And your condition, may I ask?"

"Really, you men are so dreadful inquisitive; it is quite like the thing they used to have in Spain—you know—dear me—the people in black—the—really I'm not fit for anything, my memory is so bad; I mean the Inquisition. Oh dear me! I had almost forgotten your question. I am unmarried. I suppose I ought to call myself a spinster, but that is such a dreadfully ugly name."

I don't think I felt quite comfortable, when I looked at that stout female nodding and smiling at me from the other side of the fire-place, and I began to wish that somebody else were in the room. However, the only thing to be done was to get on with the work, and, in as dry official a tone as I could muster, I asked her age last birth-day.

What was my embarrassment when, instead of directly replying, she drew her chair round full face to me, and exclaimed, "How old should you take me to be?"

"Well, really," I stammered, horrified with the inquiry, "I do not think I could possibly guess."

"Then try."

I looked at the red face and the voluminous form, and mildly ejaculated, "Not more than five-and-thirty."

"That is extraordinary," she exclaimed, in a delighted tone; "that is exactly what all my friends tell me, but I am older than that. I can't tell you though; no; really I must; I must write it down."

I handed her the schedule, in which she inserted the information, and returned it to me, saying, "Of course, I know you will read it; you men are such quizzes. Oh! now don't pretend you won't. There! I declare, if you have not read it now!"

"You may rely upon my——"

"I don't suppose that you are any better than the rest of your sex."

I almost trembled as I gazed on my companion, smiling and nodding in a greater degree than ever. I endeavoured to recollect the precise place I had put my hat, while I blandly asked her rank, profession, or occupation?

"There now, I knew how I should be puzzled; papa, dear papa was quite right, I am sure I don't know what I am; I have some houses you know, and some funds in the Bank; and then you know there is some money my [illegible] lent to somebody; and that's all. Oh! no—then I have some railway shares."

"A freeholder and proprietor of houses," I remarked, writing it in rapidly.

"There! now you see how clever you are! You did that in a quarter of the time I took to tell you about it. How I only wish——"

As I really was getting alarmed for my own safety, I hastily interrupted her with a request for information about the servants.

"There, again! you see," she rejoined, looking at me with decided admiration, "you are so prompt and quick, I should never have thought of them; but you are so business-like, and do just what I should never do myself. Will you ring the bell please?"

I complied with the request, and almost expected she would compliment me on my prowess as a bell-ringer.

"You must be fatigued," she said, as I buttoned my coat: "pray do let me offer you some wine."

Fortunately, I had only time to refuse when Buttons appeared with the missing schedule, which that intelligent young gentleman had taken upon himself to fill up as far as regarded the servants. Hastily glancing through it, I was about bowing myself from the room, when the lady rose, and, advancing to me, said,

"Excuse me, but I am so lonely here that I should feel obliged, if you should hear of any one wishing to board, if you would only think of me."

I started; I even think I blushed. I know I stammered out something. I am certain that I snatched up my hat eagerly. I am perfectly aware that I rushed down the steps into the street. I am convinced that I walked rapidly to the nearest cab-stand, and I am sure that I did not feel quite comfortable until I was sitting before my own fire in my own chamber, about three good miles from that street. I assuredly did get the three remaining schedules the next day, but I took good care never to be seen by the "head of family" in that house. I solemnly aver that I neither left there my papers, my umbrella, nor my gloves, for the purpose of giving me opportunity of calling again; and, I equally solemnly aver that I daily look with dread at the second column of the Times, lest it should contain a notice that "If the enumerator who called at the house in —— street will call at number —— he will hear of something to his advantage."

Such were some of my experiences as an Enumerator. I might, in addition, disclose many curious particulars concerning the information to be found in some of the schedules. I might give some strange examples of the modes of filling-up the returns. I might show how British humour [illegible] in a number of the documents; but I have no wish that John Bull should lose faith in his enumerator; I have therefore, written the history of my Enumeration, [illegible] as not to [illegible] the promise of the Registrar General, when he declares "Care will be taken that the returns are not used for the gratification of curiosity."

FANCIES.

BY ADA TREVANION.

A dark and a heavy shadow;
A whisper of sighing wind;
The breath of hay from the meadow;
The [illegible] on the blind.

A bird in my [illegible] flutters,
And a child comes to my knee,
While the [illegible] murmurs;
But neither of these I see.

I gaze [illegible] far back
A [illegible]
And [illegible]
In which years have wrought no change.

A [illegible]
O'er my soul [illegible]
Thou, [illegible]
I [illegible]

I see a [illegible]
[illegible]
The [illegible]
As the [illegible] play.

I am alone, on the ocean,
A fragile and storm-tossed bark;
Through the tempest's wild commotion
Did there come a death-cry! Hark!

But you take my hands, which quiver,
And say they are lonely, [illegible];
And moonlight, with white-hued shiver,
Is lying upon the trees.

How the waves [illegible]
The [illegible] on the shore!
The storm is over: what was it
We were talking of before?

'Tis an hour for quiet gladness,
[illegible]
For my heart is full of sadness,
And [illegible] to-night.

[illegible], 1852.

HUSBANDS AND WIVES.

How often is it said, in the present day, that man and woman are falsely placed with regard to each other! According to one party, men are too strong and women are weak, and they demand that woman's prerogative be forthwith greatly increased—they would make men of them, of course. Others consider that by a different course of education, which should direct their minds to great objects, women would quietly assume a position equal to that of man, without any more active interference. A third and large party assert that, so far from men being the stronger, they have always been the victims of the other sex.

There is perhaps some truth in each of these propositions; but when we consider that men have always been the law-makers, there may be a suspicion of their having secured to themselves no small portion of the power and privileges of social life. It is so easy to make a law in favour of oneself, that we think there is a chance of the suspicion being well-founded. On the other hand, the small amount of truth which we have supposed to exist in the propositions above stated is completely swamped by the presence of a kind of injustice.

The feeling of man and woman, husband and wife, is the chain which has certain duties to perform, which of themselves combine for the mutual advantage. If men and women, when brought together by marriage, and who have to live together for the whole of their lives, would make up their minds to be as thoughtful in each other's feelings, as much disposed to mutual forbearance and consideration towards each other's feelings in private, as they appear to be when in the presence of their friends, we should hear much less about injustice and false position.

To use a common expression, what is fair for one is fair for the other: in the married state there should be the strictest equality. The husband must come down from the position of master, not that his place may be taken by the woman, but that she may be the sharer of his pleasures, hopes, and joys, as she has ever been the partaker of his pains, fears, and sorrows. There is nothing more beautiful than friendship; and the friendship of husband and wife ensures the highest earthly happiness.

Many married men consider themselves fully justified in passing most of their evenings away from home, among their companions. If this be fair for the man, it is equally fair for the woman to go out and visit her friends also. If it be contended that the woman [illegible] always a smile ready to greet her husband when he enters, it is equally important that he should bring good-humour and a pleasant countenance with him. True, he may be troubled and annoyed with business cares; but is she not troubled and annoyed, often to a greater degree, with family and household cares? with the difference that, whilst she is always amongst hers, the man by his absence from his own, whatever his cares, in some measure modify his. If it be fair for the husband to keep the purse, it is fair that the wife should know how much or how little there may be in it. There must be no secrets on either side; what the man knows the woman ought to know. In cases of difficulty woman's feelings will often suggest a better remedy than man's reason.

The task might be aided by the mutual recognition of one common purpose and object, combined with respect for differing views regarding its attainment. Generally speaking, it may be said that [illegible] want the more [illegible] of sympathy, for women more of discretion:—

> "The kindest and the happiest pair
> Will find occasion to forbear;
> And something every day they live
> To pity, and perhaps forgive."

LEAVES FOR THE LITTLE ONES.

UNCLE HERBERT'S WEDDING.

BY T. & F.

"Cousin Caroline, were you ever a bridesmaid?"

"Yes dear, several times; more often indeed than I ought to mention, if I had any expectation of being a bride."

"But were you at a wedding when you were as little as I am?" continued the young questioner, wistfully eyeing the pretty white muslin frock and blue sash which "Cousin Caroline" was putting away, in readiness for the day which Miss Emmy began to think "never would come."

"Yes Emmy, I was rather younger, and certainly smaller than you, when first invited to take part in such an important affair. I think, too, that I was almost as pleased as you are, my little girl, although it was not at a sister's wedding that my appearance was requested."

"Can you make a story of it, cousin, and tell me all about it, from the very beginning?"

"Well, I will do my best," said Caroline, laughing; "but there really is scarcely anything to make a story of, if it is to be a *true* one; neither plot, nor incident, nor wonderful adventure."

"But I do not care for wonderful adventures," said Emmy Ramsay; "I like anything that has happened to you, Cousin Caroline, a great deal better than fairy stories."

"Indeed, little pussy! Then let us put all this finery away first, and when we are comfortably settled in the summer-house I will begin at the 'very beginning,' according to your wish and my established custom."

"Oh! how nice that will be!" exclaimed the little girl, joyfully. "I shall like it so much; for when the visitors come, I am afraid there will be no time for stories."

"No, my child; Cousin Caroline will have something else to do to-morrow, and for many days afterwards; so we will make the most of present opportunities—a wise plan in graver matters than story-telling."

Caroline Seymour was, as my little readers have probably discovered, considerably older than her young companion; indeed, she had for more than ten years been almost a mother to Fanny and her elder sister Alicia Ramsay, who had lost their own dear mother when quite young. Mr. Ramsay still lived; but, as he was often away from home, his niece had the chief management of the little household, and had been the principal companion and instructress of his two daughters. Alicia was to be married in a few days, much to the delight of little Fanny, who was very partial to her future brother-in-law, James Kenyon, and looked forward to spending many happy days at the newly-built rectory, close by, which was now quite ready to be occupied by the young clergyman and his bride.

Having thus more particularly introduced the Ramsay family to my readers, it is time to follow little Fanny to the cool, shady summer-house by the lake, and listen with her to Cousin Caroline's account of her "first wedding."

"It was a great many years ago—oh! more than I sometimes believe possible, Fanny, so fresh in my remembrance are those old days—when what I am going to tell you took place. We—that is, papa, mamma, Miss Gibbs, a friend of theirs, and myself—were still at the breakfast-table in the pretty morning-room at Ashley Court, when papa all at once produced a letter from his pocket, which had been there forgotten and unopened for two or three days.

"'What is the matter, Edwin?' inquired my mother.

"'Why, wife, a great deal is the matter this time! What a stupid trick of mine! I am getting more forgetful than ever, I declare. Such an important letter, too,' he continued, glancing rapidly over its contents; 'to have kept all this time unopened, and consequently unanswered.'

"'Who is it from? What is it about?' were the eager questions.

"'From my brother Herbert; read it, my dear,' said my father, handing it to her, and looking himself anxiously around at the company.

"'Going to be married?' exclaimed my mother, with an expression of the most comical perplexity. 'Herbert married! You do not say so!' she continued, incredulously.

"'I do not, my love; but the letter does, which I suppose is to be believed, as it is not the 1st of April.'

"'Married!' echoed Miss Gibbs, mournfully, 'what a sad, sad pity!'

"'And why so? I think him a lucky fellow to secure such a treasure as he describes. Where is your pity, Miss Gibbs?' asked my father—'the lady, or the happy man? I thought you liked my brother Herbert?'

"'So I do, Mr. Seymour, and always thought him very sensible for remaining single on the dear children's account.'

"'What children! Whom should he remain single for, pray?'

"'Yours,' said Miss Gibbs promptly; 'everybody expected them to come in to his property.'

"'Then everybody is quite in the wrong, and much to be blamed for such expectations. Pshaw! nonsense,' said my father, more good-humouredly. 'Who could wish a fine, handsome, kind-hearted fellow like Herbert to keep single and desolate in that large house of his, in order to make my children heiresses at his death? Carry, my dear, you don't want Uncle Herbert's money, I hope?'

"'No, papa,' I answered at once, not quite understanding the subject under discussion, but particularly objecting to Miss Gibbs saying anything in disparagement of my dear, kind Uncle Herbert, who had always been like a second father to Charlotte and myself.

"'That's right, my child; then you will be very pleased to hear that Uncle Herbert is going to be married early in July, and wants you and Charlotte to be his little bridesmaids. Won't that be a treat?'

"I ran off immediately to communicate all this important news to my elder sister, who was just then an invalid, and generally a prisoner to the couch in our school-room. To my surprise and distress, the intelligence was received by Charlotte with a paroxysm of tears. I knew she was very weak, and thought that the announcement had been too hasty; but not that it was altogether unwelcome as well as unexpected.

"'Are you not pleased with the prospect of being bridesmaid, Lottie?' I asked, when the sobs had a little subsided.

"'I have not thought about that,' she answered, sorrowfully. 'I have been thinking of losing our Uncle Herbert; dear Uncle Herbert, who has always been so kind to us. It is very wrong of him to get married when I am so fond of him, and——'

"'Wrong? Why, Lottie, is it not very kind of him now, to ask his little nieces to be bridesmaids?' I remonstrated, rather indignantly.

"Sister Lottie gave me no answer; but, when I told her what Miss Gibbs had said about Uncle Herbert's money, she was quite as angry as papa had been.

"'No, Carry; such a thought would not have come into my head, although, being older than you are, my dear,' she observed—with the full consciousness of having three years the advantage of me in that respect—'being older than you are, I have heard people say how rich we should be if Uncle Herbert left all his money to us, as he most likely would do if he died unmarried. We do not want his money; but oh! Cherry, it will be horrid when he gets a wife.'

"'Perhaps she will be somebody very nice; she ought to be,' I suggested, 'and then we should love her too.'

"But Lottie shook her head obstinately: 'Nobody could be nice enough for Uncle Herbert; and then, even if she were, why, don't you see, Cherry, Uncle will care all the more for her and so much the less for us?'

"This was quite a new idea for me, and not at all a pleasant one, Ernny; for I was very very fond of Uncle Herbert, as I have already told you.

"'And shall we never go to stay with him again? never have any hay-making parties and blackberry gatherings?'

"'Oh! no, there will be an end to all that sort of fun, of course,' said Lottie, decisively.

"This was a very melancholy prospect for the future; I did not like it at all, and, influenced by my sister's arguments and persuasions, had arrived at the settled conviction that we should neither of us approve Uncle Herbert's choice, and should both resolutely refuse the invitation to be present at the ceremony, in the capacity of bridesmaids.

"'Did you hear her name?' inquired Lottie, when we had come to this praiseworthy determination, and were rather cheerful in consequence.

"'No; I know nothing more than I have told you, for I ran off before anything was said about the lady.'

"'She's a horrid fright, I dare say,' said my sister decidedly.

"'Poor lady, who is it you are abusing so unmercifully?'

"We both started at the voice. It was Uncle Herbert who spoke. Not able to understand why his letter had met with no reply, he had found his way over to inquire the reason and receive the congratulations which he expected from his brother's family.

"'Well, who is the "horrid fright," Lottie?'

"But neither Lottie nor I could give a satisfactory answer to this query; we both hung our heads and looked foolish.

"'Well, well, I will not tease my little favourites, or tell Miss Gibbs what you think of her,' said Uncle Herbert, good-humouredly. 'I am too happy to make mischief. Your mamma told me you had heard the news; have you not a kiss, or a word of congratulation for me, you monkeys?'

"He took me on his knees, and seated himself on the couch by my sister.

"'Heyday! what now; why what is it all about? Have you [illegible] [illegible] from laughing, for a change?'

"'We never quarrel, as you ought to remember, Uncle Herbert,' said Lottie indignantly. Then, after a pause, she added, in somewhat distinctly accents: 'We wish you every happiness, Uncle Herbert; but we would rather not be bridesmaids, thank you!'

"Her lip was still quivering, and I quite expected another burst of tears.

"Some inkling of the real cause of our discontent seemed to dawn upon Uncle Herbert, for he immediately began to dilate upon the charms and accomplishments of the lady who was soon to be our aunt, and how anxious she was to make the acquaintance of his two dear nieces; such a good kind aunt, to which we were obliged to listen, with an amount of interest which we tried hard to conceal. In fact, when the long talk was over, and Uncle Herbert had assured us again that our visits at the park would be just as frequent, and he just as kind to us as ever, we were both much anxious to be introduced to the original of the portrait which was shown to us, and looked anything but a horrid fright.

"It was agreed that when Lottie was strong enough we should drive over with Uncle Herbert to the pretty cottage in which she was then living with quite an old lady, her grandmother, who, as we were told, was a very kind old lady, and particularly fond of little girls.

"Uncle Herbert stayed with us a week, and was, if possible, more merry and full of fun than ever, so that we quite forgave him for going to be married, and rescinded our determination of absenting ourselves from his wedding."

"'And did you like the lady who was to be his wife?' said Ernny anxiously.

"'I have loved her people so much, Ernny dear. We were great friends from the first happy day of our meeting to the last sad hour when I closed her eyes for ever.'

"'Oh! Cousin Caroline, did she die before marrying your Uncle Herbert?'

"'No, dear; not for many years afterwards. We had a merry, happy, wedding party, with nothing to mar the joy and contentment of any one of the few guests assembled to take a share in the ceremony. There were handsome presents in abundance, for the bride had long been an occupant of that pretty little cottage, and had won the friendship and esteem of all around her, from the children of the village school to the nobles of the Manor Hall and Park, who had insisted upon performing a father's part, in giving her away at the altar. Though an orphan for some years, my new aunt was neither penniless nor friendless, and the most fastidious could find no reasonable objection to Uncle Herbert's choice. So he carried her from her home amidst the blessings and good wishes of all, and the bells rang a merry peal after them; whilst we young ones, loath to lay our pretty dresses on one side, resolved upon finishing the day with becoming festivities. We made the cottage walls re-echo our joyous laughter, chasing each other up the old oaken staircase, or hiding in some of its many odd nooks and corners; we danced on the lawn, we rambled through the woods and shrubberies of Manor Hall, doing, in fact, whatever the whim of the moment prompted us to do; the dear old lady, whose guests we

ever, letting us follow our own bent, and entering heartily into our innocent enjoyment, although I know she must have grieved sorely for the young girl whom Uncle Herbert had stolen from her."

"And who was the old lady?—her grandmamma, Cousin Caroline?"

"Yes, dear; they had lived together since my aunt was quite young—a little girl I mean; and, of course, it was hard to part from her, even for a few weeks, and though she had promised to leave her cottage and live in Uncle Herbert's beautiful house, for the sake of being near her darling, it was not quite the same as having her all to herself, in a home of her own. There now, we have talked long enough, Emmy, and I must not tell you about any more weddings to-day."

"Thank you, Cousin Caroline; it was a very nice story; but I want to know a great deal more than you have told me."

"Do you, you curious little puss? I declare you are never satisfied. I see the carriage in the distance though, so we must be moving towards the house, and see about tea. Papa and his companions will be quite ready for it, I am sure, after so much shopping. What questions must I answer on our road? What is there you particularly wish to know?"

"Well, tell me whether you and Cousin Charlotte often stayed with your Uncle Herbert and his wife?"

"Yes, dear; we lived at no great distance from them, and one or other of us was a constant guest at their house; for my aunt was unfortunately very delicate, and was often glad for one of us to relieve her, in a great measure, of her household cares and duties. Papa and mamma never said, 'No,' if Uncle Herbert came over with a petition for 'one of the girls' to return with him. At first, of course we were too young to be more than companions to Aunt Herbert; but time slipped on quickly, transforming us into young women and housekeepers."

"And when did Cousin Charlotte marry?"

"Years ago; just when I had almost resolved never to be a bridesmaid any more. My father and mother died soon afterwards, leaving Cloudy passed into other hands, and then——"

"Then what happened to you?"

"Why, then a little girl, a very delicate baby, came to Uncle Herbert's house, and I was asked to live there, and help to take care of her."

"And did you go?" asked Emmy, looking perplexed and bewildered at this statement.

"Yes, Emmy, and never left her again. Eight years afterwards, just eleven years ago this last spring, another little baby girl was put into my arms by Uncle Herbert, and I must silently as I kissed it, for that baby had no mother; she had gone home to the holy angels, leaving me the charge of her two children. You, my Emmy, and dear Alicia, can best tell if I have striven to do my duty by them."

Emmy looked up dubiously; then, suddenly throwing both arms round cousin Caroline, exclaimed,

"I see it all now; you dear, dear cousin Caroline; you have been telling me about my own papa and mamma, only you have called papa Herbert Seymour, instead of Horace Seymour, and made him your papa's brother, instead of Aunt Seymour's. I meant to ask you a great deal more about him, but I know all that I want to know now. I wondered you never told me the name of the lady he married. I wish we had a portrait of poor mamma. I should so like to fancy her. Was she fair, like Alicia?"

"See, and judge for yourself, my child," answered Caroline, leading the little girl to the dining-room, in which a substantial tea was already prepared.

"Here is an exact resemblance of your poor mother, as she looked on her wedding-day!"

"Oh! how lovely she must have been! But why was the picture never here before? Is this the portrait papa has always wanted to find, since the miniature which I never saw was lost?"

"Yes, the artist who painted it died before it was sent home. Many of his pictures were stolen, this amongst them; but it was recently discovered, exposed for sale, in a shop-window, and here it is, fortunately, just in time to smile down upon Alicia and her wedding guests. May her blessing rest on both my children then and now," said cousin Caroline, fondly.

"Ah! I hear papa's voice; run and meet him, and send Mr. Kingsley to me. When the wedding is over, and the house quiet again, I will tell you some more 'true stories of your dear mamma.'"

Boswell's Introduction to Johnson.—They met in the back parlour of Davies, the bookseller's shop, in Great Russell-street, where Boswell, "inquiring as gentlemen," according to his own account, had endeavoured to drink tea. Boswell saw Johnson through a glass door communicating with the shop, and Davies whispered to Boswell, "Don't tell where I come from," recollecting the doctor's hatred of the Scotch. "Mr. Boswell, from Scotland," said the incorrigible old actor, archly. Let Boswell tell the rest himself, for no one but himself can do his own sensations justice. "Mr. Johnson," said I, "I do indeed come from Scotland, but I cannot help it." I am willing to flatter myself that I meant this as light pleasantry to soothe and conciliate him, and not as any humiliating abasement at the expense of my country. But, however that might be, this speech was somewhat unlucky, for, with that quickness of wit for which he was so remarkable, he seized the expression "come from Scotland," which I used in the sense of being of that country, and, as if I had said that I had come away from it or left it, retorted, "That, sir, I find is what a very great many of your countrymen cannot help." This stroke stunned me a good deal, and when we sat down I felt myself not a little embarrassed and apprehensive of what might come next. Having thus commenced his intimacy, the young Scot soon found his way to No. 1, Inner Temple Lane, where Johnson then lived in chambers; and thus began that acquaintance to which the world owes the most telling piece of biography ever given to an English public.—*The Queen of Society.*

OUR LIBRARY TABLE.

SOMETHING FOR EVERYBODY; OR, A GARLAND FOR THE YEAR. By John Timbs, F.S.A. (London: Lockwood and Co., Stationers' Hall Court.)—The title of this volume fairly expresses its contents. Full of curious and varied crumbs of information such as fill only in the way of men of letters, it is impossible to turn a page without falling on a fact or anecdote new to the generality of readers. The harvest of a long season of literary labour, of extensive reading, and personal observation and consideration, is here neatly garnered; for, as our readers are aware, many valuable volumes of the same character have already appeared by the same prolific and indefatigable compiler. Such books, though they do not take rank with original works, are frequently, as is the case with the present volume, infinitely more useful than a large majority of those which are; bringing, as they do, the curiosities of literature from the upper shelves of libraries and other difficult places, to the fire-side, and the sunny window-seats of family drawing-rooms; letting young readers into the quaint customs of the past, throwing light on almost-forgotten sayings, giving meaning to phrases the origins of which had well nigh been forgotten. Thus we learn that the absurd practice of making April Fools is supposed to have originated in the festival which was held at the time of the vernal equinox, or "first day of the month" of the Jews; on which day, according to their traditions, Noah sent the dove out of the ark on its bootless mission. Hence the sending and sending persons on fruitless errands on the first of April—a jest still maintained in many places, and exceedingly enjoyed by young people. So we find Mystery, perpetuating by pantomime, the memory of remarkable events which could not otherwise have been preserved. In this way, as we all know, arose the miracle-plays of the Roman Church, in which the people were taught the principal events of the Old and New Testaments by seeing them acted by the priests. And even subsequently to the art of printing, the vulgar have been prone to continue this mode of commemoration; and which the wearing of oak leaves on the 29th of May, in remembrance of the restoration of Charles II., and the still popular processions of Guy Fawkes, are amongst the latest illustrations. We had supposed ourselves in possession of a goodly quantity of the old-world lore issued in these pages; but Mr. Timbs's volumes cast throw light occasionally on these and similarly, and even on Strand and Footpaths themselves; and will prove of real value even to literary seekers, who will here find themselves spared the trouble of much labour and research on a great variety of matters. Speaking of the yule-log, our author tells us, that, as the servants were entitled to ale at their meals while the log lasted, they usually endeavoured to get as large a one as the hearth would admit of; and he adds, that Ingestre Abbey, near Shrewsbury, was burnt down, during the times of the civil wars, through kindling too great a yule-log. In Herefordshire, where some of the Roman and feudal customs are, or were lately, practised, Mr. Timbs tells us:

On the eve of Old Christmas Day are lighted thirteen fires—thirteen (representing) in a circle, and a larger one round a pole in the centre (the Virgin Mary). While these fires are burning, the farm-labourers witness the brightness of the Apostles and Virgin, drawn from some shed, into which they lead a cow, on whose horns a large plum-cake has been stuck. The cider labourer, taking a pail of cider, addresses the cow thus:

> "Here's to thy pretty face and thy white horn!
> God send thy master a crop of corn—
> Both wheat, rye, and barley, and all sorts of grain!
> And next year, if we live, we'll drink to thee again!"

The cider is then thrown in the face of the cow, who, by a toss of the head, generally throws the plum-cake on the ground. If it falls forward, it is an omen of a good harvest next year; if backward, that it will be unfavourable. This ceremony is kept at which is usually kept up till the next morning.

The first part of this ceremony reminds us of one which we heard of in Shropshire. On Christmas-eve, the colliers in the neighbourhood of Coventry have a custom of making a cake of clay, in the centre of which they place a large candle, with fifty or more smaller ones around it. This, when lighted, they carry to the threshold of every door, and, kneeling down, sing around it. This they call a 'star;' and the greatest devotion is offered to the appearance of the bright one in the East, that went before the shepherds of yore to Jerusalem. There seems some reference in this custom to that named there in the Herefordshire ceremony, and yet a faint likeness between them. With the colliers it serves as an occasion for obtaining money to drink-money. Mr. Timbs proves the use of the Christmas-tree to be of much older date in England than we have been accustomed to suppose it, and reminds us that Stowe, in giving an account of a great storm on Candlemas Day, more than four centuries ago, speaks of the standing-up of a standard-tree on Cornhill, which was full of holme [holly] and ivy for Christmas.

And it is thought (observes our author) that the Christmas-tree may be traced, as a symbol long anterior to the Christian era, namely to that cradle of civilisation, Egypt. The palm-tree is known to put forth a shoot every month, and a spray of this tree, with twelve shoots on it, was used in Egypt at the time of the winter solstice, as a symbol of the year completed.

The palm-tree spray of Egypt, on reaching Italy, was imitated by the tip of the pyramidal

&c., and was decorated with lighted tapers, in honour of Saturn. On the other hand, in Germany (from which country we have undoubtedly brought the revival of the custom of dressing Christmas-trees) they are as many pyramids as trees. They are formed of slips of wood, arranged pyramidically, on which the tapers are arranged, with green paper laid amongst them in imitation of leaves. Amongst other little-known local customs connected with Christmas, we are reminded that

Dr. Stukeley said, only a century ago, "On the eve of Christmas Day, at York, they carry mistletoe to the high altar of the Cathedral, and proclaim a public and universal liberty, pardon, and freedom to all sorts of inferior and even wicked people, at the gates of the city, towards the four quarters of heaven."

What a mingling have we, in this ceremony, of pagan rites with a conception of Christian principles! Amongst other singular customs,

"More honour'd in the breach than the observance,"

mention is made of "Crack-nut Sunday," or the Sunday next before the eve of St. Michael's Day, when

Within the memory of aged parishioners of Kingston-upon-Thames, the congregation in the parish church were accustomed to crack nuts during Divine service. Young and old folks alike joined in the cracking. [illegible] the oddity was not peculiar to Kingston, for [illegible] [illegible] Vicar of Wakefield, one of the parishioners, "They kept up the Christmas carol, and [illegible] knots on Valentine morning, ate pancakes at Shrovetide, showed their wit on the first of April, and religiously cracked nuts on Michaelmas eve."

Yet, with due deference to the learned writer, there is a great distinction in cracking nuts on the eve of the saint's day, and cracking them during the service at church on the Sunday before; and so we are led to think that the oddity was peculiar to the pretty river-side town. Of such amusing and interesting details our readers will find a rich feast in the volume before us. "The May-day," "The Well-dressings," "Mothering Sunday," and a host of other graceful and pretty fashions, are either dead or dying out before the utilitarian spirit of the Present, which marches on, overturning and throwing on one side all that is not entirely sensible and strictly necessary; as if God himself had not sprinkled poppies and blue-bells amongst the growing corn; so every day is rendering more precious these records of the past, with which soon very few of us will have any personal acquaintance.

Magnet Stories, No. 36. "Lost in the Wood." By Mrs. Alex. Gilchrist. (Groombridge and Sons, Paternoster-row.)—Mrs. Gilchrist's addition to the Magnet Stories fully sustains the character of the series. The remembrance of the childhood of their elders is always delightful to children; such details bridge the distance between them, and awaken sympathies which no other themes can do. To hear of what mamma or papa did when they were little children, to know that they, too, had their tasks and troubles and advantures like themselves, creates a new bond of sympathy between them, bridges the years, and makes the childhood of their parents identical with their own. How merrily the little ones press ours; how closely they lean against us, listening to such reminiscences—which Nature herself, as they are over the present and gone [illegible], designs to be one [illegible]! We [illegible] of green fields all the [illegible].

The Life-Boat: a Journal of the National Life-Boat Institution. (Wm. Clowes and Son, [illegible]-street, Charing-cross.)—We do not take up this journal with a view to its literary merits. It possesses more stronger grounds for public support in the simple fact that it registers the valuable and heroic services of boats, men by whose aid this, perhaps the most noble of all our public institutions, for the rescue of distressed humanity, is rendered actively efficient. If the majority of the dead and the preservation of the service be considered, not even the majority of [illegible] [illegible] can equal in its [illegible] exigence the almost hopeless horror of shipwreck on our coasts, where the violence of the sea and the rugged nature of the coast [illegible] denies all but the merest chance of escape to the stranded vessel at her ordinary boats. Should the disaster happen in the vicinity of one of the Society's stations (of which there are 1[illegible] on the coasts of the United Kingdom), no matter how high the sea rises, how heavily the wind raves, or the breakers roar among the rocks, a crew is always waiting to man the life-boat. Even [illegible] volunteers, and hazard life and limb in the endeavour to save the perishing sailors, to whom, but for their providential succour, "no help cometh." What was the prospect of those who annually perished by shipwreck on the narrow seas, and on the coasts of the United Kingdom, before the registration of such dismal statistics, we have no means of knowing. At present, notwithstanding the improvement in our mercantile navy, the system of certificated officers, excellent charts, light-houses, light-ships, buoys, and all other appliances which philanthropy and science have introduced—life-boats, Manby's apparatus, life-belts, &c., &c.—no less than 700 human beings are annually drowned on the shores and in the waters of the United Kingdom alone. During the past winter I find the number of persons saved by the boats of the National Life-Boat Institution to amount to no less than 303, and the loss of the wreck of the "[illegible]," on shore on the *North Skeet Rocks*, Boulmer, Northumberland, does not give the number of the crew saved. It is, therefore, with much regret, notwithstanding individual donations and bequests, that we find the committee ordering the sale of £1,[illegible] stock from the funded capital of the Institution. The outlays of the institution are ever in advance of the receipts, and yet, from all the several parts of Great Britain constant requisitions are being made for larger boats, at new cost, or the establishment of boats at new stations; while a constant drain, in the shape of current expenses, contracts the utility of an institution whose claims are, or deserve to be, in the widest and grandest sense of the phrase, National.

JOURNAL OF THE WORKHOUSE VISITING SOCIETY. (London: Longman, Green, & Co.) —This number opens with some very interesting extracts from the Report of Her Majesty's Inspector of Schools for Pauper and Vagrant Children, from which we gather that the condition of the children and the conduct of the schools are daily improving. The account is, for the most part, of a very hopeful character. A letter on military training of boys in the workhouse schools, from the Master of the Wolverhampton Union, is worthy of attention; as is also Miss Louisa Twining's answer to the questions of the Commissioners to inquire into the State of Popular Education in England. This lady suggests, in order to avert the evils of large numbers of children herding together without family affections or any attempt at their cultivation, first the appointment of a superior class of persons over district and workhouse schools, and secondly the maintaining a certain amount of protection to the girls after they have left school. The following passage is well worth quotation:

> With training schools wanted urgently for boys for the army and navy, for labour of all kinds in the colonies, where they would be gladly received, in Britain, and for girls as servants equally at home and abroad, why should there be all this vast waste of material, and a loss inflicted to fill our workhouses? For as long as our workhouses are what they are, and seem intended to be by those who describe those there—places of degradation—it must be fatal to bring up children in the daily contact, if not familiarity with all those classes who make it their home.
>
> G. A. W.

*** We have not received either the first part of "The Englishwoman's Journal," or "The Odd Fellow's Magazine" for notice this month.

AMUSEMENTS OF THE MONTH.

The past month of August has, as is usually the case, brought but little novelty with it to theatrical matters; and as four of the leading theatres are closed, we have little to descant on. At the

ADELPHI,

"The Dead Heart" has been drawing well during the last few weeks; but by the time this sees the light will probably have receded from the bills. At the

HAYMARKET,

Which flourishes irrespective of "seasons," and never appears to close its doors, "My Lord and my Lady" have been very attractive personages.

THE OLYMPIC

Closed on the 18th (on extra night for a benefit).

THE STRAND,

Deserted by its company, has been taken possession of for a few nights by Mr. and Mrs. Howard Paul.

THE PRINCESS'S

It closed, to reopen shortly with a new play, entitled "Playing with Fire," and "Othello," Mr. Fechter being the mighty Moor. At

THE LYCEUM,

Which has opened for "an autumn season" under Mr. Falconer, has been produced from his pen, a new and original comedy, called "Woman; or, Love against the World," and it has been very favourably received. The following is a sketch of the plot: *Geraldine D'Arcy* (Mrs. C. Young) has married from devotion a young Englishman, *The Hon. Mr. Ardin* (Mr. H. Vezin), and the union becomes, in consequence, much ridiculed. The gentleman stays so long at Trebe (the scene of the adventure) that his London friends become alarmed and despatch *Mr. Lumley Jones*, a fashionable man of the world (played by Mr. W. Lacy), to bring him back. Meanwhile, *Ardin* and *Geraldine* have been secretly married. But one *Lady Harriet Wilmington* (Miss Murray), who admires *Ardin*, informs *Geraldine*, in her husband's absence, that the marriage is illegal; whereupon *Geraldine* leaves him—he returns, finds her fled, and travels about himself for three years. In the interim, he becomes *Lord Lindengrove*—and she *Lady Lettice Mountjoy*. To sum it up briefly, several meetings and explanations ensue, and "all ends," as the storybooks say, "happily." The comedy, well written and of smart and elegant dialogue, was well received. It is to be hoped Mr. Falconer's autumn season may prove remunerative, though it is a bad time for London amusements.

W. R.

THE TOILET.

(Especially from Paris.)

FIRST FIGURE.—White muslin dress. At the bottom of the skirt a goffered flounce, surmounted by a puffing bouillonné, having a double head, with guipure insertion in the middle, and narrow ribbon run in it. Low body, covered with a short square cape, trimmed like the skirt and plaited. Sleeves, with three puffs and a flounce, surmounted by insertion. A mauve silk slip under the dress. A Tuscan hat, with white feather; [illegible] gloves; mauve silk [illegible] bordered with black velvet.

SECOND FIGURE.—Robe of sky-blue silk; trimmed at the bottom with a plain bias-cut band of white French crape, surmounted by a white chicorée. Body in the waistcoat style, trimmed like the skirt. Sleeve half-wide with elbow, finished with a white satin cuff, ornamented with a chicorée to match the skirt.

Under-sleeves and collar of embroidered muslin. Muslin skirt, with graduated flounces. White crape bonnet, trimmed with white roses and myosotis. White marquise parasol. Glacé gloves.

The vogue of flounces continues, but we see a crowd of other garnitures. Here a deep flounce, with a plaited heading; there several flounces, surmounted by, or even, a bouillonné. A very popular style of ornament is a coloured band of plain silk, of a brilliant contrast with the colour of the material; another, not nearly so general, is made by putting on a deep bias fulled as high as the knee, and divided at intervals by rosettes, buttons, or bands of silk or velvet.

Barège dresses are frequently made with five or seven narrow flounces. White muslin robes are in great vogue for elegant dress at the watering places, where they give many soirées dansantes; in which case nothing so well replaces a veritable robe de bal. They are garnished with embroidered flounces, or with goffered volants de Valenciennes, or bouillonnés; in short, caprice is the order of the day, and everything pretty and graceful is the fashion. Dresses of barège, silk grenadine, and tarlatane are also much employed on the same occasions. Corsages are made both high and low, according to the material, and the purpose of the dress. Wide sleeves and those with elbows and ruches are preferred. I spoke in my last letter of the revival of muslin shawls and mantelets—these are always fresh and convenient, especially for the toilet de campagne. Black shawls of embroidered cashmere and garnished with lace are very much worn; but we see a great many rather shawls of silk grenadine, with satin borders and embroidered in the corners. Grey paletots and burnous have a constant vogue, and the same may be said of the black silk pardessus.

The autumn models of confections do not exhibit any material change of fashion.

PASSING EVENTS RE-EDITED.

The great event of the past month has been the Social Science Congress at Dublin, where amongst the many other interesting subjects discussed, that of employments for educated women was introduced. Hitherto, we confess that as a looker-on we really have not perceived any definite advancement of the question. Miss Blackwell's example appears to have awakened but little enthusiasm amongst the cultivated women for the study of medicine as a profession, chiefly, we believe, because the women whose intellectual and mental power would fit them for this calling require no precedent. As in the case of Dr. Elizabeth herself, each woman carves her own way in the world, and requires no guiding. The inclination for such an exceptional study, as women are at present educated, must be intuitive. Mrs. Crizand tells us that the wood-cutting school at Islington failed, because the pupils all married; but should this have been a reason for preventing fresh pupils benefiting by a knowledge of the art? If we remember rightly, a less pleasing reason was given by the Committee of the School of Design; and the want of due attention and perseverance was alleged at South Kensington as a reason for giving up a class for teaching women-pupils the art of wood-engraving. In the course of

Mrs. Grenville's paper we observed a remark, that the difficulty with regard to educated women does not lie in the obtaining of employment, but in the manner of obtaining the remuneration, which, to be acceptable, must be offered in such a way as will not do violence to the refined mind and feelings of gentlewomen; and proposes a society to be constructed by ladies and gentlemen, who would appear as a go-between between the employer and employed—so that the payer and payee would not at all appear. Really, if these gentlewomen looking for employment are at the very outset ashamed of the money which is to render them independent, the sooner we cease to pity them the better. They remind us of Lady Morgan's old gentlewoman, who, compelled to sell mutton pies, was wont to carry her basket into back alleys and unfrequented places, and after the faintest possibly uttered "Mutton pies!" ejaculate, "I hope to God that nobody hears me!" Was Lady Morgan ashamed to take the money she had earned of her publisher? Is Rosa Bonheur degraded by being paid for her pictures? Do the host of lady vocalists and others lose caste because they are paid for their services? Our lady friends, with such claims to work for, had better seek to raise in them a right feeling of the dignity of labour, even where gentlewomen are concerned. If these claimants to a share of the labour market are themselves ashamed of the very end they have in view, what earnestness can they throw into their pursuit? Active minds may suggest and even act for them; but without individual interest and stimulation what amount of excellence or perseverance will be obtainable? There is nothing derogatory in painting in oil or water, in ornamental designing, colouring photographs, wood engraving, and lithography; the degradation is in being paid for the work; while the artists are lingering and thirsting for the remuneration, for the very sake of which they have undertaken it. This affectation is really as vulgar as it is pitiable. Miss Bessie Parkes' scheme of emigration for this class of women meets with our best wishes. It is sensible and practicable, and offers the only means of maintaining a balance between the sexes in a country where the excess upon the female population is always increasing. While upon the subject of the employment of women, we may observe that one of the last bills brought during the recent session of Parliament was one on the part of Lord Shaftesbury for improving the condition of women and children in factories. His lordship spoke of the long hours (from 6 to 9), of the tender years at which these little ones are set to work, either at home or in the establishments. He also asserted that the minds of both are undermined by their slavery, to the utter neglect of home and children. As a commentary on this system, which deprives the children of the mother's care, and consigns the youngest to a nurse, and the rest to the contamination of the streets, we have the case of the child-murderers at the Chester assizes, the revolting details of which might [illegible] Exeter Hall, with worse than at Tongatabu, or the Fejee islands.

During the past month we have to record the loss of the good Sidney Herbert, whose deeds as a statesman, a philanthropist, and a Christian gentleman, have added new brightness to his own beautiful and, to Englishmen, sacred names. Another name familiar to us appears upon a tomb, that of Madame Catherine Hayes; she died at Sydenham from the bursting of a blood-vessel; but all who saw her during the past winter must have noticed the fading bloom of the sweet cantatrice.

We go out of our way to chronicle the pleasure we received in listening to a fine lecture by W. Preece, Esq., at the Greenwich Lecture-hall, on the evening of the 26th ult.; the subject "The [illegible] and [illegible] of Science." With taste, and the necessary attention to the art of declamation, Mr. Preece has every element of success. The materials of the lecture were excellently chosen and cleverly arranged.

C. A. W.

ANSWERS TO CORRESPONDENTS.

POETRY accepted, with thanks: "The Path by the River;" "The Traveller's Dream;" "The Summer Rain" is rather unfinished; "Kate," an obscurity in the sense of the last verse stands, for the present, between us and this poem. Will our valued contributor kindly oblige us with an amended copy?

POETRY declined, with thanks: "Reunion;" "On Her Majesty's Visit to Ireland;" "Hope;" "Ministering Angels."

PROSE received: "A Queer Adventure;" "Canova;" "The Old Water Gap;" "A Mistress of Fleming."

"All in the Wrong" shall be replied to in a few days.

"F. M., M.D., Cork."—We returned this gentleman's tale by return of post, but have received no further directions regarding the MS., which we shall gladly return on receipt of stamps for the purpose.

PROSE received and accepted: "Lost and Found Early;" "A Word for Old Age."

"[illegible]."—We regret, at the last moment, to be obliged to defer the continuation of this tale till our next number, when it shall appear without fail.

Printed by [illegible] and Tuxford, 346, Strand, London.

OLD SWEET.

(A Staffordshire Story.)

"Thee'lt come whome soon to-night, father?" said Mrs. Lloyd, anxiously. "To-morrow's Sunday, and thee minds what thee promised the parson."

"Grand-dad's a-goin to take me to church," put in little Polly Lloyd, with her mouth full of porridge.

Whereupon Mrs. Lloyd turned round reprovingly upon that young person, with "Hold thee noise, and ate thee [illegible], do, then!" administering a slap by way of emphasis.

"Nay, wench, don't be so sharp with the little 'un," said the old man. "Her is goin to church with Grand-dad, if her's a good girl, isn't her. Drink thee porridge, my child, and don't cry. Hast put a bit o' candle in the lantern, Poll?"

"Thee won't want the lantern to-night, father," the woman answered, still coaxingly. "Thee'lt come back straight from th' All, and not go to Wood-green, to-night! Thee'lt be whome again before it's dark."

"I tell thee, give me the lantern!" said the old man doggedly. "It'll be dark afore I get away from th' All. The master always keeps me a long spell talking; besides I want to see our Milly on the way, and she'll, as like as not, have one o' them praying fellows there, and thee can't get a word in till he's holloed himself out o' breath. I want to see Milly about them pigs."

The woman, with a sigh, reached down the lantern from its hook, and brought a thick walking-stick from a corner. "To-night and Milly to-morrow," she said.

"Her won't talk about pigs of a Sunday, nor I am neither," said the old man, with a half-laugh; "her won't even work a bit o' work of a Sunday, let alone bargaining for live pigs."

As he spoke, he was putting the string of the lantern round his neck.

"Be sure they take care o' the money," said the daughter.

"Don't thee fret thyself."

"And thee won't go to Wood-green!"

"My word!" cried the old man, striking his stick, angrily, on the paved floor, "will thee never have done with Wood-green? If a man does, once in a way, take a drop o' yale too much, is it always to be thrown in his face? Didn't I tell thee, wench, I was coming home straight from th' All? What more dost want?"

He had not told her anything of the kind, nor would his promise, on that subject, have been worth much if it had been made. However, he had been a man of his word on all other matters through a long life; and so on this Wood-green subject he always managed to save his conscience by some such equivocation as the present. The Wood-green temptations, though irresistible, would have lost half their compulsion had he been conscious of having told a downright lie in yielding to them. The asking whether one has not made a promise—the "Didn't I tell thee?" is very different from absolutely making a promise.

As the old man stepped out into the street he met his daughter's husband, Abram Lloyd, black and grim-begrimed, coming into his tea.

"Where be'st goin?" asked Abram.

"Goin for the money, lad," answered the old man. "And I, may be, shall look in at Milly's on the way about them pigs. Good-night, my lad."

Abram, coming in to his wife, said: "He's off to the old place again." And so there was some talk between husband and wife upon the subject of "yale," and little Polly, listening with ears too obviously open, received another slap, ostensibly for having spilt porridge on her pinafore, really because Mrs. Lloyd felt instinctively that the child ought not to have heard those reminiscences of grand-dad's discredit. The uneducated have a quick sense enough of any breach of right, but they cannot discriminate nicely as to the manner of mending the breach. Slapping little Polly for spilling the porridge certainly did not wipe from her memory the conversation about Grand-dad and his "yale."

"He'll fall into the Park Pool, and be drowned, some o' these nights," said Abram, in conclusion. "That's what'll be the end o' him."

Abram had finished such conversations many times before with precisely the same form of words. Being slow of thought and speech, he always had a stereotyped series of sentences for any subject that came up often. The saving of the painful conception of ideas, and of the slow labour of translating them into words, is an object with a sluggish nature. The trouble of remembering what one has thought and said before is as nothing to that of inventing. Nevertheless Abram afterwards took to himself credit for the gift of prophecy in having uttered these words on this particular night. "I says so," was Abram's explanation, whenever the story of "Old Sweet" came up in after-years. "Them was my words."

Meantime old Sweet trudged away up the street, the bare basket, as yet unlighted, hanging from his neck, and his thick stick beating time to his footsteps as he went. A hale, hearty old man, white-haired and ruddy of complexion, with a light grey eye scarcely crow-footed at the corner, a kindly smile, a thin-lipped mouth firm of shape, but a little twisted from the habit of tobacco-chewing. His tall, broad-shouldered figure was hardly bent; his legs were nimble enough; he swung his arm as he went; and when a neighbour called to him as he passed, he turned his head quickly, not bringing his whole body round, as a feeble old man does. Clearly a man wonderfully strong for his age. Still, one who knew him might see signs of the incipient weakness in his face and figure. His gait was not so steady, his legs though nimble were unsteady, his hand was tremulous when he stretched his arm out.

The neighbours, standing smoking at their doors, all had a word for the old man as he passed up the street, and a word about him when he had passed.

"He won't walk so steady when he comes back," said one.

"I wish I were in his shoes," said another. "Nought to do but to take the money and to drink it."

"Broad is the gate and narrow is the way," cried a lately-converted methodist, with a heavenly energy that more than made up for the misquotation; "and sure he's in that road, and the devil has a safe grip o' him."

"Nay, brother," said an elder of that church, "none o' us be perfect. Old Sweet has led an honest life for sixty year, and no man has had aught to say against him from his youth upwards, save concerning this weakness for the drink. We should pray for him, brother. Lookee the good he gets for his soul Sunday at the church. I fear the parson preaches a many more souls to hell than he opens to heaven. Still it don't become us to judge a fellow-creature."

While they talked, a little toddling girl from a cottage higher up had seized the old man's hand, and was trotting by his side, prattling to him as she would have prattled to her own father.

Old Sweet, at his sturdy pace, soon left the houses behind him, cheering his small companion with the gift of an apple as sturdy-cheeked as himself. The house where he lived with the Lloyds was a little way out of the small town of Hedgebury, on the Bulimbon-road. The Hall, whither he was going, was in Hedgebury, belonging to the greatest man of the place, Squire Thorne, a man possessing much land in those parts and many coal mines. Abram Lloyd was body-collier in one of these mines. But old Sweet had worked for Squire Thorne—for him and his father before him—for many years and in a more domestic capacity. He had been chief gardener at the Hall. Not very long back, however, the young Squire had pensioned him off, Sweet being on the verge of seventy, and, further, being obstinately wedded to the old-fashioned ways of gardening, which his master wished to travel with the new. Thus Sweet was pensioned off, and a more scientific son of Adam was installed in his place. This pension he always received on the Saturday night, and that was his business at the Hall on the night in question.

On his way he had to pass by one end of the Park Pool. The Park Pool, which belonged to Squire Thorne, as almost everything in Hedgebury did, was of considerable extent, of irregular shape, broadening here and narrowing there, and, though for the most part shallow, having holes of great depth in places. The Bulimbon Road bounded one end of the pool, and this end was reckoned to be the deepest part of it, insomuch that it was always a bugbear to the mothers of small children, and was thought to be a dangerous place, as we have heard, for people returning from public-houses at night.

When old Sweet reached the end of the Park Pool he stopped for a minute, and, standing on the grassy edge, looked out on the expanse of water. From this point the pool seemed of great extent. It stretched away for perhaps a quarter of a mile, and then a slight bend hid the boundary of the further bank. There was a small rocky island not far from the road, with low trees growing thereon and dipping their branches into the water, and beneath their overhanging branches, half buried in the rushes, a boat was moored. Water-fowl were sailing rapidly to and fro, leaving sharp, dark lines on the white water in their wake, or rising suddenly for a short flight, making clearly-defined widening circles in the spots whence they rose and where they alighted. The sun had set, and the sky was already beginning to lose its rosy tint. The trees and the meadows on the borders of the pool were becoming every moment more indistinct in detail, more sharp in outline, coming out as flat dark masses against the light sky. In the distance mists were rising, concealing yet more the line of the further bank. The water was perfectly white, save where the shadows from the island and the boat sank about their—shadows and their substance mingling without sign of division, just as we see them mingle in so many of Turner's pictures. The water was so white that it seemed a gap in the landscape, and the island pinnacled on, its shadow looked like a column rising up from an immense depth.

I cannot tell whether the old man felt any influence from the twilight scene. He stood, as I said before, for a minute or so on the grassy margin by the road-side, looking across the apparent void, and then stooping drew his stick idly to and fro in the deep water lapping at his feet. Another degree of darkness came upon the landscape suddenly, as if a veil had fallen between the dim light and the earth, and old Sweet shook the water-drops from his stick and proceeded on his way.

Cottages began to appear along the road, and soon the road became a street. This was a portion of Hedgebury known by the name of Hell Road. Here lived Milly Whiteman, the other married daughter of Sweet. Jem Whiteman, her husband, was by trade a gun-lock filer, and he was just turning out of the shed which served for his shop, when the old man came up.

Jem was holding by the arm a small boy, who [illegible] in a [illegible] manner. Another boy, black-haired and pale, evidently Jem's son, from the strong likeness between them, followed at the heels of his father.

"What's the lad been a doin', now?" quoth the old man, somewhat indignantly; and Jem proceeded to explain that the culprit had been playing the truant from his work all the afternoon. Jem sprinkled his discourse profusely with Bible-phrases, and more than hinted his opinion that the boy he held by the [illegible] was possessed by the devil.

This unlucky youngster, it appeared, was Abram, the son of Martin Lloyd, and so nephew to Jem Whiteman and grandson to old Sweet. He was apprenticed to his uncle to learn the gun-lock filing trade, much to his own disgust, for he evidently was an idle boy, who delighted in mischief rather than work.

The grandfather, however, was disposed to treat that young rascal leniently.

"Thee 'rt a bad lad," he said, shaking his stick, but speaking in no very harsh tone; "but thou'lt never do so no more, wilt thee? Let'un go, Jem, this time. Boys is but boys, and he's only young. I doubt I didn't love work much better nor him at his age."

The pale black-haired boy looked shocked at his cousin's escape.

"Thee never play'dst truant in thy life, Hiram, didst thee?" the old man said, contemptuously; adding, under his breath, "Thee never hadst the spirit for it."

The fact was, the old man had no strong liking for Jem Whiteman or his son. Jem was a great man among the methodists—a class-leader, even a preacher on occasion—and for the methodists old Sweet had a supreme contempt. He had a notion that they were, for the most part, a poor-spirited lot, certainly not so steady and upright as those who attended the church, or those who attended nowhere. Even his daughter Milly lost something in his esteem from this cause; and this good woman felt this, and bore it as a cross that it was meant for her to bear.

Milly, hearing her father's voice, came to the door, and with her a little girl, the exact counterpart of the pale boy with the black hair. The boy was objectionable, the girl pretty and lovable. Often what we dislike in one we like in the other, though it is not easy to explain why. Milly loved her father with her whole soul. It grieved her tender heart that he was not a methodist. If he could but be brought into the right way! This weakness of his with regard to Wood-green was the great thorn in the flesh to her. How she prayed, how she wrestled with the Divine Power, about this besetting sin of her father's, is not to be written about lightly here. She loved him all the more tenderly for this fault. So it is—that human weaknesses, not strengths, call forth in us the deepest, sweetest love. Often she found tears when she thought of the [illegible] old man [illegible] of his honour. There is no love like that of a mother for the helplessness of her child; and Milly's love for her father had something of this in it.

The old man felt the depth of this love and [illegible] upon it, as men always do. Milly could say more to him than Mary Lloyd could—her entreaties and remonstrance came straight from the heart, and she could no more help uttering them than feeling them; but the father [illegible] her in his answers as he never thought of answering his other daughter. Mary's periphrases he answered with equivocations; Milly's plain heart-utterances he met with [illegible] confessions and with jests.

The old question was settled in a very few words. Then Milly came down the steps and took the old man by the hand. Little Esther retired into the house. Little Polly Lloyd would have listened and looked with all her eyes and ears. Mrs. Lloyd would have [illegible] Polly for the [illegible]. Milly, at the same time, knowing why father had, bitterly [illegible] herself.

"Oh, father dear!" she said, "you will not go to Wood-green to-night? Promise me you will not! Oh, to see you as I saw you last time, reeling up the street! Oh, think of the sin!"

She put her pale face close to his red cheek, and stroked it so that his [illegible], as if in pain.

"Thee be'st but a poor fool, wench," the old man said. "Them Methodies have turned thee brain. A mug of good malt would put a little colour into thee own white cheek, and a little courage into thee heart. Dost 'ee think I be goin' to put myself under the thumb o' them praying fellows? I tell thee what, the more thee sayest against it, the more I'll take my own way. There's no sin in drinking a drop of a Saturday night, and no man has ever seen me drunk. If I get a little bit merry, why that's good for the health, and don't hurt me nor nobody else."

There was more talk of this kind from her and from him, and then she desisted.

"There's rag at the door an thee please,

father?" she asked, as he left. "Don't forget!"

"No, lass; I'll rap," he said; and so went on his way.

Night was setting in. There were lights in the windows here and there, and shadows of latticed panes chequered the street as he walked up it. He stopped in the light of one of these windows, and pulling out his big watch looked at the hour.

"My word!" he muttered to himself, "I shall be late at the master's;" and the sound of his stick beat quicker time after the moment's pause.

The gate which opened into the Hall stables was but a short distance beyond Hall End. When he turned in there, the court-yard, under the shadow of its ancient trees, was utterly dark.

I have related a series of very trivial incidents, no doubt, in the foregoing paragraphs; but it sometimes happens that trivial incidents are remembered and treasured up as of great moment. The last few hours of a dying friend stamp themselves in our memory for ever—each word, each grasp, each change in the pale face comes back to us through all our life in its due order and with an awful significance. People remembered afterwards every word they had spoken to old Sweet on this night, and every word that he had spoken in return. They remembered how he had looked, how he had quickened his pace here or slackened it there, how he had stood for a minute gazing up the Park Pool dabbling the end of his stick in the water. Some said afterwards that they had noticed a strange expression in his face—a sign as of one marked for death; and some recalled sayings of his on this night—sayings which had struck them at the time as having a mysterious meaning; words of doom uttered all unconsciously by him, but awfully fulfilled in the end. The little girl who had trotted by his side on the Barleston road treasured up that incident till her dying day, and in virtue of it always claimed pre-eminently the office of telling the story of old Sweet. His daughter Milly never forgave herself for not having besought him on that occasion more earnestly to keep away from the public-house at Wood-green. She had felt the inward call to speak words of power, to wrestle with resistless strength, and she had stifled that call and had spoken weak words of her own devising, instead of those which it had been put into her heart to pour forth.

Squire Thorne kept the old man in talk for some time, and then dismissed him to the kitchen to drink a mug of the Hall ale. The warming influences of that quite put to the rout any vague notions he might previously have had of returning straight home. His lantern was lighted, and, when he turned out of the stable-yard gate, he took the direction opposite to that of the Barleston-road—the direction which led to Wood-green.

* * * * *

Milly White'ss, in default of other success, had succeeded in persuading her father to rap at her door as he returned from that terrible Wood-green-inn. This had become a regular custom, and the old man, however advanced his stage of drunkenness might be, never failed to give this sign that he was safe so far on his road home. Most times when Milly heard the rap she would get out of bed, and throwing open the window look into the street, seeing, on moonless nights, the retreating light of the lantern flickering and flaring and staggering on its course down the Barleston-road. Though the sin of her father always smote her, though she felt that each new drunken fit added to the burden which must one day bring down a just retribution, still it was a relief to know that the old man was safe so far. There was the great danger of the Park Pool yet to be passed it was true, and Milly always wished most earnestly that the Park Pool had been situated on the other side of Hall End, so that the rap at the door might have told her that that danger too was once more escaped; but every foot of ground got over in safety was something to be thankful for, something to encourage the hope that the long-suffering mercy of God was not yet wearied out.

On this night, Milly heard her father's uncertain footsteps a little past twelve. There was a pause of sound, and then a shuffling of unsteady feet upon the steps, and then the sharp rap of the stick. Milly got out of bed, and was soon enough at the window to say "Good night, father," before the old man was beyond earshot.

"Good-night, my wench," he shouted huskily, as he lurched away down the street. These were the last words Milly ever heard him speak; and she was very thankful all her life-long that she had heard them. It was almost like a death-bed leave-taking.

Milly shut the window, and got into bed again. Jem was snoring loudly—a snore usually melodious, not unlike the voice with which he led the chapel-choir. Milly still listened to her father's retreating footsteps, till they were altogether lost in her husband's snores. She lay with closed eyes, picturing to herself the old man's progress. The light of the lantern danced like a will-o'-the-wisp through her fancy. She saw it playing on the hedges and on the rutted road, and now flashing up into the thick darkness of the sky. This will-o'-the-wisp light with the lingering echoes of the heavy staggering feet, led her step by step along the road old Sweet was travelling. Now he neared the Park Pool. She saw the flash of the lantern on the glistening waters; she held her breath. The danger would be over in a moment. But suppose he should stagger too near the brink? suppose his feet should catch in the long grass? Just that she might feel the relief more keenly when she dismissed such fancies, and assured herself that now the danger was past, she gave way for the moment to imagining the worst. Yes; he tripped in the long matted grass, he caught at the branch of the hazel-bush overhanging the pool, and missed it, and with a struggle half-recovered his balance, and then with uplifted hands grasping the air fall over. She heard the plunge, she heard the hiss of the extinguished light, she saw the dim white struggle in the blackness. . . . . No; she dismissed the scene from her fancy. He had passed the Pool, and was now rapidly nearing home. Thank God for all his great mercies! this one more added to so many!

The beatings of her heart were becoming more quiet; she was repeating to herself the comforting words of some favourite hymn; she had turned her head sideways on the pillow and was addressing herself to sleep, feeling that now the danger was past. Suddenly there was the rap upon the door again—loud and sharp and very distinct.

"Jem! Jem!" she cried, waking her husband, and was out of bed and at the window in a moment. All the street was dark and quiet—nothing to be seen or heard—only a something that she felt—a shiver and a curdling of the blood, and a pain gnawing her heart.

"What ails thee?" Jem said, a little querulously, clutching up with a yawn.

She could not persuade him that she had heard the rap again. It was a dream, it was fancy. No, he was not going to strike a light and go opening the door at that time o' night. "Get thee to bed, old woman; that's the best thing thee can do. It's mighty hard that a man can't have his sleep quiet when he works hard o' days."

"Then, I'll go myself and see, Jem," she said trembling; and striking a light with much difficulty from the old flint and steel contrivance, she went down in her night-dress and opened the door, and, putting the light forth, gazed round. There was nothing to be seen or heard.

* * * *

When the morning came, Milly half-believed that she had deceived herself as to that second rap. Things appear so different at midnight and at dawn! Still she had a lurking dread that something might have happened to her father. Of course, she believed in signs and warnings; it was of the very essence of her religion to do so. The only literature that she read—the Methodist Magazines of that day, were brimful of supernatural stories. If it had not been her fancy, what did the sound portend?

So Milly hastened to dress herself, and before she saw to any of her household matters she set off for Abram Lloyd's house in the Harborne-road. Her fears seemed to her so fanciful in the daylight, that she encouraged them as she had encouraged her imagination to picture that terrible scene of the Park Pool the night before. She felt so sure they were absurd, that she experienced a kind of enjoyment in keeping them up, until the moment when the certainty of their groundlessness should dispel them entirely.

If any tragedy had taken place at the Park Pool during the darkness, there were no signs of it now. The sheet of water lay breathless in that exquisite serenity of early morning. The dead pallor of the evening twilight had given place to the tender colouring which follows the dawn; there was a tremulous flush coming and going upon the surface, which one might liken to the flush which trembles through the pure skin of an infant.

As Milly paused a moment, she saw a man advancing towards her along the Harborne road. It was Abram Lloyd. That painful leap of the heart, which comes when after suspense we find our fears on the verge of realization, when, clinging to the last straw of hope, we ask inwardly "Then can it be true?"—that leap of the heart made Milly start forward with clasped hands.

"Hast seen aught o' the old man, Milly?" Abram asked.

"No! is he not at home?"

He had not returned home. Abram was on his way then to the Hall End, and then to Wood-green. Probably the old man had slept at the inn there. Hope of that, however, was dispelled by Milly's telling how she had said good-night to him through her window at a little past midnight.

Soon the whole town of Hedgebury was up in arms. The news that old Sweet was missing spread like wild fire. Every child knew it before breakfast-time. At the houses of Lloyd and Whitehouse, at the stables of the Hall, at the Park Pool, men and women congregated. But the inn at Wood-green was, above all others, the favourite place of resort. "Mine host" did a great stroke of business on that Sunday morning. Old Simon had been a good customer at "The Dog and Shadow" all his life, and even in his disappearance he befriended that house. Men, who would on no account have entered beneath the swinging sign on a Sunday morning under ordinary circumstances, found old Sweet's disappearance an excuse not only for entering, but for renewing their potations when the first glass was drunk out. Again and again the landlord told the story of the old man's departure on the previous night. "Ten minutes before twelve Mr. Sweet had left "The Dog and Shadow." He (the landlord) had lighted his lantern for him. Mr. Sweet was not what he should call 'on,' certainly not. Mr. Sweet could stand good wholesome liquor as well as most. He was just comf'table—what he called comf'table—ready to tumble into bed when he got home, and sleep straight on till daylight; but still firm enough upon his pins. Would have backed him to go to Harborne, and there, the eight miles in two hours, and been as fresh as a daisy at the end of it. Never knew Mr. Sweet to be drunk in his life. Had seen him a bit 'on' on occasions, but last night Mr. Sweet didn't take his usual quantity by a pint."

A deputation of the church-going population went to the "parson" on horseback. Another deputation, from those who were of the Methodist persuasion, sought their own special pastor. The parson, though he was in the midst of reading through his sermon, started up at once, greatly interested in the matter. He became at once the leader. The smith who had hitherto

him walking in a groping, sluggish way, not to walk with a will under his direction. There were open coal-pits; there was the Park Pool. Sweet might have fallen into either. There was the Old Pit not even fenced round; there was Mike's Pit with a broken fence; there was Trowbridge's Pit, which had been arched over, but of which the arching had fallen in. Sweet might have wandered from his way and fallen in to any one of them. All lay round about his road. The deep end of the Park Pool by Buckstone-road must be dragged. The pits must be tried. They must be careful in trying the pits. If there was water in the Old Pit, they must drag that. Let them lower a candle down the other two before anyone ventured. While the men were to this, the lads might search every hedge and ditch round about. Old Sweet might be lying somewhere with a broken leg.

"Come on, my men!" cried the parson, and he himself headed the party who were to drag the end of the Park Pool.

The Methodist minister, who was found praying that words might be put into his mouth for that morning's discourse, was not so ready in practical expedients as his brother of the church proper. He was inclined to point a judgment of God in old Sweet's disappearance. The divine mercy, outraged so often, had failed at last. The old man had gone down to the pit with all his sins upon him: a warning—a standard warning to such as ye, who spared. Then, that view of the question being exhausted, the next thing that presented itself to the good man's mind was prayer. Let us pray for our erring brother; let us pray that our end may not be like his; let us pray for anything or everything, so long as we pray. Whether he prayed for Sweet living or for Sweet dead was not clear to the minister; though, had it struck him that he might be praying for the dead (that unpardonable sin!), his prayer would have been shorter and less eloquent.

The Methodist minister spoke bitterly of the Parson afterwards for having profaned the Sabbath in that unholy practical work of his. A blind leader of the blind, indeed! Each hated each other as only those who differ in religious matters can hate. The parson honestly believed the minister to be a hypocrite and an idiot. The minister was the most truthful guileless of men; if he had a plenitude of conceit, he had, nevertheless, intuitions deeper and higher than any the parson had ever dreamed of. On the other hand, the minister thought the parson worldly and wicked, a sort of half-devil, who misled the people which entrusted themselves to his teaching. The parson was a man of sound morality and excellent sense; he taught his flock lessons of stealing nought, which were as good as gold in comparison with the gilt tinsel of the mystical minister.

Up to church-time and a little later the parson laboured with the men.

"I'll forgive you for not coming to church to-day, my lads," he said, just before he rushed off home for his surplice and his half-read old sermon.

Neither he nor the Methodist minister had many hearers in that morning, and those there had were ill inclined to be attentive. The parson shortened his sermon and threw the briefest pauses, being so anxious, as his congregation, to learn what tidings there might be of the missing old man. The minister did not seem to shorten the sermon. There was a great outpouring of groans on that day, it was said afterwards, which, being interpreted, signified much bygone and weeping and ejaculation; with perhaps some softening of hitherto hard hearts. Old Sweet's probable death was loudly pronounced to be an express warning sent from above to unrepentant sinners.

The end of the Pool by Buckstone-road was dragged, the coal-pits were searched, but no signs of the old man were discovered by the men engaged in those operations. The lads whom the clergyman had set on to search the hedges and ditches were more successful. Stuffed into the end of a drain they found the old man's lantern; and scattered about a field close to the Pool they picked up some shreds of grey felt which might be fragments of his hat.

About three days after, his stick was found under a hedge, a long distance from the Park Pool, between Wood-green and Hell Batt, so that if, according to rumour, he had been that stick to knock at Milly's back, it must have been carried back by someone to the place where it was found. On the stick were some dark stains.

* * * * *

My Hedgebury legend would not be complete unless I related how old Sweet was found. Indeed the sexton of Hedgebury church, who told me the story, and who showed me old Sweet's grave, began his relation with the finding of the body.

"I've heard tell, sir," he said, "how, many a year gone, the parson and the clerk were once left to finish the churchin' between 'em in full service time. All the congregation walked out, man, woman, and child."

The emptying of the church was caused by the discovery of old Sweet's body. On a Sunday some five or six weeks after the disappearance of the old man, little Abram Lloyd, apprenticed as it will be remembered to Jim White, his uncle, rushed into the church, midway in the litany, crying out "Father, grand-dad's found!" and then, addressing himself more generally to the congregation, "Old Sweet's found!"

There was a stir, and the people rose. Those at the door slipped out. Then there was a rush, and not a soul stayed behind save the parson and the clerk.

Little Abram, it appeared, having shirked going to chapel under pretence of accompanying his father and mother to church, had escaped to join some friends of his, the place of rendezvous being a field bordering the upper end of the Park Pool.

Here, the boys sending ducks and drakes in

the water, had perceived far out a floating something which the wind drove slowly towards them.

The floating something turned out to be the corpse of old Sweet. He was [illegible] appearance in the water, and by [illegible] the boys recognised him. Instantly they took to their heels and ran away.

From examination of the body, it was evident that the old man had been murdered. His skull was fractured; his money and watch gone. The corpse must have been thrown into the Park Pool high up towards the farther end; and thus it was that the men who had dragged the end by the [illegible]-road had failed in finding it.

Old Sweet's murderers were never discovered.

THE GREEK SLAVE.

BY EMILY JANE WALLER.

Unloose these heavy chains, that hold
  A form that once was free as thine;
Unbind these fetters—set me free—
  And bid the slave no longer pine!

In days long past, and ne'er again
  To cast their [illegible] o'er my soul,
I roam'd as free as mountain wind
  Where proud Ionian waters roll.

In fairest Greece, my native land,
  When [illegible] the [illegible] [illegible],
When silver moons and shining stars
  Look'd down from skies of deepest blue—

Then, [illegible] the [illegible] of [illegible] [illegible],
  When [illegible] the many-colour'd flow'rs,
Or [illegible] the [illegible] [illegible] [illegible],
  In [illegible] [illegible] the hours.

The [illegible] [illegible] that [illegible] me lay
  [illegible] [illegible] of [illegible] [illegible],
Of golden [illegible], [illegible] [illegible],
  The king's days [illegible] Greece had known.

Then, when these fetter'd hands were free,
  I wand'ring roam'd the hills among,
Or rov'd the calm and silent shores,
  Where Aspro winds his silver stream.

And now, e'en now, when soothing sleep
  Has press'd these weeping eyes to rest,
Fair visions stealing o'er my brain
  With soft emotions fill my breast—

Fair visions of my native land,
  Her sleeping vales, her streamlets bright,
And free in sleep, I pace again
  On lofty Pindus' tow'ring height.

To Grecian shores my busy thoughts
  Return again, in sleeping hours—
No more a slave, in sleep I roam
  O'er Grecian hills bestrew'd with flow'rs.

Ah! let them hold in stronger chains
  And [illegible] [illegible] [illegible] [illegible] hands,
And cast their iron fetters round
  This [illegible] frame, in closer bands.

Their [illegible] I [illegible]—their [illegible] [illegible]
  With calm indifference I [illegible];
The heart can ne'er a slave be found;
  The heart, still throbbing, still is free!

THE PATH BY THE RIVER.

BY ADA TREVANION.

Do you remember, 'mid the moss,
  A white path like a thread;
Through branching ferns, which waved across,
  And to a river led?

With flowers on [illegible] [illegible],
  And [illegible], which made
A glory in the summer sun,
  And [illegible] in the shade.

A giant tree, long prostrate lain,
  Bridged the blue waters o'er;
Hard by, laburnum's golden chain
  Was blent with sycamore.

And, resting 'neath them, you might see
  Each happy living thing—
Gay butterfly, and drowsy bee,
  And wild-bird on the wing.

I have a gentle memory
  Connected with the scene,
Of one with lips of rosy dye,
  And eyes of sapphire sheen.

The willow basket on her arm
  Was over-brimmed with flowers;
And from her flushed face beamed the charm
  Of radiant summer hours.

Wreathed bindweeds, graceful leaves and bells,
  Were mingled 'mid her hair,
With blue-eyed speedwell from the dells,
  Foxgloves and lilies fair.

She did not for grave looks reprove
  Her song, blithe as a bird's;
Too used to meet with kindliness
  To dread ungentle words.

She vanished, with ambrosial smile
  Like those of long ago,
Which left me after a brief while
  Whitened amid Life's snow.

But sweet and pleasant thoughts of her,
  And that calm sylvan place,
Oft to my lonely heart recur;
  A dream of summer grace!

BRITISH SONG-BIRDS AND THEIR NESTS.

There are many things which emigrants from our own fair islands to our British southern colonies, Australia, New Zealand, India, &c., miss, and for which, in their exile, they long with heart-sick desire; but, amongst them, two are pre-eminent. They miss the varying verdure of the trees and hedge-rows at the different seasons of the year, and they miss the sweet notes of our singing-birds.

Here, in our own land, the changes from the wintry aspect of the trees, with their bare branches and lichen and ivy-clad trunks, to the delicate many-tinted greens of spring—then to the full deep summer verdure, and from thence by slow degrees through all the rich autumnal hues of purple, and red, and brown, and yellow, to the falling leaf, and the dark leafless winter barrenness—produce a never-failing delight in the mind of him who is accustomed to notice the aspects of Nature; especially if he be also accustomed to trace the hand of the Great Work-Master, and to glorify Him in His works. But in Australia, in New Zealand, and even in India, there are no such changes to be seen. It is true that the gorgeous tintings of flowers, and insects, and birds, in those lands, far exceed anything that we see in England and Scotland; but the dark and monotonous green that pervades the country all the year through, however suitable to those hot climates, is very trying to the Englishman's feelings. And so it is with regard to the song-birds. The labourer, who has been sent at early dawn, as he went to his work, to hear the rich warbling notes of the thrush and blackbird; the trilling song of the skylark, as it rises high into the blue vault above him; and the sweet low notes of the wood-pigeon; and to listen, in the evenings, to the

"Liquid sweetness, long drawn out,"

of the nightingale—is sadly cast down when he misses all those sweet familiar sounds in the land of his adoption. There is a story told of one man who had taken out a skylark, which he kept in a cage, and it is said that men would walk miles to hear it sing; and rough country-men, wild and rude as they seemed, shed tears as they listened to its sweet notes. Surely, then, that God has bestowed on us Britons so rich a gift in our woodland minstrelsy. Let us look a little at the habits of our different species of song-birds, and learn about their times and seasons, their modes of building their nests, and hatching, and feeding, and educating their young ones.

The blackbird, or merel, and the thrush are to be reckoned as amongst our earliest singing-birds. Nests, with eggs in them, have been found as early as the first week in January. The usual time, however, for blackbirds (Merula vulgaris) to pair is in February or March, and the thrush (Merula musica) is a little later; commonly towards the end of March. The blackbird usually selects a low bush, or stump of a tree, a few feet above the ground, for the site of its future nursery; though occasionally an outhouse, or a heap of sticks, or a wall or tree covered with ivy, is chosen; and there Madam Merula and her husband make preparations for their coming progeny. The office of Monsieur appears to be that of cheering his wife by his song; for it does not seem that he does much, either in collecting materials for the nest or in arranging them when collected. That is Madame's affair, and carefully and skilfully she performs it, gathering moss, stalks of grass, roots, small twigs, and frequently dead leaves, and most delicately weaving them into a deep round nest, like a bowl with edges curving inwards, and large enough to contain herself and her family, even though it should consist of four or five children, and to make them a commodious home until they are able to fly. In this nest she then deposits four or five eggs, usually of a dull light blue, or greenish brown colour, mottled with reddish brown, the markings darker and closer at the larger end. The eggs, however, vary much in colour and in size. Having laid them, Madame takes her seat on them; and there, for thirteen days, she keeps close quarters, never leaving the nest save to feed.

And whilst she sits, let us first notice the wonderful instinct with which God has endowed all birds. Never does the nest of one species of bird differ from others of the same species, or so closely assimilate to those of other species, as that it may not be known by a skilful observer to what bird it belongs. Also, it is a known fact that the nest is always built in time to receive the eggs destined to be placed in it, no bird being ignorant of its own requirements, nor too lazy nor dilatory to carry out the necessary operations for meeting them. And so it has ever been. If the nest of a blackbird built in Adam's time could be obtained, we should no doubt find it exactly of the same architecture, both in respect of material and form, as those of the present time, and neither worse nor better constructed: for the knowledge of the art of building is not an acquired, but an inborn, principle in the bird-mind.

At the end of thirteen days, out comes the brood. Probably one or two of the eggs may have failed, but usually three or four young birds begin to open great wide yellow mouths, and give ample employment to both parents in finding food for the ravenous appetites with which all young birds are furnished. In a few weeks the young are fledged, and then the parent-birds lead them out into the world, never again to return to the nest. Yet they still keep them under watch for a considerable time after they have taken them abroad.

I was visiting at Faringdon, in Berkshire, toward the end of April this spring, and happened to catch sight of a family of young blackbirds having been discovered in a low box-hedge exactly under the drawing-room window of the house in which I was. I was not long in paying a visit to the settlers, whom I found all at home. Madame was in bed with her family, and did not disturb herself, as I gently put aside the twigs of box, and stood face to face with her. The young birds—three in number—were so closely covered with her wings that I could not see a morsel of one of them; but the mother-bird was a picture that I would not willingly have missed seeing. She lay all spread out over the nest, with her pretty head laid on one side on the edge of it, very much in the position that a cat assumes when pleased, turning the underside of the throat up, and glancing with the clear bright eye that was visible confidingly at me. I visited her more than once, and found her in the same position; but later in the day I got a sight of the large, almost fledged birds, over which she had sat—and the next day the whole party had left the nest.

It was curious to observe how entirely the young were left to the charge of the male bird after they left the nest. I never once saw the mother in company with her young after they came abroad; but the father and all three young ones might be seen every day, and all day long at intervals, hopping about in the shrubbery, the beautiful jet-black bird, with his yellow bill and feet, and keen yellow-ringed eye, followed wherever he went by three little dim brown birds (for during the first year of their lives the birds, whether male or female, are of the colour of the female, which is a dull brown) hopping after him. He would drag up huge long worms out of the turf, so long and large that he often nearly fell backwards when they eventually yielded themselves to him. These great worms were a delight to the little creatures, who all gathered round him, shrieking and crying, and fluttering their little stumpy wings, but never attempting to lay hold on the prey until papa had cut it up with his sharp bill into several portions, which he presented in turn to his children, and then went in quest of more. But I observed that he never put the food into their mouths, as it is the custom of sparrows, and chaffinches, and other small birds to do with their young.

I have been much in the habit of watching and feeding the birds, which congregate in great numbers on my lawn, and have been often much amused by watching the small birds feed their young, and not only feed, but discipline them. A whole family of sparrows, consisting of father, mother, and four young ones, had their home in my garden last year, inhabiting a hole close by my sitting-room window; and as they were well fed many times in the day, and wholly unmolested, they of course became very sociable. As soon as the young could flutter down to the ground and back to the nest, they were brought out at feeding-times, and it was wonderful to see what quantities the little things contrived to eat. They soon began to pick for themselves, but this did not content them; for with open yellow mouths and piteous cries did they follow about their poor parents, who on their side seemed as willing to cram as the little ones to be crammed. But if any danger was near—a cat or any suspicious-looking object, such as a chair where there was usually none—the parents would place the young in a row on the railing, or on the branches of a little shrub-tree that stood at a safe distance, and evidently tell them not to move; for at such time not one of the young creatures ever left the very spot on which it had been placed. The parents would then venture to snatch up the food, in spite of the alarming object, and hold even the sides of the young when they saw them emerging, with tempting lumps of soaked bread, or boiled rice, in their bills; yet each remained in its place, and was fed in turn.

But once I witnessed a curious scene. The four little ones were placed in a row, as I could see them from a gravel-walk, much like a class of children in a school, and the parents came and fed them in order, one after the other. As I watched them, however, whilst the feeding-bird was gone for fresh supplies, I saw the young gentleman who had been fed at the top of the class, slip round behind his brothers, and take up his place at the bottom; no doubt with the view of surreptitiously obtaining a double feed. But he was mistaken: mamma found out the trick in a moment, and instantly struck him off the perch down to the ground, and then hovered over him and scolded in a most amusing manner; and after a time, youngmaster went back, somewhat crestfallen, to his old place. I have seen a mother go backwards and forwards eight times with food to the same little bird. The seventh time she was intercepted on her way by another bird, and the food taken from her; but she returned at once and fetched more.

The blackbird feeds on berries, fruits, insects, and worms, and is a solitary bird, frequenting thickets and woods, chiefly where there are evergreens, such as fir, holly, &c., and where there are perennial springs. They are cautious and timorous birds, and easily alarmed; yet our Faringdon family did not seem to mind our visits to the nest—probably because we were very cautious in our approaches, and careful not to talk near them.

The thrush, or throstle (called by the Scotch, "mavis"), is distinguished amongst our singing-birds by the clearness and fulness of its note. Its song is exceedingly sweet and exceedingly varied; moreover, it lasts very long, beginning very early in the year, and lasting until quite the end of summer. Late in the evening and early in the morning may the thrush be heard singing from the trees. It is a social bird, and comes freely about our habitations all the year through. I have seen them, three or four at a time, come to pick up the bread-crumbs, &c., that had been thrown out both in the spring and summer, but even more frequently in the winter, when their tracks in the snow may be known by the impression of the whole foot and legs, which is left to the knee-joint; and a deep trail, made by the bird's long and strong tail-feathers, marks its whole progress. The female builds her nest generally in bushes, and mixes a little earth or clay with the dry grass of which it is chiefly composed. She lays five or six eggs, of a pale blue colour mixed with dusky spots.

The skylark, or laverock (*Alauda arvensis*), is, and deserves to be, conspicuous amongst our singing-birds, and must be characterized as the only bird that chants whilst on the wing. And glorious is its song as it springs from its nest, and rises higher and higher, almost perpendicularly, and by successive springs, to a height beyond our sight, singing as it rises, and pouring forth such a gush of cheerful song as is unequalled by any of our warblers, and then drops down as if exhausted, but in fact only to sing again.

"Upsprings the lark,
Shrill-voic'd and loud, the messenger of morn;
Ere yet the shadows fly, he, mounted, sings,
Amid the dawning clouds, and from their haunts
Calls up the tuneful nations."

Larks build their nests on the ground, consequently their eggs are often destroyed by stoats, weasels, &c.; and moreover, that wicked interloper the cuckoo often breaks into the nest, and, turning out the true tenant's eggs, substitutes her own for them. Yet, in spite of these dangers, larks abound in the land. The eggs, of which the hen bird lays from three to five, vary a good deal, but are usually of a greyish hue, with a tinge of purple or green; and they are commonly placed with their smaller ends towards the centre.

The skylark is about seven inches long; the feathers reddish brown, dark in the middle, with pale edges; the neck of a reddish white, spotted with brown; the breast, belly, and thighs white; the tail brown, and forked. The lark is known throughout Europe, and in Germany there is a tax on them (they being delicious eating), that has been known to produce as much as 6,000 dollars in one year in the city of Leipsic alone—so says Mr. Bewick, in the last century. The nest is placed in a hollow scraped in the ground, usually under the shelter of a clod of earth or bunch of herbage. It is made of grasses, and perhaps a few leaves, the coarser outside, the more delicate within. The male bird brings the materials, and the female arranges them.

"The daisied lea he loves, where tufts of grass
Luxuriant crown the ridge; there with his mate
He founds their lowly house, of withered leaves
And coarsest spear-grass; next the inner work,
With finer, and still finer fibres lays,
Rounding it curious with his speckled breast."

GRAHAME.

The nightingale (*Philomela luscinia*), the very king of songsters, though common in England, is unknown in its northern counties, as also in the extreme western counties, Devonshire and Cornwall. In Somersetshire nightingales are very numerous. They are not particularly pretty birds as to colouring, their hue being on the upper parts of a rusty brown, inclining to olive, and below of a pale ash colour. But we see them so seldom, that it is not very important whether they are pretty or not; the delicious, gushing, thrilling notes of the nightingale are enough attraction for any one bird to possess. It seldom sings between the months of August and May. During those winter months it is supposed to visit the more distant regions of Asia. But this is uncertain, the famous bird of the East (the bulbul) being now considered not to be identical with the European nightingale, whose district extends from about 33 to 56 degrees north latitude, and from 54 degrees east longitude to about 10 degrees west longitude, including the extreme North of Africa and Arabia on the south, and the South of Norway and Sweden on the north; its most western limit being the coast of Spain; whilst on the east it includes Turkistan and Persia.

It is a solitary bird, never uniting with others, but hiding itself in the thickest parts of the bushes, and singing chiefly in the night. It eats berries, ant's-eggs, and small worms. The nightingale is said to feed on the glowworm, but probably it is only as it would on any other small grub or worm that comes in its way. They begin to build in May, and almost always on the ground, in some natural hollow, amongst the roots of trees or of a hedgerow. Their nest is loosely put together, of dried stalks of grass, bits of bark, and roots, &c., and is lined with fine grass and hair. The eggs are of an oval form, and dull olive colour, and from four to six in number. The male and female sit on them in turn, and the young, when hatched, hop about on the ground before they can fly, returning to the nest when tired.

The following description of the song of the nightingale is so just, that I cannot myself describe it so well, and will therefore give it as I find it:—"The leader of the vernal chorus begins with a low, timid voice, and he prepares for the hymn to Nature by essaying his powers and attuning his organs. By degrees the sound opens and swells; it bursts with loud and vivid flashes; it flows with smooth volubility; it faints and murmurs; it shakes with rapid and violent articulations; the soft breathings of love and joy are poured from the inmost soul, and every heart beats in unison, and melts with delicious languor. But this continual richness might satiate the ear; the strains are at times relieved by pauses, which heighten dignity and elevation. The mild silence of the evening heightens the general effect."

But though not uniting in flocks, nightingales in great numbers frequent the same woods, and may be heard answering each other from tree to tree, until all the air is filled with melody.

I have heard them singing around the house in which I was, and heard them singing all the night through, until the very sweetness became fatiguing to me, and I longed for silence!

The poets fail not in praises of sweet "Philomel." Indeed, the nightingale and the lark have more verse from them than any other birds. Milton speaks of the former as "smoothing the rugged brow of night," adding—

"Sweet bird, that shunn'st the noise of folly,
Most musical, most melancholy!
Thee, chauntress, oft the woods among
I woo to hear thy even-song;
And, missing thee, I walk unseen
On the dry, smooth-shaven green."

And the sweet "lady" in "Comus," that lovely embodiment of feminine purity and unfailing faith, sings—

"Sweet echo, sweetest nymph, that liv'st unseen
Within thy airy shell,
By slow Meander's margent green,
And in the violet-embroider'd vale,
Where the love-lorn nightingale
Nightly to thee her sad song mourneth well."

But though not equal to the nightingale, yet the song of the wren is not to be despised; and though I must necessarily give precedence to the singing birds of greater note, I must not neglect to notice our smaller warblers—the wrens, the linnets, and, above all, the sweet summer and winter minstrel, the redbreast. None of the small birds deserve our praise more than the dear little Kitty-wren (*Sylvia troglodytes*). It is a tiny creature, not more than three and a half inches long; a merry little reddish-brown thing, with dark cross-barred back, and brown bill. It braves our severest winters, as do many of its companions, and its sprightly note is heard cheering, for it sings quite late in the evening; and even in the midst of a fall of snow its little voice may be heard. It builds a cosy little nest, large, however, in proportion to itself, as the wren needs accommodation for a large family, for it lays seven or eight eggs, and in some cases even a dozen or more have been found. Very early in the spring Kitty takes her mate, and soon thereafter, in some fork of a tree close to the trunk, or in a clump of ivy, or in some other snug, dry corner, she builds a beautiful spherical nest, with a domed top, and a neat little round entrance at one side. The outside of her nest she forms of fern, and moss, and grass, and small matters of that description as near like the surrounding things as possible. She makes the walls of her house very thick, and lines the inside with hair or feathers. Kitty is fanciful in her choice of a site for her home, and varies the materials according to circumstances; but what I have described is her usual style of architecture. Nests have been found, however, at the tops of honeysuckle and raspberry-bushes—in the latter case the nest being made of the leaves of the tree—in hay-ricks, [illegible], [illegible], on branches of wall-fruit trees, and holes, [illegible] being made occasionally of the holes previously tenanted by sparrows and swallows; one has been known inside that of a swallow, and another in the old nest of a thrush; and, again, in the newly-finished nest of a sparrow, &c. &c. One has been found in an old bonnet, and [illegible] amongst some peas in [illegible] [illegible], and another in one of the [illegible] of the [illegible] at Winchester. In some corner or other, then, wherever she has built her nest, the wren lays a quantity of the prettiest little whitish eggs, speckled and spotted with pink crimson; and, whilst she sits on them, her good husband feeds her until her little ones are ready to share the food he brings. Twice in the season does the wren build, lay, and hatch. If the nest is disturbed, however, it is ten to one that it will be forsaken and a fresh one built; and this two or three times, if successive nests are disturbed, or the young handled.

The linnet (*Fringilla linaria*) is common all through Europe. Its song is lively and varied. The bird is so easily tamed, and its favourite food being "linseed" (whence the name linnet), which is easily procured, it suffers less from captivity than other wild birds whose natural food cannot be supplied them. When confined with other birds the linnet learns their song.

The chaffinch (*Fringilla cœlebs*) sings very sweetly, though its song is short, and not much varied. But then it is such a beautiful bird, and is possessed of such pretty manners, that its very little song obtains much praise and favour. And the same may be said of both the goldfinch and the bullfinch. A little young hen-chaffinch on one occasion got into my house, and was seen fluttering in the staircase, unable to get up the steep steps with its feeble little wings; and my servants not [illegible] there [illegible] [illegible] catching the little creature, apparently not having in its helplessness sufficiently to measure the spring by which she wanted to escape it, until it had become more quiet. It was of course re-caught and released by its parents, who soon took it up the lawn and [illegible] trees. From that day until the end of the season the little delicate young bird came daily to feed at [illegible]; but never once did I see her without her father—the great, strong, beautiful bird never allowing his little daughter to depart from his side, but, following her closely, and watching over her with the tenderest care, so as never to lose sight of her. Could the little thing have told her father of the peril she had been in, and from which she had so narrowly escaped? It looked very like it.

I am sure no description of the redbreast is necessary. In town and country, in summer and winter, it is too familiar a friend to need description. Every country has it, though distinguished by a different, yet always by a familiar name. In Finland and Sweden it is called Tomi Lideng; in Norway, Peter Ronsmad; in Germany, Thomas Gierdet; and with us, Robin.

The robin feeds on worms, caterpillars, &c.,

and shows by his wintry habits that, though at these seasons forced to live chiefly on berries, and to eat crumbs, yet that he greatly prefers a little animal food; for, if you throw out a bone or a bit of meat, robin never touches a crumb until he has secured and eaten the meat. The same may be said of the tom-tit. It is very amusing to see the little sapphire and apple-green gems, with their varying plumage and bright eyes, pick a crooked bone, and observe how they climb about it, and seem as if they stuck to its surface, whilst they clean out every particle of meat from its crevices. I have seen two or three of these lovely little birds on the same bone, whilst the grass around them was studded with thrushes, and blackbirds, and chaffinches, and robins, and sparrows, until it seemed alive; and the rush of wings, when the whole bevy was dispersed by fright of any kind, was quite startling.

HARRINGTON GRANGE.

BY LOUIS SAND.

Chap. I.

The Master of Harrington.

"And now, Meg, I shall be at home always, to tease and worry you. Sour old Meg! And won't I have the chairs all about! And won't Flora rummage and make a litter!"

"I wouldn't care about that, if you'd liven up the master a bit, Miss Amy."

"Papa! But he won't let me. He doesn't like being disturbed. Only to think of no more school, Meg. Nothing to do but please myself all day long, and tease you, and worry papa!"

"You'll soon get tired, Miss Amy. You'll find it lonesome enough, I doubt."

Lonesome! That was a new idea. Miss Amy went back to her book, thoughtfully; and Meg, looking at her for a moment, turned away, muttering something about a "miser."

It did not look like a miser's house, by any means. Old it was and quaint, and had been in the Harrington family for hundreds of years; but though the furniture was old-fashioned, it suited the rooms; and the lawn before those quaint windows was smooth and green.

"Why should I be lonesome, I wonder?" murmured little Amy.

A whine was the only answer, and two minute paws intruded themselves upon the open book.

"Aye, it's all nonsense; isn't it, Flora? You and I are going to do as we please, and be as happy as the day is long: won't we? Lonesome, indeed!"

All the neatness and order apparent just now about the old house was the result of Meg's suggestions, and in preparation for Amy's reception as no longer the school-girl at home for her holidays, but mistress of the house; and all that Meg suggested she had full leave to carry out, if only her master was left in peace—yet he was called "Harrington the Miser."

Shut up from day to day in a grim room, which Amy had named "The den;" rarely visible except at meals, and not always then; the name of "miser" had been fixed upon him, and clove to him. His household was limited to this one old servant, Meg, and a boy who suffered under her; and when he was asked for money he gave it, but always with a caution. He had never thought of his daughter as anything but a child; he knew that she must grow up sometime, but the knowledge had never troubled him till one morning his old servant forced her way into his den, and stood before him sturdily, resolute to be heard.

He looked up at her then with his usual dreamy gaze, taking her presence as an annoyance, and wondering how soon she would rid him of it.

"Always thus—always!" said Meg. "It wasn't used to be so: and see now the years it has been growing upon you!"

The Master of Harrington heard, without seeming to hear; his gaze wandering round the dusty shelves which held his treasures.

"Now that Miss Amy is coming home you must change it, master. You must come out and talk to her. Think how lonesome it will be for a young thing, after being always among merry companions."

Mr. Harrington sighed. He wished Meg would let him alone; but she wouldn't. He knew her of old, and she was privileged. Well, well, he would see what could be done. She was asking him no light thing, but he would try.

And perhaps he did try; perhaps it was too hard a thing to ask of him: at any rate, on the first morning of Amy's return, Meg encountered him after breakfast, as usual, with his hand on the door of that grim room.

"I thought, sir——" said Meg.

"Aye, so did I. But I can't do it, Meg. It's too late."

And he shut himself in. He would have fastened the door, but the lock had grown rusty, and wouldn't turn.

Then Meg advised Amy to break into his retreat, telling her it would be good for him to be dragged out, and made to leave off his old habits.

And behold in that silent, musty den, the only atmosphere in which he was at ease, a merry voice and a light footstep, rousing the echoes and the dust in wonder at such an invasion. And a soft cheek was laid against the old man's furrowed one.

"Oh, Pappy, what a gloomy den! What a sober old bookworm! Mayn't I come? You never can be angry!"

The Master of Harrington was sorely troubled. He fidgeted nervously, and looked away from the mischievous blue eyes.

"Amy," he said, at last, "you have been amongst a great many friends."

"No, Papa. Not all friends."

"But some of them were."

"I don't know," said Amy, musing; "I think not. I was just sorry to leave them, but far more glad to come home. No, I don't think they were what I should call friends."

"But I wish them to be. I mean," added the poor bookworm, "that I wish you had some one to stay with you, dear, and be merry with you; for—don't think me unkind—I can't have this [looking round the walls] to myself and—the past."

"Then I may never come?" said Amy, sorrowfully.

"My darling, it is not a place for you. When I come here, all miserable and alone, think what it will be for me to have a sunbeam always ready to shine on me. But I cannot change my habits, Amy. You will not let that trouble you?"

"I don't think I could, Papa," said the sunbeam, thoughtfully. "I am so happy, I don't know what it would feel like to be troubled; so I must go, and leave the doctor in his den! But, Pappy dear, I don't want any friends, to come and make me amuse them; I would rather not. Good-bye."

What is that man a miser wants? "Hoards of gold," say the greedy and dissatisfied men who talk of him sometimes at the Inn down below: "strong boxes full; crisp notes, that crumple deliciously in his fingers; and bright heaps of yellow gold. Well, and a pleasant thing to find, too; but a miser can't enjoy it. He's only half a man, being him!"

Chap. II.

An Invasion.

"Plenty of work if I want it—which I don't; plenty of nice books to read; Floss to play with and talk to—what can I want?"

And little Amy stood at the window, and peeped round the curtain.

"There they are again, Floss!"

And Floss leaped upon the window-ledge, wagged a small tail, and cocked a pair of pert ears, as much as to say "So they are!"

"I wonder who they can be?" said Amy.

But Floss could not tell her that.

"This is the third day I have seen them, and I know they are sketching this house. A dear old place it is, too, for a picture. How I should like one! I'd hang it up in pappy's den, opposite him; that he may have something to look at prettier than those musty shelves. I should like to rummage in that old den, and make a mess of it. Floss!" said Amy, emphatically, "the result of it all is, I want to look at that picture. I daresay it's only a daub, like Miss Jones used to do at school, and then the drawing-master touched it up till nobody knew it again. Yes, I dare say it is a daub. He doesn't look like Miss Jones, though. Perhaps he can draw really."

So Amy, having nothing better to do, sat down with her sewing in her fingers, and began making a pretty little romance about the two strangers. They were not married; but going to be, perhaps. Very likely the drawing was all a sham—only a pretext for getting a walk together alone. But where did they come from?"

"Miss Amy," said Meg, coming in, "there's a lady wants to beg a glass of water."

"Tell her we don't give anything at the door, but if she will walk in I'll see about it."

"She's with a painter chap," said Meg, not at all disturbed; "and he's got a seat, but she hasn't—just like men. She looks tired to death."

"Let her rest in the hall. A painter chap!" said Amy, springing up and peeping through the window. "It's that lady, I declare. Why, Meg, he is taking this house!"

"I guess he'd rather let it alone."

"A picture, Meg—a grand picture—of the old Grange, to hang in your parlour, when you have one. Shouldn't you like to see it?"

"Not about this lady!" said Meg, gruffly. "Am I to ask her in?"

"In! What, here? to Floss and me! But I don't know what to say to her."

"What was the use of your going to school, then? Didn't they teach manners?"

"Couldn't she go into the other room, by herself?"

"I should say not."

"Well, then, ask her; and say the [illegible] talk, for I'm busy."

"Wherever is the History of England gone? and my French Grammar? Oh, and the inkstand! Everything will walk off just when I want it."

"She's gone to ask the gentleman," said Meg, coming back, "and she will be very glad to rest. Miss Amy," whispered Meg, "they're grand visitors from Wilsdon."

Grand visitors! If Meg had wanted to drive all idea of "manners" out of Amy's head at once, she could not have hit upon a more effectual way of doing it. What was she to say to grand people? She began to think about her governess, who had once entertained a baroness, and who spoke with familiar feeling of several Peers of the realm. But then her governess was such a very upright majestic figure—how could poor little Amy be like her?

She took up Floss in her arms, in her per-

picture, and then, with some idea that it wouldn't be proper, she put him down again, and as she did so, her bonnet came off, and her hair fell all over her shoulders. And there was the "grand lady" looking at her.

"We are much obliged to you, Miss Harrington. My brother is so anxious to finish his painting that I did not like to complain, but I am very tired. This house is a beautiful subject for a drawing."

"I thought it must be that you were sketching," began Amy, eagerly; then, remembering how she had been told at school that it was vulgar to look out of the window, she stammered and blushed.

"I cannot sketch," said the lady. "It is my brother."

Then Amy ventured something more, and wished most heartily she could get away to arrange her hair; but just at that moment the bonnet again, and Flora, evidently thinking the net had been constructed with an especial view to his private amusement, was using it in a very improper manner indeed.

"Oh, Flora, Flora!" cried Amy, again darting to the rescue.

As she rose, she encountered the lady's eyes looking down upon her with a peculiar expression, and blushed again.

What a beautiful face it was! yet it was perfectly white, not having a vestige of colour, except in the lips. But Amy was thinking how foolish this self-possessed stranger would think her; how childish and awkward. She could find nothing else to say; nothing in the world in the corners of her brain; she could not think how the stranger could sit there so calm and easy, while her own pulse was all [illegible] with nervousness.

There was a long silence, broken at last, but not by Amy.

"My brother is ready, I see," said the stranger. "May he come in? Perhaps you would like to see the sketch."

"Oh, that I should!" And Amy started up eagerly. When the portfolio was placed before her, she could think of nothing, not even the stranger artist nor his sister, in her delight at the old Grange, which looked at her familiarly from it.

"My dear old window!—and the cedar, that beautiful cedar tree! and Flora too! I knew [illegible] you got Flora? If Meg could but see it! No, this is not like Miss Jones's drawing."

The artist and his sister exchanged glances.

"Any one was welcome to see it."

Amy looked round at the voice, thought of the demeanour her governess had recommended before gentlemen, and became demure.

"And now I must thank you for taking me in," said the lady. "I am Eleanor Vere, and this is my brother Philip. We are staying with Lady Harding, at Wilmore."

Miss Vere offered her hand, and Mr. Vere bowed; and little Amy watched them away from behind the curtain.

"My brother! Then they are not married, or going to be, and I was all wrong!"

"And only think, Meg," said Amy, skipping into the kitchen—"only think of my hair being all down, and my net off! That was Flora! wicked Flora! What will papa say to my grand visitors, I wonder?"

"Miss Amy," said Meg, coming close to her, "was it Vere you said the name was?"

"Yes, Eleanor Vere. Why, Meg?"

"Then I wouldn't speak of it before him, dear."

"But why not?"

"Oh, it's something long ago. He's not one to be raking up old rubbish to tell you; but don't you say that name to him now, don't! It'll be sure to bring on a bad fit. Tell him they were visitors from Wilmore, if you like; he never speaks about names."

"Very well, Meg. But oh, such a beautiful picture! I wish he were a real working artist, and would sell it; only I have got no money!"

Chap. III.

Lady Harding and her Guests.

I will not describe the hall of Wilmore, its park, the magnificence of its gardens, or the pinnacled church which the ancestor loyally [illegible] over it. Some descriptions may be all very well, but it seems to me impossible for word painting to convey to another mind the effect produced by the original upon your own. The beauty of a landscape comes to you with a peculiar power, because you are happy, and look at it through a happy medium; so you run on, painting it in your enthusiasm; while Miss Jones, who is not happy, and who cares nothing just at present for scenery, says, "What a fuss about a few trees and a bit of sunshine!" and turns over indignantly to find the thread of the story. Perhaps those pages, passed over so indignantly, contain your pet piece of composition—the best bit of writing in the book; but it doesn't matter for that. Miss Jones is reading a tale, and has no fancy for being cheated out of it, or inveigled into studying descriptive composition. Like a hungry cheeky schoolboy, at a feast of tea and plum-cake, if you talk to him in the most eloquent and kindly language, he will wish you would be quiet or go away, that he may eat his cake in peace.

But if I am not describing scenery, I have been guilty of a short digression—pardon.

"Pardon it, Philip," said Lady Harding.

She is speaking of one of pictures; but Philip Vere turned to the speaker, laughingly. The little coup of coffee, with a splendid morsel of bread-and-butter to each, were being handed round, and Lady Harding, having established herself in her own peculiar corner, looked with languid complacency on the assemblage of guests who were staying in her house. Not with a view of considering how she could best entertain them; "So," said Lady Harding, "I make it a rule to invite several people at once; all remarkable for something. I can manage it, and then they amuse each other. I am not equal to the task of amusing visitors."

"Eleanor tells me you have a sketch of the old Grange. Produce it, Philip."

Philip obeyed.

"Ah, it is a good subject, well treated."

"Thank you," said Philip. "By the way, why isn't it called Wilmore Grange? The village is Wilmore."

"It was once, I believe; but the Harrington family is a very old one—older than ours, Philip. The head has been called 'Master of Harrington' for centuries; and there is this peculiarity about it—the property is not entailed, but, by a sort of tacit consent, descending from branch to branch, it is always left to the next male heir of the name, if there is no son of the house, in order to keep the Harrington name [illegible]."

"And this man is a widower?"

"Is he?" said Lady Harding, absently. "Poor Amy!"

"You knew her, then?" said Eleanor.

"Knew her, my dear!—she is dead long years ago! Yes, I did know her; she was very dear to me."

"Ah, his wife, you mean. I wonder," continued Eleanor, carelessly, "that you, aunt, with your passion for lions, do not cultivate the daughter."

"Lions! What, little Amy! Is it come to that? But I forget how the time passes. I used to be fond of little Amy when she was quite a child, but the intercourse had been broken off, and—but I thought she was at school."

"We saw her, however," said Eleanor, turning away indifferently.

Lady Harding looked round her guests again, languidly. They seemed well amused. There was a Miss Goddard (née Arabella), who could talk of nothing but airs, tenors, mezzo-sopranos, registers, and key-notes. She was at present engaged in a duet from "Traviata" with a Mr. Mello—also great on the subject of registers. There was a Miss Florence Harris, an authoress, and a Mr. Sackville, a poet, besides several lesser stars, who twinkled feebly beside those of the first magnitude.

"And so what is little Amy a lion, Eleanor?"

"Who? what? Miss Harrington—I had forgotten her existence!"

"Eleanor is wrong," said Philip Vere; "at least you must not look at these people, and fancy Miss Harrington has any claim to their distinction. She is as beautiful as sunshine, and as bright!"

"I should like to see her again," mused Lady Harding. "Her father used to accept my civilities towards his daughter, if not to himself. Eleanor, my dear, I am so dull! Come here; and Philip, take your drawing away. We must have Amy Harrington to stay here a few days; a fresh face is worth anything. Have you sent out the invitations for the fifteenth?"

"I believe so, aunt."

"Well, then, write in my name. Now, you know, I am graciously put here and do it."

"No, no, Eleanor, nothing about Lady Harding's compliments; begin, 'My dear little Amy.' You know nothing about it, I tell you!"

Eleanor Vere looked up in astonishment; her usual languid face was flushed, and her delicate hand trembled.

"Upon my word," she said, "you are strangely excited about this little schoolgirl!"

"Well, well, do as I tell you, my dear. She is to come for the fifteenth, and the carriage shall be sent for her."

Eleanor finished the note, and forgot it. She went up to Philip, who was turning over a book of engravings to the music of "Il Trovatore," with correct accompaniment by Mr. Mello.

"It will be worth something to see that little bit of nature here," said Philip, not looking up.

"What are you talking about? Oh, that Harrington again!" And a look of annoyance crossed Miss Vere's face.

"I am sure you want something companionable, Nelly."

"I am sure I don't. Did I ever want anyone but you? I wish that man would leave off playing!"

"Now, Eleanor, am I to be visible at this bal or the fifteenth, or am I to stay painting in the White?"

The "White" was a little room arranged as a studio, purposely for Lady Harding's nephew, under her own surveillance.

"You can't paint at night."

"Beautifully."

"Now, Philip, don't be disagreeable. What should I do amongst all these people without you?"

"Well, then, be good, and don't put on that overwhelming air of pride, because you have heard the same tattle a few times. Do you know what I heard Miss Harris say the other evening?"

"No, nor care."

"Then you ought. She said—not meaning it to reach my ears; but I can't help having long ears, you know—'Not even the piercing eye of genius can discern aught but the fossilized remains of a heart in the narrow precincts encrusted by the repelling exterior of the cold and haughty Vere'!"

Eleanor's face softened.

"Meaning you, Philip?"

"Meaning you, Eleanor!"

"I am so sorry!"

They both laughed.

"I know you would feel it, Nelly, with your superb exterior—"

"Repelling and cruel—you mean!"

"With your face and figure, what a pity it is you can't sing like Miss Goddard, or write like I can!"

"Philip, with your strong voice, and developed muscles, what a pity you don't play like Mr.

Mella; or bluster like Sir Thomas, your uncle!"

Sir Thomas Harding, I am sorry to say, had retired, according to his wont, to the library, where he was sleeping peacefully, with a handkerchief over his head.

"Sing!" exclaimed Eleanor, scornfully—"sing, Philip! as if you would like me to show off as Miss Goddard does! Such trills and quavers and gasps! I can play the 'Dead March in Saul,' and certain other things, to please myself; but I don't care for that sort of quiver and dash!"

"My dear aunt," said Philip, taking his sister up to Lady Harding, "do you know that I have a new lion for you? Nelly can play the 'Dead March in Saul'!"

"Saul! Saul who? Who did you say was dead, Philip? You are so strange."

"Why, you have been down amongst the dead men yourself," said Philip. "There, Nelly, don't be vexed; I won't do it again."

"Did you send that note, Eleanor?" asked Lady Harding, rousing up. "No, really, here it is still. Do have it sent, my dear."

So little Amy was put into an extreme flutter one morning by a delicate pink note, the contents whereof caused her to jump up and work off a little superfluous excitement in a very animated game with Flora, that piece of [illegible], enjoying it quite as much as his mistress. Then, once again, was there an intrusion into the den, and a pair of soft arms round the "doctor's" neck.

"I couldn't help it this once, Papa. A letter from Lady Harding—do read it!"

Mr. Harrington rubbed his eyes, read it, and looked at his daughter.

"To go and stay at Wilmore—eh? And her ladyship promises to take you under her wing, and see that no one runs away with you? So you want to go, puss?"

"If you think the puss wouldn't be very much out of her element amongst such grand people!"

"Nonsense!" said her father, sharply; "the Harringtons are as good as the Hardings, though they choose to live in a different style. But, as the style is different, have you got any finery?"

"Plenty, papa. White muslin dresses of the most extensive character!"

"Very well; you must go, sometime, I suppose; and I would as soon trust you to Lady Harding as to any one, although——. There, be off, and enjoy yourself."

Then Mag had to be told, preparations to be made, and Flora cautioned about his good behaviour during her absence, and all day long the little school-girl was in a state of excitement vacillating between pleasure and dread, laughing outright at the thought of what her old governess would say, if she knew it, and her schoolfellows. And then she wondered whether there would be a footman behind each chair, with a white napkin round his arm, and a white wig, as she had read about in some novel; and last, but not least, she wondered whether she should be very much frightened! Then came the day, and the carriage, and she shrank up into a corner of it, laughing again to think what a morsel of a creature she was in this great lumbering thing! For she was a little bit frightened, too; and the little fit increased as the distance from Wilmore Hall lessened; and at last she began to wish most heartily that she dared tell that fine coachman to turn back and take her home again!

She did not then, however; and when Lady Harding herself met her in the Hall, took her two hands, looking into her face eagerly, and kissed her cheek, she felt better, but much astonished to see that there were actually tears in the eyes that looked at her so kindly.

"My child, your mother was my dearest friend, and you are so like her!"

Then, drawing Amy's hand within her arm, she took her to her room, still showing traces of that emotion which had astonished Eleanor Vere.

"Now, my dear, shall I send my maid to you, or will you ring by-and-bye?"

A maid! Amy opened a pair of puzzled eyes, and smiled.

"Oh, no thank you, I never have any one to help me."

Left alone, she began to speculate instead of dressing. "How odd, not to be able to dress oneself! I think I'll have Mag for a lady's-maid. How she would stare in that queer [illegible] of hers if I were to tell her so!

And so mamma was Lady Harding's dearest friend! How I should like to know what that is, I mean how dear a dearest friend is! I don't think I ever had one. I used to hear them calling each other dear and dearest, at school, and the minute after they would be quarrelling. That wasn't like Lady Harding. I can't fancy her quarrelling with any one. I wonder what the ball will be like. If I can only keep near her I shan't care. She is so kind."

CHAP. IV.

THE BALL.

This was Lady Harding's way of entertaining the children of her neighbours, instead of the more orthodox and more frequent dinner party. "A ball is fatiguing enough," said her ladyship, "but as for a dinner party, I never can, I never will consent to take my place at such an ingeniously contrived instrument of torture, as a fashionable, formal dinner-table in my own house."

It so happened that little Amy, bewildered by the novel circumstances around her, lost herself from beneath the wing of the hostess, and could no where distinguish that kindly face which she was so anxious to keep near her.

There was Sir Thomas, the very picture of a

jolly, fox-hunting country gentleman; and he, passing the corner which this school-girl had selected to shrink into, under her painful consciousness of being alone among strangers, made a mental memorandum to ask his wife who that pretty little girl was, on the sofa there, playing with her fingers.

For Amy, a stranger amidst upwards of a hundred people, seeing the floating muslins and other light drapery, relieved by the less abundant black cloth, enjoying the scene quietly in her own fashion, had suffered some portion of her dreamings to wander back to the old Grange, and her hand, which the baroness said she was playing with, was in reality engaged in stroking a [illegible] Flora.

Then the music! Such soft, beautiful music! It came to her like a dream. The moving figures and the gentle hum of voices only added to the visionary haze creeping over her; and when a voice spoke to her, she started and blushed painfully at the consciousness that her eyes were full of tears.

"My dear child!" said Lady Harding, sitting down beside her.

"I—it is all so beautiful," stammered Amy; "but indeed I did not know I was being so foolish."

Already there was an air of languor and weariness about Lady Harding, which made the little school-girl ask her, innocently, why she took so much trouble, if it tired her. And her hostess, smiling at such simplicity, told her it was a duty she owed to society.

Then a solemn gentleman, with a moustache, being brought up to Amy, requested to solicit the honour of her hand for the Lancers.

"Dancing," thought Amy. "Did they call that dancing?" The ladies walking about the room languidly, as though they were painfully conscious that a certain space must be got over somehow, and did not know how to do it with the least trouble to themselves; and the gentlemen, walking also, twirling moustaches, and bowing themselves into bad triangles, with a manner as solemn as if they had been the ghosts of former dancers, and knew the vanity of it."

"Fond of dancin—ar—?" asked Amy's partner, bending his superb head devotedly, to catch her answer.

Amy replied that she was very fond of it, whereupon the gentleman, satisfied that he had done what England expects every man to do, became silent again, and vouchsafed no more.

After him came a boy of an awkward age, who generally affected partners double his own height, but whom Lady Harding presented to Amy with an idea of mutual fitness. This young gentleman stammered a little, blushed, was extremely interested in the toes of his pretty boots, and talked a good deal of amiable nonsense.

On the whole Amy was rather fond of him, and glad when he put her down upon a lounge near the piano, where the talented Miss Goddard and her confidant Mr. Mello were preparing to electrify the audience with a burst of melody.

But where was Eleanor Vere all this while? Gone up with Philip to the White, to see a little "effect" which he told her he had thrown off to gratify her.

It was merely a face, half hidden in the brown curls that fell about it, bending down to look at a picture; and on the table whereon the picture rested, a dog with pricked-up ears and head on one side, also engaged in contemplating it.

Eleanor turned away impatiently.

"An artist's eye you know, Nelly; I couldn't help recollecting it."

"Why did you bring me here for nonsense, Philip? Come down, we are being rude to my aunt's visitors."

"Much you care for them," said Philip, looking at her. "Why, Nelly, I really thought that sketch would please you. You say there is nothing like nature."

"Except art. Stop, Philip, here is another 'effect' for you."

Eleanor paused in the doorway, with her hand on his shoulder. A little group had gathered round the piano, where Miss Goddard and Mr. Mello had been giving the duet "Parigi o cara" to an admiring audience, and the lady, turning to bow her acknowledgments for the hum of thanks, had caught the expression of little Amy's face, and seized upon her. She was "quite sure she was musical! A musical face, was it not, Mr. Mello? Did she play—sing—did she prefer Verdi, Beethoven, Mozart, or—"

"I don't know anything of Italian," said Amy, frankly, "but if it would make me sing like you, I wish I did."

"Now if that is not nature," said Eleanor, "it is a bit of perfect acting—[illegible], Philip, which is next best to nature. Look how pleased Miss Goddard is!"

"Acting!" repeated Philip.

Miss Goddard was charmed, delighted. Amy must sing something. Not know Italian! That was very sad—German, perhaps?

No. Amy shook her head.

An English ballad then, or Scotch. Nothing was so delicious, she quite doted on them.

"Amy," said Lady Harding, turning over the music books, "Do you know 'Auld Robin Gray?'"

Yes, Amy knew that.

"Ah, charming!" said Miss Goddard, as Lady Harding placed the song on the piano. "Do you accompany yourself, or shall I?"

"Herself, please," said Lady Harding, gently.

There was silence for a moment when the song ended; Eleanor and Philip went nearer to the piano, and then Lady Harding drew Amy away from Miss Goddard's rather [illegible] raptures.

"Amy, did you ever sing that for Walter Harrington—your papa, I mean?"

"Yes," said Amy, wondering at the question. "But only once, for it brought on a bad fit."

"A bad fit! What is that?"

"I don't know," said Amy, sorrowfully.

"They say he has an affection of the heart. Is that very serious?"

Lady Harding half smiled.

"I will ask you that some years, or indeed months hence, little Amy. Already I perceive that Mr. Mello is wounded."

"Wounded with what, I wonder," thought Amy, looking at him. "Not with a rose, at any rate; it is a pity he does not use one."

Turning her head at this moment, she caught Eleanor Vere's eyes fixed upon her. Amy started forward, eagerly; but there was a little flush in her cheek as she drew back chilled, from the haughty indifference of Eleanor's greeting.

What had she done? Why was Miss Vere so different? She had been kind and cordial enough that day at the Grange.

Again Miss Goddard took possession of her, but Amy's eyes followed Eleanor, wistfully.

"I am charmed with you, positively. Do you know any of the choruses in 'Martha'? No—what a pity! Well, we must teach you. I make a tolerable alto, and Mr. Mello—isn't he delicious?—a first-rate tenor. Ah, you are looking at that proud Miss Vere. Is she not perfectly revolting?"

"Revolting!" echoed Amy, in amazement. "Why, it is the most beautiful face in the room!"

"Beautiful! oh!" said Miss Goddard, with a grimace; "some people think so, I believe; but I don't. And she is eaten up with pride and self-conceit; far too good to associate with common-place people such as we are."

"Eleanor," said Philip, "Miss Goddard is giving you a character; prejudicing her new plaything. I am sure of it; I shall go to rescue your friend and your name."

"Stop, Philip!" exclaimed Eleanor, haughtily; but he was gone.

"Miss Harrington, I have to confess that I am no dancer; but if you will walk through a few of these intricate and beautiful figures with me, I shall be very much obliged to you."

Amy rose, and Miss Goddard threw "You wicked cruel creature, you!" after him, assuring him that Amy and herself were fast friends for life, and he would not separate them.

"That is friendship at first sight, I suppose," said Philip, speaking low. "It is strange how confidence grows upon one; but do you know I once caught myself believing a speech of Miss Goddard's? Shall I tell you what it was?"

"If you please."

"That she saw genius in my face, and fame and fortune in my future."

"Does she flatter everybody?" asked Amy, remembering the speech which began "I am charmed with you."

Philip laughed. "Thank you; then you think that was flattery. Well, I suppose she does."

There was a question which Amy longed to ask, but she was afraid it would be rude; and, after all, what did it matter to her?

"If you will promise not to think me dangerous," said Philip, who had been watching her face, "I will tell you unasked. Yes, I am an artist by profession, inclination, and for daily bread. Was not that what you were wondering?"

"Yes," said Amy, absently.

"You are looking at my sister. She has been my constant companion and champion ever since I was shut up in a dark closet for saying that 'Mother's Spelling-book' was a bother. And so you like dancing?"

"I like everything."

"Miss Goddard and friendship at first-sight included?"

"I do not dislike Miss Goddard," said Amy, laughing. "I don't think I should choose her society, but she is the only one here who has taken any notice of me."

Philip's face clouded. What he might have been going to say remained unsaid, for the beautiful and intricate figure began, and he was obliged to move. Walking about with her after it was over, he came upon Eleanor and Lady Harding in close conference.

"What treason now?" asked Philip.

"A picnic to Wilmore Castle," said Lady Harding, languidly. "I have done my duty in suggesting; it is for you to carry out. You know I always expect my guests to entertain each other."

She made room for Amy, however, with an air of interest which none other in the whole list of her acquaintance was ever favoured with.

"As you like everything, Miss Harrington, there is no need to ask your acquiescence," said Philip; "and I can answer for Eleanor, can't I, Nelly?"

But Miss Vere was gone.

THE OLD WOMAN'S SORROW.

The days again are lengthening; I sit in the quiet room
With only the fitful firelight chasing away the gloom;
And my eyes keep gazing idly upon the vacant chair there,
Till the world's wealth would I give to see him in that vacant chair;
That as I used in the old times, I might kneel by his side again,
And, with my arms around him, tell of all my grief and pain.
Since he was taken from me, to the grave so dark and cold,
From the failing heart and the weak frail arms that so vainly strove to hold!

Yes, I try to humbly speak the words, and not even in thought repine;
Thank God he is gone to his quiet rest, and that lonely grief is mine!
Perhaps we had been wiser, if in early youth he went;
But more deeply sad is the parting of two lives together spent
From the bloom of their youth's glad morning to their evening's dim decline!
Ah! until a long unparted day, dear husband, was thine and mine!
I saw not thy form drooping—noticed not that thy hair grew gray;
Ever dear, ever near thee, I watched not thy slow decay.

I saw not thy countless failing; thy eyes were the [illegible];
Each knew not that each was changing, until strangers called us old.
Since you left me, all my heart is still, and I [illegible] have grown;
Ah! yes; the [illegible] in a world of my own.
I am thinking, [illegible] thinking, of the time so long ago,
When the sound of your voice would stir my heart and make my young cheek glow.

I am [illegible] of our happy [illegible] years:
Of the many joys and griefs we shared—of the [illegible] hopes and fears.
To tell them my [illegible] story, alas! were of no avail;
How would they learn a lesson from the old woman's idle tale?
What would they care that we first began in our childhood's happy day?
What would they feel that our children, one by one, were taken away?
What could they know of our sorrow, when the last of them was flown?
Or how closely we drew together when we were left alone?

Worn away to a thin, bright thread, is the wedding ring I wore;
Worn away to a thread as frail is the shadowy life I bear!
I [illegible] the world's wealth away I would freely give,
To see [illegible] in that [illegible] chair and know that thou dost live.
Yet, not so, not so: it were better far from this weary being free,
That thou shouldst not return again, but that I should go to thee.

BESSIE.

Be Kind.—Kind words, lately, and with [illegible] the small ministry of social life, [illegible] of considerable value, but in the aggregate forming the wealth of [illegible]. They are the "[illegible]" which keeps the machinery from rusting, [illegible]. They are the dew that refreshes and beautifies the otherwise arid fields. They are the [illegible] of this [illegible], dreary world.—Old Jonathan.

THE TRAVELLER'S TREE.

BY MRS. ABDY.

"The Ravenala is a tree which grows in Madagascar, and other parts of the East, in thirsty localities, attaining a great height. Its large leaves, when pierced at the base, afford a kind of water fit to drink, and hence it is known as the Traveller's Tree."

The wayfarer passes—how gladly he sees
The [illegible] of beautiful trees!
Lo! [illegible]
Some [illegible] cool, tranquil shade;
They cheer him awhile on his lone, weary way,
Yet the thirst that consumes him they fail to allay.
Oh! fair Ravenala, he searches for thee,
And eagerly welcomes the Traveller's Tree.

Thy thick-clustered leaves a rich treasure enfold,
A [illegible] than silver or gold;
The wayfarer watches with eager delight,
The pure sparkling waters spring forth to his sight.
Refreshed by the draught so [illegible],
With vigour renewed he proceeds on his road,
Still [illegible], earnestly, hoping to see
That boon to the weary—the Traveller's Tree.

The wayfarer's trials are [illegible],
And yet one experience [illegible] his eyes?
From fear and [illegible],
How oft have we [illegible] nature [illegible] and [illegible],
And sought [illegible] spirits, [illegible] and glad,
Whose genius and wit have [illegible] our way,
And strewed it with flowers [illegible],
As those [illegible] dropped from the blossoming tree!

But long the fresh flowers had their charms in our eyes,
We turned to the haunts of the gifted and the wise;
The light spells of fancy we [illegible] to discard,
And sought our enjoyment in Knowledge alone.
How gladly from Pleasure's vain scenes we retired,
The calm [illegible] of study were all we [illegible];
That tree of [illegible] to be
Around at the foot of the sheltering tree.

Yet, something was lacking; we thirsted to find
A nature [illegible], gentle, and kind,
Still [illegible] Life's rough, tedious journey [illegible],
Our trials to share, our [illegible];
We found it—such gifts [illegible],
And soon [illegible];
We found gentle Sympathy's [illegible],
The wayfarer's blessing—the Traveller's Tree!

Though Genius may proffer its sweet, blooming flowers,
And Knowledge exult in the wealth of its stores,
Nor wisdom nor wit have the power to impart
Such comfort to sorrow as Kindness of Heart;
There, only, the [illegible],
That [illegible];
There, only, can Life's weary wanderers see
The true Ravenala—the Traveller's Tree!

CONCERNING A GENTLEMAN, AGED SIX.

BY JOVEN.

Passing a quiet evening at the house of a friend not long ago, I was much taken with the graceful winning ways of the young gentleman who is to serve as my text. He had those large, full, tender eyes that boys sometimes have; was very good-looking withal, seemed to know it in a dainty conscious way, and came up to you as one who expected to be petted, and almost knew that he deserved it. Falling asleep as the evening wore on, he gave the prettiest little apologetic look on waking up, and retired to his rest with a courtly gravity that was somewhat funny, but thoroughly loveable and charming.

Now our party was a very quiet one, but it kept thoroughly London hours. *Domestic* London hours, I mean; not Ball-room London hours; so that I think the ladies had retired soon after one o'clock, or at some such early period of the evening. An inveterate smoker or two remained to enjoy the tranquil weed, and to "chew the cud of sweet and bitter fancy." I, who was to sleep in the house, lit a pipe, whose ludicrously small size and generally low character have rendered it the mockery of a large circle of acquaintances, and then joined in the conversation with the bland volubility that is preeminently my characteristic. It was past three o'clock when my friend showed me up-stairs to my bed-room. "Let us peep in on young Fred," said he. Very stealthily we opened the child's door, and saw—

No! Nothing in particular. This is not a romantic tale. He had not been assassinated, poor little fellow! he was not sitting up in bed, reading Mr. Buckle, bless his little heart! (I mean Fred's little heart: not Mr. Buckle's). It had been a warm night: the little fellow had partially kicked the bed-clothes about, and he lay there, curled up across the bed, in the quaintest manner. He was sound asleep, breathing very tranquilly; and on his face there was a smile like an angel's. One could not look at him without thinking of those grand lines of Wordsworth:—

> Not in entire forgetfulness,
> And not in utter nakedness,
> But trailing clouds of glory, do we come
> From God, who is our home!
> Heaven lies about us in our infancy.

Surely he saw angels in his dreams. Surely he remembered the home from which he had only strayed six years.

I got to bed that morning with feelings that had been somewhat strange to me for some time past—feelings that go back, say twenty years, to the time when, without any of this child's beauty or grace, I had yet slumbers as sweet and as sound, with a mother to watch them who has been in a Devonshire grave-yard for a long time now—for a long and weary time: forgotten often, never remembered but with thoughts that "lie too deep for tears."

We all know that hour, when people die, and when people dance; when the night is dead, the day unborn; an hour cold and dreary even in the height of summer. I fancy that an almost audible shudder goes through the great city at that hour. It was very sweet to see that child sleeping! Throwing up my window I saw a redness in the east; ere long the heavens were bright and burning with the vivid dawn; and the dawn seemed to shame me, to reproach me, to accuse me.

Do none of my readers know the sensation—a sensation well nigh as tragic as one can have—of looking at a sunrise with jaded eyes, as it ushers in another day to be wasted? It comes upon you, sometimes, at a ball. You have been dancing, laughing, flirting: into the crowded room comes the terrible morning light, seeming to ask, "And what will you do with me?" I may be a nervous man—in fact, I know myself to be so; but at this sight, at the thought of this question, all the life of the ball is dead to me. The music jars upon me. The dances seem unmeaning, almost ghastly. Go into your study with this impression keenly and cruelly fresh upon you: I think you could write Hoffmannesque stories of a sufficiently wild character! But the pen will not work; the words come sluggishly, and the heart sinks. The brain is dull through the very intensity and passionate speed of its working. You have more in you than you can express. Let us even go to bed; and the brain may write its own poems—poems that will never get to printer's ink.

There are men—aye, and women—who take opium to *get* dreams! Is there no drug that can stop them? Cannot we bid this wonderful life of ours *halt* for a moment? Tearing through us like Heaven's lightning, thoughts, fears, and fancies come and go. The "machine" cannot rest. Yonder boy is sacred: only the purest and tenderest thoughts as yet are his. And *we*? Like the waves of the sea in a blind cavern (the simile is an old one), crowding thoughts and phantasies stir restlessly within us, even as we sleep. I think of those waves—how they may wash a corpse upon the rocks: and our brains? Thoughts of dear dead friends seem to be flung against us. The trick of the eye, the cadence of the voice—things that, waking, we could never remember—all these come back to us, solemnly and sadly, in the night. Dear old friend, for years forgotten, in the whirl of daily life—dear old friend, lying dead in an Indian grave—I can hear the merry laugh again as when we played cricket together; hear the cheery voice again—the voice that was so brave and hopeful; see the eyes that looked out at the future with so keen and eager a glance. And in a moment, he passes away. There comes another visitor. No, old friend: not less dear are thine now than some few years back, when I sat down on a gravestone in the churchyard, on your wedding-day, writing hurriedly some few lines of verse—weak enough I doubt not, but warm from the heart. I can remember very well that long farewell pressure of the hand that had been so often clasped in mine, and was never to be clasped in mine any more. We were about the same age; we were neither of us very strong. He would never own his weakness—never quite believe in it; he kept to his work, and he could work like ten. At last he broke down of a sudden, and the news came to me as I sat in my room, one morning, too ill to go to London, that he was dead.

Fresh forms crowd round me in my dreams. Little sisters whom I never saw in life come to me now. A brother, wonderfully gifted, whose name, had he lived, might perchance have been ere now a household word; and whom I could have so fondly followed at a distance, proud to hear men praise him; he comes again—sometimes very fondly and kindly, sometimes angry and passionate with the sufferings, both of brain and body, that killed him ere his time. Ere his time? The time was good; for it was of his Father's choosing. He, for one, has reached his journey's end: he, for one, will never faint upon the hot road in the summer noons—never miss his way upon the dark path in the winter night. And as this Image also departs, I awake, feverish, unrefreshed, with strange sounds dying away, as what we call "reason" and "common sense" come back—strange sounds, that seem to come from an unending distance, and yet to be close at hand—strange sounds, that are indeed echoes of the dead years. . . . .

Some few hours having elapsed since I saw little Fred asleep, into my room struts little Fred awake, the bright eyes looking brighter than ever, and the sweet voice sweeter. I protest that a child's morning laughter is an absolute tonic, and helps to set one up for the day. This little Fred, entering my room when my cold splashing and sponging are over, and when I am tranquilly fixing to my shoulders that badge of respectability, a black coat; this little Fred, with queries as to my "corps," with ardent imitations of the British volunteer; this little Fred, placing his arms with due rigidity, holding up his head with due determination; this little Fred, with twenty little drolleries and vagaries, ever accompanied by his own running commentary of boy-laughter—I vow that he quite chases away all the sad solemn shapes that have been round me in the night. A wonderful magician is this young gentleman of six! Strange powers of exorcism has he! I—who feel myself now to be growing rather an aged Wizard, who is not in possession of a magic wand—I do loyal homage to the Boy. The day long, I cast imaginary horoscopes for him. Poor little Fred! the Knickerbocker days—days of childish prettiness, petted by Mamma, petted by everyone with a heart—must pass away. I soberly try to picture to myself the Future of the child.

And behold, I am aware of days of gloom. Clouding troubles cast their shadows before. Here is little Fred's first great grief, rapidly drawing nigh. As thus. His Father has driven away, after the parting "tip," and little Fred is inducted into his first school. Is there a dreariest feeling? Yesterday, we wanted to go to school. There seemed a kind of dignity about the act. No more feminine pettings; we are getting too old to be kissed by ladies before company; it is time that we should mingle with other boys. To-day, we see the other boys, and grow somewhat terrified. There is an amount of rudeness about the other boys to which we are unaccustomed. One other boy, apparently the wag of Dr. Sapius's establishment (where pupils are fitted for a professional career—where every attention is paid to their moral and religious training, washing extra), makes remarks, of a humorous but disparaging character, about our personal appearance. He does not scruple to express his conviction that we ought to be clad in crinoline; that our face was lent to us by our youngest sister, and that our real name is Susan. His toadies (those toadies! always toadies!) have the indelicacy to laugh. We don't meet with the slightest sympathy. The other boys ravage our property; inquire, with unblushing rudeness, about the profession of our father and our pecuniary means; and, regarding us as a new source of excitement, play practical jokes. We had grown tired of being petted: now, our hair is pulled, ink is upset over our dainty garments—we are as a butt to all.

"These things don't occur in well-regulated schools!" Don't they! There comes a day, not long postponed, on which we have to do battle with Charley Tickle, the Wag. That other boy's lex-talionary (in which there is no real fun, you know) becomes absolutely insufferable. We challenge him to combat. We stand up, in position, against him. He is cheered on to the deadly encounter by the voices of his stupid admirers. He appears well acquainted with the art of boxing. When we rush in at him wildly like "Uncas" (about whom we have been recently reading), he deftly parries our vague blows. We grow confused; we are knocked down; we are picked up; we are in a wild rage, but in a very impotent one. Actually, when he slips in a forward lunge, when we might "hit him a good one," we simply give him an open-handed slap in the face—as if we were Susan. Susan—to that he recovers himself, laughingly, and, ere we can be well upon our guard, administers one —two! It seems three years (it is actually six minutes) since the battle began; and now it ends—in our discomfiture, in our defeat!

When we recover from the confusion of the fray, and from the shame of our vanquishment, the first thing we become aware of, is that good-natured chap, Charley; addressing me not as Susan, but as "old fellow," and laundering, with such appliances (as of cold [illegible]) as were at hand to reduce the black eye which he has just inflicted. Soon after which Charley is our famous friend. You have no idea, Mamma, of that boy's talent for boxing. It is a fact that Doctor Swipe, having discovered a certain caricature, could not refrain from laughing at that boy's fun, even though he caned him!

And I think, little Fred, that, after all, your schooldays will be happy enough. Boys are terrible cruel, sometimes (my own character, at the age of ten, was an aggravated mixture of the Emperor Nero and the late King of Naples, with a few characteristic tricks suggested by the assiduous study of Ojibbeway torture); but there is a [illegible] that disarms them. As a rule, it is only the Unpleasant Boys who get severely treated by their brethren. The Unpleasant Boys who tell tales, who are mean with their money, who bully the children—punished are these: and why not?

Little Fred, it is with the blush of remorse on my cheek, that I ask you to behave well towards the unfortunate gentlemen who will teach you French! The shameful cruelties—aye, cruelties—which I have seen inflicted on French masters, appal me even now! The British Boy—when he is a bad one—knows how to torture; the French exile has to learn how to endure!

Little Fred, I would speak unto thee very seriously. Amongst these gentlemen (for such they are, despite their beggarly wage, despite their threadbare coats) who teach thee to conjugate "aimer," there are grand men, my Frederick! There are men who have given up fortune, social position, social enjoyment, for a principle; men who have been in prison for saying boldly; men who have had escapes from prison; men who have wandered in the woods of South America, obscurity and gallantry; men who have fought upon barricades, and in the wild confusion of street-battle, many years before you or I, my Frederick, first saw the light. My heart bleeds, sometimes, when I think of such men—of their lonely lodgings, cheered only by the old [illegible]; and of the slaughtering, silly cruelty with which their pupils vex them. An exile's feelings are easily touched, soon hurt. A foolish word, spoken out without any thought of unkindness, may cause a big-hearted man to wince, in a pain very acute and intimate.

Lo, it is the year 1874! The present writer is a dweller in Bohemia, as a British merchant (quite safe?) and I'll [illegible] to him little Fred, aged nineteen. Description of little Fred: Eyes full, penetrating; visage long; curly moustache long, black. And has it come to this? Here is my cherub of 1861, and in the lips of him is an abominable Havanna! In the soul of him? Let me hope, not cynicism; let me hope, not weariness, disappointment, doubt. He calls me "old fellow," does little Fred; treats me as a well-meaning man of middle age, but one who is behind the times; and he takes me to places of amusement. What will they be like, I wonder, in 1874? Will there be an Armenian playing King Lear? Will negro melody still retain its hold upon the British heart? Will there be music-halls extant? Will comic vocalists still express a wish that they were with Nancy? or state, with a glaring disregard to truth and accuracy, that they are "Old Bob Ridley, oh!" Will there be acrobats? Yes, there will be acrobats, and there will be gorillas—live gorillas; and the excitement of the day—"the Great Sensation" of the day—will be a single combat on the tight rope between a young gorilla (from the river Gaboon) and M. [illegible], the eminent French acrobat, who inherited all Blondin's popularity on the untimely and lamented death of that performer in the Crystal Palace, in 1862? . . . . . Frederick, my son, these things do not delight me. Even in 1861 I was "bored" and wearied by them—albeit Leotard at Cremorne is a sight worth seeing. But in 1874? My son, I will rather accompany thee to Wimbledon, paying the fare for both, and see thee shoot at various ranges.

Two important influences—amongst many others—bear on the British Boy in these days. Influence number One, that of "Sensation" Novels; Influence number Two, that of Cadet Rifle Corps. It needs the second to check the first. Years ago, Doctor Arnold warned his boys against novel-reading overmuch. Masters like Arnold (and such will remain) might very profitably repeat the warning, with additional emphasis, in these present days. Walter Scott did good: He gave strong but healthy food to a Boy's imagination. He cannot be read too much. The grisly Red Indian novels of the day can do little else but harm, and cannot be avoided too carefully. I am much grieved [illegible] to see the popularity of such books as those of Gustave Aimard. Without one atom of the descriptive power and the deep feeling for natural beauty possessed by Cooper; without even the dash, [illegible], vivacity of Capt. Mayne Reid, these books yet seem to be universally read by boys, and liked by them. Come out, my British Boy, from amidst this French phantasmagoria of scalping: come out, and read Ivanhoe! come out, and go to the drill.

I (in 1874) am right glad, Frederick, that thou hast obtained a prize. Thirteen years ago, I remember me that thou didst essay to wield a rifle. It was too big for thee; aye, blush not at the recollection, Frederick; for thou wert then but six years of age. Even then, I did prophesy thy future [illegible]. . . . And Frederick, Frederick, [illegible], who won the [illegible]?

It is idle. I grow short. I [illegible] the looking-out for my grey hairs. Tobacco—the which I am still madly addicted—is curling its fumes around me, when I hear a rap. I lay aside the precious magazine, which is still extant and flourishing; which has Novels by the Author of "[illegible] Morley," worthy the high promise of that powerful tale; which has Essays by J. A., thoughtful, earnest, and scholarly as of old; nay, to which "Jones" himself—in the "stupid season," when the clever writers are out of town—is still allowed to contribute; I lay down, I say, that periodical on hearing the postman's rap. Three letters.

1. A Comic Song is required by Monday next.... But I am too old to write Comic Songs.

2. Mr. Snip would feel obliged by the settlement of that little account. I dare say he would. It is only natural that he should.... poor man!

3. As I live, *wedding cards!* Mr. Littlefred, Mrs. Littlefred, née Pershouse! I do remember me: 'tis *the Lady in Blue!* Well, Frederick, if you *will* marry on six hundred a-year, do so. Take the consequences. *Be* destitute, my Boy. If evil times *should* come, I—who am single, and have no incumbrances—will cheerfully provide the chops.

* * * * *

Doctor Young observes that

"We take no note of time but by its loss:
To give it, then, a tongue, was wise in man."

This is one of the most harmless remarks ever made by a British Poet. *Et hinc*, the tongue has spoken. It tells me that it is high time to close my desk.

Not dreaming of school battles—still less of 1874 and rifle triumphs, or of 1878 and wedding-cards, little Fred has been long asleep. I should like to look in at his room, before I go to my own!

BALLOWMERE.

(A Tale, in Four Chapters).

BY ALFRED GRANDCHAUFF.

CHAP. I.

"Where are we now, guard?" was my ejaculation between sleeping and waking, as the train slackened its speed, and the lights of what appeared to be a town of considerable size flickered dimly in the distance.

"N——n-T——, sir," replied the green-coated functionary, an announcement which I received with no little satisfaction; for I had scarcely quitted my seat since leaving Euston-square, and although fond of travelling, and no grumbler, still I maintain that the iron highway, although the quickest mode of locomotion, is, at the same time, the most tedious, and that a day spent in a railway carriage, except in very pleasant company, is, oftener than otherwise, a wearisome day. Why I had left my snug bachelor apartments in ——Square, and undertaken a journey of some three hundred miles, at a time when most sane people do not wander far from their own firesides, unless compelled to do so, it is not so easy for me to explain without considerable circumlocution. However, while the tickets are being collected, and that interminable coal train, which now blocks up the line, moves on and makes way for us, I may as well give you my previous reminiscences of the place, or rather of the last and only night I ever spent there, for of the place itself I saw little or nothing.

Without being very particular with regard to dates, I may say that it was certainly more than ten, but less than twenty years since this visit took place. I was then making my *début* as a traveller—in fact, commencing the first trip which the kind solicitude of my friends would permit me to undertake alone.

Escaped from the thraldom of my worthy pedagogue's birch, the "ugly weeds" (Campbell) tailed coat, having been donned for the first time, instead of the ingenious jacket, my head well stored with good advice and [illegible], and my pocket comfortably lined with golden portraits of our most gracious Sovereign, a second Alexander in my own estimation, I had begun that march in which the world in general was to be surprised and conquered, although with bloodless weapons. And my second day's march led me up the Tyne (Campbell speaks of a "march over the mountain wave," and so I suppose I may do the same), the voyage having been accomplished in a vessel, which, probably on the "lucus a non lucendo" principle, had been named the "Velocity," on account of the extraordinary length of time which it generally took on the passage. But peace to the old boat! It has since gone to the bottom of the German Ocean, and far be it from me to "drag its frailties from their last abode." From the bluff old Captain, and steward, I received every kindness; and acting on the advice of the latter, a native of the wilds of Strathspey, I betook myself, upon landing, to a quiet, comfortable, unpretending hotel, in a quiet, comfortable, unpretending street, in which to pass the night. I remember very well the words in which my Celtic friend directed me to this house, as they contained the first and last attempt at a joke that I ever heard from a steward on board ship.

"They ca't the 'Lamb,' sir; but ye need na fear being fleeced at it for a' that." To the "Lamb" then I went, and although internally there was everything to render any man of moderate desires as comfortable as need be, still to me the hours passed wearily enough. Incessant rain prevented me from going out, and thoughts of the happy home which I had left so recently as "the old house at home" prevented me from appreciating very enthusiastically the pleasures of solitude. Indeed my case had reached such desperate straits, that I had begun to play a game at bagatelle, right hand against the left, when the door of my apartment was gently opened, admitting (there must be a heroine in every tale, and mine comes in here perhaps as unexpectedly to you as she did to me), a lovely girl, nine or ten years of age, who addressed me with all the frank innocence of childhood: "Oh, if you please, sir, mamma thought you would be so lonely here this wet evening; so she asked me to come and amuse you." Rather a drop this, for Alexander the Second! Had the good lady marked the juvenile conceit of her temporary guest, and taken this method of administering a mild and perhaps necessary rebuke? I do not know; but in my momentary vexation the word *impudent* had almost escaped my lips—almost, but not quite; for a second glance at my little visitor convinced me that, on her part at least, there was no intention to give offence; and my resentments, although sometimes sudden, being seldom long continued, we became, in less than five minutes, the best possible friends. The abnormal game at bagatelle was exchanged for the less exciting pastime of "jackstraws," and in this very innocent recreation, relieved by occasional snatches of conversation, which would scarcely interest the reader, the hours passed away, until, between ten and eleven, I found myself getting very sleepy, and my little playmate fast asleep. Next morning, before taking my departure southwards, I again saw my young friend, Mary Lennox, and we said "good-bye" to each other, I honestly believe, with more regret than older friends generally experience in similar circumstances. My vanity, however, was subjected to a slight wound on our parting, as well as on our meeting. I had offered her one of my cards—yes, to be sure, I had cards with my name, for the first time, not Master, but Mr. Alfred Grandchamps, engraved upon them in the most approved fashion. My self-satisfaction with my ancestral name of Grandchamps was a very marked trait in my character. I was no vulgar Brown, Jones, or Robinson, requiring the help of either names or prænomen to distinguish me from the innumerable gentes (vide Adams's "Roman Antiquities," and let the non-classical scholar remember that I don't mean gents) of the Brown, Jones, and Robinson class. No; the Grandchamps of that ilk, to the younger branch of which family I belong, had, once upon a time, quartered their arms with the Viponts and the Bruces, and although now rather in the shade, having lost their broad acres, through their fidelity to the doomed house of Stuart, still plumed themselves on their patrician origin. If, as the poet facetiously tells us, "the grand old gardener and his wife smile at the claims of long descent," my paternal uncle, Walter Montieth Grandchamps, certainly did not, and, although unpropitious circumstances had obliged him to pass in a dingy Glasgow warehouse instead of in the senate or the camp, each ten-pound note which he transmitted to his affectionate nephew was accompanied not by the grumbling inquiry, "What will he do with it?" but with sundry plain hints that the fewer of his bank notes might not only to leave a reasonable supply of the circulating medium at command, but to show the world in general that they really had it. "Common people," the dear old man used to say, "may economise at second-hand stationers, and save a shilling or two at ready-made tailoring establishments; but our family, my boy, must never condescend to such things." Judge of my chagrin then, when little Mary said, as she looked at my card, with an arch smile—which, although harmless enough in a child, is apt to get somewhat dangerous to the careless by-stander, when the child begins to be a woman—"Well, Mr. Grandchamps, you are a very nice man, and I mean to work you a pretty little purse to keep your shillings in, before you come again." That horrible pun on my name, and that sly hint that I was rather too fond of hearing the rattle of the gold pieces in my pocket! Who could bear two such indignities without retaliation? Not I, and so a hearty, [illegible] smack on the face avenged the insults.

"What!" exclaims the horrified Mrs. Dickscowitz, "do you dare to commence your adventures by telling us that you raised your hand against that defenceless innocent?"

Softly, my dear lady! it was my lips, and not my hand, that inflicted the chastisement; and I dare say you remember well, in the days of "auld lang syne," when Dickscowitz was yet a bashful young man, the various little arts by which you contrived to provoke him to behave in the same reckless manner. So you may cease so to proclaim aloud; for your virtuous daughters, the Misses Dickscowits, are evidently beginning to get interested in this particular view of the subject of capital punishments, and you may depend upon it that I shall say nothing to shock either them or you.

I believe there was a tear in little Mary's eye as the vehicle that was to carry me forward on my journey dashed down the narrow street, and for many a day the "Lamb" and its inmates were often in my thoughts. But the years rolled on, no matter how, with me; and although I frequently speculated on the probable fate of my kind friends of a night, and kept resolving until the thing became a sort of mania in my mind, that I would go and revive old acquaintance with them, I had never done so. How many years longer I might have resolved and hesitated, I do not know, but a simple circumstance at length brought about the long-intended research. My worthy friend Dr. Bolusdose, happening to call upon me on a little matter of business, took the opportunity of saying to me at parting: "Why, Grubbchopps, you look sadly ill, through keeping so closely to your studies as you have done for some time past. Throw away those horrid papers, and take a week's, or, better still, a month's holiday in the country somewhere."

"In the country at midwinter?" I replied. "Why, Doctor, you are surely mad. Where could I go? What could I do?"

"Go anywhere you please—do anything you please—you will be sure to find something to interest you; and when you return we shall have much pleasure in listening to your adventures. You always assume the character of the recluse by fits and starts, and for the present you have had enough of it. Away then into your desk with the romance, or whatever it is, [illegible] premature [illegible], the world will wait a little; and mark me, sir, I have given you some valuable medical advice for nothing; and, if you refuse it, such another haul is not likely to be offered you twice in one lifetime."

Here, then, was just the opportunity I had been waiting for—I needed relaxation and something to interest me. Grand excuses these for pressing upon an expedition, which, in other circumstances, might be regarded as ridiculously Quixotic. With me, to resolve is to act, and in less than two hours myself and my portmanteau were whirling away from the "Babylon of bricks" at the rate of forty miles an hour. Here we are now, however, on the platform; and if the reader is by this time sufficiently interested in the fate of Mary Inniers to wish to know more of her, let him follow me, and perhaps he will not be disappointed.

At the waiting-room I easily ascertained, by consulting a Directory, that the "Lamb" still continued to be numbered amongst the hotels in N——, but that it had changed landlords since my last visit. "The Lamb, Old Clinton Road, James Lindsay"; such was the entry, and, accordingly, towards the Old Clinton Road I directed my steps, beginning by this time to think that I had entered upon a thoroughly wild-goose chase, but determined to make the most of it. I had no difficulty in recognising the old house again, nor in finding my way into the very room where I had sat with Mary nearly fifteen years before; and he who at mature age has revisited, for the first time, some spot hallowed by the recollections of joyous youth, will understand my emotions, as that room, in which each object, although long forgotten, assumed at a second glance a familiarity almost painful, like the "banquet-hall deserted" of Erin's bard, called back from the dead past many a phantom vision of pleasures gone, and hopes for ever fled. But my moralising was speedily interrupted; for, obedient to my summons, mine host, Mr. Lindsay—a goodhumoured burly Northumbrian—presented himself at the door, begging, with his best bow, to know what might be the gentleman's commands. The question was rather perplexing, for I really had not made up my mind in which way it would be best to prosecute my enquiries; however, I explained, off-hand, that I had been attracted to the house because I had spent a very pleasant evening there many years ago, that I thought it advisable to counteract the injurious effects of a long, cold journey by indulging in a glass of hot brandy-and-water, and should be glad if he would join me in that and a little friendly chat for half-an-hour or so.

The invitation was at once accepted, and I had no difficulty in leading the conversation to the former inmates of the "Lamb." Mr. Lindsay had known "old Inniers," as he called him, for many years, having been in the habit of frequenting his house on market days before coming to settle in N——, and sympathised most heartily with him in the misfortunes which had befallen him.

"Had he then been unfortunate?"

Yes, he had. Ten years ago he was in very prosperous circumstances, and had realised a few thousand pounds upon which he intended to retire to the country in his old age, but by a series of unsuccessful speculations he had lost all. It was more remarkable, too, that this had happened to him, seeing that the most [illegible] investments were recommended to him by such a judicious gentleman as Mr. William Blandon. No one could understand it. This Mr. Blandon had lost his father at a very early age, his mother being left almost entirely unprovided for, and Mr. Inniers had kindly taken charge of the boy's education, and placed him as clerk with a respectable stockbroker, who, after a few years, received him into partnership. Of course he was very grateful to his benefactor, and always ready to advise him as to what speculations were safe or unsafe; but all was of no avail. In a few years poor Inniers was a ruined man; and although Mr. Blandon had done everything he could to avert the calamity, the final crash came at last. But Inniers, although ruined in a pecuniary sense, was not dishonoured; for, with the small sum which he received from the present landlord for good-will and fixtures, he paid all his creditors to the full, although by doing so he left himself almost penniless. Since then, however, he had again begun to prosper. His kind friend had lent him a sum sufficient to stock a small farm, in a remote part of Buckinghamshire, on the proceeds of which, coupled with the profits derived from a country inn, a good deal frequented by tourists in the summer months, he was enabled to secure a comfortable home for himself and his daughter Mary, now his chief solace; for she was his only child, and he had been a widower for many years. The money advanced by Mr. Blandon had all been repaid more than a year ago, but the parties still continued on the most friendly terms, and were just about to be united in closer bonds. In a very few weeks Miss Inniers was to become Mrs. Blandon, and everybody said it was a most disinterested match on the part of the gentleman, inasmuch as although he could scarcely find a fairer, he was justly entitled to look for a wealthier bride." * * * *

Such was the substance of James Lindsay's first conversation with me, but I was only half-satisfied with it in my own mind, and a little adroit cross-examination soon led him to reveal a good deal more of his real sentiments.

* * "Whatever others might think, he had no very high opinion of Mr. Blandon, always suspected something wrong in the background with such plausible gentlemen; and, although it was needless to say so without proof, had no doubt whatever but that he had been well paid by more bubble companies than one, for acting as a respectable sort of decoy duck to assist in catching such stray unsuspecting birds as Mr. Inmers. Neither did he think that Miss Inmers cared anything about her wealthy suitor. She might be induced to marry him, since her father, now far advanced in years, dreading lest she should be left an unprotected orphan, very much wished her to do so; she might, perhaps, believing him to be the kind friend that he had always appeared to be, feel a certain degree of respect for him; but love him as a husband ought to be loved—never. Poor Harry Greenbank, though absent for many a long year, was not yet forgotten.

"Harry Greenbank—what, a former suitor?"

"Yes; that was the most melancholy part of the story. Generous, daring, and open-hearted, he had early won the heart of Mary Inmers, with the full approbation of all parties concerned, and for a year or two it seemed as if with them 'the course of true love' would, for once, 'run smooth.' But exuberance of animal spirits and gay companions sometimes led him into excesses which could scarcely be justified, and at last Mary ventured to remonstrate with him, at the instigation of her friends—more strongly, perhaps, than she would otherwise have done, and told him that if such things occurred again they must part for ever. He, poor fellow, promised amendment, and, better still, kept his promise, until one evening, about six months afterwards, when invited to meet a pretty large party at the 'Lamb,' on a birthday occasion, he reeled into the room in a state about which there could be no mistake, and, after a few minutes, fell senseless on the floor. It was a painful shock to all, but a terrible one to *her*; and, although he might have been forgiven—for more than one suspected, and said that some cruel snare had been laid for him that day—he never asked forgiveness. His first act, on returning to consciousness next morning, was to write a brief note to Mary, bidding her an eternal farewell, as he knew she would never care to see him again; and another to his uncle, who had supplied the place of a parent to him, full of the most passionate expressions of affectionate gratitude, thanking him for all that he had done for him, and all that he intended to do, but at the same time intimating that all search for him, for a long time, at least, would be in vain. And all search for him was in vain. His uncle, whose constitution had been shattered by a long residence in India, died soon after. Although of unassuming and somewhat eccentric habits, Mr. Greenbank, sen., was supposed to be possessed of considerable property; but what had become of his riches no one knew. Of course there were various absurd conjectures afloat respecting the old man's will; but the only parties who, if it had pleased them to do so, could have given some information on the question—the well-known solicitors Messrs. Gregson and Sharpley—maintained an impenetrable silence. True they had, from time to time, advertised for the missing Harry, in the most widely-circulating newspapers; but beyond this nothing could be learnt from them. One of their clerks, however, who had once been in the employment of Mr. Blandon, and was now lying in a very dangerous state, had once or twice, when under the influence of gin—as was, unfortunately, too often the case with him—been known to mutter certain vague hints to some of his companions about what he knew of old Greenbank's affairs. Once he said that he could tell well enough why Blandon wished to marry Miss Inmers, but that he would never be permitted to do so, and that Harry Greenbank might yet return to enjoy his own. But in his sober moments he always studiously avoided the subject, and would never admit that he had made any such statements. The fact was, that through some imprudence on his part while in Mr. Blandon's employment, that gentleman had the poor clerk completely in his power. That he hated his former master there could be no doubt, but it was equally evident that he feared him too.

The half-hour which I had purposed spending with Mr. Lindsay had been already protracted to two hours before I was put in possession of these facts, which I have endeavoured to detail as succinctly as possible. We had, by this time, become quite friendly and confidential. He was evidently much interested in all that concerned the Inmers family, and I took no pains to conceal from him that I was the same.

"Where then," said I, at last, "is this place where you say they are now? How can I get there?"

"About sixty miles from this, in the wildest corner of Bleakmountshire. The railway will take you to the county town of Bleakmount; from Bleakmount to Craighallow there is a mail-cart, with seats for a few passengers once a day. After that you must either hire a conveyance or walk (it is only a few miles) to Mr. Inmers's place, the 'Percy Arms,' at the lower extremity of Ballowmere. But, sir, are you really going there? I wish you would, although I scarcely know why."

"Yes, I believe I shall go. You know I have medical authority for wandering for a week or two, and from your description of that part of country I should like to see a little of it, even had I no other motive. If I can do no good, at least I shall do no harm, and I hope that all will come right in the end; [illegible]-

tion, do you try to induce that poor clerk of whom you have been speaking to make a full disclosure of whatever secret affecting the interests of any of the fallen countries he may be in possession of. If necessary, you can communicate with me by letter; and on my return I shall be sure to see you."

"Thank you; I shall attend to what you say. And do you know—although I scarcely like to say so, as it may be only my fancy—I actually thought that I saw Harry himself not many days ago."

"You did!"

"Yes; I was standing looking out into the street from the window of this very room, at an early hour in the morning, when my attention was drawn to a man evidently disguised, who was gazing at the house with fixed attention. My first impression was, that it was some one calculating the chances of being able to commit a burglary; and I was just about to throw up the sash, to let him know that he was watched, when he moved away as if suddenly alarmed. It was then that his general figure and gait reminded me strongly of Harry Cruikshank, and I have never been able to dismiss the fancy; for fancy I suppose it was."

"Perhaps not, my good friend. We may be nearer than we imagine to a full solution of all these mysteries. Meantime, good night."

"Good night, sir. A pleasant and prosperous journey to you. I'm glad to have seen you; and, however things may turn out, I hope that when ever you come to R——, you will not forget me."

"Depend upon it I shall not, Mr. Lindsay." And with a shake of that huge hand as hearty as if we had been bosom friends for twenty years, I took my departure.

* * *

"Well now," thought I, as I wended my way back to the Station Hotel, "where will all this end? How is it, that although amongst the thousands with whom we come into contact in the course of our lives, there are few in whom we can ever feel any interest beyond what is excited by the mere circumstances of the hour, we still here and there meet with one, in the most apparently accidental manner, between whom and ourselves there is some indefinable sympathetic chord, that seems at times to draw our destinies together whether we will or will not? What was there about Mary Ireson, that should have caused her to dwell in my memory during all these long years, when many who have been once my most intimate associates have passed from my world, forgotten 'as a dream when one awaketh?' What is it that is hurrying me now into this remote nook, as anxious to rescue her from this William Blunden, whom I believe in my heart to be a hypocritical scoundrel, as if my own sister were in jeopardy? I do not know; but I must away to Blackmonthshire to-morrow, and be guided by what I may learn there, as to my future proceedings. It will not do to introduce rashly.

'Nec Deus intersit, nisi dignus vindice nodus;' but if I can find an opportunity of cutting one of the folds of this complicated knot, I shall not regret my journey. And when I return to London, I shall have an adventure of some kind to tell my good friend, Dr. Smoothcut; but whether of joy or of sorrow the day will declare.

Chap. II.

Several years ago, whilst wandering in that remote, and almost depopulated part of Sutherlandshire, "where," as Sir Walter tells us,

> "Beneath the northern sky
> Chides wild Loch Eribol his caverns hoar;"

I met with an old Highlander, who propounded to me a theory of cosmogony, that might well have startled Humboldt. Seeing my eye directed to the rocky masses that lay piled in wild confusion all around us, the aged Celt exclaimed:

"Aye, sir, this out-of-the-way bit of creation was made late upon Saturday night; and so there was no time to harmise it."

This quaint observation recurred to my mind several times during my cold ride in the open mail-gig from Blackmonth to Craighallow. Along that line of road the harmonising process had evidently been neglected. Here and there, where least expected, some wooded dell, or cultured valley, which when clad in the verdure of summer might have proved a most grateful retreat from the strife of senates and the din of camps, opened up before us; but had Pan himself been my fellow-passenger during those three tedious hours, compelled like me to offer a purely passive resistance to the incessant pelting of sleet and hailstones, I do verily believe that he would have longed for the comforts of the bar-room of some greasy Athenian tavern, in preference to this vaunted Arcadia.

"Only another hill or two, sir, and then we shall be there," was the reply which the driver gave to my oft-repeated questions regarding the distance to be travelled; and yet as I had made up my mind that, for some reason or another, the Fates had doomed me, like Sisyphus of old, to alternate for ever between up hill and down, as explained. "There," from the gruff voice beside me, and a hand pointed triumphantly to some twenty or thirty houses perched amidst precipitous crags, like eagles' nests, conveyed to me the welcome assurance that the last stage was now nearly finished. To avoid mistakes, I may as well state candidly, that if any one should take up a map of England or Scotland, with the expectation of finding therein the exact latitude and longitude of what guide-books would denominate "the highly romantic village of Craighallow," he will most certainly be disappointed. I have my own reasons for allowing a certain degree of mystery to veil the real names of the places where the events which I am about to desall took place. What right have I to rob Loch Katrine and the Trosachs, even for one year, of the tribute offered by thousands of devotees to the shades of Douglas and his Helen? What right have I to put Roderick Dhu's nose out of joint by opening a rival concern a hundred miles or so nearer to the metropolis? I know I shall soon have a deputation from the enterprising directors of the Trytton Junction Railway waiting upon me, with some statements as to the enormous profits to be derived from running excursion-trains, during the summer months, to the station nearest to Ballowmere; or perhaps with a proposal to open up a branch line to the very borders of the lake. But I must listen to their terms before I try to reconcile my conscience to the scheme. That, I believe, is the orthodox way of commencing a railway speculation; at least it is what a casual acquaintance of mine—the well-known Mr. Grassman Dunbrown—recommends me to do, and his experience in such matters is not of yesterday.

But to our tale. I left myself—where was it? Oh, just drawing up before the "Grouse and Trout Hotel," at Craigballow. I have no doubt whatever but that, in the proper season, both grouse and trout are to be had there in abundance and perfection; but as that season had not yet arrived, I was obliged to content myself with an improvised repast, of which I had no reason to complain; and surely John Gough himself would have winked at that stiffish tumbler of whisky-toddy, by means of which I banished the chills of my mountain ride. The appearance of an unknown stranger at this season of the year excited some little surprise, as I could gather from some sundry snatches of conversation which I overheard amongst the domestics, and this surprise was increased when it was ascertained from the name and address engraved upon my portmanteau that I had come from London. A Londoner in Craigballow in January was indeed regarded as a *rara avis*; and it was rather amusing to me to hear the various conjectures which were thrown out regarding Mr. Grandchaupp and his probable business there. The general impression seemed to be that I had come on her Majesty's service, to endeavour to bring to justice one or two parties who were suspected of being extensively engaged in illicit distillation in that neighbourhood; and this belief was considerably strengthened when, shouldering a light knapsack, I sallied out, with an intimation that it was somewhat uncertain when I might return. Following the directions which one of the natives gave me in his own peculiar dialect, respecting the most direct route to the Percy Arms, I crossed the old bridge with its single arch, that spans the Ballow, and turned briskly into a footpath amongst the heather, which I was assured, although somewhat rough in one or two places, was more than a mile nearer than the ordinary highway.

I suppose that, in order to take my stand as the narrator of incidents worth listening to, I ought at this juncture to lose my way, and wander for hours in the dark, amidst mountain precipices, or to be attacked by a band of smugglers and imprisoned for the night in some dismal cave, with a pile of human skulls for my pillow; but fortunately for me, if not for you, nothing of the kind occurred. The lengthening shadows warned me that I must not loiter (as I felt tempted to do) to admire the grandeur of the surrounding scenery, but I saw enough to make me determine upon a more minute survey at no distant period. The deep black waters of the Ballow rolled below me in sullen silence, as if gathering strength for their terrific struggle in that dark ravine below. And the dull incessant roar borne upwards from the opening of those huge chasms told how fierce the contest they had to encounter there before being resolved into the tranquil bosom of Ballowmere.

Just as I was beginning to hesitate a little about the landmarks which had been laid down for my guidance, a "gentle shepherd," with his pipe (a real *cutty* and black as charcoal), met me, and, learning my destination, very civilly offered to conduct me; but as the smoke from the chimneys of the "Inn" (as he called it) was now plainly to be discovered against the twilight-sky, I dispensed with his services, and allowed him to pursue that search after his shepherdess, which, from sundry little decorations about his person, I more than suspect, the sly fellow was bent on. I soon after reached the margin of the lake, and, keeping along that for nearly a mile, found myself at last in front of an old but tastefully-constructed building, with neatly-thatched roof, which, if skilfully photographed so as to introduce a little of the background-scenery, might easily be mistaken for a fine specimen of a Swiss cottage—and this was the Percy Arms.

Although it is a pretty generally admitted maxim that wherever you see an outward notice that entertainment may be had within for those who require it, you are at liberty to enter with the same freedom as you would your own house (if you should happen to have one), I must confess that I felt a strange fluttering a little to the left of the fourth button of my waistcoat as I stood before that antiquated porch. However, I walked boldly in, and, pulling the bell-rope in the entrance, was informed by the servant-girl who answered the summons that she thought that I could be accommodated with supper and a bed, although they seldom had visitors at that season of the year; and that she would go immediately and make further inquiry. The result of this inquiry proved satisfactory in the extreme; a bright fire soon blazed upon the hearth, and a nice shoulder of mutton was to be ready by nine o'clock. Having ascertained by consulting my watch that that would not be for nearly four hours, the question then was whether I had better introduce myself at once, or wait, like Mr. Micawber, until something should "turn up" to bring me into notice. Something did very soon "turn up" to distract my thoughts from the solution of the difficulty; for from the regions below came the unmistakable tones of a hurdy-gurdy, accompanied by peals of merry laughter; and not a little astonished was I to find that one of those sub-aqueous which, when in my student life in —— Square, I had sometimes anathematised in phrases not perhaps to be met with in any of the theological works of the day, had followed me even here! I determined to go and have a look at the unexpected intruder.

Groping my way through a dark passage at the foot of the stairs into the kitchen, whence the sounds of revelry proceeded, I found the greater part of the household, and a clod-hopper or two from the neighbouring farms, assembled around an ebony-coloured son of Africa, who, having laid aside his instrument, was now gratifying the spectators by executing one of the dances of his race—a feat which he performed with a drollery, grace, and agility which might well have caused Rice's "Jim Crow" to blush for his laurels. The good people thinking that I should, no doubt, be as much interested in the exhibition as they themselves, kindly made room for me in one of the front seats, which chanced to be an old settle near the chimney.

My entrance did not make much visible difference in the movements of the dark skin. Having eyed me with a little surprise at first, he bowed to me with a grin, as much as to say, "You'll give something handsome, no doubt," and then went on as before. At the conclusion of the performance he entered pretty freely into conversation with me after his own fashion, but I do not think that even Jeffrey or Brougham, in their days of triumph at the bar, would have made much of him in a cross-examination. I felt some real curiosity to know what had brought him into that remote region at a time when he could not expect to make such an exposition either very pleasant or very profitable; but his only explanation was, "Been to Blackmont Fair. Why not gentlemen of colour make professional visit to the provinces as well as white gentlemen?"

With this explanation I was obliged to be content; for the girl whom I had first seen at this moment returned from the parlour, saying that Miss Inmara (the first time her name was mentioned in my hearing—she was at home then) had sent him this—the this being a silver coin—and had also directed her to give him some refreshment before he started for Craighallow, where it appeared he intended to pass the night.

"Thank missy; but which is missy's room? Me serenade her some night before leaving to fulfil my engagements in de metropolis. Young ladies dey dote on de serenade."

"Oh, the bow-window over the garden; but you had better not go there late at night, unless you wish Cæsar here [pointing to a formidable-looking mastiff] to tear you in pieces! He's so fond of his mistress, that he won't let everybody come near her in the daytime without asking their business; so I don't know what he might do at night!"

"Nebber fear; me know how to make good dog quiet. Intelligent dog soon tell African gentleman from English thief! Here, Cæsar."

The dog sure enough seemed inclined to meet the advances of his sable visitor with sentiments of reciprocity. What was the witchcraft used I do not pretend to say; but the occupants of the kitchen expressed no little surprise at seeing the brute that had never been accustomed to tolerate any familiarity on the part of a white man, unless after a very matured acquaintance, submitting himself without the slightest symptom of dissatisfaction to the caresses of a nigger!

Returning to my room after this little episode, the old question returned again; but this time I had made up my mind what course to pursue, and taking a card from my case, I wrote on the back of it as follows:—

"Miss Inmara has probably forgotten, long ago, even the name of the lad who spent a very pleasant evening in her society at the 'Lodge,' N——, in the summer of 18—. He has never forgotten the kindness shown to him on that occasion, and very much wishes, after so many years, to be allowed an opportunity of expressing his thanks."

"Here," said I, to Isie—for that I had discovered to be the name of my waitress—"be good enough to take that card to Miss Inmara." And as the girl seemed somewhat mystified as to what the purport of my message might be, I added, "I believe I had the pleasure of seeing her once, although it is now a very long time ago."

The shrewd Isie promised to execute my commands at once, and it only remained for me to wait the result with patience.

I daresay some of our city belles will set me down as a very presumptuous puppy, for thinking that any young lady would admit me to her society on such slender grounds as these. But I really cannot help such insinuations—and, if the truth must be told, I care very little about them. Integrity of purpose is a better passport than a hundred flattering letters of introduction. I remember very well what occasion once the Honourable Mrs. Priestley took lest her daughters should form improper acquaintances; yet, after all, that fresh bouquet of princely lineage, who carried off Miss Cecilia Priestley from her devoted admirer, the unexceptionable young curate, turned out to be a profligate swindler, who, to his long catalogue of crimes, had now added that of bigamy! Everybody pitied the poor victim—I did so most sincerely. But who shall say that the stroke was altogether unmerited? If there was duplicity on his one side, there was, to use the mildest terms, considerable want of caution on the other; for neither Colonel nor Mrs. Priestley, nor even Cecilia herself, took the slightest trouble to explain that the lady's income could not be anything of what it was represented to be. Had they done so, the sagacious Mr. Blackham was far too knowing to have embarked in such a piece of business but unprofitable roguery. Each party had thus something to conceal. Innocence was not quite so innocent as it seemed to be, otherwise this idea would never have defaced the countenance of the house of Pinnahy[?]. Virtue is undoubtedly sometimes made the dupe of Vice; but this generally happens when, as in the instance just referred to, she has first proved false to herself.

Let no one, however, suppose that I have given this explanation as if I were a prisoner at the bar, trying to make out the best possible plea on my own behalf. I need no such exculpation. I had come between three or four hundred miles with the express design of seeing Miss Ianetra, and believing it to be morally as well as mathematically true, that between any two given points a straight line is the shortest line that can be, I determined to follow the straight line instead of the curve. From what I knew of young ladies in general, I scarcely thought that my request would be complied with without some deliberation; I did expect to succeed eventually, but my impression was, that the aged landlord himself would probably come, in the first place, to try to ascertain something of the character of his guest; and he [illegible] I could have no objection. In this conjecture I was mistaken — very agreeably mistaken. That light quick step can't be [illegible], and yet 'tis scarcely possible that—yes, it was even so. Innocent, and confiding in that innocence, meditating no wrong, and fearing none, the same arch, guileless smile, which I remembered so well in the child, still irradiating her face, Mary Ianetra stood again before me. The suddenness of her appearance, I must admit, confused me a little; but my embarrassment was only momentary, for, as she extended her hand, she said gaily, "So you have never forgotten us altogether, Mr. Grindlestripp[?]. Who could have thought that a promise, ten years unfulfilled, would be thus unexpectedly fulfilled at last!"

"Indeed, Miss Ianetra," I replied, "you gratify me more than I can tell; but you also astonish me. It was quite natural that I should remember you; for few are so callous as to forget, under any circumstances, those who have treated them as you did me—although, of course, I was too proud to own it then—when separated for the first time from the dear familiar faces that have guarded their childhood; but I had no hope that I should be welcomed as a long-expected stranger, and indeed rather feared that, on receiving my abrupt message from him, you would conclude that the governors of the nearest lunatic asylum were very likely to find one of their inmates missing in the morning!"

"Well, from what I remember of the gentleman, I think I can answer for it that he does not belong to the class which is usually designated 'dangerous.' If it were natural for you to remember me, it was equally natural for me to remember you, as we had not many such visitors at the Lunch[?]. Poor mamma often talked about you even in her last illness, and seemed to have a presentiment that you would some day or another come to see us again; and in that presentiment I have always shared. Would you believe it, scarcely ten minutes before you came in, when examining the contents of an old drawer, which had not been opened for years, I found the little purse which I worked for you according to promise a few weeks after you left us? Here it is—rather old-fashioned, I fear, by this time; but is it not a very remarkable coincidence that it should have turned up upon this particular morning?"

"It certainly is; and yet our lives are full of such coincidences, which, although apparently trivial in themselves, may nevertheless be not without their meaning. Some such have marked my journey hither, and you must not laugh at me, Miss Ianetra, if I say that I have a very firm persuasion that this journey, so long meditated, and so long delayed, will not be eventually destitute of some memorable incidents. You remember what grand achievements I meditated in olden times, and how I fancied myself sometimes, like some knight-errant of old, to rescue captive princesses and spell-bound maidens; and you see that I still occasionally indulge in day-dreams of chivalry. Should you, then, be haunted by the dread of any possible or even imaginary evil, tell me of it, and try what sort of a knight-errant I shall prove myself to be!"

Although I spoke in a sportive tone, I soon regretted the abruptness of my last remark. I have said that the face of Mary Ianetra still beamed with the guileless innocence of childhood; but it scarcely needed a second glance to show that sorrow had been there as well—that sorrow, however, which, unaccompanied by guilt, destroys none of the finer sensibilities of our nature, but rather imparts to all a refined, though chastened loveliness. It was very evident that I had touched a sensitive chord. We read of—

"A tear so limpid and so meek,
It would not stain an angel's cheek!"

And surely of such a nature were those pearly drops which, in spite of all her efforts to restrain them, my incautious words had caused to fall thick and fast. This was, indeed, a distressing change from the merry mood[?] in which our conversation had commenced; but, after all, it was, perhaps, better that this little outburst of feeling should have occurred at the time it did, as it was the means of very materially strengthening the bond of sympathy between us. "[illegible]" I did what I could to calm that sorrow, which [illegible], and not always then itself, was altogether sincere, and possibly [illegible] her tranquillity, and made many apologies for what she called her foolish weakness—anything, she said, that vividly recalled the remembrance of her dear mother, as seeing me again had done, affected her deeply—and besides, she had other trials.

"Yes, I replied," I know you have."

"Indeed! I did not think it possible that you could have heard anything about us, unless some fairy good, like those of whom you once told me such marvellous tales, has been carrying information to you!"

"If my informant was a fairy, he was certainly a very substantial one—much more so than those good creatures are generally represented to be; but have you never thought of inquiring how it was that I came to know where to find you?"

"I had quite forgotten that; but now of course I am most anxious to learn how it was; and as you must know something of what a woman's curiosity is when once aroused, you will not be so cruel as to keep me in suspense."

"Certainly not. I found a new tenant at the Lands, but in honest James Lindsay I believe I also found a friend. He it was who told me where you had gone, and several other things as well, which interested me very much."

"Oh, Mr. Lindsay! I always liked him very much, and I believe I was something of a favourite with him; but he surely did not tell you all?"

"Yes, Miss Innes; feeling assured that I was to be trusted—as I flatter myself he did—and seeing that I was not actuated by mere prying inquisitiveness, the good man told me unreservedly all he knew, and all he thought."

"All?"

"Yes, all; and you must not, indeed you must not, be displeased with him for speaking, nor with me for listening!"

The subject, which it would have been so difficult under ordinary circumstances to broach, having in this manner, as it were, broached itself, we very soon found ourselves discussing, with all the freedom of old and intimate friends, certain matters in which it is proverbially difficult, and I fear proverbially dangerous, too, for a lady to receive even an intimate friend as a confidant. I am not going to detail minutely the conversation which ensued. It will be sufficient to state that Mr. Lindsay's information turned out to be quite correct. There was no attempt to disguise or conceal that. Mr. Blandon, who had spent a day there quite recently, had told her that intelligence had reached him, in reply to repeated inquiries, that a young man answering the description of the missing Greenbank had been drowned in attempting to cross one of the rivers in a remote part of the United States, and that from various links—trifling, perhaps, when taken separately, but forming when connected a powerful chain of evidence—there could be little doubt about the identity. He had not dared to press his own suit personally with Miss Innes, but he had been politician enough to secure the services of a far more successful pleader, in the person of her aged father, who, now that there could be no hope of ever again welcoming the lost Harry, took every opportunity of urging her to bestow her hand on one whom he firmly believed would be to her a true and tender protector, when left, as she soon must be, a lonely orphan. The struggle was a severe one with poor Mary—filial affection and gratitude to a supposed benefactor on the one hand; on the other the certainty that the fetters that would bind her to her wealthy suitor must be those of gratitude, not of love; and sometimes even now, although "instant gone and instant gone," "still, small voice" of hope whispering in her ears, "the lost may yet be found, the absent may yet return."

"I am sure," she said, after a rather long pause in our conversation, "all we have in this world we owe to Mr. Blandon, and I should be ungrateful not to wish and pray for his happiness; but this is too much."

"Too much indeed, Miss Innes; never let the simple possibility of such a sacrifice being required at your hands torment you again. I have not seen this model of disinterested benevolence; but, from what I have heard of him, I have certain suspicions of my own regarding his real character, which I may some day be able to verify. I do not know if you have ever doubted whether or not there might be another face behind that fair mask, but I do know that you cannot love him, and surely no consideration on earth will ever induce you to vow and promise to do so.

"No," I added, resuming my original lively manner, "the Grandchamps, you know, are all gifted with the wonderful second-sight, by virtue of which I can see, and that, too, before twelve moons have waned, the wedding guests assembled. I see the proud triumphant smile of the bridegroom, as he turns for one moment from the blushing bride to acknowledge the compliment of the old shoe, which one of his friends has thrown after the carriage which is to convey the happy pair to the nearest station on the Utopia and Fairy-Land Railway, but that is not the smile of Mr. William Blandon."

"Oh, nonsense, Mr. Grandchamps; but (and here the little hand, which had rested passively in mine, trembled violently) do you really think that he is still alive? I had schooled myself to think of him as one who had passed from earth for ever (at least I thought that I had done so), for blank despair is sometimes less painful than racking doubt; but I will not deny that your words sound like the echo of some of my own late waking dreams. I know you have spoken kindly, but have you spoken wisely? Is it not foolish—is it not wrong then to indulge in delusive hopes, which are altogether unwarranted?"

"Is it foolish, Miss Lenora, or is it wrong to believe in a superintending Providence, whose hand is sufficient to bring back the wanderer and to heal the broken-hearted, whose prerogative it is to balance the weighty scales in which are meted out the just rewards of right and wrong, which no mortal hand may carry to do? I believe (the various steps which have led to that belief I need not, at present, recapitulate) that the friend and lover of your childhood will yet be restored to you, and, though it is scarcely my province to attempt the part of the moralist, I also venture to predict that if such happiness should be in store for you, you will be gradually led, in after-life, to look upon those dreary years of sorrow and trial as a wisely-appointed ordeal, the necessity of which you will then, somehow, be enabled to understand, although you cannot understand it now. What is future is always uncertain, and, although the gathering cloud may sometimes almost fill you with dismay, try if, in the midst of the murky gloom, you can catch a glimpse of the "silver lining.""

"Good advice, which I am sure I shall try to follow as far as I am able. And now I must leave you; but remember you have promised to take breakfast with papa and me in the morning. You should have seen his surprise when I showed him your card and message; for many a quiet laugh has he had at mamma and me when discussing the probabilities of your ever revisiting us; but I am sure it will be a real pleasure to him to make your acquaintance."

"And the pleasure will be as great on my part as on his. I mean, you know, to take a week or two with you, if you will allow me; but, before beginning to explore this magnificent region, I expect to be favoured by you with a list of the places best worth seeing, and the legends connected with them, for each spot here looks as if it must have its legend."

"A few months later I could perhaps direct you, or even guide you to some localities that would interest you; but I fear very much that in this wintry weather the most agreeable scenery that I can show you will be found in the immediate vicinity of our parlour fire."

"Thank you. I shall be pretty sure to be found in that neighbourhood about nine o'clock to-morrow; and now good night, for I fear I have been selfish in detaining you so long."

"Oh! no; but now I must really go. Good night, and pleasant dreams of your lady-love; for, in spite of all that you have said to the contrary, I know there must be such a reality somewhere."

"No, Miss Lenora, 'the sainted maiden,' the lost Lenore, has gone, and nothing remains for me but the hideous black raven, croaking its everlasting "never more.""

"And how about the silver lining?"

"Faint perhaps, but still there."

The door had closed upon Mary Lenora, and left to myself I cannot say that my meditations for the first few minutes were of the most pleasing character. I had, in fact, carelessly unlocked the "skeleton chamber," which I fear is to be found in most breasts, however well it may be concealed; but, as the phantoms which revealed themselves there have nothing to do with our present tale, they shall not be paraded to leave their prison-house. And, although the fact may appear exceedingly shocking to certain young ladies of the sentimental-class, it is a fact, nevertheless, that the appearance of supper upon the table very quickly restored me to my usual equanimity. Some one has remarked that you can never find at any given place the particular article for which that place is specially celebrated, unless it be coals at Newcastle, rogues in Chancery-lane, and shrimps in Billingsgate. Let the author of that assertion order a hot joint of Blackmountshire mutton at the Percy Arms after an exhilarating walk across the moors, along with a moderate supply of that glorious porter, nicknamed "bitter beer," and I venture to predict, that before he has half finished his repast he will have added another exception to a rule, which I admit to be generally correct.

An interesting old volume and an excellent cigar kept me up until a late, or rather, perhaps, an early hour, and, on looking out of my window, after retiring to my room, I was surprised to see a man, whom, although partly hidden by the garden-wall, I soon recognised by the light of the moon to be no other than our old friend of the hurdy-gurdy, standing with his eyes fixed intently on the other end of the building. What could it mean? He had certainly promised to serenade the lady, but nobody believed that he would do it; besides, his instrument was nowhere visible, and altogether his attitude was, to say the least of it, somewhat suspicious. Determined if possible to ascertain what his object was, I was proceeding to open my window in order to speak to him; but this was not so easily done as I expected, and startled by the noise, he walked off with a rapid but firm step—a step, I thought, that scarcely corresponded with the colour of his face—and was soon lost to sight in the adjoining thicket. Strange! I thought. Yes—everything around me is strange to-night; but, as I sat and mused on the events of the last two days, I could not help in some way associating the disguised watcher that had appeared to James Lindsay, opposite to the Lamb, in the early morning, with the figure which I had just seen gazing up so earnestly, in the clear moonlight, at the dear window over the garden.

(To be continued.)

THE QUEENS OF NAPLES.

BY ANTONIO NICOLO.

(*Author of "Ten Years in the Dungeons of Naples.*")

Search the history of the world; fix your eyes upon the pages concerning Italy, dwelling especially upon the stories of the lives of the Queens of Naples; and the result of such a perusal will be, that the name of the Queen of Naples has been fatal to almost all those who have ever borne it; and, commencing with Constance, we will endeavour to prove the truth of what we have just stated.

She was the only legitimate descendant of the royal Norman line, and the wife of the Emperor Henry VI., who, after the death of William II., of Sicily, had a legitimate pretension to that crown, and attempted to obtain it by force of arms. The Nobles of the Two Sicilies, however, disdaining the German yoke, had elected for their king Tancred, the natural son of Roger the Second, joining him with all their hearts, and yielding him all the assistance in their power. In 1190 a war was engaged in between Henry and Tancred; but the latter was beaten, and compelled to a precipitate retreat from the Neapolitan dominions. Constance, however, fell into the hands of his enemies; when she was sent in chains from Salerno to Sicily, to Tancred, who generously restored her, without ransom or condition, to her husband.

The unhappy Queen Sibilla was the wife of Tancred, the conqueror of Charles VI. of Germany. In 1194 Tancred died, leaving as a successor to his crown a helpless boy, who was unable to defend it. Charles, who in 1190, had been defeated, again invaded the Kingdom of the Two Sicilies, and this time took possession of it. The wretched family of Tancred, surrendering themselves, upon promise of favourable treatment, were sent into Germany by the savage conqueror, who detained them in long captivity, and deprived the youthful King of his eyes.

Elena was the wife of King Manfred. In 1265 a battle was engaged in on the plain of Grandella, near Benevento, between her husband and Charles of Anjou. Manfred, betrayed by his army and subjects, was killed, and his corpse mangled and torn in pieces. The Queen was besieged in Lucera, made a prisoner, and shut up in the Castle of Dell Uovo, where she happily died without having heard of Conradin, her son, being carried to the scaffold, and the rest of her family expiring amid the most excruciating sufferings.

Queen Lancia was the widow of Robert, King of Naples, the son of Charles II., and the chief of the Guelph party. Having no offspring, Robert bequeathed his crown to Joanna, his niece; and when he died the new Queen oppressed the widow in a thousand ways, who was obliged to shut herself up in the Convent of Santa Croce, and died there.

The name of this Queen Joanna is abominable in history, and her end not less infamous and horrible. She ascended the throne of Naples in 1343; married Andrew of Hungary, who was assassinated in the solitary Convent of San Pietro, she herself being an accomplice in the murder. Publicly acknowledged as a Messalina, on account of her debauchery, she was twice besieged by her own subjects and driven away from the kingdom. She was bereft of her sons, who died, one after the other, in their infancy. Four times she was a wife, and four times a despised and disgraced widow. She was unhappy in the selection of those upon whom she bestowed her benefits. For want of an heir she adopted Charles of Durazzo, who, alarmed and offended by her fourth marriage, declared war against her. Naples was conquered, and Joanna taken, imprisoned, murdered, and her body exposed to public ignominy in 1382.

Margaret was the wife of Charles of Durazzo. The widow of Louis of Hungary invited King Durazzo to a private interview in her royal palace in Hungary; the King went, and was there treacherously murdered in the presence of the Queen, by assassins whom she had concealed there on purpose. In consequence of this murder Margaret was confined in Gaeta in 1386.

Constance, of Clermont, the poor and virtuous Queen wife of Ladislaus, the son of Charles III., was the heiress of the most opulent noble of Sicily, and was asked in marriage by Ladislaus on account of her immense dowry, which contributed to maintain him on his throne. When he had dissipated her fortune, and the death of her father left him nothing more to hope or to fear from his influence in Sicily, he repudiated her, and obtained in 1392 a Papal bull from Boniface IX. to annul his union with her. She was thenceforth insulted in the presence of her rival, reduced to a poor and private position, placed in confinement for three years, and finally compelled to marry the Count Andrea, of Capua, one of the favourites of the King.

Joanna the Second was the sister of Ladislaus, and ascended the throne of Naples in 1414. She has left in history a page stained with the most shameful and scandalous vices of which a woman is capable; so that when the Neapolitans wish to name a woman of bad character, they call her "Queen Joanna II.," as if they could have nothing worse to say to her. She was devoid of all mental energy and talent, and the slave of [illegible] passions, which seemed to strengthen in intensity as her advancing age increased the shame of indulging in them. She married James of Bourbon, Count of la Marche, who, in reward for having obtained a kingdom, gave her, in return, [illegible], domestic war, and sorrow. His first acts were to deprive her of the royal authority, her [illegible], and put to a cruel and an ignominious death, Jacopo Pandolfello—the first minion of Joanna, a young man of five-and-twenty, of low birth, and with the solitary recommendation of a handsome person—and to imprison and subject her for one year to a rigid state of durance. She was then rescued from her guards, in a popular tumult, and compelled to besiege and expel her husband from the kingdom, who died in a Franciscan Convent in France. Being without offspring, or the hope of having any, she adopted as her heir Alfonso of Aragon, King of Aragon and Sicily, who, jealous of her power, came to an open rupture with her, arrested her second minion (she could not remain without one), Sir Giovanni Caracciolo, besieged himself in her palace, and compelled her to summon Sforza to her deliverance. Scarcely was she delivered than she substituted (1423) Louis of Anjou for her heir; but this substitution proved not useful to him [illegible]. After ten years of peace, in which she was tyrannised over by Caracciolo, even beyond the [illegible] of a minion's love, and doubting in his safety, she sought refuge in the confidence of the Duchess of Sessa, the [illegible] of which was painful to him. This new favourite [illegible] her weakness to anger against Caracciolo, awakened her apprehensions of his designs, induced her to permit his arrest, and obtained a pardon for all those who assassinated him in the same royal palace. This very Duchess afterwards took the part of Alfonso, and obtained from Joanna a secret revocation of her adoption of Louis of Anjou, which was of no use to him. She at length adopted Regnier, brother of the Duke of Anjou, and died utterly worn out in mind and body in 1435.

Isabella was a princess of great spirit and the wife of Regnier, to whom Joanna had bequeathed the kingdom of Naples. On the death of the latter, Alfonso of Aragon immediately made his claim upon her kingdom, and [illegible] by the force of his arms. Unhappily for Regnier, he was at that time a prisoner to the Duke of Burgundy, and Isabella hastened to Naples to maintain the rights of her captive lord; but she brought with her neither treasure nor soldiers. She supported with difficulty the unequal combat against the King of Aragon, but yet prolonged it for three years, when her husband, having effected his release (1438), joined her. When the troops began to desert, and his possessions were gradually wrested from him, until the city of Naples alone remained in his keeping, the Queen Isabella escaped from the kingdom with her children. Shortly after, the troops of Alfonso entered Naples by surprise, through a deserted aqueduct; Regnier then escaped also, and, perceiving the hopelessness of a further struggle, he finally abandoned the kingdom to his rival, and joined the queen, bringing her the sad news of the loss of a crown in 1442.

Another Isabella was the wife of Frederick, who ascended the throne of Naples in 1496, on the death of Ferdinand the Second of Aragon. She was exiled and imprisoned in France, in 1501; then escaped and took refuge in a small convent in Ferrara, where she was miserably supported by the charity of some [illegible].

Two other queens, the last of the proud dynasty of Aragon, were, one after the other, imprisoned, starved, and shut up in the small castle of the [illegible].

Caroline of Austria (nicknamed Peppa), a woman whose ambition caused a river of blood to be shed in the kingdom of Naples, was the first wife of Ferdinand I. of Bourbon. She was three times a fugitive, despised, [illegible], and cursed by the people; and she died of a broken heart, in exile.

Caroline Murat, sister to the first Napoleon, after a short reign, descended from the throne of Naples and returned to France, only to hear of her husband being shot at Pizzo, in Calabria, by order of Ferdinand the First.

Clementina was the first wife of Francis the First, who ascended the throne of Naples in 1825. This queen was always unhappy. After her marriage she was a long time delayed in Austria by the [illegible] of war. She at length reached Naples, during the French invasion, and shortly after was obliged to fly with her husband to Sicily; finally dying, in her 30th year, of melancholy and a broken heart.

Maria Christina, the good and sainted queen of Ferdinand the Second, of cursed memory, was his first wife, as well as his first victim. Abused by her husband, after her accouchement in 1836,* and frightened by a duel which was about to take place between the King and his brother Charles, she died after a few days, regretted by all who knew her.

Maria Theresa of Austria was the second wife, and is now the widow, of Ferdinand Bomba. She was, as a queen, cruel and sanguinary, like her husband, and hated by the people to death. When Francis the Second granted a constitution to save his dynasty, she, to escape the popular fury, was obliged to fly from the Capital, and shut herself up in Gaeta for several months, and then leave for Rome, exiled, despised, and accursed by all.

The young Queen Maria Sophia was destined to close the list of the queens of Naples.

* When well enough to get up after her accouchement, the King, playing with her in his room, as she arose took away the chair where she had been seated; so that when she went to sit down again, she fell on her back. The King beginning to laugh, she felt indignant, and said— "Your Majesty has just played the part of a Lazzarone!" Upon which, Ferdinand gave her a severe blow on her cheek—an insult she only [illegible], but ominously.

Scarcely had she married Francis II. (who was brought up to be a Capuchin) when she was put into mourning by the death of her father-in-law. As soon as she was a queen, Garibaldi upset the throne of her husband, and, being shut up in Gaeta, she suffered the shame and grief of a defeat; and, after a reign of one year, in the very hour in which Cialdini entered Gaeta, she left the Neapolitan shores, never, it would seem, to see them again.

This historical sketch speaks too plainly of the sad destiny of the Queens of Naples; and it cannot be considered anything else than a piece of good fortune for the Princesses of Europe, that the line of the Queens of Naples has finished, and that of the Queens of Italy begun.

LEAVES FOR THE LITTLE ONES.

FERGUS AND HENRY.

BY HANNAH GRAY.

"Fergus, my dear, do you know that you are acquiring a very bad habit of striking and beating your little brother for the merest trifle? Some day you may cause a serious accident, and hurt him severely. I shall be compelled to chastise you if this goes on long. I have not yet told your dear Papa, because I do not like to vex him, when he can stay with us at home so seldom; but—"

"Oh no, Mamma! dear Mamma!" exclaimed Fergus, with a burst of tears. "Indeed I do not mean to be a naughty boy; and if you will only not tell Papa, I will not be so any more. Only kiss me and forgive me, Mamma, and smile upon me as you used to do!"

That night the little boy added to his usual evening prayer these words—"Please God help me to be a better boy to my little brother!"

But although Fergus wished now and then to be a better and kinder boy, and even tried a little to be so, he did not try very hard; and poor Henry, who was a most amiable child, still received many an undeserved thump and blow. Nurse did not like to tell; and it happened that Mrs. Linton was very much engaged for a considerable period, so that nothing of this came to her personal knowledge, and she really thought Fergus had improved in his temper.

One summer-day the little boys were playing on a large grass-plot surrounding the fish-pond in front of the house, and which towards the middle sloped down on all sides to the edge of the water, where swam various pretty ducks of foreign breeds. Usually the two children were not permitted to play on this grass-plot; but to-day they were considered quite safe; because not only was their careful nurse watching over them, but their mamma herself, her fair face shaded by a large garden-bonnet, was fishing with a rod and line, beneath the shade of a drooping willow that stood between them and the water, in the company of her friend Miss Frances Hughes. Papa likewise, at home on one of his brief holidays, sauntered along a path near the fish-pond, now and then turning his frank and noble countenance towards his dear boys, and smiling upon their gambols with all a father's love.

"Mamma! Mamma!" cried Fergus, "do turn your head, if you please, and look at the funny man!" And he clapped his plump, chubby hands.

This "funny man," the object of Fergus's admiration, was a portly Dutchman, with a noble paunch, constructed so cunningly of gutta percha, that he could roll to any extent without permanently swerving his natural position; always returning, like the wise man out of the depths of misfortune, head uppermost. The Dutchman had dangled, like a ripe fruit, from the last Christmas-tree, and Fergus had gathered him, and had possessed him ever since. But with prudent foresight Mrs. Linton had put him away for awhile; and he had only been brought out this sultry afternoon to keep the children quiet on the sunny grass-plot.

"Look, Mamma! look, Papa! look, do, please, Miss Fanny!" called out Fergus again, as the Dutchman commenced another somersault. "I do think he is funnier than ever!"

"No! me!" cried little Henry, extending his dimpled finger to give the toy a push—"me do it, Fanny!"

"No, not you! Let him alone!" said Fergus. "He is mine, and you mustn't play with him."

Henry, however, persisted with baby perseverance; and Fergus, raising his hand in a fit of passion, gave him a blow that sent him rolling down the slope of the grass-plot.

Nurse jumped up, with lips as white as death; mamma, glancing round, caught a glimpse of her darling baby's peril, and uttered a terrified scream. Little Henry rolled on over the smooth, slippery grass with accelerating motion, and fell with a dull splash into the deep water. All was confusion and dismay; and when Mr. Linton turned from his extended promenade at the further end of the gravelled path, he beheld his wife leaning far over the brink of the fish-pond, her taper, jewelled wrists and hands extended gleamingly from its depths, and the nurse and her friend Miss Frances struggling with her to prevent her from madly following her precious baby into the suffocating waters.

The father divined, rather than saw, what had

occurred. To throw off his coat, and rush to the rescue, was but the work of a moment with the strong, loving man. Little Henry was caught as he rose to the surface, close to a group of pure white water-lilies—well was it for him, that he had not been detained in the tangle of their roots and branches; as it was, he was only partially insensible. His papa bore him tenderly to the house, and he was soon stripped of his wet garments, and warmly cradled in his mother's arms, while her tears of joy bedewed his curly head.

But my young readers will naturally ask, "Where is poor Fergus? What has become of him all this time?"

That was more than anyone could tell, when at last they could turn their attention from his little brother to look for him. The boy had disappeared, and they almost began to fear that he might, in a fit of childish terror and remorse, have thrown himself into the water. However, before they could resolve to make preparations for dragging the pond, Jemmy—a man who helped in the little farm-yard attached to Mr. Linton's estate—came up to the house to say that he had seen Master Fergus in the Deep Lane about the time the accident must have occurred. This Deep Lane ran on one side of the house, and led to a somewhat extensive wood. It was a lonely place; but, as the man had often seen him there, gathering chickweed and groundsel for his canary-bird, he did not think much of it, and went about his business without speaking to him.

Mr. Linton immediately went in search of the child. The lane was narrow and winding, with a high bank and hedge on each side, hence its name. The anxious father passed turning after turning, looking round each hedge and bush, in the hope of seeing his child; still no Fergus appeared. At length, very far on, near the entrance to the wood, he found the toy which had been the occasion of the sad occurrence. This determined him to go on, and to enter the wood. The trees were thickly planted, and it was dark and gloomy even in the full daylight. Mr. Linton passed anxiously between the stems of the fir and beech-trees; and at length he thought he perceived, in a little hollow cleared of underwood, the glimmer of a scarlet sash. He hastened to the spot, and there indeed was his poor boy crouched close to the ground, his cheeks and hidden in his little hands, over which his brown curls fell dark and dishevelled.

"Fergus! dear child!" exclaimed the father, in his tender, vibrating tones—"rise up, and come with me, my dear boy. Your little brother is safe, and all will be forgiven!"

Fergus yielded to the kind force that was exerted to raise him. "Oh! Papa," he cried, throwing his arms round his father's neck, and bursting into a passionate flood of tears—"oh, Papa, I am so glad! I meant to die here, and never, never come home again, if I had killed Brother Henry!"

Mr. Linton, notwithstanding the agitation he had passed through, could scarcely forbear smiling.

"And did our dear boy think that Papa and Mamma would make no search for him to bring him back again, even if his wicked temper had killed his poor little brother? No, no, we love him far too well for that; and we hope to see him endeavouring, with all his heart, by God's help, and for the sake of the love we bear him, to get rid of this wicked temper, which causes so much unhappiness. Will my Fergus promise me this? Only to try, really and with all his might, remembering that this day's blessed sunlight had nearly set upon a Cain's murder!"

Fergus still sobbed and wept, as though he would never be comforted; but he made a solemn promise to his father, though feebly and with broken words—and he meant it too. And so great is the success of really trying, with one's heart in the attempt, that, although many weeks did not pass without the occurrence of other childish altercations, and the little boy's hand was again lifted against his brother more than once, the memory of that dreadful day arrested the blows before they descended. By degrees the habit of quick anger itself was cured; and now that Fergus Linton has grown a man, you cannot perceive, on his calm and thoughtful brow, any trace of the turbulent passions that disturbed his early childhood.

THE WORK-TABLE.

COLLAR AND CUFF IN FRENCH EMBROIDERY.

Materials: Fine Scotch Muslin, and Messrs. W. Evans and Co.'s. Embroidery Cotton, No. 24.

This new and pretty style of embroidery is remarkable for the ease and dexterity with which it is worked and for its effective appearance when finished. The rosebuds and leaves are formed by making very minute dots, three stitches being taken precisely one over the other to make one dot. The line of dots round the collar are worked in the same way. The small leaves are worked in satin stitch; the little sprigs and eyelet-holes are simply run and sewed over, and the edge worked in button-hole stitch.

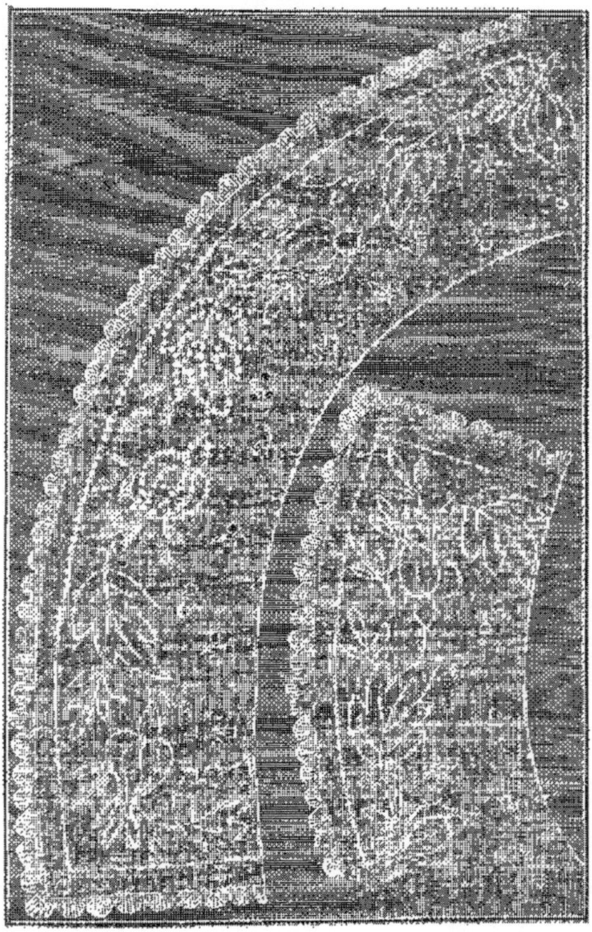

HANDKERCHIEF CORNER.

To be worked to correspond with the Collar and Cuff.

A SLOW COURTSHIP.

Long engagements between lovers are usually looked upon as unadvisable and imprudent; and it is certain they not unfrequently come to an unsatisfactory termination. An old song says—

> Happy is the wooing
> That is not long a-doing;

but this seems to point to the other extreme; and, as all extremes are of questionable tendency, it may be assumed that this also ought to be avoided. Hasty courtships are commonly ill-fated. Being made without forethought, they bring together persons of ill-assorted tempers and dispositions, disappointment follows, and is soon followed by bickerings and disagreement; which, growing sometimes unendurable, compel the parties to seek deliverance from their differences through the convenient agency of the Divorce Court. Long engagements are not subject to any of these evils, but they have perils of their own, which it is desirable to avoid if possible; and the readiest way to avoid them is to refrain from entering into such engagements. This is, no doubt, very simple and obvious advice; but it seems to be the best for the occasion, and, if more generally adopted, its effects would be to lessen the anxieties and disappointments arising from deferred hopes and expectations, by which youth and beauty is so often worn away, and the pleasant inheritance of many lives is blighted.

Long engagements, however, are not always matters of design or pre-intention. People do not enter into them deliberately, but are led into them by circumstances beyond their personal control, or fall into them, as it were, unawares, by the habit of postponing a serious responsibility for which they desire to be, perhaps, too fastidiously prepared. A man wishes, before marrying, to be assured of a competence, to get reputably established in business, to attain a higher place in rank, in some way or other to secure a good provision, and a fair prospect for the future. To achieve this object generally requires time, and if its achievement be considered a necessary preliminary to the matrimonial contract, the latter, of course, must be put off until the first has been secured. It may seem at the outset that there need be no very great delay, but circumstances transpire which render the postponement still desirable; something does not succeed as was expected, and more time is requisite, either to renew the experiment or to try some other venture; and thus an engagement, never intended to be long, unexpectedly falls into that category, from its fulfilment being repeatedly deferred, out of regard to some more immediate convenience. The persons concerned meanwhile wait more or less patiently; in some instances with no diminution of attachment, and in a reasonable course of time get comfortably married. In other cases the delay is prolonged till one or the other becomes tired of it; and then the one dissatisfied either abruptly marries somebody else, or the other, who has grown indifferent, quietly drops the acquaintance, heedless of succeeding consequences, which may include a possible action for "breach of promise," with a scale of damages varying from one farthing to a thousand pounds, according to the views of an enlightened jury respecting the amount of injury sustained by the aggrieved party. What seems strangest of all is, that some of these broken-off matches are afterwards patched up again, the rejected or neglected lady or gentleman becoming consort to the former lover in a second marriage, after the death of the partner to whom preference had first been given.

A curious instance of a long engagement terminating disastrously, and then subsequently renewed and consummated in wedlock, is furnished us in the case of Mr. Thomas Gent, a notable bookseller at York, who flourished in the last century, and who is well known, by name and reputation, to the antiquaries and bibliopolists of the present day. Whether truth is really more interesting than fiction—even as it is declared to be much stranger—must for the present be left among disputable questions; for though the critical judgment would probably affirm the proposition, the public taste would seem to determine the matter the other way, the readers of fiction being manifestly out of all proportion numerous, when compared with the readers who delight in matter of fact and history. Leaving this as a question that remains to be decided, it may yet be said that incidents and circumstances which have actually occurred have a certain measure of interest attaching to them, in some degree calculated to recommend them to the attention of all who take pleasure in realities; and, without disparagement to the superior charms of fiction, may sometimes not improperly be set forth in the way of literary representation, for the sake of such interest as they happen to possess. The history of Mr. Thomas Gent, and his remarkably slow courtship, has been thought worthy of commemoration in memoirs written by himself; and it has had the honour of being related, in an abridged form, by Southey, in "The Doctor," where, as a pleasant episode, it may at any time be read by the studiously disposed—that being presumably the only class of readers ever likely to get through so ponderous a book. The story being amusing, and having the further advantage (such as it is) of being true in all its details—besides being curious as an illustration of deliberate courtship almost unexampled—it seems, to our fancy, well worth telling over again for the benefit of general readers; for such, that is to say, as are not likely to read "The Doctor," and, still less, to peruse a page of Mr. Gent's autobiography, in which place only, so far as we are aware, is any record of it to be found. Let such gently-disposed readers as are inclined to go along with us, bear with a few sentences of dry introductory narrative; and then we trust they will find what follows thereafter tolerably entertaining.

Mr. Gent appears to have considered himself descended from the Gents of Staffordshire, though he himself was born in Dublin; his parents being worthy people resident in that city, in humble circumstances, but above the ranks implying poverty or meanness of condition. They brought him up in an honest, creditable manner, giving him the best education they could afford, and then, that he might have the means of earning his own bread in the world, apprenticed him to a printer. According to his account, his master was a coarse brutal fellow, who treated him with exceeding harshness; so that after enduring three years' service, and feeling it intolerable, the lad was induced to run away. He left Dublin with little more than a shilling in his pocket, got on board a ship, and was landed at Parkgate, to seek his fortune. He made his way to London, where he soon obtained employment at his trade, and gave satisfaction to his employers. After four years spent in different situations, he was invited by Mr. White, of York, to fill a place in his printing-house, which he considered it his interest to accept. A situation in Mr. White's establishment was at that time desirable, that gentleman being King's printer for York and five other counties, and having always, from the scarcity of provincial printers, a large share of business. There was not then a single printer in such large towns as Chester, Liverpool, Manchester, or Leeds. The trade was centred almost entirely in London. Mr. White had been made King's printer as the reward of his patriotic daring in printing the Declaration of the Prince of Orange, when all the London printers had refused to be concerned in so dangerous a piece of business; and if the Revolution had not succeeded, he would probably have lost his head as a rebel against his lawful sovereign, James II. As it did succeed, he became King's printer, and flourished as a highly prosperous subject under King William, making an honourable fortune from the profits of his business; to assist him in which he engaged Mr. Gent, in the spring of the year 1714. By the terms of the engagement, Mr. White was to pay his assistant eighteen pounds a year, and to furnish him with board, washing, and lodging; in addition to which there was an extra guinea allowed to bear the young man's charges on the road, in travelling from London to his destination. It was Gent's intention to travel by the carrier—a man of the name of Crofts, whom he describes as "a very surly young fellow as ever I conversed with," and he offered him twenty shillings out of his guinea as payment for the journey; but the carrier, it seems, "would have five or six shillings more;" so, rather than comply with his demands, Thomas resolved to venture forth on foot. He relates that the carrier set out with his horses on the Monday, "and the next morning," says he, "being the 20th of April, 1714, I set forward; and had, as I think, walked three miles, when a gentleman's servant, with a horse ready saddled and himself riding another, overtook me, and for a shilling, with a glass or so on the road, allowed me to ride with him as far as Caxton, which was the period of his journey." The rest of the way Mr. Gent appears to have walked, the whole time occupied in travelling being five days and a half.

He arrived at York about twelve o'clock on Sunday, and proceeded directly to Mr. White's house. The door was opened to him by a personage whom he styles the "fond maiden," who is now to appear as a prominent figure in the story. "She ushered me," says he, "into the chamber where Mrs. White lay something ill in bed; but the old gentleman was at his dinner, by the fireside, sitting in a noble easy-chair, with a good large pie before him, and made me partake heartily with him. I had a pinion in my cloak-lining, which I pulled out to stop my frock; at which the old gentleman smiled, and pleasantly said, it was more than he had ever seen a journeyman save before. I could not but smile too, because my trunk, with my clothes and eight guineas, was sent about a month before to Ireland, where I was resolved to go and see my friends had his place not offered me as it did." We thus perceive that Master Gent was already a person of provident and prudent habits, and gave promise of becoming a prosperous man in his generation.

He was every way satisfied with his new situation, and was altogether as happy in it as he could reasonably wish to be. Besides living very comfortably with Mr. and Mrs. White, there was a further attraction derived from the presence of the "fond maiden" before alluded to, whose pleasing looks and interesting ways and propriety afforded him delightful matter for private meditation. As soon as he had earned money enough, he supplied himself with new clothes, in place of those that had been sent to Ireland, in order to cut a smart and agreeable figure in her sight; and in his intervals of leisure he sought as much as possible to enjoy her society and conversation. In a variety of ways he seems to have insinuated himself into her favour, and endeavoured indirectly to make her understand that she stood very highly in his estimation. He was, however, extremely wary in saying anything to her that could be construed into a definite expression of feeling. He was, no doubt, in love with her in a mild, unobtrusive fashion, but not deeply enough to declare himself unmistakeably. He wished her to remain single on his account, but he did not wish to commit himself to any positive engagement. If she would wait till he should be settled in business, and required a wife to complete his household, he might then be disposed to marry her; but he did not like to bind himself to this conclusion, lest peradventure he should in the meanwhile meet with somebody else whom he might happen to prefer, or who might seem more desirable to him as a helpmate. Thus matters stood between them at the end of his first year's service under Mr. White, and in this uncertain state they parted; Master Gent resolving, before renewing his engagement with his employer, to go and visit his friends in Dublin.

His hesitation of mind, and his general feelings towards the damsel, are quaintly depicted in his autobiography. He evidently went away against the grain, and yet was too irresolute to speak the word which might have made both himself and the lady happy. Acknowledging his departure, he says, "What made my departure then uneasy, was through respect of Mrs. Alice Guy, the young woman who I said first opened the door to me, upper maiden to Mrs. White, who, I was persuaded, in letters, had the like mutual fondness for me. She was the daughter of Mr. Richard Guy, schoolmaster at Inglebeck, near Lancashire; had very good natural parts, quick understanding, was of fine complexion, and very amiable in her features. Indeed I was not very forward in love, or desire of matrimony, till I knew the world better, and consequently should be more able to provide such a handsome maintenance as I confess I had ambition enough to desire; but yet my heart could not absolutely slight so lovely a young creature as to pretend I had no esteem for her charms, which had captivated others, and particularly my master's grandson, Mr. Charles Bourne, who was more deserving than any. However, I told her (because my resolution should not anticipate her advancement) that I should respect her as one of the dearest of friends; and receiving a little dog from her as a companion on the road, I had the honour to be accompanied as far as Bramham Moor by my rival."

The rival was probably glad to see him safe off out of the way, the fair Alice being now left to his own unobstructed attentions. We shall see that he made good use of his opportunities during the other's absence. As to Gent, he went on, as he purposed, to Dublin, where he was received by his parents with all the welcome accorded to the Prodigal Son. He had not been prodigal, but his unexpected return, after his long absence, seemed like a restoration of the lost. They had no fatted calf to kill; but there was probably a fair supply of whisky flowing, and a genuine display of Irish rejoicing. Thomas, however, was not content to be long dependent on their hospitality. He soon obtained a journeyman's situation in a printing-office, and began to earn his own living. Being always a good workman, he would doubtless have got on here with his customary good fortune, had events not been unfavourable to his continuance. But it was soon apparent that Dublin could be to him no abiding city, owing to the circumstance that he had once before left it without authorized permission. His old master, from whom he had run away as an apprentice, hearing of his return, thought he had now a good opportunity of reclaiming him, and making him serve the remainder of his time. Accordingly, as Thomas was going home one evening from his work, he was suddenly pounced upon by a couple of officers, who took him into custody. There being some irregularity in the proceedings, he, after a brief detention, regained his liberty; but, to avoid being reclaimed by a more formal process, he was compelled to take refuge in concealment. His father and a brother-in-law meanwhile offered the master a fair sum for his release; but this not being accepted, there was no remedy except in flight. So, as Thomas about that time had received a letter from Miss Allen, of York, saying that he was expected there, thither he resolved, out of pure regard for her company, to direct his course. The little dog, however, which she had given him, he left behind. "I let the rascal stay," says he, "with my dear parents, who were fond of him for my sake, as he was of them for his own; nor was he less pleasant by his tricks to the neighbourhood, who called him 'Yorkshire,' from the country whence I brought him."

After his return, Gent remained some months at York, and then went to London, hoping to earn more money there than he was able to do in the country. He was very careful and saving; "but yet," says he, "could not perceive a prospect of settlement, whereby to maintain a spouse like her as I judged she deserved; and I could not bear the thoughts to bring her from a good settlement without I could certainly make us both happy in a better." Seeing no immediate chance of this, he applied himself industriously to business, that he might be prepared for any opportunity of establishing himself that should happen to occur. He got on prosperously, and had the honour, in the year 1717, of being made Freeman of the Company of Stationers; and in the same year he became citizen of London. Now that he was beyond his reach, his tyrannical old master in Dublin was willing to compromise on account of his unfulfilled apprenticeship, and offered to accept five pounds for his discharge. This enabled Gent remitted, and thus became absolutely free both in England and Ireland, for which he expresses himself in his memoirs extremely thankful.

"And now," says he, "I thought myself happy, when the thoughts of my dearest often occurred to my mind. God knows that it is but too common, and that with the best and most considerate persons, that something or other gives them disquietude, or makes them seek after it." Odd as it may seem, the obvious inference from this is that the "thoughts of his dearest" did not contribute to his happiness, but tended, on the contrary, to disturb his peace of mind. But we must suppose this was because he could not yet consider himself in a position to justify matrimonial proposals; and it can be readily imagined, that as time went on, he began to feel the awkwardness of his situation. Three years had passed since the beginning of his acquaintance with the maiden, and all this time the courtship had been rather implied than definitely explicit on either side. There was an evident liking between them, and they were ready to come together whenever circumstances should favour the conjunction; but circumstances having been hitherto adverse, they still remained apart, with as little apparent probability of being united as at the beginning. At length a chance occurred to him which seemed likely to render their marriage possible. A partnership in a business at Norwich was offered him, and he accepted it, and made preparations for removing to that city. But, unhappily, a few hours afterwards there came a mournful letter from his parents, saying that they were grown very infirm and helpless, and desired to see him once more before they died. It is to Gent's honour that, out of regard to his parents's wishes, he immediately gave up his engagement at Norwich, though he had already taken his place in the coach for the journey. He went to live in Dublin, thus abandoning all chance of any present settlement, and, as a consequence, indefinitely postponing his hopes of union with his beloved, who was beginning, we fancy, to be a little weary of the prolonged delay.

Though Gent acted under an impulse of natural duty on this occasion, he confesses that he was not without some cause for self-reproach. "I wrote," said he, "a lamenting letter to my dear in York, bewailing that I could not find a proper place as yet to settle in; told her that I was leaving the kingdom, and reminded her by what had passed that she could not be ignorant where to direct if she thought proper to do so; that I was far from slighting her, and resigned her to none but the protection of heaven. But sure never was poor creature afflicted with such melancholy as I was upon the journey. My soul did seem to utter within me, 'Wretch that I am! what am I doing, and whither going? My parents, it is true, as they were constantly most affectionate, as indeed they are, especially in the advanced years, peculiar objects of my care and concern; but am I not leaving England, the Paradise of the world, to which as any loyal subject I have now an indefeasible right—but am I not also departing, for aught I know for ever, from the dearest creature upon earth? from her that loved me when I knew not well how to respect myself—who was wont to give me sweet counsel in order for my future happiness—equally partook of those deep sorrows which my tender love had occasioned—was willing to undergo all hazards with me in this troublesome life—whose kind letters had so often proved the healing balm to my languishing condition, and whose constancy—had I been as equally faithful, and not so desirous of being improved through too many perplexing doubts—would never have been shaken, and without question would have procured the greatest happiness for which I was created!'"

These self-reproaches, for which undoubtedly there were some grounds, made him seriously ill on the road. His situation just then was certainly a very hard one. Nobody can well blame him for the sacrifices he was making to his sense of filial duty; and yet every one must regret the neglect which he was treating the amiable young woman who was so sincerely attached to him. But he obviously could not fulfil his duty to both parents and sweetheart; and who shall say which he ought to have preferred? When duties thus come into collision, so that one cannot be performed without the other being neglected, it is very difficult to decide which shall be done, and which shall be left undone. Most people would take the course that most coincided with their inclination. One cannot easily tell to which of the two courses before him Gent was most inclined, had he acted from feeling instead of duty; but it is certain he took that which went most against his interests; so that, if there be merit in self-sacrifice, his conduct must be considered meritorious. His employment in Dublin was far less profitable than what he had had in London, though love for his parents rendered him contented, "and took all thoughts," says he, "of further advantages away." Such, at least, were his feelings in his sober and reasonable state of mind. But, unhappily, there were times when he was influenced by other moods; and on one of these occasions he fell into a temptation which induced himself of a sudden to give up the claims of parental duty to the contrivance of a comparative stranger—"Mr. Alexander Campbell, a Scotchman in the same printing-office with me, getting me in liquor," says he, "obtained a promise that I should accompany him to England, where there was a greater likelihood of prosperity. Accordingly he so pressed me, and gave such reasons to my dear parents that it was not worth while to stay there for such small business as we enjoyed, that they consented we should go together." This consent, however, was given very reluctantly. "Their melting tears," he says, "made mine to flow, and bedewed my pillow every night that I lodged with them." His mother seems to have attributed his desire to leave them to his anxiety to be united to Alice Guy. "What, Tommy," she would say, "this English damsel of yours, I suppose, is the chiefest reason why you slight us and your native country! Well," she would add, "the ways of Providence, I know, are unsearchable; and whether I live to see you again or no, I shall pray God to be your defender and preserver!"

Thomas avoided any formal leave-taking, as an ordeal which he had not courage to go through. "I thought it not fit," says he, "to accumulate sorrows to us all, by returning any afflictive answers; but, taking an opportunity whilst she was abroad on her business, I embarked with my friend once more for England."

Having obtained employment again in London, his time and thoughts were almost wholly engrossed in business, to the oversight of all other interests and considerations. He had by no means forgotten or given up his Yorkshire damsel; but so little had he communicated with her of late, that her heart was growing sick with hope so long deferred. He was not yet prepared for setting up an establishment of his own, suitable to his ambition, and adequate to the merits of the lady who was to grace it with her presence. As Doctor Southey observes, he was provident overmuch; and indeed this he acknowledges, even when endeavouring to excuse himself. "All that I had undergone, I must confess," he says, "I thought were but my just deserts for being so long absent from my dear (it had now been an absence of some years); and yet I could not well help it. I had a little money, it is very true; but no certain home wherein to invite her. I knew she was well fixed; and it pierced me to the very heart to think, if through any miscarriage or misfortune I should alter her condition for the worse instead of the better. Upon this account my letters to her at this time were not so amorously obliging as they ought to have been from a sincere lover; by which she had reason, however she might have been mistaken, to think that I had failed in my part of those tender engagements which had passed between us."

The Greeks were ten years besieging Troy before the town was taken; and for nearly as long a period Miss Alice Guy endured the faint-hearted courtship of her hesitating and irresolute lover before the strongholds of her affection were shaken, and she showed signs of surrendering to the solicitations of other wooers. But the most constant of women, courted in such loose, negligent fashion, must needs give way at last. No one of them can be content to hold herself perpetually in waiting for a man who does not know when he intends to come for her! Mr. Thomas Gent no doubt meant, in perfect good faith, to fetch the lady Alice when he was ready for her; but meanwhile she was left in the dreariest uncertainty to await his quite arbitrary convenience. No wonder that at length she tired of it.

As usually happens in such cases, she showed most signs of tiring just as he was making more than usual efforts for bringing things to a satisfactory conclusion. He had purchased quantities of type and other printing-office properties, gradually adding still further to his stock as his increasing means enabled him, and had formed the resolution to make a venture in the world somewhere on his own account, with the gentle Alice for a partner. He says that she at first encouraged him in the enterprise; leaving us, however, to infer that something intervened which made her think less favourably of their prospects. He does not say that she ever really discouraged him; and the truth appears to be that he still hesitated, and that his own resolution all along was only half-hearted. His purse being much exhausted by the purchases he had made, he went on working for further supplies; by-and-bye he bought a new frame, and otherwise added to his stock, whereby his fund of money was again diminished, and more had to be earned before he could conveniently carry out his project. So Gent laboured on, working partly on his own account, and partly for the master under whom he had been serving, occasionally employing journeymen to help him through, and in one way or other so overtasking his strength by excessive diligence as to be in danger of breaking down from the fatigue. All this while Alice Guy, in the tenth year of her engagement, was still left waiting; Thomas, nevertheless, comfortably imagining, and taking it for granted, that "things would so fall out that after some little time he should have occasion to invite his dear to London."

Notwithstanding his own lukewarmness, he had perfect faith in her continued constancy. His confidence in his own attractions must have been unlimited; since, playing loosely at that wide distance, he seems to have backed himself against all comers with the certainty of going in at any time to win. Time, however, which is always "working wonders," was unexpectedly preparing for him an extraordinary surprise. The reader shall have it as he himself relates it, and will so, perhaps, most thoroughly realise his situation. "One Sunday morning," says he, "as my thoughts were [illegible] by a little boy at the end of the lane, there came Mr. John Hoyle, who had been a long time in a messenger's custody in [illegible], for reprinting The [illegible], under direction of Mrs. Powell, with whom he wrought as journeyman. 'Mr. Gent,' said he, 'I have been at York to see my parents, and am but just, as it were, returned to London. I am heartily glad to see you, but sorry to tell you that you have lost your old sweetheart; for I assure you that she is really married to your rival, Mr. Bourne!' I was so thunderstruck that I could scarcely return an answer. All former thoughts crowding into my mind, the consideration of spending my substance in a business I would not have engaged in as a master but for her sake, my own misfortune that had occasioned it, and withal that she could not in such a case be much blamed for mending her fortune—all these threw me under a very deep concern."

There are not many young ladies, we fear, who will be much inclined to pity him. He himself was aware that he could not expect much sympathy. Not the less did he feel his disappointment as a real and serious misfortune, rendered all the more intense since it might have been prevented. There being nothing for it, however, but to submit to fate, he consoled himself as well as he could, by making it the subject of poetical contemplation, and produced a copy of verses which he entitled "The Forsaken Lover's Letter to his former Sweetheart"—a doleful ditty, in which he represented himself as being most cruelly and shamefully jilted and ill-treated. A copy of this was given to a friendly printer, who printed and sold many thousands; in consideration of which he offered the author a price for copyright; though, as Gent observes, "as it was my own proper concern, I scorned to accept of anything, except a glass of comfort or so." Needing comfort so much, he might, perhaps, be justified in accepting anything of the kind falling in his way; but he could hardly be excused in taking so large a poetical licence as he seems to have ventured on, by describing his abandonment. Indeed he overdoes the thing by misrepresentation. We have Southey's authority for saying: "If the Forsaken Lover's Lamentation had been sung about the streets of York, Mrs. Bourne might have listened to it without suspecting that she was the treacherous maid, who, for the sake of this world's splendour, had betrayed her only sweet jewel, left him to languish alone, and broken his heart.

Fearing that none would be false, then the

Gentlewoman would never have whispered to him that it was [illegible]. Thomas [illegible] closed his complaint with the desperate determination expressed in the ensuing stanza:

Now to the woods and groves I'll be ranging,
Free from all scorns I'll rest with my grief;
While birds are singing and sweet notes [illegible],
This pleasing concert will yield me relief.
Thus, like the swan before its departing
Sings forth its dirge in melting strains,
My dying words shall merit the kind powers there
To pity my fate, the most wretched of swains.

It was thought proper for disappointed lovers to write in this strain in those eighteenth-century days, and accordingly Master Thomas fell into the fashion; but he had no notion of doing what he pretended. He neither went to the woods, nor died; but shortly entered into an engagement with a printer's widow, to take the management of her business—"being the more willing," we are told, "to enter into the service of this gentlewoman, since he was disappointed of his first love." The widow was a most agreeable person, a sea-captain's daughter, and had been educated at a boarding-school at Hackney; she had been twice married, and was the mother of two children, one by each of the two husbands. Master Thomas much admired her, and would have been very well content to accept her, with her flourishing business, in lieu of his lost Yorkshire maiden. "I thought her," says he, "worthy of the best of spouses; for sure there never could be a [illegible] economist, or sweeter mother to her dear children, whom she kept exceedingly decent. I have dined with her; but there, as in reason, I [illegible] what was fitting for my meals; and her conversation, agreeable to her fine education, almost wounded me with love, and, at the same time, commanded a becoming reverence. What made her excellent carriage the more endearing was, that I knew I could never expect to behold my first love at York; though I heard, by travellers, that not only she, but her husband used to inquire after me. Indeed, I was sensible that Mr. Bourne, though a likely young man, was not one of the most healthful persons; but far from imagining otherwise than that he might have outlived me, who was then worn to a shadow. But, see the wonderful effects of Divine Providence in all things!"

[illegible], for they are very wonderful indeed! if we assume, with Thomas's presumption, that the hand of Providence is to be seen in what follows, [illegible] interfering with an especial view to his convenience. It seems an odd sort of providence which goes to deprive a woman of her husband, that another man may have the opportunity of marrying her! Why Providence should have any particular reasons for preferring to see Gent living in wedlock with Alice Guy to Mr. Charles Bourne, one cannot very readily comprehend. The probability seems to be, that Providence was thereabouts indifferent, in such a matter, respecting either. Quite otherwise, however, was Mr. Thomas Gent's persuasion, as is evident from the manner in which he tells his story. "It was one Sunday morning," says he, "that Mr. Philip Wood, a quondam partner of Mr. Midwinter's, entering my chambers, where I sometimes used to employ him too, when slack of business in other places. 'Tommy,' said he, 'all those fine materials of yours must be moved to York!' At which wondering, 'What mean you?' said I. 'Ay,' said he, 'and you must go too, without it's your own fault; for your first sweetheart is now at liberty, and left in good circumstances by her dear spouse, who deceased but of late.' 'I pray heaven,' answered I, 'that his precious soul may be happy: and for aught I know it may be as you say, for, indeed, I think I may not trifle with a widow as I have formerly done with a maid.'" The news, in fact, though coming unexpectedly, had the immediate effect of re-kindling his old affection, and of engendering possibilities to be realised, under different conditions, which the marriage of the lady had for the time being put out of the question. But judging rightly, that if he intended to renew his suit in the present state of circumstances, it must be in a very different fashion from that in which he had formerly conducted it, he proceeded at once to take the measures which seemed requisite to success. It was obvious that this time no slowness could be tolerated. It must be a swift decided business, to be gone through much after the manner of a business contract, without indecision or hesitation. Perceiving this, he lost no time in arranging his plans, settling his affairs conformably to the purposes now before him—which was that of marrying the widow of Mr. Bourne, taking it evidently for granted that his proposals would be sure to be accepted.

"I made an excuse," says he, "to my mistress (meaning the printer's widow whose business he had been managing) that I had business in Ireland, but that I hoped to be at my own lodgings in about a month's time; if not, as I had placed everything in order, she might easily by any other person carry on the concern. But she said she would not have any beside me in that station I enjoyed, and therefore should expect my return to her again; but respectfully taking leave, I never beheld her after, though I heard she was after very indifferently married." Being in the secret, we know very well that he never intended to return; yet there were probably some reasons why he did not like to tell her so. His whole proceedings were clandestine, as if he deemed it necessary to slip away "on the sly," and get married before anybody was aware of the transaction. "I had taken care," he adds, "that my goods should be privately packed up, and hired a little warehouse and put them in, ready to be sent, by sea or land, to where I should order: and I pitched upon Mr. Campbell, my fellow-traveller, as my confident in this affair, desiring my cousins to assist him; all of whom I took leave of at the Black Swan, in Holborn, where I had paid my passage in the stage-coach, which brought me to York in four days' time. Here I found my dearest once more, though much altered from what she was about ten years before that I had not seen her. There was no need for new courtship; but decency suspended the ceremony of marriage for some time, till my dearest at length, considering the ill-consequence of delay in her business, as well as the former ties of love that passed between us by word and writing, gave full consent to have the nuptials celebrated." And performed, accordingly, they were, "in the stately cathedral," the very day of Archbishop Blackburne's installation.

So, after all intervening accidents and turns of fortune, Mr. Thomas Gent is at last united in lawful wedlock to his first love. Having got, as he fancied, the desire of his eyes, he now expected to be happy. His notion of a wife seems to have been that she would make it her constant object in all respects to please him; that she would have no will of her own in any way opposed to his; but that she would meekly wait upon his wishes, and submissively attend to his commands. Now, whether it was owing to his having married a widow instead of a maiden, it is certain he did not find the lady so conformable to his notions of things as he had expected. Those long years of severance had not only wrought changes in her appearance, but changes also of another sort upon which he had not calculated. "I found," he says, "her temper much altered from that sweet natural softness and most tender affection that rendered her so amiable to me while I was more juvenile and she a maiden." She was none the less "sincere" than formerly, but she had contracted what he calls "a presumptive air and conceited opinion," which made him imagine (having noticed it also in others) that "an epidemical distemper prevailed among the good women to rule themselves and families; or, if not prevented by Divine Providence, to prove the sad cause of great contention and of disquietude." The good lady, during her previous married life or widowhood, had surrounded herself with a set of "pretended friends, spunging parasites, and flatterers, who imposed on good nature," to the serious damage of the household; and it was much to Gent's annoyance that she persisted in keeping up acquaintance with these people. Instead of the delightful conjugal life his fancy had prefigured for him, he declares his days were "embittered with the most undutiful aggravations," and that everything was rendered uncomfortable to him. Mrs. Gent would persist in having her disagreeable parties, which he abominated, thinking that so much lavish expenditure would bring them to untimely poverty. He charges his wife with using "[illegible] provoking arguments" in contending with his objections; and altogether he lets us sufficiently into the secret that she did not turn out the perfect angel he had expected her to be.

Nevertheless, he bore his lot with tolerable patience. "In this conjugal captivity, as I may term it," he says, "I was fully resolved, likewise in a Christian sense, to make my yoke as easy as possible, thereby to give no offence to custom or law of any kind." Not being able to shape his condition to his mind, he brought his mind to accommodate itself to his condition. In this way, after a few early bickerings and contentions, Gait and his wife lived on together very passably. They discovered that, after all, they had many tastes and interests in common, and these they appear to have tacitly agreed to cultivate for their mutual satisfaction. So, upon the whole, their married life—after the romance was all knocked out of it—passed on not uncomfortably: a quiet, yet strong attachment grew up insensibly between them, which sufficed for such emotional cravings as yet clung to them. For, in truth, the romance had all gone before they were married: it had evaporated during that slow six years' courtship—leaving their respective natures in that calm unimpassioned, and shorn of its most subtle and refined attractions—as happens, and will always happen, whenever the idea of marriage is entertained by man or woman as one of intentional calculation, and deferred beyond the limits of a reasonable postponement from considerations of mere worldliness. If you want the bloom and beauty of affection, marry while the romance is on; if marriage be only contemplated as a business contract or transaction, entered into for the joint convenience of the parties, it may be desirable perhaps to wait till the romantic element is extinguished, when it can be acknowledged that the object wanted is simply a partner in business, or a companion in society. The present veritable history illustrates the inconvenience of losing the romance; showing how what might have been a generous and beautiful attachment, had it been earlier followed out to its authentic issue, became, through the slow and cold process of a long engagement, a mere tame and common-place relationship, founded on conventional interests, but scarcely graced by a particle of sentiment. The inference seems to be, that long engagements have a deteriorating effect on the affections; and that whoever would maintain the integrity of true love must be loyal to its inspirations, and never fail to cherish it as the highest prize and blessing which human life can offer in mitigation of its many cares and troubles.

LEAF AND CLOUD BEAUTY.

BY EDWIN GOADBY.

Apart from the special value Mr. Ruskin's works possess for the art student and critic, they have always other and more common attractions, opening pleasant by-paths out of even severest technicalities, and charming away from noisy toiling town all who will read his pages and receive his lessons. The last volume of "Modern Painters," now some months before the public, is no exception to this rule, but provides so special a feast that we are tempted to re-spread it, making such additions and reflections in so doing as may help to present matters in an interesting form. He invites us into the country; and surely with so cheerful yet pensive a seer we can spend a pleasant hour. "Come with me," he says, "and sit and listen, on this green turf or grey rock; I have neither reed, pipe, cithara, nor curds and cream; but here are leaves and trees, and yonder are the clouds—the 'Angels of the Sea.'"

We cannot refuse. We lift the latch, and, though beneath our own roof-tree, we have learned the best, saddest, most enduring lessons; still there are many we may learn beneath the palace-dome of Nature, where no classic tomes can awe us from their shelves, and no ghostly memories stride between us and the objects of our study. For we must study even here where most men think least of it, and are merely content to enjoy and luxuriate as in the very lap and bosom of remunerating intelligence. Our roof-tree! Yes, Nature has given us many; and it is concerning these fair springing arches, and their veiling flowering broods that come between us and the sky, typifying our own life in its solidity, passion, and perishing, that we have to learn as well as to unlearn.

Strange notions, I dare say, we have of leaves and trees, to begin with, like our Hindoo, Persian and Greek predecessors. "Man," says the "Veda," is like unto a high tree; the hair is his leaves, the skin his bark, the blood his sap, the bones his hard knots." But casting aside all the fables of Zeus and Ormuzd, and their creation of man from trees, what we have to do is to recognise a certain human element, so to speak, in their beauty and development, leaving all knotty questions of sap and pith and albumen to be solved, as best they may be, by hard-headed botanists and Linnæan professors. Our first notion of a tree is rather a queer one. It has hairy tubular roots, a composite stem, divers boughs, and multitudinous fans waving to and fro in the air, called leaves. The roots fix it fast in the ground, the stem supports and builds the boughs, and the leaves supply it with the necessary grace, and robe it with greenness and delight. So far we know, and see too frequently enough. But the history of a bud, a leaf, or a branch, is as deep and mystical as the building of a pyramid, the carving of a palace, or the life and times of a Cheops. Herein we have a fruitful source of the most refined and elevated pleasure, and cannot realise half the joy the prisoner of Fenestrella found in his cherished Picciola.

Dividing the leaf orders into wood-planes, living in speechlessness on the ground, as lilies, and leaving no other memorial than bulb or root; and building-plants, raising themselves into edifices above the ground, and consolidating and enlarging year by year, Mr. Ruskin divides the latter again into builders with the shield, and builders with the sword. The nomenclature is rather fanciful, but has the merit of accuracy and descriptiveness. Builders with the shield are those who, by expanded leaves, cover and nestle the young buds beneath them, and grow in places where they can minister to the comfort and delight of man. Those with the sword, on the contrary, live in savage condition, and have their leaves like swords, and their sturdy limbs in the spring of a group of them, hardy and fearless. Most trees belong to the first class; the pine has come in not so as the representative of the other.

It is with the shield builders we have to do just now. Pluck a small branch, beyond where it has just burst out from last winter's growth and left an eye-ward bend. You will find the branch smooth, the leaves opposite or alternate, as the case may be, and at the terminal end a small cluster of leaves forming a rosette if it be a rhododendron branch, a quatrefoil if a horse chestnut, and a cinquefoil if an oak. Underneath each leaf, and sometimes above, are small projecting points, which the leaf guards and shelters. This will be the bud of next spring, and will begin its beautiful unfolding as soon as it has undergone the chemical change whereby a certain amount of saccharine matter is developed. Observe that every pair of buds tries to set itself at right angles to the pair below. Both hazel and laurel buds have the power to conquer this change next year; but as this would make a merely mathematical tree, various influences operate upon them to cause accessions, hindrance, and even death. It is not every bud that can command space and light, and sooner than rudely infringe upon a neighbouring bough, it will twist this way and that, turn up or down, feeling its way out with joy and affection, as though it possessed reason and human regard. We shall have to remark this again by-and-bye.

But now the leaf is to be formed and unsheathed, and here new laws and beauties appear. Accidents operate to make changes and deviations in shape and size, yet always subordinately with the great heart-law they all follow obediently and lovingly.

Nature will not suffer herself to be bare and unvarying; so almost every class of tree has a different leaf-system and different shapes, no two leaves being at any time exactly alike. All more or less strive to approach the model of the central or main sceptre leaf in the terminal group; but it alone is a perfect rosette, while they are straggling-sided, and occasionally there is by being longer on one side than on the other. And now let us mark one or two points in their position. First, we shall find that the leaves of a branch, almost invariably fall away from the terminal or uppermost group in graceful expansions of symmetry; since that place can hold little grace, and space for expansion during the ascension of the year depends. Second, that the leaves at the end of the spray, by a most beautiful process, unravel and form their clusters at different heights one above the other, so as in no way to impede one another, and present the most striking obliquity of form. The beauty resulting from this successive climbing of clusters can only be fully seen in studying an oak, chestnut, or ash spray. Third, the springing back of the leaves upon their stems, and the gentle deflection of the stem, or stalk itself, where it issues from the bark, the one being the cause of the other. Attention to be noticed in drawing them in their right poise and position. These three laws operate universally upon all leaves, and to their modifying and effective influence much of their gracefulness and delicate beauty is owing. Each cluster of leaves presents the general aspect of a family group, all animated by the tenderest regard for each other, never crowding nor overlapping in all their courses, never willingly impeding each other's growth, but full of a tender and exquisite sensibility; all wanting light and air, yet all following the law of liberty that Kant has laid down for us sterner men, in his "Metaphysic of Ethics"—"So act that the use of thy freedom shall not circumscribe the freedom of any other." There is no fighting, no shuffling for place; but all is order, method, most beautiful symmetry. And here Mr. Ruskin, actuated by the desire he acknowledges further on in the same volume, of bringing everything to a root in human passion or hope, and tracing every principle of painting to some vital or spiritual fact, takes occasion to compare the disposition of leaves in the crowded fringe of large trees and the more open and scattered sprays of smaller ones, with the same falling into place amongst men. "When the community is small, people fall more easily into their places, and take, each in his place, a firmer standing than can be obtained by the individuals of a greater nation. The members of a vast community are separately weaker, as an aspen or elm leaf is thin, tremulous, and directionless, compared with the sparlike spring and firm substance of a rhododendron or laurel leaf. The laurel and rhododendron are like the Athenian or Florentine Republics; the aspen, like England, strong-trunked enough when put to proof, and very good for making cart-wheels of, but shaking pale with epidemic panic at every breeze. Nevertheless, the aspen has the better of the great nations, in that, if you take it bough by bough, you shall find the gentle law of respect and room for each other truly observed by the leaves in such freedom way as they can manage it; but in the nations you find every one scrambling for his neighbour's place."

Now, noting all this beauty and distinctness of plan and outline, we come upon the great faults of both the old master and their modern imitators. Never having studied leaf law or leaf history, they knew nothing of the aspects we have so briefly indicated, and cared that their public should know still less. A mere sleight of hand, mechanical trickery with the brush, or "niggling," as it is called, sufficed to show in a rough blundering way all that such men as Hobbima and Ruysdael cared to paint. Their very ignorance, unfortunately, passes with many for wisdom, and their neglect of nature for devotion to art! We are told that even the single painting of a leaf cost Titian to "thoughtful trouble;" Leonardo did it "very nearly, trying hard;" Holbein, "three or four times, in precious places highest wrought;" and Raphael, "it may be in one or two crowns of saint or angel." In brief, to all over-earnest, over-innocent young Pre-Raphaelites, Ruskin gives this bit of pithy and seasonable advice, "If you can paint one leaf you can paint the world."

But we have not done with the leaf. Goethe was the first to suggest the idea that a leaf is the unit of botany, and that every part of a plant is a transformed leaf to meet a new condition, and this has given rise to many similar discoveries both in botany and osteology. And in one of Addison's earliest papers in "The Tatler,"* when he would satirise imaginative philosophers, he makes his dreamer to tell him that he had seen a forest of numberless trees which had been picked out of an acorn; and if his own vision was but more minute, he himself might find a miniature oak in an acorn, pluck from that tree another small acorn and it would contain another tree, and so on, almost infinitely. Addison's was fiction, but Goethe's was better fact. The occurrence of this law is shown in the bough of a tree, which only accident, caprice, and internal laws of growth and accommodation, prevent from following out the precise form set forth in the terminal leaves and buds, each terminal or portion one, and each lateral one, tending to grow itself into trefoil, quatrefoil, or cinquefoil, as the case may be. It may be but dimly seen; but there it is, plain and discoverable. It is seen more directly in the fact that every leaf not only helps the tree to grow outward and upward, but is itself attached by minute fibres to the very roots, as it were, adding to the thickness of shoot, branch, and trunk, and thus making it a genuine leaf-monument. Every leaf has thus acted its part, and, according to its size and strength, has wove its little strand of cable, as a spider his thread, and sent it down by the side of the springing tower by a marvellous magic irresistible! "The fall of a granite pyramid from an Alp may perhaps be stayed; the descending force of that silver thread shall not be stayed!" Who, after this, shall dare to reckon his thoughts, his influence, his example, as nothing in the family, the town, the nation? Who say, "I am nothing—nobody—and must be content." Thus by its leaves the tree builds both head and trunk, fruit and shaft, prudently beginning as a sapling by a careful looking to all his several branches, by a prudent seeing to the rights of that first-born central bud, that must keep right on and upward whilst the lateral ones droop, change, and die. By an observance of all the laws of symmetry and force on the one hand, checked and balanced by those of variety, freedom, and loveliness on the other; until, as brood after brood drops in kindly largesse, the trunk grows massive, the roots deeper, the boughs more spreading, and ever in beautiful vicissitude, the quiet monuments have deep lessons of love, and hope, and working for you and me, and all men. We may sport or sleep beneath their boughs, and their wild wind-harps will breathe us dirge and ditty, wet-chant and life-psalm. Lowland trees shall teach us soft and winning lessons; and the pines that fledge the wild-ridged mountain, moulding the character of Swiss peasantry and Scotch Highlanders, have sterner and sadder teaching.

A few words on motionless leaves. Their beauty is of a chaster, humbler cast than that of their brothers and sisters of the free air. Fringed and cleft that our feet shall not hurt them, but vend them into more delicate forms, they are star-shaped, heart-shaped, spear-shaped, arrow-shaped, that they may fix our wandering eyes and excite our wonder. They grow where their very existence is a self-abnegation, an existence for others, covering our flower beds with greenness, our blank walls with colour, our ruins with freshness, and our very sand-heaps with pleasantness. As mock lichens and variegated grasses, like so many miniature forests or dwarf arcadias, they cling lovingly and enduringly to blanched ruins, towering stones, and dripping walls. In sadness and sunshine, in sober gray and bright green or red, they weave the dark, classical tapestries of the hills. They are earth's first gift and her last, full of wistful eloquence and modest beauty—"trees for the builder's yard, flowers for the bride's chamber, corn for the granary, moss for the grave."

The beauty of clouds is vaster, grander, and more imposing than that of leaves and flowers, lilies and ranunculuses. It will awe, hush, soften, and make eloquent even the most obdurate. A wild sunset crimson, a dense down-crashing thunder-cloud, and a bright fleecy flock of angels' down, have charms and force for the most unpoetic minds. For there is a human pathos about clouds. They typify man's restless heart and head. Their restlessness is a symbol of his passion; their infinity, a prophecy of his aspiration; their colours, an expression of his fancies; and their frailty, a preacher of his in-

* No. 119, January 12, 1709.

passion. The Scandinavian Edda even makes them of a human giant origin. When Ymir was dragged into the void, called "Ginnunga-gap,"

"From his brain
Were the [illegible]
Clouds all created."

There is also mystery. The clouds remove the last veil from us, soften the blue air into warm beauty and tempered brightness, cling in crowns and robes of mist about our hills, and patter with joyful drops upon the thirsty fields and dusty streets. They stayed the "pillars of cloud" and "pillars of fire." Above all there is mystery, endless, unfathomable. The old question in Job comes to us again in its weird solemn tones, "Knowest thou the balancing of the clouds?" Why are they so light? How do they balance and yet not sink beyond our vision? How do they contain so much water, and yet move like airy balloons and silk-coloured argosies? Why does not the lightest puff of wind burst their spherical globules of air and water, if such they be? In what does their coherency consist? heat or electricity? And their shape—Who hollows them into bergs, rolls them into pavilions, spins them into webs, and dashes them into foam? Why do they now float on, flat and wool-like, unbroken and unchanged? Why be laughed away by morning light, and gather again when the Sun goes off his rule and away? Why hold up the crimson curtain for Nature's evening pageant, and then in brightly [illegible] and peace-[illegible] over his grey [illegible] and grave? Here is mystery enough to make our imagination, tempt our reason, and humble our heart: much we know, but more we must be content not to know, accepting as our answer the reply Plotinus the Mystic has put into the mouth of Nature: "It behoves thee not to disquiet me with interrogatories, but to understand in silence, even as I am silent and work without words." Assuredly there are many lessons and many warnings for us, coming in the soft foldings and convolutions of the clouds.

Let us study their nature. We will begin with the soft cirri of the upper air. Height is the first thing we note concerning them, and calm reigning stillness. As they never touch or cross the highest mountains in Europe, they must form above an elevation of 15,000 feet, and it is this that gives them such serenity. They are mostly indicative of serene and settled weather. Various and shifting as they are, they have a symmetry of their own, and beginning with a few fibres increasing in length and tenacity, a silent law of growth moulds them into transparent bars, fading into weariless vapour, and drifts them into silken plumy streams [illegible] as [illegible] veils. Their sharp edges are always shadowed, whilst their farther ones are soft, melting, imperceptible. The two kinds, the hairy and the plumy, continually intersect each other with a most beautiful effect, containing all the grandeur of medieval scrolls and Alhambra courts. Their multitude also gives an impression of infinity and sublimity. They undulate into ripples and divide into flocks, forming what is commonly called a mackerel sky. On a winter morning's sunrise, by a moderate calculation of their ranks, Mr. Ruskin tells us that he arrived at the fact that there were no less than 50,000 of them in the field of sight. Their voluntary union into flocks was noticed long since by our poets. Milton sings—

"Of some gay creatures of the element,
That in the colours of the rainbow live,
And play i' the plighted clouds."

And their slow silly movement and silent resignation of the wind are sweetly rendered by Shelley—

"Underneath the young grey dawn
A multitude of dense, white fleecy clouds,
Were wandering in thick flocks along the mountains,
Shepherded by the slow unwilling wind."

In the middle, or central cloud region, the great masses of cloud are formed, grouped for general purposes under the term cumuli, from their piled-up and supposed manner of building up by vapour from beneath. And here in the very outset we are met with the first difference. The cloud flocks seemed to own the power of the wind; but these cumuli, although in reality impelled by the same power, nevertheless appear to move in haughty independence, and stand out and rotate as though possessed of an independent will. Hence they are called by one author "cloud-chariots," and in the lesser ones floating beside them, and the thin fleece trampled out before them, as by hoof of fiery steeds, the description is well borne out. Diana herself might range the cerulean round in such delightsome manner. And they grow from chariots into larger fields and flying continents. They imitate on the grandest scale our own mountain ranges, boiling up in Titanic energy, toppling into avalanche, rending into chasms, and glittering into crevasse and glacier. Miles upon miles of coloured cloud, they rear their mountains into pinnacles, and expand our wonder almost into idolatry. Their pictures are marvellously beautiful. Now a cup-cloud will hang about some lofty peak, as in imitation of earthly reality; and then a tiny cloudlet will sail along their snowy hollowed valleys, touch a moment the glittering top, and then, watching the wind, turn away in play. Range after range they stretch in wildering beauty, heightening for us the infinite unfathomable beyond, and filling our hearts with [illegible] [illegible] figures—

"High on some lofty cloud-cliff, harp in hand,
Singing the sun to sleep, or there he lays
His head of glory in the rocking deep."

Ancient artists, but very imperfectly succeeded in representing, or making any adequate show of these cloud mountains; nor have modern ones done much better. Only Turner in his "Babylon," "Pools of Solomon," "Lake of Como," and others, has succeeded in doing them anything approaching to justice. He has, if Mr.

Ruskin be trusted, fairly caught their infinity, and therefore their most glowing reality. "For," he says, "we may be sure that what is not infinite is not true." "The moment that we trust ourselves we repeat ourselves; and therefore the moment we see in a work of any kind whatsoever the expression of infinity, we may be certain that the workman has gone to Nature for it; while, on the other hand, the moment we see repetition, or want of infinity, we may be certain that the workman has not gone to Nature for it."

To the lower region, although by no means exclusively so, belongs the nimbus or rain-cloud, and all forms of haze and mist so difficult to render in painting, so common in nature, and so various and beautiful in effect. They are much nearer to us than the cirrus, owing to which we have much of their diversified phenomena; and their colour is a monotonous grey, or warm ash-brown, growing inky and sulphurous if there be thunder about, or flashing into jagged fringes of white when the forked rain floats in a columnar body. Their velocity seems greater because of their nearness, and they writhe and twist and spin as if instinct with unwilling speed. In the Alpine valleys they are seen with splendid effect, careering round and round the principal heights, clinging like dark veils to the leeward side of jagged cliffs, or dancing in wild joy of phantom shape and delirium, or piling themselves up like colossal soldiers in muffled bivouac and tented sleep. Yet they have more peaceful aspects, more benignant moods. Soft, silken coloured, brightening as they bloom, creating strange paradises and hanging gardens for us, and marshalling into bright ranks of fleecy pinnacles, as typifying the harvests of joy and plenty they are commissioned to produce. Ruskin beautifully calls the rain-cloud the "Angel of the Sea." Beautifully are its wings coloured, not with ashen grey and looming black, as we too often think, but with more various hues than either cirri or cumuli. Rose-colour, purple, amber, steel blue, and soft mistiness of gold, tint and dye their softly-laden wings and dewy plumes. Light, reflected, refracted, and gathered up into curious shades and fanciful rays, seems to be the cause of their colour. But it is when struck by the sun on their under-surfaces that the rarest assemblages of hues are developed. It is to this fact that we entirely owe the rich colours of our sunrises and sunsets. How much heat, and the vapours it creates, may help to produce the grander and more extended scenes, seems at present uncertain; but in both Africa and India the sunsets are unparalleled for their depth and beauty of colour, sometimes covering half the visible heavens, and coming back in unison reflections from the very East.

Here, then, is a grand field for our British painters. Leaves and clouds, all of which we have in abundance and variety. All foreigners agree in calling our island "the foggy," and the rain-cloud is rarely absent from our skies, rushing down in thunderous volleys upon Scotch hills and Yorkshire moors, or distilling in gentlest drops on plain and meadow. Here, too, Turner was at home. If he could not enter into the spirit of the pine, he has caught the innermost one of soft rain-cloud, wild storm-cloud, and shrieking typhoon. Not unfelt or unimaged was the rain-cloud to the Greeks. For them, as it should for us, it had meanings, mystical, beneficent, and terrible. All to them were sea-angels sprung from Nereus and his children—and Graiae and stormy Gorgons, Iris the crocus-robed, and Medusa, the fierce freezer into stone with her cold, fanged, serpent locks; Chrysaor the angel of the lightning, and Pegasus the angel of the wild fountains, the winged racer of earth and heaven. Leaves, trees, and cloud had meanings for them, mystical, paganish, simplicities, childish if you will; earth, ocean, air, were peopled with bright gods our colder wisdom has scattered and destroyed. But that wisdom which makes us forget that their beauty is diminished or less meaning, that age has not tarnished their hues, nor the vicissitudes of earth altered the garments of heaven, is a wisdom that comes ill from a people who are the Greeks of to-day, and who find no truer art-priest than he whose heart is so noble and whose aims are so pure.

THE KING AND THE POTTER.—"In 1588, Henry III., then King of France, finding he could no longer withstand the clamour for Palissy's execution, and reluctant to sacrifice the old potter, whom he had known and respected from his boyhood, visited him in prison. 'My poor Master Bernard,' said the King, 'I am so pressed by the Guise party and my people, that I have been compelled, in spite of myself, to imprison these two poor women and you. They must be burnt to-morrow; and you, too, if you will not be converted.' 'Sire,' replied the fearless old man, 'you have often said that you feel pity for me; but it is I who pity you, who have said, "I am compelled." That is not speaking like a king! These girls and I, who have part in the kingdom of heaven, we will teach you to talk royally. The Guisarts, all your people, and yourself, cannot compel a potter to bow down to images of clay!' Not many months afterwards, the two fair girls were led to the stake, singing praises to God, as they received their crowns of martyrdom. A year later, in 1589, in his eighty-first year, Bernard Palissy, the potter, died in the Bastille."—*The Art of Doing our Best.*

OUR LIBRARY TABLE.

GREAT EXPECTATIONS. (London: Chapman and Hall.)—If Mr. Dickens's name did not stand alone on the title-page, we should be disposed to attribute much of the conception—even some of the execution—of this story to his friend and fellow-writer, Wilkie Collins. For a long time now these novelists have been accustomed to write together. The Christmas numbers of "Household Words," jointly produced by them, showed year by year a gradual assimilation of the two styles. At first the difference was broad and marked; the least critical of readers could assign to each writer his own chapters. But, after a Christmas or two, readers began to be puzzled in such investigations. Which was Mr. Dickens and which was Mr. Collins came to be decided mostly by the choice, not the execution, of the scene. No longer we wondered at the monstrous joining together of black silk and [illegible]; the [illegible] had disappeared, and if the physiologist could still detect in the delight of gods and men a suspicion of the fishy [illegible] and tail, he confessed that these anomalous monsters had been reduced to their lowest possible rudiments. That this assimilation of the two styles was a great gain to the joint story is evident enough. Whether the influence of the one writer upon the other, when exhibited in works written separately, is a gain or a loss, it would occupy more than the space at my disposal here to discuss. The influence of Collins upon Dickens was very much greater than that of Dickens upon Collins. If we compare this last book with the early sketches by Boz, we see how great is the change, and further that this change is all in the direction of the Romantic school of which Collins is the English chief. Collins's books on the other hand show simply a steady progression in the one line which his genius had marked out for him. Dickens's influence upon him is to be found only in treatment and phrase—in a spice of sentimentalism, in a solemn aping of jocularity utterly repugnant to his manner of thought—never in conception either of story or character. Still, though we attribute much of the change in Dickens's writing to Collins's influence, we must allow that the change is by no means in opposition to his own genius, and that his bias in this direction would have shown itself had Collins never written. Dickens began by professing an extreme naturalism. In his earliest sketches and in Pickwick, he describes only such scenes as came under his own notice. The lowest phases of life, the ordinary places and people and characters—these he set before himself as models from which to paint. To say that he painted them truly would be to say only a truism to everybody now. We all know his manner of observation. Seizing upon some external point or trait in a man (Wemmick's post-office; Jaggers's finger-biting, hand-washing, boot-creaking; Joe's whisker-feeling; Mrs. Gargery's apron; the same [illegible] as thirty years ago), and never getting deeper than that, [illegible] it to something [illegible], and ever after mistaking that in which he has [illegible] it for the thing itself, and trying off into the most astonishing mechanical [illegible]—we all know this manner by heart; and we all know that his characters are not men but highly-painted puppets, though sometimes a homely truth is spoken out of their wooden mouths which startles us as if a stick or [illegible] spoke. Professing extreme naturalism, he was the most unnatural of writers. Professing to draw the most familiar portion of the world around him, he lost his way and got into a world which was the most extravagant burlesque of that he had left behind, a region whose inhabitants habitually made harlequins and pantaloons and clowns of themselves, where pantomimic transformations were continually occurring, things becoming men and men things, and one thing becoming another, until all was a chaos. The absurd [illegible], he was the master of [illegible]. The [illegible] side of the [illegible] he looked upon [illegible] as [illegible], as the public [illegible] the [illegible]—he saw the grand grave upon their visages, and strove to paint the grotesque of it. He had the keenest sense of a certain harmony and likeness between all things in heaven and earth; but trying to express it, instead of showing how all things were parts of an universal whole, he made each other than it was. That a writer, whose [illegible] to paint the commonest phases of life, should be [illegible] by his imagination into inventing an altogether ideal world, with inhabitants unreal as the shadows in Plato's cave, is a fact that would seem at once to separate him broadly from the naturalists. Dickens's first fame, as it seems to me, was a [illegible] fame. He will never live because of his truthful representations of society, or because of his insight into human character, or because of his photographs of the manners and customs of the time. So long as his books do live, it must be from other and more opposite causes. His original wit and talent of grotesque and exaggerated description caught the public ear by their strangeness at first; and people instantly attributed to him a power of depicting low life, because they happened to be low-life puppets who were exhibited in this new species of writing. But among thoughtful persons his fame will rest by no means on his [illegible] for describing simple nature high or low, but on his literary art. We must pass on to the book in hand. Briefly let us write, that, comparing "Great Expectations" with the "Sketches by Boz," we should pronounce "Great Expectations" to be the legitimate offspring of Dickens's true genius, and the sketches to be mere abortional fruits of an immature tree. In the legends introduced into his earliest works, in "Oliver Twist," in a "Tale of Two Cities," we may trace, step by step, the overshadowing of false sentimentalism by active sensationalism. However much Wilkie Collins has influenced him, it has been not against him with the grain. This romance of "Great Expectations" is a little too much like "The Woman in White." It would be difficult to point out the precise points of resemblance. If analysis of both plots were placed side by side we should find that that of the later book was even carefully rendered different from that of the earlier. Still the stories are of the same kind, and affect us in the same manner. As "Hans Vernon" could not have been written unless "Transformation" had been written, so, though in a less degree, this book could not have been written unless "The Woman in White" had been written. The readers of "All the Year Round" must begin to feel this painfully. The plot runs thus: Pip, hero and autobiographer, has no connexion by blood with any of the characters who keep on the scenes of the piece. Pip in early childhood succours an escaped convict, feeding him and procuring a file for the removal of his fetters. This convict, afterwards transported for life, grows rich abroad, and in gratitude devotes all his riches to the service of Pip. The first volume brings Pip up to the crisis when it is made known to him that he is heir to a great fortune at the hands of some unknown benefactor. In the meantime Pip, brought up as a blacksmith with the husband of his sister, has been introduced to an eccentric maiden-lady named Havisham. Living with her is a beautiful girl, called Estella. With Estella, Pip of course falls in love. He has always thus hoped that Miss Havisham will do something for him. When he hears of his good fortune he at once decides that Miss Havisham is his benefactress. Jaggers, Miss Havisham's lawyer, is the medium chosen by the convict to convey his good intentions to Pip. Jaggers, Miss Havisham's confidential man, is established as Pip's guardian. Jaggers, seeing Pip's supposition, never gainsays it by a word. Moreover, Miss Havisham herself, seeing the same, fools him to the top of his bent. He is made to believe that Estella is intended for his wife. This Estella, Miss Havisham (a person who has been jilted when young) has educated to revenge her injuries upon the whole race of man. Pip is one victim; moreover, Pip serves to Miss Havisham as a thorn in the sides of her hungry relations, who are eager after her wealth. The second volume finds Pip a gentleman, in London, believing Miss Havisham to be his benefactress, regulating his behaviour with an eye to her satisfaction, and with an eye to his future wedding with the charming Estella. Most of the scenes in this volume are irrelevant, and the conduct of the story is disappointing. We are introduced to some impossible people, after the manner of Dickens; the volume is a series of episodes having little bearing on the main story. We might have expected a contrast of luxury and extravagance here to the old blacksmith life—a preparation by exquisite sensitiveness of honour and position, and so forth, that should make the discovery of the convict-origin of his wealth felt with the greater force. We find nothing of the kind. Pip does not enter high life; he gets but moderately into debt; his morals do not become exquisitely sensitive. He of course cuts Joe, the blacksmith (what else could he do?, particularly when instigated thereto by Estella); and he comes to look upon those youthful meetings with the convict as the black spot in his life—the one action thereof which makes him unfit for the companionship of Estella. Volume the second ends with the return home of the convict, who, having escaped, enters England at the peril of his life. The convict discovers himself to Pip as his secret benefactor; and thus Pip is saddled with the hiding of this terrible monster, and finds all his air-castles blown to the winds. At the same time, Estella becomes engaged in marriage to a rejected enemy of Pip's. Volume the third (by far the best portion of the book) is occupied with the account of Pip's hiding of the convict, his attempts at escaping with him, and the final capture and death of that unhappy person. The suspense and excitement is kept up, from beginning to end, with admirable skill. There are episodes here too, but all of the horrible kind; and these, whether intentionally or not, help on the excitement of this part of the story. Miss Havisham is rescued from burning by Pip. Pip is tied up hand and foot by a bloodthirsty villain, and is threatened with death. (By the way, though as a short story this scene would be excellent, it is thoroughly out of place here.) The plot, such as it is, evolves itself in this volume. A man named Compeyson, an old accomplice of the convict, now inimical to him, turns out to be the person who had formerly jilted Miss Havisham. Estella turns out to be the daughter of Mr. Jaggers's housekeeper. More wonderful than all, the convict turns out to be Estella's father. That such a series of dismal coincidences does not appear very ludicrous to the reader says much for the skill of the story-teller. Finally, Pip goes abroad (all the convict's wealth having been confiscated to the Crown), and, returning after an absence of many years, meets Estella—a charming widow—among the ruins of Satis House, Miss Havisham's former residence. We are led to suppose that they lived happily ever after. Now, we cannot praise this plot. The queer coincidences with regard to Estella, her papa and mamma, cannot be put down as anything but most impossible absurdities. The account of jilted Miss Havisham and her wedding-cake is stolen boldly out of Mr. Wilkie Collins's brains. For all this, the story goes well. The suspense of the last volume cannot be surpassed. A man who can make us hold our breath cannot be denied literary skill. Let us bow to that, and let others discuss the absurdities, each for himself. As for the characters, those who know Mr. Dickens's that world, and can translate the ghosts thereof into the real flesh and blood of this world, will discover in Mr. Jaggers a notable creation; also in Joe Gargery they will discover some glimpses of a human soul that will be like enough to blind their eyes with tears. The book as a story is utterly inferior to "A Tale of Two Cities." The lovers of fun will find but little [illegible] in it; but to those who respect the magical art which can stir their blood by mere words, this book will seem to have in it elements of a higher success in that art than Mr. Dickens has yet achieved. J. A.

JEST AND EARNEST; OR THE LUDLAM PAPERS. By Godfrey Turner. (*Kent & Co., Paternoster-row*, 1861.)—Those who know how vast a quantity of excellent writing lies buried in obscure and forgotten "back-numbers" of magazines and periodicals, will be glad to hear that another clever man has ventured to plunge into those dust abysses, and has returned with a bookful of charming tales and essays. The anonymous system which so generally prevails in English journalism has perhaps prevented Mr. Godfrey Turner's name from being so well known to the reading public as it deserves to be. It is the name of a gentleman with a very keen eye, a very clear head, and a very warm and generous heart. All these qualities of his will readily enough be discovered by the purchasers of his book, and it is in the hope of adding to the number of that class that we pen the present notice. Mr. Turner, in the very outset, has chosen to adopt a name which is connected with somewhat mixed associations, not all of the best or pleasantest kind: "the impressions here recorded, the ideas set down, the opinions advanced, the sentiments avowed, are Cockney sentiments, Cockney opinions, Cockney impressions, Cockney ideas." Mr. Turner should know best, but we cannot willingly take him at his word. Of late years the "Cockney school," which began by somewhat exaggerated rhapsodies about Nature, which was thrilled with rapture at the sight of an Alderney cow, and went into dithyrambic ecstacies whenever it met a dandelion—has rushed into the other extreme, and devoted itself to the notable task of cataloguing furniture and photographing the kitchen-dresser. It has become characterised by what we may term a sterile abundance of details. Very husky in its pathos—somewhat vulgar in its humour—it is not a school to which Mr. Turner could ever belong. His ideal of art is a much higher one—his literary style is a much purer one—than we generally meet with. Loving London as he does, and loving her with a love that has been born of a very intimate knowledge of her ways, his heart is yet warm towards the old simple country life; and the general polish and accuracy of his writing reveal the conscientious endeavour of an artist. His subjects, indeed, are chiefly city ones; but he himself exclaims, towards the close of a very graphic and vivid sketch of a London fire—"My picture, be it observed, is a picture and not a photograph." Herein lies one cardinal merit of many of his essays. They have a central thought in them, to which their details serve simply as illustrations. Without such a central thought or sentiment, a descriptive essay becomes a kind of Marine Store-shop. We can give no higher term to many productions of the so-called Cockney-school, which weary you with particularities and perplex you by the unnecessary exhibition of a hundred things in which no mortal takes an interest; and we cannot too earnestly repeat that with productions of this stamp Mr. Turner's writings are by no means to be classed. The "Jest" and "Earnest" of his book mingle very pleasantly together, and are separated by no arbitrary line of demarcation. They lie side by side, and the varying moods of the author's mind find rapid and skilful expression without too much heed of arbitrary conventionalisms. Mr. Turner's humour is not of the mere punning stamp. It belongs, as a rule, to the class of *true* Burlesque. Burlesque—the statement may be new to many admirers of Mr. Byron—Burlesque does *not* require elaborate distortion of the English tongue, and should in no case consist mainly of that. Mr. Turner's "Charade"—one of the happiest of his efforts—makes us laugh at the genuine fun without making us shudder at the fate of some unhappy polysyllable torn, twisted, and tortured into a vulgar phrase. Again, whilst Mr. Turner knows how to be humorous without grinning through a horse-collar, he knows how to be pathetic without throwing himself about in spasmodic agonies. Very tender and delicate, and all the more touching through their absence of exaggeration, are many passages scattered through his essays and stories. This book is not one to be fairly judged by extracts. Carefully writing *within* his strength, he has produced few of those startling paragraphs which are known, we believe, as "bits of fat." He writes quietly, equably, with no lack of vigour, but with no ostentation of it. When he paints London scenes, he does not blind you with glaring colours; when he tells you a simple story he does not weary you by metaphysical refinements. Earnest he is, but his earnestness, like his humour—like his pathos, is unobtrusive. That he has the strength within him for higher things than any contained in this volume, few will doubt who peruse the book to its close, and few who begin it are likely to halt midway. We can very honestly commend it to our readers as one of the most charming volumes of its class that it has been our good fortune to meet with, and we sincerely hope that we shall soon have the pleasure of hearing from Mr. Turner again. We quote a few sentences from "Palliser", as fair specimens of Mr. Turner's ordinary style:

OF [illegible] [illegible], AND SEVERAL OTHER VAGABONDS.

Banjo-twanging and burnt-cork-besmirched; clad in absurd garments—in special swallow-tail coats, short of waist, long of skirt, and [illegible] of buttons; extravagant in the matter of shirt-frill, also of collar, likewise of hat, brooch, and eyeglass—who is it now that lasts before us on the pavement? [illegible]yah, yah, yah! (the reader will kindly supply a [illegible] [illegible] chargeable by [illegible] of [illegible].) This is the Minstrel of modern Civilisation. Something, [illegible], and [illegible] [illegible], [illegible] singing "Mary Blane," or the later [illegible] [illegible] "Hoop de dooden doo!" All the clown, [illegible] and [illegible]—all his care and all his pride—all his everything beside—"Hoop de dooden doo!" All his life a dreary laughter-making, in its own [illegible], [illegible] and [illegible], "Hoop de dooden do!"

What shall be said of him—of Pulliam I mean—[illegible], and politically? What figure does he make in the Census returns? Is he liable to Income Tax, under Schedule A or B? Would it be proper to admit him to the Franchise? Has he a right to any opinion on the point, himself? What is his relation to the Mr. [illegible] view of Progress? Who is he, in short, when [illegible] at home? I can't say. I don't like to think. I may have my [illegible] ideas on the subject, but would rather not disclose them. A [illegible] popular [illegible] was [illegible] him yesterday, not in a complimentary manner, at a street [illegible], where he was, in very threadbare motley, [illegible] a [illegible] [illegible] in the neighbourhood of the Strand. The [illegible] of the two players, [illegible] the [illegible], passed to his acknowledgment. "Stop a bit," he said, looking sternly in the face of his [illegible] brother; "stop a bit," he said, in a hoarse, very [illegible] kind of voice, "don't laugh;—I was one of you once!"

It was a just rebuke, and a [illegible] [illegible]. It was, perhaps, more. The instinct of the Vagabond spoke out there, I think. The "profession" (as English actors like to call their [illegible] guild) has become a deal too respectable. Let us hark back again the old Vagabond theory, by all means and for all sakes. Let the poor player, as of yore, be typical of life in his brief [illegible]-coming and going, in his exits and his entrances, in the [illegible] parts he has to play, in his little hour wherein he frets and struts, in his [illegible] meaning. "The best in this kind," says [illegible] [illegible] Theseus, in the [illegible] [illegible] of all dramatic pieces—"and if I were manager of a theatre to-morrow, I would have the words inscribed over my proscenium;—" The best in this kind are but shadows, and the worst are no worse, if imagination amend them."

THE TEN YEARS' DIGGINGS IN CELTIC AND SAXON GRAVE HILLS, IN THE COUNTIES OF DERBY, STAFFORD, AND YORK, FROM 1848 TO 1858. By Thomas Bateman. (London: J. R. Smith, 36, Soho-square.)—It is very rarely that a reviewer sits down to his task under more melancholy circumstances than those present. The earliest copies of the book above mentioned had only just reached the hands of the author's private friends when they were startled and saddened by the announcement of his death, after a few days' illness, and in the prime of life. But, though thus short, it had been a life so industriously employed, as to gather up into it many admirable results and worthy labours. A country gentleman, of large fortune, and residing in the loveliest portion of the Peak of Derbyshire, Mr. Bateman did justice to his inherited means of an antiquarian character; and in a particular department, that of British ethnology, lived to win an European reputation. He did for his native county of Derbyshire what Sir Richard Colt Hoare did for Wiltshire, and the Rev. Bryan Faussett and the Rev. James Douglas did for Kent. Indeed, he did more. They, except in a single case or two, did not preserve the human relics they disinterred, whilst their successor, thoroughly well acquainted with comparative anatomy, preserved these [illegible], arranged them in his museum, where together they form a splendid collection, and as [illegible] have been visited by the chief foreign and English ethnologists. But the services Mr. Bateman's labours is rather for an age to come, when scientific men and thinkers shall from this and other storehouses of the kind, obtain such inductions as to race and physical progress, as may be of the utmost value to science and sociological studies. Mr. Bateman's father preceded him as a barrow digger on the Derbyshire moors; but, dying in 1835, his labours were continued by his son. The result of the earliest of these is recorded in the "Vestiges of Antiquities in Derbyshire," published in 1848; whilst the volume before us gives the result of explorations since that date. In the spring of that year, a barrow was re-opened near Arbor-low, the great Druidical temple, which is to Derbyshire what Stonehenge is to Wiltshire. The uppermost interment had been broken up by the plough; but the original interment was presently reached, in a kind of [illegible] [illegible] or enclosure, formed by ten shapeless masses of limestone.

The persons thus interred (says Mr. Bateman) consisted of a female in the prime of life, and a child of about four years of age; the former had been placed on the floor of the grave on her left side, with the knees drawn up; the child was placed above her and [illegible] behind her shoulders; they were [illegible] and covered with [illegible] bones of the water-vole or rat, and near the woman was a bone's [illegible], so [illegible] [illegible] [illegible] with the more [illegible] interments. Round her neck was a necklace of variously shaped beads and other trinkets of jet and bone, [illegible] ornamented. The various pieces of this compound ornament are 420 in number. Altogether the necklace is the most elaborate production of the pre-metallic period I have seen. The skull, in perfect preservation, is beautiful in its proportions, and has been selected to appear in the Crania Britannica as the type of the ancient British female.

The following is a picture of an interment, that carries us back in imagination to the most primeval times.

Underneath the large stones lay the skeleton of a man in the prime of life and of fine proportions, apparently the sole occupant of the mound, who had been interred whilst enveloped in a skin of dark red colour, the hairy surface of which had left many traces both upon the surrounding earth and upon the verdigris or patina coating a bronze axe-shaped celt and dagger, deposited with the skeleton. On the former weapon, there are also beautifully distinct impressions of fern leaves, handfuls of which in a compressed and half-decayed state, surrounded the bones from head to foot. From these leaves being discernible on one side of the celt only, whilst the other side presents traces of leather alone, it is certain that the leaves were placed first as a couch for the reception of the corpse with its accompaniments, and, after these had been deposited, were then further added in quantity sufficient to protect the body from the earth. Close to the head were a small black lump of jet and a circular flint; in contact with the left arm lay a bronze dagger with a very sharp edge, having four rivets for the attachment of the handle, which was of horn, the impression [illegible] of that substance being [illegible] around the rivets."

In the summer of the same year a tumulus was opened, which contained, amongst other things,

A small incense-cup, or miniature vase with a lid to close it, measuring altogether two inches high [illegible]. When found it was [illegible] but still retained, inside, remains of thread [illegible]. Close to it were two bronze pins or broken needles, and a [illegible], some of which [illegible] with a small [illegible] plated with silver and engraved with a [illegible] pattern, near which were two [illegible] implements of [illegible]. Many pieces of burnt [illegible] were found in contact with these relics, which were probably the remains of a basket in which they were placed at the funeral.

These few extracts will suffice to show the very interesting character of this volume, which, in connection with Mr. Bateman's previous work, "Vestiges of the Antiquities of Derbyshire," is of the utmost value to the antiquarian and ethnologist. The results of all these varied diggings, in pottery, gold ornaments, bronze work, and other relics, are carefully preserved in the Museum at Lomberdale, many of the skeletons beautifully articulated, and the whole forming a noble monument of the patient research and untiring industry, of one whose death will be [illegible] his generation.—R. M.

The Englishwoman's Journal. (19, Langham Place, Regent Street; Kent and Co., Paternoster-row.)—The September part of our contemporary contains, amongst other interesting matter, an abridged account of the proceedings of the Social Science Congress in Dublin, or, rather, of that department of them, in which the ladies connected with the journal appeared. We are glad to find our own view of Mrs. Overend's proposal, occurring simultaneously to a correspondent of the E. W. J.—who signs herself "A Member of the Committee of the Association for the Employment of Women," and who indignantly repudiates the idea that ladies who seek employment are ashamed of their labour, and justly observes that if they do so they are not fit to be trusted with work—an opinion in which we very sincerely agree with her. Mrs. Plant's paper on "The Institutions of History" is an exceedingly interesting one. Our favourite subject, in a literary point of view, "Trees in their Season," is not yet finished, but continues its pleasant rambles [illegible] agreeably. Eden is never described but Adam is introduced; so it is impossible to speak of the Fruits of Civilisation, horticulturally considered, without reference to the introducers and [illegible] growers of them, with all the various anecdotes in connection with their ancient and modern history. So the theme lengthens as it proceeds, and we must say that, long as it has been continued, we shall be sorry when it is concluded.

Magnet Stories: The Shepherd Lord. By Julia Corner. (Groombridge and Sons, Paternoster-row.)—In this very pretty story our young friends will find the interesting facts of the life of the "good Lord Clifford" embodied; him who, having suffered thirty years for the sins of his father, distinguished as "the butcher," who in cold blood murdered the boy Earl of Rutland, a lad of fourteen years of age, was subsequently restored to his title and estates, and won by his virtues the happy title by which the people have remembered him. Miss Corner is so intimate with historical facts, and so well known to the youthful public, that her name is a promise of pleasant reading. In the present tale she has used so slight a thread of fiction to combine the real occurrences of the past, that the "all truth" which childhood so eagerly asks for, is really found in the principal and most interesting details of this story.

THE TOILET.

(Specially from Paris.)

Fancy Toilette.—White muslin dress, the skirt trimmed with a number of narrow flounces placed on the bias, and surmounted by a headed flounce traversed by a puffing, in which a ponceau ribbon is run. Body gathered. Round waist. The sleeves have two puffs and four frills on the shoulder. Duchess-sash of white ribbon, bordered with ponceau, or whatever colour may be run in the skirt trimming. Tuscan hat, trimmed with a wreath of cherries and a black velvet bow. On the hair a Greek net of [illegible], with loops of ribbon.

Second Toilette.—Dress of [illegible], check pattern, green and blue. On the skirt a headed flounce as high as the knee. The corsage which

558

descend the bodice are whirlpool of green and blue ribbon. Body high, with a waistband and [illegible], [illegible] half wide, plaited at the top. The whole trimmed with ribbon crosses, like those on the skirt. Muslin collar and under-sleeves. *Bonnet* of the same material as the dress. Bonnet of white crinoline, trimmed with blue ribbon and white roses.

The continued warmth of the temperature, which, while I write, is almost tropical at Paris, has very [illegible] the preparations for splendid autumn toilets; and [illegible] [illegible] [illegible] with flowers, and robe of gauze, either flounced or spangled, continue to form the most charming toilets. These skirts are either trimmed with flounces, or made with a triple of skirts falling one over the other. Robes of plain white muslin, or of muslin embroidered, are worn over either white or coloured transparents, and are universally popular and becoming.

Then there are white piqués, and piqués coloured [illegible] or [illegible]; the [illegible] [illegible], silk and [illegible] grenadines, poplinettes, [illegible], and a host of other pretty materials, for industry is always making fresh efforts.

A new addition—the [illegible] [illegible]—is very graceful, whether of silk or ribbon. It has bodice [illegible] made, fastened with fancy buttons, which may be in [illegible] or [illegible], and forms a corselet in front, fastening at the side with two ends [illegible] with lace or quilled ribbon. The [illegible] is made in two shades, which may be black and violet, [illegible] and white, mauve and white, according to the shades of the dress, or that [illegible] in the toilet. I recommend it as a very graceful innovation, breaking up the uniformity of white robes, and transforming a simple and [illegible] into [illegible] toilette. One sees the most charming and elegant robes at the various balls. Here are two or three models for you: A simple robe of white [illegible] trimmed by a deep flounce, surmounted by a full ruche of [illegible] [illegible]. Corsage draped behind and before. In the hair a [illegible] of [illegible], and a ball of white [illegible] on the other. Again, a robe of very thin [illegible] muslin, the flounce lined with rose-coloured [illegible]. The other, and I have done. A robe of sky-blue silk, with six little flounces at the bottom of the skirt, each flounce [illegible] with a [illegible] of white silk; these flounces [illegible] the robe on one side, where they are finished with a bow of ribbon. The corsage is a bertha of folded *tulle illusion*, [illegible] with blue ribbon velvet; this [illegible] is surrounded with two little flounces to correspond with the trimming of the skirt, [illegible] by sprays of rose foliage, with a large full-blown white rose on the bosom and on the shoulders. Sprays of [illegible] [illegible] and their foliage, also decorate the ornaments that traverse the skirt. The coiffure is of [illegible] roses, disposed à la Grecque.

With this very radiant toilet we observed a magnificent Arab burnous of white Algerian tissue, with great [illegible] and [illegible], white and gold.

The form of bonnets has not changed with the commencement of the new season, but the ornaments offer infinite variety. The bonnets *à la Marie Stuart* are much in vogue. A pretty bonnet for demi-toilet is composed of [illegible], upon the front three [illegible] of blue [illegible] ribbon, at the side a tuft of blue [illegible], and [illegible] of the same flowers in the interior. Another, of white [illegible] ornamented with roses, with [illegible] and strings of black [illegible], is simple, but effective.

PASSING EVENTS RE-EDITED.

Philanthropy has just now taken a turn in the direction of creatures that really cannot help themselves, and are therefore not likely to be rendered more feeble and [illegible] by [illegible] [illegible]. It is pleasant to find practical men engaged in the destruction of ignorant prejudices, and proving that nothing is ultimately gained by working against Nature; that the [illegible] of creation is established in the most apparently trivial as in the mightiest of the Almighty's works, and that literally a sparrow cannot fall to the ground out of the appointed time but that defects in the great system follow. For a long series of years farmers have carried on a war of extermination against certain members of the animal world. Owls, weasels, stoats, sparrows, and moles have been regarded as their special enemies, and a price has been set upon their lives. Even [illegible] [illegible] songsters, the blackbirds and thrushes, because they sometimes stained their mellifluous throats with juice of cherries, or dipped their beaks into the luscious pear, were shot down without mercy; as if their cheery whistling and mock-notes wild were not an ample payment for the tax [illegible]. In vain men of science and humanity pointed to the [illegible] of the mischief compared with the services and the delight they rendered. The bleary eye of ignorance saw the birds pecking the buds in spring, and the marks of their dainty beaks upon the ripe fruits in autumn; but they could not understand how much of the crop had been preserved to them by the soft-billed songsters, who had destroyed few buds indeed compared with the myriads of destructive insects of which, if left to their natural work, they would have cleared the trees. In some districts, twenty years ago, the matter was not left to private [illegible]; but the churchwardens, on behalf of agricultural villages, [illegible] to pay so much per dozen for sparrows' heads; so that the destruction of these useful little birds to the wise economy of Nature was, in some seasons and in some localities, almost general. Birds in the open way were ruthlessly destroyed, and these, the greatest checks to the increase of insect-life upon the earth and under it, being in a large proportion removed, the real destroyers to corn-lands and orchard-produce have of late years so materially injured our field and garden-crops, that even thoughtless persons have begun to inquire the reason of it. In France the question has received public attention at the hands of scientific men, who have fully established the services of the sparrow, the song-birds, and other hitherto ill-used animal-friends of man; and have claimed for them, on the most practical grounds, the consideration and protection of gardeners and agriculturists. The publicity given to the inquiries of the French Commissioners has had the effect of ventilating the subject in our own provincial papers, and I find extracts from the *Gardener's Chronicle*, *Journal of Horticulture*, and other similar works, circulating up and down in country districts, all bearing evidence to the active use of hedgehogs, toads, moles, blackbirds, thrushes, and sparrows, in keeping down the rapid increase of slugs, snails, caterpillars, earth and wire-worms—the favourite food of the moles.

A practical gardener, writing in the *Journal of Horticulture*, states that he has seen a pair of sparrows with a second brood pass eight times in nine minutes from some gooseberry bushes which were infested with caterpillars to their nest, each time with caterpillars in their bills. "The insects had attacked the bushes in great force, about the first of August; on the third he perceived the sparrows busy with them; and by the eighth the caterpillars were all gone." This witness in favour of feathered friends has a kind word also for other small fry hitherto scorned and trapped wherever they could be caught, and ends his letter by saying: "We have also eight or nine hedgehogs, and about twenty toads, under glass"—an effectual guard against the depredations of beetles and other insects in green-houses.

In France another subject of great interest, in a social point of view, is being mooted and written about; nothing less than the propriety and ultimate necessity of introducing the ancient method of disposing of the dead by cremation instead of burial. Having ourselves suggested the propriety and utility of such a mode of returning earth to earth, five years before the appearance of the brochure which has awakened the attention of the French and American savants to the subject, we may be permitted to ask of our readers a dispassionate and unprejudiced consideration of the subject. The space already occupied in cemeteries and grave-yards in Great Britain is enormous, while in proportion to the increase of the population will be the increase of these silent territories, the existence of which in the neighbourhood of crowded towns, however we may plant them with trees, or make the hillocks of decay gay with flowers, are simply reservoirs of malaria and disease. We live in days when the mouldering and expensive funeral-parade wholly unnecessary for the reduction of the corpse to its primitive elements. Chemistry has simpler methods, and less repugnant to the public mind, which, after all, can never have realised the abhorrent process of this reduction in the tomb, or surely the quick, innocuous, cleanly transfer of our mortal particles back to the lap of Nature would seem a thousand times preferable to the slow, unspeakable and utterly loathsome disintegration of the grave. Almost everyone professes to be indifferent as to what becomes of the body after death. "It is unimportant," we have often heard it said, "where I am laid;" but we should like such persons to go one step further, and in the cause of health and economy of space for the living, bequeath their remains to be disposed of by cremation, and thus add the weight of intelligent example in breaking down the prejudices of the less liberal in old-established forms and ceremonies, since the difference of interment and cremation, after all, consists in so little.

C. A. W.

ANSWERS TO CORRESPONDENTS.

"The Summer Past," and "Sonnet," not up to our standard.

Poems received.—"A Quaker Burial;" "The Living Toys."

"Law of Marriage."—We decline to introduce the subject.

"The Monk's Mantle."—Pretty, but not up to par.

"Beauchamp."—We regret to tell this gentleman what we are sure his biographer is not—a hero.

P.S.—*In consequence of the temporary absence of the Editress, further answers to Correspondents are unavoidably postponed.*

Printed by [illegible], London.

MY FIRST PORTRAIT.

(By the Author of the "Photographer's Story.")

People who go out of the beaten road, wandering away to right or left, up any of the pleasant by-paths, are sure to be looked upon askant by those relations and friends who, stiff-necked, can see no thoroughfare save that where the crowd jostles and the dust rises. Probably friends and relations are in the right. A good man, in a good [illegible], should follow at the heels of something that precedes it. That is the height of its [illegible] breeding. It is only your cur who leaps the hedge and takes to the lanes. Nevertheless, for curs, there are loadstone mountains at the end of these lanes, which they cannot resist. The well-conditioned dogs do not feel the power of the magnet; the attraction for them is in the heels of the well-conditioned dogs preceding. The well-conditioned are the wisest.

I have gained little money and little fame by taking to the by-path. My uncle was senior partner in a large linen-drapery establishment. The linen-drapery business was the line of life cleared before me. Whether from the designs of the prints in stock (I think not, however, there was little in them to induce it in those days), or whether from the elegant attitudes of the young men in attendance behind the counters (I think not; I drank disgust of them, above all, drove me into the by-path), I early in life, became passionately fond of drawing. This taste was encouraged in me while a boy. My cleverness in that way was praised, and the taste fostered. When I produced a portrait of my little sister, true and yet untrue—true in giving an abstraction of her, untrue in that every detail of the face was wrong; for I did not know how to draw—when I produced this, my uncle gave me half-a-crown. I have the early sketch by me still (as I have the finished painting, the story of which I tell here), and I wonder that the obtuse man who praised it could see in it any likeness whatever to the original. It represented the notion of my sister which I had in my own mind—a possibility such as she might have been, but certainly was not. My sister ran away with a [illegible] counter-jumper. The sketch which I retain, ill-drawn as it is—Well, it could not have done that.

When I grew beyond the boy, and was just beginning to feel the weight and dignity of the name assumed by me, then I was told that I must put away this childish thing, and take to the linen-drapery counter of life. I feel again, as I recall that time, an echo of the cruel pain that I felt then. I have been stricken by no such sore wound in all my life since, the grief and the shame, and the uncertainty as to whether the talent which had come to be my sole aim might not be, after all, the mere childish pastime which they called it!

However, I need not dwell on this early struggle. Through strenuous opposition I became an artist; I took to the lane. Stones were thrown after me according to the desert of a cur. Still I met with friends. A local artist saw my sketches and took me by the hand; then I got to London, and found the kindest of friends in a great painter there. I became a student in the Academy; I went to Italy for three-quarters of a year; finally I set up as an artist in a tiny studio, in a quiet street not far from Rathbone Place, where the colour-sellers dwell. It is of an incident of my early days there that I now write.

Having taken to this by-path of the artistic profession, I was acknowledged by my friends, and [illegible] with their advice. The only part of the artist-profession which paid was portraiture. It was not so lucrative a trade as linen-drapery, but still portrait-painting might be made to pay. To this I must apply myself; all else was child's-play. Everything is child's-play which does not bring in so much money for so much work done.

I kicked against the notion of portrait-painting. Had I not my grand ideas to work out? The transformation of Medusa, the golden hair changing into serpents, the divine beauty into fatal horror? Isabella, from "Measure for Measure," in the fury of her chaste rage? [illegible] the strong, stricken with the weakness of a helpless jealousy? Virginia with the first blush called up by lewd eyes on her child-face? Peter weeping bitterly? The Christ in his garden agony? I kicked against the notion of portrait-painting.

While I yet resisted my fate, my first commission for a portrait came to me. The sketch of my Medusa was on the easel. I had been at work on it that morning, and had hit upon the indescribable expression of face of which I had dreamed for so long. The face changed as you looked at it: it was all beauty; it was all a-gleam; it was all horror; the golden hair glided and [illegible] into snakes; the warm loving light of the eyes died in the cold magnetic fascination; the sweet lips stiffened into fear, into pain, into

fluids, into a devilish composition. I was in the hour of my triumph, gulping down tears—for I did shed tears, as I think imaginative people mostly do in such moments.

Just at this time a carriage drove up to the door of the house where I lodged; I had heard it rumbling up the quiet street. The cessation of sound startled me from my reverie, and brought to an end my hurried gaping at and [illegible]. A lady was descending from the carriage as I looked out. I had no suspicion that she came to visit me. I had not yet entered upon portrait-painting, and my studio was visited by few people save brother-artists.

The small maid-of-all-work flung open my door, forgetting to knock in her trepidation.

"Please, sir, a lady wants to see you."

The lady had been left upon the stairs, but before I had time to answer she had entered.

"Good morning, Mr. Musgrave," she said. "I wish to speak with you professionally."

The door was closed, and the servant had gone. I was busy in clearing a chair for the lady to sit down.

"I would rather walk up and down," she said; "I can speak more easily so. You paint portraits?"

Here she stopped suddenly opposite my easel, and I remained silent while for a full minute she stood gazing on my "Medusa."

"What a ghastly face!" she cried. "What is the subject?" Then, without waiting for an answer, she went on: "You have imagination, I see. I don't care for the subject of the picture. You never saw that face; none could have seen it; and yet it is true. I recognize a truth in it. I interpret it according to my own fancy; so would everyone else. It has a thousand meanings; but the secret of it is just this, that there is a real touch of humanity in it."

The lady spoke in a rambling manner, as she walked restlessly to and fro. Her accent was slightly foreign, though she spoke very quickly, as people seldom speak a language not their own. Her thoughts seemed preoccupied. She appeared as if she were accustomed to talk fluently while thinking of other things. She gesticulated with her hands, and her features had a wonderful mobility, while her eyes remained dreamy and vague. She was tall and slim, and straight as an arrow; elastic, and full of exquisite life to her finger-tips. The blood came and went in her face; her nostril had changeful intonations like a voice; her black hair stirred and waved as she moved; her beautiful hands (she carried her gloves in one of them)—this, fine, long—were more expressive in their ambitious soft suppleness and contradictions than most people's faces. I never saw any person to whom the body was so little an encumbrance. It seemed merely the expression of the life-principle. She gave me an idea of spiritual sense, that she did not strike one with that intolerable obtrusion of being dressed and hidden and fettered and tortured, by which one is instantly stricken at sight of all other persons. Dress, whether of sordid flesh or diaphanous drapery, fell away from her, and left her disengaged!

"You have imagination," she said; "have you the mystery of it? Can you give it rein, and at the same time keep it well in hand?"

I stammered and blundered in answer. I felt a very secondary person in my own studio. Brought down suddenly from my enthusiasm, my pleasure in Medusa found and snubbed by this exquisite vision of life, I was bewildered and confused. This woman, with her profusion of picture, made me feel no longer a genius, but a clown.

"You paint portraits?" she asked again, still pacing up and down.

"No," I said; "I am not a portrait-painter. My aims in art are higher and bolder."

She gave a swift glance round the room. On the walls, on easels, on chairs, leaning against the wainscot, or tumbling from portfolios, were my sketches.

A motion of her hand asked me "What are these?"

"Not a single portrait," I answered.

"*All* portraits," she exclaimed with an emphasis of the first; "every one."

She pointed to a Virginia; to a Miranda, dreaming of Ferdinand; to a Marguerite, [illegible] in the church; to an Angelo, his cold blood blazing into burning lust; to a Leontes, racing by jealousy; to an Œdipus, looking his last upon the light of day.

As I explained, she said of each one, "A portrait."

I had never before observed a peculiarity—I suppose an imperfection—of my artist-talent. All of those sketches consisted of one figure only. I had not the power then, I have not the power now, of painting a dramatic scene. I should never have thought of painting the lewd eyes of Appius in the same picture with the blush on Virginia's face. Appius might have been a separate study; but the two persons, even though they thus came together as immediate cause and effect, I could not have painted upon the same canvas. I honestly confess that I approve of my own practice. An ordinary picture is to me but a collection of incongruous figures. The passion of one creature is enough to fill the whole soul of an artist while he bodies it forth. Having perfected the one figure, when he passes on to others the tone of his mind has changed—he paints in a different key. Even the sight of the complete figure, the knowledge that face is separated from face by only the space of a few inches, that drapery crosses and commixes with drapery—this knowledge would utterly prevent me from concentrating my powers on the new passion and the new figure. The crimson of Virginia's face would tone down the bestial fire in the eyes of Appius.

In the concentration of thought entirely on one passion and one face, each picture of mine was, in a sense, a portrait. As my lady said, pointing to one after another, "A portrait—a portrait." She particularly struck me forcibly for the first time.

"I want you to paint a portrait for me," she went on, as she resumed her pacings to and fro.

I was silent. The temptation was great. To have painted this glorious woman would have created a new era in my art-life.

"You must devote yourself to your work," she continued. "You shall name your own price—a hundred guineas, five hundred guineas, what you like. But until the portrait is complete you must put your hand to nothing else."

"I do not want money for such work," I answered, and I spoke from the heart, and not impulsively; as an artist, not as a young man. "I would give you money to let me paint you, if I had money."

"My poor boy!" she said, with a beautiful compassion for my enthusiasm. "It is not my own face that I want painted. It is the face of a dead man."

In my surprise I was silent for a time. Then I said, earnestly, "I will do what you will—yes; I would do anything for you."

"A dead man—a dead man—a dead man," she repeated to herself as she went to and fro.

"I am to paint," I asked, hesitatingly—"I am to paint from the—the corpse?"

"No," she answered. "Buried long ago, and lying hundreds of miles from here."

Again surprise made me silent.

"You have a likeness of him—some miniature or chalk sketch, or—"

"None," she cried. "Why should I come to you, if I had a portrait of him already?"

After a long pause of consideration, I said: "What, then, do you wish me to do?"

"You think me mad," she said. "I do not wonder at it. You have not thought of the possibility of this as I have. But it is possible; it can be done, and shall be done, and you must do it. Listen!" she went on, silencing me with a motion of the hand. "Do not speak until you have thoroughly grasped this notion. You are to paint the portrait of this dead man, whom you have never seen, whose dead face you cannot see, of whom there is no likeness left. The sole record that remains of him is one little lock of hair."

I was full of bewilderment and amazement. I had passed through extraordinary vicissitudes of feeling in the interchange of these few sentences. The sudden giving up of all my determinations against portrait-painting, the delight in anticipation of painting so exquisite a creature; the disappointment of this anticipation; the shock on the supposition that I was to paint from the face of a corpse. I cannot describe how the contrast affected me, between my first hope of having for my model this woman so beautiful in the fullness of life, and the idea of copying the stark dead face. Lastly, the blank astonishment and dismay that the lady's first explanation caused me—all these conflicting emotions struck me dumb and helpless.

"It is impossible," I said, at last. "You ask what neither I nor anyone else can do."

"It is not impossible," she cried, with another emphasis of the slender foot. "This dead man has more life for me than you have. I can see him now more plainly than I can see you. All the world is full of him to me. I see glimpses of him in other people; I hear echoes of his voice in other voices; I distinguish a foot-fall like his among all the thousand foot-falls of the streets. Pictures on canvas and on walls take for me the outline of his features. His face starts out of the darkness; his figure haunts me in long avenues of dreary country places. In crowded rooms, I see his reflection in the glasses. What do you talk of life and death? For me this man alone lives, and all others are ghosts."

"You can draw?" I asked. "If ever so little, you can draw?"

"Not a stroke. I have tried to learn .... Should I come to you if I could do for myself what I demand of you?"

"You must learn to draw," I said. "I will teach you."

"I cannot learn," she cried vehemently. "That is denied me by the curse of God. Do you think I have not tried all means before I sought out you? I have had better masters than you can be. You are not to be my tutor, sir, but my slave. I will have you do this thing for me."

The lady was in the right. It was more impossible for me to disobey her commands than to attempt the impossibility she commanded. After vainly combating the impracticability, I came to the business inquiry, how the thing was to be done.

"Are there any relatives of this dead man whom I can see?" I asked. "Anyone with any faintest resemblance to him?"

"None."

"Any chance likeness of him in another person? Chance likenesses are very common."

"None; at least none that can serve your purpose."

"Impossible!" I said again.

"You artists, whether you write or whether you paint," she broke out bitterly, "you artists pretend to a magical insight. You conjure up an Othello, and you say this is the man whom Shakespeare saw—this, and no other. This creature of a poet's brain, which never had an existence, which comes to you through a few antiquated words, half of which you cannot understand, this shadow of a shadow you fashion forth. Look at your own pictures;—Miranda you call this one, Marguerite that; and you say that they are the veritable creatures which Shakespeare and Goethe brought into being. I tell you to paint a man who really lived on this earth. I am here to be questioned—I am here to cross-examine—to tear out of my heart every word he ever spoke to me—to tell you what he was to me. Because I saw him entirely. That is nothing; I tell you to paint him so. I knew and know him. Look into my eyes; your insight will find something of him there. Look at my hand; it has clung to his until some form and soul of his must be left indelibly behind. Look at my smile; I learned the trick of his in days gone by. Listen to my voice, transpose the treble into bass; mine is an echo weak echo of his. Take me as I am—I am not my own, but his: I am a part of him. I am your book; study me. I will describe; I will answer ten thousand questions. I will sing to you the songs that he loved, I will read to you the reading that he approved, I will tell you of our talk, I will show you his letters, you shall see the one lock of hair. I say that it is *not* impossible; and you *shall* do it."

I can give but a faint impression of the torrent of her words here. I have put into her mouth but stilted common-places. I cannot help it. Her rapid utterance was not so much language as vocal thought. As one saw in her neither drapery nor flesh, but life; so one read thought and passion, not speech, in what she uttered.

"Now, you will paint me this portrait," she said, with recovered calmness, after a long silence.

"I will try," I said.

"I will not ask you to be secret. I will trust you. I am more certain that you will not betray me than if you had sworn the most solemn oaths. The first thing to tell you," she continued, "is my history; how I came to know this dead man, what we were to each other. There is that in the dead face. You must be told it."

I cannot disclose the details of her story. There were no names mentioned. I never learned her name. The story was a sad, not an uncommon, one: A young girl sold to an old man for money; a guilty love; the passenger had gone to India, with his regiment, and had died there, shot through the heart in battle, about a year before. This was all.

"There is *that* in the dead face," she said, and, as I write it, I recall Tennyson's description of Lancelot:

"The great and guilty love he bare the Queen,
In battle with the love he bare his lord,
Had marred his face, and marked it ere his time.
Another sinning on such heights with one,
The flower of all the west and all the world,
Had been the sleeker for it; but, in him,
His mood was often like a fiend, and rose
And drove him into wastes and solitudes
For agony, who was yet a living soul."

The lady, after her first burst of passion, went on with a wonderful calmness. Her strange determination had evidently been formed for a long time, and she had thought out all the details with a morbid acuteness. The story told, she drew from her bosom a locket, in which was a curl of light brown hair. She confided to me, in the next place, the Christian name of the dead man. He could have had no other name save that, it seemed to her; this was another link in the chain of circumstantial evidence.

She described to me accurately his person, his manner, his tastes. She had the talent of describing. The picture that she had in her mind she could present to another. How she did this I cannot tell. I have said that the thought came through her language so vividly that one took no note of the words. Her description was like a sketch. But not only by voice, but by action of undulating hands, of emphatic foot, of all the light and shadow of her expressive face, she gave life to the image she sought to impress.

A shadow gathered itself together before me, dim, vague; its features shrouded, its figure wrapped in gloom—an indistinct form, but still a form. As by long study of a poet's writing one feels his creation gradually coming forth—such and no other, having a personality entirely its own; so a new image, distinct from all others, began to rise in my imagination as she spoke. How true or how false I cannot say. When two men read the same poet precisely alike! What poet has ever said to the artist, "You have made my creature visible to others as I see it."

On this first day she was careful, I think, to give me only a general idea of the man I was to paint—the history, the name, the light brown hair, the description of him as a whole. Just as a lover, seeing his future mistress for the first time, carries away with him a vague impression of her as separated off from all the other girls, and yet scarcely knows the colour of her eyes or the contour of her cheek; so I gained at this time but a general impression of the person she described. The lover learns afterwards his mistress by heart, trait by trait, line by line; and thus I learned this terrible figure, until at length I could see nothing, paint nothing, but the one face.

The lady's carriage returned for her. She shook hands frankly with me, saying, "I trust you. Remember you put hand to no work till I come to you to-morrow morning. Think of my portrait; dream of it; let it never leave your mind for a moment!"

When the sound of her carriage had died away I turned from the window, and took down my Medusa from the easel. What a change had come over me in the short time since I sobbed over my success in her beautiful terror! That picture was turned towards the wall. I sat down before my blank easel, thinking, thinking. The lady had had no need to say, "Let it never leave your mind for a moment."

"A spirit passed before my face. It stood still, but I could not discern the form thereof." So it is written in the book of Job; and such a terror of the formless presence as came upon the seer there came upon me. All day, whether in the streets or at home, I was haunted by this shape, "If shape it might be called, that shape had none." I was eager to grasp it; to force it to give up to me its hidden lineaments; to assume some definite form, false or true. I could not and dare not. I longed to take my pencil and compel out of this shadow some visible presentment. The commands laid upon me by the lady prevented this. I had entered upon the work. I felt that this was a first stage that must be gone through. I had laid aside the notion of impossibility, and felt the artist's all-absorbing and patient desire of success. To think—that was all I could do as yet; the time for working had not yet come. All night I dreamed of it; never for a moment did it quit definiteness. There it lay, an embryo—to grow into form only through painful and weary time.

I say that I had given up the notion of the impossibility of the thing. To a reader of this story, laying the case plainly before him, this will seem absurd. To hire out and discern a dead woman at the price of so many guineas would be understandable; but that, after consenting to undertake this work, I should permit myself into belief of the remotest hope of any success, must seem incomprehensible. The reader argues from a different stand-point to that which I occupied. The project once entertained, the previous notion of its impossibility was shut out. What had taken its employ was the consideration henceforth, not the uselessness of employing any means at all. I was, as it were, in a dream, which, though logical in its own boundaries, could be fitted on to no premises of the daylight world—not an uncommon state of mind with the artist.

At the same hour on the following morning the lady came again. We met as old friends, and the entreaty of each upon the business in hand.

"You have obeyed me?" she asked, with one of her sad, winning smiles. "You have not been painting?"

"I have obeyed you; and will obey you to the very letter in all you command me."

"You artists," she said, "as I have read and know, have your early simple lessons in the drawing of the human face. There are distinct types of face, markedly distinct from each other, to one or other of which, or to some recognizable blending of which, all human faces may be assigned. These types you remember by mere simple lines, which of course you keep by heart. Now, draw these for me."

This I did, and from the hasty sketches thus made, one was selected and put aside as the primary type (without individuality, without expression) of the face wanted.

Again she spoke of the "temperaments." Of these she had read in some old book, and said she believed in them as guides in the matter in hand. In coloured crayons I made another series of sketches, and from these again one was chosen and put aside.

The day was far spent by this time. While I had been sketching she had been impressing on me prominent points of the history told in brief the day before. Of the family of the dead man, of the manner of his bringing up, of the scenes in which he had lived, of the changes which he had gone through, she spoke, giving me, according to her belief, not words, but her own thoughts.

When she left, she again laid her commands on me that I must on no account attempt to draw the face—to draw it at all—as yet. One day intervened before her next visit. During that space I had in some sort assimilated, as I remember, my first day's direct impression with the sketches selected on the second visit.

Again, at the next sitting, I drew sketches. The passions, we artists, she had heard, had definite expression for each passion—coarse and general hints, no doubt, but still having in them some truths; such a downward curve of the lip for such a passion; such a contraction of the eye-lid for another; such a wrinkling of the forehead or puckering of the cheeks for another.

I sketched all the old crude formulas—mapping out of the emotions into hyperbolical figures, not unlike the mapping out of the stars on a celestial globe. Then I softened down these exaggerated signs. I illustrated by my own old sketches. I showed the difference between love in the face of a Miranda and of a Juliet. I contrasted the base jealousy of a Leontes with the demoniac possession of an Othello. I put side by side child-Cleopatra blushing under the first gaze of Antony, and Virginia. Degrees of passion trembling into coarseness; the virtue that is vice; the love that is hate; the pride that is shame—such subjects were out of our morning's lesson.

Then we passed on from the fleeting expressions of passion, which pass over the countenance like shadows over hills, to that settled resemblance which any one passion long obeyed will stamp upon the features. Child-Cleopatra, in her quasi-innocence, was contrasted with the brazen harlot in whose lap Antony bartered away his life.

Upon the chosen type of face, these fleeting expressions of passion, these settled impressions of passion, were tried. Something came out of this. "So he looked at such a time"—and the incident was told. "Not like that—this—rather. Now it is better." All this; and the dead face seemed to stir within its grave.

* * * *

I cannot write the history of day by day. The ingenuity of my patroness in gathering together every smallest detail which might help to bring home to me the character and the person of her dead lover, is the most marvellous quality that I have ever known.

One day she brought a collection of engravings—some old and shabby, some new and tawdry, some scarce and fine, evidently a collection made through years, gathered together month by month, from all places, and with always the same object. In some figure in each of these there was a certain likeness to him—here the position, there the turn of the head, there the eyes, there the smile. And these scraps of likeness she had the rare power of making me see, showing me in what the likeness consisted, where it began and where it ended. These scraps she would make me copy again and again.

Another day she brought a portion of his

letters. She showed me the writing and the differences in it, according to the varying rapidity of it, and according to the emotions influencing him while he wrote. Here was a letter blotted with tears; another full of the wildest gaiety; another acrid with jealousy and distrust. She read these letters to me, changing her intonations. "Thus he would have spoken this. So he would have flung his arms about. This is something like his laugh."

She read to me books that he had liked, and told me the observations he had made upon certain passages. She sang to me songs that she had sung to him—told me how this had made him solemn, this brilliant and gay—how this had always filled his eyes with tears. One song in particular was his favourite; and this she was constantly crooning. To me, now, that strange episode in my life comes back set to the music of this song.

Day after day passed by. Almost every day, never suffering more than one day to intervene, she came to me. Whether true or false, I gradually created in my imagination a distinct picture of the dead man. Every story she told of him fitted itself to this image. In my dreams I seemed to have revelations of him. The creation of my brain was complete. More distinct than of any ideal character, was the image now impressed upon my mind. Not with the passion of one especial moment upon him—the crimson blush of Virginia, the transforming agony of Medusa, the wretchedness of Leontes eyeing the "paddling palms"—but as a veritable human being, to be portrayed, when the time came, under influence of any passion, or at ease from all.

Hitherto I had been commanded to abstain from attempting the portrait. At last the converse fiat was issued. For one week the lady was to remain absent; at the end of that week, she was to see the portrait.

I painted my picture, and the lady came. A burst of tears; an agony of wringing hands and bowed head and writhing body; not a grieving woman, but grief itself. The portrait was a failure. Utterly unlike. All the labour and the pain thrown away. No hope left.

* * * * *

Yet it came to be acknowledged, after the first shock of disappointment, that my unfortunate picture was not *totally* unlike. It was impossible, after all my study, that it should be so. There were portions of it in which some echo, some far-off shadow, of the reality was to be discovered.

We set to work with renewed hope.

I thought it strange then, I think it strange still, that my failure in the first attempt was so great. I knew very much more of this man whom I had never seen, than of any person whose portrait I have since taken. I knew from a thousand sources of chance likeness, of imitation, of description, of shrewd conjecture, of flashing intuition, what this person was like. What do portrait-painters usually paint but the best clothes of their sitters? The glossy coat and spotless shirt-front are not more mere dress than the sunny smile and the prim mouth and the dull wateriness of the set eye. I knew this dead man, his strengths and his weaknesses, his loves and his hates, his great sorrows and his great sins. Of no other people whom I have painted have I known more than that they had such a facial angle, such features, such a blemish to be toned down, such a half-beauty to be petted into completeness.

However, we set to work a-new. I painted now with the lady by my side. Why should I dwell on the details of this time? I can give no idea of how the portrait was painted. It is sufficient to say that I did at length succeed in achieving some faint and distant likeness, having more of death than of life in it—a galvanised ghastliness of expression, a cruel rigidity of outline, a sickly pallor of colour—yet being, as some distorted reflection of the reality, recognisable by my monitress.

When this was achieved, I learned for the first time that a sister of the dead man was alive, and in London, and to be seen by me. Why had this not been told me before, I asked. Because the sister was unlike the brother, I was told, and would have been of no service to me until this time. One look only of the sister claimed any kinship with the brother's countenance. Under sudden surprise there was a lifting of the eyebrows, a compression of the lips, a steady glance of the eyes, which I should now be able to seize upon and appreciate.

How I was to see the sister was in this fashion: There was a *déjeûner* about to be given at some grand house on the river-side. For this the lady obtained a voucher for me. Here, she undertook to show me the sister, and to call up in her face the expression upon which I was to seize.

I went to this *déjeûner*. The lady pointed out to me by a silent gesture and a momentary glance of the eye the woman whom I was to observe. This sister was a blonde, handsome, haughty, impassive. A crowd of young men surrounded her whereseover she turned.

I never lost sight of this woman. My lady too hovered in her neighbourhood. My lady, as the other, had a crowd of worshippers about her. They seemed to me two rival queens.

I had no enjoyment in the scene. The incongruity of seeking in the midst of this frivolous gaiety for the expression of a dead man's face was constantly present with me.

The afternoon wore away wearily. I was conscious of my shabby clothes and my haggard face, so different from those of the men around me. I felt on an equality with my lady as we laboured at our terrible work in my little studio; here I felt how far we were separated. She trifled with the men, she smiled upon them, she talked and laughed and listened. Her eyes were brilliant, her colour went and came. She whispered, she sighed, she coquetted.

I was dissatisfied. I thought of the painted death-in-life upon my easel. I thought of the reason we were both there; and I mistrusted and misjudged her.

Suddenly she turned upon me her eyes. She rose from her garden seat and crossed over to the blonde sister. My lady extended her hand, and smiled a winning smile, and spoke soft words. On the face of the other there came the look I was to watch for—a lifting of the eyebrows, a compression of the lips, a steady glance of the cruel eyes. She put aside the extended hand, swept the ground with a low bow, and passed on. My lady turned to me with a crimson face, waving dismissal.

That was enough. The one look completed for me the picture studied for so long.

* * * * *

And now to end my story. The portrait was finished. My money was paid me. On the next morning the lady was to take away the picture.

The lady never came—why I cannot tell. On that morning a lady in high life died suddenly; whether my lady or not I do not know, for I had never heard her name.

THE LAND OF THE LIVING.

BY MRS. ABDY.

"Beautiful was the reply of a venerable man to the question whether he was still in the land of the living: 'No; but I am almost there.'"

Not yet; though the fiat I feel has gone forth,
 Not yet has the summons been spoken;
The frail, feeble link that connects me with earth
 Not yet has been shattered and broken.
The kindred and friends of my earlier years
 Have long in the churchyard been lying;
I fain would depart from this valley of tears,
 And pass from the land of the dying.

A few of the friends of my manhood are spared;
 Alas! they are dull and repining:
They talk of hopes withered, of talents impaired,
 Worn spirits, and vigour declining.
I suffer like them—yet I do not complain,
 For God the assurance is giving
That soon shall I lay down my burden of pain,
 And haste to the land of the living.

I weep not for those whom on earth I loved well,
 They are only removed to a distance;
The shroud, and the pall, and the funeral knell
 Were their passports to deathless existence.
Like them, may I soar to the realms of the blest,
 And join in the angels' thanksgiving;
In the land of the dying sink calmly to rest,
 And wake in the land of the living!

"THOU ART THE WAY, THE TRUTH, AND THE LIFE."

BY BEATRICE.

By each sting of daily care,
Each anxiety I bear,
By the struggles of a heart
Loath with worldly joys to part,
By the inward longing love
Of a purer life above,
Lord, I truly hope and pray
Thou art teaching me the *way!*

By each hand of burning pain,
Trampling fierce o'er heart and brain;
By each flood of bitter tears,
Bathing all life's fevered years;
By the throes of anguish born
Of forgetfulness, or scorn—
Severed bonds of love and youth—
Thou art teaching me the *truth!*

By the closely-knitted sod,
Over those long gone to God;
By the nearer touch of woe,
When the mocking head lies low;
Through the "hidden path" I tread,
Ever by thy mercy led,
Trust I still amid the strife,
Thou art leading me to *life!*

KATE.

BY ANNE A. FREMONT.

She loves me truly, my noble Kate!
 Her pure eyes fondly look in mine,
And the vile rust of pride and hate,
 That in the world-struggle will somehow twine
 Round the human heart, and choke divine
And purer feelings, dies fast away,
As her head on my throbbing breast I lay;

Yes, well she loves me, my charming Kate,
 Her brown eyes tenderly glance in mine,
And, clasping her hand, I feel that fate
 Has one bright star that will calmly shine,
 Though adverse winds and black clouds combine
To blot it from out my darken'd sky,
And my heart gains peace from her loving eye.

Aye, thine is love indeed, dear Kate,
 When my soul to earth too fondly clings,
Thy very presence doth elevate,
 It unto purer heavenly things,
 Like the close-heard beating of angel wings;
As woman to man should ever be,
Help-meet, counsellor, is Kate to me!

ROSE CHERI.

Early, very early, on a summer Sunday morning, in 1855, I was wandering near one of the hidden country roads about Paris, when a gracious—oh such a gracious—lady passed me, the shadow of the trees above adding a new beauty to her sweet presence. The face was as fair and open as that of a pure English girl; the blue eyes, just turning towards grey, were full of that grave gentleness which tells of troubles long since past, but not ungenerously forgotten, while the entire countenance seemed wholly in harmony with the peaceful Sunday nature all around.

This lady carried a Book of the Hours, as she glided, rather than walked, past me; and I saw that the hands which held the volume were exquisitely beautiful and refined.

A moment and she was gone, nearer than I by every step, to the village-church—the old, broken, ill-patched Norman church.

I knew her face somewhere; the recollection was not painful, yet assuredly far from joyous. Who was she? A public character I felt sure. The calm, self-possessed, shy way in which she had passed me would have told me, had I never seen the lady before that divine morning, that she was accustomed to audiences more important than one unobtrusive fellow in a lane.

Who was she? First, where was I? At Passy! Ah!—it was Rose Chéri, the lady who has done more to raise her profession of actress into reverence and good repute than any comedian before or since the date when she conquered the Parisian public.

It is only six years since I saw her; and then she was but thirty. Thirty—and she had been famous through ten pleasant years—and now she is dead! That gentle right hand, which seemed to speak, it was so gracious, will no more help the sick and poverty-stricken people of Passy. She would go into a sick-room, and confer as much good by her own pleasant and cheerful presence as she bestowed in substantial charity.

"All the poor at Passy knew her." This is her best epitaph.

And how did she die?—this gracious actress; this kind, beneficent lady? By tending her little child through its illness. The anxiety and toil she had to endure during this little one's malady paved the way to diphtheria, and this cruel and occult disease has killed Rose Chéri in the very perfection of her life.

We have here in England such prejudices against the private characters of French actresses—and perhaps only too justly—that it were unjust to let the occasion of this great comedian's death pass without some notice of a life which has done much to ennoble the French stage, and prove that the woman who respects herself, no matter what her place be in this world, will by most men be respected. Rose Chéri had this advantage over Rachel: she was loved and reverenced; Rachel was never reverenced. Both dead, men compare their remembrances of the two women, and perhaps pray Heaven that they may themselves keep virtuous.

About thirty-five years ago, a troop of nomadic actors and actresses overran a small theatrical French circuit. The troupe had this in common (though whether it was an advantage or not may be a question) they all belonged to one family—the Cizos. The courageous leader of the little band was Jean Baptiste Cizos, who was at that time about twenty-two years of age. However, he was not alone in the directorship, being very materially helped in his small state-dignity by Sophie Juliette, his wife, who, being several days older than her husband, may have considered herself more than justified in exercising that wifely control, and admirable management, to both of which qualities French wives have a tendency, to the benefit or disadvantage of the husband as the case may be.

Jean of course played all the "leading" business for gentlemen, Sophie every character for the "leading lady;" Madame Sophie's two pretty sisters played seconds and thirds to Madame Sophie herself, while the husbands of these sisters stood similarly disposed towards Jean Baptiste. These six, together with fathers and fathers-in-law, mothers and mothers-in-law, and several old relations, made up the troupe; which certainly gained this honourable distinction, that people spoke quite as well of them, if not better, behind their backs than they did before their faces; for the entire family persistently clung to the belief that debt was disgraceful.

In the various histories of Rose Chéri which abound, there are no more pleasant chapters than those devoted to praising this straightforward family company of comedians. If the receipts were good—ben, the dinners were good also; if the house presented that beggarly account of empty benches which makes a manager's face so blank as they are, the family took onion-soup and very plain bread; and instead of complaining of this fare, they flavoured it with that hope which is almost as good as a king's feast.

We, in our conventionality, pity roving actors and their aptitude at finding lean purses in their pockets—if ever they carry purses at all; but let us think of the hope ever present in the midst of these little groups of wanderers, together with the exciting change from day to day, and perhaps if we weigh our monotony and daily comfort against the happiness of the strolling players, they will not cause it to kick the beam.

To continue: The Cizos were happy even when they were unfortunate. Nor were they often without means; for as the theatre is an institution in France, the chief opponent the little company had was fine weather, when, it being equally a French institution to get all the sunlight possible, the theatre was deserted, and the fields were dotted with impromptu pic-nic parties; at which times Jean, royal-impressario as he was, either took cheap pleasure also in the fields and woods, exhibiting them to the little company as though they were new plays to be studied, or—be painted; for Jean was no mean artist, and his palette was frequently his refuge from an attack of managerial misfortunes.

The first child given to the strolling manager and his wife was Rose-Marie, the heroine of this notice. The mother (whom we need not say was far above average womanhood since her daughter grew to be so noble a creature), though an actress, would not succumb to the French plan of putting children out to nurse. She would and did suckle her first-born: the cradle was always brought down to the theatre, a place found for it at the wings, and madame would always nurse it between her "calls." This pleasant custom gave birth to a most preposterous anecdote when Rose Chéri had become the rage. It was declared that on one occasion the child was not only brought down to the theatre, but left there, and the loss was not discovered till the family were half way towards their next encampment.

What! would a mother forget her little one, and her first-born, during a journey of some miles? Preposterous. There is not a matron in the four kingdoms will believe such a statement.

Before she was five years of age, "well-rounded" as the French say, Rose Chéri had been before the footlights; beyond which her little blue eyes, and dance, wavy hair, created infinite emotion amongst all the women who saw the child. The plain, simple, country people liked to see her dance, and delighted to hear her lisp the few words of a ballad; but that which enraptured them was the child's smile. They always frantically applauded the smile.

Do you know that smile of a fair, blue-eyed, little innocent coquette of five? No! *Eh bien*, your social education is not complete.

So great was the success of the little child, that the entire infantine body of the last generation of this travelling company of comedians were drilled to appear before the public. But nobody approached little Rose Marie in popularity. None of her cousins, neither her brother nor sister, could shake the popular fealty; and had she not been charitable almost as soon as she could stretch forth her hands, the other little ones would never have possessed so many bouquets as they did; for in French provincial theatres, of even the commonest kinds, the bouquet is an institution.

Two or three years being past, the Cizos children absolutely aspired to opera-comique; and the more comic the opera the more the young mothers of the audience were moved to tears—tears in French provincial and perhaps metropolitan theatres being sufficiently prevalent.

But meanwhile Madame Cizos' common-sense was not asleep. The children might be very admirable in opera-comique, but that was no reason they should not be able to read and write: so Rose Marie, and the other little ones, were regularly marched off to the parish-school of any place at which the company had pitched their gay tents. The little ones had as many different schoolmistresses as audiences. This variety must have been delightful!

School over, madame taught her little ones to work and cook, and look after the house, and even their landlord's garden: for perhaps the honest lady knew that half the carelessness and disorder of life is but the necessary fruit of a badly-managed childhood. The honest couple Cizos seem to have devoted themselves to that work which is, perhaps, the very justice and poetry of marriage—the unselfish and unceasing endeavour honestly to raise the children above the social state of their parents, to do their duty by the little ones, knowing that the parents rather than the state are answerable to heaven for its human gifts.

Another year or so, and the wise, homely mother, projecting herself into a future in which her eldest child might fail as an actress, had the little girl taught music: so that had Rose Chéri, when she had grown up, failed as an actress—as child-comedians too frequently do—the girl would not have been without a profession. Rose Chéri owed that debt which even her love and reverence could not repay—the gratitude a child feels towards an unselfish, wise mother.

So for years the little ones gained their bread, and partly that of the parents. Sometimes they played in "real" theatres, at other times in barns, elegantly got up with evergreens and lime-tree branches; while on one especial occasion the children performed in Delavigne's tragedy, founded upon the massacre of Edward the Fourth's children, on a stage which under ordinary occasions was a billiard-table! The tragedy was followed by "Tom Thumb"—also played by the tragedians. These young people were not proud, and never threw up their parts, as some of their ill-governed elders are, it is said, in the habit of doing. "The Swiss Cottage" was a great favourite. Imagine the fair-haired little child marching on as a drummer, and singing that tremendously martial couplet—

"Vive le vin, l'amour, et le tabac
Voilà, voilà, voilà le refrain du bivouac."

Little Rose Cizos was Proteus. She was ready for any rôle. A drummer to-night, on the following evening she helped the big people in the choruses of "Masaniello" (imagine "Masaniello" in a barn!) and did, perfectly unaided, the whole of the affecting ballet in the first act of that work—though as a rule this performance at the grand opera commands the service of twelve important dancers, to say nothing of the entire *corps de ballet*.

The charming "at-home" condition of the little company at this time is delightful to contemplate. On one occasion a very wet holiday has induced Manager Cizos to post the particulars of a performance for that evening. Suddenly out comes the evening sun. The sky is blue, and there is not the shadow of expectation of an audience left. Under these circumstances what is to be done? The theatrical ukase has been promulgated; managerial honour demands that it shall be carried out. What is to be done? Bah! the honest company of players and the bucolic audience are hand in hand. "Come," says Monsieur le Maire—that great personage in little French towns—"Come, you and the little ones often amuse us; let us amuse you for once. Bring everybody out into the fields, and we will dine like one happy family."

To close the door of the theatre, down comes the bill, and the children have a run in the fields, which must be quite as delicious as singing in even the most charming comic or grand serious opera ever composed.

There is another delightful little anecdote of this primitive dramatic life. A little piece is "in full activity," as our authority has it, when Anna, Rose's sister, remembers she has forgotten a letter she ought to have in her pocket. The poor child trembles, and confides her trouble to her elder sister Rose, who immediately exhibits much mental disturbance. And what then happens? All the simple country audience are in a taking, and the most active making himself the least unimportant, in a grandiloquent speech addresses M. Cizos on the part of the auditory, and hopes nothing is the matter. M. Cizos, in an equally grandiloquent speech, informs the audience of the truth, with the gravity of a Roman senator announcing a defeat.

"What, is *that* all!" says the spokesman. "Let her go and get it, and *begin all over again!*"

This was done, and the audience never applauded more heartily than on this particular evening.

Such was Rose Chéri's life. By the honesty of her parents, it was her happiness to reap the harvest of being admitted into the purest French society, and here it was the future actress must have acquired that knowledge of refined life which made her such a perfect lady on the stage, and possessed her with that beautiful ease and captivation of motion which was as natural to her as her gentle, loving face.

It was about this time that the stupid pun was made which induced the father to change the young actress's name. "Cizos" has precisely the pronunciation of the French for scissors ("*ciseaux*"), and somebody in the pit, after seeing the sisters Rose and Ann play in a dialogue, was witty or stupid enough to cry out, "*Quelle jolie paire de ciseaux!*" (Cizos) "What a pretty pair of scissors!"—which calembourg so disgusted the father, that he decided Rose should appear in future as Rose Chéri—a term which, it need not be said, is of very common use throughout France amongst the members of a family.

The first intimation the father had of the coming greatness of his daughter was given by the composer Loïsa Puget, who saw her in a little piece long since forgotten. The lady urged Jean Cizos to take his daughter to Paris. His heart beat, but his countenance fell, as he scanned the paltry means at his disposal. Frankly he told Loïsa Puget of his want of means and of patronage. The lady smiled, then gave him an introduction to one of those despots of the French drama, a Parisian manager. And so the family realised their little all, and came to Paris.

Before that Paris director are spread out all the weak, or impassioned, or foolish provincial criticisms, religiously gathered and believed in by the simple and not over-talented father and mother. But monseigneur is not moved to read any of them—in fact, he seems to grow grander as he looks on these feeble records of past successes. However, monseigneur the director allows the young person to make an attempt. The permission is of no great value, but the Cizos believe Fortune herself is in the house!

A fortnight after Rose Chéri made her first appearance upon the Paris stage, under unusually disadvantageous circumstances, in a worn-out piece by Scribe, and in a character created by a dashing actress. The poor child had never been dashing. She had been true to a deep, sweet, loving nature. Timid, modest, poorly clothed, the little provincial was received coldly by the public of the great "Gymnase." The style was utterly new. Style has no set rules; the public are capricious often, yet conservative as frequently, and Rose Chéri failed signally. She played a second night—was then dismissed.

As with Rachel so with Rose Chéri—both failed utterly on their first nights, and on the very same stage. Her failure was a terrible blow to the poor family. They had staked their all upon this chance, which, with sickening hearts, they saw fade into nothingness. They were utterly without means in the great city. They could not return to their old provincial haunts, and, singularly enough, this very indigence was the indirect means of saving the family. Unable to quit Paris, the hapless father made frantic efforts to live, to exist within its walls. Theatre after theatre was tried in vain; all the doors were closed against the poor girl, and Samson even told her she had everything to learn. Here once more existed a similarity between Rose Chéri and Rachel; for Samson had said precisely the same thing to the beautiful and terrible Jewess.

On the father struggled. They must live, and Rose was the only one of them with sufficient talent to gain bread in the capital for the unfortunate family. *Bread*—yes, that is the literal term; for only after the most desperate efforts did the father obtain what can hardly be called a preengagement of his daughter at the theatre in which she had already appeared.

There is a kind of theatrical position common to Paris theatres of which we know nothing in London. When an actor falls ill or out of temper in our theatres, some one and a book becomes his substitute. In Paris there are always retained subordinates, who play what is called the "en cas;" that is, the actor or actress is expected to learn all the rôles which he or she could by any means play upon an emergency; and thus, by these means, the absurdity of "reading a part" is never committed. Rose Chéri was engaged to play the "leading lady en cas." Her salary was fifteen shillings a week. The poor child had never passed the theatre in which she had made her début without weeping at its failure; now, once more belonging to it, she wept for joy.

She set to work to study all the chief lady rôles of the Gymnase repertoire.

Six weeks—six long weeks passed, and she had not appeared on the stage. Suddenly a Mdlle. Nathalie fell out with an author who had just produced a piece for the Gymnase; and, as a consequence, she would not continue to play the character created for her. She did not especially say "I won't go on the stage;" but, as she was taken ill precisely five minutes before the time at which the curtain was to rise, the inference is that her indisposition was rather wilful than physical. In continuo there is no time to re-make the bill, and so the stage-manager posts up the scheme of stairs to the fifth-floor on which the Chéris live. Rose has studied the new part, with little hope of making it available, but without despair.

The unknown little actress, at fifteen shillings a week, has saved the polite Gymnase from a riot, though not from a "misunderstanding." It is necessary to apologise for the substitution of the future queen of French comedy, in the place of Mdlle. Nathalie. Nathalie the public for some minutes will have. Useless is it that the manager says the lady is ill. A stout gentleman in the pit contradicts the assertion that he has just seen her in an open carriage. Manager says stout gentleman has been "the victim of a mistaken identity." Public sides with stout gentleman, who is victorious. "But the piece will be played," says manager; "a young person will play Mdlle. Nathalie's character." "Bah!" says public, "we will hiss your young person." "If she merits it," says astute manager; "if not, you are too noble, gentlemen" (manager does not say also "ladies," thereby inferring he is quite sure they are not counting any of the distribution), "you are too noble to refuse your approbation."

Here public applauds manager. They would hiss him were they told that their satisfaction arose from the fact of his having got the better of them. We mortals are such contrary human creatures.

Meanwhile, here is poor little Rose Chéri, aged seventeen, trembling behind the curtain.

Happily, Henriette, the *rôle* in question, is in tears and sorrow when she first appears on the stage, and the public applaud, slightly, as the good acting, which is absolute reality. The public listen. Gradually the young lady gains confidence. The sweet voice we all know so well grows brighter, and is heard to exquisite advantage; fear gradually passes away, and the people begin to murmur of the purity of look, and smile, and movement of this new actress. The public have seen nothing like it. Mdlle. Nathalie is known, to say the least of it, and that elder lady is absolutely audacious; whereas this new comedian is like a daughter or sister speaking and speaking before one.

Then those gentle blue eyes tremblingly look towards the public; the smallest boldness. At last, all her movements—that paralysis of power—gone, she begins to use the speaking right hand, which has never yet had a rival.

The first act ends, and the manager says: "Very well."

All the Claque are there, "looking about sharp," for they know how much depends on this night.

In the second act Rose Chéri is more than herself, if that can be. In studying the part she has found interpretations which Nathalie would have despised. These she gently lays before critic and the public.

But they would not look before the curtain rises. At the end of the second act comparisons with Nathalie have ceased; she is less skilled in the character, they say, than the new actress.

Well, at the end of the play there was another act—enthusiastic, not malignant. All the house was calling for the "new actress."

"What is your name, dear child?" says the manager. He did not even know her birth.

"Rose Cizos," says the victorious girl.

This name the manager protests against.

"They called me Rose Chéri in the provinces," she says.

"That will do," returns the manager, and he goes before the curtain, speaks in the midst of a dead silence, a roar of applause follows his words, and "Rose Chéri" is given to the world.

Nathalie gets well again in no time, rushes to the theatre, and vigorously demands her character back again. She has lost the battle though; but, riotously indignant in defeat, she appeals for restitution to the law, which, more candid than polite, tells mademoiselle she has been treated very properly.

Then the managers of all the other houses came trooping after Rose Chéri—all those who had turned from the pleading father and daughter were now, figuratively, at the young actress's feet. Even the great French Comedy sends its ambassador up those five flights of stairs; but he came down them with little satisfaction.

"Name your own conditions," says the ambassador.

"I shall not quit the Gymnase," said Rose Chéri; and she never did. No money, no interest, not even Royal entreaty could draw her from the theatre in which she made so great a name.

Her fame spread with greater rapidity, and within three years of her *début* she received a thousand pounds from Mr. Mitchell, of the St. James's, for a six-weeks' engagement, which, by the way, nearly sent Scribe into fits; for that autocratic author would have his Gymnase pieces played, and was satisfied with no casts in which Rose did not shine.

She never left the Gymnase. She loved it. She married the director of that theatre, M. Montigny, and when evil days fell upon that house during the revolution of 1848, she sold her jewels to keep up its prestige, worked night after night for months throughout the provinces, and regularly sent her gains in order to maintain the credit of the house.

It is impossible to describe Chéri's acting. The character that she most victoriously created, in late years, was the *Baronne d'Ange*, in Alexandre Dumas's fils' play of "Le Demi-monde." As all my readers know, the heroine of this play is a fallen woman of high intellect, who seeks to raise herself, by marriage, to a respectable position. In this savage yet pitiable endeavour she is foiled by Olivier de Jalin, the very photograph of the new school of better-ordered young Frenchmen. It is beyond the pen to give a sketch of Chéri's treatment of this character. Her will, her shame, her despair were wonderful; her defiance of Olivier was terrific; her concealed reverence for his honesty in opposing her hopeless ambition the most touching and natural performance imaginable.

Of Mde. Rose Chéri's exquisite and pervading beauty all men who ever saw her must speak with reverential love. She was gloriously pure to look upon: there was always a sweet sadness in her gayest smile (when she let her true nature display itself), and there ever seemed to be tears in her voice. She was by no means sentimental, but she knew she had a soul—a fact of which some actresses may, perhaps, have no idea in their own individual cases.

Then her hand—it was a perfect creation in itself. To one accustomed to watch her acting, it forestalled the words she was about to utter. There is a portrait of this gracious lady, in which her right hand plays a beautiful part. It is drawn delicately toying with the exquisitely fine chain round the neck. Perhaps there is no pose so trying as holding that member before the breast. As you look on this portrait, you feel that if that undulating gracious hand were hidden the work would lose one of its chief beauties.

And this gentle hand loved to do the most womanly of women's work—to tend the sick, and help the poor, and fondle little children.

Dead, passed away, is Rose Cheri. No more are the children to kneel by her side; no more is she graciously to smile upon and cheer an invalid; dead that gentle lady I saw passing through the sweet summer air to the old church. That "peace which passeth all understanding" seemed to be with her as she walked. Died, tending a sick child; buried midst weeping women, and little children, and many hosts of strong men, who go out from the great city to crowd about her grave and softly cast the autumn flowers on her coffin.

Peace there must be with her, gentle lady!

And this woman? She was a French actress, one of a despised class. She was loved and reverenced throughout France. There have been greater actresses; never purer. Other actresses have created intense terror and emotion; her mission it was to inspire peaceful love, and good-hearted, earnest gentleness.

J. R. Ware.

ONE HAPPY DAY.

BY ADA TREVANION.

In the sky the sun was shining,
On the hills the landscape lay,
When I left my weary [illegible]
For a long, bright, idle day.

Draped in gold were the laburnums,
Lordly chestnuts hung in flowers;
And the [illegible]
In the wood [illegible].

In each green copse sang the throstle;
Gleamed each white stream like a bride;
And the first flush of the heather
[illegible] moor and mountain-side.

When the mists melted from the heavens,
And the air was [illegible] sweet,
[illegible] was the [illegible],
With its snowy, leaping feet.

And beneath the dark pine branches,
Which shut out the garish day,
In the midst of the green dimness,
Soft and green the moss-beds lay.

Then came twilight. O that twilight!
Its remembrance thrills me yet!
Through twilight and [illegible]
Many suns have risen and set.

When the western hills were glowing,
And the stars, before unseen,
Took their places in the blue heavens,
Trembling into light serene;

When the evening bells were chiming
Over all the shadowy land,
Seeming as if they were whispering
That the past was near at hand;

Has my memory served me truly?
Did Love whisper at my ear,
Thrilling every sense with gladness,
And a faint, delicious fear?

Yes! My heart keeps one spot holy,
Like the [illegible];
Weary words and [illegible]
May not [illegible] upon its calm.

For my bliss was not [illegible],
Though its glory passed away;
Sadness, freedom, and affection,
All were mine that happy day.

Ramsgate, 1860.

LE PUY, HAUTE LOIRE.

(*Continued from page 180.*)

A carnival at Le Puy doubtlessly presents nothing new to one habituated to that gay epoch in Italy; but to those who, like myself, have only witnessed the calm attempts of northern festivities in that season, a short sketch of it may not be altogether uninteresting. On the Sunday, Monday, and Tuesday before Lent every one is allowed to run riot with his senses, and merriment amongst the lower classes, too often degenerates into debauchery, on account of the disguise that seems to take from them the responsibility of rational beings. Thus all day long groups of [illegible] non-descripts lounge about the streets, accosting all on their passage, entering shops without buying, under fantastical pretences, and performing divers other eccentric feats, to the apparent great amusement of their sober fellow-townsfolk.

So great was the [illegible] before my windows throughout the day, that I could do nothing but watch the masked actors, philosophize on human folly, and then laugh with the rest. Place [illegible] is the preferred resort of those motley personages. At the sound of a horn they assemble a host of boys, make them what I take to be very witty speeches from the [illegible] they carry; then a shower of apples or [illegible] from upon the juvenile audience into a scramble and uproar, until silence is again imposed by the orator; and renewed eloquence has again the same effect, and that much to the delight and profit of the [illegible], whose stalls are soon emptied, and who in their turn indulge in an extra pint or two of [illegible] to fête the Carnival. But the prettiest sight to me was the aspect of the children arrayed in fancy dresses; now a "Marquis" of three years old; now a young peasant girl in Italian costume; now a bold "Zouave" of six; now a gendarme so youthful—all rosy and smiling with pleasure at the sensation they caused, as they walked along with their no less delighted mothers. The cavalcade, however, is the grand affair, and really a pretty sight it was to me, who had never seen anything of the kind before, for it far outdoes the procession of the "bœuf gras" in Paris, and preparations are made for it during many weeks before the day. This cavalcade represented the entry of a king into the good town of Le Puy in the middle ages. First came a row of horsemen in the costume of trumpeters, sounding their instruments with martial boldness, their horses clearing the road for the coming royalty; a band of music in fancy uniform succeeds; then the clattering of steel is heard, and a body of warlike cavalry appears, lances in hand. They slowly march on, and are soon followed by officers on foot, who, with their staves, keep back the throng. Then appears his Majesty arrayed in gold embroidery and velvet, and seated on a white steed richly caparisoned, whose stately walk makes the monarch's plume [illegible] gently undulate at every step; his portly demeanour also denotes his importance in his own esteem. His court follows him, all clothed in the richest [illegible]—velvet costumes that seem to have been worn by lords and knights of yore, but which I am told were new for the occasion. The young men in the town spare no expense for this ceremony, and will pay as much as a hundred pounds, sometimes more, for their attire. The royal suite was followed by several open carriages and cars, on some of which reclined Venus, Cupids, and other gods and goddesses of the heathen mythology, amid flowers and verdure; others represented ancient armies, composed of negroes and monkeys, which appeared to amuse the crowd immensely, while cavaliers in velvet costume, each carrying a long pole, from the top of which a long bag was suspended, gathered for the poor by presenting the pole at every window at which a face was to be seen. Of course, a prodigious multitude accompanied this parade, which was Sunday afternoon's amusement. A masked ball in the evening terminated the day. The Monday and Tuesday were similar, and on Wednesday morning, when the faithful flocked to church to have ashes put on their foreheads, in sign of humiliation, a few lagging masks and a host of "rag-a-muffins" [illegible] about before my window what they called "Mardi gras"—a stuffed object, which was thrown into the river. This ceremony they style burying "Mardi gras"—Shrove Tuesday. Thus ended the carnival.

But at mid-Lent this [illegible] recommenced again for a day, and many masks loitered about the streets and caused a little excitement amongst the people, the children again appeared in their fancy dresses, and then all was hushed down for Passion week. "It is then you will see a splendid ceremony," said Madame D. to me, whose only aims to convert me is the magnificence of the Roman-worship, the splendid processions, and the wonderful modern miracles—the three very last things that could have any effect on me in religion. However, the thunderbolt to my Protestantism was to be the touching ceremony of the Thursday before Good Friday. There was so much "poesy" in it, she said.

The day arrived. Madeleine was in despair: it rained hard all day, and the poor penitents had to walk bare-footed through the streets, which were thus rendered dirtier, if it is possible, than what they generally are. The disagreeable weather ceased towards evening, and at about eight o'clock my maid called me to the window, where she had for sometime been on the watch, and, issuing from a very dark street opposite me, I beheld the most extraordinary sight imaginable. Between two rows of tall white figures, their faces completely concealed by their white hoods, each carrying a lighted torch, walked another white figure personating the Blessed Saviour, bearing a huge cross—Madeleine whispered to me that it was only in paste-board—under the weight of which he panted, limped, and at intervals fell exhausted, but was immediately urged on by the lance of another white figure, representing a Roman soldier. Then followed numerous similar personages, counterfeiting Christ's disciples; the two thieves carrying their crosses, &c. &c. A priest brought up the rear. All were bare-footed (except the priest), and a dead silence reigned around. As they slowly advanced across the Boulevard, a light appeared at every window. Madeleine knelt down, made the sign of the cross, she also holding a light in her hand. From several houses women brought pillows, which they placed on the passage. Then the procession halted. A supposed St. Veronica approached, and wiped the cross-bearer's face, whose features, the legend says, remained imprinted on the napkin. The priest knelt down on one of the pillows, turned towards the pretended victim, mumbled a prayer, crossed himself, and the procession continued its course. This train of lawless spectres, in the silent gloom of night illumined with torches, produced a most unearthly effect, and quite horrified me; for, methinks, that to a Christian, the sacrifice of Christ has something so sacred in it, that mortals ought to shrink from parodying it.

"Are those men monks?" asked I, of Madeleine.

"Monks!" answered she, laughing. "Oh! no, Madame: they belong to a congregation of 'Penitents;' and are workmen of the town, who will finish the night at the public-house, rest assured. I have a cousin who carried the cross last year, and who returned home afterwards so intoxicated, that he quarrelled with his wife, and turned her out of doors."

While we were commenting on the sight we had just witnessed, a Monsieur M. and his wife came in to spend the evening with us. They both joined in our disgust, and affirmed Madeleine's statement as to the sequel of this penitence. "Besides," added Mr. M., "to all the religious fêtes here, and without which they would find but few performers."

"But let us leave the penitents to their glory," continued he, "for I am come on purpose to give you an account of my journey into the mountains, dear Madam, according to promise; and if I have not been in a village buried in snow, I have at least walked over one.

"I wanted to gain a small village near the Mezenc, the highest mountain in France, and, after innumerable difficulties across the snow, I perceived that I could go no farther on horseback; so leaving my horse in charge of my servant, I proceeded on foot by the path indicated by long poles driven into the ground on purpose to guide the traveller in winter. The poles gradually disappeared, and both I and Fox (a Newfoundland dog; it is the fashion in France for dogs to have English names) became very much puzzled. No village arose within our view, but pyramids of snow on all sides. Fox in particular could not understand the thing in the least, and eagerly looked into my face for an explanation. We wandered about for some time, until Fox seemed to be of opinion that we had better return, and I at last was obliged to side with him. Just then a mountaineer appeared, coming towards us.

"'Where is "Les Estables"?' asked I; 'I have been in search of it for this last hour.'

"'Well, sir,' answered the man, 'you may look for it another hour, and you will not find it; for you are now walking over it. The village has been buried under the snow for this last month, and will very likely be so for two months longer.'

Can you imagine such an existence? Three months under the snow? Three months shut out from the world, without a glimpse of the blue sky above? Methinks I never could support such an imprisonment. But thus are the inhabitants of many villages in the mountains doomed to pass their lives. They provide for the inclement season, and lay in stores of provision for themselves and their cattle, which are sheltered under spacious houses built on purpose. They dig paths from their houses all leading to the church as soon as their interment is effectuated, and thus they find means to communicate with each other. Should one of them die during this period, they are obliged to bury the corpse in the snow until liberty returns. Is it then surprising that these disinherited children of Nature become brutalized, as I am told they are, and that for the least offence they strike each other with knives, and that assassination is a common thing between them, although they generally have a great respect for strangers? Their superstition also is unbounded, nothing being too absurd for their credulity. And, strange to say, in spite of their hardships and misery, they cling to these barren mountains as a miser to his gold, and rarely can one be induced to quit them. They will listen with eager curiosity to the glowing scenes of wealth and prosperity that you may depict to them, and their fertile imaginations will elaborate visions of really the riches of distant climes; but, although they also love to hoard up in their little way, yet they seem rooted to the rock on which they were born, and nothing can withdraw them from it. Such I believe, however, is the mountaineer in general.

"After I had regained my horse," continued Mr. M., "we turned our steps in another direction, where the snow had not been so powerful, and in a village a few miles from Les Estables we found the inhabitants in great dismay; the postman had been attacked by wolves, and had only by miracle escaped. I found him greatly excited in the midst of the villagers, and of course as soon as I arrived he had to recommence his narrative, which is as follows:

"'I set out this morning early, as usual, on my daily rounds; and when at some distance from the village, I found, to my great consternation that I was accompanied by a wolf on either side, and, 'Bonne Vierge!' I was without a stick! the sight of which will sometimes keep a wolf in awe, for when alone he is a fearful coward. I walked on, recommending myself to Our Lady and to all the saints in Paradise, my ferocious escort dodging me, now appearing, now disappearing; now approaching, now retiring, keeping my blood in one perpetual ebb and flow of heat and cold, until I at last arrived, unmolested and thankful, to the village, where I distributed my letters and remained at least five hours. The 'gendarmes' being out, and I deeming my wolves long since gone, after such a lapse of time, set out to return home. I, however, took the precaution of borrowing a stick. Alas! I soon perceived, to my horror, that my calculation had been in vain, and that my foes had awaited me. One life-long hour I walked, my blood curdling in my veins, swinging my staff about, and repeating I cannot tell you how many Paternosters and Ave Marias; for the thought of entering the pine wood almost made my heart cease to beat, as there the monsters could draw near me unseen. I entered, and then could see them gradually pressing me in on either side, every step bringing me closer and closer to their jaws, until a few yards alone separated me from one of them, I could now at intervals see his glaring eyes between the trees shining on me with greedy hunger, making my whole body shudder again. He seemed on the eve of springing; my staff alone retained him; and, in my fear of him, I had almost forgotten the other, when I heard a sudden rush on my other side, and, O my God! a paw was on me. With desperation I struck the beast off with my staff: a howl rent the air, and both animals were upon me. Then began the struggle of life and death. Right and left I struck with frantic force, and howl after howl followed my blows; more and more furious became the exasperated beasts, while my strength gradually failed, and I felt that all was over for me. With a supreme effort, however, I still hurled my staff about, when—oh! I shall never forget it, a third wolf came rushing down the path. A cry of horror escaped me, my eyes swam before me, and I fell. At that instant a fire-arm was heard, then a second, then a third, and two gendarmes galloped up. The three monsters rushed howling away with rage, and here I am, neighbours, safe and sound, humbly beseeching the Holy Virgin never to make me pass such a moment again. The inhabitants of the village I had left, fearing for me, had related my adventure in the morning to the 'gendarmes' on their return home. They had immediately galloped off after me, and happily in time; for a moment later, and I should never have related my sufferings to you.'

"We all warmly pressed the hand of the poor fellow," continued Mr. M.; "heartily congratulating him on his narrow escape, while his wife and daughter hung over him, crying with emotion and joy.

"Early the next morning the whole village was on the alert: a troop of peasantry, armed with guns and staves, went in pursuit of the wolves, and before I left I had the satisfaction of seeing them return with the carcasses of two out of the three, which the sportsmen brought home in triumph, to the great joy of the villagers, who made quite a holiday of their victory—a victory which is also rewarded by government; and I left them all drinking and dancing to their hearts' desire, the old postman scarcely convinced yet of his escape, so near had he seen himself to the jaws of death, and few indeed have been so fortunate; for, alas! a year rarely passes without the mountaineers in these parts having to deplore a human life, besides the ravages amongst the cattle caused by these greedy visitors.

"But enough of snow and wolves for this year, all that having long disappeared, except on the mountains, whose hoary heads still sparkle in the sunshine, and seem to bid defiance to the most caressing beams, and to resist alone the amorous voice of Spring; for, in every direction, dormant Nature is aroused, and the air vibrates with notes of love. Every tree and bush has started at her cheering call, and shows its embryo buds ready, after a few more puffs of her balmy breath, to burst forth into all the verdant splendour of renovating May. The busy throng, too, now fluttering and chirping on every spray, as if impatient to find a nuptial bower, will soon warble with joy and song amid the tender leaves, that the feathery tribe deem no doubt there on purpose to shelter and conceal their mysterious loves. We "pocous," resembling so many bees long shut up within our hives, swarmed forth at the first gleam of sunshine. Prisoners whose chains were at length burst asunder, we hastened to inhale the first breath of liberty; and yet winter has not been severe here, and if intense cold reigned for a few days, we were afterwards compensated by weather that at times forced me to open my windows in the month of February. We have only had one fall of snow; and as for rain, we have not had it more than twice during our sojourn here, but then it fell in torrents, until complete streams poured down the streets from the high town, and Place Martouret was almost inundated. We are told that this is always the case, and that perhaps we shall see no more all the year, without it be a thunder-storm or two, that are generally very violent. The rich inhabitants are most of them already gone to their "chateaux" or country seats for the summer, most of them at a short distance from the town. Those who cannot indulge in such a luxury, possess what they nominate their "vigne" (vineyard)—a small piece of ground, where they amuse themselves cultivating the rebellious vine, that never really ripens under the sun in the environs of Le Puy. In this enclosure is built a small house, sometimes a mere hut, and here the little bourgeoisie spend their Sundays all summer long. Provided with a prodigious omelette—they have a particular taste for that delicacy, as well as for pork in general, which makes that animal so to speak the dearest of all meat—and with an immense loaf of bread, the whole family sets off regularly every Sabbath morning for the [illegible] of their leisure; the roads are literally filled with them. There they revel in the charms of music, dance, and good cheer, stimulated with the pleasure which every thorough-bred "ponot" feels, in the [illegible] thought that every drop of wine he drinks at his "vigne" was produced on his own ground; that it is, in a word, "vin du cru," of the extraordinary quality of which I have already spoken. Every Frenchman is fond of making a noise in the world; never mind how, as long as he does make a noise; this is why I think they are so fond of the drum, and that even in their very churches a drum may sometimes be heard; but the "ponots" show fully appreciate that instrument, on which he greatly excels in general, and a "vigne" might as well be without the genuine "vin du cru" as without a drum, with which the environs resound on all sides. This musical instrument is sometimes accompanied with the "ophicleide," a deep-mouthed brazen monster, that outdoes the drum if possible in noise, and to the sound of which they dance the "bourrée," or national dance—a graceful and pretty figure, when well executed, as I have seen it in society. With such harmony, the "ponots" may well join the rest of their countrymen in their depreciation of English music—much to my amusement, as may be supposed.

As we have neither "chateau" nor "vigne" to receive us, we are obliged to content ourselves in exploring the wild [illegible] that surround us, and which we do daily. But before visiting the country, we wished to pry into a few more nooks and corners of this curious place, which interests us beyond measure, and the other day we again mounted the high town. We passed before the grand entrance of the cathedral, and soon arrived amid sombre-looking convents and black walls, to the little village of Aiguille, picturesquely reclining on the opposite flank of Mount Anis, in front of the perpendicular rock whence it derives its name, and commanding a view of a graceful turn in the valley that winds round "Our Lady's Mount." This village is separated from Le Puy by the great "séminaire" or college for young priests. A most delicious shade [illegible] with its gardens [illegible] and beautiful, though somewhat limited, view consisting in [illegible] of the valley, through which runs the gentle Borne, decked on either side with trees, interrupted here and there by an antique ivy-clad bridge, over which the water-kissing ash hangs its branches. Far up the valley, on the margin of the Borne, may just be perceived the black rocky isle on which stands the ruin of the impregnable Château d'Espaly, once a stronghold of the protestants. On the opposite side of the river [illegible] a small meadow, then a corn-field, and then on the declivity, which gradually ascends to the "Plain of Ronzon," with its avenue of trees that seem to touch the sky, are scattered the vineyards of which I have spoken, under the denomination of "vignes." A [illegible] of this [illegible] also to see the noble ruins of Polignac of which I shall speak hereafter. In the gardens of the "séminaire" are several [illegible] stones, which antiquarians suppose to have been inhabited by the Druids, and which certainly are of Celtic origin.

But to return to Aiguille, in its quaintness. We saw on the [illegible] a very curious little monument called by the inhabitants "The Temple of Diana," the only edifice of its kind in the Haute Loire, and they are very rare anywhere. It belongs to the eleventh century, is of an octagon shape, with a semi-circular apse joined to one of its sides. The vaulting formed of eight planes that surmount the building is pierced in the middle by a circular aperture. Many curious [illegible] decorate the walls, and the interior is supposed to have been once ornamented with fresco paintings. Some are of opinion that the heathen Diana may have been adored in an edifice on that spot, as tradition says, and that the Knights Templars constructed the present building, on account of a Greek cross that surmounts the principal door. However, the most probable conjecture is, that this graceful little temple was nothing but a place for baptism when baptism by immersion was practised, which ceremony ceased only, in these parts, in the 14th century. In the 17th century this edifice was turned into a chapel, and dedicated to St. Clare; but it was again abandoned before the Revolution in 1793, and was unmercifully used as a hay-loft, until the town of Le Puy purchased it, and will, I trust, restore it again to public worship, for it really would be a great Vandalism to let so elegant an antiquity fall into decay and ruin. As we were examining this Temple of Diana, a village matron approached us, and pointing to a lowly cot near us—"There," said she, "there is where Crozatier was born, and there is where they are now weeping for him!" We thanked her, and turning towards the humble home she had shown us, we took a peep into the birth-place of the glory of modern Le Puy, the great sculptor and founder, of European celebrity, Crozatier, whose name is so blended with the name of Le Puy, that I think his eventful history might find its place in a chapter of these sketches, and will give it in my next, it being too long for this.

BY THE RIVER.

Quiet River! in the sunlight flowing,
  All my cares I cast upon thy breast;
Bear them with thee whither thou art going;
  Leave me here a little while at rest.

Sleep, my heart! Awake my languid senses;
  Grasp the events that close about thee lie;
Grasp the Present. Saddest of the tenses
  Is the Past—the Past that cannot die.

Softly, swiftly, deep between its rushes,
  Glides the tawny river with a sound
As of one who, swaying gently, hushes
  Baby-eyes to [illegible] sleep profound.

Through this drowsy undulating hammock
  All the noontide hollow, hushed and whist;
Indistinct the myriad insects murmur
  As a landscape trembling through a mist.

Little shrieks of happy children playing
  In the meadow just beyond the stream,
[illegible]
  Muffled come, like noises through a dream.

Birds and bees, and all the tiny voices,
  Peopling solitudes of grass and wood,
[illegible] with folded wings and [illegible] pauses,
  Chastened to the river-music's mood.

Peace! Save when the nightingale [illegible]
  (Stabbing almost to the inmost soul),
In a sudden agony that thrills
  Nature with a pang of [illegible].

Sleep, my heart! The passionate thrills are dying
  Down the panting air. The [illegible]
Of the gliding water stills the sighing,
  Soothing, [illegible] vibrations, low and long.

* * * * *

While I dreaming lie, the river riseth,
  Swelling as a chord of music swells,
All unheeded till the change surpriseth
  Languid senses in their sluggish cells.

One by one, black barges up the river
  Soundless glide, like shadows from the sky;
Lifeless, passive, stirring scarce a shiver
  On the tide which bears them helpless by.

Wearied sleep the children in the meadow,
  Slumbering [illegible] among the withered grass.
Ah! an emblem! . . . . (Thus I solve the shadow
  Lest the [illegible]), Let the moral pass.

Tumbled lie the children, flushed and heated,
  [illegible] in [illegible] hay;
And the haycart by a hedge-row seated,
  Rest, upon the middle of the day.

Out of depths of calm a wind upspringeth,
  Rising, falling, strengthening by default;
As a [illegible], whispered, [illegible], ringeth
  Forth at length upon an air [illegible].

All a-ripple stir the shady spaces
  Under heavy branches; gloom and gleam
Fight [illegible]
  Where, through rifted foliage, beams on beam.

Sunlight flashes on the bending grasses,
  All [illegible] the drowsy [illegible];
[illegible] in the airy [illegible]
  Through the woodland on to wavy [illegible].

But the river, when the wind down-sweepeth,
  Pales as one who pales in sudden pain,
When a ghastly, sweeping sickness creepeth,
  Creepeth round the heart and round the brain.

All its placid breadth a-tremble quivers,
  Like broken eddies whirling round;
All its monotonous music shivers
  Into jangled fragments of sweet sound.

Dies the wind; and now the river [illegible]
  Like [illegible]
Never [illegible]. Dumb its ancient [illegible],
  [illegible] in the [illegible] of deep [illegible].

Till, at last, the tide [illegible] turning,
  Back the disenchanted waters flow,
Heedless of their upward course, and yearning
  Towards the marshes stretching far below.

One by one, black barges down the river
  Slow return, a sad funeral train.—
Wake, my heart! The waters back deliver
  All my cares, my cares, to me again.

June, 1861. J. A.

Sir William Jones.—Without neglecting his old friends, Latin and Greek, Jones was, [illegible] years of age, an [illegible] linguist. With French, Spanish, Portuguese, and Italian he was perfectly familiar, and revelled in the varied literature of all these continental languages. To these he added [illegible], Greek, and Hebrew, Arabic, and Persian. Nor was Jones in any one language a superficial student. The mere acquirement of a foreign tongue was of little use, unless it could be at once followed by a careful study of the literature connected with it, and a close comparison of the manners and customs of the nation speaking it with those of other races, especially with his own. To read was one thing; to apply that reading and turn it to practical use, was another.—*The Art of Doing our Best.*

BALLOWMERE.

(A Tale, in Four Chapters).

BY ALFRED GRANDICHAUPP.

Chap. III.

True to my promise, I presented myself next morning about nine o'clock at the family breakfast parlour in the Percy Arms. Both father and daughter received me with the utmost cordiality; and, although I had never seen Mr. Lismore before, there was something so transparently guileless about the venerable old man, that I did not feel the slightest embarrassment on my first introduction to him under such peculiar circumstances. Miss Lismore presented me as their old friend Mr. Grandichaupp. As an old friend he received me; and as old friends mutually pleased with each other we were soon engaged in an animated conversation around the blazing urn. No allusion was made by either Mary or myself to those matters which had principally occupied our minds on the previous evening; neither did I think it expedient in the meantime to say anything about the dark stale-night wanderer. I had, however, fully determined to keep a little more strict watch on the mysterious personage; and was not without hope of being able to find some trace of him in the course of the day. It was almost necessary for me to return to Craighallow, as I had left my portmanteau at the Bridge and Trout; and, thinking that he of whom I was in search had most probably gone in that direction, I was anxious to lose no time in following in his track. But such a proposal was at first strongly opposed by my host and hostess, on account of the most unfavourable state of the weather. The wind had increased since yesterday to a perfect hurricane, driving before it the spray from the lake, and the large rain-drops with a fury which few men would care to brave. Mr. Lismore offered to send a gig or horseman for my "impedimenta," hinting that, being unacquainted with the country, I was, perhaps, scarcely aware of the nature of the task I was imposing myself. But I silenced all objections by telling him that a great part of my life had been spent amongst mountains and moorlands in weather as stormy, and that the tempest was generally as agreeable to me as the sunshine. I added—what was certainly in a measure true—that it was just the very morning which I should have chosen of my own free will for the kind of walk before me, and that it was exceedingly considerate in the Pluvius Apollo of the weather-office to have obliged me in the way he had done!

Finding me thus resolute, my friends withdrew their opposition, and even admitted that, if instead of crossing the moor, as I had formerly done, I kept close by the lake and river-side, I should find some objects the sight of which would amply repay me for the temporary inconvenience of a drenching.

"I know nothing," said Miss Lismore, "in Rhuskennanshire to equal the Lyn of Ballow, even as I have been accustomed to see it, on a quiet summer evening. To-day, in the flooded state of the river, it must be still more grand; and you are very fortunate in being able to visit it under such favourable circumstances, although I fear the ague or rheumatism which may be expected to-morrow will not be found quite so agreeable."

"Oh, never fear," I replied; "I am proverbially unpropitious to any inconveniences, and shall be nothing the worse for exchanging the civilities of the season with the water-spirit of the Ballow."

"Make my compliments to that deity, if you should chance to meet with him, and say that, when spring returns, I shall be sure to wander up to his domains again!"

"Happy god! with such a message as that I shall surely not forget him in spirit!"

Impatient of any further delay, I was quickly threading the narrow, romantic path by the side of the lake. I found it much more sheltered than I had expected; but, had it been otherwise, I could not have failed to enjoy the scene around me. As a pedestrian in the regions of Belgravia or Rotten Row, I have often envied those darlings of fortune that have rolled past me in their lordly equipages, looking as if this earth were too vile for them to tread on; but, with my foot on the mountain-side, and the music of a hundred mountain-rills in my ears, I have never envied any man except him who, from sunrise to sunset, could outstrip me in scaling the crag or breasting the torrent—and that man I have seldom seen.

I am not going to attempt to describe the Lyn of Ballow. Many men can "look upon Nature with a poet's eye"—that is no very extraordinary gift; but it is altogether a different thing to be able to depict Nature with a poet's pen. Scott, I know, can show you by the light reflected from his pages most that is worth seeing, from Cape Wrath to Tweed, without the assistance of Mr. Cook and his admirably-arranged excursions. Byron can transport you, in your easy chair and slippers, to the placid Leman and the misty Jura; but these, with here and there another, are the giants whom we all admire, but whom the warning contained in a certain well-known fable should render us exceedingly cautious how we attempt to imitate.

And yet how many have neglected the warning! England, worse than Egypt of old, has of late years been visited with the plague of frogs—yes, puffing, croaking frogs, plaguing the public, plaguing the publishers, plaguing the reviewers, plaguing their friends, plaguing, in short, everything and everybody except, perhaps, the grocer and tobacconist—plaguing even these, sometimes, after the manner of the Glasgow professor of the last century, who obstinately persisted in having his books issued of such a size, that a single leaf of them was found to be too big for a pennyworth of snuff, and not big enough for "three bawbees' worth." I have before me now the poems of my old acquaintance Mr. Mythville Sophristis, bound in most unexceptionable green, with the author's name in gilt letters on the back—a dainty volume, in which, as Sir Benjamin Backbite says, in the "School for Scandal," "a neat rivulet of text meanders through a meadow of margin;" and it can do this new candidate for the bay-leaves no harm to hear a few plain-spoken words regarding his previous lucubrations, especially as a certain class of critics have been flattering his vanity by describing them as replete with "thrilling touches of sentiment!" and "exquisite pictures of nature."

With regard to the "sentiment," or whatever is intended to be understood by that somewhat ambiguous word, we have only to remark, that the country-lad who, after finishing the ordinary course of instruction at the village school, finds himself unable to discourse more eloquently on the tender emotions than our friend Mythville has done to the damsel who most unaccountably happens to frequent "the same lovely walks" as he does, at the same "delicious sunset-hour," justly deserves to be made the laughing-stock of all his brother bumpkins.

The "pictures of nature," so far as we can ascertain, consist principally of those commonplace observations which anyone would naturally make regarding the objects around him when passing through some pretty country lane, or near some old rookery, on a fine autumnal evening—considerably disfigured, be it remembered, by the hammering process which they have had to undergo while being converted from natural prose to unnatural jingling rhyme. But it is when our young author attempts to soar that he exhibits the most pitiable failure. As long as he sticks to "ivy-clad towers," and "gently-meandering brooks," we can just endure him; but when he meditates anything greater, his weakness becomes at once apparent; his majestic forests dwindle into the faint ghost of some suburban shrubbery; his cataracts you can produce for yourself any day of the year by turning the handle of the parish pump! I speak with more sincerity, Mr. Sophristis, than those friends of yours who have, as a matter of courtesy, written you those pretty, but very cautiously-worded notes of congratulation which you are so fond of exhibiting; while at the same time they have abused you in private in good set terms for compelling them to buy such rubbish! And I tell you, that it is useless in you to try to describe Nature; because Nature in her "grandest moods" you have never seen. If, instead of shivering over that fire from October till sixty something, you will go forth with me (but it must not be in the sunshine!) to one or two spots that I could name, by the swelling billow and foaming tarn, you shall there be obliged to admit in what an extent you have caricatured what God has created; unless—as I fear very much, in spite of all your fine talking, would be the case—you should be more interested with regard to the state of your livernous wrapper, and "patent paragon umbrella," than with the sublimest works of the Eternal. No, my little Mithville, you can never climb the two-peaked mountain. Rest contented, then, to admire the grandeur of its summits from some fitting corner in the valley below; and do not, I beseech you, do not attempt to deluge the world with a second flood of that weak, washy, mediocre trash which the Roman satirist declared, two thousand years ago, to be intolerable alike to gods and men and booksellers' shelves!

After this little digression on a subject not materially connected with our tale, I shall hurry as quickly as possible over the remaining portion of my walk to Craigballum. As I approached the Grouse and Trout, I knew, by certain sounds that reached my ears, that my search was not to prove fruitless, and that I should at least have the means of ascertaining whether my suspicions were correct or otherwise. The landlord seemed somewhat at a loss to know what to make of his erratic guest; but I satisfied his curiosity by simply telling him that I had spent the night with some old friends of mine—the Inneraray—and that, thinking the morning a very favourable one for walking off a slight cold caught during my ride on the previous day, I had strolled out to see what the Bellerie looked like in its flooded state, and to give directions regarding my portmanteau, which I wished to be sent on, when convenient, to the Ferry Arms.

"Well, sir, there are few of our visitors, or indeed of our natives either, who would have cared to face what you have done this morning. However, you don't seem as if it would do you much harm; but, as you have had a liberal allowance of one kind of moisture, sir, won't you step into the bar here with me for a minute or two, and try a little of a different sort that I think I can honestly recommend?"

"Thank you; I believe I may safely do so. You seem to have some merry revellers below; and that blazing peat-fire appeared so inviting as I passed the window, that I felt very much inclined to try to find a place beside it for a few minutes."

"Oh yes, there's a nigger chap there who has been hanging about the place for some days. I don't know well what to make of him, for it is not often that we see such gentry in these parts. However, he's a comical sort of a fellow in his way, and as there are a good many loungers about the village to-day who can scarcely get about their occupations, and one or two farmers from a distance who have put in here, as the sailors say, from stress of weather, the presence has been very welcome. If you think you would enjoy half-an-hour in such company, we can, if you please, go down together."

We went down together, and I was soon as much at home with the bluff countrymen, in the kitchen of the Grouse and Trout, as I had been on the preceding evening in the corresponding regions at the Percy Arms. The "nigger chap" recognised me at once, and returned my salutation with a low bow and a grimace; and it was not long before I had an opportunity of carrying out the plan of operations on which I had determined. Having discovered that one of the country farmers was well acquainted with Mr. Iemers, I talked to him about the family for some time; and then beckoning the negro towards me, asked him if he would allow me to fill him a glass of old ale to refresh him a little after his extraordinary exertions, and continuing, as it were, my conversation with the old farmer while I poured out the sparkling beverage, I remarked, "Yes, Miss Iemers is certainly a very charming young lady, and is just about to be married to Mr. William Blandon—a most respectable citizen of N——." And then presenting the glass, I immediately added, "Here, Cæsar, or Pompey, or whatever your name may be, drink health and happiness to Mr. William Blandon and that young lady who was so kind to you last night, beneath whose window you afterwards offered up the *dear-bought serenade*!"

"*Rem teligeram.*" To use a very vulgar phrase, "I had hit the right nail on the head," and hit it with a vengeance. Lamp-black and burnt cork an inch deep could not conceal the Saxon blood that boiled in that indignant flesh! I was now sure of what I had suspected before; but not wishing to call the attention of the company to the exact state of affairs, I contrived by an easy manœuvre to drop the glass on the floor, breaking it, of course, to pieces; and, in the slight confusion that followed, it was no difficult matter to whisper, in a now eagerly attentive ear, "Mr. Henry Greenbank, I know you well now, in spite of your disguise, although I never saw you before last night, nor you me: contrive to meet me alone outside as soon as possible, for I have much to tell you that you will be glad to hear."

Mr. Greenbank (for it was indeed he) made no further effort to conceal his identity, but replied, in a low, agitated voice, "Who or what you are, or by what inexplicable means you have gained the information regarding me that you seem to be possessed of, I know not; but it matters little—I am Henry Greenbank, and I will meet you where we can converse alone, in a few minutes, as soon as I can do so without exciting the suspicion of these gaping clodhoppers!"

"Do so. Depend upon it, I have sought you for your own good, and that of another; and I have good news to tell you."

"Then it was not true what you said about Mary—I mean Miss Iemers?"

"No, it was not. You must forgive me for practising that ruse in order to satisfy myself that my conjectures were correct; but we must separate for a little. I shall walk on towards the old bridge—follow me as soon as you can."

We very soon afterwards met in a retired spot beyond the bridge, and I related as briefly as I could the whole story of my acquaintance with the Iemers family. Mr. Greenbank did not interrupt me, even by asking a single question, until I came to talk—as I did, unreservedly—of Mary's long, unchanging devotion to himself; and then, dear reader, if ever you have had to communicate a similar piece of information to a muscular young man of five-and-twenty, I think you will agree with me, that the grasp of the hand which rewarded you for your trouble, although no doubt very gratifying to the feelings, was at the same time somewhat trying to the flesh!

"If what you tell me be true," said he, "let us hasten at once to the Percy Arms, or let me go alone; for you must require some rest after your battle with the tempest this morning."

"Oh no. I am quite ready to accompany you; but excuse me if I ask you whether or not you have seen yourself in a mirror this morning? I do not know what Miss Iemers's views with regard to negro-emancipation may be, but if 'Pity the poor African!' is to be your plea, we had better return for the hurdy-gurdy, to give additional *éclat* to the scene."

"Hang it! I had quite forgotten this ridiculous disguise. What a figure I must look, to be sure! It will take me an hour or two, I am afraid, to render myself presentable, as the European portion of my wardrobe is deposited with a faithful old friend who lives five miles further up the Ballow side; but if you will stay and refresh yourself at the Grouse and Trout until I can get there and back, I shall not loiter by the way. I have something to tell you of my own adventures in this neighbourhood which will astonish you, perhaps still more than anything you have yet heard."

"Tell it me as we go along then. The sky is brighter than it was, and I must be allowed to accompany you, at least for a mile or two. I can then return and order dinner at the Grouse and Trout for us both—don't frown, in your present ecstatic state, at anything so vulgar as a good dinner—and afterwards I shall be at your service."

This plan was adopted, and Mr. Greenbank's narrative, in something like his own words, was briefly as follows:—

"You know the cause of my sudden departure from N——, but you do not know of the malicious plot (for such I now believe it to have been) by which I was entrapped on that fatal day. Mr. William Blandon and I, although acquainted for many years and in the habit of seeing each other very frequently, had never been on what is called intimate terms. I, along with others, certainly believed him to be a very good man; but his apparent goodness always repelled rather than attracted an impulsive character like mine, and, although I respected him perhaps more than any of my friends, I was always glad to escape from his society. On the morning of the birthday-party, I had to call upon him on some business-matters, and could not help thinking that his reception of me was far more cordial than it had ever been before. After business, he pressed me to take a glass or two of wine. Then, he had just been getting in some foreign spirits, which were said to be of a very superior quality; he was not much of a judge himself: would I favour him with my opinion? Accordingly we visited the cellars, and, after tasting the contents of more than one or two casks, a letter was brought to him by the servant in attendance, summoning him, as he said, to York Assizes, on an affair that would admit of no delay. It was most unfortunate; still, if I had the rest of the day to spare till six o'clock, I might assist him out of the difficulty. I had the rest of the day to spare; and Mr. Blandon explained to me that one or two gentlemen from Scotland with whom he had been recently associated in the formation of a new joint-stock company, were to pass N——, on their way from London to Edinburgh, that day, and had promised to dine with him at an early hour, and remain until the departure of the north mail, a little before six. It would seem very inhospitable to send them to a hotel, but there was nothing else for it, unless I would consent to stay and do the honours of the table in his absence. I had no objections to urge to this arrangement. The Mac-somethings arrived soon after; and Mr. Blandon, after making the best apology he could under the circumstances, committed them to my care, with a private intimation that they came quite far enough from the north to prefer whiskey to claret after dinner. In my novel capacity of host, I felt myself in duty bound to accommodate myself as much as possible to the tastes of my guests. Their tastes lay in imbibing toddy about as fast as the servants could supply us with hot water, from the moment the cloth was removed until a few minutes before the departure of the mail—and the result you know.

"When I left N——, I had no definite aim beyond the usual resource of the reckless and desperate in all ages—a life of dangerous adventure on the ocean wave. Fortune, they say, must be assiduously followed by those who would win favours. The reverse was true in my case; for the more I tried to shun the fickle goddess, the more she followed and smiled upon me. At Liverpool I met with the captain of a vessel belonging to a highly respectable company in New York, with whom I had a slight acquaintance; and after telling him as much of my story as I thought necessary, he at once consented to take me with him for one voyage as supercargo, and to give me every opportunity of gaining experience in my new profession. Although formerly merely an amateur, still I was no novice in nautical affairs; and before we had crossed the Atlantic, I deemed myself fully qualified to take the position of mate on another ship belonging to the same company which was to sail in a few days for the West Indies. I eagerly accepted the appointment; and, before we had been a week at sea, a terrible collision occurred—of which I daresay you must have read the accounts at the time—on which occasion the measures which I took while my superior officers were overcome with panic (and one of them, at least, with brandy) were considered to have been the means of saving a valuable cargo and many valuable lives. I was thus brought prominently under the notice of the owners, and before another voyage, the captain and I exchanged places, or rather, I took his place, and he was dismissed, with a very severe reprimand, from the service of the company. But this was not all. The senior partner in our firm invited me to spend a few days with him at his mansion, in the neighbourhood of the city, during which time he so won upon me by his almost parental kindness that I told him my real name and the whole of my history. From that time, whenever I was not at sea, he insisted upon my making his house my home; and on his death, which occurred a few months ago, he bequeathed to me almost the whole of his fortune, with an earnest request that I would return and see whether it were still possible for me to do anything to gladden the hearts of the friends of my childhood.

"You are probably aware that, before leaving N——, I wrote to my uncle, Mr. Joseph Grimshank. Of course he could not reply, as I gave him no clue by which I could be traced; but the first thing I did, on maturer reflection, after landing at New York, was to endeavour to open up a communication with him by means of Mr. Blandon, whom I then thought the most likely person to assist me. I begged Mr. Blandon to assure my uncle, if he thought that it would be prudent to do so, that my devotion and gratitude to him were unchanged as ever. I even ventured to request him to discover whether Miss Linners showed any signs of relenting; and left him to use his own discretion as to how much he should communicate to her of what I had written. Mr. Blandon's reply was left at the address I had given him during my second voyage, but it was far from being satisfactory. My uncle had died without even mentioning my name. Miss Linners would not suffer the slightest allusion to be made to her former intimacy with me, and was (at least report said so) about to be married to a gentleman who had quite recently formed her acquaintance. Such was the tale, cautiously worded and cunningly interspersed with professions of sympathy and condolence, by which the hypocritical scoundrel endeavoured to deceive me, and by which, for years, I was deceived. Sometimes, it is true, when the hurricane swept our decks, and the ship rocked like a child's plaything on the crested wave—when the timid "shrieked," and the brave "stood still"—the figure of Mary Inmore would appear, to interpose between me and destruction, gently reproaching me for ever mistrusting her, and beckoning me to return. I scarcely know when I first began to doubt Mr. Blandon's good faith towards me. I am not naturally suspicious, and it was long before I could admit to myself the possibility of my having been deceived. When, however, my kind benefactor in very plain terms hinted his suspicions that I had entrusted my cause to a false friend, and afterwards rendered me, in one sense at least, independent of the world's smile or frown, I determined, in compliance with his last wish, to return at once to England. On arriving at N—— I learnt, by some cautious inquiries in the neighbourhood of The Lamb, that Mr. Inmore had fallen into difficulties, and that he and his daughter (still unmarried) had retired into Blankmontshire. I at once resolved to follow them, and tried hard to persuade myself that it was best for me to go in a straightforward manner and beg that the future might yet be allowed to atone for the past. But it would not do. That such was the most proper course for me to adopt, I did not doubt; but the simple possibility of a cold reception from Mary Inmore was more than I could bear. She might be even now engaged to another, and to meet her under such circumstances would be to inflict unnecessary torture on one—perhaps on both; I must therefore be better acquainted with the real position of affairs before I presented myself, or if possible without being seen, and know without being known. It was then that the idea of assuming this ridiculous disguise suggested itself to me. I had once taken the part of an African minstrel with considerable *éclat* at some private theatricals at New York, and that character appeared as suitable for my present purpose as any other. The metamorphosis was soon effected; and after one long look at the window of that little room in The Lamb where Mary and I had spent so many happy hours together, I took the train for Blankmont, carrying with me a light hurdy-gurdy, and an old knapsack containing a somewhat more presentable dress, to be used if required. You are aware, perhaps, that a considerable part of my youth was spent in this neighbourhood, and that Mr. Blandon's widowed mother still resides in a small cottage about four miles higher up the river. I remember having seen her frequently with the late Mrs. Inmore when I was a boy, but of course I had no intention of making her my confidante; but I thought that I knew where to find one man able and willing to aid me, and to him I resolved to make myself known. This was an old gamekeeper in the employment of Lord P., who first taught me the use of the fishing-rod and fowling-piece, and in whose company I have from time to time spent many a happy day in pursuit of the speckled trout and mountain hare. He is quite a character, this same John Irvine (or Jack-o'-the-Hill as he is generally called), and although I must not urge you to accompany me all the way to his lonely hut to-day, I hope, when we have more leisure, to have the pleasure of introducing you to as fine a specimen of the true 'Natty Bumppo' type as you perhaps ever saw. Well, as chance would have it, when I arrived at Craighallow, Jack was standing amongst the idlers at the door of the inn. He little suspected who I was, and as it did not exactly suit me to introduce myself to him there, I contented myself with cutting a few capers such as you have witnessed, endeavouring at the same time to discover what his movements would be for the night. Nothing could be more satisfactory. He was to proceed homewards, accompanied for the first mile or two by a friend, in about an hour. My plan therefore was to saunter on before, and meet him after his companion and he should have parted company. The sun went down before I had got far on my way, but a brilliant, cloudless moon well supplied the place of the lord of day; and as the distant shadowy outline of many a familiar spot appeared before me, my spirit rose for the time superior to all the perplexing difficulties which harassed me, and I abandoned myself without reserve to the happy memories of youthful years. Having wandered some distance from the direct route, in order to deposit my musical instrument in an old hiding-place among the rocks, the entrance to which was known only to a few, I was just about regaining the highway, singing, as I walked along, some verses of a favourite old ballad, when, to my consternation, I heard my name pronounced, with a start of bewilderment, by a traveller who came abruptly in sight from the opposite direction. I had disguised my face effectually enough, but not my voice, and Mr. William Blandon (for he it was), by the sense of hearing rather than of sight, had instantly recognised me. It was an embarrassing rencontre on both sides; for although Mr. Blandon welcomed me with a great affectation of delight, I could not help suspecting from his manner that my sudden appearance was anything but agreeable to him; while, on the other hand, my own schemes were thus prematurely disarranged. There was no help for it, however; and after I had told him as much as I chose to do respecting my present position, and assured him that my arrival was known to no single individual except himself (on which point he seemed to be particularly inquisitive), he accounted for his presence there by saying that he was returning from a hurried visit to his mother; and proposed, as he had only just time to catch the mail-gig from Craighallow to Blankmont, that I should walk back a short distance with him. I did so; and now we have come to the place to which I wished to bring you before entering upon the climax of my story. What remains to be told will now be more intelligible to you."

Although I had not ventured to interrupt Mr. Greenbank until he himself made this voluntary pause in his narrative, it was impossible not to be very much struck with the aspect of the locality to which we were approaching. A narrow foot-path, shut in on both sides by rocks and thick brushwood, had brought us to the base of a cataract below which the river Ballow separates itself into two streams, the larger of which immediately enters a subterranean passage, through which it flows for nearly a quarter of a mile. I had heard for some time, with no little astonishment, the roar of the unseen waters almost beneath my feet, and it was with a feeling akin to awe, that I now drew near to get a close view of that whirlpool, black as Acheron, through which these waters disappear from the light of day. There is a tradition amongst the mountaineers, that nothing that enters this whirlpool, to which they have given the name of "Devil's Gully" can ever be seen again; but this is not strictly correct, for the remains of a poor countryman, who was once precipitated into the abyss, were found a month or two afterwards below the junction of the upper and under currents; but had it not been for some shreds of clothing which still adhered to the limbs, no one would have supposed that the crushed and mangled mass had ever borne a human form. Mr. Greenbank allowed me to gaze for a few minutes into the frightful chasm, and then continued:—

"When Mr. Blandon and I reached the point where we are now standing, we both paused, as if by a natural impulse, to survey for a few moments, in silent admiration, the spot which had been both the charm and the terror of our childhood. The river, swollen by the melting of the snow on the hills, was at least four or five feet higher than it is to-day. I suppose you have heard of the *blarney stone* in Ireland, and the extraordinary virtue which it is said to confer upon the lips that press it. Well, that stone beneath your feet there also has its virtue. Whoever touches it with his right hand, stooping in such a manner as not to bend the knee, between the hours of sunset and sunrise, shall obtain the wish nearest to his heart. In conformity to the superstition, I was just in the act of placing my hand upon the stone, when a violent, I cannot now by any stretch of charity call it an accidental, push from behind sent me headlong into the gully. Aye! you may stare at me with incredulity; but, difficult as you may find it to believe, that the arm which a few minutes before had been intwined in mine in apparent friendship, could thus be raised to hurl me to destruction, it is true nevertheless."

"If I appeared incredulous, Mr. Greenbank, depend upon it, it was not for the reason you imagine. I was prepared to hear and to believe any villany of that man; but that you were once *there*, and are now *here* (unless a miracle has been wrought for your salvation), I know not how that can be."

"My escape may indeed be regarded as miraculous, and had the river been in the same state then as you see it now, my fate must have been inevitable."

"But did you not say that the river was considerably higher that night than it is to-day?"

"I did; and to that circumstance, under Providence, I owe my safety. This may seem an enigma to you, but its solution is easy enough. The subterranean aperture was not sufficiently large to admit the whole volume of water, and the surplus fluid (as a lecturer on hydrostatics might term it) flowing onward between, but not under the rocks, carried me along with it into that stagnant pool behind those trees. When, half-choked and bruised, I succeeded in struggling from the mud, it was to find myself alone. Blandon had hurried away as fast as he could. I have no doubt he believed then, and still continues to believe, that his murderous purpose had succeeded; but some how, when he least expects it, he shall yet be undeceived. I have little else to tell you. Jock o' the Hill received me as one risen from the dead, with the most passionate manifestations of delight, and nursed me with every care, and no little skill, through the two days' illness that followed that dreadful night. As soon as I was able to travel, I was obliged to hasten to *Liverpool* on some business which my partners had entrusted to me, and this having been satisfactorily concluded, I returned to this neighbourhood a few days ago. I have never been able to catch even a distant glimpse of Mary Inmore through all my masquerading, and had fully resolved before seeing you, that this day should be the last of such nonsensical foolery. I am ashamed that you should have caught me practising it; but you must remember that love, like insanity, often assumes most unaccountable phases, and when a little cold-water has removed these stains, let the remembrance of them vanish too."

According to the arrangement which had been agreed upon, I left Mr. Greenbank at some distance from Jock o' the Hill's abode, and returned to order dinner, and wait his arrival at "The Grouse and Trout." He very soon joined me there, just as I expected to find him when dressed in his proper costume, as handsome a fellow as ever stole the heart of maiden fair. The landlord, good man, had no idea that the gentleman, behind whose chair he now stood with obsequious politeness, was the same whom he had entertained in his kitchen a few hours before, and amused us not a little with a doleful account of some robberies that had taken place on the previous night. He, himself had lost ever so many fowls, and a whole cheese had been abstracted from Walter Begg, the carrier's cart, in an adjoining yard. "It was that nigger chap, gentlemen, you may depend upon that. I never liked the looks of the fellow; but to come into my house after plundering me as he did, that was a stroke of impudence, which I should scarcely have expected."

I could see that Greenbank winced a little at this attack upon the honesty of his "alter ego;" but, putting the best face upon it, he asked, with a roguish twinkle of the eye, whether or not the authorities had been apprised of the vagabond's proceedings, and advised that they should be applied to without delay. As, however, the authorities in Craigtallow consisted only of an old constable, who had been laid up for six weeks by an attack of rheumatism, there was little hope that the matter would be brought to a successful issue. Although neither of us felt any great desire to linger over the wine, the shades of evening had once more begun to thicken around us before we left the Grouse and Trout. In spite of the impatience of my companion, I had contrived that it should be so, as I did not wish our approach to the Percy Arms to be observed from a distance, thinking that some caution would be requisite in introducing the long-lost stranger. The day that had been ushered in by fierce tempest was succeeded by a night calm and serene: fit emblem of that sacred repose, which the Angel of Peace sometimes breathes upon the stormy passions that agitate the human breast!

Mr. Greenbank spoke but little on the way, and I shall not attempt to describe his emotions, as each foot-step brought him nearer to her with whom he now once more hoped to realise "his earliest and purest dream." About half-a-mile from our destination, when passing a cottage, the interior of which could be seen by means of the light which issued from the window, he seized my arm with a sudden start, exclaiming at the same time, "That is she." I turned my eye in the direction indicated, and there, beside the decrepid old woman who occupied a seat close to the low logs that burned on the hearth, stood Mary Innes, speaking the words of consolation and of comfort, all unconscious how closely, in her case, the shadowy sands of night and morning were approaching each other.

Whispering hurriedly to the strong man, who now trembled like a reed beside me, to go on a little way beyond the first bend of the road, so that I might have an opportunity of acquainting Miss Innes of his arrival, and assuring him that as soon as they met I should go forward to make the same announcement to Mr. Innes, leaving them to follow us slowly or as quickly as they pleased, I knocked at the door, and scarcely waiting to be invited, entered the lowly dwelling. I was proceeding to explain to Miss Innes that I had seen her through the window, and thinking that she might perhaps feel a little timid at walking home alone, had ventured to offer her my escort, when the old woman, who, although blind, must have had the sense of hearing developed in no ordinary degree, interrupted me with—"But there were two of you, I know by the footsteps, that stopped before the door: where's the other?"

"Yes," I replied, looking at Miss Innes, "I had a friend with me; he is waiting for us not far away."

Did she suspect from my manner who this friend really was? It must have been so, else why that blood mounting so rapidly to the cheek? why those meek eyes turned so beseechingly towards mine, as if to say—can it indeed be he? The secret would not keep. What words I employed when we left the cottage I cannot remember, but Mary was speedily informed that her lover, kept away from her by a bone fund for five long years, had at length returned, having no reason to blush for any single act of his since he was last by her side; and one minute afterwards all the sorrows of those five dreary years were forgotten in that long embrace. But a stranger intermeddleth not with joys like these. Such transports of happiness as I witnessed that night by Ballowmore are rarely granted to mortals here below; and it is well that it is so; for, were it otherwise, man would be so contented with the present, that he would never sigh for a future Eden.

—

Chap. IV.

"Let me have a cigar with you in your room after you have finished those letters which you say must be written to-night," was the request which Mr. Greenbank made of me, as I rose to leave the supper-table, at which, after the first raptures of welcome had subsided, we had been discussing, after the fashion of ordinary mortals, the natural bearings of the various incidents recorded in the preceding chapters.

"Most certainly," I replied. "As soon as you are at liberty, that is" (with a sly glance at Mary). "If you ever should happen in this world to find yourself at liberty again, come up to me, and try the soothing influence of a weed, after the somewhat exciting events of the day."

"But you said, a little ago, that you had thought of a plan by which that wretch Blandon can be visited with the punishment most justly merited by his crimes, without having recourse to legal measures; won't you enlighten us a little on this point before you go?"

"No; my plan requires some consideration, and must not be submitted for discussion prematurely. I shall, however, be prepared with a rough outline of the programme by the time you come up."

"And am I not to be admitted into your counsels?" said Mary, looking so proud and so happy; "you surely could not be so cruel as to keep me in the dark."

"Certainly not; but we must proceed constitutionally, you know, in this matter. Mr. Greenbank and I, acting as the Lower House, must pass a bill of "*recent pleasure*" against Mr. William Blandon. Mr. Innes shall represent the Upper House, and give it his sanction; and you, Miss Innes, assuming the functions of Royalty itself, must afterwards affix your sign-manual to the decree of your loyal and loving subjects."

"It seems, then, I am to have about as much of my own way as Queens generally have; but although her most gracious Majesty is not to be permitted to take part in your deliberations, I suppose it will be quite constitutional for her to open Parliament in person, in one hour from their time, in the hall, where it will hold its present sittings—No. 4, Percy Arms, Hinkinsonshire."

"'The throne shall be ready for your Majesty's reception, and may Monarch never wear a more uneasy crown than that which will then be placed upon your brow.'"

I had given it as my reason for leaving the room that I had letters to write, and such indeed was the case; but they were not of such a nature as to occupy me more than five or ten minutes, and might have been delayed till later; but I knew that Mr. Inmers would retire early, and, remembering the proverb about the number three being in certain cases rather awkward, I thought it prudent, as well as considerate in me, to withdraw for a time. My correspondence was soon finished, and I then sat down to have what the Dutch metaphysicians would call "a downright good think" about the practicability of the scheme which had suggested itself to me in the course of the evening, when we were discussing some additional facts connected with our story which had come to light during the day. It is time that these facts should be detailed, and I cannot do so more intelligibly than by transcribing, verbatim, a letter which Mr. Inmers received that afternoon from the eminent solicitors, in N——, to whom Mr. Greenbank, sen., had entrusted the management of his affairs:

N——, January 11th, 18—.

SIR,—We have the honour to inform you that in terms of the will of the late Mr. Joseph Greenbank, bearing date Feb. 12th, 18—, your daughter, Miss Mary Inmers, will, under certain provisions afterwards to be explained, be entitled, on the 12th proximo, to the sum of £80,000, should Mr. Henry Greenbank, the nephew of the testator, not appear before that time. It was the wish of our client that the nature of his will should not be made public, in the event of the continued absence of his nephew, until the expiry of five years; but we were also intrusted with a discretionary power in this matter; and we have thought it best to anticipate, by a few weeks, the communication which we should then have had to make to you. The reason for our doing so is as follows:—The clerk who was employed in drawing up the will of Mr. Greenbank, and who is now lying dangerously ill, has requested the clergyman who visits him to inform us that, under [illegible] circumstances, he disclosed the contents of that will to Mr. William Blandon, and that he has reason to believe that Mr. Blandon has been, and is now endeavouring to take some unfair advantage of Mr. and Miss Inmers by means of the information thus obtained. Of course you will know best what importance to attach to this statement; but we thought it only just to the late Mr. Greenbank, to you, and to ourselves, to let you know of it as soon as possible. We have despaired of ever hearing anything further of Mr. Henry Greenbank, and are obliged to conclude that the report which reached us some years ago of his death must have been correct; but full details respecting the property named above, the [illegible] and amount of interest accumulated since 18—, shall be forwarded to you in our next.

Trusting that we shall continue to possess the patronage of Miss Inmers and yourself,

We are, Sir,

Your obedient servants,

GRIGSON AND SHARPLEY.

John Inmers, Esq.

Here then was the true key to the disinterested motives which had influenced the saintly mock-brother. Knowing that Mary Inmers would come into possession of £80,000 if young Greenbank, whom he had always hated at heart, as one likely to thwart some of his favourite plots, remained out of the way, or could be kept out of the way for five years, he thought that such a stake was worth almost any risk; and what he risked to gain it, we have seen. The same post which brought this letter from Messrs. Grigson and Sharpley had also brought one to Miss Inmers, from Blandon himself, in which he informed her that he had now received certain information that their dear young friend had not survived his departure from N—— more than a year, and urged her more earnestly than ever to name the day on which he might hope to obtain the desire of his heart cherished for years, concluding with a few attempts at something like the pathetic, copied, if I am not greatly mistaken, from an old work entitled "The Universal Letter Writer."

It was much more than an hour (I never expected anything else under the circumstances) before my meditations were interrupted; but they came at last, with many apologies for their long absence, declaring, of course, that they had no idea of how the time had passed. Mary did not stay with us long; it was very late; besides, she knew that I had some project which I wished to discuss alone with her Harry, and, like a sensible girl, she soon left us to ourselves. No sooner had she gone, than my friend, adopting the Homeric method of plunging at once into the middle of a subject, exclaimed: "Well, now, Mr. Grumbleton, what is to be done? Is one of us to hurry off to N—— to-morrow morning, and have Mr. William Blandon arrested for the attempted murder of one Henry Greenbank, on the 17th of last month?"

"I have thought of that; but I fear it will scarcely answer. In the first place, a publicity would thus be given to many things, which neither you nor Miss Inmers would like to see flourishing in a prominent position in all the newspapers in Hinkinsonshire; and, in the second place, knowing the cunning of him with whom we have to deal, as well as his hitherto unblemished reputation, and knowing also how easy it is to give to facts a false colouring, which may for a time mislead even the most cautious, I doubt very much whether, with simply your word against his, any jury would convict him upon the capital charge."

"Well, I agree with you there; but could we not have him indicted for attempting to gain fraudulent possession of certain monies, the property of one Miss Mary Inmers?"

"Worse and worse. You forget that your

uncle's wealth, by the terms of the will, is yours, not hers, except as much, from the tenor of Messrs. Gregson and Sharpley's letter is would appear so; but, besides, it is scarcely likely, you know, to offer your hand to a young lady, even although she should be "seised or possessed" of fifty thousand pounds. No; I have thought of all these plans, and one or two besides. Horse-whipping, for instance, or ducking in the nearest pond, are no bad expedients, under certain circumstances; but here, I think I know of something better."

"And what may that something be?"

"You remember that Mr. Blandon has written to Miss Imrie, earnestly begging her to fix the day for her nuptials?"

"Yes, the impudent dog, I know he has."

"Well then, let her fix the day."

"Fix the what? I say, say, sir, are you mad, or do you wish to drive me so?"

"Neither, my good fellow, I do assure you; and if you will hear me to the end you will probably agree with what I say. I was going to advise that Miss Imrie should fix a day—and that an early one—for her nuptials. I did not mean that she were to take place on the same day; although we must, for the success of our scheme, allow the dear man to harbour this delusion in the mean time. Don't you think that when the critic comes we can find a bridegroom without having occasion to trouble him? and won't he just be not a little piqued to find that he has come all this distance merely to have the pleasure of seeing Miss Imrie, and the creature for which he has bartered his soul, pass into the keeping of his old friend, Mr. Harry Greenbank?"

"Ah! now I see what you would be at. Bring him here, thinking he is going to have Mary, and then snapping him just as he is about to clutch the golden apple. Really, Greenbank, the idea is worthy a master; 'Quaint measures are necessary,' as old Dr. Dowdy used to tell us, and I think I owe much something of this kind in [illegible] part of our proceedings when Mary and I each see it every morning; but don't you fear that there may be some insurmountable obstacles in the way?"

"No, I think not. I shall endeavour to secure Mr. Imrie's approval and co-operation. Mary, I think, I may safely leave to you. We must, of course, take care that Mr. Blandon does not visit the Percy Arms before the wedding day; that I think will be easily accomplished; for, secure of his prize, he is not the man to care much about the pleasure of saying pretty things to the lady before the time. Such friends as we can depend upon may, if necessary, be admitted into the secret; and any business that may require to be attended to in N—— I daresay I can transact for you, if you will intrust me with it. I met this Mr. Sharpley, of the firm of Gregson and Sharpley, on the continent some years ago; a pleasant companion he was amongst the Alps, and I shall be very glad to renew my acquaintance with him. I think we had better take him into our confidence. I understand it is usual here, as in most parts of Scotland, for marriages to be solemnized in private houses instead of at the public altar in the church. This is also in our favour, and altogether the thing seems perfectly practicable."

And the more we talked of it the more practicable it seemed; so that before we separated for the night we were quite sanguine of a successful issue. When I met Mary on the following day, her "womanly conscious" blushing cheeks revealed to me very plainly that Harry—who had been with her for half-an-hour alone—had not pleaded his cause in vain, and that little opposition would be offered by her. Mr. Imrie—feeling keenly, as those who never attempt to deceive themselves must always feel deception practised upon them by another, especially when that other has for years been regarded as a true and valued friend—hesitated a little at first; but I succeeded in convincing him, by arguments which seemed satisfactory to myself, that as Mr. Blandon's crimes were such as would scarcely be reached by the arm of the law, we were perfectly justified in the course we intended pursuing.

Mary would not consent to write to Mr. Blandon herself; I therefore undertook to compose an epistle, which should be afterwards transcribed and signed by Mr. Imrie, to the effect that his daughter had at length consented to name the 15th of next month for her marriage. And I flatter myself that, if the proper use of language be, as the French diplomatist said, to conceal one's real sentiments, my missive was a masterpiece in its way—"Pour encore! [illegible]" The best of it was, it had the desired effect; and the conspiracy—no, we must not call it by that ugly name; I mean the legitimate combination for the purpose of inflicting a severe moral chastisement upon one in every respect deserving of it—rapidly hastened to its consummation.

I spent a few days in N—— with Mr. Sharpley, who heartily approved of all that we intended doing, and declared that nothing should prevent him from seeing the dénouement at the Percy Arms. He had taken such good care of Mr. Greenbank's property while that gentleman was absent on his travels, that he thought he had a right to be present at the wedding—besides, what better opportunity could he have of congratulating his client, and giving an account of his stewardship.

James Lindsay threw up his cap, with a shout like that of a schoolboy who has received a half-holiday, and laughed—such a laugh!

"Where it most sparkled no glance could discover—In lip, cheek, or eye—for he brightened all over!"

I did not ask for an introduction to Mr. Blandon; but I did insist on his being pointed out to me in the street, or rather, I succeeded in painting him out to myself; for I had formed so correct an idea of that gentleman's appearance, that I had no difficulty whatever in recognizing the original. "Yes," thought I, as he walked past me, "that self-satisfied simper becomes you well here; but you little know what a mine is ready to explode under your feet! Wait till I get you into Blankamptshire!"

And at last the day came. Eleven o'clock was the hour fixed for the ceremony to take place, and a few minutes before that time, a chaise, drawn by a couple of prancing greys, drew up before the Percy Arms. Mr. Sharpley, Captain Morrison—a Peninsular veteran, who had retired on half-pay to his native glen, and was on very intimate terms with Mr. Inmare—James Lindsay, the Presbyterian clergyman who was to officiate, and myself, along with a few neighbours and friends, were assembled in the most commodious apartment in the house to receive the bridegroom expectant, and performed our part so well, that to the last moment he had no suspicion of what was about to happen. As is not unusual on such occasions, a few moments of rather embarrassing silence succeeded, and then all eyes were turned towards the bride, who entered leaning upon the arm of her venerable parent. Mr. Blandon, animated surely—villain as he was—by some emotions nobler than those which earth's glittering dross inspires, as his eye rested on the lovely figure before him, made one hasty step forward, as if to place himself in his proper position in front of the clergyman; but before he could take a second, the hand which he thought would in a few minutes be his for ever was clasped in those of Mr. Henry Greenbank, who, on a preconcerted signal, had thrown open the side-door behind which he was concealed, and now stood boldly confronting the man whom the interposition of Providence alone had prevented from being his murderer. For a few moments the stockbroker appeared to be utterly paralyzed; and I have no doubt actually believed that the ghost of the murdered Harry, like that of Banquo of old, had come as an unbidden wedding-guest; but the looks of scornful defiance which met him on all sides, and the hearty welcome which the true bridegroom received, convinced him at length that it was no vision, but a reality which startled him. He felt that those eyes had "*speculation*" in them, and that the terrible game at which he had been playing was irretrievably lost. And as this consciousness forced itself upon him, no pen can describe that look of cowardly terror and baffled malice! I have seen men rendered so hideous by vice, that you could scarcely call them human; but I never saw a fiend incarnate till the hour in which the mask was suddenly torn, before my eyes, from the face of the smooth-tongued hypocrite!

After struggling for a time, as if it were for words to utter some curse of vengeance, he turned to leave the room; but we hemmed him in on all sides, so that there was no escape; while Mr. Inmare addressed him in the most solemn manner on the enormous nature of his guilt; and concluded by saying that one of the reasons which had influenced him in allowing him to be brought there that day was, that he might see and know that there is an Eye above all, which continually watches over those who seek its protection, and an arm of might that will not suffer the machinations of the wicked to triumph for ever. It was then intimated to him that after the ceremony he would be allowed to depart. What his thoughts must have been, as he heard the vows uttered and the blessings invoked, I do not pretend to tell; but as soon as it was permitted him to do so, he slunk away like a hound that had received the lash, no one honouring him with a word, except that I whispered to him, in low, but audible tones, as he passed me—"Be very careful on your journey *not to go too near to the Devil's Gulley!*" But although we had guaranteed him against personal violence, it was not so easy to restrain the fury of the crowd outside. Jock o' the Hill, who was aware of most of the circumstances narrated above, was determined that the popular voice should at least be heard on the occasion; and the moment Blandon showed his face outside, he was received with such an outburst of yells and hisses as must have rung in his ears for months afterwards. The post-boy, who had been induced to refuse to carry him back, declared point-blank, in an accent which showed that he had received his early training considerably south of the Tweed, that it was enough for him to be able to say that he'd driven Satan once in his vehicle, and that he was not going to try the experiment a second time! The victim was therefore obliged to walk to Craigbal-low, followed by the infuriated mountaineers, who, if the truth must be told, gave him some more tangible proofs of the estimation in which he was held than mere words could have conveyed. The lesson might prove a salutary one to him; but I scarcely expect that it will be so; for, although such men as he may gnash their teeth in unavailing regret that their designs have been frustrated and their villanies revealed, seldom, indeed, is it granted to them to realise the import of that holy word—REPENT!

It were needless longer to protract our tale. Harry and his better angel are away to some spot in that fairy-land of which we have spoken. Their healths have been proposed in an appropriate speech (I need not say by whom), and duly honoured in a flowing bumper; Captain Morrison has sung his best, in fact his only song—

> I'll be his, and he'll be mine,
> The braw braw lad of Gala-water,

and the wedding guests are about to separate; Mr. Inmare seems to miss his Mary, but he does not murmur; because he knows that in a few weeks he will take up his abode with the young couple in the noble mansion which they have purchased at no great distance; where, also, a hearty welcome, a fishing-rod, and a gun—three no contemptible blessings—are always to be reserved for me. To-morrow I return to my books and my bachelorhood; trusting, dear reader, that you have not wearied during the short time that we have lingered together by Ballowmure.

CHURCHYARDS AND EPITAPHS.

BY MERLIN.

PART III.

"I like that ancient Saxon phrase, which calls
The burial-ground God's-Acre! It is just;
It consecrates each grave within its walls,
And breathes a benison o'er the sleeping dust."
LONGFELLOW.

This
Is the house of God:
Come to it as often and as early as you can;
Enter into it with joy and gladness,
And
Behave in it as in the presence of God,
With all due decorum and devotion.

The time approaches rapidly when this and similar inscriptions will no longer be read by the village youth as they enter the house of God. One by one new churches rise up with spires pointing to Heaven, unlike the grey old towers from whence the starling and jackdaw have for centuries welcomed the morning light. New ones rise, and old ones are renovated; but nevermore these words of kindly warning are renewed upon the old, or written on the new. It is only the thoughtless who can see this wholesale sweeping away of the customs of our forefathers without some regret: there is something to reverence in them, if only because they were the things our sires daily contemplated. For ourselves we confess, in spite of modern innovations, to a warm love for these simple churches and customs of our ancestors, and cannot but feel a loss of something dear to us, when, after an absence, it may be of only a few years, we find the church walls we left once grey with lichen and moss, and covered with the rudely-formed hieroglyphics of men whose earthly frames have crumbled into dust, with sharp edges, and smooth stones neat and prim, and a new-fashioned door where the old porch stood. Half the looked-for joy of "coming home" depends upon seeing them again; yet think not, courteous reader, that I prefer the oaken high-backed pews and ill-convenienced ways of their days to these; it is not that, so much as an estrangement from their spirits, for one cannot so easily realise, though only in fancy, their habits and probable appearance in a place they never knew, as in one whose every particular was fastened on their memory.

It was a sweet October afternoon, with here and there a leaf flickering through the air, when, after breasting a hill that left me breathless, I entered the old stone porch of a village church to copy the lines placed at the head of this paper, and to rest myself upon the worn seats of red sandstone, so wisely provided for the traveller to rest, as it were under God's wing. A man of middle-age was sitting there, with his staff between his knees, upon which he rested his sharp chin; he too was scant of breath, though I knew he had not climbed the hill; but the hard lines and sharp angles of a face that had evidently once been round and comely to look upon told sufficiently of his quick snatches and short existence. Half the delight conferred by my long rural walks depends upon the opportunities that occur of talking with village people: let those who find time heavy on their hands try this, it will give them many a pleasant hour and teach many a wholesome lesson; at least it has me. A little ineffectual ray of sunlight stole through some yew trees into the porch, and played about his face; but they only served to deepen the expression of pain and disease.

"A beautiful autumn day," said I, opening my conversation by the aid of that obliging topic the weather, and taking out a pencil to copy the lines.

"It be, sir, very fine," was the reply.

"Been ill long, sir? you seem weak."

"A good o' time, sir, and very weak;" and he paused not for words so much as breath, and again resumed speaking slowly, with a rest between each sentence. "Ever sin' last winter; but it war comin' afore then; years agone now."

"Indeed," said I, to fill up a gap; "and cannot the doctor do you good?"

"Nay, I count they can't mend me much; I took a cold; they ca'd it summat else; but it war a cold, as it didn't leave me kindly like."

"Live in the village?"

"Ay sir, ay, in on a thae cots, as stand back fro the road yonder. It's a good kind o' the squire, and shows a good heart, he's given him for the rent sin I war took, and the gentry's all kind, and sends me bits and sups fro their own tables, and blankets—it's very kind, sir."

"That it is, and you're right thankful too."

"Happen so; but they won't be thanked. Miss Hester, sir, that's squire's daughter, says I shant goo to the parish, though there be them as say it 'ud be best: but I don't like the thoot o' that. You see I worked as long as I could, and we'd a large family to keep. Ony how, some's grow'd up now, and helps us all they can, but it aint much; ony it's the spirit to do't if they could."

And the sick man wiped away a tear with his rough flexible hand, leaning back against the wall.

"And they all did well; all but Mark, poor lad. When I used to lay awake o' nights, I often made to myself a pictur like of him comin' home a better man; but it 'ill be too late now for me," and he paused again and tried to hide another tear, though he might have been proud of it rather than ashamed. I saw he had more to tell, and did not speak. Presently he continued: "He took to poachin' wi' a rough set in the town. It's no use to repent, but I've often thort if he'd stayed wi' the rest on us he'd never ha' done it, and the first night as he went out, they was took, and some transported; but the squire got him off, if he'd leave the country. So he went to sea, an' it's three years now, sin' wi heard on him: eddication warn't easy then as it is now, and he couldn't write you see, may hap he's gone there afore me (pointing up to the blue sky), and so be I'll see him soon: he was right at heart, ony it was the wild fellows o' the town as spoilt him."

It was sad to see the pale man, and to hear him talk thus, pausing at every sentence for breath; but it seemed, as he afterwards said, a "relief like to talk about things;" but here he was interrupted by a violent cough that shook him terribly. Before he recovered, a little red-faced girl came tripping up the neatly kept path, to fetch him in and carry his cushion, made on purpose for this seat, where he often sat for hours in the summer. He seemed so weak when he rose to go, I could not but offer my arm, and, leaning on me, we slowly went down the path together. On either side were grassy mounds and tomb-stones of yesterday and to-day. Pausing before one of them, marked only by a little foot-stone, he said, "That's the place; Will lies there, and before another summer I shall too." I could not bring myself to speak of a hope I knew could never be realised, and he did not speak of this with regret, like he had of Mark. I saw him seated in his cottage, and asked his leave to call when I came that way again. (Oh! let us never use discourtesy to the poor!) To which he answered, "Do, sir, do; for it's cheery to have a stranger to talk wi'; if I arn't gone I'll be happy; thank ye kindly for to-day, and God bless yo!" Under pretext of showing me where the keeper of the church keys lived, I took the little maiden with me. I wanted the man's name, that I might send what little I could spare of worldly wealth to "Miss Hester" for his use; she would best know how to supply his needs. With the keys in my hands I went back to copy epitaphs, somewhat saddened by the old man's converse.

I did not call again; for, passing through the church-yard only a few weeks later, I saw the sod was newly turned upon the grave he had pointed out, and knew his spirit was beyond the limits of my world, and that there were no more fears of the poor-house, or of want, for him—a worthy son of toil, who had bravely fought life's hard battle; fought it and conquered, without swerving from the ranks. His life had been a manly voyage against the adverse wind and tide of fortune, with no rudder but his own weak arm—no compass but his own unflinching will; yet had he won the victory, and gone down in peace to receive his reward.

Let us return to the epitaphs: Here is one we take from that over-stocked acre in which we were holding converse; but it is not so much the verse as the device above it I would ask you to consider; it was new to me, though it may not be to you. However this may be, it is a most emblem for a gentle maiden's death—this pillar of whitest marble, from which the top has been roughly knocked off, as indicative of the life brought to an end just when its fairest promise was held out. The verse below the name runs thus, and, though without great merit in a literary point of view, is sweet and appropriate; perhaps its greatest failing is that it would be more consistently applied to an infant than a maiden verging on womanhood:

> This lovely bud, so young and fair,
> Call'd hence by early doom,
> Just came to shew how sweet a flower
> In Paradise would bloom.

All who have lingered to read the inscriptions upon grave-stones, more especially in rural places, must have observed the frequent repetition of one verse, almost as universal as the names of families, of which, in a by no means extensive parish, I have counted a dozen or more stones, all bearing one name, and often the same epitaph. This was particularly the case in the church-yard on the hill, of which I am now writing, and the two following verses were there over and over again—in the remotest corner and down by the footpath—on stones that had as yet no touch of moss, and on others which the closest inspection would only enable you to make out here and there a letter; just sufficient to know that it was only one of those upon a more ancient stone, and that the time spent in removing the moss (which, by the way, is just in full bloom, and more than ordinarily plentiful and beautiful after the summer rains), and striving to decipher the dim characters, was just so much lost time. The first of these, commencing, "Afflictions sore," is too hackneyed for quotation. The second was as follows:—

> Friend after friend departs;
> Who has not lost a friend?
> There is no friendship here of heart,
> That finds not here an end.

There was one more, recurring very often, though not so frequently as the above:

> He was a kind and inoffensive friend,
> Peaceful in life and happy in his end;
> Harmless in words, and in his dealings just,
> A constant friend, and upright to his trust.

These are repeated here merely to illustrate the not over wise custom among the villagers of H * * * h in attributing the same virtues to so many individuals, among whom there could not be so near a resemblance as to warrant this repetition. It is with pleasure we turn from these to one of a more than ordinarily feeling and manly tone; it is copied from the obscurest corner of a new cemetery, and the stone is void of name or date:

> Here, with her sleeping
> Babes, resteth in peace
> an excellent woman,
> A most devoted wife
> and mother,
> And a faithful follower of
> Christ her Saviour.
> Stranger! tread lightly;
> Speak reverently;
> Go imitate an example
> Fragrant with the
> Most precious memories
> To him who knew her best!

How rapidly that cemetery, which was but yesterday the play-place of happy children, is filling with the dead! It seems but a day since its green sod and gravel-walks were consecrated, with pomp and ceremony. It is but a few years, and yet there are but few houses in the dark city behind that have not brought some from among their number hither; and we see everywhere, among the green shrubs and newly planted, heaving mounds, and stones telling that "The grass withereth, and the flower fadeth;" and that "Frederic" is "not lost," but "gone before;" and Thomas, beloved son of the above, has "changed Time for Eternity;" or that Mary has "put off incorruption;" and desires that "Ye be also ready, for ye know not when the Lord cometh." Or of the tender child, who was to her father as "the sun is to the day;" who "suffered long and was meek," but "is now where pain and suffering are no more." These, and such as these, are the epitaphs current among our contemporaries. One by one, as the old stones are removed or their inscriptions become unreadable, the old and often ludicrous lines become extinct. With pleasure we mark the good work Education is doing, and which prevents their repetition.

In the cloisters of Worcester Cathedral, on an otherwise naked stone, we read this word of gloom:

> Miserrimus;

What a dark history may not the imagination shape from it! Through how much sin and remorse must the man whose dust lies beneath have passed, to merit so dark an epitaph! Happily there are few lives utterly desolate, and these only known to such as are burdened with the weight of unatoned-for and undiscovered crimes.

Hitherto, kind reader, we have been diffuse; gossiping among the tomb-stones rather than fairly writing off the epitaphs for your perusal, our purpose here not being to classify and arrange into various sections the epitaphs we have copied, so much as to present you with a fair estimate—or, rather, sample—of our English churchyards and their tombstones, taking them as they exist; and thus, as in the following pieces of verses, we wander and pause, now by a stone of to-day, and then by one upon which the rain and snow of centuries have fallen, stooping to trace the dim old capitals, or the illuminated letters of to-day's writing, and now, by way of "conscience-work," we proceed rapidly from one to another, leaving the readers of the page to make, as is most in accordance with their individual character, a commentary for themselves.

Since the publication of the first part of this paper our attention has been drawn to others of a similar nature in contemporary magazines, but their examples being gathered from different localities, and the subject being differently treated, we do not think this consideration sufficient for the abandonment of our original design. Nor do we, as has been suggested, see any reason why the names of obscure individuals should be here produced, or even the places in which the epitaphs are to be found named, unless in cases like the following, when they will help out the point of the lines in question. On Jane Pitt, of the Level, 1779.*

> Here lie the remains of a worthy old queen,
> As good a companion as ever was seen;
> At the LEVEL she dwelt in every one's heart
> Till death at her majesty LEVELL'D a dart.
> Kings, princes, and peasants, at his summons must fall,
> For death the great LEVELLER, LEVELS us all.

Or the following:—

> Esther Greene—a bitter, sour weed,
> God never loved her, nor increased seed.

It is only in cases like these, where the name, or circumstances in life, give rise to the epitaph that name or other description is not out of place.

---

* We extract this and several of the following from an interesting volume by John Noake, Esq., entitled "The Rambler in Worcestershire," in which will be found much curious information relating to the churches, &c., &c., of that county.

Twenty years I was a maid,
Two months I was a wife,
Five weeks I was a mother
And then I lost my life.

Our next speaks well for the connubial bliss of one Mary Ford—

Here lies the body of Mary Ford,
Whose soul we hope is with the Lord;
But if for hell she's changed this life,
It's better than being John Ford's wife.

And reminds us of another we quote from memory—

Here lies my dear wife, a sad slattern and shrew,
If I said I regretted her, I should lie too.

Here is a specimen of orthography early in the 16th century—

Here Death triumphs, and take us al must dye;
Thus we triumphe to Christe by Death to flye
To live to dye is not to dye; but live
To dye to follow in blessed life to give.
Aske how they liv'd, and thou shalt know their ends.
They dyed saintes to God—to prove true friends.

My anchor's cast—
My warp's on shore—
And here I lie
'Till there's no more,

is pithy and appropriate for the grave of a thrown waterman. We give our next to puzzle the reader as it has done us: it is copied from an antique church tile—

Think man thi liffe may not ever endure,
That thou dost thi self of that thou art sure;
But that thou kepist unto thi sectur care,
And ever hit availe thee hit is but aventure.

Our friend is gone before
To that celestial shore;
He hath left his woes behind
He hath all the storms outrode,
Found the rest we toil to find—
Landed in the arms of God.

There is an attractive conceit, if I may use the expression, about the following verse, which impresses the lines on most memories:

Pope hold asserts (some think the maxim odd)
"An honest man 's the noblest work of God."
If this assertion is from error clear,
One of the noblest works of God lies here.

Here is a Bacchanalian's verse—

To tell a merry or a wondrous tale,
Over a cheerful glass of happy ale,
In harmless mirth, was his supreme delight,
To please his guests or friends by day and night;
But no fine tale, how well soever told,
Could make the tyrant Death his stroke withhold.
That fatal stroke has laid him here in dust,
To rise again once more with joy, we trust.

"A little girl," says Mr. Noake, "walking in a Parisian cemetery, and reading, one after another, the praises on the tombstones, exclaimed 'I wonder where all the *sinners* are buried?'" And well, too, might we so exclaim in almost every acre of burial ground; for the tombstones of wives, husbands, daughters, sons, friends, M.P.'s, shoemakers, poets, blacksmiths, warriors, and rural constables, all teem with unnatural, overdrawn, and frequently nonsensical inscriptions written in their praise, as though all the world conspired to out-Herod Herod in this particular, or to wipe out the slanders they did not fail to speak while they lived, by more objectionable praises after death. Every county book has its store of these, all in the same high-flown laudatory strain. From these generally worse than worthless effusions we select one that will repay perusal. We commend it to the reader as the only one we have found among many of a similar nature, worth the trouble of copying.

In this sequester'd grave, this humble stone,
Guiltless of art, adorn'd by truth alone,
Thy virtues, lov'd Eliza, here may show,
And paint the sources of a husband's woe.
What if no scenes of busier life appear,
With dazzling radiance, in thy brief career?
Thine was the zeal that shunned the general gaze,
Thine the mild lustre of domestic praise.
Five fleeting years in joys connubial past,
Four pledges of delight, too pure to last,
Prov'd how brightly in more lengthened life
Had shone the FRIEND, the MOTHER, and the WIFE.
Charm'd by thy temper, by thy example fir'd
No more the youth life's giddy course desir'd.
O! How without thee shall the path be trod,
That leads to life, to virtue, and to God!
Yet shall my soul his high behests obey,
Whose bounty gave, whose justice takes away;
Nor e'er my grateful heart forget, that he
Ow'd thee to Heaven, who owed his heaven to thee.

A REFORMING QUEEN.—Isabel of Spain was quick to discern objects of real utility. She saw the importance of the new discovery of printing, and liberally patronized it from the first moment it appeared. She had none of the exclusive local prejudices too common with her countrymen. She drew talent from the most remote quarters of her dominions by munificent rewards. She imported foreign artisans for her manufactures; foreign engineers and officers for the discipline of her army, and foreign scholars to imbue her martial subjects with more cultivated tastes. She consulted the useful in all her subordinate regulations; in her sumptuary laws, for instance, directed against the fashionable extravagances of dress, and the ruinous ostentation so much affected by the Castilians in their weddings and funerals. Lastly, she showed the same perspicacity in the selection of her agents, well knowing that the best measures become bad in incompetent hands.—*Women of Worth.*

HARRINGTON GRANGE.

Chap. V.

The Picnic.

You know what it is, my dear reader, to be staying at a country house with a number of other guests, all disposed for enjoyment; where everything is well ordered, and goes smoothly; where you have nothing to do but be amused. You know how quickly the days will seem to have passed when you look back upon them, as Amy did this fifth morning of her stay at Winmore. First there had been the ball, then the pleasant languor of the day following; music, instrumental and vocal, agreeable conversation, then an evening of charades, then something else. Prominent amongst the pleasures there was the visit to The Wilds, under Lady Harding's escort; and now, in all the beauty of this summer morning, there was the genial bustle of preparation for the picnic to Winmore Castle.

"My good young people," said Lady Harding, feebly, "you do not expect me to join you. I really am not equal to it. As I am Miss Harrington's stern guardian pro tem., I shall manage for her, and the others will please themselves. Can you ride, little Amy?"

No, Amy thought not.

"Then Eleanor shall drive you in the pony-carriage. Do you hear, Eleanor? Then that is settled. Good-bye. I hope you will enjoy it."

There had been but one drawback to Amy's happiness, and that was Eleanor Vere. Sometimes she would speak to her; but if she did, it was in an even, cold tone, that differed at once from the familiar she lavished upon the other visitors, and from the tone she used to Philip. But always she treated her with a silent indifference, or a marked and haughty politeness. And now she was to drive with her alone to this picnic.

Little Amy looked into her face wistfully, as they sat in the carriage together; she would have liked to ask why all this was, but then she had no right to ask it. Miss Vere was studiously polite. Even now she pointed out places of interest in the neighbourhood, with the precision and formality of a guide-book. Why should Amy complain? Philip was there to meet them when they arrived at the place fixed upon, and with Philip and his sister she climbed the hill to the castle. There was plenty to say about that. Had he sketched it? Could he tell how old it was?

"No, but he could ask Miss Hunt."

That lady, however, turned on him an eye that was loaded with deeper things, and could not be brought to bear upon his childish questions. "When in that courtyard rang the clatter of horses' hoofs, and the ring of the mailed footsteps; the clang of the sword, and then the swift whizz of the arrow from its bow, or, in later times, the heavy boom of the gun!"—that was how Miss Hunt's thoughts were occupied. "And to think, in that noble pile—majestic in its fall—the hand of the great destroyer, the scythe of the hoary king, Time, as it sweeps over the battlements, touches the bower of the noble lady, who had there looked out for the plume of her lord; and striking the forms of lord and lady, reduced them to their kindred earth! Such, and so fleeting," sighed Miss Hunt, with a great sigh, "is the strange and mysterious thing which we call 'life!'"

And on the brow of the hill stood Mr. Hackville, the poet; his own lofty brow bared to the breeze; his long hair flowing behind him, and his eye "in a fine frenzy rolling."

"They were sensible people in those days," said Mr. Hadley; "they had music at the daily board."

"Yes," responded Miss Goddard. "Feasting the soul as well as the body; or, rather, rendering the earthly feast spiritual."

"I wonder could one get up that turret in the distance?" said Philip Vere, who, having rejoined Eleanor and Amy from the group, was beginning to tire of these somewhat high-flown reflections.

Miss Goddard came down out of the clouds immediately, called him a "rash thing," and challenged him to assist her in scaling the turret spoken of.

They trooped off together, large and small stars, and a little figure appearing cautiously from behind a buttress, watched them with a smile.

"Now I am by myself, now I can get a bit of that moss for Papa. I saw some just like it in an old book of his. If I had asked them to get it, they would have laughed, and talked such queer stuff that I never can understand it. I suppose it's clever; but Papa is clever, and he never talks like this to me. Perhaps it is because I am so stupid. Now, if I can but climb high enough!"

Struggle on, little Amy, one step more, and the tempting bit is reached. A step more on the rotten old stones, and a hand loosens its hold to grasp the dangling treasure. And the stone, careless of consequences, slips comfortably away from under the feet which have trusted to it, and crashes, in spasmodic leaps down the steep side of the hill. And Amy is down also, lying on the grass.

One little cry—only one—and then her lips are bitten hard to keep in the evidence of pain. She must get up. Oh, if she could only get up before they all come back again!

"I cannot stir!" murmurs Amy.

"Keep quiet," says a voice beside her, so gently that she does not even start. "Do not attempt to move an inch!" And Eleanor Vere, passing her arm round Amy's neck, drew her gently nearer to the rain.

If it had been anyone else—even Miss Goddard—but to terrible Eleanor!

"I am very sorry," began poor little Amy; but she stopped. The arm that had been passed round her drew her into a close embrace, and the haughty Eleanor was kissing her forehead and her cheeks.

Amy had not seen, but Eleanor had, that less than one foot's difference in her fall and she would have rolled, as the stone did, down that precipice to the very bottom.

"I have sprained my ankle," said Amy, looking into the face bending over her, and wondering at its ashy paleness, no less than at the tenderness to herself; "but I don't mind it, indeed, if you will just help me to get up. I know it is sprained, because I did it once before."

"You must do as I tell you," said Eleanor. "Lie here quite still for a moment. The carriage is down there, below; you will suffer Philip to carry you to it. Hush—I will tell Mr. Sackville, and make him keep the others quiet with a recitation—he is fond enough of it," said Eleanor, unable to resist the sneer even now. "No one shall tease you but Philip and myself."

"But there is no need—I cannot bear to take you away," said Amy, distressed.

Eleanor stopped her, almost harshly.

When she came back again with Philip, neither of them spoke; but he lifted her like a child, and took her down the hill to the carriage. I am not sure that he would have minded if the hill had been longer, or even if no carriage had been at its base, and he had been obliged to carry her all the way.

"There; now I must leave you to Nelly, and go back," said Philip, half hoping he should be ordered to get up behind.

"Yes," said Eleanor, busy with the shawls, with which she made a sort of lounge for Amy. "Go back, and tell them there has been an adventure, and I have borne away the heroine. Is that right, little one?"

Amy looked up, gratefully.

It was not the words, so much as the altered tone and the look on Eleanor's face, that made her turn away her head, and think that, after all, she would rather bear the pain of the injured foot than go back to the morning, when it was well.

Eleanor drove home in silence, thinking perhaps of what might have been but for that over-ruling Providence which men call chance. She made light of it to Lady Harding, before Amy; but the former, covering her with gentle caresses, insisted that she should not be shut up in her own room, as she wished, but should come to the drawing-room. There was a sofa, just fitted for such a case; and Eleanor would be nurse, would she not?

"I want no nurse," pleaded Amy. "It is only tiresome you know, Lady Harding; and it will be so long getting well, I think I had better go home at once."

"That is how she treats us, Eleanor," said Lady Harding. "Home, indeed! Do you think I should suffer an invalid to go out of my house?"

"But I am not an invalid."

"Do you wish to go?" asked Eleanor; and Amy, looking into her face, gave way, and confessed that she did not.

That evening—placed on the couch in the drawing-room, Lady Harding having left her, and Eleanor alone sitting there beside her; while the ghosts of the dancers filled the room, mixed up with the castle the bit of moss, the rolling stone, and the fall—a thought came to Amy, suddenly, and she cried out: "Oh, Papa, Papa!"

"You shall write to him yourself," said Eleanor. "Yes, he might hear all sorts of things, and be frightened. Rumour never tells the truth."

The letter was written and sent. Eleanor took her place again, and the blue eyes, which were wont to be so mischievous, fixed themselves upon her.

"You are very kind to me," said Amy, timidly.

Eleanor's hand was on the brown head in an instant, stroking it.

"My dear little Amy," she said, shuddering; "you don't know all."

"All what?"

"You don't know that one step—the breadth of my hand—further to-day, and you would have been crushed to pieces."

But Amy's gaze never flinched.

"I saw when Mr. Vere lifted me up, and I am very thankful. But yet I think I would go through it again—for this. I like to be cared for. I *mean* it. It hurts me when people—beautiful people like you—are so cold and proud."

Eleanor's only answer was a caress.

Chap. VI.

Round the Sofa.

In the darkest corner of the spacious drawing room, with Eleanor beside her, and twilight gathering over them, little Amy rested, in the half-sitting, half-reclining posture, for which some of the modern couches are so favourable.

Sir Thomas came up and blustered, wanting to know what they were all about, to leave her alone in the rain. When he was a young man he should not have done such a thing, he knew. He thought the rising generation of gentlemen a sad falling-off. Nothing but poetry and music and metaphysics would do in these days. Honest, old-fashioned field-sports were out of date—they were even voted vulgar and coarse! Worse than that—he now found that chivalry was gone out too; and as for that attention and respect towards ladies which had characterised his younger days, where was it, when a party of young fellows went roaming about an old ruin, and left a young lady to help herself at the risk of her life—eh?

Lady Harding drew him away, with a gentle "My dear Thomas!" And Miss Goddard rushed upon Amy as furiously as her muscular hand was wont to clatter up and down the keyboard. "Was she hurt much? Any bones broken? How well she bore it—quite a heroine!"

Mr. Mallo had floating through his head the first few melancholy bars of "Wilmore Castle, a Requiem," when it occurred to him awkwardly that as no one was dead a requiem would not be quite à propos.

Miss Harts bent down her hooked nose, and whispered an incident of Spartan fortitude, which dealt in such unpleasant images that Amy felt a little uncomfortable under it; and Mr. Sackville, looking upon her with a hazy, far-off gaze, which seemed to pass through her into the mysterious future, had composed the three first stanzas of "The Dirge of the Castle," and was going desperately through the alphabet in search of a rhyme for "agony," which he couldn't find anywhere.

"And now," said Miss Goddard, playfully, "shall we indulge in a little music, or will it be too much for the invalid?"

Whereupon Amy looking distressed, Eleanor begged to assure her that Miss Harrington did not consider herself an invalid, and was particularly fond of music. Then the chandeliers throwing down their soft radiance, the piano became again the cynosure, and the sofa in the dim corner was deserted.

"I have a note for you," said Lady Harding, coming up to Amy, and putting one into her hand. "It came enclosed in one to me from your papa. I think he may trust me even with his Sunbeam. Such a name as that is worth earning, little Amy."

"I am sure everyone is too kind," was the grateful response. And Amy's eyes sought Eleanor; but she was leaning silent and abstracted over the back of the sofa, and Philip was with her.

"I shall tell him you have already achieved greatness," continued Lady Harding, lightly. "All my visitors are glad of an adventure to talk about."

Amy silently folded the little note from her father—nothing but a few kind words, but precious, as such words generally are; and Philip Vere, bending over, put something before her.

"I hope you will forgive me, Miss Harrington, if it is not the right place."

"My moss! Oh," cried Amy, her eyes sparkling—"how could you do it?"

"Then you are angry—you did not care about having it?"

"Angry! Oh, thank you! It was for papa. But how did you know what—? You must have told him, she said, turning to Eleanor. "Why did you?"

"I only told him you slipped in trying to reach a bit of moss," said Eleanor. "Was there any harm in that?"

"I am so sorry!" began Amy.

But she was not allowed to finish, for here ensued a furious attack from Miss Goddard, who insisted upon Amy's sofa being moved nearer to the piano, and into a better light. Amy, however, ventured to announce a preference for the dim corner; and Eleanor said decidedly, "She is better here."

"Oh, certainly," said Miss Goddard, with a slight tinge of temper in her tone, "if you say so. I am aware that my claims are but feeble compared with yours. I only thought it might be dull; but Miss Harrington is fortunate in her guardians."

Philip went away with her to the piano, and again Amy was left alone, except for Eleanor, who took the vacant chair at her side, and began arranging the pillows.

"You are very good to me," said Amy, again, wistfully.

"And you are not to say that," replied Eleanor, "unless you want to drive me away."

For the strong feelings hidden beneath that cold exterior had been stirred powerfully, and Eleanor gave way to them, wondering at herself while she did so. Philip's constant companion, caring for no one but him, the circumstances which had surrounded her childhood were peculiarly favourable to the growth of that sarcastic bitterness which tinged all her intercourse with strangers. She could just remember her mother, and she knew that that mother's life—at least her married life—had been one unbroken effort to shield herself and her children from cruelty and oppression. And down deep in Eleanor's memory were the days that followed her death—when they, the brother and sister, feeling that now there was no protector, clung together, and hid themselves from their father's presence and his servants; when, one day in particular, a blow aimed at Philip fell upon his sister; and he, seeing it, sprang like a little tiger to avenge it; when they were both imprisoned in separate closets, and half-starved; but it seemed that nothing would kill them! And then came England, Lady Harding, and kindness. Eleanor could never forget that; but her disposition had been tainted and embittered, and it refused to recover. She clung only to Philip. Believing that there was nothing but hollowness and unreality in those with whom she casually associated, her manner in general almost justified the pedantic strictures of the authoress, Miss Harts. But for Amy Harrington, if a bitter speech or a sarcasm had ever come to Eleanor's lips, it never left them. She could not tell why, but it was impossible to think of Amy as she thought of others, or address her in her usual repelling manner. She had detected herself feeling a strange interest in the little school-girl when she saw her first at the Grange; and ever since, watching her with an attention which would not slacken, though it annoyed herself and distressed its object, there had come to her at times a softening towards this one bit of nature in a motley group—an attraction towards her which she could not shake off. She had accused herself of folly and weakness, of injustice to Philip—for was not she all he had? and of inconsistency—for had she not told him repeatedly that she cared for no one but him? But, "if you would love another, do him a kindness," is an old axiom; and on the day at Wilmore Castle had broken down the barrier which Eleanor Vere set up. And now, lingering day after day by Amy's side, she struggled no more against the impulse, but gave way to it, all the more warmly for the vigorous opposition which had gone before.

The foot would be well soon, and then Amy would go back; besides, the period fixed for their own visit was almost expired; Eleanor did not like to think of that.

Miss Goddard sneered, and gave forth innuendoes which fell as harmlessly on Eleanor's ears as the trills and grupps of her marvellous duets. Miss Hartt recited to Amy the story of Damon and Pythias, of Orestes and Pylades, of pius Æneas and his fidus Achates; and finally, coming down to modern times, in charity to poor little Amy's ignorance of the classic lore which stored her own mind, the simpler story of the grand and beautiful life of the Llangollen Ladies. And Miss Hartt was not sneering. If her language was high-sounding and pedantic; if she was dubbed, with her blue spectacles, hooked nose, and large mouth, a strong-minded woman and a "blue," she recognised beauty when she saw it; and for aught I know, under all the pedantry and conceit, the hooked nose, the queer-shaped garments which she affected for the sake of peculiarity, there was in her heart, in one corner, dim perhaps, and out of sight, a little door labelled "Woman's love."

And Amy thanked her, simply, for her stories, saying she liked the Llangollen Ladies best, because the other names made her think of school-days and of ancient history.

Verily she was nothing but a school-girl. Yet, for all that, in Walter Harrington's den, conned over studiously and anxiously, there was a plan even now for her future, of which, happily for her, she knew nothing.

It was such a pleasant life at Wilmore, and everybody was so kind to her. As for Eleanor—"I know now," thought Amy, "what I wanted to know the first night I came here; when Lady Harding said mamma was her dearest friend."

She was in her usual place in the corner, alone; but Eleanor was making her way to her, and the music was going on as usual.

"I know all about it," thought Amy, looking at Lady Harding's languid face and wearied attitude. "But she did not look like that then; she was younger, and not so tired; like Eleanor, perhaps, only not so beautiful."

Amy turned with an involuntary movement to Eleanor, and put her hand into hers.

"Ah!" she said, softly, "I am so glad I slipped that day, getting the moss."

"Amy, Amy!"

"I am. I have never known what it is to be unhappy. I used to hear them talk about it at school, but I don't know what it feels like. I was a little uncomfortable the first few days here; because, do you know, I began to think I must have done something wrong. I am not used to people's ways, I have seen so little, and am so ignorant. But now I am happier than ever."

Philip, lingering unseen in the shadow, heard the words, and saw the caressing movement; and there was a cloud on his face as he met Eleanor's eyes fixed upon him suddenly. With a motion for silence he left the room quietly, as he had entered it. He had been less in his studio lately, less occupied with his painting, and more frequently with his sister. Perhaps he had gone away, now to ask himself why this was, or to make resolutions for the future. At any rate, it was not to take any more active measures for redeeming lost time, for Eleanor, mounting the stairs to his Whim, some time afterwards, found him in anything but an attitude of application. He was sitting at his easel, but not painting. One elbow rested on his knee, and his head on his hand. He was idle.

"Oh Philip, Philip!"

"And oh, Nelly! Well, what am I to be lectured about now?"

"Idleness, perhaps. You know you deserve it."

"Didn't we come into the country for a holiday, and to repair my health, damaged by hard work? But I am not idle. Will you allow no time for conception and arrangement? Oh, I assure you the picture which has been growing before my eyes is beautiful enough to make the fame of the youngest artist, Nelly."

"Not excepting the unlucky Giles, whose Academy picture you cut up so scandalously?"

Philip did not answer, and Eleanor went up to him.

"Philip," she said firmly, dropping her light tone, "we have never had any secrets; do not let us begin them."

"What now?" asked Philip uneasily.

"You have fallen in love with little Amy Harrington."

He looked up at her with an attempt at a laugh.

"I think it is you," he said.

"My little darling!" murmured the cold and haughty Vere. "Yes, I never knew it was in my nature to care for any one as I do for her. She does not love you, Philip. If she did I might be jealous, even of you—think of that; but she does not. I cannot think of trouble coming to one so sunny and so happy."

"Why should it? You say she does not care

for me," said Philip, walking up and down the room. "How do you know?"

"How do I know? Trust a woman for finding that out. I do not say she never would, but, as yet, she has not thought about you. She cares for you; my dear little Sunbeam! She would lie a-basking in the shine ever; to fold in the shadow of a strong love. But you, knowing your own resolution," said Eleanor, pointing to the easel, "why disturb her, Philip? She has never seen the shadow of trouble; how will she go through the world?"

"Flowers must be bruised before they give out their strength," said Philip; "and if there is trouble for her, she will bear it nobly. But why talk of her to me Nelly, knowing, as you have just said you do, that here is my mistress [illegible] daubs, these blotches of colour. I cannot have a divided aim, you know."

"Then shake off this folly, and work," said Eleanor.

"What good advice, and how easy to follow! Is that all? Wouldn't you advise my going back to town out of harm's way, and will you come with me?"

Eleanor bit her lips.

"If you like, Philip."

"What, still decided! Come Nelly, it is very ungrateful of me to play at bitterness with my best friend. We both remember my resolutions, and how grand and noble they sounded; how easy they were to make. I know your advice is meant well, and it may be good; I cannot tell.

> "The reason why I cannot tell;
> But this I know, and know full well,
> I do not like thee, Dr. Fell!"

Dr. Fell representing your advice, and not you, Nelly. Well, I will try, then."

And Philip turned his [illegible] face to the easel.

"And if Philip tries," thought Eleanor, "I know the firmness and perseverance of his nature; he will succeed."

She thought of his past enthusiasm, of his noble devotion to art as a profession, not so much because he must live, and work to live, but because he had an idea of perfection which he had never yet seen realised. He had set this before him; working steadily, already his name was in many mouths, coupled with words of praise. "Rest," said Philip, "absolute labour is necessary for what I have proposed to myself; my aim is not to equal, but to excel, and that, not for the sake of triumph, but for Art itself." She thought of all this; of how he had said that no other affection must come in, to interfere with this aim: that he must live for that, and that alone; and—could Eleanor Vere suffer a taint of selfishness to creep into her pride for her brother?—the thought of Amy's young life, as it was now, unruffled, and of the love which the little school-girl had given to her. Use she [illegible], if it was one, was something like Walter Harrington's efforts to leave his beloved den. Philip still sought his sister, and lingered where he might hear Amy's voice, if it was not addressing him. The flowers, too, which he had been in the habit of bringing in daily for her, were not forgotten, but given in silence, with a glance at her guardian, Eleanor, that was almost pleading. There was a change in his manner, however, and Amy saw it, and pondered over it, uneasily. He was Eleanor's brother; he had been very kind to her, constantly; had she done something to offend him, that he was so distant and reserved? Once she was on the point of asking Eleanor; but instinct, or some dim feeling of self-consciousness, checked her.

"Sir Thomas has but a poor opinion of the art," said Miss Goddard, who was nothing to music an amateur of the pen's. "He utterly despises the fine arts; but let not Mr. Vere think so savage; is not painting one? He is one of us, in spite of himself."

"How do you know there is any spite about it?" asked Eleanor, laughing.

Two months ago nothing could have equalled the superb scorn with which she would have received this speech—classing Philip with these [illegible] amateurs! But Amy had improved her already.

"Oh, because you are both so proud," replied Miss Goddard. "And Mr. Vere, in particular, thinks he is a great genius; and means to astonish the world."

"So he is a genius," said little Amy, indignantly.

"Ah, you believe in him. Well, I acknowledge you ought to know more about him than we do; you monopolize most of his society."

"Now I wish you were at the piano," thought Eleanor, watching the blush that rose over Amy's face. "Is that Mr. Sackville's poem?" she said, turning to the romancer. "Have you read it?"

"You want to change the conversation, then," retorted Miss Goddard. "If I thought so I should be glad. I never dared to indulge in the possibility of your having a vulnerable point before. Let me see; it was genius in general, and Mr. Vere's genius in particular, I think; I shall try to remember. And here he comes, to answer for himself. Your battle has been well fought in your absence, Mr. Vere," said the lady, retreating.

Philip's face flushed as he advanced, eagerly; but Eleanor told him it was all nonsense, and, if he wanted to know particulars, he must go to Miss Goddard. Amy never even looked up.

"This will not do," thought Eleanor; "already she is beginning to tremble, like a frightened bird, at the sound of his footsteps; and I can see the colour come when he speaks to her, and the pulse beating in her temples. Oh, Philip, Philip!"

Once again Eleanor found him in the almost-deserted Whim, dreamy, as before, idle at his easel.

"Again!" said Philip.

"Oh, Philip! I have no right to interfere, I know; but——"

"Well, I give you the right. Speak, Nelly! What is it now?"

"Oh, Philip! be honest now! You deceive yourself. Why halt between two opinions? Either win her, or else keep away. How do you know the misery you may bring upon her?"

Philip's eyes glistened.

"A nice opinion you have of your brother! I am honest, and I do not deceive myself. Give me a few more days, and then I promise you I will work harder than ever for fame and fortune."

"You have both, Philip."

"Not enough. I am grown, suddenly, greedy. I must work hard and be ambitious, and gain money."

"What for, when you have enough?"

"Nelly, Nelly, be satisfied! You have done your duty. If I tell you that those noble aspirations of ours were mere moonshine; that the endeavour to satisfy a human heart with fame and pictures is like filling a hungry man's mouth with chaff—what do you say to that? If I tell you that the fame and fortune I speak of winning are but secondary hopes; that the first and greatest is so bright, Nelly, that——"

Eleanor put her hand over his mouth, suddenly.

"That will do, Philip. I see it all."

Going down from him, she encountered Lady Harding, who stopped her, anxiously.

"Eleanor, do you know what Roger says?"

"What report?" asked Eleanor, calmly.

"These chattering people. Come here, into my room; I have something to tell you."

TO A DONKEY.

Ignoble beast! too oft art thou
Libelled [illegible]
Who walk erect, with stolid brow
[illegible] features.

They call thee stupid, thou [illegible],
And boast progenitors [illegible];
While by their words and deeds [illegible]
Their brutal nature [illegible].

Let others thy [illegible],
And tax thy sturdy frame with blows;
To sift thy merits is my aim,
And all thy hidden [illegible] disclose.

What though thy bray in loudest note
No sense of melody conveys;
My muse shall willingly devote
A rhyming tribute to thy praise.

The [illegible] may not be thine,
With plodding pace thy highest [illegible];
Thou [illegible], nor stable fine,
With [illegible] thy needs.

Yet, when with stout and [illegible] sides,
In park I watch thy [illegible],
As little infants on thee ride,
I [illegible] must think thee worth a [illegible].

Hard is thy lot, a [illegible] drudge,
When, with a [illegible] load [illegible],
Thy driver [illegible] thee with a grudge,
And thwacks thee with [illegible].

Poor beast! I have oft, with pitying eye,
[illegible] thee tread the roughest ways,
When tail [illegible] thy [illegible] try
A [illegible] will to please.

Distrusted both by old and young,
Thy [illegible],
[illegible] with his tongue,
Because thou'rt but an ass [illegible].

Thou hast not [illegible], like [illegible] of old,
Whose [illegible],
Thy [illegible] with a [illegible],
If he can do a [illegible].

Yet, patient under every wrong,
[illegible] thy [illegible];
For though endowed with [illegible] strong,
Thou [illegible].

Thy [illegible]—
It was [illegible], in strength of [illegible];
To win, the [illegible] of [illegible]
By simplest final weapon done.

Thus far thy [illegible],
To wipe the stigma from thy name;
[illegible] may [illegible],
Or not, my purpose is the same.

And when along the [illegible]
I see thee [illegible] with [illegible],
I'll greet thee, with this [illegible] pledge
To [illegible] thy [illegible].

[illegible]

[illegible] was always an early riser. Happy the man who is! Every morning day comes to him with a virgin's love, full of bloom, and purity and freshness. The youth of nature is contagious, like the gladness of a happy child. I doubt if any man be called old, "so long as he is an early riser and an early walker." And oh! youth!—take my word for it—youth, in dressing-gown and slippers, dawdling over breakfast at noon, is a very degraded, ghostly image of that youth which sees the sun blush over the mountains, and the dews sparkling upon blossoming hedgerows.—[illegible].

THE WORK-TABLE.

ROSE-BUD PATTERN FOR WINDOW CURTAIN IN NETTING AND DARNING.

There is no style of window-curtain for the drawing-room more elegant and distinctive than that which is produced by the combination of netting and darning, it being recommended equally by lightness and richness. Our illustration is arranged for working on the square netting, which may either be executed by hand or purchased by the yard; the latter being the imitation of the former, manufactured by machinery, and much used by ladies who have not leisure for large undertakings of this kind. The rose-bud pattern now given will be found to produce a very handsome effect. The portion consisting of the separate rose-buds and leaves is for the body of the curtain, while the running pattern is for the border. Care must be taken in the darning that the stitches should all be carried one way, or the beauty of the work is much impaired. The cotton for the darning should not be very coarse, and the squares should be well filled in, as when these precautions are not observed the work when washed has the appearance of being rough and irregular. The advantage of this pattern is that variations can be made in it to suit the taste of the worker. The border may be worked as stripes at regular distances; or, if there is an object, the sprigs can be placed further apart. This pattern is also very handsome for anti-macassars."

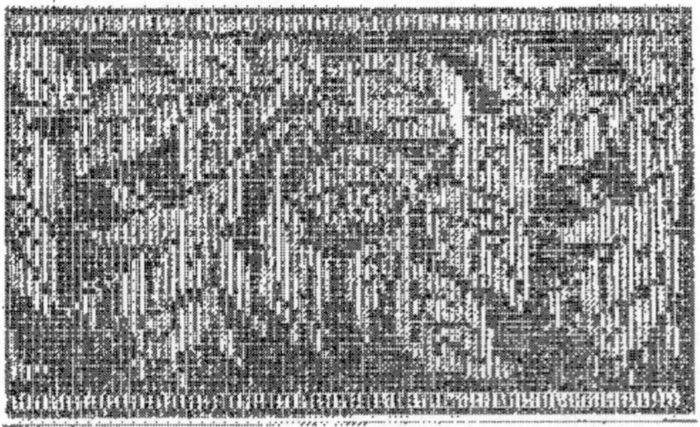

The materials used for this work must be the Boar's Head Crochet Cotton, No. 4, 8, or 12, of Messrs. Walter Evans and Co., of Derby.—Ed.

SOCIAL ETHICS.

(A Letter to the Editor.)

Dear Madam,—A subject of very grave importance was, a short time ago, introduced to public discussion by a letter in the Times, which purported to be the production of "Seven Belgravian Mothers;" I say purported, because it has since been repeatedly asserted in many high places that that letter was written by an ingenious member of the staff attached to the establishment in Printing House Square. Half London was at the time of its appearance "out of town"—exploring the mountains of Switzerland, or studying the habits of anemones and zoophites among the rocks of the sea-coast. There was a general dearth of interesting subjects for the daily press, and therefore it is more than probable that this discussion did not originate with seven English mothers, but with one writer of considerable penetration, who saw that, once opened, it would serve to while away the dreary weeks of the dull season. It is highly improbable that seven Belgravian mothers should get up a little joint-stock company of their own for the express purpose of indicting a letter to the Times, deploring the forlorn condition of their spinster-daughters. But, from whatever source it originated, the importance of the subsequent discussion is the same. Even supposing the whole of the flippant correspondence which followed to have been the fabrication of the one brain, it could not materially alter the position of the question. Thirdly, because it is a fact that a vast number of middle-class professional men do not marry, if at all, till late in life, and consequently there was some ground for such a discussion. Secondly, because having occupied a prominent place in the *Times* for many days, it also, in the natural course of events, assumed a prominent one in the mind of the nation, and, to a certain extent, in the whole of the civilised world; and, thirdly, because the subject did not terminate in the columns in which it originated. The leader, in which the whole of the correspondence was summed up, was a masterly one; but it did not, as its writer could have done, point out, in clear, unmistakeable language, the evils which must result if the desire for high professional and social position, or "keeping up appearances," is to go on increasing the number of late marriages. But there were in it some very noble expressions of feeling, such as the following: "We should be slow to believe that the majority of either sex in the world of rank or fashion know so little of true love that they cannot bring themselves to start from small beginnings, to climb the hill together, as all who do not inherit wealth and position must, and as all who would appreciate the full value of the conjugal tie would choose to do." These are wise words, dictated by a pure and manly feeling, very different from the character of the "correspondence," which was throughout carried on in a tone of levity unworthy of the subject, unmanly and undignified. The controversy, I should have said, has been, from first to last, confined to the upper and middle class sections of society. The arguments first put forth were that certain Belgravian mothers found it impossible to make "suitable" marriages for their daughters. To this it was replied that the class of men referred to were prevented from marrying—because they could not afford it—because they were selfish, and unwilling to give up their bachelor pleasures—because the cares and duties of married life would interfere with their rise in their profession; and lastly (worst argument of all), because of the existence of a certain great evil, to which, happily, I need not further allude than to say that throughout the newspaper discussion the extent and character of that evil has been greatly exaggerated. The arguments against reasonable marriages, which have been so strongly dwelt upon, are calculated to increase,—not to diminish—what is admitted on all hands to be a deplorable phase of modern society.

The transition of the discussion, from the columns of the newspapers to the pages of our contemporary magazines—the *Cornhill* and the *St. James's*—was an easy and natural result. The *Cornhill* for September first took up the subject, under the title "Keeping up Appearances," to which "Respublica" replied, in a letter to the editor of *St. James's*, entitled "A plea for Hymen." "Keeping up Appearances" has been very widely condemned as "specious" and "malicious"; but it is nevertheless a fair statement of facts and a truthful representation of the opinion entertained by the majority of professional men who are averse to early marriages. But its arguments were open to the objections subsequently raised against it by other writers than "Respublica." Domestic happiness was in all cases to be made subservient to professional distinction, and it was taken almost for granted that after marriage it was impossible for a man to rise either in the social or professional scale. Inasmuch as it did this, it was, of course, injurious to the true interests of humanity and the world. According to its showing, the pure atmosphere and tranquil enjoyments of a home, the calm happiness that attends upon a man surrounded by a loving wife and children, was quite a secondary consideration, and it was utterly impossible that he should work hard and be capable of great achievements if he had them. "Many an enterprise of great pith and moment has been greatly crippled by a happy marriage, and a large family of fine children. Many a victorious career has been cut short by baby-fingers." These are the arguments of "Keeping up Appearances." The clergy, who, among professional men, are so often pointed out for their poverty, are here brought in as evidence, and their want of the means to enable them to live in a state according with their position as scholars and gentlemen is unscrupulously attributed to early and "imprudent" marriages. The clergyman's position, as a poor man, is sketched, and we are shown what will be the result of his owing money to the butcher, the baker, and the tailor, in a very forcible way. But it is cowardly and mean to say that his poverty is the result of his marriage, or that "the whole nature of the man is changed under such pressure, and nothing but the gradual degeneration of conscience saves him from being unscrupulous." I have been fortunate enough to enjoy the acquaintance of many clergymen and ministers. One of the happiest, noblest, and most godly men I ever shook hands with, was a minister, with a wife and several children, living upon a very small salary; but he prepared his children for the university, and managed to send them to a Scotch one. You might have searched six counties round, and not have found a man more universally loved, more happy, or more fortunate in his relation with the world. I am happy in the belief that there are hundreds such among our clergymen, who educate their own sons, and do their work none the less efficiently because they are poor, and who never do suffer a "degeneration of conscience." Is it fair to lay their poverty at the door of early marriage? What is to be the result, if clergymen are to wait till they have an abundant living before they can marry? May they not wait from twenty-five to thirty, and from thirty to forty, in fact till all the prime of life is past, and still be only curates? If it is within their power to rise and to obtain high preferment, depend upon it they will do it none the less for having an ardent loving wife and an increasing family of children to aid and stimulate them. It is not possible or desirable that all men should be at the top of the ladder. If we have architects, we must also have masons, and the masons must preponderate. I would urge that man is not ennobled by the distinction he attains in any work, if to obtain it he sacrifices the first law of the nature which originates the happiness of his life. The layer of the stone upon the pillar is equal with the architect. His sphere of life is capable of as great results. I am not in favour of a man who is discontented with his position in the social scale marrying at all; because, if he does, he must suffer the mortification of seeing his children in their early years subject to his own condition; But I am in favour of a man fulfilling to the utmost his opportunities, and being content therewith. A certain degree of happiness and comfort are essential to any nobility in life; without them, the nature of a man becomes perverted and misanthropical, and the whole current of healthy thoughts and good impulses dies within him. Let every man take the standard of his own capabilities, and employ and extend them till they are made the utmost; but he will not do this by remaining single, forming existence in one particular branch of pursuit by only [illegible] his nobler qualities and life in it. Wealth, strength, position in society, any one of these he may get by this; but will he, as a man, be the best and fullest that he might have been? Readers who have read "Keeping up Appearances," read also "Concerning Men who might have been made more of," by A. K. H. B., in Fraser for last month. There is no direct connection of subjects, but there is a certain general similarity of questions in which we are all deeply interested. We rise from reading "Keeping up Appearances" with the feeling that we have spent an hour with a cold, hard-natured man, who has no perception of colour and beauty. We rise from the perusal of "Concerning Men who might have been made more of," with the feeling that we have spent an hour in company with a man whose perceptions of truth and beauty are of the keenest and clearest, and who has also enabled us to perceive it. The one is the nobleman, the other the serf. It is sad to have it brought home to us that we might have been made much more of. It is very solemnly "A. K. H. B." tells us so; but we feel the better for the knowledge; we feel prepared to work for nobler ends, and to enjoy more worthy rewards, if we can but bear in mind his great lesson; and after that, if we can also bear in mind the doctrines enunciated in "Keeping up Appearances," oh how miserably poor their cold conventionality and false teaching will seem! It needs a master-mind, like that of "A. K. H. B.," to set this social question before the world in its proper and true colours. Great as was my enjoyment of his last thoughtful though and yet solemn essay, I must confess that I was disappointed when I found that he had not written of this vexed question.

"A Plea for Hymen" successfully refutes the assertions of the Cornhill essayist. There is (always remembering that it is a woman's writing) as little nonsense in it as possible. The arguments are full of good sense; and it is, all points considered, the best paper of the kind which the discussion has elicited. Man is not the same machine he is made out to be. His affections are not like the steam of a railway-engine, that can be turned off for a day, a year, or for ever. The affection which the man bears to the woman is the great moving power of his life, before which all others bow. Exceptions there are, but in the vast majority there is no other source of impulse so powerful; and as you ascend in the scale of intellect, it will be found to increase rather than diminish. Does it follow, as a natural consequence of early marriage, that men shall be unfit for [illegible] study, and its reward. A prospective marriage will never be half so great a stimulus to them as the actual possession of a wife. Do those who remain single till they are far advanced in life attain the highest places? Do they make the largest fortunes, or achieve the grandest results? The history of the whole world, from the beginning of time, answers No. The same history shows us hundreds of instances in which men have waited and waited, till the young hearts grew cold and the [illegible] sank into a misanthrope. "Early marriage," says "Respublica," in concluding her letter, "is rarely prejudicial to a man. The young clergyman will be as ready for self-sacrifice, the young barrister for study, the medical man for devotion to his duty, with a wife as without one; and, with a true wife, he will be a far happier man than he can possibly be as a bachelor. Did a soldier ever shrink from the breach because he had a wife at home? I think not; for married men would generally rather die than incur the contempt of their wives. When a man has completed his quarter of a century, and a woman is of age, each is ready for marriage; and with a moderate income, unquestionably, marriage should not be shrunk from; for, after these ages, a member of either sex, still single, is in an unnatural state, losing happiness by by, which should be in actual possession."

It must not be supposed, from the passage I have quoted, that "Respublica" is an advocate of marriages on the attainment of suitable age in all cases; a directly contrary opinion is expressed in the commencement of her paper. But the names of many eminent men, living and dead, who married early, and yet won for themselves in after-life the very highest places in literature, science, and the practice of law and medicine, are cited as proof that marriage does not prevent men from obtaining professional distinction.

All this does not alter the fact that men do not marry so early by twenty years as their fathers did. All that can be written, all that can be said upon the subject, will have no effect in altering this; it is a question upon which the individual alone can judge. Twenty writers in as many years would not induce twenty men to marry. The arguments that will make them do this must come from *within*; all that comes from *without* will be like wheat sown upon the broad highway. It is to be lamented that it should be so, for it is a direct perversion of the laws of Nature. It is a struggle between social and natural laws, in which, for the time, the victory seems to be with the social. Its effect, if it should continue, cannot fail to be highly prejudicial, not only to the happiness and content of the nation, but also to its population and its wealth. Ambition has always had her votaries; but hitherto it has not been deemed impossible to enjoy the love and comfort of a home and wife, and still develop a talent to its highest capability.

There are other flaws in the social code beside this, that are acting strongly against marriage. Before speaking of them, I would say that only the basest of men would desire a woman to relinquish a home in which she had been used to comforts and luxuries, to share privation and drudgery. What a man should have to offer a wife must depend upon individual circumstances in every case. A ploughman, if he have but the rude furniture of a country cottage and wages varying with the seasons from ten to sixteen shillings a week, is in a position to marry: probably his children will get little or no education, but, unless he lose his health and ability to work, he will not breed a race of paupers. A mechanic, if he has not constant employment; a surgeon or barrister, if they have not an established practice, would not be mad enough to ask a woman they loved to marry them. If they did, she would, no doubt, be brave enough to risk her happiness and help to aid them by love while they did achieve their work; but, in ninety-and-nine cases out of every hundred, dispassionate friends would step in, and prevent the consummation of such madness. There can be no general standard of what a man in any grade of life shall possess, to entitle him honourably to marriage. Every case is special, and must be specially judged; but taking the hypothesis which has been set forth—if the ploughman is to wait till he has a farm, even of two acres; if the surgeon is to wait till he is a physician; the barrister till he is a Q. C., and the author and the artist till they have established reputations—what will be the end? In a hundred years, where will England be? Why the prophecy may be almost realized, and an enterprising New Zealander may be packing his sketch-book, ready to come over and sketch—not perhaps the ruins of St. Paul's Cathedral, but the dark desolation of a half-depopulated city.

Conventional class-distinction and wealth, with but one exception, have never obtained so great a sway in the world as they now hold here in England. The respect which is paid to wealth and position is growing into a national evil, which becomes more deplorable every year. It would, of course, be unnatural to suppose that the educated should make associates of the illiterate; or, that there should not be distinctions between various grades of men. These are barriers that will never be broken down, however desirable it may seem that they should be. If they were it would lead to the elevation of many—to the polishing of many a rough diamond. It is not to be expected that men should give a man credit for talents he has not proved himself to possess; but it is very hard that a man should be forced to sacrifice his affections and the happiness of his life because he cannot command a certain elegance of life and luxurious manner of living, or was not born to a certain rank. This is by no means an exceptional result of what modern society produces: If the Belgravian mothers who have reason to complain had not sought to make "suitable" matches for their daughters—if, instead of educating them with a view to an expensive "establishment" in life, they had left alone match-making, and exercised no undue control over their inclinations and affections, what different results might have followed! By all means, let our daughters and sisters be accomplished. There is nothing on earth so beautiful as an accomplished girl of pure taste and unaffected nature. But do not teach them that it is a degradation to themselves and to their family to cultivate homely household ways, that many things beside marriage may put them in need of. Do not teach them that there is a class beyond the pale of which they cannot step without disgrace, or that they will lose any womanly dignity by marrying a man, with whom, in the early years of his married life, even shillings may be of great consequence. Very little is really necessary to either happiness or nobleness in life, and a woman can have no holier work than that of aiding a man struggling up-hill or teaching children their alphabet. If daughters are to be educated as expensive puppets, with a becoming scorn of domestic cares; if they are to love only at a proper time a proper man, not of their own choosing, or chosen from an extremely limited "set," where there is but little variety, then will mothers still lament and daughters still remain single!

I am not arguing for unequal marriages: I am not blind to the productive usefulness of the observance of existing social laws; but I cannot fail to see in some of those laws the root and ground of the evil which has, after smouldering for a long while, burst into open flame, and been attributed by false theorists to causes that were and are utterly powerless to produce the effect. I know that it is deemed highly imprudent to attribute any evil to existing social relations established among the classes into which the community is divided. Possibly I ought to know better than to venture an assertion to the effect that many men do not marry because the girl they would like to make their wife has been educated for a higher "style" than they could afford. I do make it nevertheless, for I have known instances in which it has been the case, and am well aware that there are thousands of similar cases occurring every year. There are many men here, in this great centre of modern civilization, who have a "void in their hearts" that only marriage could supply. Men who could support a wife in honourable independence, who are deterred from marrying because the woman they love would not, if she were willing, be allowed to link her life with theirs. If they succeed—if ten or fifteen years hence they have raised themselves, and the lady is still unmarried, they may venture to ask her hand. But the years of warm, fresh love will have flown by never to return. It can be no matter of surprise then mothers and daughters should equally regret that they remain unwed. A woman's life is different to a man's—a woman is the greatest sufferer from anything that delays the commencement of her career as a wife. The position of unmarried women, after the attainment of a certain age, in their father's house and in society, is far from an enviable one. It is, in fact, one to be pitied as much as it is to be regretted. The duties, the responsibilities of a wife and mother are so essential to the happiness of women. Their enjoyments are limited, and I can fancy how dreary and dark the stately halls, the fashionable dinners, and the whole routine of life is to a woman to whose heart the long-deferred hope has brought sickness. Whatever laws exercise a tendency to depreciate marriage are a great evil. Tennyson wrote :—

> ...... either sex alone
> Is half itself, and in true marriage lies
> Nor equal, nor unequal: each fulfils
> Defect in each, and always thought in thought,
> Purpose in purpose, will in will, they grow,
> The single, pure, and perfect animal,
> The two-cell'd heart beating with one full stroke.

Every man whose name is conspicuous among the illustrious dead for purity of thought or high principle has seen in marriage the consummation of manhood, in love the purest attribute of life, the surest link between God and man.

I shall close my letter with another quotation from the noble conclusion of "The Princess." I have elsewhere said that all writing can have no effect in making men marry, but I have the fullest reliance that the laws of Nature, though they may be violated for a time, will assert themselves through every impediment human nature can offer, and, resting upon this faith, I will take leave of a subject that cannot but be painful to contemplate.

> I loved the woman; he that doth not, lives
> A drowning life, besotted in sweet self,
> Or pines in sad experience worse than death,
> Or keeps his winged affections clipt with crime.
>
> * * * * *
>
> The woman's cause is man's; they rise or sink
> Together, dwarf'd or godlike, bond or free:
> For she that out of Lethe scales with man
> The shining steps of Nature, shares with man
> His nights, his days, moves with him to one goal,
> Stays all the fair young planet in her hands.
> If she be small, slight-natured, miserable,
> How shall men grow? but work no more alone;
> Our place is much: as far as in us lies
> We two will serve them both in aiding her—
> Will clear away the parasitic forms
> That seem to keep her up, but drag her down—
> Will leave her space to burgeon out of all
> Within her. Let her make herself her own
> To give or keep, to live and learn, and be
> All that not harms distinctive womanhood.
> For woman is not undevelopt man,
> But diverse: could we make her as the man,
> Sweet love were slain: his dearest bond is this,
> Not like to like, but like in difference.
> Yet in the long years liker must they grow—
> The man be more of woman, she of man;
> He gain in sweetness and in moral height,
> Nor lose the wrestling thews that throw the world;
> She mental breadth, nor fail in childward care,
> Nor lose the childlike in the larger mind;
> Till at the last she set herself to man,
> Like perfect music unto noble words.

I am, dear madam, yours truly,

UN' GIOVINOTTO.

LEAVES FOR THE LITTLE ONES.

FURZEBANK LODGE, AND ITS OCCUPANTS.

BY T. S. F.

"Not gone yet, Mrs. Chipps! Why I shall never believe you are going till I see 'A room to let' in that little window up there."

"Well, no, ma'am," said Mrs. Chipps, dropping a curtsey, and looking almost ashamed of herself, as she added, "I do find it so very hard to leave this place, Miss Sharp, ma'am. I make up my mind every day, but, somehow, I haven't the heart really to say Good-bye; and I keep writing and telling my dear daughter I'm coming, and they keep writing to know when, and——"

"And you cannot fix the when?" said Miss Sharp, smiling, as excited little Mrs. Chipps paused for a moment to take breath.

"Well, ma'am, I really cannot; but I think it must be next week, now. If they would only give me till next week, I think I could get off by then, now that Mrs. Fripps is nicely again."

Mrs. Fripps was a poor deaf dress maker, who lived in the room below Mrs. Chipps; being, in fact, that tender-hearted little body's landlady. And Mrs. Fripps, having had a severe illness recently, her lodger had been a most unwearied and careful nurse—as Miss Sharp quite well knew; but that good lady had not time for her usual gossip with Mrs. Chipps; so, bidding her call and say Good-bye, when she really was going, she went on her way, through the little church-yard, just recently laid out and planted, much to Mrs. Chipps's delight.

Miss Sharp, having given a hasty glance at the shrubs which she intended watering that evening, went on to the broken-up ground, which was to contain a model parsonage and parsonage garden in the course of time; but, just then, presented a scene of chaotic confusion. There, as Miss Sharp expected, was the object of her search—Mrs. Bernard, the clergyman's widowed sister, and joint owner of the Lilliputian estate, of which she was taking a survey.

Miss Sharp had studied "the plans" with considerable attention, and knew quite well that the study—Mr. Williams's own room—was to be on one side of the porch; the dining-room on the other, facing the road, and almost immediately opposite her own residence. She knew, too, that the drawing-room would look out upon the church-yard, towards the east window, and that climbing-plants innumerable were to decorate the outer walls, in spite of the architect's remonstrances; in fact, Miss Sharp was a great friend both of Mr. Williams and his sister, and took a warm interest in all that concerned them, quite agreeing with Mrs. Chipps in her ideas of the "nice young minister," and that "sweet Mrs. Bernard."

"I thought I heard the rustle of your ample skirts, Anna. Have you come to give me another piece of your valuable advice?" inquired Mrs. Bernard, turning towards her friend, and away from the spot where a well was about to be.

"No; no advice this time—a piece of news instead: The Fentons have come, and Miss Nisbet with them."

"Come!" exclaimed Mrs. Bernard, in consternation; "and I was not there to meet them. I am so sorry! I have been waiting for my brother. He must have been detained at one of the cottages. I will walk to the Lodge at once. If you see him, send him after me, will you?"

"Yes; and I hope I shall see him, for I think I have heard of a situation for Reed."

"Oh! have you? He will be so glad. You must tell me all about it when I return. I must lose no time in welcoming my old schoolfellow and her charges."

So whilst Miss Sharp goes in search of the clergyman, to tell him that Reed has a chance of the under-gardener's place at the Fenton's, if he applies at once, and Mrs. Chipps returns to her solitary tea in that one room, which she has long considered her home, and loves accordingly, we will follow Mrs. Bernard to Fernbank Lodge, and the new arrivals whom she was so anxious to welcome.

The luggage was just being unloaded, as Mrs. Bernard arrived; and Miss Nisbet and Nurse Turner were giving directions, and seeing to the placing of the several boxes.

"I have not come to interrupt, but to help you, if I can," said Mrs. Bernard, after the first warm greetings had been exchanged. "Can I not be of any use?"

"Well, if you do not mind holding this sleeping baby for a few minutes, I will just see, with Phœbe, about the nursery being in order, whilst Turner is busy unpacking."

"Dear little thing! pray give her to me. How soundly she is asleep! But where are the other children? I long to know them all."

"You can watch them from the window. They have just asked leave to run into the garden, till nurse is ready to put them to bed. They will be quite safe, as Flory is with them."

"Flory" was a sedate, prudent little maiden, fast merging into a "young lady," and highly enjoyed having charge of the little ones, and exploring the nice garden, of which they had heard so much. A very charming place it was; quite different from the London squares, to which they had all their lives been accustomed as their only playground. Here was soft mossy turf, a beautiful well-kept lawn, and a nice little paddock, too, to play about in; and the trees, acacias, elms, and sweetly-scented limes, they were so high and so spreading that Gertrude almost twisted her little neck off with looking at them. Then there were more flower-beds than she could count, well-stocked with flowers enough to delight sister Flory's heart; for Flory dearly loved the "lilies of the field," and all other beauties with which our beneficent Father decks his children's earthly home.

Little Charlie and his still smaller sister May were in perfect ecstasies at the daisies and buttercups, springing up so abundantly in the paddock; but prudent Flory, afraid of the dew for their little feet, and Nurse Turner's scolding at damp boots, would not let them go on to the grass, or let them gather any flowers that did not grow close to the gravel-walks, till to-morrow.

"Charlie hope to-morrow come soon, Foy," said the little fellow, turning reluctantly away from the scene of attraction and temptation, in obedience to Nurse Turner's summons to bed.

And whilst they are sleeping soundly, wearied out with the journey and excitement, all but Florence (who thinks and thinks of the joys of a country life, the actual fulfilment of her wildest dreams, till sleep is an impossibility), I will say a few words, by way of introducing the new occupants of Fernbank Lodge more particularly to my young readers.

Florence, Gertrude, Charlie, and May were not the only members of the Fenton family—although by no means unimportant ones—there was the "new baby" already briefly alluded to, who had dethroned "Baby May" from that dignity, after a brief reign of fourteen months' duration. And what a large, good-tempered prodigy, that new baby was! and how pleased

Charlie and May were with it! If Nurse Turner had let them, I think they would have kissed it to death, in their extreme love and affection. Lily was baby's real name; but it was one very rarely required for domestic use.——All these, with Miss Nisbet the Governess, and Nurse Turner, and Nurse Turner's niece and assistant, were to occupy Fernbank for a few months, whilst Mr. and Mrs. Fenton were on the continent; whither they had recently gone for a little change of air and scene, much needed by both papa and mamma. The latter had but just recovered from a very serious and protracted illness; and Mr. Fenton, after many years of hard work, had at length become possessed of a comfortable independence, through the death of a distant relative, late the owner of Fernbank.

A son and daughter accompanied them in this excursion; but the former was to remain, with his tutor, at one of the German universities; and Miss Fenton, mamma's companion and sister Flory's ideal of perfection, having long been emancipated from the school-room, and "quite a woman," was not unlikely to leave the happy family-circle altogether ere long, so could not bear to be separated from papa and mamma, now that there was a governess in some measure able to supply her place with the younger ones.

Those younger ones woke up early, in their new home, on the following morning; awoke to the unaccustomed sounds of the birds singing beneath the windows, and the poultry cackling in the yard. Flora and Gertrude shared the same room—a large, comfortable apartment, which Flory intended should look more home-like when all her treasures were unpacked, and a few of her elder sister's drawings decorated the walls—improvements which impatient little Gertrude was anxious to set about at once, much to her methodical companion's discomposure.

The two sisters presented a striking contrast in their "little ways"—those little ways which are such very important indications of character.

"I wish, dear, you would go on brushing your hair, or dressing yourself—or doing anything, in fact, but littering our room!" remonstrated Florence.

"But I really cannot, Flory. You must not be so angry, and so prim and old-maidish; and *I must* just unpack that one little box for you. I can dress afterwards."

"You will not be in time for prayers, Gertrude, if you do. See, you have pulled your hair all down again whilst you have been talking, and there are your own things all littered about. Do attend to them first, there's a good girl! Besides, I do not want the ornamental unpacked till the useful is settled into right quarters. Where could I hang a picture now, Gerty, when every available nail is monopolized by your clothes!"

"How cross you are! and how badly you treat me, Flory!" said Gertrude, ruefully.

"Ah! yes; I know I am a tyrannical elder sister, but there are some things I must have my own way in, dear! and arranging my own property is one of them. However, if you put your property straight first, and go on steadily with your dressing now, you shall help me by-and-bye if you are good."

"By-and-bye I shall be at lessons," pleaded Gertrude.

"Suppose Miss Nisbet should be too busy to give any lessons to-day, what would you say to a holiday, Flory darling!"

"A holiday! a holiday! I will do anything for a holiday!" was the delighted rejoinder.

"Well, then, make haste and come down stairs. See, I am quite ready to go and look after the little ones; and Miss Nisbet will be making breakfast directly."

"Dear creature! Tell her that I'll be down before—before she can say 'Jack Robinson,'" rejoined Gertrude, giving a vigorous twist to her long black hair—the hair that never would come smooth without a great deal more trouble than Gertrude liked to bestow upon it.

"I shall not deliver such a decidedly improper message, you naughty child! Good-bye, and do not dawdle."

That day was indeed a holiday, so far as Gertrude was concerned, to her intense satisfaction; employed by the elders of the party in getting things in order, by the juniors in giving as much unnecessary trouble as they, in their pleasurable excitement, could contrive to do. Nurse Turner was too busy even to scold, and Florence too occupied in making arrangements for everything in her room to have a suitable place, to keep order out of it; so Gertrude led the little ones into all sorts of scrapes and mischief, for which they finally paid the penalty of going to bed early, being threatened with remaining there for a week, deprived of their clothes, on account of the mess they had made of them—a punishment which little May did not understand in all its significance, and of which Master Charlie did not entertain the slightest dread; indeed, he seemed at all times of opinion that clothes were useless encumbrances, to be slipped out of and abandoned upon every possible occasion. What he would have thought of a Turkish bath I am not prepared to say, but he certainly did consider a common air bath, accompanied with gymnastic exercise, as decidedly enjoyable and beneficial.

"The children," inclusive of Gertrude, who was thoroughly tired out, being then safely disposed of, Miss Nisbet and Flory started for a little stroll in the cool of the evening, the former having promised to call at the Rectory as soon as they had leisure. Florence was quite ready for an exploring expedition, eager for a sight of "the village," and a little more conversation with Mrs. Bernard, to whom she had only spoken a few words on the previous evening, but of whom she had heard so much from that lady's old schoolfellow, Miss Nisbet. Although there had been little intercourse between the two in later years, there was a time, of which Florence knew nothing, when Miss Nisbet had been engaged to be married to a near relative of Mrs. Bernard's, who had died from the effects of an accident. It was long before poor Miss Nisbet recovered the shock of his sad death sufficiently to resume her duties as a governess, and even now she was often very delicate and unnerved, and found teaching hard work when Gertrude was not in a tractable humour.

Cutting off the corner of the furze-covered common, on the borders of which their residence was situated, Florence and her companion turned into the main-road, leading into the village.

"Oh! there is the church, with its new tower that papa told us about!" exclaimed Florry. "How pretty it looks peeping from between the trees! Do you not think so, Miss Nisbet?"

"It is very nicely situated certainly, but I cannot say much for the beauty of the building, with the exception of the tower; the chancery windows are so small, and the roof so disproportionately expansive. Excepting in an architectural point of view, however, I will not quarrel with the little church, so conveniently situated for our accommodation."

"I wonder who lives in those cottages," observed Florence, as they passed the last, excepting that inhabited by Mrs. Chipps and her family. "Oh, look, what a pretty little boy there is on that door-step; do let us stop and speak to him."

Miss Nisbet stopped at Florence's request, but the little curly-headed fellow was rather too shy to face the two strange ladies, so ran in to his mother and sisters for protection.

"What is the matter, Georgie, dear?" was the inquiry, as the flushed cheeks were buried in "mother's lap."

A whisper about "two pretty ladies" was followed, almost immediately, by the entrance of the pretty ladies themselves.

"I hope you will excuse our intrusion," said Miss Nisbet, in a voice that was in itself an apology; "but, seeing your door open, I have ventured in, to ask if you can direct me to Mrs. Bernard's; we are quite strangers here."

"Our minister's sister do you mean, ma'am?"

"Yes."

"She lives with her brother, ma'am, our good clergyman Mr. Williams; it is just five minutes' walk, if you turn to the left and keep along the high-road. It is close to the timber-yard—anybody will tell you the house. My husband has gone to speak to Mr. Williams, or he would show you the way. He's been out of a situation some time, and is going to try for one at Fernebank Lodge."

"Oh, indeed," said Miss Nisbet, smiling. "Well, I hope, for your sake, he may get it. Good evening, and thank you for the direction. I shall soon find Mrs. Bernard's, I dare say; excuse my intrusion."

"No intrusion, ma'am, I'm sure; pray don't name it," said Mrs. Bond, dropping a curtsey, and trying to make Master Georgie take his fingers out of his mouth and "thank the young lady pretty" for a penny which Florence had contrived to put into his hand for a cake.

Both Mr. Williams and his sister were at home, and received their visitors very cordially, making Florence, who was only shy for the first five minutes, soon feel quite at her ease with them. She was quite delighted with their tiny drawing-room, half blocked up though it was with mediæval-looking furniture, and still more so with the little garden, in which Mrs. Bernard worked so hard, and took so much pride. As for the clergyman's sister, Florry thought her governess had not said half enough in her favour. Mr. Williams talked more to Miss Nisbet, to whom it was his first introduction, although he had long been familiar with her name and history; but Florence watched him slyly, and came to the conclusion that he had a very pleasant and what she called "good look about him," and he did not frighten her by being very sober and grave, as she had fancied all clergymen were obliged to be, whether in or out of the pulpit.

The brother and sister were very much alike in their personal appearance, both fair, with broad and rather prominent eyes; both with hair that nearly matched the eyes, and each had a pleasant smile and an agreeable, easy manner. They were extremely attached to one another, and, since the termination of school and college days, had rarely been separated for any length of time. Even during the brief period of Mrs. Bernard's married life, they had been near neighbours, Mr. Bernard having been assistant curate in the same parish with his brother-in-law.

So Mrs. Bernard, as the daughter, widow, and sister of a clergyman, was, as her friends called her, a most thorough "parsoness" herself, and quite as much listened to, in matters more especially within her province, as if she had been Mr. Williams's wife.

Mrs. Chipps did occasionally observe to Miss Sharp that it was "a pity that their dear young minister could not find a wife among so many nice ladies," but as Mrs. Chipps found it impossible to select the right one, perhaps Mr. Williams himself laboured under similar difficulty.

* * *

Weeks went by very rapidly with the inhabitants of Fernebank Lodge, who daily became more attached to their new home, more interested in, and better acquainted with, their neighbourhood and its residents.

Lessons were once again resumed, and a snug little room leading out of the conservatory and looking on to the gayest part of the garden, was converted into a school-room.

Here, Florence worked hard and resolutely at German exercises and French grammar; and Gertrude toiled daily over the sums that would not "prove," the ill-sewn seams and puckered work which Miss Nisbet felt compelled to unpick.

Poor Gertrude! it was quite sad to see those saucy, mischievous eyes clouded over with tears; but her governess could not be trifled with; and what she knew Gertrude, with a little pains-taking, could do, she insisted upon having done.

She was a dear, coaxing, loveable child, with all her idleness, whom Miss Nisbet felt strongly tempted to pet and spoil, instead of correcting; but she knew that Gertrude would grow up a very useless and, perhaps, unlovable woman, if allowed to have all her own way now.

So Gertrude was compelled to put her things away, when she had done with them, instead of littering her own and every other room in the house; was not allowed to romp in the garden when lessons were unlearned, or to sit down to dinner with hands that had been making "dirt pies" for little Charlie, without having been subsequently introduced to soap-and-water.

Despite all these daily trials, however, Gertie was a very happy child, forgetting her troubles so quickly, that Florence could scarcely imagine she really was as "miserable" as she represented herself, and appeared to be, when in disgrace with Miss Nisbet, or scolded by nurse.

Charlie and little May, under the influence of the fresh country air and the abundance of rich milk they consumed, were becoming such wonderfully healthy children, that they were always being stopped, when Nurse Turner took them into the village, to hear complimentary remarks on their improved appearance.

Miss Clinga had become decidedly attached to them before finally taking her departure from the neighbourhood, but she really had left at last, and was not very likely to come back again. But the children had other friends in the Lane, always on the look-out for them when they passed. Master Charlie generally stopped at Mrs. Reid's, to shake hands with her little boy, or show him the last new toy which "good sister Flory" had bought for him. Florence spoiled these little ones dreadfully, but nurse Turner's strictness probably counterbalanced all injurious effects of her treatment.

Miss Sharp was another great friend of Master Charlie's, also Miss Sharp's good-natured cook; the latter had once given him and little May a piece of cake as they went past Miss Sharp's garden-gate, and, as the young gentleman never forgot a favour conferred upon him, he never caught sight either of Miss Sharp, or her cook, without the observation, "Charlie doin' to have a piece of cake now"—a prophecy which generally brought its own fulfilment.

The new parsonage, meanwhile, progressed rapidly towards completion, and Florence, who took a great interest in it, looked forward to the time when Mr. Williams and his sister should be still nearer neighbours to them, with considerable impatience. She was always finding some excuse for a visit to Mrs. Bernard, tolerably certain of a hearty welcome from that lady and a pleasant chat with her brother, if he were at home and not busy with sermon-writing.

Mr. and Mrs. Fenton quite approved of and encouraged this intimacy, and Mr. Williams and his sister were frequent and welcome guests at the Lodge.

Florence often assisted her eldest sister in the work she did for the poor of Mrs. Bernard's district, and occasionally accompanied her to the school, at which Georgie Reid's sisters and other little people from the "Lane," were daily attendants.

Georgie's father had obtained the situation of under-gardener at Mr. Fenton's, and was often the bearer of a piece of cake for the little boy, or some "barley-sugar" which Charlie, at Gertrude's suggestion, would save for him, out of his share of that delicacy.

Poor Charlie! it really was a great exercise of self-denial, "barley-sugar" being a special delicacy, bestowed upon him only when he was a very good boy indeed; had not scratched his nurse's face, pinched baby, or pushed little May down and sat upon her—events which occasionally happened when Master Charlie, to use his own phraseology, "had a passion."

But Charlie's passions were never of long duration, and everybody was so glad to hear the welcome words "Kiss Charlie; Charlie's good now;" that his misdemeanours were not treated very seriously.

One day it happened that Mrs. Fenton and her eldest daughter, having gone for a long day's shopping, to buy those indispensable "wedding things," which would so very soon be needed, Miss Nisbet had accepted an invitation for Florence, Gertrude, and herself, to spend the afternoon with Mrs. Bernard.

An afternoon with Mrs. Bernard was always a treat to the girls! there was sure to be some unexpected amusement of riddles, puzzles, engravings, or books to look at, and plenty of merry conversation; particularly if Mr. Williams were there. So the two girls started off, in high glee, at the appointed time.

"I want to call in the Lane for a few minutes, my dears, to speak to Mrs. Reid about some work; and I have something for that poor invalid lodger in the next house; so you can go on, and I will follow as soon as I can. Mrs. Bernard will be expecting you, if I should be detained longer than I hope to be."

Neither Florence nor Gertrude objected to this arrangement, and were very glad they had not waited when they found a whole hour had slipped by, without any sign of Miss Nisbet's appearance.

"My brother is also out longer than I expected," said Mrs. Bernard. "Sarah, has your master been in since he went to the post for me?" inquired she, of the servant, who just then came in with the tea-tray and those particularly nice rock-cakes, for the manufacture of which Mrs. Bernard was famed.

"He came in for a minute, ma'am; but was sent for, all in a hurry, to Mrs. Reid's."

"Anything the matter, Sarah?"

"I don't know for certain, ma'am; but I think something is wrong."

"Miss Nisbet was going to call there, I know.

I hope nothing has happened to dear little Georgie," said Florence, anxiously.

"Might I just put on my bonnet, and run round there, Mrs. Barnard?" she added.

"I think, my love, you had better remain quietly with your sister; but if you will both excuse me, I will go and ascertain what is detaining them."

"And you will send for me, if there is anything I can do," pleaded Florence.

"You shall know directly what is the matter, should there be any trouble; and, if you can be of any use, I will not fail to send for you."

"Thank you: do let us know soon, I so hope there is nothing wrong with Georgie."

Florence's great happiness was to "be of use," and she could not wait very patiently till Mrs. Barnard's return. Gerty caught sight of her at last, but Mr. Williams and Miss Nisbet were with her: they all looked very grave, and Gerty was quite sure that Miss Nisbet had been crying. Gerty was not mistaken, and I am very certain that she, poor child, would have cried too, if she had been in Miss Nisbet's place.

Poor little George Reed had met with a very serious accident. He had unfortunately crossed over the road, thinking that he caught sight of Nurse Turner and her charges, and before he could get back again to his usual play-ground—the door-step—he was knocked down and run over by a horse-and-cart, and the poor little fellow's leg was broken. Miss Nisbet, who was passing just as the accident occurred, was the first to reach him, and render her assistance in lifting him up and carrying him in, to his mother. The little sufferer, stunned by the shock, was quite insensible, has his poor mother could not believe that he was really alive, he was so white and still when laid upon his little bed. Miss Nisbet went herself for the doctor, who lived close by, and sent one of the neighbours off for Mr. Williams.

"And is he very much injured, will he live?" inquired the two girls, eagerly.

"We hope so," replied the clergyman, cheerfully; "there is every chance of his doing well; but poor little Georgie must make up his mind to be a cripple all his life."

Gertrude's eyes filled with tears, and Florence's voice was very husky as she almost whispered—

"Miss Nisbet, are they going to take his leg off, do you think?"

"That has been done already; the worst is over, thank God! The dear child behaved so bravely."

"I think we shall do no good by talking any more about it at present," said Mr. Williams, who noticed that Miss Nisbet looked very pale and exhausted; whilst the two girls were struggling hard to repress their tears.

"Little Georgie is in better hands than ours, and our good doctor will be sure to take every care of him. We must ask him to give you young ladies permission to see his little patient as soon as ever it will be wise to do so."

Many weeks, however, elapsed before they were allowed to visit the little fellow; for George Reed's recovery was much slower than had been at first anticipated. He did get tolerably strong at last though, and received a great deal of kindness from all the inhabitants of Fernbank Lodge.

Little Charlie Fenton often called with sister Flory, with some nice fruit or flowers, for "the poor boy who had only one leg;" and all the neighbours in the Lane, young and old, were very kind to him, and invented occupations and toys for his amusement.

* * * * *

It is a long time now, since all these things happened; for Charles Fenton—a tall, healthy, powerfully built young man—is now a very enthusiastic Volunteer, with whom, attending "drill," is one of the chief duties of life. A few years back he went home to see the old folks at Fernbank, and to assist at sister Mary's wedding, and then he did not fail to call on his staunch friend and admirer, "Georgie" Reed; and found him, as usual, hard at work at basket-making. Very pretty fancy goods he has for sale, and a very thriving trade is carried on in that little cottage of his, where he and his now widowed mother live together. Their cottage is close to the parsonage—the "new parsonage"—in which Mr. Williams—no longer a "nice young minister, although still a very popular one—has been "settled" for many years.

His sister has gone to her rest, but in her place is one who works as heartily and as lovingly in the parish, and takes as much interest in school and church as ever Mrs. Barnard did; for Mr. Williams, at length, startled the neighbourhood by appearing one morning in his own church as a bridegroom, and the bride he had selected was Miss Nisbet, once the governess at Fernbanks Lodge.

PREVENTION OF SEA-SICKNESS.—Let a person on shipboard, when the vessel is heaving over the waves, seat himself, and take hold of a tumbler nearly filled with water or other liquid, and at the same time make an effort to prevent the liquid from running over by keeping the mouth of the glass horizontal, or nearly so. When doing this, from the motion of the vessel, his hand and arm will seem to be drawn into different positions, as if the glass were attracted by a powerful magnet. Continuing his efforts to keep the mouth of the glass horizontal, let him allow his head, arm, and body to go through the various movements—as those observed in sawing, planing, pumping, throwing a quoit, &c.—which they will be impelled, without fatigue, almost irresistible to perform; and he will find that this has the effect of preventing the giddiness and nausea that the rolling and tossing of the vessel have a tendency to produce in inexperienced voyagers.—*Athenæum*.

OUR LIBRARY TABLE.

EDWIN OF DEIRA.*

That Mr. Smith has abstained from closely following the legend of Edwin of Deira as generally related, is a matter of little consequence. These early personages are not historical but mythical, and the poet has full right to deal with the vague stories regarding them as seemeth good to himself. But not the less for this will he have to run the gauntlet at the hands of critical readers, as to the propriety and expedience of the changes he has introduced. This poem is grounded, doubtless, on the legend told by Bede. We happen to have no Bede at present by us; and so cannot consider in detail the changes made by the poet. But there are changes here which must strike anyone at all conversant with the legend. Why is the Christianizing of the king taken wholly out of the hands of his Christian wife? Why is the coincidence in time of the birth of a child to him with the attempt upon his life, never mentioned? The slow influence of a wife, constantly strengthened by the presence of her ghostly comforter, was surely a more natural means to affect the softening of the king's heart, than the sudden entrance upon the scene of the theatrical chorus of priests. Again, the greatest stress is laid in the old story on the impression produced upon Edwin by the synchronizing of the birth of his child and of the murderous blow. This impression was natural enough, and one can conceive how wife and priest would turn it to their own good purposes.

However, Alexander Smith has, doubtless, better reasons than we can divine for these and other alterations. The conversion becomes more miraculous; the Christianizing of Northumbria is made to represent in some sort the Christianizing of all England, by the judicious mingling of the two accounts of the conversions by Augustine and Paulinus. The story of the pleading pontiff, dear to our childhood, comes in close proximity to the grand story of Coifi. We get the effective banding of the priests together with the terrific demolition of the heathen temple. Perhaps this crowding of tableaux is better art than the quiet painting of a woman's influence, and the shadowing forth of the impression produced by a strange coincidence upon the mind of a sick man.

Having begun with carping, we may as well finish our fault-finding before we turn to the beauties of this poem.

In the first place, then, it is incomplete. It begins as a heroic biography (so to speak) of Edwin. It takes up, half-way through, the idea of the Christianizing of England. Edwin ceases to be hero and becomes only an instrument to the new purpose. The prophecy of the Shape does not sufficiently connect the first part with the last. No one who had not read of this Shape in the original legend, would pay much attention to its appearance in the first book of the poem. Edwin's heroic history ends with his reconquest of his kingdom and his marriage to Bertha. He grows morally after that time (and glimpses given us of this growth are well done) and at length turns from the false heathen gods to the true. Taking Edwin still for the hero of the poem we want to see how he is affected by this change of religion—how it upheld him in the reverses and sorrows which old legends tell us he afterwards sustained. But the Christianizing of him and his kingdom being performed, there is an end. We are told in effect that he lived happy ever after. For Edwin's sake the poem should either have terminated with his marriage, or have carried him on through an afterlife set to music very much more high and solemn than any here.

If on the other hand we take the Christianizing of England as the chief theme of the book, we find that through the first half there is no mention of it, no allusion even save in the dim prophecy of the Shape. We find the heathen knights practising all the Christian virtues, perfectly satisfied with their gods and having no conscious craving for a belief purer and higher. Moreover, it requires a better preacher than Alexander Smith to show forth the excellence of the Christian idea. White robes and swinging censers and psalmody are but poor persuasions to the grasping of a new faith. Mr. Smith has attempted to make his priests speak the words of inspiration which they must have spoken to transform men's souls and convince their intellects; but Mr. Smith had, on the whole, better have remained silent. The entire scene of the Christianizing is to us revolting—not more here, however, than in the original legend, for the speeches of the priests are closely copied. The selfishness of Coifi, the doubt and darkness of Ella, are surely incentives to conversion not of the most orthodox kind. The savage destruction of the ancient temples, to the infinite fear and horror and distress of the blind multitude, seems to us a sad first-fruit of the new religion.

Looking at the poem in either light we find it incomplete. Taking it as it is, we see in it a blending of two poems into one.

Mr. Smith is unfortunate in the choice of his subject. The appearance of "Edwin of Deira" so soon after that of the "Idylls of the King," provokes comparison. Very nearly Tennyson's equal in some lighter matters, Alexander Smith

---

* By Alexander Smith. (*Macmillan & Co.*)

is infinitely beneath him in this deep, solemn, moral insight which sanctifies the true poet, and sets him apart from all other men. This "Edwin" seems the more ambitious, remembering the "Idylls." How purely ideal appear the wonder-working words of Paulinus to the sorrowing words of Arthur in "Guinevere," embodying the very essence of Christianity!

Let us turn to the pleasanter part of our task. Comparing this with the previous poems of our author, we find a progress greater than is commonly made by a poet in so short a time. Tennyson's advance from "Claribel" to "Guinevere" has been the work of many years. Alexander Smith has advanced faster than Tennyson. His "Life-Drama," with its "sprawling suns" and general spasmodics, was not written so very long ago. The language of "Edwin of Deira" is noble and simple—not showing, it is true, anything like the exquisite simplicity of the "Idylls", but still a sure progress in the same direction, from glittering words and conceits to deeper thoughts and feelings. We get, now and then, good terse lines here, such as would not shame some of our older giants.

Of similes Mr. Smith is still profuse. We cannot imagine what injury the sun has done him that he should put it through so many unimaginable tortures. The skill, too, that treats the light or the wind, or anything and everything, is made to do unremarkable duty. But in the wildest moments our poet does not now give us absurdities. He does give us many of the most exquisite similes that have ever been written. Tennyson could not write some of the best similes that Smith has written; but (dare we pronounce the blasphemy?) Tennyson could not write some of the best that Smith has written.

Again, he has a great power of description, of word-painting. And this is not only by laborious detail, but often by a single touch of colour, like the "nuncios rose" of Shakespeare's [illegible]. Ruskin expatiates somewhere, rhapsodising about some picture of Turner's, on three hair-breadth strokes of vermilion laid on the light side of a distant building. Four strokes would have spoiled the picture; any other kind save hair-breadth strokes would have spoiled the picture. The three hair-breadth strokes prove the genius—and we have the three hair-breadth strokes more than once in this poem.

But of a higher order than this power of outward description, whether by subtle selection or accumulation of details, is the power of uttering simple heart-truths, of touching the string which, girdling the whole earth, vibrates throughout its length to the simplest touch, stirring all nature. Of this power Alexander Smith is not destitute. Tennyson has it, perhaps, in greater measure than any other poet since Shakespeare; and we are not to look for the depth of Tennyson's sympathetic insight here. But still this soul of the true poet is to be found clearly stamped upon "Edwin of Deira." Take a passage or two, chosen somewhat at random. For instance, of the impossibility of estimating the full happiness of love—

I know that I am happy; I know not
How happy—and I may not ever know;
I am as one engirded in a realm,
Whose wide unskirted boundaries and shapes
He will not have encompassed round about
When he is hoary grown. (p. [illegible].)

Again at page 97—

The primrose smile
Lord of a happiness, unknown, unshared,
Which e'en in all his heart's first years and years—
Unmeasured as the shapes of hills.
When one climbs to the [illegible]!

Of love coming down from its solitary heights to mingle in the world of men—

Seen in love's eye within the heavens above;
[illegible] [illegible] [illegible] than [illegible] by a cloud
Of daily duties? Love's [illegible], dreams
From out the pride and passionate ways of youth,
In pursuit! [illegible], providently sown,
A few drops sprinkled in each common [illegible]
Wherewith the human table is set forth,
[illegible] all with heaven. (p. [illegible].)

Of the healing of sorrow by time—

For now the grassy mound of Ragnar's grave
Had grown a portion of the accustomed world—
Familiar as the shapes of distant hills,
And hardly moving sorrow in one than theirs. (p. [illegible].)

Again—

The [illegible] grave
That ever more kept green that [illegible] of [illegible]
Unto the [illegible] level of the world. (p. [illegible].)

Again, in "Torquil and Oona"—

Though not for us that tender mood of grief
Where the red naked grave that jars and stings
Fades from its shape, and, growing less by time,
Melts in the mass of long-familiar things. (p. [illegible].)

Of the reticence of men's friendship—

The noble love that lives in manly minds,
That is ashamed of its own tenderness,
And hides itself in deeds—would not be said,
And [illegible] [illegible] and dies. (p. [illegible].)

Again—

We are men,
Not women, and our hearts should never dwell
Upon our tongues. (p. [illegible].)

Of Ebertildye—

I bring no spies deer for thought and man
That wear strange clothes and speak with foreign
 tongues;
Such hospitality befits a king! (p. 118.)

Such passages as the above rank higher than any simile however exquisite,—than any piece of word-painting however minute.

In the drawing of character the poet has no great skill. Edwin himself has no personality; Bertha might be any other good and fair girl and wife and mother. Hagan is distinguishable from the rest of the heathens only by name. The treacherous instability of Redwald is scarcely delineated.

The best portion of the poem is that which paints the married life of Edwin and Bertha. The description of the child, and of the parents' delight in it, is really exquisite.

To sum up: it is not a great poem, but there is some very beautiful poetry in it. In plan and in the drawing of character it is utterly deficient; nor does Mr. Smith show a power of rising with his theme to a due solemnity and majesty. It is a poem from which one will be inclined to cull pretty passages: it is not a poem one will be inclined to read again.

J. A.

Biographical Portraitures; or, Sketches of the Lives and Characters of a few Illustrious Persons. By John Leaf. (London: Jones Hammond, Paternoster-row.) —The stories of good and great men's lives never pall. We cannot have too many of such histories; and, for those whose means will not afford the high price of the original memoirs, the ready sketches of them, concentrating (like these before us) the governing circumstances and principal events, detailed and amplified in their proper relation. To compile and condense is by no means the easy task that the inexperienced imagine. Judgment and careful analysis are necessary in the mere preparation of materials, in order to select the most characteristic and interesting of them; and, subsequently, there is the assimilating factor in the writer's mind, so as to impart to them a distinct arrangement, and to infuse them with his individual style. In the volume before us Mr. Leaf has taken care to render the personalities as varied as possible; Haydn, Felix, Daniel De Foe, the Dauphin (Louis XVII.), the Duke of Kent, Cornelius Agrippa, Dr. Kitto, and Thomas Campbell are the illustrations chosen. And though we may take exception to one or two of these, as scarcely coming within the meaning of the first phrase of our notice, the variety and interest of the work are all the greater for their presence. Amongst the most entertaining of these memoirs are those of Cornelius Agrippa and Dr. Kitto, the first of whom figured so long as a magician in mediæval history, but whom the painstaking research of Mr. Morley has proved to have been simply a laborious scholar, anxious to acquaint himself with the secrets of Nature, "and studying, as a means to this end, magic, cabalism, and astrology. He was an earnest lover and seeker after truth, opposing his intellect and learning to the teachings and fables of the clergy. "Their bigoted and perverse representations of sacred personages are not to be credited," he says. "All the recent Martyrologies and professed legends of the saints are full of such prodigious lies, that they make Christianity a laughing-stock in the eyes of Jews, Turks, and Infidels." Of course a man who previous to the Reformation ventured upon such declarations as these could hope but little toleration from the Churchmen; and accordingly, though the son of a noble house, we see him driven out from place to place, misrepresented, subject to losses; his whole life, indeed, full of "shifts, perils, and disappointments." "A diligent student," he made himself familiar with almost everything that was then called learning. He had mastered the scholastic philosophy, and, in the way of secret speculations had made himself acquainted with cabalism—a method of mystically interpreting the Scriptures—to say nothing of the various works in Greek and Latin literature, which were then beginning to obtain attention among scholars. Armed with this knowledge, Agrippa goes forth to gain a footing as a man of letters, and make the world wiser by his expositions. He is ambitious of becoming the protégé of Margaret of Austria, Maximilian's daughter, who is Mistress of Dôle and Burgundy, and celebrated for her love of letters, and her bounty towards learned men. Received as an orator, with admiration, the University of Dôle bestowed on him, at twenty-three, the degree of Doctor of Divinity, and Agrippa fancied himself already assured of the favour of Margaret, and on the high-road to fortune and preferment. He marries, settles down to authorship, and produces a curious work on magic. Our author gives us some curious quotations from Agrippa's curious, but tasteless.

Magic altogether [says Mr. Leaf] it may be said to embody, in a sort of occult system, the natural science, metaphysics, and mystical theology that were current among the learned at the time when it was written. Indeed, magic is defined by the author as the whole knowledge of nature—the perfection of all true philosophy. In his character of magician, therefore, Cornelius Agrippa was simply an inquirer into the natural and divine significancy of things, and an expounder of their occult or hidden virtues. This, and not any art of conjuration, was what he understood and meant by magic.

But the Friars and Monks thought differently. Heresy and the black art are subsequently laid to his charge, and even the admired orations are condemned, and their author denounced in the presence of the Mistress of Dôle, as a "Judaising heretic." So Dôle is forsaken, to

it was wont to be called, till its capture and spoliation by a French army, in 1678, changed its name to that of Dôle la Dolente, became so in earnest to Cornelius Agrippa, who had to retire from the face of his clerical enemies, and seek employment at the Court of Maximilian. In 1510 we find him *attached* to an embassy from the Court of Germany to that of Henry VIII., and resident as the guest of Dean Colet (the friend of Erasmus, and founder of St. Paul's School), at Stepney, then a pleasant suburban village, famous for its pretty scenery and the scented penny-royal that overspread the adjacent common. We have not space to follow the fortunes, or rather misfortunes, of Agrippa; now on the field of battle, now amongst his books, but ever pursued by the enmity of his co-religionists the priests, whose tenets and conduct he condemned openly, but whose creed he had not the courage to abjure. He had been knighted on the field of battle, made Doctor of Medicine and Law at Paris, twice married and twice a widower, threatened by the Inquisition, excommunicated, bereaved of his second wife by the plague, just as her virtues were enlisting the Princess Margaret to seek her, and his own pecuniary and worldly difficulties appeared to be surmounted. The Princess Margaret, whose patronage he had so much desired, bestows her friendship on him, and shortly after dies. His salary from the Court of Charles V. is in arrears, and, on various pretexts, withheld from him; his children literally hunger whilst he follows the Emperor with his vain suit. At length the affair is adjusted through the intercession of the Archbishop of Palermo—his debts in course of liquidation, a humble salary ensured him, and reinvigorated in hope and circumstances, the poor man tempts his fate a third time, and marries a woman who turns out faithless and infamous, and from whom, after three years of misery, he succeeds in getting a divorce. Once more attacked for his heresies (to which the Monks added the crime of dealing with familiar spirits), the Emperor (who sides with the Monks) leaves him no choice between recanting his writings, or the loss of salary and his Imperial protection. Agrippa will not recant, and, without money, overwhelmed with debt, we find him driven from kingdom to kingdom, till, finding a refuge in a friendly gentleman's house at Grenoble, he dies there, worn out, at forty-nine years of age, with disappointment, sorrow, and disgrace.

Agrippa (observes Mr. Leaf) was no pretender of any kind, but a true man, faithful to his insight and convictions, and, in so far as he taught error, teaching it only as a scholar imperfectly informed. He was a wiser and more purely religious man than any of his enemies—a truth-seeking, candid-minded, earnestly aspiring man, such as few were in his age and country.

Henceforth the occult science has lost one of its greatest names. Mr. Morley has let in the daylight on all that was mysterious in the life of the so-called magician, and his seven demons turn out to be faithful dogs; his wonder-working implements, his books.—The life of Kitto presents us with a very different phase of social history, and marks the progress of literature, and its influence on the times and men, very remarkably. More than three hundred years had intervened between the birth of Cornelius Agrippa Von Nettesheim, at Cologne, and that of John Kitto, the journeyman-mason's son, at Plymouth; yet, in the face of low birth—of poverty—of the difficulties which the utter and complete loss of hearing placed in the way of communication and sympathy; in spite, too, of the mistakes of friends as to the best means of settling him in life; the natural tendencies of his mind, the conscious power within him, leads him to his true vocation, and establishes him, at thirty, as a scholar and a man of letters. His passage to this preferment has been by no means an easy one. An accident at thirteen years of age shut out from the poor boy for ever that fifth sense, by the loss of which the powers of his mind were to be so strengthened and concentrated.

Never more did John Kitto hear the living voice of man or woman. Henceforth the world lay round him in dull monotonous silence! Nevermore when the spring advanced, with its choral burst of joyous birds, did he hear tidings of its coming. The murmuring brooks ran noiselessly, and the delicious cadence of waving trees fell all inaudible upon his stricken sense. The solemn chant of waterfalls and ocean-tides, the anthems of the mighty winds in winter, the silvery trilling of leaves on summer nights, the march of a tempest over plains and forests—all these had lost their power to move him with a thrill of awe or pleasure.

But the poor boy, who had hungered and thirsted for books as soon as he had learned to spell through them, fell back upon them with an interest painfully intensified. At home; in the workhouse; as a shoemaker's apprentice, he never lost sight of the grand hope and aim of his existence—the accomplishment of learning. All the stray halfpence, all his crude efforts at art (for we find him painting halfpenny pictures for this purpose), are hoarded and devoted for no other end but to buy books; and when at length the hard usage to which he was subjected, as apprentice, induced him to complain of it to the master of the workhouse (who had always been a friend to the lad), his written statements to the magistrates, by their correctness of diction, astonished the bench, and led to his release from his indentures and "ulterior measures for his advancement." We cannot follow the lad throughout the various changes of circumstances and occupation which intervene till we find him engaged with Mr. Charles Knight, the publisher, and recognized as a man of great and various information, master of many languages, and, having travelled in the

East, familiar with oriental customs—a circumstance that decided Mr. Knight to ask his assistance in preparing a pictorial Bible; but the specimen commentary which he produced had the effect of transferring the whole work to his hands—"a work which has made him celebrated, and upon which the distinction he has gained in literature may be said principally to rest." The whole details of the Doctor's life are so full of interest, and are so agreeably described and arranged, that this memoir alone is worth the purchase of the book. It offers another example for a future edition of "Self Help," and proves how valuable in time becomes the habit of accumulating facts and observations. Little by little seems to have been the principle on which John Kitto acted—a principle that cannot be too much impressed on young people, and which proves in almost every instance, but especially where knowledge or wealth are the objects of attainment, infallible. We congratulate Mr. Leaf on the very useful and pleasant work he has performed, and repeat that such books cannot be too well known and studied. The good sense and intelligent admiration of what is really worth admiration and preservation, in individual character, and the selection of the characters themselves, are proofs of the author's fitness for his task, and make us desirous of meeting him in other similar undertakings.

PERIODICALS.

THE ENGLISHWOMAN'S JOURNAL. (19 *Langham Place, Regent Street; Kent and Co., Paternoster-row*). — The October number of our contemporary contains the usual quantity of articles, upon the usual subjects. "Margaret Beaufort," a pleasantly-written paper of historical biography, is completed. The Report of the Society for promoting the Employment of Women contains a paragraph which we reprint for the use of our lady-readers. A well-known London tradesman, on an application to him to take a woman as an assistant, replied, "Ladies have this matter in their own hands. If every lady, as she came into my shop, were to ask to be waited on by a woman, we should be obliged to supply one." Surely, if, instead of signing addresses, the upwards of two hundred ladies of influence who did so were simply to act upon the tradesman's suggestion above-quoted, it would save time, and be far the most direct way of bringing about the desired substitution of women for men-assistants, in drapers' and other shops where ornamental and other light articles are sold. We are happy to learn that the success of the Victoria Printing Press is established, and also that active measures are being taken to organize a system of "Emigration for Educated Women." The "Black Country" is, we fear, too true a picture of the social condition and moral wants of the district it treats of. "Helps to the Doctor" suggests co-operative societies of women to take upon themselves the care of the sick. Our readers must read the article for themselves, and form their own judgment of the feasibility of the plan. Such associations, to be of any practical value in their several localities, must first submit to be trained to the proper performance of their self-imposed duties; otherwise, we fear, instead of being "Helps to the Doctor," they would very likely be found hindrances.

THE ODDFELLOW'S JOURNAL. (*Manchester.*) —A very pleasant contribution to this number is Mr. Hardwick's sketchy paper, "Our Jerry." The familiar Y. B. N., in an article entitled "A Voice from a Sisterhood," touchingly reveals the claims of superannuated governesses. Mr. Edwin Goadby's "Advice Gratis" is an amusing essay, on a subject of universal prescription, and which our sometimes own contributor has very cleverly handled. The remainder of the papers, however interesting to members of the fraternity, are not so in a literary sense.

THE RELIQUARY. (*London: John Russell Smith, Soho Square. Derby: Bemrose and Sons, Irongate.*) — Let no one run away with the idea (which the editor, Mr. Llewellynn Jewitt, tells us is rife in some circles) that this Quarterly is either "a Popish, or at least a Puseyite," publication. It is simply a literary depository for relics legendary, biographical, and historical; which relics, for the present, are all collected in one county—Derbyshire; to the history of which the learned editor and his coadjutors are adding, from time to time, much interesting information. In spite of the excellent illustrations, in themselves exceedingly valuable, as preserving the forms of many antiquities which otherwise would be lost to the future, we regret that the high price of the work must necessarily limit its circulation, and, in fact, confine it almost to the locality from which it emanates. The present number contains some interesting papers, on antiquarian and other matters.

JOURNAL OF THE WORKHOUSE VISITING SOCIETY. (*London: Longman, Green, and Co.*) —The value of this society appears to increase from month to month, and, indeed, can scarcely be over-rated. Forming a link of communication between the public and that great body of alms-men and women, the inmates of our workhouses, all that concerns the aged, the sick, or insane, and the children in them, are constantly made the subjects of discussion. Upon the theme of workhouse education we have a paper by Miss Louisa Twining, whose active interest in the subject is well known. It points out the different systems of education provided by the Poor Law, and states the main objections to them. This lady advocates, and on very just grounds, the education and training of the children apart from the contaminating influence of the adult society within the house. She would supplement the improved district and county schools with homes for destitute girls, who, under existing circumstances, are herded with the utterly depraved. The paper was read in the Educational Department of the Social Science Congress at Dublin, 1861. Another most interesting and affecting paper, read in the Social Economy Department of the same meeting—The Sick in Workhouses, by Frances Power Cobbe—we very earnestly direct our readers' attention to.

THE TOILET.

(Specially from Paris.)

First Figure.—Black velvet dress in the Princess style, richly decorated with fancy silk trimmings. Lace collar and under sleeves. Bonnet of pink crape and black velvet, ornamented with roses. Inside a bandeau of black blond and a large rose on the right.

Second Figure.—Dress of deep-blue French moire; body high with a waistband. Sleeves, with turned back cuffs, open at the side. On the skirt and cuffs are insertions of black guipure enclosed between very narrow plaitings of blue ribbon. Tulle collar and under-sleeves, black lace [illegible], *jupon* under-skirt, with a wide hem and a deep border of small plaits. Cashmere cloak. Bonnet with a white tulle crown, sprinkled with [illegible]. Front and curtain maroon velvet. On the front a maroon feather. Inside blue velvet flowers; velvet strings.

Third Figure.—Toilet for a little girl six years of age. A striped silk frock. *Pardessus* of a woollen material, trimmed with bands of velvet. Nainsook collar and under-sleeves. Tudor hat of black velvet, decorated with a [illegible] feather. The hair is gathered in a Greek net of *grenadine chenille*.

In home toilet, and at friendly evening parties, this style of head-dress continues in favour. For dinner parties, two *coiffures* in hair merit distinction. The one for a young lady of thirty is a Greek *coiffure*, style [illegible], with a [illegible] falling on the neck, and a [illegible] of black velvet. The other is adapted for a girl of eighteen, and is also a *coiffure* Greek, but of the Hebe genre, with curls and ringlets *frisées* flowing on the neck.

Flowers powdered with aluminium are very much worn, both in bonnets and head dresses. Simple robes are garnished with a plaited trimming; it may be of silk, in striking contrast with the colour of the dress, or of the same material. The plaits are often five, six, and eight inches in height; they are sometimes made with a double heading, bordered with silk.

All self-coloured **robes** are bordered with black velvet.

I have seen some very pretty specimens of evening dress, which may be useful as models. One, a robe of white muslin, for a young lady, has a succession of narrow flounces placed one [illegible] as high as the knee, and surmounted by a [illegible] deep flounce, headed with a [illegible] traversed by a [illegible] transparent. *Corsage* low, with *fichu La Vallière*, garnished with ruches. Sleeves *bouffantes*, demi-long, and [illegible] pointed. Another robe, of blue muslin, is precisely the reverse of the preceding one in its decoration. A deep flounce is set on at the bottom, and is finished with a heading, above which six other narrow flounces are placed. Low body. *Fichu* rounded [illegible], with ends crossing on the bosom, of the same material as the dress. Sleeves full, open, and pointed.

For demi-toilet take the following: a robe of royal [illegible] white and black, trimmed with [illegible] flounces [illegible] with black, almost as high as the knee. *Corsage* low, with a high chemisette of plaited muslin, garnished with black ribbon; sleeves gathered at the top, large and open at the bottom.

360

Imp Mariott

Black and white continue in favour for dress bonnets; one, just composed, is a capote of white tulle, drawn over black silk, with a bavolet of black silk, and a great puff and ends of black ribbon, containing a bouquet of Gloire de Dijon roses, with foliage of black velvet.

The toilets announced for winter are very rich, but very simple; and the same rule will apply to bonnets.

AMUSEMENTS OF THE MONTH.

There have been some novelties produced during the past month in the dramatic way. Of these, the chief is at

THE PRINCESS'S,

Where "Othello" has been produced, Mr. Fechter enacting the mighty Moor. We shall in our next give a detailed criticism of his performance, and will merely say now, that the reading is a brilliant but unequal one, nothing particularly fine occurring till the third act, where the genius of this original actor shows itself. His chief defects are too much colloquial familiarity in the delivery of the text, and his foreign accent. But beauties and blemishes are scattered throughout his impersonation, which we will more fully enter into hereafter. At

THE ADELPHI

Nothing new has been produced.

THE HAYMARKET

Has been varying its tone by presenting tragedy, Mr. E. Booth having been performing Shylock and Sir Giles Overreach. He has met with much applause, his elocution and stage business being very good, superadded to his correct and vivid readings of his parts. Of him we shall speak in detail in our next.

THE ST. JAMES'S

Has re-opened under Mr. Wigan's rule, with the adapted Comedy, "A Scrap of Paper," and is well filled.

THE OLYMPIC

Has put forth a new play, unlike its usual staple, in consequence of the illness of Mr. Robson, who has now, however, we are glad to hear, nearly recovered. At

THE LYCEUM,

The Comedy "Woman" has been still running, with good audiences, and we accept the stability of a piece as a proof of its popularity.

THE STRAND

Has brought out another burlesque of Mr. Byron's—"Esmeralda," perhaps the best in dramatic construction of his pieces of this class. The usual play upon words and parodies, dances and dresses abound in it.

DRURY LANE

Opened on the 24th with great promise of representations of Shakespeare, sustained by Mr. Phelps. Here we must conclude, but next month shall present our readers with a more elaborate criticism on the various entertainments.

W. H.

PASSING EVENTS RE-EDITED.

Whatever tends to foster habits of foresight and economy in a people, tends also to the growth of self-reliance and the self-respect which is its fruit, and is an advance step in their civilisation; just as the *trusting* to extraneous help (prospective or actual), friends, the "Charitable Requests Board," or any other form of unearned pecuniary assistance, moulders a man's heart at the core, and takes out of him the moral pith and back-bone, in the strength of which alone he walks upright, and feels the healthful vigour of independence. Mind, I speak of "trusting" to extraneous help; for there are times when the friendly grip of another can alone save us from the quicksands of some sudden calamity or turn of fortune, and we should sink but for outside assistance. The conditions are wholly different, and everyone can point their separate examples.

The man who is content to accept gratuities for earnings, accepts a down-at-heel condition for life. He may have "greatness thrust upon him," but he never achieves it; he may inherit a fortune, but he never wins one. If his position shuts him out from such probabilities, he sneaks his way through the world, with just provision from day to day, content to have his short-comings to his family made up to them by anyone who will relieve him of his responsibilities; and is, to all appearance, as satisfied

as a browsing sheep to any need of foresight for the future. Such a state of things is by no means uncommon amongst our industrial classes—even to men in full health and occupation. An almost total want of ordinary prudence and frugality characterizes them as a body, when employed, and as total an abnegation of self-dependence as soon as a mill stops, or a blast-furnace is quenched. Any step, therefore, that helps a man to a sense of higher social duties than is involved in the mere earning of daily-bread—that promises, with the help of a little self-denial, to set him beyond the need of charity in sickness or old age, is one to be rejoiced at; and, as such, we congratulate the public upon the accomplished fact of Post-office Saving Banks.

A penetrating mind may discern something more in their establishment than a paternal Government's desire to encourage thrift and foresight in the working-classes; and, remember, that the man who holds Government-securities for his savings, gives the best security to Government for his loyalty and love of order. Men who have saving-bank books to fill, will neither be anxious for strikes nor any other form of public rupture, and in this view of the case the whole nation is the gainer.

"But," it may be said, "savings-banks have existed for years, and the advantage in the shape of interest to the depositor is still greater than under the old system."

There were, however, under the old system, such things as occasional robberies, a dishonest secretary, or defalcations on a greater scale; and a savings-bank has occasionally collapsed, bringing ruin to hard-working or aged men and women, who had no hope beyond that little hoard and the gloomy portals of the work-house. In the post-office saving-banks, however, the money is as secure as the Government; while the investing and withdrawing of it are simplified to a degree previously unimagined.

Under the old system, a deposit could only be made at certain hours, on certain days of the week—a book had to be purchased, and, the deposit being made, could not, under any circumstances, be withdrawn short of a fortnight's notice; while the depositor had frequently a long distance to walk, to pay in or draw out his money. All this is now obviated.

On the first day these banks opened, I found the post-mistress of the district in which I am living quite radiant with pleasure at having had thirteen depositors in the course of the forenoon.

"You see, ma'am, the men must pass the post-office somewhere or another in their way to and from work, and as they are at liberty to make the deposit at any one of them, and at any hour from nine o'clock till six, and may put in as little as a shilling if they please, and have nothing to pay for the book, you can understand it is a great temptation to a man to make a beginning—and I do hope——"

"And so do I, Mrs. Post-mistress—that, the beginning once made, may lead from shilling deposits to pounds; and that the system of post-office saving-banks, scattered throughout the length and breadth of the kingdom, may help to produce those habits of frugality and carefulness, of which, in the aggregate, the working-classes are so negligent."

A little pamphlet, published by Emily Faithful and Co., at the Victoria Press (for the employment of women), in Great Coram-street, and sold at 5s. per hundred, will put any readers in possession of the whole system, and enable them to spread a knowledge of it amongst their workpeople and all with whom they have any influence.

C. A. W.

ANSWERS TO CORRESPONDENTS.

Poetry received, with thanks: "Clothilde;" "The Ash Tree;" "A Night and Morning;" "Hey Gwenn."

"Laura."—We think the author of the [illegible] capable of better things. Will he try again?

Prose received and accepted: "Jessy;" "The [illegible] We Bid;" "Living Tone."

Declined, with thanks: "A Chamber's Burial;" "Gardens of our Forefathers"—the society of [illegible] on the "[illegible] of Antiquity," already published.

Gertrude.—Our talented correspondent must bear with our silence with regard to his proposition a little longer. The first chapter received. "A Posthumous Letter" in our next.

M. H. H., Newbury, Berks.—Whatever papers this correspondent may send us shall meet with attention, and, if suitable, acceptance; if otherwise, they shall be returned on receipt of postage-stamps for the purpose. We really must be excused prescribing the style of our correspondents' writings, though we shall be glad to judge of her own; these papers, whatever be their merits, are not adapted to our pages. We are not in want of a continuous tale.

Poems received, but not yet read: "Miss Cam;" "Here I won my Victoria Cross;" "A Memory of our Darling Alice;" "Eighteen Years Married."

Printed by Rogerson and Tuxford, 246, Strand, London.

A POSTHUMOUS LETTER.

(By the Author of "Kaleun Morley.")

[I do not know any more pleasurably painful duty that a man can be called upon to discharge than the revision of the papers of a deceased literary friend. The very lineaments of the mind, still communicating life and activity to that of him who reads, only recall the more vividly the irrevocable dissolution of the hand that wrote. It is this life in death—this communion without interchange—this sympathy without acceptance—this one [illegible] which is yet so unutterably [illegible] alike, that causes the performance of this duty to be accompanied with the most strange intermingling of pleasure and pain of which a man can well be susceptible. It has lately been my melancholy pleasure to revise and arrange—not with any view to publication—the literary remains of one who was once my fellow-student, and, up to the hour of his death, my most intimate friend. During the last year of his life we were both abroad; in different parts of the world, however, and with different objects—I, in Paris, in a professional capacity; he, in Egypt, in search of health. I heard of his death only two months after his return to England. We had corresponded faithfully up to this time, and his letters from Egypt were most minute and full of interest. In one of them, however, he had alluded to an adventure which he said was so strange that he would keep it for our next re-union. It was not our happiness to meet again, and I often wondered, after hearing of his death, what could have been the nature of the story he had in reserve for me. In looking over his Egyptian journal the other day, I came upon a loose manuscript which I read with much interest, as it contained apparently a narrative of the very adventure in question. I cannot account, however, for the circumstance of its not being incorporated with the rest of the journal. It is in the form of a letter addressed to myself; but whether it is a recital of the circumstances exactly as they occurred, or whether the story is only founded on the original adventure, amplified into what was intended to be a literary amusement for our two selves, must in the mean time remain a matter of doubt. The following is the story referred to, which I have been kindly permitted by the relations of the deceased to submit to the public, on the simple condition of altering the names of the persons concerned.]

You remember, Willie, how you and I used to discuss the character of that mysterious fellow Drepier, and think it about as difficult a subject of psychological analysis as ever was operated upon by our truculent intellects, sharpened as they then were by hourly disputations on all the insoluble problems of metaphysics. You remember his incomprehensible isolation from his fellow-men, and the utter futility of all our efforts to learn anything regarding his origin or his personal circumstances. You remember the defiant contempt with which he treated all friendly advances, and the special hatred towards me which his looks so evidently betrayed, as year after year he found himself second to me in the list of honours. You remember how we oscillated from disliking to pity, from pity to disliking, and from disliking to pity again. What his object in life might be was a problem to his fellow-students, compared with which the "Sartor Resartus," and all the other mysteries that we dreamt of in our philosophy, were tangible and luminous. His only passion seemed to be for distinction, and even this was often belied by his capricious abandonment of study at the very time when he was gaining on the only antagonist he had to fear. I sometimes fancy he must have been of noble parentage, but unacknowledged. Surely by none but the scion of a noble house could such face and figure belong. Had the pride of a princely race stooped to the queen of a gipsy tribe, it would have been a fitting solution of the Drepier mystery. And then, his rooms! Do you remember what speculations were built upon it, when we learned that instead of humble lodgings like those of most of our student class, this great Hidalgo inhabited a suite of apartments in —— Hotel, Princes-street?

I suppose you will hardly believe me, Willie, when I tell you that there is a circumstance connected with my acquaintance with him in Edinburgh, which I have never told you of. After you left, having no other bosom friend to vent my affections upon, I actually found myself looking daily more and more to the side of pity in regard to the Drepier subject. By a series of little kindnesses, all in the way of class business, the first of which were met with sullen indifference, that gradually warmed into something better as the series accumulated, I positively succeeded in thawing him, to the [illegible] amazement of all who beheld the miracle. I got so far into his better sentiments in a day or two, as to discover that he would not object to a little female society, and found very little persuasion necessary to induce him to accompany us one evening to the Armours'. We passed a very pleasant evening, Draper proving himself much more talkative than I could have previously given him credit for being. I was so secure of Mary at that time, that I did not feel in any great measure of inconvenience to yield her society entirely to the stranger, and to confine my attentions to Mrs. Armour and little Jane. To my surprise Draper suggested to me next day that we should renew the visit as soon as possible, which we did, and, as stage-books say—"same play as before." Next day he was absent from his class. This, you remember, was an unusual thing for him; and when I found the same to be the case on the day following, I felt so anxious regarding him, that after class hours I called at his hotel to see if anything were the matter. I was surprised to learn that he had not been seen since the last evening we had spent at the Armours'; in fact, I thought I was looked upon with something not very far from suspicion when the waiter told me that I was the last man in whose company he had been seen. I returned in a state of considerable anxiety to my lodgings, and pondered over the circumstance for some time; but hitting upon no satisfactory theory, I betook myself to my usual refuge. After filling the room with the accustomed smoke of three or four pipes in unbroken succession, I had risen and opened the window, when, just as I was in the act of turning round to resume my seat, I became suddenly aware of Draper standing before me, pale and haggard, and regarding me with a look of intensified hate that was absolutely fiendish. "What devil," he gasped out, "sent you to blast the only two hopes I ever had?" And before I had time to protect myself he had planted a blow on my chest that stretched me breathless on the floor. I heard him close the door with a wild laugh, after which I became utterly unconscious, and continued so for several hours. When I again came to myself I was lying with my head beneath the open window. The snow was falling fast, and huge flakes were settling on my face, where they melted and mingled with the blood that was flowing from my mouth. I felt a dead chill all over me, and it was only after a series of vain efforts that I was able to crawl to the bell-rope. I need not trouble you with any details regarding my subsequent illness, which lasted about a fortnight. Next time I saw Mary I learned from her that just before paying me that disagreeable visit Draper had called at the house, had sought and obtained an interview with her, and had made her a formal offer of marriage. Mary of course told him in the gentlest possible manner of our engagement. He muttered something, it seems, and rushed from the house, from which, I suppose, he came direct to my lodgings. I told Mary nothing of the circumstance at the time, as I thought it would only vex her; and I concealed it from you, as I fancied you would blame the unworthy jealousy which had led to it. But something tells me, Willie, that the time is not far distant when whatever you have loved in me will become [illegible], and when the thought of blame will find no entrance into your heart. To tell the truth, I trace back my disease to that unlucky blow. It was not till sometime after Mary and I were married that I became aware that the effects of it had settled down on me, and that the strength on which I had prided myself was on the wane. Ah, Willie, may you never know such sorrow as mine was when I led Mary back to the home of her childhood, and turned away to seek that which I knew too well was lost to me for ever! I had almost murmured against Providence when I counted up my wrongs and forgot that if I went abroad at all, it must needs be—alone.

It was necessary that I should narrate the above, before you could fully enter into my feelings in what follows. I am about to tell you of the strangest and most awful adventure that ever varied the tenour of my life. It would seem as if it had been ordained that though my life was to be a short one, there was yet to be crowded into it the concentrated experience and discipline of many years. Is it not good that it should be so? Is it by time, or by the result that we shall be judged? Is the fruit-tree that [illegible] to be held in dishonour because of the barren [illegible]? There is no set time for ripeness and maturity. If mine be summer-fruit, shall I murmur because it is gathered in its freshness before such as need the mellow suns of Autumn?

As I told you in a former letter, I arrived at Thebes on the 14th of January. I had been upwards of a fortnight exploring the wonders of Gournah, the Memnonium, Medinet Haboo, Luxor, and last, and grandest by far, Karnac, before I allowed myself to visit the wonderful old tombs that honeycomb the mountains separating the "Lybian suburb" from the desert. You know that my tastes are sepulchral, and though I was well prepared before coming to Thebes to delight in the [illegible] of temple-glories, the tombs of the kings were what I kept to the last, as by far the most interesting of all the sights with which Egypt could tempt me. It was a long and dreary ride up a long and dreary valley. It was in the very depths of solitude that these grand old monarchs chose to lie down, each one in his glory. How easy, with the same sun looking down on the same glaring hills, to fill the valley with the long winding processions that, thousands of years ago, bore successive dynasties to their long resting-places! How easy to conjure up the whole funeral pageantry filling these fearful solitudes with the crimson glory of dead majesty, the placing of the royal mummy in the chambers of the hills, and the [illegible] return of servile [illegible] to take a new yoke of bondage!

I spent the greater part of the day in the tombs known as Belzoni's and Bruce's. You have read too many books of Egyptian travel to require that I should describe them to you. But oh, Willie, there is that which books cannot give—that intensity of realisation which the immediate presence of [illegible] so delightfully [illegible]—what translation of our whole

belong to past ages, that proved the delicious rapture of a victory over Time itself! Sitting in the heart of the earth, surrounded with the grand emblems of monarchies that lie buried in the farthest records of human history, shut in and overarched with rocks richly hardened with the typical language of ancient worship and rigid ceremonies, gazing on the hollowed sarcophagus on which the eyes of the royal occupant alone were to gaze when the cycles of ages should bring about the glory of resurrection—here (and I say it with reverence) I felt one day as a thousand years, and a thousand years as one poor day. How poorly the mortality of the world's oldest kings [illegible] upon you now! I was a living man in the nineteenth century of the reign of grace, and I held in my hand the cerements that had wrapt a royal corpse when this world that we call old was yet in its early prime! The monarchs that ascended their royalty three thousand years ago, are not so far faded but that to-morrow they might step out round reasonably enough for a stranger's grave under a palm-tree. Surely this aspect should make a saintly [illegible] of shorter life, or at least shake the breath of impatience. I have striven hard, Willie, to learn the lessons of the tomb. It has one for you, and another for me. To you, in the vigour of manhood, it is that every turn is long; long in great action, longer still in pleasant results. To me, blasted in my youth, a mere apprentice to be stricken down with the implements of the Master ere yet I have raised one pillar that shall perpetuate my name, it is that hours, days, years, ages are nothing—Time itself but a creature of thought, a perishable garment, fit to be cast away or at once a serviceable and out of fashion. Surely both lessons are true. Then like with poetry, I shall meet the last enemy with calm.

Full of such thoughts I emerged into the daylight, and being curious fully to realise the unutterable solitude of this region of death, I sent my guides and horses back to the boat, telling the former that I would return on foot, and that I might be expected shortly after sunset. I retained a flask of wine, a torch, and wherewithal to light it, having some idea of revisiting the tombs I had just left, when the usual hour for travellers' visits should be past, and I should be free from all fear of interruption in continuing my researches. In the meantime I wandered hither and thither over the interminable series of dreary sandstone ridges that stretch away to the Libyan desert.

I had pursued this employment for some little time, when I descried one of the natives—a half-naked member of the tribe of the fellaheen—walking towards me, carrying something in his hand, that in the distance looked like a snake writhing in the agony of captivity. As he approached, I began to imagine that it was a young crocodile, some three and a half feet long, which he was holding by the tail. On a nearer approach still, I saw that it was a specimen of a class of animals which I had long wished to see, and which are popularly known as "Monitors of the Nile," being supposed by the Arabs to give warning of the vicinity of a crocodile. Its head was like that of a serpent, and the resemblance was heightened by its having a forked tongue that appeared and disappeared with the usual snakelike rapidity. In its rage, too, at its unwelcome durance, it was hissing like an infuriated dragon—of which fabulous monster only the want of wings prevented its being the express miniature. There was a diabolical beauty about it, such as Turner might have transferred to the canvas with terrible effect. Even the dreadful dragon of his Hesperides might have been a more masterly specimen of colouring and conception, but in none the combination of beauty and fury that was presented by this enraged reptile. It was in vain that it writhed and twisted, it could not reach the hand of its captor, who was by this time imploringly holding it out towards me, and offering it for money. Anxious to possess the creature, I presented the Arab with a few piastres, which he accepted without demur. The difficulty now lay in the delicate operation of conveying it from one hand to another, as I found that he objected to my wish, made known to him by signs, that he would carry it for me to the boat. In the mid act of transference the little wretch made such a violent snap at our hands that we both instinctively let go, upon which the reptile made off in one direction, and the Arab in another, the latter doubtless fearing that the money would be reclaimed. I shouted after him, but he soon disappeared, and I saw him no more. When I turned round again in the direction that the monitor had taken, I saw its scaly form just disappearing over the ridge of a sand-hill in the direction of the river. Making a rapid circuit I soon found myself in front of him; but seeing me he wheeled round, and struck out for the desert. I followed of course. Sometimes I lost sight of him for a little, and invariably on coming up with him again found him making for the river, until the sight of me sent him round again to the west. I suppose he travelled farther from the water than ever Nature intended him to go; for by the time I lost sight of him his pace had considerably slackened. At length, when I was within twenty yards of him, he disappeared behind a large fragment of rock. I made my way to the spot as fast as possible, but my enthusiasm was considerably damped on finding that I had miscalculated the dimensions of the stony impediment, which, with the exception of a small opening at the bottom through which the monitor had crept, was deeply embedded in the sand. I tried in vain to turn it from its position by main force, and then, being determined if possible to have some reward for the labours of the chase, I set to, with might and main, to remove the sand. It was slow work. Every handful that I removed was only the signal for another quantity to roll down and more than fill up the momentary vacancy. I felt conscious, however, that the loose sand was a much less serious obstacle to the displacing of the stone than the original material, which seemed to me to have been closely packed on purpose to baffle any attempt at its removal.

After working nearly a couple of hours, I again tried the effect of force, and found to my great delight that the huge fragment was yielding, and after pausing to collect my strength, I succeeded, after a severe effort, in turning it fairly over. I was completely blinded, and all but suffocated, by the shower of sand that followed its removal; but, on recovering my eyesight, I was agreeably surprised to find myself standing at what seemed to be the entrance of a great cavern, into which a steep flight of steps, almost covered by the sand that had just fallen, promised safe access, and a reward more than equal to my labour. I paused a moment to arm myself with equanimity in case of disappointment; for the idea of a discovery had flashed upon me at once, and had spurred my pulse to a pace at which Dr. Sangrado would have shaken his prophetic head. I had guessed at once that this was the entrance to a tomb hitherto undiscovered; but I suffered myself to revolve several possibilities, such as of its being unfinished, of its being only a natural cavern, with an artificial entrance, but of no definite Egyptian character, &c., &c., in order that there might be no reactionary regrets should my first idea turn out to be erroneous. I soon saw, however, from the depth and precision of the intaglios on the walls on each side of the staircase, that this was a relic of the purest Pharaonic period; and though I could not read the hieroglyphics fluently, I had sufficient experience in deciphering them to see that the long series of cartouches, which in column after column was continued to the foot of a flight of seventy-two steps, was in reality the pedigree of the occupant of the supposed tomb, and contained, moreover, certain astronomical references to the relative positions of Sirius and the sun, in connection with certain events then recorded, which, I could not but think, would, when made known to the scientific world, prove of the utmost value in settling some of the much disputed points of Egyptian chronology. At the foot of the steps were two doorways, over the edges of which was the usual Agathodæmon, a representation of a winged globe supported by asps. On the under-side of the stone lintel, instead of the sacred Scarabæus which I had more than once seen in such a position, was the figure of a crocodile, the limbs of which were represented as ornamented with bracelets, the ears with ear-rings, and the neck with a necklace.

Having now come to the real point of exploration, I lit my torch, and entered the cavern by the larger doorway with the greatest caution, in which vitrone the pits in the tombs at Gebool had given me a lesson. The hall in which I now found myself was not very remarkable either in point of size or beauty. It was about twelve feet square; the roof, which was embellished with stars on a blue ground, being supported in the centre by a single square pillar, on which, as on the walls, were the usual sepulchral paintings representing the process of embalming, the funeral boat, the judgment scene, &c. What I particularly remarked, however, was the frequency with which the crocodile was represented in connection with the royal cartouche. In every instance in which the prenomen, name, and titles of the monarch were given, came some reference to the crocodile. Provoked by curiosity to hard mental labour, I at length, by severe use of the small knowledge of hieroglyphics which I possessed, succeeded in making out, to my own satisfaction at least, such titles as the following:—"High-priest of crocodiles;" "worshipper of crocodiles;" "tamer of crocodiles"; "friend of crocodiles";" with other designations purporting that he had also been the leader, the guardian, and the charmer of the reptiles in question; and finally, and highest honour of all, brother of their king!

I was now quite prepared for the second hall, which was very large and beautiful beyond any of those I had visited in the tombs of Belzoni and Bruce. The roof, which was similar to that of the first hall, was supported by twenty-four enormous columns, that had been hewn out where they stood, into as perfect specimens of Egyptian art as those which stand in the Memnonium or Karnac. Sixteen of these had capitals representing the lotus-bud; the remaining eight were in imitation of the full-blown lotus. These pillars were smoothly covered with some species of composition, and on this was painted what might have been the entire archives of a kingdom, so great was the space, and so beautifully minute the hieroglyphics which covered it. The walls of this hall, covered with a similar composition, were embellished with a series of brilliant frescoes, representing various events in the life of the king. The colours of these were as bright as one could well imagine them to be on the day when the artist first introduced the living monarch to see and admire his future resting-place. One picture represented him as kneeling before a crocodile, which was ornamented with chains and earrings like that I have already mentioned, and offering it geese and various kinds of fish. In another he was seen leading a huge crocodile by a golden chain; in another sitting before the altar of Sevak, the crocodile-headed god, with his hand in a crocodile's mouth. In short, crocodiles seemed to be the tale and burden of this monarch's life. All round that immense hall he was feeding them, decorating them, training them, riding on them, sleeping on them, worshipping them, embalming them, and attending them to their burial.

But, in my eagerness to discover more, I did not stay to examine these very minutely. The general impression of magnitude of space and immensity of labour was sufficient in the meantime. I hastened on, therefore, where another door-way invited into a third hall. Here I found myself in a gloomier region, but one which, when examined, excited in me far more astonishment than all the brilliant colouring with which I had just been dazzled. Imagine a hall about a hundred feet by sixty, with its walls entirely covered with immense polished slabs of black granite, so exquisitely placed, that it was quite impossible to detect the line of junction. Four rows of square columns, twelve columns in each row, likewise cased in polished granite, supported the roof, on which was a profusion of astronomical symbols. But the wonder was this; in Bruce's tomb I had seen hall after hall, each of which presented in painting a complete chapter of Egyptian life. The whole of this, and much more, was here crowded into one room, and was cut into the granite in mezzo intaglio, such as might almost have become a signet-ring. Each of the pillars represented a science or an art. One side of the hall was covered with what seemed to be the history of the nation from the remotest times; the second with its mythology, and the third with— what think you?—thousands and thousands of times repeated, in bewildering myriads, that almost drove me distracted, the dread emblem of Eternity—a serpent, tail in mouth, forming a perfect circle! When I had passed along the dark colonnade, with the intention of examining the fourth wall, I found myself at the edge of a pit at least twenty feet deep, and stretching across the entire breadth of the hall. At the bottom of this lay, to all appearance dead, the beautiful little fugitive that had led me to such unexpected pleasure. Beyond the pit, all was naked, calcareous rock—a strangely sudden conclusion to the polished granite and exquisite art I had just been surveying.

Where, then, was the sarcophagus, which my imagination had been painting to itself from the very first? Where was the royal mummy, the brother of the king of crocodiles, for whose glorious repose this was the destined tomb? . . . . I had read not a little about Egyptian discovery, and I felt at once convinced, on seeing this abrupt incongruity, that here was an illustration of the old stratagem of hiding the inmost sepulchral chamber, by having before it a curtain of natural rock, to deceive the intruder by leading him to believe that the pit terminated the excavation. I was a little disappointed, notwithstanding this conviction, as I felt that I should have liked to reach the climax of discovering at once and alone; whereas, now, I foresaw the necessity of returning to my boat without having completed my explorations, and of delaying a whole day, probably, before obtaining the requisite material, human and otherwise, for crossing over the pit and breaking down the partition of rock. I was turning, almost fretfully, away, when I observed, in the pillar against which I had been leaning, that the under-slab of the granite in which it was encased had fallen partially away from that immediately above it, the aperture being sufficiently wide to admit my hand. No one can have a more thorough horror than I have of the Vandalism of which so many of our tourists are guilty in defacing and destroying the priceless vestiges of antiquity. Yet in this case curiosity predominated over all compunction, and by main force I wrenched the granite from its position; though, I must confess, my conscience severely reproached me, when the huge mass, from which I narrowly escaped as it toppled over, broke into several fragments as it fell into the pit.

But good came out of the evil. Before me was a narrow staircase, down which I immediately descended. As I had half-divined, it led to a passage under the rock-curtain, and in a few moments I was in the inmost hall of death!

There, before me, was the royal sarcophagus! It was of oriental alabaster, covered with shapes of rarest art, and placed on the backs of four immense crocodiles of polished granite. The figures on the sarcophagus were in alto-relievo, and represented forty-two gods welcoming the soul of the king with crowns and precious gifts. Savak holds him by the hand, and seems to be relating his virtues to the other divinities. On the lid a chapter of the great Funereal Ritual was beautifully carved. The hall was of the same size as the first I had entered, and its walls presented the same scenes, but in very delicate basso-relievo instead of painting. The whole was by far the most beautiful and entire specimen I had anywhere seen of Egyptian art.

And now I found time to take a large draught of wine, and to reflect on my good fortune. I had made a discovery; beyond all doubt I had made a discovery. How often, Willie, in mentally facing the inevitable result of my disease, had I felt my chief regret to be that I was leaving behind me nothing that was complete! I felt, on such occasions, that I had neither strength nor time to write a literary work, that could stand by itself as a complete and finished memorial. At such times came over me the longing desire to do some one great deed, the renown of which would embalm my name. Anything—anything but the fragmentary and merely preparative efforts of a youth divided among many pursuits. Was not this, then, all I could desire? Was it not complete? And now, this tomb, like Belzoni's and Bruce's, would be known by the name of its discoverer. In far-off years, perhaps, Mary would come upon my name in works of Egyptian travel. You would see it with pride attached to my donations in the British Museum. This astronomical discovery in reference to Sirius would cause much wonder among the learned, and produce great results in chronology. . . . . . Do you blame me for such thoughts? Do you blame me for magnifying my position, when I reflected that, through century after century—ay, millennium after millennium—the dark, lonesome hours had flitted, unperceived, through those solemn halls, and that the first light that had fallen on their gloomy wings was the flickering ray of the torch I bore in my hand? Of all the myriad million eyes that had seen the sun since this monarch fell asleep, mine were the first to gaze on the hallowed mysteries that darkly glorified his long repose! Of all human sounds that since then had fled into the infinite of space, from the roar of battle to the song of childhood, my own footfalls were the first to startle the echoes of silence that brooded over his slumbers! . . . . Oh, kingly soul, by what invocation shall I bring thee from the depths of primal time? This solitude is thine own! I [illegible] thee in it. I would know the secret of thy being, though it should blind the eye that looks on it! Hark! I dare to strike upon thy battle-sounding hall! Where is the revenge of violated majesty? To-morrow I shall bring the world to gaze upon thee; to expose it, and yet to mock thy grand solemnities; to carry thee away to classify thee as a thing of science, a subject of learned curiosity and cheap amusement! Dost thou not blast me? I brave thy presence! My foot is on the neck of the [illegible] thou didst adore! Where is the wrath of insulted [illegible]? Or, if thou art insensible to insult, can adulation reach thee? Oh, king of the great, pride of the elder-born of Time, vouchsafe a word, a sound, a sign! Is not this thine own temple—these thine own glories? Where, if not here, wilt thou manifest thyself from the depths of the eternity in which thy mighty soul sojourns? I stand on the threshold of the eternity; the fleshy integument is fast disentangling itself from my soul; I am not, now, altogether of earth! Let me, then, but see or touch the fringe of thine imperishable vestments, that the secret sense of immortality may steal through me if only for a moment! . . . . Had I evoked myself in a dream, or is that shadow on the wall the moving reflex of a real form? Ha! have I raised thee, then? But this shadowy similitude confronts me not! I am not afraid to front thee! One moment to nerve my frail mortality, and now I come to thee, face to ——!

Draper, as I live, mocking at me with the laugh of hell! He was gaily dressed in brilliant oriental costume, and was armed to the teeth. He had grown a large beard, and was altogether so completely metamorphosed, that I might almost have taken him for the monarchical personage I had so madly invoked, had it not been for the pistols in his girdle, and, what startled me much more rapidly from the frenzy into which I had wrought myself, the same look of devilish malignity which had so often haunted my dreams since the night of the fatal blow. He was standing in the dark doorway, with his arms folded across his breast, motionless and mysterious as the great old statues that guard the halls of Egyptian temples. I held my torch towards him, to make sure that this was not the fancied creation of my own excited brain; but it only changed the dark scowl into a glare of fierce rage. We stood fronting each other for some time in silence. Mine were anything but forgiving thoughts. Before me was the man whose unreasonable spite and whose rash hand had dashed the cup of life from my lips, when it was brimful of the ruddy elixir of hope, and had left me only the dregs. Was I not to avenge my own wrong? Should I not gather all my remaining strength for one retributive blow, if it should be the last movement of my soul? . . . . "Vengeance is mine." Yes, but should I not constitute myself the instrument of it, since the favourable occasion was granted for me? By the memory of my perished hopes—by the broken heart of my young affianced wife, I must crush him to the ground!

He seemed to guess my thoughts, and was the first to break the unnatural silence.

"Let us have it out fairly, Maggregor. You shall cross my path no more. Fate seems to send you on my track to blast all my fondest projects. I will dare Fate itself, rather than be for ever annoyed by you. The discovery is mine, and I will be first in claiming. This is the grave of one or both of us. Take your choice of these two weapons."

I was somewhat shamed, I confess, by the chivalrous generosity which led him to forego his advantage, and place his enemy on equal terms with himself. Maddened as I was with the thought of my wrong, and fearfully ready to constitute myself the minister of my own vengeance, I could not fight under colour of such a cause. Perhaps the discovery was his. I suggested as much. You know if I am a coward, Willie; so I may tell you that I did suggest this, but that it was only to pave the way to stabbing his conscience with my real wrong, and to showing him that I had grounds for "more solid claim than this" for aiming at his life.

"You are a coward, Maggregor," he replied tauntingly. "If this is your first visit to this place, then you are not the discoverer. I have lived in this country since I left England. I have adopted the life of the East, and there are those here who serve me as their chief and prophet. From them I the other day obtained a knowledge of this tomb, which they had all sworn to keep secret from Europeans, since, besides the Egyptian monarch in the sarcophagus there, a venerable prophet of their race is nevertheless buried within it. I did not know, however, and I do not believe that they knew, of the existence of the hall in which we are. This, I suppose, is your discovery. I intended to keep the secret until I had taken extensive plans of the whole excavation, and then to submit them to the savans of Europe. Now, however, you have interfered with my triumph. But you shall not think it if my hand be true. Your cowardly evidence will not avail you. Choose your weapon; but give me this in the first place. I dread no treachery when I see the gleam of yours."

Saying which, he snatched the torch from my hand, and fastened it where the heads of two of the [illegible] all but met.

A coward!—I who was thirsting for revenge! I who, I thought, did well to be angry, and to risk the dregs of my life to punish the crime which I knew too surely human law would never reach! I hurled reproach on reproach, curse upon curse, until frantic at seeing that the villain only smiled at my vehemence, I seized one of the pistols which he held towards me; and it would have been short work with either myself or him had he not grasped my hand with such force that I could not wrench it from him. "Stay," he said; "let it be fairly done. Promise me on your honour—probably your last words—that you will take no unfair advantage?"

I did promise, and was at once put in possession of the weapon of which I had made choice.

"How shall we time ourselves?" I asked.

"Well suggested," replied he coolly. "Let me see. . . . Yes. I'll manage that too. Meantime I throw myself on your honour."

Restoring his pistol to his girdle, he put his hand into his breast, and produced a small phial and a piece of paper. He next saturated the paper with the contents of the phial, remarking with a grim smile as he did so, "A little chemical knowledge is invaluable to an eastern prophet." Having then pulled out a long gold thread from the hem of his loose robe, he suspended the paper from the neck of one of the crocodiles; after which, taking the torch from the place where he had fastened it, he took up his station by the side of the sarcophagus, with his back to the wall, and directed me to place myself in a similar position at the opposite side of the chamber. I did so, at first at a loss to explain his movements, though, I must say, putting implicit trust in his honour.

"Take your aim now, Mengunger," said he, "while you have the light. I shall not move from this spot. I shall drop the torch and extinguish it with my foot. Whenever that is done the paper will blaze up. Fire when you see the flame. Are you ready?"

I had no sooner answered that I was, than the torch was dropt, and in another instant we were in darkness, save for the strange phosphoric gleam that danced on the paper, and that only rendered the darkness more visible and horrible.

These were fearful moments. The very coolness and formality of Dauphet's proceedings had again calmed me down. Yet I was so bewildered with the strangeness of the whole train of circumstances that I could hardly reason. It was all so new that I felt myself utterly removed beyond the pale of accountability. I felt for a moment, as I have sometimes felt in sleep, that it only required a strong effort of volition to cast off the horrible dream. But no; it was no dream! What was this in my hand? Why was my heart beating as if it had burst my guilty frame, and were forcing its way out? Was it this that my hand was raised to slay? Back, back, distracting thoughts! The demons of my past is there!

Up shot the flame, and two pistols flashed instantaneously. Dust and smoke, and a noise as of innumerable thunders pealing through endless hollows. With the last flicker of the paper I saw Dauphet reeling. I did not pause to feel if I were myself hurt, but dashed forward towards him. The ground yielded beneath me as if an earthquake were rocking the foundations of the earth. I clutched at the sarcophagus, threw myself on it, and the next moment, amid dust and falling fragments of rock, and the rumbling noise of a thousand echoes, felt myself hurried downwards into some unknown abyss. The sudden shock of the sarcophagus striking against the bottom threw me headlong forward, and for awhile—I know not how long—I lay deprived of all sensation.

Consciousness returned long before I recovered the power of motion. It seemed to me that I was no longer in the flesh, and that my soul was resolved into some dark element, itself a part of the blackness of darkness. And had I been launched into the unknown, with the burden of murder on my soul, that was to weigh me down for ever! . . . . The crash of another fragment of rock falling near me sent a convulsive quiver over my frame, which made me feel that I was still in the body. Gradually I recovered sufficient strength to move my hand towards my flask of wine, which I had not emptied, and which luckily was still safe. After a draught of the wine I felt considerably reinvigorated, but this only increased my perception of the horror of my situation and of the deed I had done. All my angry feelings were gone, and I could think of nothing now but the soul of Dauphet by me hurried before God with all its irrevocable guilt unpardoned. How was I to meet him? as meet him one day I must. But was he really dead? I had not heard even a groan. Perhaps, like myself but a few minutes before, he was lying stunned by the fall, and I guiltless of his blood.

Catching at this thought, as the last glimpse of possible happiness that should save my last days from the blackness of remorse, I gathered all my strength, felt for the ground, and, having reached it, moved cautiously about in search of him who had so lately been my foe. I felt that I could now give my life cheerfully for him, even for enough of breath in him to pronounce my pardon and to pray for his own.

After a few steps I came upon what seemed to me a large heap of stones. Suddenly remembering that I had still the means of light about me, I set fire to it, and in an instant the whole was in a blaze.

I was utterly unprepared for the new scene that burst upon me. I found myself in a hall, seemingly of endless length, supported by a double row of massive columns. Between both columns was the mummy of a crocodile. From most of them the cloth had partially fallen, so that wherever I turned, the mocking grin of monsters met me, and it seemed to me, in my frenzy, as if they were rejoicing with the joy of fiends over my deed and my doom. And, worse than all, a few feet from me lay poor Dauphet, still and motionless, with his bloody face turned towards me, his closed eyes and lips appealing me with speechless reproach! For the moment I felt realised within me all that I had ever read of the damning horror of a murderer's conscience. I stood transfixed, knowing that I could never fly from the hell within me. And the blaze went down, and the darkness came over me; and I felt as if I could never again wish to see light.

Was I to die here, then, and the slain man

and the slayer to lie here together, till the trump of doom should wake us to mutual and everlasting reproach! . . . . Another thought flashed on my darkness. Had I really killed him, or was he not perhaps killed by the fall?

Even in the horror that had overtaken me when the sight of his body met my eye, I had not failed to observe that the remnant of my torch was lying beside him. I soon found it, and having lit it, set about the awful task of examining the corpse, to see if I were indeed a murderer or no. I found that the back of the head was completely knocked in, and close beside it lay a sharp fragment of rock, against which it seemed to have struck. I would fain have made no further examination, as I could hardly bear to look upon the ghastly spectacle; but the thought that perhaps he was dead before this happened compelled me to search more minutely. To my infinite relief I discovered that the bullet had lodged in the fleshy part of the left thigh, where I could still feel its presence. Let strict moral criticism find me, if it will, equally guilty as if it had passed through his heart; still, I say, I felt infinite relief in the thought that an unexpected retributive interposition had left me only indirectly concerned in the article of death. I saw at once, on looking up and around, that the pillar supporting that part of the floor of the chamber above, on which the sarcophagus had rested, had been too slender in proportion to the immense superincumbent mass, and that the concussion produced by the discharge of the pistols had destroyed the delicate equilibrium that ages of stillness had left undisturbed. The column had fallen, and it was against one of its fragments that poor Drapier had struck.

My next thought was how to escape from this dreadful place. I saw that it was quite impossible to reach the chamber above. I explored the whole of the crocodile charnel-house, but could see no outlet. I observed in my search the remains of several straw fires, which, no doubt, Drapier had caused to be kindled during his previous visits; but I could discover no indication of the entrance of which he must have availed himself. I returned and sat me down by the dead man to meditate, and, if possible, to pray. Then it occurred to me that I ought again to search the body, to try to find some clue to his personal circumstances. I found nothing but a small sum of money and a note-book, in which, however, to my great satisfaction, I found a series of rough plans of the whole sepulchral excavation, with the exception of the hall in which the sarcophagus had been deposited. After carefully pondering these, I observed a small asterisk at the position occupied by one of the crocodile mummies. Feeling sure that this must mean something, and having already a little experience of concealed entrances, I proceeded at once to examine the spot indicated. I found it an easy task to push aside the mummy, underneath which, as I had half divined, was a passage sloping gradually downwards, but leading, as I at once suspected, in the direction of the principal entrance. I hastened back for the torch, now nearly burnt down, and rushed along the passage, which, in a short time, took an upward slope, ending in a long flight of steps that led to the smaller of the two doorways at the entrance of the cavern. In a few minutes I was in the open air, with the pure sky over me, and the unconscious stars smiling unchangeable peace, as if they saw no death and no sorrow in all the wide universe.

Utterly exhausted and sick at heart, I turned in the direction of the river. Hours of alternate walking and resting brought me at last to my boat. You will not be surprised to learn that it was weeks before I was again able to leave my couch. Many times afterwards I returned to what I thought was the spot where the entrance to the cavern had been, but to me the place seemed entirely changed. I hinted once to my dragoman that I had discovered such an entrance, on the day before my long illness. His opinion, which I suspect to be the right one, was that the Arabs, jealous of European discovery, had entirely filled up the entrance with sand, and as I might be some miles out of my reckoning with regard to the exact situation of it, in a region where a monotony of sand-hills rendered the identification of it next to impossible, I thought it utterly useless to institute any operations for its rediscovery.

And yet to think of poor Drapier lying there!

[Here the MS. ends.]

J. R. S.

THE DOG'S DREAM.

What are your dreams, my poor old dog,
  As by the blazing hearth you lie,
With twitching tail, and ears erect
  As if prepared your speed to try?
Are you among the heath and fern
  By the wild mountain's side once more,
Or gambolling by the babbling rill,
  As you were wont in days of yore?

I too can fancy back the scene
  By mountain side and gushing rill,
And dream of joys that centred there,
  And think awhile I have them still.
I see again the heather bells;
  Once more I see the bright ferns shine
Through mossy turf and tangled brake,
  And trace the steps that paired with mine.

And do you hear the well-known voice
  From distance hail you back again,
And, still obedient to the call,
  Do you come bounding o'er the plain?
Or do you look into the eyes
  That you so well had learn'd to read?
Or do you lick the gentle hand
  From which it was your wont to feed?

I too, like you, in happy dreams
  That silver voice again can hear,
Forgetful for awhile that ne'er
  Its tones my waking hours can cheer;
I look into the eyes once more
  That beam'd so much of love on me,
And feel the pressure of the hand,
  Then wake to know it cannot be.

If aught your mem'ry can retain
  When it has pass'd—of that sweet dream,
To you the fond illusion still
  A bright reality may seem.
Not so it is with me: I wake
  And the deceptive joy is o'er;
I feel my loneliness, my loss,
  My sad reality, the more! H. L.

A NIGHT AND MORNING.

[illegible]

Beneath the purple heaven's misty gleaming,
  When all the dewy flowers in sleep were [illegible],
I heard a song of melancholy [illegible],
  Whose music was as old as is the [illegible].

The ancient elms which grew beside the meadow
  Were tossed, like troubled life, by every breath;
The one dark yew-tree in the bell-tower's shadow
  Was solemnly at rest, like peaceful Death.

The hollow-sounding sea moaned sad and weary,
  And the pale moon a wanderer above;
With folded hands, I sat in sorrow dreary,
  And sighed my heart away for hope and love.

But when on high the god of day appearing
  Dimmed the dusky grey with rosy streak,
I met the breeze o'er hill and dale careering,
  And let its cool kiss dry my wetted cheek.

The skylark's song trilled from the gate of heaven,
  And happy sounds came from the waving wood;
Night's chain of silence far and near was riven,
  And all awoke with praise who toiled for good.

I gathered up the sighs which heaved my breast;
  I gave my doubts and murmurs to the air;
From rose-bush near I broke a stainless blossom,
  And o'er its beauty bowed in trusting prayer.

And so I went my way, with footstep lighter,
  O'er dews which spangled garden, field, and grove,
I felt, through faith, that my life-path was brighter,
  Though morning brought to me nor hope nor love.
  [illegible], 1851.

HER GRAVE.

And love shall pour full circle yet,
  In spite of partings and of tears,
And joy be like a jewel set
  In life, [illegible] by years;

But toiling with a fuller faith,
  With higher hopes, with deeper trust;
Treading with firmer steps the path
  That leads unto the good and just.

The soul shall wake, and live once more—
  And not in vain, O not in vain—
To win the crown that fancy wore
  When coming years, like fields of grain,
Were still before us, and the task
  Seemed but to reap and gather in,
And when to love was but to ask;
  When but to love it, was to win.

Ah! me, the grave has long grown green;
  The stone itself is rich with moss,
And all the years that since have been
  Are heavy with a love and loss;
Comes the air with trembling sound,
  Voice-like whisperings as of old;
The summer twilight deepens round,
  Grey shadows gather fold on fold.

And there the grave of her I loved—
  Alas! she never bore my name,
Yet not the less she lived and moved
  The first, the dearest, in Life's frame;
The graceful girl of summers back,
  The woman forty years agone.
Do human hearts or break or crack:
  Ah! no: the brave ones still live on.

And, true to love as true to life,
  To live in sunder pain and grief,
And, O, not breathe the name of wife;
  But to be worthy brings relief.
Love lives and lasts without return;
  Another's then?—alas! not so.
Death comes, old flames anew may burn—
  I love the girl of long ago.

I love the woman once a child,
  My playfellow in far-off years,
Grown earnest, who, with accents mild,
  And eyes so blue, so full of tears,
Bade me farewell; but could not heal
  The deep'ning wound herself had made;
Oh! if to love were to be loved,
  Life's sunshine might exceed its shade.

And I have lived my life away;
  I will not deem I lived for naught
While yet through memory sunbeams play—
  While still my days with toil were fraught.
Though love is much, it is not all,
  And life holds yet a second good;
And manly voices loudly call,
  And work is worthy of the soul.

And I have worked, and years have passed;
  My time of pause is drawing near;
I entered first, I bring at last
  My all of manhood to you here:
Here 'mid the scenes where we have play'd;
  Here near the church beside the yew,
Where first we met, laughed, parted, prayed,
  I come to lay life down by you.

H. A. C.

THE CALICO-PRINTER OF JOUY.

In the course of this year (1755), a grave question occupied the French Chamber of Commerce. Up to that time the false policy had insisted upon a monopoly of flax, as being a native product, to the utter exclusion of cotton, either raw or manufactured, as a material for which money had to be exported. But, on the other hand, as the female world of France rightly insisted on wearing the graceful fabrics of India and British looms, a contraband trade, too profitable to be put down by the severest measures, had sprung up as a natural consequence. In such a dilemma French legislators began to doubt whether it might not be both wiser and more profitable to import raw cotton for manufacturing purposes, than to send twenty millions of francs yearly out of the country to pay for foreign fabrics, to say nothing of the poor wretches, about three hundred in number, whom revenue-laws annually sent out of the world by the rope or the galleys. Such a point as this would appear to admit of no discussion in our own days of free trade; but at that time popular prejudice in favour of monopoly raised so strong an opposition-party that the battle proved doubtful and long. Not till 1759 did an edict of Louis XV. revoke the old laws, and authorise the manufacture of printed cotton fabrics.

Curiously enough, while England had owed the introduction of this branch of industry, sixty years before, to a Huguenot driven out of his country by the revocation of the edict of Nantes, the French stood indebted for the naturalisation of an art which might seem indigenous to their soil, to a German Lutheran, Christopher Oberkampf by name. Christopher was a working calico-printer of the Rhine, a grave thoughtful youth, then about twenty, who had the year before (1758) made his way to Paris, his knapsack over his shoulder, with the intention of pushing on beyond the Pyrenees into Spain. On Oberkampf's arrival at the French capital, however, the important question then pending struck him at once, and, with the true instinct of a man born to make his fortune, he determined to stay where he was, and await the results. By the time it was decided in accordance with his hopes, the young calico-printer had formed his plans, and had also, by dint of hard work and self-denial, amassed a little capital of twenty-five louis. A younger brother came over to share his fortunes; a fellow-workman joined them, and the three set heartily to work to realise the ambitious project of establishing the first printing-ground in France. The preliminary step was to find a locality suited to their enterprise in the environs of Paris, and Oberkampf fixed at once upon the valley of the Bièvre. At a point, about three miles from Versailles, where the valley widens, the village of Jouy clustered round its church on the river-bank. A double range of hills, wooded up to their summits, shut in the little hamlet from the world. At this spot, and up the windings of the valley, as far as the eye could reach, the river crept through meadows, enlivened now by a few dwarf trees, and anon by lonely poplars, which served as landmarks. The village was poor, almost unknown, the landscape dreary and unpromising; but to Oberkampf it presented the great requisites, water, space, and low wages. A cottage—or, rather, a hovel—with a piece of marshy land sloping down to the river, was to be let. He first hired it, and forthwith commenced operations. A more primitive manufactory had hardly been set up, since the day when kelp and sea-sand were first fused into glass on the open beach. It was just as well that the future millionaire had no money wherewith to buy furniture, for his cottage would scarce suffice to hold the implements of trade. The dye-vat had to be set up out-of-doors, and boiled after the fashion of a gipsy's kettle. At night Christopher spread his mattress on the printing-table where he had toiled all day, and slept the sleep of hard work and honesty.

By the end of the first year, in spite of heavy drawbacks, and unaided by the mechanism which has since so greatly facilitated calico-printing, Oberkampf had contrived to issue between three and four thousand pieces, and had established a reputation for the beauty of design and superior finish of his goods. Still, for some time, fortune would hardly consent to smile upon the German's industry and perseverance. His first partner had brought him to the brink of bankruptcy; the second involved him in a law-suit. Then came an inundation, which well-nigh swept away the cottage. And, finally, when the success of his works had enabled him to import experienced Swiss and German workmen, the little industrial colony, with its chief, were denounced as suspicious persons and heretics, and, but for the protection of the seigneur of Jouy, a wise and liberal man, would have been driven from the place. Yet by dint of patient labour and indomitable resolution, Oberkampf surmounted every difficulty as it presented itself, and by the close of 1767 might fairly be said to have conquered fortune at last. In that year the calico-printer signalised the opening of a new factory he had lately built, by throwing into the market immense quantities of an entirely new description of prints. The ground was white, covered with a small running pattern of coloured flowers. Each province had its peculiar hue and style, so that, as the manufacturer proclaimed, every peasant woman in France might be able to choose a dress to suit her fancy. These prints were the celebrated Jouy mignonnettes, of which old French ladies still speak with affectionate regret. Their material was good, the colours fast, the charge—no trifle in such a speculation, especially with our neighbours across the channel—highly [illegible], and the price within the means of the humblest purchaser. The manufactures of Jouy speedily became favorites, both with high and low. Marie Antoinette and her ladies adopted them when they masqueraded in shepherdesses; songs were made in their honour; and the light tasteful fabrics soon brightened every village-dance, fête, and wedding throughout the country.

The rapid sale of these new cottons justified their projector's sagacity. He had made the capital discovery that—as many years afterwards he told the Emperor Napoleon—the secret of success lies in ministering to the tastes and requirements of the many. But at the date of their first issue Oberkampf would hardly have imagined that his [illegible] were destined one day to stand between himself and the guillotine. During the Reign of Terror, in 1794, when some enemy had denounced the German as a royalist and monopolist to the Committee of Public Safety, one of the chief arguments which saved him from a summons before the revolutionary tribunal—equivalent to an appearance on the scaffold—was, that his establishment, by supplying fabrics at once cheap and good, had been a public benefit to the people of France. That terrible magistracy not only dismissed the charge, but issued an order whereby they took the "citizen Oberkampf" under their especial protection.

Fortunately for the inhabitants of Jouy, at this epoch its municipal power was in the hands of "the patron," as Oberkampf—now recognised as a benefactor both by his neighbours and workpeople—was affectionately styled. Through his influence order was maintained in the community, and personal safety and security of property were guaranteed to its inmates. The hamlet, thus living peaceably from day to day, and held between its hills, as in the hollow of a mighty hand, from the storm of passion and anarchy which overswept France, offers one of those pictures upon which the mind delights to dwell. Surely, if ever the wisdom and energy of one man availed his fellow-creatures, it was when this noble-hearted foreigner, throughout that turbulent time, kept the little valley tranquil; kept its rivers unstained by human blood; kept his hundreds of dependants in a calm and wholesome round of daily task and daily fare. Nor was this work of a true philanthropist fulfilled without great personal sacrifice. For four years, dating from the close of 1792, commerce and manufactures were alike paralysed in France. At the beginning of the crisis, Oberkampf called his people together, and told them that they were not to him mere instruments of his prosperity, but fellow-labourers; and promised that, for so long as they kept to their employments, and he was able to pay their wages, the works should never be closed. And nobly he kept that promise. During those years the establishment paid its workmen in full, and only paid them in the depreciated paper-currency of the state when the panic of that terrible season had withdrawn metallic currency from circulation. Nor was the beneficence of its chief limited to his workpeople. Throughout this time of scarcity, he, with his family, lived as frugally as in the days of his poverty, that they might more effectually relieve the distress about them.

Towards the close of 1795 the long period of commercial stagnation had been finally tided; but it left Oberkampf a poorer man by sixty-four thousand pounds. "Our money is not lost; it has been well laid out on the spot where it was earned," he remarked on this occasion. "We have saved a whole population from ruin."

In the following year, as if to indemnify "the patron" for so serious a check to his fortunes, cylinder-printing was introduced into the manufactory of Jouy, and gave at once an enormous impulse to its prosperity. Impressions from the cylinder proved clearer than those obtained by the old method, and one machine did the work of forty-two block-printers.* A chief source of our manufacturer's success was, that he identified his own career with that of scientific progress. He kept up a close intercourse with the scientific men of Paris, and every fresh appliance, whether in chemistry or mechanics, was adopted in his establishment. The chemical part of his business Oberkampf had deeply studied; and the manufactory was not without its laboratory, where his nephew, aided by the counsels of Gay Lussac, and other great chemists, made several important discoveries and improvements.

Under the Empire, the fortunes of Jouy reached their climax. Its veteran chief had lived to see his children's children rising about him, and was the head of a whole colony of relatives, whom he had summoned from time to time to share his success. The whole district smiled with a reflection of his prosperity. Its population had been nearly quadrupled, homesteads had risen in every direction, as if, as said the people, they had sprung from the soil, while the thickets of [illegible] and unwholesome marshes were transformed to the emerald and gold of corn-field and pasture-land. Oberkampf had, in these late years, successfully realized his gigantic scheme of taking the raw cotton, and bringing it, in his single establishment, through all the separate processes by which it becomes muslin or calico. From his factory, by far the largest in the Empire, the old man looked back with affection to the cottage on the borders of the Bièvre, where, half a century before, he had made his first essay. And this grain of mustard-seed, the tiny capital of one-and-twenty louis! The profits of the firm for 1805 were more than sixty-six thousand pounds!

* A cylinder-machine of the present day, which requires only one man to regulate the rollers, and a boy to supply the colour-troughs, does the work of nearly two hundred block-printers.

A great day, and never to be forgotten in the annals of Jouy, was the 20th of June, 1806. On that morning a gendarme, booted and spurred, rode through the village, and up to the factory. Arrived there, he announced a message from St. Cloud, which he must deliver to M. Oberkampf in person. Before the gendarme rode back through the hamlet, his errand was spreading from house to house like wild-fire. "The Emperor was expected!" In half-an-hour Napoleon, accompanied by the Empress Josephine, arrived. He was conducted over all the buildings, inspected the different processes, after his usual rapid fashion, keeping up meanwhile a running fire of questions. Many of his queries show imperial acuteness, not a few betray imperial curiosity, and read uncommonly like some which Peter Pindar's George the Third put to Whitbread. One graceful tribute to the true greatness of the manufacturer Napoleon did not forget to pay. On taking leave, the Emperor, in the presence of the assembled work-people, and the village population which had gathered about the factory, unfastened the Cross of the Legion of Honour he himself wore, and bestowed it on Oberkampf, emphatically saying "There is no man in France more worthy to wear it." All Jouy felt itself decorated in the person of the "patron;" the people received this honour done to him with an enthusiasm which moved Josephine deeply, and the Imperial couple drove off amidst some of the heartiest blessings which ever greeted their ears.

The invasion which overspread France in 1814 put an end for a time to manufacturing industry at Jouy. Here the presence of a *foreign* army in the capital was so severely felt as to compel a stoppage of the works. Hardly had tranquillity been restored, when the battle of Waterloo in the following year brought the allies once more to Paris. Again labour stood still, but the manufactory was not deserted. Crowds of the poor, *feeling* comparatively safe under the protection of their patron, forsaking their homes, encamped with their little possessions in the spacious buildings, as in a caravanserai. Then, after some houses in the neighbourhood had been destroyed, and there was hourly fear lest a detachment of the enemy might set fire to the factory, the brave old man lost courage. His chief apprehension was not for himself and his family—their fortunes were secure—nor even lest he should experience the bitterness of seeing the work of his life-time perish before him. The sight of these fugitives and his own dependents unmanned Oberkampf. "This is more than I can bear," he cried repeatedly; "if they burn down the factory, what is to become of my poor people and their little ones!"

His fears were not realised, and peace soon restored things to their accustomed routine. But the shock had been too great for Oberkampf, his health visibly gave way, and he died in the autumn of the same year, at the good old age of seventy-seven. The rapid development and concentration of the same branch of industry in Mulhausen and other French towns sapped the life of the single establishment of Jouy, and after the founder's decease its prosperity declined. All the buildings, except the principal one, now converted into an India-rubber manufactory, have disappeared. Still Oberkampf is not forgotten; the main street of the village bears his name, a pillar marks the spot where he was decorated by the hands of Napoleon, and the old people of the place dwell fondly on "the good days of the patron!" Nor will his memory, as that of a benefactor, be suffered to die out. To perpetuate it, his family and friends have invested a sum, from which the poor receive liberal alms of food and clothing throughout the winter months. Many years since, one of his daughters bought the little cottage by the Bièvre, had it enlarged, and endowed it as a day-home, where orphan children, and such whose mothers are unable to give them due care, are collected, to be taken care of and taught. As the population is scattered, a children's omnibus, supplied by her charity, goes its round for the little creatures every morning, and takes them back at night to their friends. It was thought at once noble and feminine, and worthy of Oberkampf's daughter, thus to consecrate the scene of the infant fortunes of her house as a perpetual blessing for the little ones of Jouy.

MISS JENNY CAW, AND HER CHRISTMAS BOX.

Chap. I.

It was Christmas Eve, in the year 1834, and Miss Jenny Caw sat in the dusk of the December twilight before her small bright fire, contemplating the glowing embers with a thoughtful countenance. The snow had been falling all the long dreary day, and lay thick on the shrubs and evergreens of her little front garden, weighing down the leafless branches of the gnarled apple-trees in the orchard adjoining, and making the grand old hollies into so many sheeted ghosts. The steep, narrow path had been cleared from the cottage door to the garden-gate; but the lawn on either side was obstructed by great snow-drifts, that lay heaped up against the south hedge, driven there by the incessant raging of a keen north wind. Of "rude Boreas," however, and his "railing," Miss Jenny had heard almost nothing in her snug little parlour, sheltered by the gable of her neighbour's barn. So she had been sitting quietly by her fireside the whole afternoon, while the storm raged over the "wide, white world" without; and alternately doing a little nothing, and idly gazing on the fire, with her plump chubby hands folded lazily on her lap, she had by degrees fallen into a gloomy humour, very unusual with her.

"Miss Case!" suddenly said a sharp voice at the door, while a small withered visage, much marked by the small-pox, and surrounded by the wide border of a scrupulously clean cap, protruded itself through the half-open doorway; "Miss Case! if you please, ma'am, you never rang for your tea; and I'm sure 'tis time you had it, and candles too, ma'am."

Miss Jenny roused herself from her reverie with a sigh. "Very well, Martha," she quickly replied to her old and much-indulged servant. "Very well; bring in tea and candles whenever you like."

"Whenever I like! ma'am; but with all respect to you, it is whenever you like. And what would you fancy for tea, ma'am: an egg, or a blocter, or a bit of ham? The tea is already made, and standing on the hob; and you can have it in immediately."

"Thank you, Martha," replied Miss Case, "I do not think I care much about anything. Pray give yourself no further trouble, but just bring in the tea and a loaf and butter."

"Now, ma'am," said the old servant very earnestly, "I must say that is very foolish of you, not caring to have a good meal, when you had so long a walk this morning, and no proper dinner after it. The truth is, you care about everyone else but yourself, ma'am."

Her mistress smiled kindly. "The truth is, Martha, I have had many sad thoughts that seem to take away my appetite this afternoon. I was thinking what a different Christmas I used to spend when my own dear mother and sisters, who are now angels in Heaven, and——" She broke off abruptly, and with her eyes fixed on the glowing embers, appeared to retire within the sanctuary of her own pure heart, where the beloved objects she had lost lay spiritually enshrined.

"Martha," she resumed, after a pause, "did you send that wine to the poor woman who had twins last week, and the elder-syrup to little Eliza Schofield, who has such a bad cough, and that nice bit of chicken and the old linen to Lucy Rhode; and——"

"Yes, ma'am, I done it all," replied the servant tartly; "and it aggravates me the more that you forget to think of yourself this cold day, when you have done your best for others. But I forget that I am losing time all this while; and as you will not give any orders, I shall just have my own way."

So saying, the honest woman brought in candles on a waiter; and, having closed the shutters, and drawn the crimson moreen curtains, she made up the fire and departed. Speedily there arrived a savoury odour from the little kitchen opposite; and in five minutes more the old servant re-appeared with a tray containing the teathings, a plate of buttered toast, and a small dish of delicate fried ham with a couple of newly-laid fried eggs in all their white and golden glory. A tiny cut-glass basket, containing amber-coloured honey, and a small plate of the same material, heaped with transparent jam, completed the repast, so fitted to tempt a languid appetite. Miss Jenny shook her head at her officious maid, but sat down nevertheless to the tray as if she meant to enjoy her meal; and Martha, after remaining a moment near the table, to watch her mistress begin to eat, much as if she had been an ailing child, quitted the room better satisfied.

The good little spinster, left to herself, sipped her tea, trifled with a slice of ham and an egg, tasted the jam, and then desisted, and gazed into the fire as before, sighing. It appeared to her as if she had some vague presentiment of approaching danger or annoyance. She pushed away the tea equipage, with the food almost untouched, and was just stretching forth her hand for her netting, that she might make a pretence of working as before, when she was startled by a light tapping at the outer-door.

There was no reason in the world why good Miss Jenny should start and tremble at this very common sound. She had no duns to fear—her simple dealings at that country place being all on the ready-money system; nor had she any fine-lady acquaintances to be horror-stricken at finding her in the act of drinking tea at half-past five o'clock in the afternoon. Neither was she in any painful state of expectancy as to the arrival of a long-looked-for relative or friend from any distant part of the world. All these probabilities being non-existent, there was no rational cause whatever for her trembling, nor could she give any plausible reason for it herself. So she placed it all to the account of her "nerves." "Dear me!" she thought, "how nervous I am becoming, to be sure!"

Martha did not appear to have heard the summons that had thrown her mistress into so unusual a state of trepidation, yet it was not repeated; and Miss Jenny, who had risen from her chair, and was listening with most unaccountable anxiety, remained still in suspense. She thought of answering the door herself; and then, as the moments elapsed and no further sound was audible, she once more sank into her easy chair.

"What a foolish creature I am!" she exclaimed. "It was only a runaway knock, after all. A pretty idiot I should have appeared, opening the door this inclement evening, for some mischievous boy to laugh at, round the corner!"

But scarcely had she resumed **her** musings over the fire, than Common Sense whispered, "You are aware that your only near neighbour has no children, nor any inmate likely to play you a trick; and it is extremely improbable that any mischievous person from the village should come abroad on such a night as this, and take the trouble to grope his way across the bridge, and over the common, and all along that lonely lane among the snow-drifts, merely for the purpose of giving an undeserved fright to a harmless old maid like you. Besides, the knock had nothing of the character of a runaway knock about it; it was hesitating, timid, and evidently achieved for a purpose. I am afraid, my good creature, I must trouble you to ascertain whose your servant is, or to go to the door yourself, merely to see if any poor freezing creature be there, requiring your succour this dismal night. Come! come up! a little draught of air will do you good."

"Very well, I will go," replied Miss Jenny to her honest menace. She dallied no longer with her dreamy indolence, but throwing a shawl over her shoulders, and taking up one of the candles, she stepped forth into the little lobby, and thence to the outer door. This she opened without further hesitation, and met a blast from the north-wind, that extinguished her candle. Thus consigned to almost utter darkness, she could nevertheless distinguish, on the top step of the narrow flight, rendered dimly perceptible by the whiteness of the snow that had drifted into the porch, what appeared to be a square box of tolerable size. Just then Martha began to bustle about in the kitchen.

"Come hither!" cried Miss Jenny to her tardy maid; "and bring the lantern with you," she added, stooping down and passing her hand over the square object on the step. "Now, just lift this box into the house—but stay: we might as well take a look down the path to see if we can discover any trace of the individual who brought it, and left it here in this strange way!"

And in fact, on throwing the light of the lantern as far along the pathway as possible, there was still visible a double row of footsteps—the marks of some one who had approached and returned, and which had not yet been effaced by the snow.

"It is of no use going down to the gate to look for them, ma'am," said Martha. "No one would linger there longer than they could help, such a night as this. It is a wonder any-one could be hired to deliver the box!"

"It certainly is," replied Miss Jenny. "Bring it into the parlour at once, Martha, and let us understand what it means."

It was not so easy to do this as Miss Jenny expected. On a closer inspection of the lid, a small card was discovered in one corner; and on this card were scrawled, in an almost illegible hand, the following lines—

A Christmas Box
For the honoured
Miss Jenny Case.

"Well!" exclaimed Martha, "if this is not a peculiar way of making you a present anyhow! They might at least have stayed in our kitchen a bit! I had just stepped out to the wood-shed for some fresh logs for the kitchen-fire, or I would have gone quick to the door when they knocked, and caught them. What sort of a knock was it, ma'am?"

"Light and gentle," replied her mistress. "Just so." And she gave a specimen of the mysterious summons with her dimpled knuckles on the wainscoting. "But do not you think your best plan would be, Martha, instead of standing there lost in speculation, just to open the box and see what it contains? You perceive that it is only tied across with string, and there is little force to be used."

"And that is strange too, ma'am, and suspicious as if it contained nothing very valuable! And only look, ma'am, the lid is bored full of gimlet-holes!"

So saying, she applied her bony fingers to undo the string, when suddenly there arose a stifled cry within the mysterious package. The two women started and turned pale, and Martha lifted up her hands and eyes.

"It is"—whispered Jenny, in terrified accents, which testified that quite another idea had occurred to her than that to which she gave utterance—"is it a puppy?"

"A puppy!" replied the matter-of-fact Martha, somewhat disdainfully—"a child, more likely! Poor wee thing! poor deserted babe!"

And she eagerly stripped off the cording and raised the lid; while Miss Jenny dropped into a chair that stood conveniently near, trembling all over. Martha lifted a double piece of flannel that lay beneath the lid, and behold a fine child, about five weeks old, opening its tender mouth for another cry.

"The brute! the unnatural brute!" exclaimed the old servant, with a burst of honest indignation. "Here is a deed of Godfrey's mending, I suppose, and then packed it in here! The brute of a mother! the unnatural murderer!"

"But it is not dying, poor thing, is it?" faintly inquired Miss Jenny, who had not yet ventured to look into the box.

"No, ma'am, no; but a little drop more of the snow, and it would not have been here now, seen in the body, poor angel!"

"I cannot say I wish it had been so," mildly remarked Miss Jenny. "Poor little dear! I always was so fond of infants. Put it on my knee, Martha, that I may have a good look at it!"

Martha raised the baby very gently, and placed it on her mistress's lap. "There, ma'am; 'tis a fine child, you see, and decently dressed, simple, and clean. Oh! what a heart the mother must have had to part with it!"

"This is no common case of child-desertion, Martha, that you may depend upon, for observe how nicely the box fitted it to the bed. Poor creature! perhaps she could maintain it no longer. Let us examine its clothes and the articles in the box, that we may, if possible, discover some clue to the parents. Surely we shall find some marks or names."

But nothing of the kind could they discover; and as the infant appeared to be recovering its senses very fast, and began to cry with all the strength of a powerful pair of lungs, Martha hastened to set some milk on the fire to warm for it. When the milk was ready, and properly diluted with water, Miss Jenny, good soul! insisted on trying to feed the hungry babe herself; although, as she declared to Martha, she had not touched an infant for more than twenty years. But she succeeded very well, nevertheless; and the baby being so satisfied, fell into a peaceful slumber, its head resting on the shoulder of its kindly nurse.

"And now, ma'am," said Martha, placing herself right opposite her mistress, with her arms folded firmly across her chest, "what do you intend to do next? There is no workhouse or foundling hospital in this out-of-the-way place."

"Do, Martha!—why keep the poor dear with me, to be sure," was Miss Jenny's quiet and ready reply. "I have enough to live on, thanks to a merciful Providence; few relations, and none of them very near or dependent upon me, as you know, Martha. Therefore I will keep this infant, to be the comfort and may-be the prop of my old age; and God enable me to do my duty by it!"

The old servant knew her mistress well, and saw that no opposition would be of any avail. "Just like you, ma'am, never thinking of consequences," she remarked, gruffly. "But—but—what will—the—neighbours say?"

"What can they say, Martha? You are at liberty to tell them all the facts of the case. I know they have a little gossip, and like to think evil rather than good; but I defy the most inventive of them all to make anything out of this against either you or me."

Miss Jenny, in her singleness of heart, was very confident; but quite mistaken, as we shall see hereafter.

* * * * *

On the same morning, while the foregoing scene was taking place in Miss Jenny's secluded cottage on the hill-side, there entered into the little church of the village, half a mile off, a tall slight woman, attired in a black bonnet and veil and a large cloak, who could scarcely sustain herself on her trembling limbs. Divine service had already commenced, and several people raised their heads from their prayer-books to watch her feeble gait, as she walked slowly up the side-aisle. Being shown into a pew, the stranger apparently remained in deep devotion during the remainder of the service. There were not wanting those that thought they remarked sobs, and almost heard the convulsive shake her slender frame at many parts of the prayers; and when she raised her face after the final blessing, the front of the pew where she had leaned was wet with tears. She took a cheap lodging in the village for the night, and left early the next morning, having contrived to baffle the numerous attempts of her prying hostess to learn something of her history. One who remarked her setting forth said her departure indicated that she went up toward the hills, in the direction of Miss Cow's cottage; but it is certain that she visited no person in that neighbourhood. Nothing more was heard or seen of her, and she gradually faded away from the remembrance of the villagers.

It was no long time before a singular or unprecedented circumstance, but it evidenced the power of prejudice in that small narrow-minded [illegible] country place, that all Miss Jenny Cow's friends and acquaintances of the genteeler sort began to look shy upon her, so soon as it was ascertained that she had really taken in and adopted a foundling child that had been mysteriously left at her door. They shook their heads, and remarked one another of the frequent absences of the little spinster, on pretence of visiting her friends in Wales, where she occasionally spent months at a time. One of these visits she had only recently returned from, and they had fancied her looking slightly thin and anxious. All agreed that it was quite impossible that Miss Jenny would burden herself with the care of a young infant from motives of pure benevolence alone. We have said "all"; but there was one exception—a timid widow, who possessed rather more of the charity that "thinketh no evil." She faintly said that "she didn't know, but she was not quite sure that she would not have done the same, had a poor innocent baby been left at her door in such inclement weather." But this charitable person was soon talked down; and, although she continued to visit Miss Jenny for a time, she at length yielded to the general opinion; which was that Miss Jenny, if she had possessed a due regard for propriety, would have consulted with the vicar of the parish as to the disposal of the child; but that, having declined to do so, she was not exactly a proper person to be intimate with.

So poor Miss Jenny, greatly to her astonishment, and somewhat to her sorrow, found herself gradually left alone save with regard to her humble friends among the peasantry. These still welcomed her step at their doors; and thought her bright eyes and buxom figure one of the pleasantest sights they could see, these cold winter days. But Mrs. Warrington of Elm Villa, Miss Penelope Cleaby of Ivy Cottage, and their circle of small gentility, passed Miss Jenny in the village street with averted heads, or bowed coldly from a distance, or with a prim recollection of the manners of their superiors in rank and fortune, contrived to be "not at home" whenever the innocent offender, scarcely yet believing in her banishment to the northern Coventry, presumed to call upon them as formerly.

"I told you so, ma'am," Martha quietly observed, when her mistress complained to her of the altered manner of those whom she had once deemed her attached friends. "I always said it would be so, ma'am, if you remember."

"You did, Martha, and I did not believe it; for I could not have conceived that the good people about here could be so uncharitable. However, as it is so, I must bear it patiently, and endeavour to hold myself above caring for my neighbours' prejudices; for I certainly do not intend to abandon this unfortunate babe to the mercies of the world. My innocence will be declared in His own good time, in the sight of all."

"You are right, ma'am, as you always are," was the crabbed but startling Martha's unexpected reply. The old servant wiped a tear from her eye, and gazed with a smile of maternal tenderness upon the infant lying in her lap, and cooing as it played with her bony fingers.

Now the truth was that this sweet little neglected bud of humanity, wafted as it were to their threshold by the wintry breeze of deepest poverty or maternal indifference, had grown to the hearts of both mistress and maid, until they would sooner have parted with any other treasured thing that was theirs than have consigned their protégé to the tender mercies of the parish conclave.

Chap. II.

A golden atmosphere broods over a picturesque Eastern city, and glances with reflected beams through the windows of a large building in a narrow irregular Eastern street—a refuge for maimed and suffering gallantry, for brave enduring hearts fainting in mortal sickness, more fell than sword or musket, more devastating than bursting shell or ploughing cannon-ball. Through the loopholes and portals of this extensive building issue sounds and scents of agony and sore disease. Ever and anon, from beneath those low and gloomy portals come forth the silent dead, borne away in sorrowful though scanty procession to their solitary graves in alien soil, far from the fond hearts that beyond the tideless Mediterranean languish for tidings from the loved and lost.

Within the lugubrious building of which we speak, on narrow pallet-beds ranged in a double row down long rooms, recline a number of suffering beings, laid low by wounds, by fever, or by the lingering dysentery of neglect, exposure, or semi-starvation. It is the quiet hour of the afternoon. A few sleep; to some the nurses (Englishwomen, in many cases, of birth and breeding, and nurtured amid far other scenes) are gently ministering; others lie feebly gazing around, upon their companions in misfortune, or occasionally reading a few verses from the Sacred Record, or a page of a tract or book that the good ladies have given them. They are uncomplaining sufferers, yet many of their sufferings might have been avoided, and that the British public know by this time; and the British Lion is rousing up its great generous heart for the benefit and efficient assistance of these brave and faithful heroes.

At the extreme end of the second ward a sick soldier has been talking to another, who lies on the next pallet, of his wife, his affectionate wife, to whom he had only been united one short year before he was summoned with his regiment to the Crimea, to fight the war of justice in the East. He is a noble-looking fellow, though frightfully reduced by his wasting disease; and his dark hollow eyes beam with tenderness as he talks of his "Maggie."

"But I am very miserable about her just now," he says, stifling a sob. "I just heard that she and her babe were doing well, and that as soon as she could get about, she thought of going into service, and saving the money she was receiving on my account. Since then I have not had a single line from her, although I have written regularly. Poor thing! poor thing! —I cannot sleep for thinking of her. Her folks are all dead, and she frets night and day after me—I know she does; and there are times when I am sure she is dead, and the babe and all."

And here the poor *fellow* can hold out no longer, but fairly bursts into a shower of weak tears.

His comrade endeavours to comfort him.

"No news is good news, King; you know that. If your wife had been ill or dead, surely some kind body would have written to break to you the evil tidings."

King shakes his head despairingly, but endeavours to cease his crying, and dries his poor wet eyes on the sleeve of his shirt. At this moment one of the lady-nurses, who has just entered the ward, advances towards him with a pitying countenance; yet with a gleam of pleasure in it, as if she had something gratifying to impart. She is a woman past thirty, of noble presence, with a frank visage framed in thick curls of golden-brown hair, and a smile that appears to infuse new life into her patients. Sitting down by King's bedside, she gently inquires into the progress of his recovery, and then cautiously informs him that a friend from England is waiting to see him.

King opens wide his eyes in great astonishment, wondering who it can possibly be; for, as he says, none of his acquaintances at home could scrape together money for such a journey.

"Your friend has, however, come hither through all obstacles, to see and nurse you well again," replies the lady; smiling so significantly that poor King is quite puzzled. At length a thought darts through his mind; but no! it is too blissful to be true; and if his Maggie have arrived, oh! what hardships she must have passed through on her way thither! His head reels at the idea, and he turns so pale that the lady holds a bottle of smelling-salts to his nostrils.

"You are right, my poor fellow," she whispers in answer to his supposition. "A faithful wife will brave everything for a beloved husband. Your Margaret is here; and waits in my room until you can see her."

"God bless you, ma'am!" exclaims the warm-hearted soldier, venturing to wring the lady's small white hand, which is not withdrawn from his rough but manly grasp. "God bless you for ever, for all your kindness! It will do me more good than medicine to see her!"

The lady left his side, and proceeded quietly through the ward. The sick man strained his feeble gaze to look after her; for through that door by which she went out, she would soon return, accompanied by his Maggie. In a few moments she reappeared; and behind her, with [illegible] yet unstained story, came Margaret [illegible]. As they walked up the ward between the long double row of beds, the various inmates raised their heads to look with curiosity and interest on the new arrivals, for a whisper had already circulated among them as to who and what she was. The wife saw nothing, cared for no curious glances; all timidity was dead within her, all native bashfulness subdued; she was searching for her poor sick husband. Arrived at length at the upper end of the long ward, her tearful regards fell upon him. The lady-nurse moved aside; the sick soldier stretched out his arms, speechless with joy. His wife fell into them, weeping and sobbing aloud, while there was not a dry eye through all the ward.

* *

"But the baby, Maggie? You have never mentioned him—and I scarcely dared ask——"

Maggie looked down, and became very pale, while tears suffused her gentle blue eyes.

"You thought he was dead, did you, John?—and no wonder. But he is living; he is safe and well—or rather was, the last time I saw him; and he is with those who will take good care of him. Do not ask me any questions now; I will tell you all hereafter. Oh! John, what have I not suffered to come to you!"

And the sorrowing mother burst into tears, which almost appeared, even to John's not over quick perception, to have a touch of remorse about them.

"Her heart grieves her for leaving the child to come to me," he thought to himself.

"Come, come, Maggie," he said, aloud; "don't trouble yourself about anything. I am sure you have done nothing but what is right and good. And only think, Maggie, if you had not come, and I had never recovered!"

"That is the only thing that comforts me, John," she said, more cheerfully; "the thought that you will soon recover with my nursing; for no one could take care of you like your own wife. But now we must cease talking, for it is time for you to take your sleeping-draught."

And she rose from her seat, and reached down a small phial from the little shelf above the head of the bed.

"One question more, Maggie, and then I will be quiet. How is it that you are allowed to remain with me? It is quite against the rules."

"Why, John, don't you know that I have been admitted as nurse to this ward, and that I have therefore a right to stay with you and nurse you until you are well?"

"Thank God for that!"

And John took her hand between both of his, and held it in that position until he gradually sank into a tranquil slumber.

We now return from the city in the East, with its minarets and its tombs, its picturesque beauties, and its real squalor, and privation, and suffering of every kind, to the humble British cottage on the bleak hillside, where Christian benevolence watched over and cherished sweet innocent babyhood.

Christmas passed away, with its drifting snows and social amusements, and another year was born into the world—the year 1855. Then came a bitter period of frost and gloom; and then the breath of Spring loosened the fetters of all inanimate things. Leaves began to bud, and mountain-springs to gurgle merrily from their fastnesses, and small flowers peeped out through the crumbled sward, and told their still unconscious neighbours that old Winter had departed. The little birds trilled their morning hymn at dawn from every bush and tree; and then came the cuckoo, with his dusky wing and hurried flight, waking the dells and ravines to reverberate with his bell-like monotone. In the sunny nooks among the hills the hoary orchards knew his voice, and blossomed until they were clouded as it were with summer snow, filling the air with delicate fragrance. The golden-flowering gorse shone in luxuriant beauty, lending the mountain gorges with orange-like colour; and the pale primrose and modest violet exhibited their delicious sight on every bank and mossy knoll. And all this time the east wind never ceased its mutterings, breaking out occasionally into an infernal discord that rent the very elements.

But of this last feature of the [illegible] year, Miss Jenny Cow and her faithful maid heeded little or nothing, so absorbed and concentrated were their womanly hopes and cares on the plump, chubby, smiling infant, that grew every day more plump, smiling, and intelligent. Great were their mutual congratulations when at length the rosy brown plaything could creep all over Miss Jenny's neat parlour; unutterable joy on the memorable day when he tottered with uncertain steps from the protecting arms of the spinster to those of her maid. After that the [illegible] and delight of him knew no bounds. Martha would [illegible] to the market-town [illegible], and return home laden with toys and [illegible]; and Miss Jenny would attend a shopping-excursion to the same place, principally with the view of purchasing new caps, or coats, or other pieces of finery, for her darling Johnny; for she had named the little one after a favourite deceased brother. And so the time slipped away. England, in its exultant excitement, experienced a brief delirium on hearing the tidings of the fall of Sebastopol. Little did Miss Jenny guess how this important national event would affect her small household in the person of her adopted child.

"There, Martha, the water is all right." And Miss Jenny withdrew the thermometer from the tub of warm water in which Master Johnny was to undergo his evening's ablution. "Now, pop him in. How plump and rosy the darling looks to-night! Did you ever see a child of his age grow such a beauty? It would do his poor mother's heart good to see him, if indeed she be yet alive."

"Oh! ma'am," snapped Martha, "I cannot bear to hear you mention her, the unnatural creature! I do hope she will never come back for the little angel, that I do."

"So do I, Martha; for I do not know how I could make up my mind to part with my little cherub now. And yet if she does come and claim him, we must give him up to her, you know."

"Oh dear! ma'am," said Martha, "I wish to goodness you had not happened to speak of it. It is always dangerous. I feel now as if we might expect her [illegible]. Hush then, my honey! don't cry so, there's a man! Nice warm water! We will soon have done, my chicky! and then he shall have some warm milk, and go to his pretty cot. There! there's a darling!" &c., &c.

So Martha went on, prattling to the child, who vigorously resisted the treatment to which he was subjected, kicking and screaming lustily. It was a pretty picture. A brilliant wood-fire burned in the ample grate, the small logs of fir and pine sending out jets of light that were reflected from the shining tins and polished brasses that adorned the high mantel-piece and white-washed walls of the little kitchen. Near the hearth sat Martha, on a low rocking-chair; scrupulously neat and clean in person and attire, her small sharp features were softened and rendered absolutely agreeable by the beaming kindness visible in every lineament, as she held the infant Hercules in the bath, laved the pure water over his dimpled limbs, and scrubbed his golden hair till it waved in close curls all over his handsome and well-poised head, revealing in their pure beauty his broad white brow, rosy cheeks, and red curved mouth, not materially disfigured even by the lusty bawl in which he was indulging. Opposite to this group stood Miss Jenny, in a tidy black silk gown and Quakerish cap, trimmed with pale pink ribbons, that harmonized admirably with her smooth clear complexion and bright dark eyes.

"What a deafening uproar the little urchin makes when he is washed!" she exclaimed. "Can you not reduce him to order, Martha? But hark! what is that?"

The noise alluded to was a loud knocking at the front-door, that was plainly distinguishable above the cries of the child, who immediately paused to listen to the somewhat unusual sound.

"Stay, Martha," said Miss Jenny to the old servant, who was preparing to answer the importunate summons. "Take the boy upon your knee, and rub him dry in your best style, while I go to the door. Who can it be, I wonder, at this hour of the evening?"

So saying, the cheery spinster hurried off, while the infant renewed his cries beneath the friction which his nurse inflicted upon him. The outer-door thrown open, there stood beneath the little porch, dimly distinguishable in the autumnal twilight, the figures of a tall, slender woman, and a man in regimentals, the latter of whom leaned heavily upon a stick. Miss Jenny had scarcely noted this much, when the woman uttered a piercing shriek, and pushing aside our spinster with very little ceremony, begging her pardon at the same time in an agitated voice, rushed along the little passage and into the kitchen, directed thither as it appeared by the vociferous cries of the child.

Completely petrified by this very unusual proceeding, Miss Jenny remained in the doorway confronting the soldier, whom she regarded with somewhat of that awe that is inspired by a red coat in the bosoms of the timid inhabitants of a secluded parish, like that of Sedgecombe. In Miss Jenny's case, this was mingled with the misgivings naturally felt in the presence of a sturdy beggar, who knocks [illegible] at your door unexpected and appears inclined to make good his footing upon your threshold the next. Had it been possible for a policeman to be within hearing, she would undoubtedly have summoned a [illegible]; but such aid being quite out of the question, she contented herself with blocking all ingress as far as possible, without absolutely shutting the door in the face of her visitor, until she could ascertain the meaning of the woman's strange rudeness.

The soldier, for such he really was, perceived the trepidation of the little lady; and respectfully bowing, was apparently about to speak and apologise or reassure her, when his wife came sobbing and laughing in a breath along the passage, holding the child close to her bosom, with her shawl folded round his rosy limbs.

"Oh! John, here he is; he is such a beauty!" were her first broken exclamations. Then kneeling at Miss Jenny's feet, who had turned wonderingly towards her, she seized her hands, and covered them with kisses. "Thank you, thank you, ma'am, for all your kindness to my precious babe! Oh! how shall I ever repay you?"

"So it was you," said Martha, who had followed closely from the kitchen, in some alarm at having the baby so unceremoniously snatched from her. "It was you who deserted the darling, and then left him in a box at the door to perish with the cold and hunger. Out upon you!"

"Come," said Miss Jenny, recovering her composure, for she now perceived how the matter stood—"come, Martha, reserve your indignant comments, and let us all go into the parlour, and explain ourselves to one another. I suppose, my friend, that is your husband, and that you are the mother of my precious little Johnny?"

"There! husband, there! did you hear that? his very name!" exclaimed the woman, who appeared quite unable to calm herself down to any degree of quietness. "No, I cannot bear to part with him yet," she continued wildly to Martha, who wished to take him from her for the purpose of putting on his night clothes. "You do not seem to know the feelings of a mother. Let me just go and sit in your chair, and rub his little feet before the fire, and I will be as quiet as a lamb, I promise you; oh! I do indeed."

"Allow her to do as she will, Martha," said

Miss Jenny. "The poor thing hungers for her baby's caresses."

Martha appeared disposed to resent this intrusion upon her privileges, but she yielded to her mistress' determined manner; and changing their destination from parlour to kitchen, the party gathered round the bright wood fire, where the baby-boy soon fell fast asleep in his delighted mother's arms.

"He might really have remembered me," she said. "He has never been shy nor strange for one moment, the precious lamb!"

"I did not until this minute," remarked Miss Jenny, quietly. "I know you now—Margaret King. You were my neighbour at Abergavenny."

• • • • • •

severely wounded at the attack upon the Redan, invalided, pensioned, and intending to reside in the parish.

"Then poor Miss Jenny will not lose sight of this baby that she is so mightily taken up with. You are sure it is true, Ann?"

"Oh yes! Aunt, they went all through the village yesterday, inquiring for a suitable cottage, the mother carrying her infant, and Miss Jenny herself along with them. She looked as pleased as could be. And, as for the man, he is as respectable a non-commissioned officer as I ever saw in my father's regiment. Poor fellow! he looks very weak and ill."

"But Mrs. Warrington of Rose Villa, Miss Penelope Glisby of Ivy Cottage, and the rest of them, will they not think it very odd and unladylike of Miss Jenny to be so intimate with a sergeant of infantry and his wife, making quite friends of them, as it were? It will be as bad an affair in their eyes as the foundling business, Ann, you may depend upon it."

"Dear Aunt! let them be as still. I always liked Miss Jenny so dearly; and now that she is proved innocent, you know, I am sure that we can sufficiently find fault with us for doing so."

The third sister, whom we formerly alluded to as the only individual of Miss Gray's genteel acquaintance that did not suspect or condemn her for her conduct with respect to poor Maggie's baby, granted her niece's repeatedly urged request; and although their call was made with some embarrassment after so long a desertion, the forgiving Miss Jenny overlooked the widow's past coldness, and they are likely to become the best friends in the world.

John King and his family have settled themselves in the cottage with a green porch at the end of the village. Johnny is daily taken to visit his kind benefactress, who scarcely suffers him out of her sight, and has declared her intention to educate him and set him out in the world. There is little doubt that the boy stands already occupies an important position in the good spinster's will.

Most of the respectable persons in the parish, following the example of the Irish widow and her niece, have renewed their visiting acquaintance with Miss Jenny Gray. But Mrs. Warrington of Rose Villa, Miss Penelope Glisby of Ivy Cottage, and one or two more of the genteel coterie, still hold aloof. They appear resolved never to forgive their benevolent neighbour for daring, on her own responsibility and without consulting them as to the propriety of the case, to succour and shelter the friendless infant recovered of her existence and unexpected "Christmas Box."

THE HALL-SPECTRE.

(A Legend of Holgebury.)

BY THE AUTHOR OF THE "PHOTOGRAPHER'S STORY," "VILLAGE PLAYERS," &c.

"When two strong winds by hard compulsion blow,
Strake answers stroke, and woe is piled on woe!"

Delphic Oracle.

Chap. I.

The Blacksmith's Shop.

Years and years ago Timothy Redman was the blacksmith of Holgebury. His shop stood on the Harborough road, just on the outskirt of that part of the little town which went by the name of Hall End, and not so far from the Park Pool but that at night, when he happened to be at work, the light from his forge, streaming through the open door, struck upon that sheet of water, which reflected it upwards, in a faint, hazy glimmer, to the dark sky. From a distance this halo could be seen, even where the blacksmith's shop itself was hidden by the hill on which stands Holgebury Church; and men, returning from their work on a winter's night, seeing this flush which throbbed visibly with every breath of the distant bellows, would say to each other, "Tim's at work; let's go and have a bit o' chat with him."

The blacksmith's shop is always a place of rendezvous for a village population. It is the "Change of the rustics; it is the club where they go to learn their news. It is, in some sort, a rival establishment to the village inn; and men have been known to stop half-way at the blacksmith's shop, and, lingering there a session, at last to forego "the pint," for the consumption of which they had expressly left their homes.

Hedgebury, a century and more ago, was scarcely more than a village. The coal-fields in that neighbourhood were as yet but little worked, and the population was, a large part of it, agricultural. Tim Robson's shop never lacked its loungers. In the daytime there were idle fellows; there were also carters who brought a horse to be shod, or a plough to be mended, or a waggon whose wheel-tire wanted repairing; housewives brought up household kettles, to be set right; children played about the door. But, as the evening came on, the regular frequenters of the place dropped in, one by one. Men, who had been working themselves stiffly, seemed to find a soothing influence in seeing the blacksmith at work while they stood idle. On a winter's evening, especially, the shop had its attractions. The warmth and the light, and the roaring of the bellows and the clink of the hammers, produced a charming soothing to the instincts of the slow-thoughted men who were grouped there.

On one especial winter evening the blacksmith's shop was open. At the moment of the rising of our curtain Tim Robson was at the fire, blowing the bellows with one hand, while with the other he held the end of a bar of iron in the hot blaze. At an anvil on the other side of the fire stood Tim's man, beating out continually showers of sparks with the regularity of clock-work.

Tim himself was a small, thin man, with a red face and bright roguish eyes. He had a husky voice, which was very often swallowed up in a choking cough. Tim was never quite sober, and never quite drunk. He was constantly drinking; and I suppose for the very reason that he never allowed the intermission of his potations, he never suffered from the usual depressing effects of drink. Tim was always in high spirits. He laughed in spite of his cough, in spite of "the badness of his inside." Poor Tim confessed to suffering from that complaint which renders him, described by saying, "I be very bad in my inside," and which would now be recognised at once as a far advanced stage of consumption.

Tim's assistant, called Enoch, was an old man, a giant in proportions, but having as little flesh about him as a live man could possibly have. His tough, swollen muscles, and large bones, seemed bound together by nothing but an integument of brown wrinkled skin. He stooped very much, and his scant hair and whiskers were grizzled so that they were almost of the same colour as his brown-begrimed face, and faded into them with no perceptible line of separation. Enoch seldom spoke. His silence was a joke against him among the habitués of the shop—not that Enoch's companionship was by any means a common talent with [illegible]. But Enoch had a look about him which expressed wilful reticence. No one imagined "Lumpy Ned" to mean that ever-gaping mouth of his for purposes of speculation. When he spoke it was as much a miracle as if an ox had spoken. One would have as soon looked for "speculation" under the eyelids of a corpse, as in his fixed, light-blue, unblinking eyeballs. But Enoch's thin, firm mouth was always obstinately shut, and his keen eyes shot out sudden, quick glances from beneath his shaggy eyebrows, in a manner incomprehensible to the sluggish people about him. When he did speak, it was always something exactly to the purpose. Some village problem, which had been helplessly turned about and about for an hour's space by the rustic wiseacres, and left in its original state, Enoch would solve by a monosyllable. Thus it came to pass that, while Lumpy Ned and all his kind did not strike the public opinion as by any means inarticulate animals, Enoch was thought a very good joke because of his silence.

Besides these high-priests of Vulcan, there were at least a dozen men congregated about the door of the shop. Some were smoking, some whistling in an under-tone. Conversation flagged in a way that would have been terrible in better society. No doubt the exchanging of ideas is a pleasant and useful process; but when one has no ideas at the moment to exchange, it is doubtful whether Lumpy Ned's plan of not saying anything, is not as good, or better, than his neighbour's plan of saying nothing. These people do not feel the necessity of talking. Conversation is not a habit with them—scarcely more a habit than it is with oxen; and they feel no shame in keeping silence.

The fire seemed to have very much more life in it than the group upon whose figures it played. Heraclitus, was it not, who taught that fire was the first principle? There seemed some vital essence in the glow of this forge-fire, which endued with life, for the moment, even the rough walls and the heaps of rusty iron which it lit up. It transformed every stone and blackened beam, giving each a different expression to that which it wore in the steady gray daylight. It was not only the contrast of colour and the intenser shadows that wrought the change; but, in addition, there was the motion which was apparently imparted by the throbbing fire to everything on which it shone. The rough walls heaved as if with breath; the roof expanded upwards, and then contracted downwards, as if it were closing in upon the forge; here and there a glittering point gleamed like a winking eye; and along the ground the shadows lengthened or shortened with a perpetual motion as the flames rose or fell. Out through the door into the darkness the warm light streamed, flashing in the air like summer-lightning, and glancing with a more brilliant and less fleeting brightness on the waters of the Park Pool below.

On the faces of the quiescent group about the door the fire wrought queer changes. The passive, dull-intelligence of the stolid features seemed overpowered by the active, nimble in-

thickness of the glass. A flashing light will make up a marble statue into fitful life, making a wing-sandalled Mercury rise on tiptoe to his flight, or a Venus Victrix look into breathing beauty. But upon the figures of our rustics the fire had something of an opposite effect. The lines of their faces grew sterner and more rigid, the slope of their shoulders and the ungainly fall of their arms took a less human outline. They might have been men half-petrified. They might have been rudely-fashioned figures of the Promethean clay, waiting for the advent of the completing life-principle. The flickering light played about them as if it longed to penetrate within.

There was a long silence, save for the clink of the hammer and the blowing of the bellows, as we have said. Nevertheless a subject had just been talked about, which, one would think, might have awakened some interest even in the minds of the Hedgebury labourers.

"That be'st a queer sort," little Tim Barkman said, after the pause. "I suppose the sensation was what won't, to make up for being blind mostly to the things that lie close under their nose; I tell'ee I was abed last night by nine o'clock; and, more nor that, the fire here was out, and cold by seven."

"I seed it, all the same, Tim," quoth the man addressed.

"Seed what?" Tim rejoined, sharply. "Can't thee tell a plain straightforward tale, without keepin' on over and over again—'I seed it'?"

The man, Jim Sparrow by name, took his pipe out of his mouth, wiped the back of his hand across his lips, shook himself, and remained silent. He would have gone through precisely the same operations if he had been about to sing a song. I suppose it is some kind of mental screwing-up which is betokened by the above signs.

At last, when one would have concluded that he had given up the intention of speaking, he broke out suddenly, "I seed it with my own eyes! I says to Ned, 'There's Tim's forge alight at this time o' night.' We was on Hedgebury Hill, just afore you comes to the church. There was the light i' the sky, and I seed it with my own eyes, and Ned seed it too. It was exactly twelve o'clock. The clock struck as we got to the top o' the hill. I'd been over to Birkholm to our Tom's marryin', and Ned had been too, being as he keeps company with Letty's sister, and so was asked to the feast accordingly. And Ned and I was coming up Hedgebury Hill, and we both seed the light o' the forge in the sky—twelve o'clock it was by Hedgebury Church—I seed it, and Ned seed it!"

Jim finished his pipe. He had looked at Lanky Ned on ending his speech, as if with the wish of eliciting from that young gentleman a confirmation of the story; but Lanky Ned remained with his mouth open, and said nothing.

After this pause and preparation, a very bright member of the community said, "I've heard talk o' lights in the sky, of stars tumbling up there, and such-like, and I mind myself the big star, with the tail to 'un, thirteen year ago come Christmas. Squire Stokes said as it would set us alight; but it didn't, though the women was mortal afeard, and took to prayin'."

Tim, who had been in the meanwhile hammering the piece of iron he had before heated, again took up the conversation.

"Now, Master Sparrow," he said, "I'll tell thee just what I think about it. Thou hadst taken a sup too much o' the Birkholm ale. People sees double then, or sees ghosts, or sees lights, or sees anything that isn't there to see. They talk about a ghost up at th' 'All—all the servant-wenches are leavin' for it. Myself, I put the ghost down to the strength o' the Squire's beer! They say the ghost trips 'em up upon the stairs! I know it's easy enough to trip up sometimes upon the stairs, without a ghost!"

"Thee knows that right well, Tim, I don't doubt," said the bright member of the community; "but as to the ghost, they say the Squire has seen it himself. They say it's the ghost of his old uncle. He was a wicked 'un, was the old Squire. They say he hated Master Thorne mortally. If he could spite the Squire by it, he'd be mad enough to rise and haunt 'im!"

"But he left us the property," said another.

"Not he," said the blacksmith. "There wasn't a will, and so Squire Thorne came into it. Why, they're carryin' on about it in London to this day. The old Squire's madam was mighty free when he died, and she claimed everything, and said he had willed it all to her. But no will was to be found. She wouldn't turn out till they made her, and then she kicked up a mighty rumpus about it. She swore there was a will, and the parson upheld her, and so did a cousin of hers—she called him a cousin, and he used pretty near to live at th' 'All; but it's my belief she two tricked the old man. Well, the parson and the cousin swore that they had put their names to the will, and seen the old man sign it, and that everything had been left to madam. And she kept it up, and I believe it's a-carryin' on in London to this day."

"He was a bad 'un, the old Squire," put in somebody.

"He was a bad 'un," said the blacksmith. "He wasn't a gentleman. He loved low-life, and demeaned himself to hob and nob with the common people. Gentlefolks may run a bit wild, and not much harm done, if they keep company with gentlefolks. We can respect a gentleman who keeps his place all the same, though his life mayn't be quite respectable. But the old Squire got to be hated, and laughed at too. You know who his madam was? She was the wife of Ford the tailor—him who kept Page's shop before Page. The Squire used to go and drink and play cards with Ford, and the end of it was that he took Ford's wife home to th' 'All, and Ford should 'a left this part of the country. Then, at one time, there was my old master Jacob Jarrett—he was hail-fellow well-met with the Squire. Jacob had the finest game cocks in the county, and he used to be up at th' All with the Squire, cock-fighting everyday from week's-end to week's-end. I had a hard time of it with him. I never heard such a man to swear, and didn't he wallop me! I never had a penny by my wage that didn't go. And then, I said old Jacob did all the work—didn't he, though! He was always with the old Squire at one time. To think of a born gentleman taking up with a blacksmith!"

"But they fell out, didn't they, Tim?" said an old man, who could well remember the time of which the blacksmith spoke.

"I should think they did fall out," said Tim.

These reminiscences brought a glow of pleasure to the blacksmith's eyes. His present auditors had heard it many times, and they liked it all the better for knowing it by heart. It had gained a gravity and importance from being told again and again, and was listened to with attention, just as the Grecian times the well-worn story of the war of Troy, with all its time-honoured heroes, was eagerly listened to, when newer fables would excite no interest. To grasp anything unexpected and unfamiliar is an absolute pain to slow imaginations; but they are capable of experiencing a pleasure when the impressions stamped upon them by repetition after repetition is again touched upon in all its familiar details. The audience knew their cues, and were expert in prompting the blacksmith by ensuring questions or professions of ignorance in the right places.

"I should think they did fall out," said Tim; "that was about cock-fighting. Jacob had a cock which none o' the Squire's, nor none of anybody else's, could match. Well, there was some foul play o' the Squire's with the cock. I don't quite know how it was, but I know that it got beaten and cut into ribbons. There was some foul play about it, and Jacob got cheated out of a sight o' money, which well-nigh ruined him. I remember, just as if it were yesterday, Jacob coming into the shop, here, with the poor bird in his arms. He was all over blood from it. My word! how he did curse and swear! He swore he would take vengeance on the old Squire. I remember his laying the bird down on the bench there, and crying over it; for he was a bit drunk. And the bird died there, and there was the marks of blood upon the bench for many a day. And Jacob took the skin off the bird, and stuffed it with straw; but it looked like a poor scare-crow. After that Jacob never went up to th' All any more. He stuck to his business a deal better, and was kinder to his wife, and didn't lay into me quite so often. But he hated the Squire bitterly. Whenever he looked at the stuffed bird, he would break out cursing and swearing; and if ever he met the Squire, he would spit upon the ground. Not long before the Squire died, however, he sent for Jacob. I don't know what happened, but Jacob came back looking uncommonly pleased. And when the Squire was buried, Jacob put on his black clothes and followed him to the grave with the rest. For though he had been a bad un, yet he was a born gentleman, and it was his bounden duty to see the last o' him."

Tim's reminiscences had led the conversation away from the subject which originated the utterance of them. This subject, however, was again suddenly brought up. A man entered, dressed in a long black drab coat, with his chin muffled in a red woollen comforter. The long-handled crook in his hand proclaimed him to be a shepherd.

"What was up again with ye last night then, Master Redman?" asked the shepherd. "Are ye goin' to turn night into day? Were you making horse-shoes for witches' nags that night?"

"What do you mean?" asked Tim.

"Why was your fire burning at twelve o'clock last night? I saw the sparks flying out of your chimney at such a pace that it reminded me to look at 'em."

"I saw it with my own eyes," cried Jim Sparrow, rejoiced to have his story corroborated.

Tommy Redman dropped his lower jaw, so as to make his mouth a little rounder than usual.

"I was abed at nine," the blacksmith said, doggedly. "Don't you come trying to gammon me. It's of no use, I can tell you."

"Hoity-toity, man," cried the shepherd; "if you want to keep secrets, you mustn't light up your forge-fire to do 'em by. I tell you I saw the sparks flying like mad from your chimney at twelve o'clock last night. I was sitting up with my lambing yoes in the Coppice straw-yard. It did my heart good to see the light. It was bitter cold, and when a man isn't allowed to smoke a bit o' 'bacca, and can't afford a drop o' brandy, a blaze, even if it's a mile off, does his very heart good."

Just at this time the conversation in the blacksmith's shop was interrupted by a new comer. The sound of a horse's hoofs was heard, and a moment afterwards, in the ruddy light that streamed through the door, a tall, good-looking gentleman appeared, leading his horse by the bridle.

"Tim," said the gentleman, "my horse has cast a shoe. Mind you make haste, to do it the first thing in the morning."

By the scraping of the rustics' shoes, and pulling of their forelocks, as well as by Tim's bare and hasty advance, and even Hannah's cessation from work, it was clear that the gentleman was a man of local authority. It was no other than Squire Thorne.

"What's the matter, shepherd?" said the Squire; for the shepherd had still been speaking loudly when he came within earshot.

"Nothing, measter," said the shepherd, "only that the blacksmith have his taken to working at midnight. He means to get ahead of all in Hedgebury folk, and to make his fortune while we are snoring. He's a dark horse, Tim Redman is."

"What do you mean?" asked the Squire.

Then the shepherd explained more clearly.

Jim Sparrow said, "I seed it, and so did Ned."

A shadow came over the Squire's face.

"Very strange!" said he; and then, after a pause, he said "Mind you come early in the morning!" And, so, led his horse from the door, and disappeared in the darkness.

The men in the blacksmith's shop continued to talk about the midnight fire, the blacksmith himself still vehemently denying the possibility of anyone having seen the same, since no fire had been there. This at length grew bad-tempered, and began to wrangle. Then Enoch, lifting himself from his anvil for a moment, said:

"There was a fire. I saw it myself."

Chap. II.

The Hall Staircase.

"Very strange!" quoth the Squire to himself, as he led his horse along the frosty road. It was not far from the forge to his own stabling, and he had not ceased thinking about the midnight fire when he reached them. Stabling his horse there, he walked under the dark plantation towards the house. There was scarcely any light under the thick trees, though there was no misty moon in the sky, and the air had in it the keen, dry glitter of frost.

The Hall was as pleasant an old house as one would wish to see—picturesque without and comfortable within; more comfortable than our modern houses, with their lofty rooms and elaborate gildings and big window-panes; more picturesque, though it was a patched place that had come together at random during the course of a century or two, instead of being built by contract in a week. It looked well in the steady white light of the low crescent moon; many-gabled, parts coming forward sharp and distinct, parts dying away into black shadow. From a window that opened on to a low, balustraded terrace, a light came forth through red curtains. The motion and the colour of this little square of light contrasted pleasantly with the still, colourless infinity of the faint moonlight. There was just that charm of humanity and domesticity in it, which motion and colour and definite form give, as contrasted with the abstractions of higher things. The sociability, the colour of pure light, the habits of home—such imperfections are the very charm of human life.

Somewhat after this fashion our Squire moralised, I fancy, as he stood for a moment before he ascended the steps leading up to the balustered terrace. He was a man of much reading, and of a quiet, indolent life. Of course in those days such a man would be looked upon as a milksop. His late uncle, as next heir to whom he inherited the Hall, had hated him for those quiet habits. A man who did not make hunting the business of life, who thought bull-baiting and cock-fighting cruel, who did not swear and drink and bluster habitually, who took no interest in horse-racing or in the noble science of the prize-ring, was a sort of animal for which the country squires of those days had little predilection. Our Squire had been bred at the University of Cambridge, and possessing at that period but narrow means, had lived a quiet life there, and laid up much store of learning. When, by his uncle's death, he unexpectedly became comparatively rich, his first thought was, not to set up a pack of hounds or a stud of horses, but to take to himself a wife and to settle down comfortably in the house which had become his. The Hall was soon cleansed from the Augean filth which yet clung to it from its last possessor. The new Squire, a little eccentric, opened the old place, fired with the notion to be [illegible]. A little luxurious, he refurnished with all the care that an [illegible] lady and a dainty taste prompted. He carried down his books, and arranged them in the new place of the quiet library. Then he carried home his wife, and installed her as mistress of as pleasant a dwelling-place as could easily be found in those days. So at the Hall our Squire had lived a most happy life for some years. Children had risen round him. He had had few disquietudes; for the claim which the creditors of the late Squire had laid against the property had been so altogether feeble as to cause him little uneasiness. So he had lived a most happy life until within a short time of the period of our story.

There are no ghosts nowadays: even the spirits who manifest themselves by [illegible], the lifting of tables and what not, are all under rule of scientific laws, and may be fully believed in without laying the believer open to a charge of superstition. The time of the old unscientific ghosts has long gone by. If we are haunted now, it is by other ghosts than those terribly material ones of ancient days. We all have our skeletons, which come to our sleepless pillows at midnight, which dog our steps, which spoil our pleasures and [illegible] our lives and turn our hair grey, and wrinkle our faces. These skeletons clank chains in our ears, and make us echo back their groans; sometimes, too, they reveal to us hidden treasures, or discover to us most foul and wicked murders, or open out before our eyes the yellow parchments of irrevocable acts and deeds; but they are not the old ghosts. Alas! we have not the simple belief of our forefathers.

I fear lest my readers should misunderstand me. I fear lest, when I write the honest word ghost here, they should search diligently for some underlying—some hidden interpretation of the mythus. I fear lest they should ignore the matter-of-fact, and listen for the echo; waiting some more mysterious hark-out in the mystery of my ghost.

However, the truth must out. A great trouble had fallen upon my Squire recently; and the trouble was that the Hall—his home now endeared to him in a thousand ways—was haunted, haunted, if you please, in the simple old sense. Remember that I am writing of a time when no one doubted the existence of ghosts. We must project ourselves, if you please, to that time. If you can do as it is a case of objectivity—and objectivity is very clever. Seventy years ago this story of the Hall-spectre was thoroughly believed as having really happened, in the town of Hodgebury. I have it at first hand from the lips of an old lady, a native of Hodgebury, who heard the story when she was a child, and who half-believes it now.

Squire Thorne stood for a moment at the foot of the steps leading up to the terrace. I don't think he clenched his hand to his brow, or performed any unusual act of desperation; but a feeling of great wretchedness came over him. This house, so lately the one happy spot in the whole world, was becoming a place accursed. His wife and his children and his books, and the warm rooms and his beloved furniture—the [illegible] was taking them all of them by the [illegible] [illegible] in his daily cup.

"I cannot stay in this place," was his thought, as he paused before entering. "I am driven away from it as thoroughly as if that old harlot, my uncle's mistress, had got [illegible] and [illegible] about, and came with the [illegible] to turn me out."

Then he thought of all that he must leave behind. This place was full of sweet recollections. There was the little morning-room where he and his wife had sat together in the first days of their marriage—always together, keeping apart from the world in that sacred seclusion of first love; and there was the room where they had looked together at their first child in his cradle; and there was the room [illegible] where this first child had died, and lied him white and cold, with wintry snowdrops in his tiny hands—a room kept religiously the same as on that sad day, only the child lacking. Then there were other ties. For instance, what should he do with his books? What [illegible] can equal that of a new book-room—all the old books put into new places, and nothing to be found at the moment it is wanted?

In sheer desperation he mounted the steps. He entered through the window. As he appeared from behind the red curtain his wife gave a little start and shudder.

"Ah! frightened?" he said, stooping to kiss her. "We shall be afraid of our own shadows soon. What are we to do, Maggy dear?"

"I can't tell," she answered, clasping her hands hopelessly. "Mary has gone this evening, and Martha has had hysterics, and threatens to go to-morrow. The children, too, I am afraid, have learned something about it—the servants are so stupid and will not keep quiet. Little Edgar woke up crying, and would have it there was a man in the room. I was nursing. He is asleep again now."

"What are we to do, Maggy?" asked Squire Thorne.

"Perhaps the clergyman . . . ," said Mrs. Thorne. "I have heard of such—such things being laid in the Red Sea. Do you think it would do any good? We could but try."

"What!" said her husband, "the drunken, [illegible] parson! He took the part of that lying woman, and swore to her lies. He was a boon-companion of the—the—the ghost."

"Perhaps, my dear, he might have the more influence with him," said Mrs. Thorne simply.

The Squire flung himself into a chair by the fire, sighing heavily.

"I'll speak to it again to-night," quoth the Squire, quitting Horatio unconsciously, but leaving out the redundant conjunctions.

"Don't!" said his wife.

"It's very strange," continued the Squire, quitting Horatio, "but they were talking a story at the forge to-night, how the forge-fire was seen alight last midnight."

"You went to the forge then? **Did you see** anything?"

"No. But you remember what I told you last night?"

"Oh, yes. 'Go to the forge,' that was it."

Again the Squire sighed heavily. He turned from side to side in his chair, and at last took up a book which lay by him on the table. The book happened to be a Herodotus. The Squire was a scholar, as I told you before. He turned the leaves listlessly—not reading, but glancing down the pages. Suddenly a passage caught his eye.

"By Jove!" he said. "You remember our trying our fates by the Bible, my dear, before we married, don't you? *Sortes Biblicæ* they call it. There are the *Sortes Virgilianæ* too, but you don't understand Latin. Now listen to this—

'[illegible] Tegea [illegible].'

Oh, I beg your pardon: I'll translate." And thereupon the Squire translated.

It is enough, however, for the purpose of this story to give the purport of the passage. It is to be found in Book I, chapter 67, of Herodotus. It is the Delphic oracle given to a certain people who had necessity for finding the body of the dead [illegible]. The priestess prophesied that they should find this body

"Where two winds, winds **by hard compulsion** blow,
Stroke answers stroke, and woe is laid on woe."

Buried under a forge the bones were at length discovered. The two winds were interpreted to be the blast of the smith's two bellows, the stroke against stroke the mutual blows of hammer and anvil; the woe on woe was the destruction caused by the weapons forged by the smith.

"A remarkable instance of the *Sortes*," said Squire Thorne. "I will speak to this ghost again to-night, and if it answers as before I will go to the forge."

"Oh, don't!" said his wife.

"What is the time?" asked the Squire.

"Too soon yet," said Mrs. Thorne. "Take off your boots; let me help you."

The Squire, however, had made up his mind, and would not have his boots taken off.

* * * * *

At eleven o'clock the Squire went to meet the

spectre. I can imagine but cannot describe the agitation in which his wife was left. She asked to go with him, but it was an understood matter that the spectre's communications were in confidence to him alone.

The front staircase of the hall was ten or twelve feet broad; it was of old black oak, and the balusters were massively carved. At every half-dozen steps there was a little landing, and at every dozen steps the staircase turned short round, so that, as it wound up, its outline was a square. The old builders must have thought going up-stairs a very arduous performance, which probably it was, in the days of heavy drinking. The shallowness of the steps; the frequent resting-places; the stout balusters, which would bear any amount of pressure; the great width, which would afford plenty of room for a couple of helpful footmen—showed the forethought and consideration of the old architects. I have heard of a modern architect (great men they are, who let Cathedral spires come down with a crash, and are then complimented for their cleverness) who, drawing the plan of a mansion, quite forgot to put in stairs of any kind back or front, and upon being asked how the upper storeys were to be reached, replied that that was not his affair, but he should suggest a ladder at the windows.

I am digressing. You see I hang back from the ghostly encounter, and joke feebly, and pretend to feel more comfortable than usual. Well, the hall staircase was an easy one to mount by a sober person. No architect, whether ancient or modern, could have conceived an easier staircase. And yet our poor Squire found great difficulty in bracing up his nerves to the ascent. There were no Alpine Clubs at that time, or perhaps his nerves would have been in better condition for climbing.

At eleven o'clock the Squire went to meet the spectre. Closing the door upon his wife, he passed through a passage which led by another door into the great hall. He debated for an instant whether he would shut this door. He did shut it; and crossed the hall, treading nervously on only the black squares of its checkered floor. Turning the corner of a projecting wall, he came upon the foot of the staircase.

Now this staircase was the portion of the house haunted by the spectre. At the top of the second flight of twelve steps—that is, on the first floor landing—there it confronted with its ghostly presence the people who ascended the stairs.

Our Squire was a brave man, but he felt that he was just two dozen steps from an inhabitant of the other world. People have been known, certainly, to have had one foot in the grave without exhibiting the slightest concern—but the cases are a little different.

There was no lamp burning either above or below. The servants would not venture near the great staircase after dark, under any consideration. So there was no light save that which the Squire carried in a slightly tremulous hand.

He paused at the foot of the stairs, and listened. There was a very riot of sound in his over-attentive ears—it was simply ordinary silence, but at that moment it was like the roarings of the waves of a rough sea. He looked up into the darkness. A thousand prisms seemed to be scattering all their rays of many-coloured light up the broad staircase. It was simply ordinary darkness.

He was a brave man, but he muttered a prayer. Brave men have been known to pray in the moment of danger; while, I fear, other brave men have been known to swear. It depends much upon habit.

The Squire muttered a prayer, and dashed at the staircase. He was up the first six steps in two strides. Up the next six in two strides more. His light flickered—it was certainly gone—he held his breath—no; he just saved it. Then he gave himself a slight shake, and walked steadily up the remaining twelve stairs, gazing with steadfast eyes at the top.

Nothing was visible until he placed his foot on the last stair. Then, just like some figure which starts forth suddenly at the touching of a spring, the spectre was there, face to face, the eyes of the ghost glaring into his.

Now the appearance of the spectre was this: Picture to yourself the vices. You know what a cruel face is. You know what a lying face is. You know what a lewd face is. Imagine each vice inseparably blended with, or rather transformed into, torture. Here was an old wrinkled head, bald-crowned, grizzle-cheeked, in which every vice writhed in a distinct and separate pain. Fancy the word "adultery" stamped by red-hot letters upon hissing flesh; and then exchange the word for the idea and the flesh for the spirit, and you have precisely the notion which I can embodied in the spectre's face.

"Speak!" said the Squire, with a firm voice.

"To the forge!" quoth the ghost. "To the right hand—by the third beam, close under the thatch! Take the parchment, and burn it in the forge fire."

Chap. III.

The Blacksmith's Shop again.

Old Enoch had seen the fire in the forge at twelve o'clock on the previous night. He was a light sleeper—if he ever slept at all. As to his habits and customs people knew absolutely nothing. I think the Hedgebury folks were a little surprised whenever he did anything according to the ordinary fashion. To see him eat, for instance, was a sight which struck them as curious. He was one of those men (there are such in all communities) who are a little beyond their fellows. The people among whom they live generally find something ridiculous in such men. Prophets have no honour in their own country. The little boys follow them with jeers, and the adult wanderer look down upon them with pity and contempt.

The Bridgebury folks, I say, were utterly ignorant of the existence and existence of Enoch; but that is no reason why I, who tell this story, should not have an intimate knowledge of the man. Lavater tells us that, given one feature, and not only the whole face, but the whole character of a man may be made out. Chinese doctors judge of the complexion of their secluded patients by studying a large-sized little hand protruded through a hole. I myself cannot help forming an opinion of the characters of my friends from their hands. If chambermaid Maria could read a meaning in the "dry hand" of Sir Andrew Aguecheek, surely in these later times a scribe may pretend to a little advance in this science of palmistry (or whatever it is to be called). A palæontologist will decide from a single bone whether the extinct animal was carnivorous or graminivorous. Any grazier or butcher will tell you at once on what food—oil-cake or whatever one—the beef or mutton has been reared.

Given certain data, and the rest follows readily. I possess sufficient data to discover how Enoch acted on the night of which I write, although he never confided the secret to a single soul. Perhaps I have dug up a bone of his, and so inferred his diet—and here we enter upon another science. Sir Andrew Aguecheek was of opinion that "life consists of eating and drinking," and he illustrates this theory by an example, that a beef diet is inimical to the wit: porridge, too, is stated in "Every Man out of his Humour" to have a tendency to thicken the brain—but the theory may be seen worked at large in Mr. Buckle's book.

I am digressing again. I wrote that Enoch was a light sleeper; and I intend in this chapter to relate solely what Enoch saw and did. I have painted his portrait before; and having done that, I can, according to the physiognomists, deduce therefrom every important action of his life.

On the previous night, then, Enoch starting from his light sleep had seen with surprise a glare of light coming through the cracks of the shutter which served to keep out the cold wind from the place where he slept. His bed-chamber was in a small out-house adjoining the smithy. Enoch, seeing the light, turned out of his straw, and threw open the shutter, and perceived from thence that the light was streaming out of the open door of the blacksmith's shop. He slept in his day-clothes, so there was no necessity for putting himself into a dressing-gown and slippers. Snatching a bar which lay handy, he crept down the ladder in a moment, and stepped into the smithy just in time to see the bellows cease moving and the fire die away into reddening embers.

"Come out o' that!" said Enoch, but there was no answer. He expected some one to rush by him out of the darkness, but there was no sound or movement.

Enoch groped about for a candle, and found one, and struck a light. He searched every nook and cranny of the shop. No one was there; everything remained as it had been the evening before at locking up. He felt the ashes of the forge, and found them hot and still smouldering. Then he went to the door. He had put up the bar and locked the padlock himself on the previous evening. The padlock had been taken out, the bar removed, and the padlock replaced in the hasp. There it still hung, unlocked and open. He felt in his pocket for the key, and drew it forth and looked at it. Enoch shook his bewildered head and scratched it.

"I couldn't ha' done it myself?" he thought; "I couldn't ha' got up in my sleep, here, and done it, and turned in again? It's come back. They're always a-running their rigs on this."

At last, closing the door from the inside, Enoch sat down upon the bench where the gunsmith had died, blew out his candle, and dozed there till morning.

This is what had happened on the previous night.

Enoch said nothing, but ruminated on the strange occurrence all day. He did not like it at all. If such larks went on, the forge might be burnt down, which would have been the final destruction of Enoch's world. He determined to watch the next night. He had intended to keep silence about what he had seen, but when he found that others had seen the fire as well as himself, he altered his intention. To let them know that he who slept close to the spot had seen it, might prevent any further attempt.

So on the next night Enoch watched. He locked up the smithy as usual, and retired to his chamber. Then, at ten o'clock when all the village was asleep, he crept down the ladder, opened the shop-door, entered, put the bar inside, and closed the door from within. He groped his way through the shop, and ensconced himself behind the forge chimney, taking in his hand a crowbar which he had placed in readiness on that evening.

It was not an uncomfortable berth. The chimney wall was warm from the fire. Enoch cared nothing for crickets—their chirruping seemed good company to him. He sat listening to them, and to the crackling which came from time to time from the forge. Now the wind rushed down the chimney—now an owl alighted hooting on the thatch. Once a creak, occasioned perhaps by the scratching of some prowling fox—or, for aught I know, it might be the wandering spirit of Jacob's game-cock—[illegible] in the depths of the darkness. The time passed on. Enoch heard Bridgebury church-clock strike eleven.

Precisely at this moment the Squire was closing the parlour-door behind him, on his way to confront the ghost.

It might be a quarter past eleven—a minute or two more or less—when Enoch, in his hiding-place, heard the door of the shop swing suddenly open. At the same moment the bellows began to blow, and a blaze started up on the forge.

Enoch grasped his crowbar, and dashed out from his hiding-place. No one was in the shop but himself. The bellows were working as hard as they could work; the fire roared louder and louder, and blazed till the whole shop was full of light, and the frosty roof all the way down to the Fire Pool was distinctly to be traced.

Again Enoch scratched his head. He determined to see it out.

He stood looking at the working bellows, and their automatic movement struck him as being so comical, that the nearest approach to a laugh he had ever made in his life he made now. Waggishly he moved his arm up and down, in mimicry of the invisible arm which was working at the bellows, and then shook his head, and then scratched it vigorously.

"It's very pretty this," he thought; "but you'll be tired of it, my friend, at that pace, before long."

But the bellows worked faster than ever.

While Enoch still stood scratching his head he heard footsteps on the hard sand. He listened for a moment, and then darted back into his hiding-place, peeping from thence to see what would happen next.

He was ready for anything. When the bellows, which he had worked for half a life, took to working of themselves, anything might happen.

He was not in the least surprised when he saw the Squire enter.

The Squire looked pale and dazed. The glare of the fire blinded him at first after the darkness. He put his hand to his eyes. He was blue and sick and dizzy; he reeled, and then recovering himself gazed helplessly round the shop.

"To the right hand," the Squire muttered, and turned to the left, and then to the right, and then to the left again.

"By the third beam—close under the thatch." He looked up, and tried to count the beams, and could not. The roof was all one beam; or the number of beams was infinite.

He staggered up to the wall, and raised his arm. The top of the wall was too high to reach. What was to be done?

At this juncture a ladder which was leaning quietly in a remote corner of the shop was whisked from its place, and set down against the right-hand wall, just under the third beam. When the Squire had sufficiently grasped this new fact he began to mount the ladder.

Enoch's attention had been hitherto fixed on the Squire; but now he became conscious of another figure in the shop. He recognised the wicked old face well. Enoch had been a little disappointed at the entrance of only the live Squire; he felt an inward satisfaction when the ghost of the old Squire entered. The automatic movement of the bellows should presage thus much at least.

The ghost was in a state of the greatest excitement. It rubbed and wrung its hands. It absolutely danced in its eagerness.

"You wicked old villain!" Enoch said to himself, and he shook his fist at it from behind the chimney.

Meanwhile the Squire was mounting the ladder. He fumbled with his hand about and about, along the top of the wall, and could find nothing.

The excitement of the ghost below was terrific. At last, as the Squire continued to feel to and fro under the thatch without success, the ghost mounted the ladder behind him. The ghost grasped the hand of the Squire, and guided it to a hole in the thatch.

The Squire gave one shriek, snatched his hand back, and fell from the ladder. As he fell a square parchment packet flew from his grasp. The packet alighted just in the middle of the forge fire. The bellows worked harder than ever; the flame mounted higher to the roof; the ghost danced before the forge in an ecstasy of delight.

The parchment crackled and hissed and smouldered down into nothing.

Then the ghost vanished, the bellows ceased to work, the fire died out; and Enoch and the Squire (the latter lying senseless on the floor) were left alone together.

* * * * *

The Squire had never any clear recollection of that night. How he got home he never knew. Enoch kept his own counsel.

On the very next morning some people came down from London by the Harleston coach. One of them was a lawyer dressed in seedy black; the other was the widow of Jacob Everett, The Bellman's former master and predecessor at the forge. The widow came to see Tiny, and asked his permission to search in a particular part of the thatch of the smithy. Permission was granted, but the widow found nothing.

Squire Thorne had a long illness; but when he recovered he found his house free of the spectre. Beyond this he never heard any more of the claims on the property made by his late Uncle's mistress.

CLOTILDA.

(*A Reminiscence of Ancient History.*)

BY MRS. [illegible].

Clotilda was of Christian faith, a Princess wise and fair,
Striving to win her husband to her pious hopes to share;
A chieftain of the Franks was he, a man of lawless life,
Who heeded not the precepts of his good and gentle wife.

Yet still Clotilda, day by day, with sweet persistence, strove
To guide him to a gracious Lord—a Lord of peace and love;
The seed upon the barren rock and thorny ground was cast,
Yet hoped she it might flourish, and might bring forth fruit at last.

Anon, the chieftain hastened to the battle-field to go,
Eager to hurl defiance on the ruthless German foe;
But fatal were the fortunes that his hapless troops befell,
And deadly was that conflict on the banks of the Moselle.

Methinks his heart might well have quailed in weariness and fear,
Surrounded by a hostile host, no human succour near;
Yet, as with firm undaunted steps the battle-field he trod,
"Help," he exclaimed, in fervid tones—"help, from Clotilda's God!"

Behold! the German leader slain, in all his pride and might;
Behold! the chieftain of the Franks victorious in the fight.
Thenceforth, he failed not to implore the Lord's protecting care,
And loved Religion's sacred rites, and sought the House of Prayer.

Ye wives who, like Clotilda, may deplore in anxious love
A husband's cold indifference to the God who reigns above,
Like her, relax not in your zeal, nor let your efforts cease
Softly to draw him to the paths of pleasantness and peace.

He may not heed your precepts when the world looks bright and gay,
Yet may he call them to his mind in trouble and dismay,
And, with awakened faith, invoke, amid the storms of life,
The God beloved and worshipped by his dear and cherished wife!

"BETWEEN THE LINES."

Dull, our Human Story, flat, prosaic—
Common-places writ in common signs—
X and Y without an algebraic
Meaning; as we read the printed lines.

Large and clear and sharp and black the letter,
Wide and white the spotless paper shines,
And we rush along the text the better
For the spaces broad between the lines.

Children run and read, but still the story
Palleth; till at length the man reclines,
Long before he waxeth wise and hoary,
Towards suspicion of the printed lines.

Something lacking. As we turn the pages
More and more our confidence declines;
Meaningless the tedious catalogue
Writ so largely in the printed lines!

Something lacking. Here we find a riddle
Asked, unanswered; [illegible] designs—
Working whither?—broken in the middle.
Scraps and fragments all the printed lines.

Here we miss the very point of humour,
Here the pathos; till a thinker pines
For a fuller knowledge than the rumour
Told by hearsay in the printed lines.

Premises without their just conclusion;
Half a couplet here, which intertwines
Never with its sister-verse; confusion
Worse confounded in the printed lines!

Thus at last we come to learn the mystery—
How the value of the common signs,
How the context to our Human History
Hidden lies between the printed lines.

There the missing verse, the lost conclusion;
There completion of the half designs;
There the wit, the pathos, the solution—
In the spaces blank between the lines.

How to read the sympathetic writing?
Who shall teach the talent that divines
Secrets of the Soul-of-the-World's inditing,
Open Secrets writ between the lines?

Reverently turn the pages mystic
Towards the altar-flame thy heart enshrines;
All the mysteries of the text phlogistic
Start to light between the printed lines.

J. A.

A SIMILE.

BY E. A.

Deep in the shade a little brook
Goes rippling on its way;
A fair-haired child in a mossy nook
Is close by its side at play.

A little fleet of acorn cups
She launches on the tide,
And claps her hand in childish glee
As swiftly on they glide.

A little way, and many a stone
The babbling brook divide;
These tiny barks unconscious sail
Without a hand to guide.

They strike the rocks—released—and then,
All trembling from the shock,
Some slowly glide across the stream,
Some sink beside the rock!

Just as our [illegible] are minute barks
Upon life's stormy sea,
And all who 'scape the treacherous rocks
Are help'd, O God, by Thee!

THE SCULPTOR OF VENICE.

ANTONIO CANOVA.

From out of that glorious galaxy of names which adorns the commencement of this century none shines forth more conspicuously than that of Antonio Canova. The world witnessed and admired the astute political wisdom of Pitt, it listened in wonder to the eloquence of Burke, the patriotism and death of Nelson drew a tear from every eye. Wellington, the nation's hope, steadied the tottering kingdoms, and hurled from his proud summit Napoleon, who lightning-like conceived and executed most dazzling projects. But the fame of Canova burned with a steady flame, unmoved by the great events which shook empires to their base. It was no freak of fortune that raised the peasant-boy, no daring deed or chivalrous enterprise which placed him among the immortals in renown; but steady persevering industry which developed and kept in play his great talents, a constant feeling that he had not done enough, and a continual striving after some imaginary perfection which he was never able to realise—these were the moving powers which urged him to rank himself in the muster-roll of fame. From his earliest childhood he was conspicuous for the attention and application he displayed. In his grandfather's workshop never a day nor hour passed which he did not devote, in some measure, to improvement. That he had genius—aye, and a mighty genius too—there is no doubt; but had he not possessed the strength of will to persevere unremittingly, in all probability he would have remained a stone-cutter all his life, undistinguished from the ordinary workmen. His is, indeed, a name

> "To point a moral or adorn a tale."

And well it is that such men do now and then cross the stage of life. They are the commencement of the new families which step into the place of old decayed houses when they become completely shattered by the vicissitudes of fortune. The fall of the Nevilles, the Buckinghams, the Stuarts, and the Albanys is sufficient evidence of the uncertainty of position. The founders of such families were, in by-gone centuries, men conspicuous for their military powers or political wisdom, who fought their way to eminence; and so now men make for themselves names and become the originators of families, the scions of which will, in lapse of time, rank among the patricians of the land. And a proud boast it is, to be the first great man of one's race.

In a low mud cabin in the Venetian village of Possagno, the wife of a poor stone-cutter, named Pietro, was brought to bed of a boy, on the 1st of November, 1757. This infant, which was a poor sickly thing, was called Antonio, and early began to display signs of an inclination for drawing and sculpture. Pietro, the child's father, was a man of no great powers of mind or strength of character, inasmuch as he followed his occupation as assistant or partner of his father, having never been able to obtain an establishment of his own. However, soon after his son's birth he died, and, as his wife thought fit to enter again into the holy state of matrimony, the tender infant was left in charge of its paternal grandfather and his spouse. The old couple readily undertook the responsibility, and the dame did everything in her power to ensure the well-being of the child. She nursed it through the tender age of infancy with anxious solicitude, and endeavoured to train its mind for its intended occupation. She used also to entertain the boy with long legends, to hear which he would leave the clay on which he was employed, and catching hold of his grandmother's gown with his soiled fingers, would listen with breathless attention. We are afraid the only part to which the old lady objected were the spots of clay left by the young urchin on her best dress. Pasino Canova, the grandfather, was clever at his trade and a sort of genius in his way. There is little doubt that, had he possessed the advantages of education in his youth, he would have attained a respectable position among sculptors. As it was, he executed his work in the best manner, and was also capable of carving and designing for the great families which resided in his neighbourhood. He bestowed much care upon his young grandson, teaching him the rudiments of drawing, encouraging him in his earlier endeavours, and initiating him into the mysteries of his trade. Antonio passed many years as his grandfather's pupil.

The Venetian nobles are in the habit of leaving their stately palaces in Venice, and passing the summer at some rural retreat. During the fine months of the year the family of Faliero used to take up their residence near Possagno, for the purpose of enjoying the pure air and delightful scenery with which the locality abounds. The elder Canova was often employed in adorning their villa, and was held in great esteem by Signor Giovanni Faliero, whom he regarded in the light of a patron, and the young Antonio was accustomed to assist his father in these labours. His slight graceful figure, finely chiselled features, and intelligently expressive countenance, united with a modest diffidence and honest wish to please, won for him the notice and well-wishes of all. With him young Faliero, the son of the proprietor, formed an acquaintance which, while they were yet boys, ripened into sincere friendship, and which continued throughout life. The manner in which the latent talents of Canova were first brought into notice is somewhat curious, and has been frequently told.

Signor Faliero gave a grand feast to the Venetian nobility. The servants had neglected to provide a suitable dessert-ornament, and did not, till too late, discover the omission. In this emergency they applied to Pasino Canova, who, however, could suggest no remedy. The domestics were in despair. At last Antonio desired some butter to be brought, and moulding, from the unpliant mass, modelled a lion, which was placed in the centre of the table. The guests admired this masterpiece of cookery, and the master wished to know who made it. Enquiries were made, the truth came out, and the blushing Antonio was treated with applause.

Soon after this event a slight change took place in the young Canova's life. There resided not far from Possagno an artist, by name Giuseppe Bernardi, more commonly known by the surname of Toretto. To him Signor Faliero introduced Antonio, then in his twelfth year, and placed him as his pupil. Here, in Bernardi's studio, he exhibited the most unwearying industry; every thought and every wish being devoted to his furtherance in his profession. He directed his attention to gaining a complete mastery over the handicraft of his art, and does not appear to have given any proof of the high genius which was latent within him; indeed, his exertions were confined to the mechanical part of the profession, the sole intention being to make him an expert and ingenious stone-cutter; consequently it was only after the usual hours of the workshop, after a day of severe toil and manual labour, that he could give any attention to the higher branches of sculpture. However, he did his best; he never flinched. He was not one of those wayward fitful geniuses who work only when outwardly compelled; but he possessed the organ of application, and where industry is combined with brilliant talents, the most tremendous obstacles present but small hindrance to the advancement of their progress.

After remaining two years with Toretto, that artist died, and Antonio was on the point of again returning to his grandfather's workshop. He, however, possessed a good friend in young Faliero, who entreated his father to allow Canova to come to Venice, and pointed out to him the many indications of genius which he thought he had observed. The son prevailed; Signor Faliero complied, and Antonio received an invitation to the City of the Sea, with an intimation that his expenses would be paid by his generous patron, and rooms prepared for him in his palace. We can imagine better than portray with what joy the young aspirant for honours received this letter, and how his heart beat high with the transport of feelings which opened to his gaze. He was but a boy of sixteen—self-confident, still self-distrustful—but still a boy, pale, slight, and unformed. He had only his ingenuous modesty and his unfailing perseverance with which to catch the favour of the great; but the inward feeling that one day his talents would repay all obligations urged him on, and he went up to Venice a hopeful, daring, and aspiring boy.

On his arrival at this city of palaces his reception was hospitable in the extreme. His kind patron placed at his disposal every requisite of life. But Antonio, who considered his mechanical skill sufficiently good to be worthy of recompense, could not bear the thought of being altogether dependent on a stranger. Accordingly, while he gave the fore-part of the day to study in the higher branches of his art, he devoted the afternoon to working under a master, from whom he received a small sum in payment. This income, we know was very small; for, says the artist himself, afterwards, in a letter; "I laboured for a mere pittance, but it was sufficient. It was the fruit of my own resolution, and, as I then flattered myself, the foretaste of more honourable rewards, for I never thought of wealth."

The man who could utter such noble thoughts as these, and not only utter them, but feel them, was pretty sure to push his way. From his first entrance into Venice, Canova divided his time methodically—as a man of business would. The mornings were passed in study at the Academy of Fine Arts, and the afternoons as before-mentioned. In Venice a fine and extensive range of observation was opened to him, and he did not fail to take advantage of everything calculated to be of use in his profession. It was his custom to visit the theatres, and other places of public assemblage, for the purpose of studying character. He delighted to look upon the multitude of faces, note the various expressions, the diversified attitudes, and fix in his mind any countenance that pleased his fancy. Another source of pleasure was sauntering along the quays, and observing the porters as they passed along, their colossal frames and huge muscular limbs presenting models to the artist which he never permitted himself to forget; indeed, whenever he was particularly struck with any turn of the limb or play of the muscles, he would hurry home, and, while the subject was fresh in his memory, reproduce it on paper. By such means as these did the greatest modern sculptor lay the foundations of his future excellence.

As Canova, in his youth, was essentially a quiet man, a sober every-day liver, seeking no adventures, nothing scarcely is left wherewith his chroniclers may enliven their pages. His life was an uneventful life. An ordinary man would soon have sunk under the difficulties which he surmounted. His heroism was not the heroism which startles by its brilliancy; but it was the heroism which, after overcoming one obstacle, is ready to cope with and overcome the next, throughout the whole battle-field of life. It was the desire to know everything which made him eager not only after the pursuit of art-knowledge, but also caused him to become well-versed in the general accomplishments of the age. He applied himself to the study of Spanish and French, and became well acquainted with the literature of his own and other countries. Thus for seven long years the student read and worked and copied nature, during which time he astonished and delighted the Venetians by his statue of Orpheus. This, the first work of any great merit executed by Canova, was exhibited in 1776. He had long panted for fame; but so great was his unaffected modesty, that he could only be persuaded by the earnest entreaties of his friends to present it to public view. The result was unbounded applause. The most prejudiced critics were forced to admire, and admit the excellence of the work. From this time the success of the artist continued to increase. He executed several works, among which we may mention the bust of the Doge of Venice; copy of the Orpheus; statues of Esculapius, Apollo, and Daphne; &c. In his third year, he gave forth to the world his greatest Venetian effort—the group of Dædalus and Icarus, in Carrara marble. The figures are the natural size, and a close imitation of Nature. There is no attempt at idealism. Nature was Canova's mistress, indeed, art had so degenerated before his time, that it was necessary he should go straight to the fountain-head, if he wished to cleanse the stream of vitiated taste. The statuary represents the father and son preparing for the journey. Dædalus is in the act of fitting to his son's shoulders the wings with which he himself should wend his way far from Cretan bondage. Icarus holds in his hand part of the materials, as if to assist his father, but seems chiefly engaged in watching with careless indifference the efforts of his sire. The attitudes are good, and when viewed as a whole the effect is pleasing. There is, however, a great want of elevation in the work. The figure of Dædalus is such as may be seen at any moment; indeed, there is a touch of vulgarity in it. However, the simplicity and faithfulness to nature displayed throughout fully compensate for the other defects. So true is the representation that many artists suspected the group had been modelled from models formed from casts taken upon the human body in that material.

The reputation of Canova having been by this work established in Venice, it was deemed expedient for him to repair to Rome to a more extended field of labour. Accordingly, at the entrance to manhood, at the beginning of his renown, he packed up his chisels and tools, and turning his back upon the scene of his early struggles, wended his way to Rome. Here he met with a cordial reception from Cavaliere Zulian, to whom he had letters of introduction. Rooms were accorded him in his palace, and he found at once a friend and patron in the ambassador.

At Rome the enthusiasm of Canova became, if possible, even greater. It had long been his earnest wish to produce some work from heroic subjects. The contemplation of the remains of the statuary at Rome aroused within him a wish to do likewise. But the claims of poverty confined the aspirations of his genius; for without a commission he could not afford to purchase the marble from which to embody the noble forms of his heroes. At length he disclosed his views to Zulian, and received from him an order for a work, the subject being left to himself. His patron also offered to provide him the marble necessary for the undertaking. Canova, pleased beyond measure with the generous proposal, ardently commenced his task, choosing for his subject Theseus vanquishing the Minotaur. On this work he labored with unceasing attention and assiduity. He worked in secret, being desirous that no one save the ambassador should be aware of what he had in hand until it was finished. His apartments in the Venetian palace he kept closed against all comers—partly because he was aware his style of sculpture differed from that then in vogue—partly because he did not wish to be subjected to the unkind criticisms of minor intellects—and partly because when a work was seen during its progress the effect at completion was lessened, and the artist was liable to have his own industry robbed.

Canova knew that his fault was a deficiency in studied grandeur; so he viewed and contemplated and studied the works of ancient masters; went home, thought over what he had seen, worked incessantly, and finally produced the crowning effort of his noviciate. The Theseus and Minotaur established his reputation at Rome. Everyone admired it. The similitude to nature was justly admired, and the young artist felt he had achieved a triumph. The head of Theseus is quite a masterpiece. In it are expressed, as he bends over the fallen Minotaur on which he sits, those high and noble feelings which can only arise from the consciousness of having accomplished a mighty and glorious deed. The figure is in the antique, and is finely chiselled about the head and shoulders, while the head of the beast is a model of ruggedness and strength.

From this time fortune smiled upon the persevering student. Commissions poured in upon him; his acquaintance was eagerly sought by artists, men of letters, and by nobles.

There were many, indeed, who, envious of his success, carped and ridiculed, and wrote against him. These he answered with silent contempt, working quiet in his workshop, and never deigning to answer their attacks. But still the iron entered into his soul, and his modest and kindly heart was pained, that he who wished for nothing but the advancement of his art, should be exposed to the senseless jibes of ill-natured and ignorant critics. But his courage never faltered; he kept on his course, and that course soon carried him to a pinnacle at which not even the most pointed arrows of malignant envy could harm him.

In a sketch like this we cannot enter into the details of all Canova's works, and must necessarily pass cursorily over a great part of his life. From the time when he executed the tombs of the Popes (Ganganelli and Rezzonico), his life continued to be one unvaried course of success and hard work. It never changed: every day brought the same industry to the studio, even though he had workmen to execute the coarser parts. In this way he passed the next twenty-five years, honoured by nobles, princes, and all celebrities. He was Napoleon's guest; George the Third presented him with a diamond snuff-box, and the Emperor created him Marquis of Ischia, with a pension of three thousand crowns. We thus behold the poor peasant-boy raised to the highest rank by the force of his genius, in union with unflinching application and unswerving integrity. But the industry which distinguished the earlier part of his career had undermined his health, and in the winter of 1821, his stomach being out of order, and his whole frame greatly debilitated, he determined to try the air of his native place—Possagno.

But, alas! though he roamed through the well-known spots of his infancy, and drank in the breezes which fanned his childhood's cheek, no health came to the over-wrought invalid. Despite, however, his precarious condition, he determined to return to Venice before setting out for Rome. Here his illness could no longer be withstood, and he was obliged to take to his bed. His stomach refused the slightest nourishment; and, though his pulse beat regularly, his danger was imminent. But so quiet and calm did he lay, so serene was the expression of his countenance, that his friends thought death far from his chamber. Crowds besieged the entrance to his house, all eager to inquire after him, so deeply was the city affected by the illness of Italy's greatest sculptor. However, despite all the skill and learning, all the care and attention bestowed upon him, he continued to grow worse, and, after having received the last ordinances of religion, sank calmly to rest [illegible] a struggling moment without a sigh. Thus, on the 13th Oct., 1822, the great master-mind of sculpture left its frail body, and, as says Zanetti, "The august heart of Canova palpitated for the last time, and his celestial mind was closed for ever on its lofty conceptions."

He lies buried at Possagno, the scene of his early labours.

HARRINGTON GRANGE.

Chap. VII.

What gave Philip Vere the right to hang so lovingly over the chair in the dim corner, where Amy sat with her friend beside her? What gave him the right to whisper, as he did now and then? to place a footstool? to hope she was not suffering? Above all, what gave him the right to whisper—as he did once, when he was leaving her, at Eleanor's command—"Mine own"?

This: In the morning, with the sun shining upon her cheeringly, Amy, leaning on the robust arm of Sir Thomas Harding, her host, took her first walk, since the memorable day of the picnic, in the pleasure-grounds. The party at Wilmslade was thinning gradually. Miss Goddard was gone; and Mr. Blake, the poet, had departed, to woo his coy Muse amongst the [illegible] charms of scenery; to throw himself in romantic spots by gurgling streams, and struggle with the tough rhymes that would not hinge themselves. Miss Carr—with a parting injunction to Amy to study the classics, and a promise to send a copy of her next work, 'The Druidical Traditions; how far they are reconcilable with the history of the Universal Deluge'—had also bidden adieu to the shades and bowers of Wilmslade; and though a few of the lesser stars still remained to shine feebly, hoping for more distinction now that their foils were set, no one troubled Amy, or came near to watch the progress of her first essay of the threshold. But what marvel that the portly Sir Thomas, active and strong, should weary a little of his tender charge, and a good deal of her pace? What wonder that he should resign her willingly to Philip, when they met him casually at the door of a little summer-house where Amy had begged to rest? And the meeting was casual. Philip had gone there without any design or aim. Having made up his mind to conquer all, he had been wandering about in a desultory manner, restless and excited, not knowing what to do with himself, when Sir Thomas seated Amy in the very summer-house to which his anxious mind and restless steps had led him.

"Ah, Philip, this is fortunate. Then, if Miss Harrington will excuse me, I promised to see Harold, the keeper, to-day; and I had forgotten it. Take care of her, Philip; no more mischief! Upon my word, though," said the poor baronet, ruefully, "Lady Harding told me not to lose sight of her!"

"I daresay my aunt will accept me as proxy," said Philip, gravely. "I will be very careful!"

Opportunity thus suddenly thrust upon him, of course he tried first to congratulate Amy on being out of doors again, and of course failed, signally. There is no doubt that, for a sensible man and a genius, Philip Vere looked excessively foolish. More than that, the precious minutes were passing relentlessly, and he knew it; and yet his heart was beating so fast, that he could not steady his voice for the words he meant to utter. And little Amy, tired as she was, and with the weak ankle aching, got up to go; but he stopped her then, imploringly. "One word he must speak to her; would she not hear him?" Ah, if she could know how he had longed for this opportunity—how he had been hoping and fearing, and how miserable he had been, when he thought, at times, that the hopes were all false, she would listen to him, would she not?"

There is no need for repetition. What could little Amy do but hear him? What could she say but tell him tremulously, to his repeated entreaties that she would answer him if it were only one word, how happy she was? What could she do, finally, but walk back with her hand on his arm, his penitent wife, never heeding the rain in that stubborn heart, but thinking, poor little dreamer, that there never had been in all the world, and never would be, anyone so happy as she was?

Then Eleanor came to meet them, took her away from him, and led her into her own room, making her lie down, and telling her to keep quite quiet.

But there was no removing little Amy's wistful look.

"I know how it is, my darling, I know it all!"

"Oh, Eleanor," said Amy, clinging to her, passionately, "it never can be wrong that anyone should be so happy on earth. They call it a world of trouble!"

"The trouble will come time enough, little one. If happiness is sent to you, it must be right, you know."

"And you will love me—you are not vexed?"

"Vexed at gaining a little sister?"

"Ah, I never thought of that."

Eleanor bent her head for one moment till her face was hidden. In this new happiness she had been utterly forgotten?

"How foolish! how selfish!" thought Eleanor, "to expect anything else!"

"And now," said Amy, "I want to go home to papa; and no one must know—"

"Suppose my aunt knew already? No, don't look frightened; she only guesses, and no one will speak to you about it."

"But I must go home—to-morrow. It is right."

"Yes, said Eleanor, "it is right. And is Philip to go with you?"

"No, no. Not Philip at first—yet."

Chap. VIII.

Hopes and Fears.

And so little Amy was at home again.

Was that the same figure that peeped curiously behind the window-curtain at the sketchers? As she thought of that her face changed, and the shadow of the new life came over it. More old-fashioned and queer than ever the rooms looked, and yet dearer to her; the same yet changed. Even Meg's old eyes could discern a difference in her, without being able to define it. Formerly her cheerfulness was but the sunshine of an unclouded spirit; now there was something deeper in it, and there hung about her at times an air of concentration; and a soberness in her manner, which were new to Meg.

"After being few weeks away, Meg," said Amy, "he only just looked up and kissed me when I went in. I wonder what he is always writing about."

"Five weeks, Miss Amy! Two months you mean. And he was going to send for you back too," said Meg, mysteriously, "if you had not come."

"Was he! Then he did miss me. **But**, Meg, it cannot be two months."

"Do you say that, dearest, Miss Amy? When you went away it was all green, and now back now. Yes, it's two full months, but it wasn't that he missed you so much. You know he never misses anyone. Your cousin Robert is here."

"Here! Where?"

"Oh, off out somewhere now; but he'll be in directly."

"And why should I be sent for on his account?" was on Amy's lips, but she did not speak it.

She remembered Robert as a great ungainly schoolboy; and she remembered, and had a salutary dread of his sister, Janet, who used to come with him and stay such an unconscionable time, and who was always calling her a mouse, and finding fault with her. But all was so different now, it would be hardly possible to dread or dislike anyone. Flora was on her lap as usual, and her hand stroked his silky coat; but she had forgotten to ask about the behaviour during her absence, and Meg, as she went back to her kitchen, thoughtfully muttered that she "couldn't make it out."

"Maybe," thought Meg, "all the grand people, and the fine rooms, the liveried servants to wait on her, and all the grand things have put her out of conceit of the old place; and who can wonder at it? I'm sure it's dull enough for her, if the master would only think of it."

But Meg had seldom been farther from the truth in her conjectures. In the great wealth of her new happiness, little Amy was thinking more tenderly than ever of the old Grange and its inmates, and all belonging to it; particularly of Walter Harrington in his solitary den. And if sometimes, looking round suddenly upon the well-known room, she could scarcely believe that the last few weeks were not a dream from which she had just waked, it needed but glance at a certain glittering ornament on her finger to dispel the thought. But she hid that ring jealously. No one must see it yet—till to-morrow.

To-morrow! What a time it seemed! She was uneasy till her father knew all; till he should see Philip, and wonder that he, with his genius and his great gifts, had chosen poor stupid little Amy Harrington. Her reverie was broken abruptly.

"Ah, my little Cousin—at last!"

A. A.

And Robert Harrington, taking her hand—that hand bearing Philip's token—put it to his lips, and proceeded to offer a kiss more affectionate and cousinly withal. But, with her new-born dignity, Amy drew back.

"Shy, eh?" said Robert. "They used not to be like that when we jumped the sunk fence together, and went down Jones's meads. What a romp you were then!"

"We were children then," said Amy, gravely.

"And as a child, you had a tolerance for me. As a woman, though the cousinship remains, you have none! Is that the case?"

"I am very glad to see you."

"Oh, Amy, what a fib! Is that the way you show gladness? But you must give me a welcome, you know. I have a right to ask it."

Amy looked up in astonishment. Perhaps she was as nearly angry at his tone as ever she had been in her life. He was uglier than ever she thought, and more ungainly; and there was a deep perpendicular wrinkle between the eyebrows, which, though it spoke of power, did not improve his personal appearance. But Amy must have been prejudiced; for Meg called him a "fine young fellow."

"Well, what do you think of me? The improvement since you saw me, eh?"

"No," said Amy, decidedly the reverse.

Robert laughed; but it was not a pleasant laugh. Let a man despise personal beauty ever so much, it does not please him to be told to his face that he is ugly.

"'Handsome is that handsome does,' you know; and you have beauty enough for both," he said, sitting down beside her, familiarly.

Again Amy was disagreeably surprised. He had no right, cousin though he was, to take these liberties. She thought involuntarily of Philip's gentle manner and his deference, and the comparison was not favourable to Robert. He began to amuse himself with pulling Flora's ears, and making her sit up and beg; which, [illegible], she performed with much gravity and success, till Mr. Harrington came in to him, when he rose to give him a chair, and to settle Amy in her place, with great apparent attention to her comfort.

"We have been talking of old times, sir," said Robert, looking straight before him at nothing; "when Amy and I used to be called [illegible]."

"Ah, she is here again," said Mr. Harrington, as though he had only then become aware of Amy's return, "my little sunbeam! I used to wonder what was wrong about the table, but now I know. No one has run away with my sunbeam, Robert."

"Not yet, sir."

The tone was disagreeable—at least in Amy's opinion; but Mr. Harrington did not notice it.

"Is she glad to come back, or have they spoilt her at Whitmore?"

"They were very kind to me, papa," said Amy, slowly, and with a distressing consciousness that Robert's eye was upon her; "and I have been very happy at Whitmore; but I am glad you missed me, and glad to come home."

"And to find an old playfellow here, too," said her father. "Make the most of him, Amy; he is fond of us already, and goes away to-morrow."

Robert was up in an instant, to open the door for his uncle, and to close it carefully after him; but Amy rose too, and, in spite of his re[illegible] uncommonly cordial, left the room and went to her own. She could bear it no longer. Besides, she did not know whether, under the circumstances, it was quite proper she should; and his boldness puzzled and displeased her.

It would be all right to-morrow. Philip was coming, and all would be known; then, of course, her cousin would not dare to take liberties with her.

It was strange—thinking, as she did so constantly, of Philip and her father—that Meg's [illegible] as to her, not to mention the name of Vere, never recurred to her; but it did not.

To-morrow! How slowly the hours passed! Not that she wanted to see Philip again, of course, but she wanted it all known; she had felt like a hypocrite when her father said that no one had run away with his sunbeam; and she was not accustomed to have anything to conceal.

And the grin with which her disagreeable cousin received that remark! Amy had never disliked any one, but she began to feel that she might be quite capable of the sensation. To-morrow; well it came; as all to-morrows will, however wished for, or dreaded.

She rose from the breakfast-table, according to her plan the evening before, to go to her own room. Her heart was fluttering so, and her cheeks burning, she could not bear her cousin's eyes upon her.

He stopped her in the doorway; he said he was going that day; would she not give him a little of her society?

"She was very sorry; she could not."

"Not for old acquaintance?"

"Not just then. She was very busy."

Robert could say nothing about the business; but she was very timid, he knew. And when the door closed after her, he shook his fist at it, and muttered "that there should come a day of reckoning."

"I'm ugly, am I?" said Robert, standing before the glass, and smiling hideously. "I'll teach her that. I'll take lessons in pulling faces to torment her. I'm ugly, am I? She shall have cause to say so some day. Comparing me with some of the grinning puppies at Whitmore—no doubt. I know I'm not handsome; but is that my fault? I've managed to come round the old man pretty cleverly. I wonder how much he will leave her in those old bags of his. It ought to be a good round sum. How he squeezed my hand and blessed me the other day for my [illegible] for his darling! She is pretty, though; deuced pretty."

Then, Mr. Robert Harrington turned away his pleasant face from the glass, and reconnoitred his achievement of making Peggy. While he was engaged upon this gentlemanly pastime he heard a knock at the door, and an altercation in the hall; and Meg's face, very white and anxious, protruded into the room.

"Eh! Well my pretty Peggy, what is it?"

Now Robert was no favourite of Meg's, although she had at first, in her pride for the Harrington's, pronounced him a fine young fellow; but she was in a sore strait and had no counsellor.

"Oh! Mr. Robert, he says he must see the master!"

"Does he? And who may he be; a lover for Meg, eh?"

"For shame, Mr. Robert," said Meg, indignantly, opening the door. "Walk in sir, if you please."

Mr. Robert condescended to stand upright, and desist from his occupation.

"My name is Philip Vere," said the stranger.

Mr. Robert bowed, and uttered a mental anathema against the postman from Wilmore.

"I have called to see Mr. Harrington."

"My uncle is much engaged," said Robert, insinuatingly. "Indeed, he seldom sees strangers. If it is anything in which I can spare him."

"You are very kind. I am afraid, in this instance, it will be necessary that I should have a personal interview."

Robert, indulging furtively in a hideous grimace, turned to Meg, who was wringing her hands, and making other demonstrations of perplexity, and bade her show the gentleman into the study.

And Amy from her window has seen him again. Now there will be peace for her, and relief from the concealment which has lain so heavily upon her heart. She has imagined Meg's surprise at his request to see her master, and she feels that he is telling his tale to her father in the den. Not one doubt as to his reception crosses her mind; not one single misgiving; not the faintest idea of a possible rejection.

Then she saw Philip go out again, cross the lawn, and disappear without a single look back, at a hurrying [illegible]. His head was bent down, so that she could not see his face; but there [illegible] was a faint touch of disappointment that he should have gone away without [illegible] back, or looking towards the window where he would imagine her sitting. If he had, she knew he would not have seen her, but still she wished he had looked. And now, what would her father say to her, and when? There came no summons. He was thinking it over. But she must not be impatient; she half hoped he would invite Philip to stay; and now he was gone. What would he say to her?

What did he say to her?

Nothing. They met as usual at the dinner-table. Only he looked sterner, more careworn, and more absent, and Robert's face wore an expression of ill-concealed triumph. Every moment that [illegible] hope of Amy's was growing heavier, every moment the chilling suspicion in her breast increased. Her father

went away without even speaking, without waiting till they had finished; and then her only thought was how she might get away too. Robert spoke to her; but she heard no words—only a senseless jargon; and he, too, rose from the table, and said he must go, or he should be too late for the train from Wilmore-station.

"Good-bye, my little Amy," said Robert. "Next time I come you will give me a warmer reception."

Amy looked at him sharply.

"Won't she?" said Robert, turning to Meg, who was busy about the table.

"I don't know, Mr. Robert."

"You do; you know the rogue. Tell her why, if he won't. What's the use of all this hide-and-seek foolery? Tell her, I say. Good-bye, cousin."

"What is it? What does he mean?" asked Amy, in a bewildered tone.

"He means this, my darling," said Mr. Harrington, putting his hand upon the brown head, suddenly.

"Papa! I thought you were gone. Oh! papa, I must speak to you!"

"He means this—that he has asked me for my best earthly treasure, and I have given her to him!"

COCK-CROWING AT CHRISTMAS EVE.—It was formerly a belief that cocks crowed all Christmas Eve, which tradition originated from the circumstance that the weather is then usually steady and thick, and cocks, during such weather, often crow incessantly day and night. Shakespeare alludes to this superstition in "Hamlet":—

> "Some say that ever 'gainst that season comes
> Wherein our Saviour's birth is celebrated,
> The bird of dawning singeth all night long;
> The nights are wholesome, and no planets strike;
> No goblin walks, nor spirits walk abroad;
> No fairy takes nor witch hath power to charm,
> So gracious and so hallowed is the time."

The ancient Christians divided the night into four watches, called the evening, midnight, cock-crowing, and the dawning. Their expectation, with the belief in walking spirits will be remembered:—

> "The cock crows, and the moon grows dim,
> When [illegible]
> [illegible]
> Of [illegible]
> They [illegible] night, as [illegible]
> [illegible]
> [illegible]

Why are cows longer the night watches [illegible] by the cock in that scene in "Hamlet," where the [illegible]

> "[illegible]
> The [illegible], [illegible]
> [illegible]
> Or [illegible]
> [illegible]
> [illegible]
> [illegible]."

In another [illegible] "There is this remarkable circumstance about the crowing of cocks—they seem to keep night-watches, as it were general crowing-periods, at certain periods—as, soon after twelve, at three, and again at daybreak."

THE WORK-TABLE.

HANDKERCHIEF BORDER AND CORNER.

French cambric is of course the only material on which the dress-handkerchief is to be worked, and this ought to be of a clear texture. Care should be taken to select a soft fine embroidery-cotton* and a small delicate needle, as all the rest depends upon the dexterity of the execution. The spots in our design may be worked either as holes or solid spots in satin-stitch, according to taste.

If it should be wished to make the work deeper, this can easily be done by adding more rows of the holes or spots.

* Messrs. Walter Evans and Co.'s Embroidery Cotton, Nos. 60 or 80.

DRAWING-ROOM MAT, ON CANVAS,

IN BEADS AND BERLIN WOOL.

The size of this mat depending on the coarseness or fineness of the canvas makes it necessary that this should be selected according to the purpose for which the article is designed; only care must be taken that the beads employed should correspond in size, so that the threads of the canvas may be completely covered. The flower in the centre has the spot in the middle worked in gold beads, the four upper leaves being in transparent-white beads, and the four under-ones in chalk-white beads; the ground being in blue Berlin wool, enclosed within a ring of gold beads. The bands which interlace each other beyond this ring are worked the one in steel beads, the other in gold beads on a red ground. The four leaves which fill-in the corners of the mat are worked one-half in clear-white beads, the other half in chalk-white, with veins of steel beads, on a black ground. The outer border has the spots half in clear and half in chalk-white on a blue ground. When completed, the canvas must be stretched over a square of card-board and lined, a rather larger bead than those used in working the mat being taken at every stitch, so as to form a regular line of beads all round the mat.

[DRAWING-ROOM MAT, ON CANVAS.]

NETTING FOR WINDOW-CURTAINS, AND FIRE-GRATE VEIL.

MATERIALS.—The Boar's Head Crochet Cotton of Messrs. W. Evans and Co., Derby.

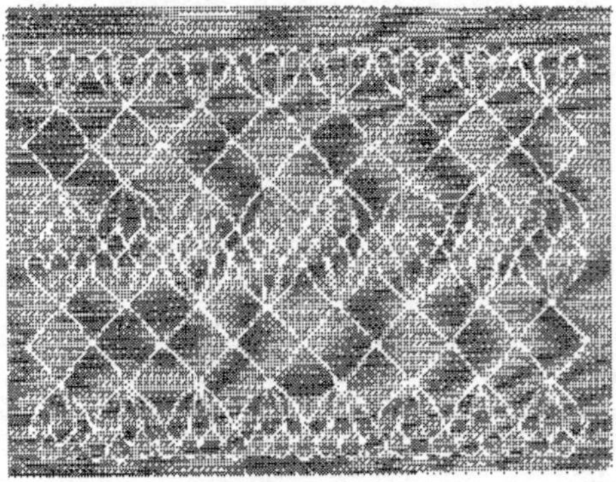

It is in the winter that works of this kind ought to be undertaken *for* the summer, so that they may be ready for use at their appropriate season. The pattern given in our illustration may be on a coarser scale if desired, but the proportions between the sizes of the two meshes must be preserved. Commence by netting a row with the large mesh. On the return-line take three stitches in one, still using the large mesh. The next row is simple netting on the large mesh. The next, which is the last row of the division of the pattern, on the large mesh, has three loops on one, which is done by passing the cotton three times round the gauge before passing the needle through, and drawing each round of the cotton tight before drawing the knot. After this, two rows on the fine mesh are to be netted. This completes the pattern, which is then to be recommenced at the first row which we have given. This pattern has a very pretty effect when worked, and it is a great improvement to an apartment in the summer-time to have the white window-curtains and the fire-grate veil to match.

LE PUY, HAUTE LOIRE.

CROSATIER—THE FOUNDER.

(*Continued from page 310.*)

We stood for some time gazing on the first home of the poor friendless boy who, from his own talent and energy, became the possessor of thousands, and of whom we had heard so much since our residence at Le Puy; for his name is cited on every occasion, so proud are the "people" of him; and so they might be, for in his prosperity he did not forget that to the people of all this, his native soil, and his generosity proved his infinite affection for it. On this spot, then, was Crosatier's early infancy spent. Here he first learnt to lisp the soft accents of his mountain "patois," the ancient "langue d'oc," still spoken by all in the Valley, and which is perfectly unintelligible to us, and which resounded the little Charles say to all his to his mother when, at six years of age, after bidding adieu to his companions and to our Lady of Le Puy, he arrived in Paris, without one single friend in the world, save that loving heart that was waiting for her boy when the "diligence" stopped in a narrow street in the capital, and who had already been there every day for the last week expecting him in vain. Six long, long years had elapsed since that heart-rending scene, to her, when she had impressed the last kiss on her baby-boy—not more than two months old; and after entrusting him to the care of the poor peasant of A[illegible], with a heavy heart had hastened to the great metropolis, whose streets her imagination paved with gold, and no sacrifice there she had been too great for her maternal love. She toiled, economised, and hoped, until at last sufficient arrived, and the sum requisite for his journey was speedily forwarded to the foster-parents, and the little Charles again felt the warmth of a mother's kiss. As she pressed him to her bosom, she vowed that every nerve should be exerted to make the world shine on him; and all her past woes were forgotten. Nor did she fail in her task, although at first poverty, alas! too frequently drew out her sanguine hopes, and checked her ambitious views for her treasure. She, however, succeeded in sending him to a good school, where he proved to be a studious lad. But it was in the public school of design that at twelve years of age he rendered himself remarkable, and carried off the first prize. At thirteen years of age he commenced the career of a carver, and soon after was employed in finishing the ornaments for the toilet-table that the city of Paris offered to the Empress Marie Louise. Indeed, such was the skill that Crosatier displayed in carving and chasing, that the Emperor exempted him from the conscription on the demand of the professors in the Imperial Academy of Fine Arts. But his mother, although proud indeed of her son, had not enough judgment to allow herself to be dazzled with phantoms of fame. She had struggled too closely with poverty, and had felt its poignancy too acutely, not to dream of something more substantial for Charles than the too often chimerical phantom of success; and she trembled at what might await the young artist entirely dependent on his own exertions for support; so that she persuaded him to embrace the art of a founder, knowing that he would excel in that career, and reap as well as sow.

From that moment every faculty was bent to the acquirement of the necessary science for his profession, and in three years he became master of almost every secret in his art, and was considered the cleverest founder in Paris. Added to great talent, he possessed an iron will, and every leisure moment that his daily labours gave him he spent in the Louvre, examining and studying the antique master-pieces with which that rich palace abounds; and often, when at home, after these visits, he would try different experiments, with the view of imitating those ancient and mysterious tints that the hand of Time spreads over metal and marble. About this time a happy chance enabled him to visit Rome, Naples, Florence, Pompeii, and other towns in Italy—which was a field [illegible] above every other. He carefully examined the antique statues that rendered his soul in these ancient halls of art, and upon his return to Paris he has-

tated their antique appearance so well, that he succeeded in deceiving the greatest connoisseurs themselves.

A duke under Louis XVIII., who passed for a great antiquarian, was particularly fond of Crozatier's society. One day, while discussing the purity of a bronze statue Crozatier had just finished, the duke declared that modern art could never attain the perfection of the ancients; "and to convince you of the truth of my assertion," said he, "I will to-morrow bring you an admirable little statuette I lately purchased at Pompeii, in a mysterious way, and which I had for almost nothing. I saw it myself dug up, at a moment when the man employed in watching over the excavations had turned away, and the workman, hiding it under his clothes, whispered his address to me as I passed. I went at nightfall, and bore triumphantly away my beautiful little Neptune, of the finest Roman epoch, which you shall see."

Accordingly, the next day the duke brought his Neptune, of the finest Roman epoch, to Crozatier, exultingly exclaiming, "Now, my dear sir, pretend that modern art can equal that!"

Crozatier took it, and, after examining it minutely, "Pray," said he, how much did your grace pay for this?"

"Only 3,500 francs," replied the duke.

"Only!" answered Crozatier, with a smile; and, opening a trunk near him, he produced several fragments of an earthen model, and after joining them together, "There," said he, "there is the original. I moulded it in 1825, and sold two copies to two Neapolitan merchants, for which they paid me 150 francs each. I thank you, my lord duke, for your very flattering opinion of my counterfeit work!"

"The duke was mortified at being thus duped; but he kept the secret, and his Neptune is still the admiration of connoisseurs," said Crozatier, after relating the above anecdote.

But love of art did not exclude from our founder's heart softer affections. Naturally timid and reserved, his sympathising soul longed in secret for a kindred spirit to blend with his: and the sweet image of a young girl he had often remarked at work at a window opposite his abode, haunted him, and presided over his most serious occupations, exciting him in his acquirement of reputation and fortune. Many very eligible matches had been proposed to him by different friends, but he refused them all: though how to make himself known even to the object of his desires he knew not.

One evening, after a day of toil and excitement, amid the burning furnaces and liquid metal which had hardened down into the Hercules in Windsor Castle, Crozatier hastened to his accustomed place at his window, whence he could perceive the beam of sunshine that penetrated his soul at every glance. It was a lovely evening, soft and balmy, even in a street in Paris when at the fifth story, and a gentle breeze wafts the exhaling breath of the lime-trees and flowers from a garden near. The window opposite was opened, and he saw two fair eyes fixed on his window. They were hastily withdrawn at his approach, while a deep blush overspread the young girl's countenance, then soon disappeared, and the window closed.

Crozatier's heart danced within him; his intelligent face beamed with joy and love; while his eyes, as if fascinated, gazed on the window for some time; but the vision did not reappear, although fond fancy saw an almost imperceptible shadow behind the white blind that shut him out of paradise. That night fairies danced round his pillow, and lulled him to sleep with melody, and more affectionate than ever was the kiss and adieu he gave his beloved mother as he hastened to his foundry the next morning to recommence his occupations. Innumerable numbers of statues continued to proceed from his moulds. The equestrian statue of Louis XIV., in the great court of Versailles; the Napoleon on the column of Place Vendome, in Paris; the Quadriga over the arch, Place Carrousel, in front of the Tuileries, all came from Crozatier's foundry.

After the inauguration of the Quadriga, Charles X., then king, sent for the sculptor Bosio, and for Crozatier the founder, and after congratulating them on their different talents, he created the sculptor "Baron," and conferred the Cross of the Legion d'Honneur on Crozatier. This was a distinction to which Crozatier, in his modesty, had scarcely dared to aspire; and as he hastened home to display his red ribbon to the delighted eyes of his mother, another image sweetly wrought itself with hers before his eyes, and rendered his newly-won honour still dearer to him.

To describe the old lady's joy and pride would be impossible. "My poor abandoned child!" ejaculated she in her joy, "Chevalier de la Legion d'Honneur!" And the tears flowed fast down her smiling face. "And now, my son," said she, wiping them hastily away, "one wish alone remains unaccomplished—one blessing more to make me the happiest of mothers. I am getting old, and would not leave you on earth alone, but would fain see you with a dear companion to partake your joys and cares. Several good matches have been proposed to you; why do you persist in refusing them all—you who are so calculated to make a woman happy, and loaded with honour and riches, too, as you are? Why not at least see whether the young girl F—— mentioned to you would not suit you? You say her family is too grand, her fortune too considerable; but have you not self-gained honours and riches in abundance—enough for a princess?"

They were in the founder's room: at that moment Crozatier's brilliant eye was turned towards the modest little window above. There she was, the spirit of his dreams, working, her lips moving as if singing.

"Mother," said he, "you are right; I must marry, for youth is fast going, and my soul thirsts to think and feel with another. Look!"

and he pointed towards the face above, "and there is that other; or I am much mistaken, (?) ask her to be mine!"

And Crozatier married his wife, during the rest of his life, proved his constant solace and greatest joy amid all the prosperity that still awaited him. His mother died happy in her son's felicity, and before even he had reached the zenith of his prosperity. One remarkable event once occurred to him during his career as a founder which, from its extraordinary coincidence, is worthy of relating. He was charged by Government, under the Restoration, to cast a colossal statue, twenty-two feet high, of the unfortunate monarch Louis XVI. For more than a week before the day appointed for the casting, Crozatier was in a state of agitation indescribable. He himself had arranged the mould, had minutely examined every detail; nothing had escaped him; and yet a something like a presentiment troubled his mind, and even prevented him sleeping. The momentous day, however, arrived, and a crowd of high personages flocked to the foundry, to enjoy the excitement that the casting of a statue ever produces. Crozatier had been there ever since daybreak, and with feverish impatience he awaited the final moment, without being able to remain quiet one minute. A cry of surprise from the spectators soon, however, made the founder smile again; and the flaming metal rushed from the furnace, falling in fiery torrents, and then slowly mounting the mould, and in a few instants the flames that poured forth from the top were totally extinguished, and the bronze metal ran over. The work was achieved. A burst of applause announced the event, and all hastened to congratulate Crozatier, who felt an immense weight removed from his bosom. Now he breathed freely, and thanked his visitors for the honour they paid him. The moment to open the mould soon arrived, and judge the horror of all present, the statue, perfect in every detail, was without a head! All were thunderstruck, and Crozatier was in despair, although he repaired the accident in a few hours, and in such a manner that detection was impossible. The poor Duchess of Angoulême, only surviving child of the unfortunate King, heard of the strange accident, and wept bitterly, it is said; and, in spite of the magnificence, she entreated the King to put it away, and not to allow it to be exposed to public view, which desire the monarch granted, and the statue never graced the place it was intended to occupy.

If I have only spoken of Crozatier as a founder [illegible], it is because he is the most known in that capacity on account of the great riches he derived from it; but he has left many charming compositions of his own, and his talents as a sculptor would alone have sufficed for a good reputation. As Crozatier advanced in age an inexhaustible desire to behold once more the native mountains seized him. He had ever manifested the greatest enthusiasm when speaking of their sublime beauty, which seemed to have made an impression on his infantine mind; and one Sunday afternoon, a few summers ago, the old peasant that still inhabits that cottage to which I called your attention, at the commencement of my history, was sitting at his door, smoking his short black pipe, and watching the young men in their Sunday clothes playing at nine pins, or at other rural games, when a handsome, well-dressed stranger, after casting a look of recognition around, approached him, and, with tears in his eyes and his voice trembling with emotion, accosted the peasant in patois. "What, Tailhère," said he, "do you not know me—me, your foster-brother?" Nearly half a century had elapsed since the two children played together for the last time on the very spot where they were now standing. Tailhère's hoary head and furrowed sunburnt face, spoke of hardships, of battles fought, and of Time's unsparing hand, although he was as poor as his parents had been before him. For some minutes Tailhère gazed with bewildered look, without seeming to comprehend who it was to whom the "gentleman" spoke; and it was long before he could thoroughly admit that the little Charles stood before him. Then what delight, as the scenes of his youth were revived! "Oh! if the old folks were alive, how pleased they would be!" but they had long since fallen asleep, as had his brother [illegible], leaving a widow and three little ones, poor things" to struggle through the world. For himself, he had fought in several actions, and after fourteen years of service he had returned home to his mountains; for, after all, there was no place like them, and he could not die happy elsewhere. Then was Crozatier obliged to relate all the vicissitudes of his life, to which Tailhère listened with transport, and sweet indeed was the sound to the old soldier and his foster-brother, as they stood together, after so many years' interval, watching the last golden rays gradually die away on the declining [illegible] opposite them, or still kindly lingering on the little chapel at the top of rock aiguille (needle rock). "Nothing's changed here," said the peasant, as he thus talked in the village, when he and Crozatier turned away from the scene that they had so often contemplated together in childhood, and that had left an indelible impression on the already poetic imagination of the artist. That was the last day of poverty for Tailhère, for every child of his [illegible] were generously provided for by the warm-hearted founder, and that for life.

In the meanwhile a missionary had been preaching at some fête in honour of Our Lady of Le Puy, and in his sermon had declared that a colossal bronze statue of the Virgin, raised on "Rocher Corneille" would insure a regeneration of the Velay, and elevate Le Puy again to its former glory. The bishop immediately seized the idea, and Crozatier was written to on the subject. He was overjoyed at the thought, and lost not a moment in calculating what so gigantic an undertaking would entail and, although his heart sank at the enormous sum requisite, which showed him that his whole fortune would not suffice, yet every penny was needed for the accomplishment of this stupendous enterprise, which he considered would be another glory to his native town. He repaired with an engineer to the spot, examined the pedestal that he knew to be cracked in various parts, so much so that iron bars had been judged necessary to bind them together; and, although both he and the engineer returned, doubting whether so heavy a bulk would not crush down the rock altogether, yet he hoped still, and examined plan after plan for success. In the meanwhile, strange to say, the bishop opened a competition without further ado, and artists were begged to send in their designs for Our Lady of Le Puy. Crozatier received his order with the rest, and, without feeling wounded at such a proceeding, he set to work to obtain a victory, for which he himself would have paid. Of course his design was not chosen, "none is prophet in his own country." It was sent back to him under the pretence that it arrived too late, although the funds to pay for the work are not yet raised. The bishop has since received a promise from the Emperor that he will award him the cannons conquered at Sebastopol. Crozatier died a few months after this, leaving money for a monumental fountain to be erected in the Place du Breuil, opposite the "Préfecture," for which he has also left the design, and which they say will be magnificent. He also has left money for the museum, and to different charities in the town, and an endowment for a certain number of young men to be sent to Paris every year to learn sculpture or carving. Thus Crozatier's name is now so blended with that of Le Puy, that I trust to gain my reader's forgiveness for so long a history—a history which I myself found so interesting.

And now, if before we return to Plain Marguerat you will descend the mountain with us on this side midway between Aiguille and Le Puy, we will pass through the Faubourg St. Laurent, whose church—an antique pile—we visited, and there saw the tomb of the famous warrior and high-constable of France, the Breton Du Guesclin, who, in the 14th century, fought against the English army, and drove it out of Normandy. He is said never to have been vanquished, but by the famous Chandos, the Black Prince's general, who made him twice a prisoner. He died not far from Le Puy, while besieging Château Neuf Randon in the neighbouring department. I was surprised at finding the tomb of an old enemy of England in this isolated place, and I saluted it with respect and awe. Me thought it was the last resting-place of a compatriot, for he was a Briton, although a French one, and his prowess against the invaders of his country proved him to have been of that stock! We did not long linger in this edifice, a dreary-looking place, with nothing else of note in it. A great quantity of beggars, as usual, burst round an image of the Virgin, and, as we left the building, a poor woman entered, and dipping her fingers in the holy-water, then offered them to me to touch, in order to cross myself as well, which is a custom in some Roman churches in the country. Two or three juvenile beggars outside the door besieged us with "La charité, s'il vous plaît," in the well-known piteous voice and look assumed for the occasion; and, as we returned home through the sinuous streets, with their paved centres, we remarked here and there a public fountain—for no house has its private supply of water—all must go to the fountains, where the assembly of servants, with their earthen pitchers, which they carry on their heads, recalled to my imagination Rebecca at the well, and I fancied what a commotion the arrival of an Eleazar would have caused amongst them, particularly if he had made a display of bracelets and other jewels, for, surely, the oriental women were not fonder of these articles of finery than the fair sex here, and the commonest neck has its gold or gilt chain, to which are suspended an enormous cross and heart of the same metal; and, as for rings and ear-rings, my Madelaine even, who is very sober in her taste, would no more think of going without her gilt ear-rings. She told me the other day that she had bought them with her hair.

"With your hair!" cried I, very much surprised.

"Yes, madame. Oh! that is a very common custom here, particularly in this country."

"And where do you sell it?" enquired I.

"In the market, madame."

A day or two after she called my attention to the window, it being market day, and, pointing to a stall we could see opposite.

"There, Madame, do you not see that long tail of hair that is blowing about in the wind?" asked she. "That is a sign that the man there is a hair-merchant; and if you wait a moment you will see him buy."

My curiosity detained me, and I accordingly watched. Very soon two young peasant girls approached, with jaunty looks almost concealed under their little white caps surmounted with a low-crowned black hat, the head-dress here. These hats resemble small hats, with a crown about two inches high. The girls removed both hat and cap, and their long tresses were let down. Then the merchant examined it, and there were a few words in bargaining, and the raven hair fell under the merciless scissors that the man held in his hands. One girl received a handkerchief; the other, a cap in return. I was truly indignant, and begged my maid never to be guilty of such barbarity while with me, saying that I would rather give her anything she might want. She stared with surprise at my indignation, and seemed to think that really English people are odder even than what they have the reputation of being, if that is possible. And I have no doubt but that she will soon require something if only to see whether I will put my promise into execution, and defend her hair.

M. B.

MY MODEL.

(An Artist's Story.)

BY JOHN D. CARTWRIGHT.

"Do you want a model, sir?"

I started, and looked up at the questioner so abruptly that I frightened her. It was early morning, and the quiet street of Pimlico, down which I was passing, was almost empty. The sunlight was streaming over the tops of the opposite houses, and the housemaids were washing the doorsteps; and the milkmen, with their cans, were the only persons to be seen, except the slender girl who addressed me.

"You are an artist, sir?" she said, seeing my hesitation, and turning her eyes away from mine.

I assented.

"And do you not want a model—a lady, sir, to paint from, such"—and she hesitated—"such as I am?"

A rich crimson blush suffused itself over her face as she said this, and I looked another way that I might not add to her confusion. It was strange, at the moment when she put the question I was perplexed because I had been unable to obtain a model suitable to the pre-Raphaelite picture I was studying. With great disappointment I had seen one after another of the many beautiful women who sit for the academicians; but none of them answered my ideal; and here, in the street before me, was a lady with the very expression of face I desired to paint, positively volunteering her services!

"I have been seeking for one," I replied, on recovering from my surprise; "but I certainly did not expect to find one here this morning."

"I should do, then?" she said, eagerly, lifting her eyes up to mine again.

"Perhaps so," I replied; "but—"

"I can anticipate what you would say, sir," she cried, interrupting me; "but let me walk a little way by your side, and explain how I knew that you wanted a model."

"Oh, certainly," I said, and turned toward Buckingham Palace. She had come from that direction, and I thought I could talk with her as she returned.

"No, not that way, please—any way but that!" She spoke hurriedly, and then blushing at this betrayal of her excitement, added, "It is so much quieter up here!"

I had no object other than that I have stated for walking toward the Palace, so I readily turned round again, and we proceeded up the street together.

It was some time before either spoke, and I occupied the interval in observing her more closely than I had hitherto done. If it were possible to present you with a photograph of her, that might describe her faithfully—words cannot. Her face was like a sweet flower of the spring, innocent and full of loveliness. Her figure was as graceful as the reed that grows by the brook, and waves at every breath of wind. No one feature was exalted to the disparagement of the rest; nor was it in their regularity that the face would be eminent, but it was the simple sympathetic expression of the whole that made its way at once to the heart of the beholder.

"If I say that I was at Mrs. [illegible]'s last night, sir," she said, as finding I did not break the silence, "you would understand how I knew that you wanted a model, and had sought for one at the Royal Academy in vain. I know the conditions, that whoever you choose must be prepared to accompany you into the country and stay through the autumn; and I am quite ready to do so if—if I shall do for your picture."

She paused, as if awaiting my answer; and, as I turned to look at her, I saw her eyes were glazed with tears, and the blue semi-circle below them told that tears had not unfrequently run down her beautiful cheeks. I did not like to act prematurely in accepting her services—she had come to me so strangely; yet it might all be explained; and I should certainly not find another model whose figure and face were so good, and so thoroughly adapted to my purpose.

"Sir," she said, "you hesitate, and I am afraid you think me very bold and unwomanly to come to you as I have done; but if I had not known you to be a gentleman I should not have dared. Oh dear! I am very miserable! I don't know what to do!"

"Will you tell me so much of your history as will explain why—why you wish to leave London?" I said.

"I really cannot, sir!" she said, drawing her veil over her face to hide the tears that began to flow; "but I am in a great deal of trouble, without a friend in London, and I must go away. Oh, if you will but trust me! All I want is to get away from some one who persecuted me, till my brother comes home from India; and then he will protect me, and reward you, and bless you for your kindness to me."

I am never proof against a woman who appeals to me in trouble and tears; and after some talk—in all of which I failed to learn anything more than that she was in great trouble, and wanted a place of refuge, for which, if I would grant it, she was to repay me by a life of gratitude—I parted from her at the door of the house at which I was staying; and smiling that the occasion of my visit was tending to conclude the arrangement for her to go with us to the country into Warwickshire.

"And you will come to me, Miss Addison, at five this afternoon?" I said, while her hand was locked in mine. "But I have forgotten to ask your name."

She took a card from her portmonnaie, and wishing me good morning, hurried down the street. In the pause between the ring of the bell and the opening of the door I watched her retreating figure. A strange interest—almost a fascination—had taken possession of me, and it was not till she was out of sight that I looked at the card she had given me. On it was engraved—

"Miss Amy Elston,"

My sister Edith and I had, from a very tender age, been the centre of each other's affections—as it does sometimes happen in a family that one brother and sister attach themselves peculiarly, to the prejudice of the others. So it was, at least, with us. Edith had entered into all my studies; Edith had accompanied me to Italy, read to me while I sketched on the banks of the Arno, and tended on me when I had the fever in Florence—as only a loving woman can do; and when we returned, and I set up an establishment of my own, Edith, still inseparable from all my doings, settled with me to keeping house. I had acquired a habit of leaving many questions for her to dispose of; and her clear judgment, as well as her affection, well entitled her to all my confidence, and to the power her opinion had in ruling my affairs. So it was nothing more than natural that I should, in this delicate question of the "model," leave it to her decision.

"What a long walk you have had, Arthur!" she said, as I entered the room, with the card still in my hand.

"I have found a model, Edith, where I least expected. Just the face I wanted, and as beautiful as Raffaelle's 'La Fornarina,' in the 'Uffizi.'"

Edith listened to my account of the strange way in which I had found—or rather the model had found me—with an interest scarcely less than my own, only smiling every now and then as I ran off into another and another rhapsody on her beauty.

"Why I declare," she said, as I finished my story, "it is romantic as a tale of chivalry! The beautiful maiden, throwing herself for protection upon the gallant knight, who seems ready and willing enough, for that matter, to do battle on her behalf. I suppose you will be presently falling in love, and come then asking me to hand over the keys!"

"Well, you see I shall have to ask you first, Edith; for I could not even engage this lady without consulting you."

"And I should think not, indeed. When a strange woman is to come into the house and dine with us, I have a right to be consulted, and to know for myself that she is a lady."

"Well, well, you will see this afternoon," I said; "and I trust we shall go down to Ashburn to-morrow; for these bright days that are slipping away so fast are very precious."

We spent the morning together, making little purchases, and calling upon some friends; but both looked toward the hour when Miss Elston was to call with an interest neither wholly equal in anxiety.

"Edith, this is Miss Elston," I said, as the door was thrown open, and the lady I had walked with in the morning entered. She was, in dress, appearance, and speech a most perfect lady. Her tearful face and modest bearing made their way at once to my sister's heart; and I saw, long before the interview was ended, that her admiration of Miss Elston was quite as great as my own. The hat had been replaced by a bonnet, that allowed the beauty of her eyes and brow to be seen more distinctly; and, contrary to my expectation, the second impression she made upon me was even more favourable than the first. If I had had the actual heroine of the story I was about to paint, I could not have been more fortunate. Her explanation to Edith was scarcely more clear than that she had given to me—She was persecuted with relentless cruelty, which she would not divulge, and she sought for a refuge with us. If we did not grant it she would have to seek it elsewhere—on the continent, she said, or wherever would afford the best hiding-place for a time.

This was the substance of her story; and at its close my sister said, "I will not do you the injustice of believing that you are doing a wrong thing; and I will not further oppress you by trying to find out what you deem it best to hide; though, as you are to go with us into the country, and will necessarily be thrown into close companionship with us, I wish it had appeared best to you to trust your secret to our keeping; it would have given us confidence; and if the wrongs you seem to suffer under are redressable, you would, I am sure, have had my brother's best assistance, and both our sympathies."

The sight of a beautiful face in sorrow and tears is not pleasant; and Edith's half-expressed wish that she would tell us how and by whom she was wronged, brought back to her face all the distress her early words had driven away.

"At Fellowfield House, Miss Elston," I said, "you will be as quiet and retired as the fireside in an evening-time. A score of houses and a church make up the entire village; and, except Mr. Withers, the rector, we have no visitors. Let me tell you, so you will not be deceived, as to how monotonous an existence you will find there. We usually rise with the sun, and are nodding-out, or had more than an hour after the sun. I paint from the early morning till four in the afternoon, when we dine; and after that we walk in the meadows by the Avon, or read till bedtime. The quiet, even life I require for my work, makes it imperative for me to live like a hermit; and so everything is managed, at Fellowfield, by one domestic and my sister, in the simplest way."

"I shall sleep in the better, sir, for all this; and shall never, never forget your generosity in permitting me to share it with you."

So it was arranged, and on the following morning she was waiting for us on the platform at the Euston Station, from whence we went to

Warwick, and on by the pleasant corn-fields of Ashore to Fallowfield House.

* * * * * * *

Very few of the many occupations men have made for themselves are so engrossing as the art of the painter; but still fewer have so pure and sweet a reward to bestow upon their followers, or offer half such inducements to the man who loves nature: for, to succeed in painting, it is not enough that you should have a correct knowledge of form, a clear eye to distinguish colour, and a ready conception of beauty; but you must also have sympathy with the thing you paint. Without this the faithful fidelity, the high poetry of art can never be rendered. You may paint a portrait, but you cannot make a picture: just as a man who cannot see all beauty, feel all misery, can never make a poet.

Few events worth recording marked the three weeks succeeding our return to Ashore; the preliminary sketches for my picture and the details occupying me, and leaving Edith and Miss Elston very much together. They had become fond of each other's society; the quiet, gentle ways of Miss Elston just according with Edith's tastes. I, too, found her society a great pleasure; and after the early reserve, so natural to the circumstances of our meeting, had worn away, we walked together many a sweet evening, when the sun was setting in all the grandeur and glory of an autumn evening. I have never, since, known autumn evenings so sweet as those. The voices of the reapers and gleaners, busy in the fields, the delight I had in contemplating my work, and, above all, the pleasure it was to interest Miss Elston, and make her forget her sorrow, whatever it might arise from, combined to complete my happiness. Perhaps I was not so disinterested in all the efforts I made to wean her from uneasy thoughts; for my greatest felicity was, in some measure, dependent upon her.

If I had had no greater reward than that which showed itself in her face, I should have been amply repaid. The blue semicircles gradually retired from under her eyes; her cheeks regained their colour, and the happiest change was evident in her whole being. Every day I felt more sure she was justified in what she had done; and my indignation against her (to me unknown) injurer increased in an exact ratio with my decreasing belief that I was doing wrong in giving her the home she had so earnestly pleaded for. Her nature was simple, affectionate, and as pure as the nature of a spring violet. It was impossible that she should do wrong; yet I wished she would tell me all—I longed so to be able to speak words of comfort to her; to assure her with my own tongue, if possible, that I thought she had done right, and to keep her from the thoughts that made her so despondent whenever she was much alone; and for this reason Edith or I contrived to be constantly with her. She had come to us like a little timid, trembling bird, that had been hunted by boys; and surely it was only the work of a true man and woman to ease her of her trouble by winning her affection. She was, as I have said, all I could desire for my picture: a contrast to Edith (who was the only other figure), and yet a by no means violent one, that could offend the most critical eye. That picture was "Effie Deans" and her sister "Jeanie." Miss Elston—or "Effie," as we used after a little while to call her—was just a prototype of the beautiful trusting and erring heroine; while "Jeanie" was almost as faithfully represented by Edith; but, as she used to say, "she had na the brown een."

By the time the leaves were falling, my picture was far advanced, and every day that served for its advancement, served also to strengthen the friendship and affection that existed between us and My Model.

In the long evenings we occupied ourselves by reading aloud the beautiful tale from which my picture had its birth, so that I might keep its spirit well before my mind. But when Miss Elston read, my thoughts were more of her than of the tale and of the fancied likeness existing between her and Effie. I could look at her when she was reading, and not disturb her; and that was why I liked her to read: not that I did not know her face. I had looked at it as only an artist who looks to draw it and take its expression as well as the lines can know a face. It was in those quiet nights, while she was reading, that I first knew I loved her. The mysterious trouble in which she had come to me, her simple loving way and womanly grace, had won upon me so stealthily that the first time it came across me that I loved her I gave an involuntary start that made her stop in the middle of the sentence she was reading, and it was many days before I could allow myself to acknowledge that I really loved her, as the one woman whom of all the world I would like to make my wife.

Edith (a woman's eyes are always keenest in these matters) knew it long before me, and, by frequent allusion to my altered bearing, sought to draw the only secret I am conscious of ever having kept from her, from my tongue. It was a long time before she succeeded.

Miss Elston had written to her brother the first week after she came to Ashore. There was one other correspondent—a lady, to whom she wrote, and from her every week brought a reply. The effect of these letters was very contrary: sometimes the result would be shown in an increase of friendliness and satisfaction; and, at others, I have seen a tear come into her eye as she has kissed Edith in bidding her good night. Sometimes I did not paint for days; that was when I was perplexing myself with questions about her past history, that I could never solve, but that kept me awake in bed many a night, in those early days of our acquaintance, before I could persuade myself to tell her of my love. It was the day following the receipt of one of these letters which had exercised a more gloomy influence over Miss Elston than any of its predecessors, that I found a fragment of a letter in my studio. I should not have noticed it, but that it lay upon a sketch I worked, and the words upon it struck me forcibly. I had often brought the letters from the village-school, which was also the post-office, and I knew it was the handwriting of Miss Elston's correspondent. The words on it were: "He is making you very miserable." They were underlined, and the paper was torn and ragged at the edge where the "here" had joined the "victory" to make "everywhere." The whole of that, and many succeeding days and nights did those words haunt me, waking or asleep. I only think in every description of handwriting that has ever been written or printed, and the tail was always in larger capitals than the rest.

I think the first time form in which I looked at the question, was in trying to discover how the fragment had got carried there. Was it possible that Miss Elston had discovered the attachment I only just knew of myself, and had taken this means—the gentlest—only means at her command of telling me not to encourage a passion that could only be attended with misery? At first this seemed probable—almost certain; but by-and-bye it was dismissed, and the real way in which it came to lie there was made clear to me. Miss Elston had read her letter in the garden behind the house, and there tore it into inches, one of which had been carried by the wind, and deposited where I found it. There seemed a kind of special Providence in this—warning me to dismiss all thoughts but those of friendship for "Effie" from my bosom; but that was impossible. I had not sought her; when she came I had not gone to work, and deliberately made myself love her. I had not gone to love, but love had come to me—taken possession of my whole being—supplanted the place my art had always held in my affections; and now love must go on to the end of the chapter. And who was he? the man who was searching everywhere for her? The first question was hardly set at rest in my mind, when this took its place. Her youth, her connection—ten thousand things rose up, to cast one of the terrible thoughts that it might be her husband. Who ever wished, like I did in disbelieve a thing he would not find twenty grounds of misgivings in? And, if not a husband, who then, and what was he? What claim had he upon that young and beautiful girl of almost childlike simplicity, who had been looking confidingly up into my face for so many happy weeks? Happy weeks! Ah! they are all over now. This question echoed again and again in my mind, until the thing became a demon of gigantic proportions, whom I saw at every turning in my dreams, pouncing down upon my Effie.

And all this while, though I often sat before the canvas, I did no painting, and the change in my manner destroyed our happiness altogether. A hundred times I made up my mind to tell Effie of my love, and conjure her to tell me the history of her past. This was what I wanted first, for I felt I could not ask her for love, ignorant as I was of her a few months before,

and meaning to me in the mysterious way she had done.

Tossed about by these harassing doubts and fears, the months went slowly by. At Christmas we made a faint attempt to be merry, but were not successful in the least degree; the only things in which I found any relief were my work and my occupations. Perhaps the relief the former brought to me resulted from the habit into which Edith and Miss Elston had fallen, of closing the windows, and I used to sit and smoke and dream away the while. But spring was coming, and there was yet much to do to the picture.

"You'll never get it done in time for the Academy," Edith said. "Never!"

And after that I worked as I had never worked before. In the kinder society of Effie and Jessie I lost my own. While the daylight lasted, and I could paint, I was comparatively happy; but in the night, when we all gathered together, I could not talk freely, as I had been before I loved her.

Miss Elston was by no means an unmarked spectator of my passion, and all I had once done to gain her affection was now repaid by her tenfold; she knew where I hid my pipe, and would fetch it; she knew what passages I liked her to linger over best; but she did all these little loving kindnesses in a strange, sad way. Her sadness, I thought, is all the better for my picture—all the worse for me.

At last my picture was done. I had never painted like that before—I have never painted like it since. It was done, and now I would tell Edith and Effie the secret that had so long borne me down.

"Now that it is finished, Edith, how do you like it?" I said. Effie had just gone out of the room.

"It is better than you have ever done before, Arthur. The same spirit that lived in Raffael, when he painted 'La Fornarina,' has lived in you while you were drawing Effie. Oh, Arthur!" she said, lowering her voice, and laying her hand upon my shoulder, "why have you tried to keep a secret—such a secret—from me? That face is almost divine, Arthur; but

"[illegible]; Love unperceived—
A [illegible]
[illegible]
[illegible]"

and your love has been a burden to you, and you would not let me help to bear it."

Edith spoke passionately; she felt that I had wronged her by keeping my secret. She was right; but I had wronged myself more, for I had suffered many hours of misery in silence, that she would have made less heavy to bear. Standing there before the picture, I told her the story she had already divined, and that night I told Effie also.

It was a past February evening; the wind was very cold, and rushing and moaning through the trees outside. Miss Elston and I were sitting alone on the hearth, and the flickering blaze from the fire were our only light.

"Have you any tidings of your brother yet, Effie?" I said.

"He said he is in England to-morrow, and will come here to thank you for your noble generosity to me, the moment he arrives."

"I am very glad he is coming, Effie."

There was a pause. I broke it.

"Effie, I have been thinking of the many, many happy days we have had together here since you first came."

There was another awkward pause, for Effie did not speak. I broke it again, and this time I spoke to the purpose.

"Effie, dearest Effie," I said, rising from my chair and crossing the hearth to where she sat, "I love you."

"Don't, oh don't say so, Mr. Addison!" she cried, covering her face with her hands.

"Why should I not? I have been loving you more and more every day since you first came to me in sorrow. I have been yearning towards you, longing to know the cause of your misery, that I might comfort and console you with sympathy and manly tender love. Till I knew you I loved my art first, best of everything; now I love only you."

She uncovered her face, and put me from her.

"Dear Mr. Addison," she said, bursting into tears, "don't—don't pain me so."

"But why should it pain you, friendless and alone as you are, to hear that I love you, as the woman I would make my wife—that I would die for you if it were necessary for your happiness? Effie, do you love another?"

"I love none other," she answered, sinking into her chair; "but I am married."

Married! Married! My senses reeled, as I heard the words; and the hideous spectre of the lover rose up like the ghost of a deadly antagonist whom I had slain in battle.

I could hear Miss Elton's low sobs, and my sister's footsteps on the stairs. She hesitated at the door; and I said, with an unnatural calmness that had succeeded the momentary storm, "You can come in, Edith," and then I sat down.

Edith, with a woman's penetration, saw at once our misery, and was silent. Oh the bitterest of those few silent moments, when no sound was to be heard but the moaning of the chill February wind, and when there was no hope in my future!

When I looked round again Effie was wiping the tears away, and when she had done, she got up and came to where I sat. There was a stool near my feet, and she knelt down upon it; my hands were resting on my knees, and she clasped hers over them, resting her chin upon them, and, looking up into my face with a sad, pitying, beautiful glance, that was very hard to bear. The firelight shone out cheerfully on us; but that was the only cheerful thing in the whole room. She never looked more beautiful and loveable than then. She wore a dress I had once praised, that fitted tight to her neck and wrists, whose narrow frills of spotless linen fell back upon the sleeve.

"Dear, dear friend," she said, "let me tell you, at last, the history I hoped never to have had to reveal to you, of my folly and another's guilt. But let me first obtain that which will be my only comfort, your pardon for the deception I have acted toward you, and the pain I have so unwittingly caused you, whom, of all the world, I most desired to please, and for whose happiness I would have sacrificed the dearest joy of my life.

"I will not linger over the history that has embittered my life, and that will have, from this hour, another deep regret attached to it; for I know it will lessen the esteem and good opinion you have had of me. Three years ago (when I was but seventeen), against the will of all my friends, I married. Unfortunately for me I was very rich, and my riches brought me many suitors, among them many worthy men, and not a few bad ones. Let it suffice to say I chose the worst."

The tears Miss Elton strove to repress arose and choked her utterance.

"I don't," she continued—"I really don't know how to tell you, Edith, what a fool I have been. It was infatuation—madness; but I loved him alone, and could no more help it then than I could make it now. I loved him, and believed he loved me too. I never doubted that his word was the truth, though I now know it to have been always false; for, unlike most men who do lie, he seemed to do it because he liked it best, and never spoke the truth even when it was easiest. My wilfulness—my disobedience perhaps merited punishment; but not the bitter, bitter misery I have undergone. Before a month was over he told me that he had married me only to pay his debts, and took no pains to hide from me his real character; and yet I loved him almost as much as ever I had done—loved him madly and blindly—while he heaped indignities upon me.

"When I went to my father's house, soon after my marriage, he refused to see me, so greatly had I displeased him. My mother was dead, Alfred was at sea, and I did not care to go to any of my old friends or some distant relatives, who I knew would take pattern from my father and refuse to associate with me. My misery was complete. Sometimes a whole week went by, and he never came home; and when he did, it was only to abuse me and make me sign a paper for more money.

"I never objected to sign those papers—never even looked how much each one represented. I only tried to allure him—to make him love me as I loved him. But it was all in vain; he did not seem to have anything tender, anything manly in his nature, and his cruelty had made me almost cease to love him; when a great change came over him, and he came to live in the house regularly, like any other man; and I thought at last his heart was turned towards me, for he seemed gentler than he had ever done before, and more like the man who first won my

him. I did everything a woman could do to make his home attractive. I learned his games at cards, that I might play with him in the long winter nights; indeed, as I have said, I did everything. But it was all of no avail, for it was not long ere I discovered what he wanted and hoped to gain by this feigned affection and alleged devotion.

"In the two miserable years we had been married he had wasted all my money. How, I did not know at the time—though I do now. I thought he must have gambled it away; but he spent it in a worse way than that. And then he wanted me to rob my brother Alfred of his property. I don't know how it came to be so, but Alfred's money and mine were so mixed up together that we never knew which was which, and either could have claimed it all. Poor Aunt Milicent, when she left it us, never knew how much misery my share would cause me, or she would have made another use of it. It had been agreed between us, before Alfred went out the last time, that we should carry out the spirit of aunt's bequest, and each take an equal share, with mutual trust in each other. I did not know then that I could possibly get his, or he mine; and I only discovered it from a letter my father (who still refused to see me) sent just in time to prevent my giving the power over it to my husband.

"Oh Edith, I do not believe that I ever deserved my father should treat me as he did. I had refused to sign the papers, and my husband had, by a great effort, kept his temper down, and asked me to walk out with him, and he said I should think better of it by the morning, for he really must have the cash to pay a pressing debt with. It was not much he wanted, and he had been so absent, so kind, that I had scarcely the heart to refuse him.

"While we were out that evening we passed my father in the street, and he would not look at me. We did not speak of the money again that night; but I lay awake all through it, trying to frame an excuse; for I saw, if he once overcame me, that he would never rest till he had robbed my brother of every shilling. In the morning he began by entreating me to give it to him. I refused, and he flew into a passion. I shudder now, and think I hear his terrible voice, uttering curses and imprecations such as he did then."

The wind had risen, and was howling round the chimneys. There did seem a voice mingling with it; but the misery of my hopeless love, and the pity inspired by Miss Elston's narrative, had heightened my fancy. It could be nothing more than imagination: still it seemed to be heard by all of us at once, for Edith started visibly, Miss Elston paused, and I looked round the dim room to see that we were alone.

"He assailed me," she continued, speaking hurriedly, "with my father's disregard; he cursed me because he had no child, and I knew not what he threatened to do unless I did as he wanted me before the night. I was resolute; determined to bear anything, everything, rather than betray my brother's trust. His conduct every day became more unbearable. Sometimes he would stay away for days and days, and then only come, half intoxicated, to heap curses upon me.

"Just at this time my father died, and, feeling more than ever the loneliness and misery of my position, I sought some of my old friends—and among them Mrs. Dean, a friend of my mother's. But I could not bring myself to tell even her what I am telling you; though I have written it in a letter to her since I came here, where I should never have been but for her kind thoughtfulness, for she suggested it to me.

"Though I had refused to give him my brother's money, I did not hesitate, when need came, to use some of it for myself. I had no other, and he would not have cared if I had starved; but when he knew that I did so he was wilder, fiercer than ever, and sometimes I had to creep away from his heavy fist, aiming a blow at me. I bore it all as meekly as I could. If I sinned greatly in marrying him, surely my chastisement has been great also; for the circumstances of my life were made utterly wretched than those recorded in the history of criminals, and I had no sustaining love to aid me in bearing them—nothing but the consciousness of my own innocence to keep faith in me through it all.

"I was at Mrs. Dean's that night when you were there, and saw you, though I did not mingle with the visitors. My heart was very heavy, and I was then nearly tempted to commit a great crime, to end my misery with my life! For I had discovered that my husband was living with another woman, to enrich whose house and adorn whose person he would have stolen Alfred's money, as he had already done mine! I saw that woman in her house; she insulted me as none but the lowest, basest of women can insult, scorn. And he—unnatural monster that he is—stood coolly by, and laughed in my face!—Hark!"

I had seen the tears glistening upon Miss Elston's cheeks by the light of the fire, as she knelt closer to me, narrating this story. But at the utterance of that last word "Hark!" her voice was not that of a woman in sorrow, but of a maniac in her wildest moment. She started to her feet. There was a hoarse voice shouting in the garden, and my dog, aroused by it, was barking very fiercely. I got up from my seat, and she threw herself upon [illegible], shrieking wildly, "It is he!—it is he!"

A moment later there was a long, loud rap, from a stick, upon the door. I placed Miss Elston in a chair, and moved toward it. Edith tried to soothe her, to recall her wider reason.

"Be still, and make the house to listen you while I live!" I said, before I left her, calling Turk—a huge Newfoundland—to my side, as I approached the door, and the latch was raised. I opened it as Edith lit the lamp.

"Mr. Addison?" said a gruff voice.

"Yes, sir," I said. "What is your business?"

He took two strides into the room; Turk growled, and kept his head against my hand, ready to obey my slightest movement. Miss Elston rose from her chair, and put one hand on Edith's shoulder.

"What do you mean by entering my house unasked? What is your business?" I demanded, sternly.

"I came to claim my wife—and that's she!"

Miss Elston gave a loud, long shriek, and fell upon the floor.

"If you attempt to advance, sir," I said, with an unnatural coolness, "I shall stop you." I looked down at Turk as I spoke, and laid my hand upon his head. With him to aid me I should not have feared a vicious ox. "This woman is under my roof and my protection. She has been persecuted—she is terrified now, and I desire that you will at once quit my house, which you have violated by an unbidden entrance!"

He swore a terrible oath, that made me shudder, and put out his arm to move me from the path to his swooning wife. Turk growled again.

"One word of mine," I said, in the same calm voice as before, "will send my dog's teeth into your throat! Attempt to pass me and that word will be spoken. This is not the hour or the place in which to claim a wife you have brutally ill-treated; therefore begone from my house!"

Expostulation, threats, oaths followed; but I kept my place, and Turk kept his.

"Unless you leave this place," I said, passion taking the place of the unnatural calm I had at first experienced, "words will not avail you, and I shall treat you as I would a burglar in the night, and leave you to the mercy of this dog!"

With another fierce oath he left the room, and I made fast the door.

All night he lurked about the house, and all night long Turk kept watch and guard, passing from room to room with an occasional low growl, just in keeping with the unnatural, desolate sighing and moaning of the wind, to which, through that long night, we three sat listening before the fire. There was such a sense of mutual confidence in keeping close together, that we tacitly remained there; the pale and sorely-troubled Effie of my picture, with her head resting on my sister's shoulder, and seldom speaking. So we passed the night.

In the morning I went to the village inn. He had been there before daylight, and waited till they arose; when he had drunk a great quantity of strong drink, and gone away. In the gloaming of the evening Miss Elston's brother came, and, after a sojourn with us of a few days, they left Ashbourne together.

* * * * * *

Twelve years have gone since that picture of "Effie in the prison" was seen on the walls of the Royal Academy. Twelve times the spring has blossomed into summer and ripened into mellow autumn since Miss Elston and her brother left Fallowfield-house. It is autumn now, and the sun is sinking below the hill, and the voice of the gleaner is loud in the field, and entering in at the open window of my studio, where this last scene I have to show is occurring.

Resting on my easel is a picture of two sisters in the cell of a prison, and before it stand my sister (still Edith Addison), my wife, and two dear children—a girl and a ruddy-faced boy.

"But, Ma," says the girl—who is, in fact, a miniature of the pale sister in the picture—"how pale and thin you were then."

"Yes, Effie dear," I take it upon myself to answer, "Ma was pale and thin and full of trouble thirteen years ago, when she first became My Model."

LEAVES FOR THE LITTLE ONES.

THE LIVING TOYS.

(From the German).

Once upon a time there lived a little boy—I wish there were more like him—who was so good-humoured, that his face was as bright and as pleasant as a sunbeam. Everything was right with him, everything pleased him; he laughed with everyone, and was universally beloved. If people did what he wished them to do, he was overjoyed; if they did not, he patiently submitted.

When our little friend—whom we will call Max—went out to take a walk in the town, he thought everything beautiful and grand, but more especially he liked the soldiers. As a regiment marched by, to the sound of fife and drum, Max would clap his hands for joy, beat time to the music, and march along with his little feet as stately and brave as the tall officers with their gilded epaulettes and clanking swords. This being the case, it may easily be imagined that of all his numerous play-things none were so dear to Max as his three boxes of tin soldiers—artillery, cavalry, and infantry—which his uncle had given him on his birthday. He would sit for hours at his little table, setting them out in battalions, making them parade, march, and exercise. Still they sometimes appeared rather tiresome with their stiff unbending forms, looking with their noses straight before them, and with the same faces every day.

It happened one bright summer's morning that Max got up earlier than usual, went into the nursery, and remained there playing with his tin soldiers for several hours. When he was tired, he went out into the garden. There he admired and caressed the flowers—he was not allowed to gather them—jumped and sprang about, and played at leap-frog over the small clumps of laurel on the lawn; always looking carefully about, that he might not tread on a worm, or injure a plant, or kick off the flower-buds with his heels. All at once he was met in an alley of the garden by a beautiful child, about his own age.

Max stared at the strange boy—and well he might; for the new comer was clothed in a robe whiter than the cherry-blossoms on the tree, and on each shoulder was a little golden wing that shone brighter than the sun. Our good-humoured friend was quite dazzled; nevertheless he remembered that his kind mamma had taught him to be polite to every one, and though his great blue eyes still remained wide open with astonishment, he mustered up courage to make a bow to the beautiful stranger, and said in a friendly tone, "Good morning!"

The child nodded and smiled, and said very graciously, "You are such a good boy, you may wish something. Let it be what it will, I will grant your request."

Max did not think very long about it. He fetched a deep breath, and then said, "Oh! if my tin soldiers would but get alive!"

Then the beautiful boy laughed, and nodded his head; he kissed Max on the middle of the forehead with his rosy lips, and flew up into the air as swiftly as a butterfly. Our little friend remained quite still, looking up, long after the wonderful child had disappeared; then suddenly recollecting himself, he gave a great jump for joy, laughed aloud in the delight of his heart, and ran straight into the house, and up-stairs into the nursery. There stood all his play-things on the round table, just as he had left them. There was a town, with a broad street of painted houses; at one end stood the church, surrounded by trees; in the street stood the infantry, while the artillery with their cannons were ranged in a circle near the church. At one side of the town Max had built a bridge with bricks, and had placed a piece of silver paper under to represent the water. The cavalry officer was already on the bridge; and behind him came the trumpeter. The remaining soldiers followed after, three abreast. All these were as stiff and upright as when Max had quitted them to play in the garden. But now, as he stepped on tiptoe up to the table, what wonders happened! The wooden houses had got bright windows, and pretty little girls and women looked out here and there. The church-doors opened wide, and through them could be seen pictures, and sculptures, and a little altar, and a beautifully carved screen; while in the tower a little peal of bells began to ring, so fine and fairy-like, that one must listen very intently to be able to hear them. The trees around the church had budded into leaf and blossom; and birds not much bigger than a pin's head hopped and fluttered among their branches, and sang most beautifully, but suddenly their voices were rendered quite inaudible, for the six trumpeters in the street began to blow their trumpets in splendid style, playing a grand new march; the officer raised his sword in the air, and called out in a small shrill voice, "March!" and all the infantry soldiers lifted their legs and marched round the table.

Our little boy stood dumb-founded before the table, and did not know what to say or how to look. All at once the artillery began to march out of their circle; the little horses with the leaden cannons neighed, ran, and trotted; the cannons rattled over the table with a deafening noise. As soon as they were fairly out of the town the artillery men took it into their heads to fire, and made such an uproar that all the birds in the trees rose up into the air with loud cries. At the same time there was a great clattering on the other side of the town, as if five hundred knitting-needles fell on the table all together. It was the cavalry galloping over the bridge. The silver paper had become real water; and a little black speck that had been upon it was changed into a boat. The brown horse of one of the tin riders turned restive, and fell splash over the parapet of the bridge into the water. Then the boatman came rowing along in his little bark, and fished out the man and the horse. But they proved too heavy for the boat; it turned over, and rider, horse, and boatman fell struggling into the stream. Then Max gave a loud scream and woke up! He had dreamed the whole history of the beautiful boy and the living toys, while he was fast asleep under the elder-bush in the garden.

At first our good-humoured boy felt rather sorry and disappointed, but he soon recovered himself, and displayed his usual merry face and bright smile. He laughed with his mother about his funny dream, and took quite as much pleasure as before in his pretty tin soldiers.

OUR LIBRARY TABLE.

Autobiography of Miss Cornelia Knight, Lady Companion to the Princess Charlotte. (*W. H. Allen and Co., Leadenhall-street, London.*)—Without the gossip of Madame D'Arblay's Diary, or the chatiness of the Widow Delany's Memoirs, the Autobiography of Miss Knight affords a valuable contribution to the future social and domestic history of the Georgian era. Her own story is soon told. The after "far-famed Cornelia," as Mrs. Piozzi calls her, who figured amongst the literary ladies of the day, as the author of "Dinarbas," a sort of *supplement* to Dr. Johnson's "Rasselas;" "Marcus Flaminius," a classical novel, which had the honour of reaching a second edition; and "A Description of Latium; or, Il Campagna di Roma," with etchings by her own hands; was the daughter of Admiral Sir Joseph Knight, an officer, we are told, of a well-deserved reputation. Miss Knight was born in 1757. Her childish days were spent in London, where, under the superintendence of her mother, she received an excellent education; and, as a girl, made the acquaintance of Johnson, Goldsmith, Burke, Sir Joshua Reynolds, and other celebrities of the day. In 1775 her father, Sir Joseph Knight, died at Harwich, where he had gone for sea-bathing. His last meal was a little frunt and a glass of wine, which his daughter brought him, and which the loyal gentleman drank to the health of the King, "wishing him out of his troubles." "After this he begged my mother to read to him 'The Sermon on the Mount,' a part of Scripture which he particularly loved." While she was reading he expired. After this sad epoch in the life of wife and daughter, Lady Knight, finding herself in straitened circumstances, and failing to obtain a pension from the Crown, left England, and, after travelling through France, finally fixed her residence in Italy. For some twenty years after their departure from England we find the mother and daughter oscillating between Rome and Naples, mixing in the best society, and seeing much of the political and prelatical sides of Italian life. But, in spite of these surroundings, Cornelia Knight remained faithful to her creed and country, nourished a hatred of jacobinical and revolutionary tendencies, and (in the language of the editor of her autobiography) was in every pulse of her heart a Tory and a Royalist. At Naples, Lady Knight and her daughter became the intimate friends of Sir William and Lady Hamilton; and when, after the battle of the Nile, the British fleet, followed by their French prizes, sailed into the beautiful bay, Miss Knight's telescope was one of the first that descried the blue ensign of the Hero. A few days later Nelson's own ship arrived, and a jubilant scene of welcome and congratulation ensued; the smooth bay, covered with boats, resounded with the strains of "God save the King," "Rule Britannia," and "See the Conquering Hero comes," airs which no English man or woman can hear unmoved in a foreign land. No wonder that the English Admiral's daughter shared in the general enthusiasm, and that when brought into personal intimacy with the victor of the Nile, who made the English Ambassador's his home, she, too, should yield to hero-worship, and exhibit her cleverness and her patriotism at the same time by celebrating his victories in verse. By the officers of the fleet she was styled "Nelson's charming Poet Laureate." An ode, descriptive of the blowing up of L'Orient, was set to music by Haydn, who, on one occasion when Lady Hamilton sang it, accompanied her on the pianoforte, and the effect, we are assured, "was grand." To such laudatory strains, Lady Morgan tells us, the hero listened with ingenuous pleasure, and would even encore Lady Hamilton when she sang them. Of these encores Miss Knight says nothing; indeed she is very wisely reticent on the subject of the unfortunate intimacy of the great Admiral and the frail Lady Emma, whose moral character she briefly states to have been a strange mixture of right and wrong. When, however, on the return of the whole party to England, the scandal became patent, Miss Knight, though with some compunctious visitings, lest her doing so should appear ungrateful, abjured her association with the Hamilton party, emphatically asserting that, at the time of her intimacy with them at Naples—for, from the period of her mother's death, she had continued to reside with them till their return to England—"there was certainly no impropriety in living under Lady Hamilton's roof; her house was the resort of the best company of all nations, and the attention paid to Lord Nelson seemed perfectly natural." On the homeward-bound voyage from Palermo the Admiral touched at Leghorn, to land the Queen of Naples and her family; and here Miss Knight passed a day with the Countess of Albany and Count Alfieri, who was very near jeopardizing the fair Cornelia, by intrusting his "Miso-Gallo" to her care, in order to have it published in England. The risk she ran of falling into the hands of the French, with his bitter satire in her possession, having occurred to him, he retracted his intention, and subsequently refused to let her have it. From Ancona, their next landing-place, the whole party visited Vienna; and here it was where Miss Knight met Haydn, who was staying with the magnificent Prince Esterhazy. At Hamburgh, amongst other celebrated persons, the fair voyager made the acquaintance of the German poet Klopstock, and his wife—a pleasant-featured, fat, fair woman, much younger than himself, and a good musician. While there the door opened, and a grave-looking personage, in full canonicals, entered the room with a Bible in his hand. He walked up to Lord Nelson, and asked him to write his name on a blank page of the book. With this request Nelson willingly complied, and the clergyman gave him his blessing and withdrew. This was the German pastor of whom Southey tells us, who, between 70 and 80 years of age, travelled forty miles, with the Bible of his parish church, to obtain the autograph of Nelson on the first leaf of it. Arrived at length in town, "Sir William and Lady Hamilton went with Lord Nelson to dine with his father and Lady Nelson;" while Miss Knight and Mrs. Cadogan—the mother of Lady Emma—put up at an hotel in Albemarle-street. That same evening Sir Thomas Troubridge, an old friend of her father, calls on Cornelia, and advises her to go to her friend, Mrs. Nepean, the Secretary of the Admiralty's wife, who herself calls the next day and relieves Mrs. Cadogan of her charge. Miss Knight's impression of her country men and women, after so long a residence abroad, is not flattering. Mr. Windham and Lord Castlereagh appear to her the two most agreeable statesmen in society. Some of the official gentlemen seemed to her conceited and coldly satirical; and she observes—

That in morning visits it was not only the same style of dress, but that nearly the same topic of conversation, the same time of staying, and the same expectations would be held by almost every lady who made her appearance.

These circumstances, after the natural and unaffected manners of the southern Italian, rendered it at first impossible for the long-absent Englishwoman to feel at home. Furthermore, she found the nation full of poverty and distress. It was, in fact, a time of famine, and of great financial embarrassment; moreover, the darkness and shortness of the days seemed strange to her, as to Sir Robert Fletcher, an old Indian friend, of whom she one day asked how he liked London. "I like it very much," he answered, "but I wish there were a little more daylight." Subsequently, the kind treatment she received from many who had known her in her early youth reconciled her even to the dark days and the strange house, "during which the days when I had been used to see nothing [illegible]." Miss Knight had left England when about eighteen years of age; she returned to it a mature woman of forty-two. She enjoyed a reputation for extensive learning and many accomplishments; she had had the advantage of the best continental society; had written several books in the stately Johnsonian style, then fashionable, though long since consigned to dusty closets and the upper shelves, if indeed they exist at all. Moreover, "she was a person of high principle, of a blameless life, and altogether a gentlewoman;" and, having intellectual gifts and influential friends, it was not strange that she should have been recommended, or have recommended herself, to the notice of the Royal family. Besides, she had the good words of the "Blue-stocking Madame," and altogether it was not singular that Miss Knight, who, during her pilgrimage, had been marked out for Court life, should become one of the attendants of the Court of Queen Charlotte, and take up her residence at Windsor. She had previously been presented at Court, and received very graciously; she was acquainted with Lady Lonsdale, a great favourite with everybody; she had also been introduced to Lord Aberdeen, and Dr. Hawley, whom Madame D'Arblay tells us, from his personal appearance, was known as "the Beauty of Holiness." She reckoned Mrs. Elizabeth Carter, the translator of Epictetus, amongst her acquaintance, who remarked with respect to women: "It is thought that the men have all the advantages over us in the world; but I think we have one invaluable advantage over them—we are not obliged to be politicians." This lady dined out every day with different friends while in London—a fact that speaks volumes not only for the number of her friends, but for the excellence of her digestion. She was then far advanced in years. In 1805 Miss Knight enters upon her situation at Windsor—an indefinite employment, for which she is to receive £100 a-year, a house rent-free, and is paid to the service of her Majesty. Her duty apparently is to be present at the Queen's evening-parties when invited, and always on Sundays and red-letter days. At this period the Princess of Wales is nine years of age, the King fast losing his eyesight, and his favourite daughter, Amelia, in delicate health. At Christmas, Miss Knight takes up her residence in the Castle, and we get occasional glimpses of the daily life of the Royal family. The Queen has her ladies, Lady Aylesbury, and the Dowager Lady Ilchester, and the ladies of the princesses, to dine with her. The King, who dines early, comes in at the dessert. Frogmore—now, as then, a pleasant place—was a favourite spot with Her Majesty. In spring and summer she liked to pass her mornings there, and to read aloud from French and English authors, while Miss Knight worked. The Queen kept a good collection of books at Frogmore, and left Miss Knight a key for Miss Knight was then a decided favourite with Her Majesty. Here it was that the Queen kept the birthdays of the Prince of Wales and the Duke of York. At Old Windsor the Princess Elizabeth (the Princess Royal), and after Queen of Wurtemberg, had a pretty cottage and garden, where she gave little fêtes in summer. At this point the autobiography breaks off abruptly, and a blank occurs in the straight diaries. The former does not commence again till 1809, and the entries are devoid of interest till the end of May, in which year Knight [illegible] to the Royal family. The mysterious attempt to assassinate the Duke of Cumberland takes place. The Duke is attacked in his bed. There is no light. The page, an Italian, who should have been within call, is absent; but the valet, Sellis, a Piedmontese, is discovered with his throat cut, a pair of old slippers of his are found in a closet in the Duke's room, and thereupon an inquest is held, and the dead valet is adjudged to be the assassin and a *felo de se*. The people, making a short cut from Hay-market to Parliament-street, pass over his grave daily; for he was buried in the high-road in Scotland-Yard. But for all this there were circumstances to throw a doubt upon his guilt; Sellis was a left-handed man, whereas his throat was cut from right to left. Sellis, as we have said, was a Piedmontese, but his name in the slippers was written in French. The page who had neglected his duty is discharged with a pension, and his brother, who had a good appointment and a family at Windsor Castle, resigns and goes away. In the meantime the Duke has been removed to Carlton House, where the Prince of Wales attends to him with assiduous tenderness, and "It was the fashion," Miss Knight tells us, "to go and see the Duke's apartments," which were left in the same state as when he removed, and visitors discovered marks of blood on the walls, and all the other evidences of a murderous struggle. But we are glad to write that the sisterly Cornelia "did not join the crowd to the horrid scene." The Princess Amelia, pale and emaciated, but still retaining her beauty, sinks day by day. However, [illegible] and the King's malady is increasing. The Princess died on the birthday of her brother, the Duke of Kent. When the King saw his beloved child the last time, she said to him "Remember me, but do not grieve for me." She had previously given him a ring, with her hair under a crystal, and her name, with the words "Remember me!" engraved within it—a gift which is said to have, even then, aggravated his mental indisposition. Her illness and death, added to the loss of Hanover, so preyed upon him that, very shortly after, he was no longer master of himself. The last time Miss Knight saw him was on the anniversary of his accession. On this occasion the whole family, with the exception of the Queen of Wurtemburg, and Princess Amelia, were present. He entered the room, the Queen holding his arm, while his countenance betrayed his excitement. It was the custom for everyone in the circle to address him as he approached, that he might recognise them by their voices, as he could no longer distinguish persons. Miss Knight could not remember what she had said to him, but "still harping on his daughter," the much-afflicted King bade her not to be uneasy for Amelia, who was well and in Hanover, where she would never grow old. I think a more pathetic scene was never penned of Royalty than is summed up to the mind of the reflective reader in the short paragraph in which Miss Knight thus outlines this last appearance which she witnessed of George III. At the end of seven years, Miss Knight was appointed Lady Companion to the Princess Charlotte, who was then growing into womanhood. For some cause or another this appointment was disagreeable to the Queen, who thwarted it by every means in her power, and never forgave Miss Knight's acceptance of it: and from this period she treated her quondam *protégée* with absolute indignity, not desiring her to sit in her presence, forgetting to invite her to dine, and always ignoring the stately appellation of "lady companion" in the very second-rate one of subgoverness; so that poor Miss Knight has quite a hard time of it with her offended Majesty, and a constant contest to maintain her position. Her description of Warwick House, which adjoined Carlton House, is not cheerful; and the life of the poor young Princess immured therein, dreary indeed. After a time, her Royal Highness is deprived of the pleasure of dining once a fortnight with her mother at Kensington Palace, and is left entirely dependent for companionship and amusement on the two ladies of her household, Dr. Short (her sub-preceptor), and her old music-master, whom she used to send for sometimes of an evening. Very limited concerts, proverbs, and small plays written for her by Miss Knight, appear to have been her only relaxations. The Princess had high spirits: all the more exuberant, probably, for the seclusion and restraints by which she was surrounded. She even exhibits a predilection for flirting; and Miss Knight is enjoined by her Royal papa to check it: especially the too *frequent* visits of the young and handsome Duke of Devonshire, whose picture hangs in the Princess's room, are to be prevented. An old but intimate friend, Miss Mercer Elphinstone, with whom the young Princess has been for some time forbidden to correspond, is still suspected to be in communication with her; for, being nearly seventeen years of age, she has the temerity to write to Lord Liverpool, requesting to have an establishment of her own, with ladies-in-waiting, &c., &c.—a requisition which it is supposed could never have occurred to her, but for the prompting of some bolder spirit outside the almost conventual solemnity and shadows of Warwick House. Her mother is suspected to have been the means of communication; and the stated dinners (at which Miss Knight is commanded never to leave the child alone with the Princess of Wales) are forbidden, and the aspirations of the Princess are severely checked by Lord Eldon, who is sent to explain the law of England to her upon the subject. The indignity to which the Princess is subjected—scolded by the Prince, her father, in the presence of her lady companion, and lectured by the Chancellor (who, when the Regent inquired what he, as a father, would have done, replied that he "would have locked her up")—threw the Princess into a low nervous fever. Shortly after the Princess's first ball (at which she wore feathers for the first time, and looked beautiful in white and silver) the Orange marriage came to be talked about; against which the Princess for some time demurred, but at length came to think the picture of the hereditary Prince "not ugly," and in the end consented to be engaged to him: upon which we have a *tableau* of the Regent papa joining the hands of the young people, in the drawing-room at Carlton House. But when the arrangements about residence, &c., came to be made, the Princess, finding that she would be expected to live in Holland (whereas she was bent on residing at least a part of the year in England), broke off the affair; and her father, with equal peremptoriness, broke up her establishment at a moment's notice, and resolved on having her under his own roof. Whereupon, the Princess, believing herself about to be made a State-prisoner, fled to her mother's; making her escape, bonnet in hand, down the back stairs, and in a hackney-coach: and was only brought back, at dawn of day, by the wise and kindly counsel of Lord Brougham, her mother's friend, under the protection of her uncle, the Duke of York. The picture Miss Knight affords us, of the pale boyish-looking Prince of Orange, who had a bad cook and gave dull dinners; whose manners, frank and good-natured, savoured more of the mess-room than the court, and whom the young English aide-de-camps slapped on the back, to the great astonishment of the officers, is rather more amusing than impressive. And when we hear that his after-conduct as a husband was not the most worthy, we are by no means sorry at the defeat of his wooing. In the meanwhile the Princess, whose "lady companion" has been treated with as little ceremony as a fourth-rate governess in a tradesman's house, is sent to ruminate upon her indiscretion in the heart of Windsor

France, and the close vicinity of her grandmother. Very soon after this, Prince Leopold of Saxe Coburg—a gentleman who is said to have only £200 a-year, which it is calculated will buy him two coats and a dozen of shirts, and who has once previously called at Warwick House, and has been seen riding in the Park, beside the carriage of the Princess, when out airing—appears as a suitor. This possible German alliance is evidently satisfactory to the Queen, who shows more affection than she has ever done for her grand-daughter; and the marriage, to avoid which Miss Knight, with a proper sense of what is due to herself, and keenly sensible of the injustice with which her services and self-sacrifice have been treated by the Prince Regent, retires to the continent. Later in the autobiography we find her visiting at Claremont House; but Hayter (to whom the Princess is sitting for her portrait) is in the room all the time. The sequel to the story of the Royal Princess is too well known to need recital. Miss Knight throws no new light upon it; indeed, throughout the whole autobiography we find prudence restraining the expression of this lady's feelings, to a degree which lessens considerably the interest of the work; which is, nevertheless (as we have elsewhere said), a valuable and highly amusing one. Our space will not permit of our following the "ex-lady companion" in her wanderings and visits to continental courts, nor can we allow ourselves to extract any of the numerous anecdotes with which she stores her journal and note-books. This accomplished lady appears to have enjoyed life to the last; she did not quit it till eighty-one years of age. C. A. W.

THE ENGLISHWOMAN'S JOURNAL. (19, *Langham Place, Regent Street; W. Kent and Co., Paternoster row.*)—A very pleasant number, with rather more variety than usual. Miss Cornelia Knight's Autobiography occupies a considerable portion of the first sheet. "The Colonies and their requirements," another instalment of the papers read at the Meeting of the Association for the Promotion of Social Science, held in Dublin, August, 1861, contains the hopeful information that in the two islands of which alone the Society possess statistical accounts, New Zealand and Australia, there is a deficiency of women amounting in the total to 155,808. "What would be the proportions" observes the writer,

"if we could include Natal, *Canada*, and Columbia in the reckoning? Of the Social success of this scheme, as exhibited in England, it would be superfluous to speak; and if the vice and immorality on the other side of the Atlantic is ever to be uprooted, it must be by some further extension of emigration, by the steady departure from these shores of our population, working out by its influence into the colonies of a body of women, infinitely superior by birth, by education, and by taste to the burden of wild, uneducated creatures we have hitherto sent abroad."

Two modes of sending out this class of emigrants are suggested: First, by payment of the whole of the passage-money on the part of the lady or her friends; and, secondly, by loan, the society advancing the entire amount, to be paid at the end of two years and four months without interest—simply requiring a good security that the money would be repaid at the end of the stipulated time. Caroline Chisholm, if we remember aright, advanced the passage-money upon the promise of her clients to repay it; and she publicly stated, that only in a very few instances was this promise dishonoured by the "wild uneducated creatures" on whose behalf her philanthropy was exercised. Miss Rye with more faith in mankind friends than experience sometimes warrants in the path of many solitary, self-dependent women, observes: "We consider the signature of this bond rather a test of character, feeling sure that there must be some radical error in that woman's life who can have attained mature age without having secured one responsible friend." Is not this conclusion rather arbitrary? One may have many friends, responsible, even in the sense of Miss Rye's phrase, to whom the very mention of a bond would be abhorrent; and there are some women, too, who would rather endure any amount of personal deprivation, than risk the refusal of a favour that is proverbially supposed to weaken friendship. It would be a fairer test of personal character, we think, if the original scheme, [illegible] by the Association for the Benefit of a higher Grade of Society, were to be carried out in its integrity. Surely, educated women should have a higher sense of honour and honesty than their illiterate sisters. Might not the certificate of the Society (dependent on the right performance of their duties) also serve as a testimonial in obtaining re-engagements for these ladies? There is another difficulty in the way of this important scheme, besides the £20 or £18 passage-money required. At present, there are no persons appointed to receive these ladies on their arrival at the Colonies; before sending any out, this should be remedied; and it is only natural to suppose that the colonists themselves will gladly respond to the efforts of the Society. A very pleasantly written paper by Miss B. R. Parkes, "[illegible] House," appears in the November number; and "Bow Church" is the subject of an interesting article.

MARGERY BROWNE: HOPE DEFERRED. By Sarah Wood. (*London: Groombridge and Sons.*)—Another instalment to the pretty juvenile library accumulating at the hands of Messrs. Groombridge. "Hope Deferred" is a simple seaside story, with very pretty bits of description here and there. Take, for instance, that of the old port of Scarborough, before its fine bay and great cliffs and salt breezes came into fashion, and when the steep and narrow streets under the hill, on which stands the ruins of the Old Castle, were inhabited only by fishermen and the owners and crews of the colliers, and a few larger craft trading to Holland. The plot turns upon the supposed loss of a young sailor, the only son of his mother, and she a widow, and the lingering, long deferred hopes of his sister, who never quite despairs of his return, though she knows (what has been carefully hidden from her invalid mother) that "Jim" had been washed overboard one stormy night, and that he counts no longer amongst the crew of the "Bonny Jean." I am not going to tell this pretty story to my young readers, but strongly recommend it to their notice.

THE RELIQUARY. Edited by Llewellyn Jewitt. (London: Smith, Soho-square.)—The "Reliquary" for October contains an interesting description of a Roman villa recently discovered on the estate of Wm. Angerstein, Esq.,—at Wellsby, near Market Rasen—of which a ground-plan, and woodcuts of various relics discovered in making the excavations, are given. An account of Throwleston Abbey, near Leek, Staffordshire, is highly interesting, and so are the "Observations on Celtic Pottery," which Mr. Jewitt's woodcuts clearly illustrate. "Stevenson" contributes a Derbyshire legend of "St. Benedict's in the Hollow;" and Mr. Henry Brockett, a paper on the singular custom of "Purse Cutting," at Newcastle-upon-Tyne, where this opprobrious act was imposed by the Corporation, as a penalty on masters of ships who had been proved to have cast ballast at sea within certain distances and depths of water. Worse than all, the culprit found the money (probably £5), which, being hung up in a leather purse in the council-chamber, he was compelled to cut; thereby acknowledging himself as vile as an ordinary cutpurse. The custom led to malpractices on the part of the Newcastle Corporation—false witnesses were suborned, innocent men punished, and it was only put an end to by the publication of "England's Grievance Discovered in Relation to the Coal Trade," a work written by Ralph Gardiner, of Chirton, (co. Northumberland), Gent., which exposed and condemned the whole system. In 1778 two cutpurses remained hanging in the Town Chamber of Newcastle, and were subsequently presented to the local Antiquarian Society. Several pages of the number are devoted to a memoir of the late Thomas Bateman, Esq., well known as a collector of local antiquities, and an intelligent contributor to various archæological works. His museum, at Lomberdale House, Derbyshire, attests to his antiquarian research and industry.

THE LAWS OF THE LAND. (No. 1, BANKRUPTCY.) Edited by W. H. Buchanan, Solicitor in the Court of Bankruptcy. (London: Houlston and Wright, Paternoster-row.) This publication actually marks an epoch in our civilisation, for hitherto we have been content to live under laws, which, originating in very ancient times, have been continually added to, altered, and amended, till the whole has (except to the initiated) become so intricate and mysterious that even intelligent and thinking men have had difficulty in acquiring a knowledge of them. Thanks to the appearance of the present work, which proposes to give a popular explanation and epitome of the enactments affecting property and persons in simple English, specially designed for non-professional readers, we have hopes that even a non-clear may comprehend all that is contained in the laws by which society is ruled and held together. The present number contains a clear explanation of the New Bankruptcy Act 1861. We shall watch the development of the work with interest.

AMUSEMENTS OF THE MONTH.

DRURY LANE

Has had great attractions for the lovers of the stage, in Mr. Brooke and Miss Avonia Jones. These distinguished artistes are seen to perfection in the play of "Love's Sacrifice," in which Mr. Brooke, as the remorseful and agonised Elmore, is very impressive; while Miss Jones, as *Margaret*, keeps the interest of the house at the highest pitch. Gifted with talent, a musical voice, and intellectual face, this young tragédienne is a valuable acquisition. Mr. Brooke's voice and impulsive and powerful style are sufficiently praiseworthy, and we strenuously advise our readers to visit the national theatre, sure that they will be repaid. At

THE PRINCESS'S,

Mr. Fechter's Othello has been the great attraction, and, in accordance with our promise, we will endeavour to express a decided opinion on it. To speak, then, as compendiously as we can, the impersonation is too domestic, or distinguished from tragic. Until the third act Mr. Fechter's acting is nothing particularly worthy of remark, but in that act, on *Iago* arousing his suspicions, the actor's genius shows itself. His start on catching himself bidding *Iago* to let his wife watch and spy on *Desdemona* is one of the finest indications of self-reproach and shame possible. In the fiercer scenes, however, he does not express the wild frenzy of passion and despair as others have done, and is decidedly too tame. Admiring, too, his performance in many things, we utterly disapprove of all the new stage-business he has introduced. His glancing at the mirror, when he comes to the line

"It is the cause, it is the cause, my soul,"

is, in our opinion, a thoroughly false, and even childish reading. Mr. Ryder (as *Iago*), and Miss C. Leclercq (as *Desdemona*), are respectively admirable exponents of their parts. At

THE ADELPHI

A new drama, by Mr. Boucicault, entitled the "Octoroon," has been produced, with, in the

opinion of most, a very doubtful success; and it cannot be hoped two pieces following will have a run like the "Colleen Bawn." We shall examine the piece more in extenso in our next.

THE HAYMARKET

Has been filled by large and laughing audiences attracted by the play, "Our American Cousin," in which Mr. Sothern (a new actor to the stage) portrays the character of a titled exquisite in so excellent and original a way as to produce, in the play-bill phrase, "roars of laughter." AS

THE LYCEUM

Mr. Falconer has produced a new Irish drama, called "Peep o'-Day," intended, we suppose, to continue the fame of the famous prototype, and it is founded on a tale of the O'Hara family. The most striking scene is the [illegible], at dark valley, where *Kathleen Kavanagh* ([illegible]) is decoyed by a forged letter, and only escapes assassination by her brother *Harry* (Mr. H. Vezin) throwing himself among the branches of a tree, and so descending a precipice to her aid. The great scene, perhaps, is the faction fight at the fair, which simulates reality very sincerely. The play, however, is much too diffuse in dialogue. AS

THE OLYMPIC

Mr. Robson has been delighting his admirers in a new farce, "A Legal Impediment," and causes unusual risibility by his ludicrous "business." AS

THE STRAND

A new comic drama, "Is it the King?" has been the vehicle for Miss Ada Swanborough's début. AS

SADLER'S WELLS

Mr. Phelps has been playing various characters with his usual genius, which especially shines in his portraiture of *Othello*. W. B.

THE TOILET.

(Specially from Paris.)

FIRST FIGURE.—Dress of maroon silk; on the skirt one deep flounce, headed and ornamented with knots of gimp. Body high, and open, with waistband. Sleeves wide at the bottom, bordered with a flounce, and decorated at the seams and on the flounce with gimp bows, to match the trimming on the body and skirt. Muslin collar and under-sleeves; the latter ornamented with plaitings of the material. Empress cravat. Résille cap of black *tulle*, with long *barbes* and red roses ornamenting it.

SECOND FIGURE.—Dress of a grey tissue, decorated with mossy cord and silk buttons. Body high, ending in two points. Sleeves open on the arm, and finished with deep cuff trimming to match. Muslin collar and under-sleeves. Bonnet of pansy silk and velvet; crown of spotted white *tulle*. For ornament, pansy-flowers and black lace. Inside the front three white roses. Blond down the cheeks. Strings very wide.

With winter naturally returns the reign of velvet bonnets; the colours most in favour, azure-blue, *pensée*, emerald, and olive-green, black being, as a matter of course, always in favour. The strings are again worn very wide; and the prevailing ornaments are blond, velvet-flowers, or tufts of feathers. The *coiffure Maintenon* of Chantilly, coquettishly mounted on a garland, is exceedingly pretty; as is also *la coiffure Pompadour*—a wreath of China blue velvet and white blond, with bouquets *jardinière*, placed in tufts on the summit and back of the *coiffure*.

For ball dress white *tulle* and white muslin are at present favourite materials. They are frequently ornamented with pinked silk trimmings, of a bright colour, placed over or on flounces of the material. One very pretty robe is trimmed with a deep flounce of the material, edged and headed by a narrow frill of pink silk. The *berthe* is formed by rows of pink cut silk, with entre-deux of the same fabric as the dress. The waist is round, with a waistband, finished with long ends and bows behind.

The *fichu Marie Antoinette* is replaced by a pelerine composed of insertion and rows of guipure. It is very short, with sleeves to match, made expressly for low corsages. The hair is worn crêpé, or rolled back with a comb, and plaits, or sometimes a bunch of curls behind. A tuft of flowers on the front of the head, and also at the back, is a pretty style of ornament.

I have nothing new to tell you of winter envelopes, which have not, as yet, materially changed in form. Muslin under-sleeves, for walking and home-dress, are all made with wristbands; the collars are very small.

I have just space to say a word of children's toilets and the *Chemise Garibaldi*, than which nothing can be prettier for either sex, at five or six years of age. They are made in flannel or cashmere of bright colours, Solferino blue or red being the favourite shades. Boys wear them with a short *jupe*, cut in great plaits under a waistband. The *jupe* is often of a grey stuff, which accords well with the jacket.

PASSING EVENTS RE-EDITED.

A French chymist has just discovered a mode of rendering muslin, lace, and all kinds of light stuffs, incombustible. He makes no secret of the process. It is merely necessary to mix the starch used in making them up, with half its own weight of carbonate of lime, commonly called "Spanish white," or "Spanish chalk." The muslin, or other fabric, is then ironed as usual, the chalk thus used making no perceptible difference in its appearance; neither does it injure the substance of the article, nor take from its whiteness.

A Miss Powell, in America, has taken up the subject of "dress for out-door work," and, after alluding to the decline of healthy constitutions among American women, which is generally attributed to inherent delicacy arising from the wear-and-tear of nerve and brain which every American person undergoes, and which, it is acknowledged, may be greatly obviated by out-of-door exercise, sensibly suggests that women are often hindered in this by unsuitable clothing. "Embroidered skirts," she remarks, "open wrappers, and dressing slippers, are not particularly suited to morning exercise or work in the garden. The case is still worse in the afternoon; a heavy rep or nice silk in winter, and the delicate organdi and barège in summer, are not improved by trending on wet gravel-paths, or sloppy pavements, or by the dust of country roads, or climbing on the stiles in summer. So we stay at home to take care of our 'good clothes,' instead of going out to take care of ourselves." "Every city woman," continues Miss Powell, who has, at least, good sense on her side, "should have a walking dress—every country lady a working dress. The walking-dress should be of stuff stout enough for all pedestrian accidents, clearing the ground as to length, with a neat dark petticoat, and kid or kid-dressed walking boots. The full-dress muslin, in a dress that has to be carried in both hands, is of little use; it is the brisk, unimpeded walk that sets the blood coursing through the veins, and brings the flush of health to the cheeks." For in-door work this advocate for healthy innovation in women's costume suggests a dress, the waist of which should give entire freedom to every muscle. The skirt, for a woman of ordinary height, twenty-five inches in length, with plain or Turkish trowsers of the same material. Every woman acknowledges the benefit of such a modification of dress, and in the actress, the skater, and the gymnast, society respects and approves of it; why, then, should it not be adopted for all industrial pursuits and out-of-door work? A gentleman present at the meeting—a sort of local Social Congress, at which Miss Powell read her sensible paper—proposed that the Empress Eugenie be memorialised to adopt a style of dress which should embody all the physiological benefits and advantages desired. We feel that the serviceable, every-day garments, that would prove a real blessing to those engaged in industrial pursuits, and to pedestrians generally, must not look to Courts for their sanction and approval, but to the practical common-sense and resolution of those who daily feel the want of some such modification in dress as Miss Powell aims at.

We are pleased to hear that the American sculptress, Miss Harriet Hosmer, will be represented in the Great Exhibition of next year by her statue of Zenobia, the "Captive Queen."

C. A. W.

ANSWERS TO CORRESPONDENTS.

Notice to Subscribers.—On the first of January will appear the commencing chapters of a new novel, by the author of "Raison Morley."

Amateur Writers.—Several amateurs having addressed us on the subject of original tales, essays, &c., we beg to say that if forwarded to us, we will give them our best attention, and, when possessing sufficient merit, the advantage of publication. Rejected manuscripts shall be sent, on the first day of each month, to the care of Mr. Allen, 246, Strand, who will return them to the owners when called for, or by post if stamps are forwarded for the purpose. But the Editor must not be expected to give her written reasons for their rejection. All contributors will please to accept this rule.

Poetry accepted, with thanks.—"Words;" "Absent Friends;" "The Confession."

"A. L.," Lancashire.—The verses sent are so redolent of pathos and true feeling that we regret the versification is not sufficiently finished to enable us to make use of them. This answer will also apply to "Time," Whitehall.

Yarbury Fields, Blackheath.—The first three lines of our correspondent's poem (which, by the way, is on a very hackneyed subject) require elucidation. We do not know whether the plural pronoun belongs to the stage or to the world, or to both of them; in which case sundry "cares" are new to us. The remaining lines are so prettily descriptive that we shall hope for an amended copy in time for January.

"Selma" is thanked for the offered verses, which are not up to the required standard. "Fair" and "there," we must remind him, are not rhymes; neither are "research" and "march," "dare" and "fancy," "works" and "jerks," still less "set" and "way." "Baby the Fifth," both in outline and treatment, suspiciously reminds us of "Baby May"—a gem that absorbs into itself every grace and loveliness of babyhood.

Publishers, Authors, &c., are invited to send their works for notice.

All correspondents requiring private answers must enclose a stamped and addressed envelope.

Printed by Rogerson and Tuxford, 246, Strand, London.

www.ingramcontent.com/pod-product-compliance
Lightning Source LLC
Chambersburg PA
CBHW021105270326
41929CB00009B/740
* 9 7 8 3 7 4 2 8 2 5 5 1 3 *